WAY

For additioन
products an S0-BWU-541
REPORTS, *see the back of the book.*

BARCODE IS ON NEXT PAGE

The December 15, 1996, issue of CONSUMER REPORTS. Volume 61, No. 13

A NOTE TO READERS

A book that's guided consumers since 1937 needs to freshen itself occasionally, and this year's Buying Guide does just that. We've redesigned it—as we have CONSUMER REPORTS—to provide an even more clear and useful presentation. We hope this makes the many pages of reports and Ratings more pleasurable and helpful.

Most of the pages of the Buying Guide are devoted to giving you the best buying advice we can on expensive purchases such as cars, appliances, audio and video gear, computers and other home office equipment, home maintenance and safety products, and some health and recreation items.

Wherever possible, those reports are accompanied by our latest brand-name Ratings, as published in recent issues of CONSUMER REPORTS, with special updates to tell you which models are still available.

In addition, the Buying Guide has some unique features:

■ Repair Histories to help you gauge how reliable a product is likely to be.

■ Product recalls gathered from the last 12 months of CONSUMER REPORTS, to help you avoid unsafe products.

■ An alphabetical listing of manufacturers' telephone numbers, most of them toll-free.

■ A directory of the last time CONSUMER REPORTS magazine published articles on various subjects and products, going back eight years.

With these thoughts, I wish you another year of sensible and satisfying shopping.

Consumer Reports
NATIONAL TESTING
& RESEARCH CENTER
TEST · INFORM · PROTECT

ABOUT THE

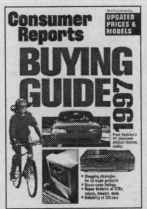

The CONSUMER REPORTS Buying Guide, the 13th issue of CONSUMER REPORTS magazine, contains the latest buying advice distilled from all our testing of the major consumer products. It's a reference work, with the information presented in a succinct and concise manner for quick and easy use all year long. The information and models in the Ratings have been reviewed and updated, with the latest infomation on model availability and the lastest prices.

The reports in the Buying Guide outline the basic information you need to consider—the pros and cons of the choices, what's new in the marketplace, likely places to find the product, what you can expect to pay, and an explanation of the features.

The thumb index gives fast access to the types of products included here: autos, audio and video gear, appliances, health and recreation products, home office equipment, and home care and safety items.

For easy reference to past issues of CONSUMER REPORTS, you'll find an eight-year index of the last full test report at the back of this book. The original CONSUMER REPORTS publication date is also given at the top of each report and each Ratings table. Back issues of CONSUMER REPORTS are available in most libraries. Some reports are also available by fax from Consumer Reports by Request; see page 353.

CONSUMER REPORTS, through its extensive reader surveys, has unique information about product reliability. In the Reliability chapter, you'll find Brand Repair Histories for products such as refrigerators, washing machines, CD players, dishwashers, lawn mowers, and TV sets. We also discuss how to go about repairing products, how long they should last, and how to assess whether they're worth fixing. See page 7.

The Buying Guide contains advice about car-buying—new, used, leased—as well as reliability information for more than 200 individual models of cars from 1988 to 1995. See the Frequency-of-Repair charts that start on page 275.

The Buying Guide collects a year's worth of product recalls, based on notices issued by governmental agencies, as published in the monthly issues of CONSUMER REPORTS from November 1995 through October 1996. See page 320.

ABOUT CONSUMER REPORTS

CONSUMER REPORTS is published monthly by Consumers Union, a nonprofit independent testing organization serving consumers. We are a comprehensive source for unbiased advice about products and services. Since 1936, our mission has been to test products, inform the public, and protect consumers.

We buy all the products we test off the shelf, just as you do. We receive no special treatment. We accept no free samples; if a manufacturer sends us a free product, we return it.

We test products in 50 state-of-the art labs at our National Testing and Research Center in Yonkers, N.Y. Our Ratings are based on lab tests, controlled-use tests, and expert judgments by our technical and research staff. If a product is high in overall quality and relatively low in price, we deem it A CR Best Buy™. A Rating refers only to the brand and model listed.

We survey our millions of readers to bring you information on the reliability of hundreds of auto models and of major products like appliances and electronic gear. Reader-survey data also help us rate insurance and other consumer services.

We report on current issues of concern to consumers. Our staff of researchers and editors brings you in-depth information on matters that affect your health, money, and well-being.

We accept no ads from companies. We do advertise our own services, which provide impartial information and advice to consumers. We don't let any company use our reports or Ratings for commercial purposes. If that happens, we insist that the company stop, and we take whatever additional steps are open to us.

Readers' letters. We welcome reader comment. Write: CONSUMER REPORTS, P. O. Box 2015, Yonkers, N.Y. 10703-9015. We regret we are unable to respond to individual letters.

CONSUMER REPORTS (ISSN 0010-7174) is published 13 times a year by Consumers Union of U.S., Inc., 101 Truman Avenue, Yonkers, N.Y. 10703-1057. Second-class postage paid at Yonkers, N.Y., and at additional mailing offices. Canadian postage paid at Mississauga, Ontario, Canada. Canadian publications registration no. 2665247-98. Title CONSUMER REPORTS registered in U.S. Patent Office. Contents of this issue copyright © 1996 by Consumers Union of U.S., Inc. All rights reserved under International and Pan-American copyright conventions. Reproduction in whole or in part is forbidden without prior written permission (and is never permitted for com-

OTHER SERVICES

In addition to CONSUMER REPORTS magazine and the Buying Guide, CONSUMER REPORTS provides other services to give you unbiased advice to help you make important choices and decisions:

Consumer Reports Cars: The Essential Guide. This CD-ROM covers new and used cars, minivans, pickups, and SUVs. $19.95 postpaid. Call 800 331-1369, ext. 173. See page 356.

New Car Price Service. Our reports compare sticker price to dealer's invoice. Call 800 269-1139. Details on page 357.

Used Car Price Service. Find the market value in your area for the used cars you want to buy or sell. See page 358.

Auto Insurance Price Service. Compare the cost of auto insurance for the coverage you need; find the best price. Now available in Calif., Fla., Ill., N.J., N.Y., Pa., and Wash. See page 359.

Home Price Service. Estimate home value, get price histories since 1990. Covers most metro areas. See page 355.

Consumer Reports Books. More than 100 helpful books in print; see page 354 and the back cover for many titles.

Consumer Reports on Health. Monthly newsletter on nutrition, fitness, and a range of medical matters. See page 360.

Consumer Reports Travel Letter. Monthly newsletter with travel values. For more information, see page 360.

Zillions. Bimonthly magazine for kids 10 and up. $16 a year (6 issues), $26 for 2 years. Write Subscription Dept., Box 54861, Boulder, Colo. 80322-4861. See page 360.

Consumer Reports by Request. Specially edited reports are available by fax or mail. See page 343.

Other media. Our information is available online through America Online, CompuServe, Prodigy, and on CD-ROM; on TV and radio stations; and in columns appearing in more than 500 newspapers.

mercial purposes). CU is a member of the Consumers International. Mailing lists: CU occasionally exchanges its subscriber lists with those of selected publications and nonprofit organizations. If you wish your name deleted from such exchanges, send your address label with a request for deletion to CONSUMER REPORTS, P.O. Box 53029, Boulder, Colo. 80322-3029. Postmaster: Send address changes to the same address. Back issues: Single copies of 12 preceding issues, $5 each; Buying Guide, $10 each. Write Back Issues., CONSUMER REPORTS, P.O. Box 53016, Boulder, Colo. 80322-3016. For back issues in microform, write UMI, 300 N. Zeeb Rd., Ann Arbor, Mich. 48106.

Consumer Reports
BUYING GUIDE

RELIABILITY

Getting things fixed

Buying brands with a good track record betters your chances of trouble-free service. You'll find the latest brand Repair Histories for big-ticket items such as TV sets, washers, refrigerators, and mowers beginning on page 11. While the data are historical and apply to brands, not specific models, they've been quite consistent over the years.

Even the best products, though, can experience problems. If a product breaks down during the warranty, the repair is usually covered. As it nears the end of the warranty—manufacturer's, service contract, or credit-card's—having even minor problems looked at can save money in the long run. Once the warranty expires,

you can fix it, have it fixed, or get rid of it.

With some products, the choice may already have been made for you. The very designs and manufacturing methods that give us better, cheaper, and more durable goods may also make some goods difficult or impossible to repair.

These products can be practically impossible to service. When they break, you have little choice but to get rid of them. Fortunately, many products are still repairable—and worth repairing.

Fix it yourself

Doing a repair yourself saves money and often leads to more satisfaction with the job. People are most likely to fix products with mechanical innards: cars, clothes dryers, mowers, vacuums, ranges, washing machines, and such. Many electronics' manufacturers advise against do-it-yourself repairs because of the product's complexity and potential shock hazard.

How-to advice. Major appliance manufacturers offer the most help to amateurs. General Electric, Whirlpool, Sears, and Frigidaire, for instance, provide technical assistance through a toll-free telephone number. GE and Whirlpool also publish manuals for amateurs. Other companies sell technical service manuals for their products, but they're not an easy read. Many books offer general fix-it-yourself advice.

Getting parts. Make sure the model number is correct. Get it from the appliance itself, not the packaging or manual. Contact the manufacturer directly for specialized parts. Most companies have a toll-free telephone number or fax line. See page 339. Some companies will sell you the part directly; others will refer you to a parts distributor.

Try local stores for common parts. Mass merchandisers like Kmart carry generic replacement parts such as carafes for coffee makers. Parts stores and appliance dealers may also have parts on hand.

Have it fixed

Repairs rank high on the list of transactions that make people anxious, but there are ways to minimize the risk.

The three basic types include: factory service, in which the company has its own service center or service fleet; authorized service, privately run businesses accredited by companies to fix their brands (the store that sells the product sometimes acts as an authorized repairer); and independents, who set their own policy.

Manufacturers typically require factory or authorized service for warranty work. The owner's manual usually provides a toll-free number to call for the nearest factory-authorized service center or you can check our listing of phone numbers by brand on page 339.

Authorized repairers sometimes earn a commission for parts, an arrangement that can lead to unnecessary replacement and higher charges. But shipping time and cost may make a factory center less appealing than a local authorized shop.

Independents can be a good choice for products that are out of warranty. If possible, get a referral.

Repairs made at home. Before scheduling an appointment, ask whether there's a "trip" charge. It includes travel to and from your home and a minimum labor charge, even if you don't go ahead with the work. Find out whether you'll pay flat or hourly rates. If the charge is by the hour, how is it billed? Billing by the quarter-hour is common.

Ask whether the repair carries a warranty. And ask to keep any replaced parts. That way, you'll know that a part you are billed for was actually replaced.

Repairs in the shop. If repairs are going to be made in-store, first get an estimate. A charge for the estimate may apply for work done out of warranty. Ask how long the repair should take. Also, find out the typical waiting time for parts. If the parts are on back order from the factory, be prepared to wait several weeks or more.

Be sure to get a claim check that shows the date your product went to the shop, and its brand, model, and serial number. If possible, get an authorized signature. Use a credit card to pay for repairs, so you can dispute, if needed.

If there's a problem. If you can't resolve a problem with an authorized repairer, contact the manufacturer's main

How long things last ———

A product's useful life depends not only on its actual durability but also on such intangibles as your own desire for some attribute or convenience available only on a new model. These estimates are from manufacturers and trade associations.

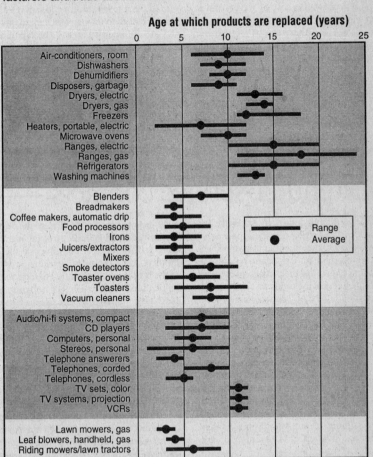

Age at which products are replaced (years)

Air-conditioners, room	
Dishwashers	
Dehumidifiers	
Disposers, garbage	
Dryers, electric	
Dryers, gas	
Freezers	
Heaters, portable, electric	
Microwave ovens	
Ranges, electric	
Ranges, gas	
Refrigerators	
Washing machines	
Blenders	
Breadmakers	
Coffee makers, automatic drip	
Food processors	
Irons	
Juicers/extractors	
Mixers	
Smoke detectors	
Toaster ovens	
Toasters	
Vacuum cleaners	
Audio/hi-fi systems, compact	
CD players	
Computers, personal	
Stereos, personal	
Telephone answerers	
Telephones, corded	
Telephones, cordless	
TV sets, color	
TV systems, projection	
VCRs	
Lawn mowers, gas	
Leaf blowers, handheld, gas	
Riding mowers/lawn tractors	

Range
Average

Source: APPLIANCE magazine, a Dana Chase publication.

customer-relations office, usually in the owner's manual, or see page 339. If you are still unhappy, complain to the Better Business Bureau and notify consumer agencies and the local newspaper.

Get rid of it

Sometimes the cost of repairs can be so high that fixing the product may not make sense. Other reasons a repair may not be a good investment: Replacement models have become a lot cheaper or are greatly improved; the product is near the end of its useful life; the brand's reliability record is worse than most others so more repairs may be imminent.

Nowhere do products become obsolescent as quickly as in the electronics industry. Solid-state components have led to products that are smaller, lighter, smarter, and—because they run cooler—more reliable. But such products are harder to service and diagnosing problems requires more expertise.

Servicers are reluctant to repair parts individually. When an integrated circuit is faulty, they replace the entire circuit board. As a result, electronic failures are often costlier to fix than mechanical ones.

One option is to extend the life of an old but functioning appliance by selling or giving it away. You may find groups that accept used goods through your town or state environmental agency or under "Recycling" in the Yellow Pages.

Even if you can't recycle it, it may still be better for the environment to send an old, energy-guzzling refrigerator to the scrap heap than to keep using it.

Extended-service contacts

With an extended warranty or service contract, you're betting that the appliance will break down after the manufacturer's warranty expires, but before the service contract does, and that the cost of repairs will exceed the cost of the contract. That's possible, but it's a long shot. Not only are products more reliable today, but they are often made in such a way that any defects tend to appear early—within the first 90 days or so, when the original warranty is in effect.

If the idea of extra protection is appealing, consider using your credit card. Buying items with American Express and "gold" Visa and MasterCards automatically doubles the manufacturer's warranty, increasing it a maximum of one year. Some standard Visa and MasterCards also offer double-warranty protection.

When a covered product breaks down, call the credit-card company for information about how to proceed. You'll need the original store receipt and a copy of the manufacturer's warranty at the time you file a claim. (Usually, you must file within 30 days of the breakdown.) In addition to their warranties, some cards toss in 90 days' worth of purchase insurance to replace or repair merchandise that is stolen or damaged.

Credit-card purchases receive further protection under the terms of the Fair Credit and Billing Act. It lets you "charge back" the purchase of an unsatisfactory product or service before you've paid the bill. You can request that the card issuer withhold payment to the retailer. The protection applies to items priced more than $50 and bought in your home state or within 100 miles of it.

Our advice is to avoid extended-service contracts. You're better off saving the money. If you feel you need protection, buy with a credit card with double-warranty protection.

Repair Histories

Every year, CONSUMER REPORTS asks its subscribers to share their experiences with various products by answering questions on the Annual Questionnaire. From that comes the automobile Frequency-of-Repair charts, beginning on page 275, and the repair histories for various brands of major appliances, electronic items, and other products you'll find in this chapter.

Repair Histories show the percentage of products in each brand that have ever been repaired, as reported to us by subscribers in the survey. They apply only to brands, not to specific models of these products. And they can only suggest future trends, not predict them exactly. A company can change product design or quality control enough to affect reliability. But over the years, our findings have been very consistent, enough for us to be confident that our Repair Histories can improve your chances of getting a trouble-free product.

Repair Histories for different product types are not directly comparable. That's because of differences in age and usage, and the years included in the graph.

Some of these Repair Histories have already appeared in the 1996 monthly issues of CONSUMER REPORTS; some are appearing here for the first time; others will be updated in 1997 issues of CONSUMER REPORTS.

VCRs

Based on more than 220,000 responses to our 1995 Annual Questionnaire. Readers were asked about any repairs to VCRs bought between 1990 and 1995. Data have been standardized to eliminate differences among brands due solely to age and how much the VCRs were used. Differences of less than 3 points aren't meaningful.

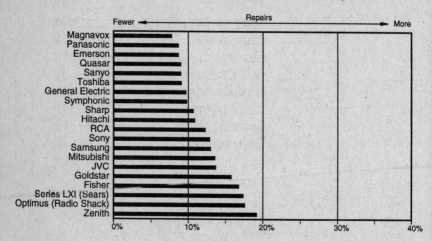

Television sets: 19-inch and 20-inch

Based on more than 76,000 responses to our 1995 Annual Questionnaire. Readers were asked about any repairs to 19-inch or 20-inch color TV sets bought new between 1990 and 1995. Data have been standardized to eliminate differences among brands due to age and usage. Differences of less than 3 points aren't meaningful.

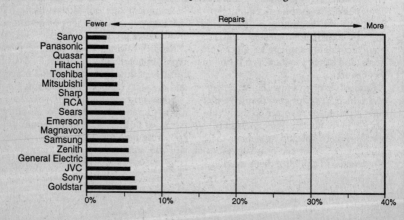

Television sets: 25- to 27-inch

Based on more than 90,000 responses to our 1995 Annual Questionnaire. Readers were asked about any repairs to 25- to 27-inch stereo, color TV sets bought new between 1990 and 1995. Data have been standardized to eliminate differences among brands due to age and usage. Differences of less than 3 points aren't meaningful.

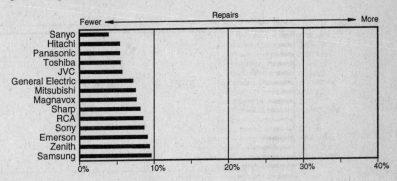

Television sets: 31- to 35 inch

Based on more than 18,000 responses to our 1995 Annual Questionnaire. Readers were asked about any repairs to 31- to 35-inch stereo color TV sets bought between 1990 and 1995. Data have been standardized to eliminate differences among brands due to age and usage. Differences of less than 3 points aren't meaningful.

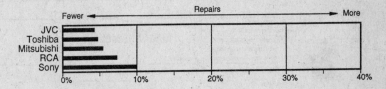

Compact-disc players

Based on almost 109,000 responses to our 1995 Annual Questionnaire. Readers were asked about any repairs to single-play or changer tabletop models bought new between 1991 and 1995. Data have been standardized to eliminate differences among brands due to age and usage. Differences of less than 4 points are not meaningful.

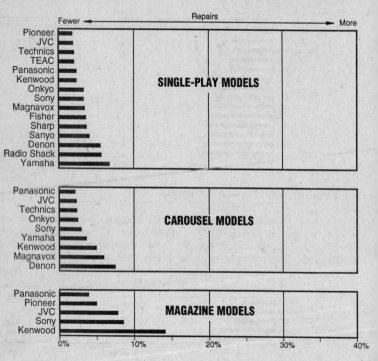

Full-sized VHS camcorders

Based on more than 17,000 responses to our 1995 Annual Questionnaire. Readers were asked about any repairs to VHS camcorders bought new between 1989 and 1995. Data have been standardized to eliminate differences among brands due to age and usage. Differences of less than about 3 points aren't meaningful. Full-sized VHS repair rates cannot be compared directly with those of compact camcorders, because the full-sized models tended to be older than the compacts.

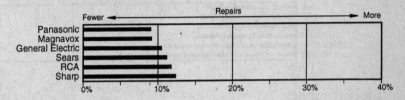

Compact camcorders

Based on more than 51,000 responses to our 1995 Annual Questionnaire. Readers were asked about any repairs to compacts (8mm, Hi8, or VHS-C) bought new between 1990 and 1995. Data have been standardized to eliminate differences among brands due to age and usage. Differences of less than about 3 points aren't meaningful. Repair rates of compacts cannot be compared directly with those of full-sized VHS models.

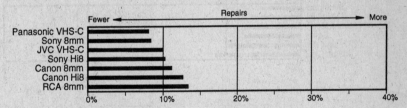

Gas ranges

Based on almost 22,000 responses to our 1995 Annual Questionnaire. Readers were asked about any repairs to freestanding, single-oven, self-cleaning gas ranges bought new between 1988 and 1995. Data have been standardized to eliminate differences among brands due to age. Differences of less than 4 points aren't meaningful.

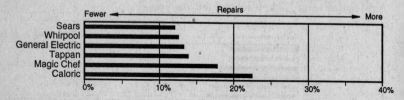

Electric ranges

Based on more than 38,000 responses to our 1995 Annual Questionnaire. Readers were asked about any repairs to freestanding, single-oven, self-cleaning, electric ranges with a smooth top or conventional coil burners bought new between 1989 and 1995. Data have been standardized to eliminate differences among brands due to age. Differences of less than 3 points aren't meaningful.

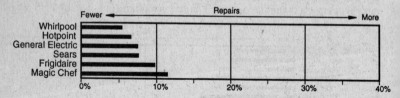

Side-by-side refrigerators

Based on almost 35,000 responses to our 1995 Annual Questionnaire. Readers were asked about any repairs to full-sized side-by-side refrigerators bought new between 1989 and 1995. Data have been standardized to eliminate differences among brands due solely to age. Differences of less than about 4 points aren't meaningful.

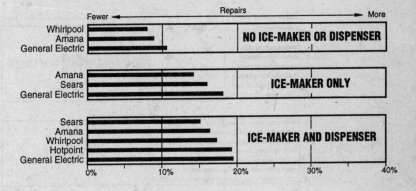

Top-freezer refrigerators

Based on more than 65,000 responses to our 1995 Annual Questionnaire. Readers were asked about any repairs to full-sized, top-freezer, two-door, no-frost refrigerators bought new between 1989 and 1995. Data have been standardized to eliminate differences among brands due solely to age. Differences of less than about 3 points aren't meaningful.

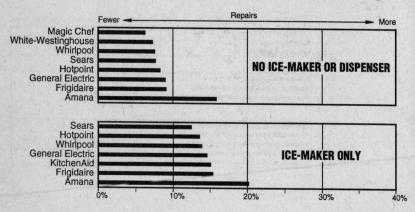

Washing machines

Based on more than 139,000 responses to our 1995 Annual Questionnaire. Readers were asked about any repairs to full-sized washers bought new between 1989 and 1995. Data have been standardized to eliminate difference among brands due to age and usage. Differences of less than 3 points aren't meaningful.

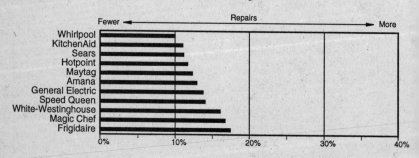

Clothes dryers

Based on more than 125,000 responses to our 1995 Annual Questionnaire. Readers were asked about any repairs to full-sized electric or gas clothes dryers bought new between 1989 and 1995. Data have been standardized to eliminate differences among brands due to age and usage. Differences of less than 3 points aren't meaningful.

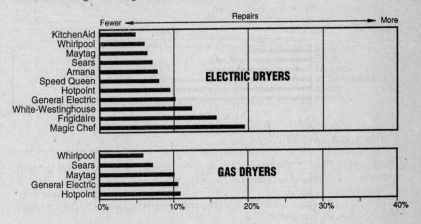

Dishwashers

Based on more than 137,000 responses to our 1995 Annual Questionnaire. Readers were asked about any repairs to installed dishwashers bought new between 1989 and 1995. Data have been standardized to eliminate differences among brands due solely to age and usage. Differences of less than 4 points aren't meaningful.

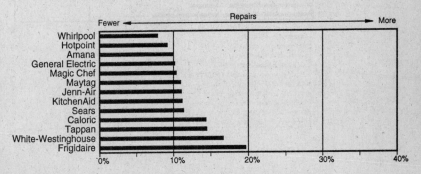

Types of mowers

Based on more than 146,000 responses to our 1995 Annual Questionnaire. Readers were asked about any repairs to manual, electric, or gasoline walk-behind mowers, riding mowers, or lawn tractors bought new between 1989 and 1995. Data have been standardized to eliminate differences among types due solely to age and usage. Differences of less than 3 points are not meaningful.

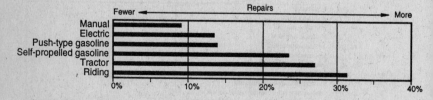

Push-type gasoline mowers

Based on more than 36,000 responses to our 1995 Annual Questionnaire. Readers were asked about any repairs to push-type gasoline mowers with a cutting swath less than 25 inches that was bought new between 1989 and 1995. Data have been standardized to eliminate differences among brands due solely to age and usage. Differences of less than 3 points are not meaningful.

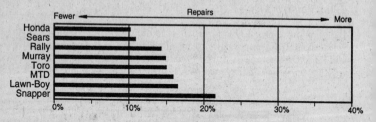

Self-propelled gasoline mowers

Based on more than 27,000 responses to our 1995 Annual Questionnaire. Readers were asked about any repairs to self-propelled gasoline mowers with a cutting swath less than 25 inches that was bought new between 1989 and 1995. Data have been standardized to eliminate differences among brands due to age and usage. Differences of less than 3 points aren't meaningful.

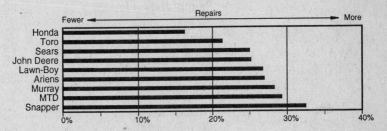

Tractors & riding mowers

Based on more than 18,000 responses to our 1995 Annual Questionnaire. Readers were asked about any repairs to tractors or rider type mowers with a cutting swath of 25 inches or more that was bought new between 1990 and 1995. Data have been standardized to eliminate differences among brands due solely to age and usage. Differences of less than 5 points are not meaningful.

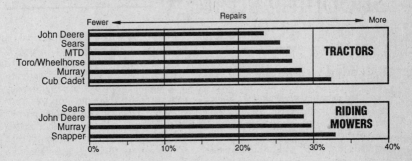

AUDIO & VIDEO GEAR

Shopping strategy

Three things to think about before you buy electronic gear.

Extended warranty?

Extended warranties are almost always a bad deal, for two reasons. First, electronic gear tends to be reliable and long-lived. If solid-state circuitry is going to fail, it usually fails early, well within the manufacturer's warranty. Entertainment gear, especially components with few or no moving parts, often lasts for 10 years or more, problem-free. Second, many extended warranties don't extend the manufacturer's warranty significantly. They run concurrently, duplicating existing coverage.

Prepare for a hard sell—stores make a lot of money from selling this paper. A better strategy: Buy with a credit card that doubles the manufacturer's warranty.

If equipment breaks, however, repairs can be costly. You can improve your chances of avoiding a troublesome product by checking our advice on brand reliability. (See the "reliability" section in each report and the Brand Repair Histories, page 11). The brand histories are based on reader experiences with actual products.

When to buy

Sales are usually plentiful during the winter holiday season, when most home-entertainment gear is sold. You're also likely to encounter sale prices in the spring, when retailers want to clear out old models to make room for new arrivals. New models of audio and video equipment are introduced during second and third quarters, and then reach retailers' shelves by summer and end of the year.

Where to buy

Specialty stores and boutiques usually boast soundproof listening rooms and good service. Expect models from high-end brands and prices close to suggested retail. Installation services are usually available.

Electronics/appliance superstores like Circuit City, Best Buy, and Nobody Beats the Wiz are hectic, high-volume selling machines. Radio Shack has recently joined the superstore crowd with its 100,000-square-foot Incredible Universe outlets. Such superstores now account for the bulk of electronic equipment purchases. They usually stock lots of models from the big, fast-selling brands—Sony, Pioneer, JVC, and the like—and may have listening rooms. Many also offer installation services. But the environment can be crowded and pressure to buy quite strong.

Don't assume that prices are always the lowest in superstores. Some items may be marked way down, while others may be close to suggested retail. Sale-priced models may be "out of stock" and have no definite arrival date.

Department stores that still sell gear offer competitive prices during sales, but selection may be limited. Sales help may be difficult to find and knowledgeable assistance in short supply. Installation may or may not be available.

Mass-merchandisers like Wal-Mart

and Kmart feature mainstream brands like Sharp, Magnavox, RCA, and Sanyo, as well as low-end brands like Soundesign and Yorx. You probably won't find separate audio components at these stores. Don't expect much sales help.

Warehouse clubs like PriceCostco and Sam's Club offer good prices, not service or ambience. Product selection is variable and limited, and brand availability changes all the time. On occasion, you'll discover great bargains on electronic gear. But service is practically nonexistent.

Mail-order operations like Crutchfield or Sound City advertise in stereo and video magazines and publish their own catalogs as well.

Before you buy from a mail-order firm, however, check for complaints with the local consumer-protection agency in the seller's state and municipality. Ask about shipping fees—they can be steep. Find out whether there's a "restocking fee," that is, a charge if you return something. And keep a record of all telephone transactions and correspondence.

Mass-market brands such as RCA, Panasonic, Sony, Pioneer, Technics, and JVC are widely available in stores and by mail, usually at substantial discount. High-end "prestige" brands such as Proton and ProScan video products and Denon and NAD audio products are sold primarily through specialty dealers, with little discounting. Most companies, including Sony and Panasonic, manufacture separate lines of entertainment gear to reach both the popular and the prestige market.

Our tests through the years have shown that prestige brands hold no substantive performance advantage over similarly featured mass-market brands. Indeed, we've found that prestige brands tend to give you fewer features for the money.

Home-theater basics ——————

A home-theater system makes watching TV more like going to the movies by surrounding you with sound.

Home-theater systems are no longer just for videophiles and film buffs. The equipment is easier to come by. Speakers are now sold specifically to augment the viewing experience. Nearly all receivers now have circuitry built in to decode special "surround" sound tracks. Large-screen TV sets often have surround-sound circuitry built in, too.

To make movies seem more real, movie theaters have long surrounded audiences with speakers that make you feel as if you're in the middle of the action. Moviemakers have devised various techniques—Dolby Surround, Lucasfilm THX, AC-3—to shift the sound according to the action. Home-theater systems recreate those effects. The principal means is through a "Dolby Surround" sound track on videotapes, laser discs, and even TV programming, played through a "Dolby Pro Logic" decoder.

In a full-fledged home-theater system, the receiver, or a stand-alone decoder processes the sound track and plays it through five or six carefully placed speakers, three in front to carry most of the action and two at the sides or rear to carry ambient background sound.

Building a full home-theater system with separate components—receiver, VCR, speakers, TV set—can easily cost upwards of $1500. The system will take up plenty of real estate in your living room, and it can be a chore to wire together. But you can often arrange for professional installation.

Though generally less powerful and less flexible than component systems, packaged audio systems promise to make home theater simpler and more compact. For $400 and up, you can buy "home theater in a box"—usually five speakers and a processor that you connect to your TV set and VCR.

You can also get big sound without installing a full-fledged system. See "Home-Theater Shortcuts," opposite.

The gear

Receiver. TV sets with Dolby Pro Logic circuitry are expensive and scarce. Most home-theater systems use a Pro Logic-equipped receiver, available for as little as $250. If you really want to approach the movie-theater experience, you'll need a receiver with at least 65 watts for all three front channels.

Loudspeakers. The left and right front speakers produce most of the sound and should be the best quality you can afford.

The front speakers should sit to either side of your TV set, far enough apart to produce a noticeable stereo effect. Ideally, the two speakers and the listener should form an equilateral triangle. If you already own a decent set of stereo speakers, they will probably suffice. For more information, see the report on speakers, page 43, and Ratings, page 56.

The center speaker carries most of the dialogue and sounds that move across the center screen. If your system's center channel has more than 65 watts of power, be prepared to buy a center speaker that's up to the challenge; many of the cheapest models are not. See receivers, page 39. The center speaker should be above or below the TV set. Many are designed to lie "flat" across the top of a 27-inch set.

Because the center speaker has to be positioned near the TV set, it must be magnetically shielded so it won't interfere with the TV set's picture. Since it's carrying mostly dialogue, the center speaker doesn't have to reach into the deep bass—unless you choose to use the "wide" Pro Logic mode on the receiver. The "wide" mode calls for a center speaker that can handle low bass (from, say, music or sound effects) in addition to the midrange and high-treble frequencies. In any case, the center speaker should come close to matching the sound of the left and right speakers.

Because the rear speakers handle only ambient sounds—applause, the din of traffic, the rumble of distant helicopters—they can be smaller and lower in quality than the front speakers. Surround speakers should go toward the rear of the room, high on the wall, if practical. They should point away from the listener to increase reflected sound, enhancing the surround effect. Almost any set of serviceable speakers will do, including a set from an older sound system. You can also buy additional satellite speakers of some three-piece systems or use an inexpensive pair of stereo speakers. See the loudspeaker Ratings, page 56.

TV set. Your present set may well suffice. It need not have fancy sound, since you'll probably bypass its speakers. (To let you do that, the set must have audio output jacks.) It need not be huge, though big-screen TV sets are more and more in demand. If you opt for a set with a screen 31 inches or larger, or for a rear-projection set, you'll need to sit far enough away so you don't see the scan lines. A rule of thumb: The closest recommended viewing distance is four times the screen size. See TV sets, page 30.

VCR. Only a VCR with stereo "hi-fi" capability can produce the sound you need. Such models now cost less than $300. See VCRs, page 33.

Home-theater shortcuts

A full home-theater setup may exceed your budget, your level of interest, or the space in your living room. If so, consider more modest alternatives. None of these rival the sound of true home theater, but all will be more "theatrical" than the sound of a TV set alone.

Fewer speakers. A home-theater system can have fewer than five speakers and still create a semblance of surround sound by using Dolby Pro Logic settings that electronically fill in some of the missing sound.

The "phantom" mode allows you to dispense with the center speaker by distributing center signals equally to the main left and right channels. You can also skip the center speaker if you use the TV set's internal speakers—but those speakers are often low in sound quality.

"Dolby 3" mode uses only the three front speakers; the surround speakers are not used. Instead, delayed surround signals are sent to the front left and right channels, creating a slight echo effect.

No Pro Logic. You can improve the stereo effect from a TV set by connecting a pair of external speakers. A plain stereo receiver can amplify the sound of any TV set, as long as the set has audio output jacks. If your TV set doesn't have those jacks, you can use a hi-fi VCR as the TV tuner, to pass the signal along to the receiver and the TV set. You won't hear broadcast TV sound in stereo unless the set itself has stereo capability or you have a stereo hi-fi VCR. Some TV sets have ambience modes, such as "SRS" or "SEq," that can create pleasing surround effects.

Sound-system basics

You don't have to pay a lot to get superb sound, and you can often get it in one easy package.

Sound systems come in all-in-one packages that you just plug in. They also come as a carefully selected and auditioned collection of individual components that take hours to wire up.

Until recently, if you took the simple road, you sacrificed a lot in sound quality. Manufacturers offered packaged systems as an option for people who couldn't afford separate pieces or didn't care enough to pick each component. Anyone serious about music would build a system piece by carefully selected piece.

That's no longer true. Today, packaged systems—rack systems, minisystems, even some boom boxes—can play music decently, even admirably. Speaker quality, amplifier power, and convenience features are the main items that push models up in price.

To know what equipment to buy, ask yourself some questions:

■ **How do you listen to music?** Listening to music for its own sake, in a quiet place without distraction, is the most discriminating type of listening. If you listen seriously, a system built of individual components is the surest road to highest fidelity, mostly because such an approach lets you choose the best speakers. The cassette deck is the other component whose quality is most likely to affect what you hear; choose one with Dolby C or Dolby S noise reduction. A CD player that's the same brand as the cassette deck can simplify the recording process. Look for enough receiver power to drive big speakers or two pairs of speakers. Overall, a component system that costs $1000 to $1500 should satisfy most people who listen seriously, though one can spend a lot more.

Even if you tend to listen while you're engaged in some other activity, sound fidelity may still be important enough for you not to skimp on speakers and cassette deck. But don't spend money on features or fidelity you don't need. Inexpensive components, a rack system, or a minisystem might do nicely. So might a large boom box.

If you listen on the go, you can get a good portable CD player for less than $100 or a radio/tape player for $50. Or consider a good quality boom box—the best of them sound nearly as good as a decent minisystem.

■ **How much can you spend?** If you are on a limited budget, consider a minisystem. Or start with a basic component system: a low-priced receiver ($250 or so) and an inexpensive CD changer ($200 or less). Spend the most you can on speakers. And shop around—discounts of 20 or 30 percent are common.

■ **Where will you be listening?** Room size and "liveness"—whether there are a lot of hard surfaces to reflect sound or soft, upholstered ones to absorb it—affect the quality of the sound. You'll need more receiver power to fill a large room or a plush room.

■ **What kind of music do you listen to?** If you like to listen to loud, deep bass—be it Bach organ recitals or Nine Inch Nails rock songs— you'll need a more powerful receiver and bigger speakers than if your tastes run to quieter music.

■ **Are you upgrading an old system?** Audio components are generally long-lived. The simplest way to upgrade an existing system is to improve on the speakers. If your receiver is more than 15 years old, it lacks digital tuning, a remote control, home-theater electronics, and other useful features found on current models. Unlike older cassette decks, some modern decks can make tapes with just a smidgen less fidelity than you'd find on a CD.

Sound-system options

Minisystem. A small system in an all-in-one package offers reasonably good overall performance. Compared with a system of separate components, it's cheaper, more compact, and simpler to hook up. Just attach a simple connector or two, plug in the system, and play. Unlike a component system, most minisystems can't be upgraded with bigger speakers or other components, nor can you add a second pair of speakers to send music to another room. Minisystems, even very good ones, are likely to deliver slightly lower sound quality than even a low-priced component system because of limited speakers and unimpressive cassette decks. Minisystems also usually lack adjustable bass and treble controls, features that help overcome speaker defects.

Prices range from $200 to more than $1500. See the report on minisystems, page 42.

Boom box. These combine an AM/FM stereo radio with built-in antennas, one or two cassette decks and, quite often, a CD player—all in a portable package that runs on either household current or batteries. Models range in weight from less than 10 to more than 20 pounds.

Smaller boxes usually have nondetachable speakers that lack the wherewithal to reproduce sound faithfully. Larger ones often come with good-sized speakers that can be detached and moved for a better stereo effect. Overall sound quality can be quite pleasing in the bigger boxes, though not on a par with a decent rack or component system. Nor can boom boxes play as loudly or as deep into the bass range as minisystems can. You'll pay more for a remote control or speakers with a better reach into treble and bass.

Prices range from about $50 to $150 for a small box; $150 to $250 or more for bigger ones. Price correlates with size and whether there's a CD player.

Rack system. Like their smaller minisystem cousins, rack systems are a package deal, but with full-sized components dressed in furniture-style cabinetry. Unlike minisystems, rack systems require assembly (the cabinet) and some wiring.

Rack systems come with floor-standing speakers, and with plenty to power them—at least 80 watts per channel. A dual cassette deck, CD player, and remote control are standard. Higher-priced models include home-theater capabilities. The size of the speakers allows good bass, which moves rack systems a notch up in quality from minisystems. Overall, the best rack systems perform on a par with and give you much of the versatility of a decent component system, but at a lower cost. Some manufacturers cut costs by cheapening the cabinets, most of which are made of plastic-covered particle board. Others cut corners by excluding Dolby C noise-reduction circuitry from their cassette decks. But unlike minisystems, most rack systems can record on Type IV tape.

Expect to pay $500 to $1200 or more. You should be able to get a good rack system for $800.

Component system. The most flexible type of system, capable of the highest sound quality, a component system is the choice for serious listeners. You can choose the best of what each manufacturer offers, upgrade individual components, or add new ones. The downside: A component system costs more and takes some effort to set up. A typical system includes a receiver, a CD player, one or two pairs of speakers, maybe a cassette deck, even your old turntable. Most receivers also allow you to hook up video equipment—a TV set, VCR, laser-disc player. If you'll be making tapes from CDs, consider getting a cassette deck and CD player of the same brand. That way, features that make it easier to tape, such as synchronized starting, are more likely to be available.

A receiver itself incorporates several components—the amplifier, a preamplifier, and a digital AM/FM tuner. Purists have long maintained that separate devices for each of those functions provide the best possible sound. While sensitive lab instruments might be able to tell the difference between separates and a top-notch receiver, human ears cannot, we find.

Expect to pay $800 for a good basic system, $1000 to $1500 for a full-featured one. Spending more than $1500 buys more features, not more sound quality—nice-looking speakers, juke-box CD player, ultrapowerful receiver, and so forth. Once you enter audiophile land, the sky's the limit.

System setup

Boom boxes are the simplest of all systems to use: If you run them on batteries, you don't even need to plug them in. Minisystems come next in simplicity; just connect the speakers and antenna and you're set. The manufacturer includes speakers that match the minisystem's receiver, eliminating some of the decisions needed to put together a component

system. Rack systems also come with speakers that are right for the system, but they require some assembly and stringing of cables.

Component systems require more decisions, including how powerful the receiver needs to be and how well it matches the speakers. Once you've figured out your component choices, shop for best price. If you can't install the system yourself, you can hire someone to do it. Our spot-check of stores around the country showed that fees for this service range from $45 to $75 an hour.

Power decisions. As a rule, the more power a receiver can deliver, the louder you can play music. To fill a living room with loud, undistorted sound, you usually need 65 to 100 watts per channel (each channel corresponds to one speaker). If you loudly play recordings with strong, deep bass or with a wide dynamic range, or if your speakers require extra power, stay close to 100 watts. For a small room—a bedroom or dorm room—you need about 35 or 40 watts per channel to play music loud. With less than 20 watts per channel, as you find on some minisystems and boom boxes, don't expect to play loud bass.

Power claims tend to be lower for Pro Logic modes than for stereo mode. Look for Pro Logic power that's even across the front—80-80-80, say. To meet Federal guidelines, manufacturers are conservative in how they rate receivers' power. Our own measurements are often higher than the manufacturers'.

Don't skimp on power. Inadequate power can do more than just reduce your enjoyment of the music. When a receiver runs short on power—when playing peaks in the music, say—it produces a harsh distortion called clipping that can damage speakers. Keeping the volume control turned down won't necessarily help; the effect can occur even when the knob is only halfway up.

Speakers/receiver compatibility. As a receiver runs, its power supply and amplifier heat up. The heat is due to the power the amplifier puts out; the amount of heat also depends on the resistance of the speakers—the impedance—measured in ohms. At a given power level, the lower the impedance, the higher the current draw and the hotter things get. Thus, a pair of 4-ohm speakers can heat up the receiver more than a pair of 8-ohm speakers. Therein lies a problem in mating speakers with receivers.

Although a speaker's impedance has nothing to do with its quality, you'll find more and more 4-ohm models as you go up in price. The mass-market brands such as Sony, Pioneer, and Radio Shack generally include a mix of speakers rated at 8 and 6 ohms. Companies like Bose and Cerwin-Vega market different lines for different retail venues, some with 8-ohm ratings, some with 6, some with 4. You'll find many of the high-end "salon" speaker lines are made up entirely of 4-ohm models.

The labels on many receivers say they shouldn't be used with 4-ohm speakers. (That restriction is necessary for a receiver to earn a seal from Underwriters Laboratories.) What happens if you ignore the label? Probably not much. But monitor the temperature of the receiver. If its cabinet gets uncomfortably hot to the touch after a half-hour's play of bass-heavy music, you're probably overheating internal parts. Turn the volume down to cool things off and think about getting a new receiver.

Positioning speakers. The best position for two speakers: an equal distance from where you'll be listening, at least six feet apart, separated by about a 60-degree angle.

With a satellite system that has three speakers, you can place the large bass module practically anywhere in the room. You'd put the small satellites in the same triangle you'd use for a pair. In a five-or six-speaker system, you maintain that triangle with the front right and left speakers and put the center front speaker above or below the television set, with the two ambience speakers angled away from you and just behind you.

These positions, of course, are the ideal. In most homes, you must put the speakers on the bookshelf or next to the couch. Experiment if you can—speaker placement can greatly affect the sound of your system. The closer a speaker is to the corner of a room, the stronger the bass. That can give a boost to a small, bass-light speaker. But putting a big, bass-rich speaker right in the corner can make the bass sound muddy or boomy. The effect of placement varies speaker by speaker.

Adding a second pair. Most receivers provide outputs—labeled Main and Remote or A and B—for two pairs of speakers in stereo mode, so that you can listen away from the receiver, in a different room. If you want to play two pairs loudly, you need a receiver with 100 watts or more per channel, since two pairs of speakers need more power than one.

In addition, some receivers are better suited than others for adding a second pair of speakers. If the remote speakers are on separate circuits from the main speakers—"in parallel"—all four speakers should behave normally. But if the extra pair are on the same circuit as the main speakers, "in series," the sound will be altered and often degraded. (Two pairs of speakers in parallel produce the equivalent of a lower impedance, which can cause the same problems that 4-ohm speakers do.)

A receiver has the preferred parallel

design if its switches and output jacks have labels that refer to three modes—A, B, and A+B—with a higher impedance noted for the A+B mode. Otherwise, you can't easily tell. A knowledgeable salesperson might be able to tell from the instruction manual. Or you can call the manufacturer (see page 339).

TV sets

If you don't need a lot of extras in your TV, you can find excellent value among 25- and 27-inch sets.

Last CR report: *March 1996*
Brand Repair Histories: *pages 12 to 13*
Price range: *$100 to $5500*

The types

Small sets. Sets with a 13-inch screen are often regarded as "second" sets, so makers tend to make them plain. Expect monophonic sound and sparse features. Price: $150 to $400.

Sets with a 19- or 20-inch screen are also seen as second sets. The 19-inch sets are made to be cheaper than 20-inch sets, with fewer features. Most lack high-end picture refinements such as a comb filter, and most have mono sound. Models with stereo sound usually have extra inputs for plugging in a VCR and a laser-disc player. The built-in sound is equivalent to a mediocre boom box. Price $200 to $500.

Mini sets. Color TV sets with screens of three inches or so remain in the fancy-gadget stage of evolution. On many models, the picture comes from a liquid-crystal display (LCD), rather than a regular picture tube. To look its best, the picture has to be viewed nearly head on. On some LCD sets, the picture is acceptable, but not as good as on tube sets. Bright outdoor lighting makes the picture all but vanish; even in shaded areas, the picture is only marginally acceptable. Sets

with a screen of 5 to 10 inches use a conventional cathode-ray picture tube. Price: LCD sets, $150 to $600; 5- to 10-inch conventional sets, $180 to $400.

Mid-sized sets. TV sets with a 25-inch screen tend to be economy models; those with 27-inch screens are usually priced higher and frequently offer more features, including picture-in-picture, special sound systems, and a universal remote control. Price: $220 to $1400.

Large sets. Manufacturers aim their 31-inch and larger direct-view sets at the home-theatre crowd. Those sets usually boast enhanced-sound systems and various high-end features, such as the ability to recall customized picture and sound settings. The largest cathode-ray-tube sets weigh hundreds of pounds and are too wide and too high for conventional component shelving. Price: $550 to $3000.

Rear-projection sets. These offer still more picture area—40 to 80 diagonal inches—but less clarity than a set with a conventional picture tube. You'll want a viewing distance of at least 10 feet for a 50-inch set, more for larger ones. Brightness and, to some extent, color vary as you change your angle of view. Large sets and rear-projection sets come with plenty of features, such as ambient sound and custom settings. Price: $1500 to $8500.

What's new

Lower prices for larger screen sizes. Now that the larger sets have been on the market for a few years, their prices are dropping. Prices for 27-inch sets we reported on in early 1995 ranged from $400 to $650; 1996 prices ranged from $350 to $500. Prices for 31- and 32-inch sets have dropped substantially. Once ranging from $1000 to more than $2500, they now start as low as $500.

Features trickle down. Comb filter, picture-in-picture, on-screen menus, MTS stereo, dark screen, flat tube—features once found only on top-of-the-line models—are showing up on smaller and less expensive sets.

New picture tubes. They're now squarer and flatter. According to our tests, the change doesn't affect picture quality.

Reliability

Among 31- to 35-inch sets purchased new from 1990 to 1995, Sony was more troubleprone than JVC, Toshiba, and Mitsubishi sets. Among 25- to 27-inch sets, more reliable brands included Sanyo, Hitachi, Panasonic, Toshiba, and JVC. Goldstar and Sony brands of 19- or 20-inch sets stood out as slightly more prone to repair. See the Brand Repair Histories, pages 12 and 13.

For advice on shopping for electronic gear, see page 22.

Shopping strategy

Most TV sets today have a picture that's close to the best quality possible under current broadcast standards. Comb filters and dark screens, which allow a set to render greater detail and produce punchier pictures, are becoming commonplace on 27-inch and larger sets.

Sound quality is more variable. In general, sound gets better as sets get bigger. Medium-sized sets (19 and 20 inches) deliver sound no better than a mediocre boom box. But TV sound is easy to improve by playing it through good external speakers. Audio outputs are common on sets 20 inches and up. Some high-end sets have an amplifier to power external speakers. For more about boosting TV sound, see the report on home theater, page 24.

The best values in big-screen TV are 25-inch sets, which sell for as little as $300, although that may change if prices for 27-inch sets drop to that level. The 25-inch sets are cheaper, in part, because they lack a lot of features common on 27-inch models. (The sets we looked at for the March 1996 report lacked a comb filter, and a few lacked the audio jacks needed for connecting to a home-theater setup.) But the picture quality of 25-inch sets varied considerably, as did that of their 27-inch cousins: The best had very good picture quality—comparable to that of the tested 27-inch models.

Don't put too much stock in the differences in picture quality you see at the store. You can't be sure that those sets are getting a uniform picture signal or that they have been uniformly adjusted.

Decide on the screen size. The world of TV sets is organized by screen size, which ranges from a few inches to more than six feet. The 27-inch size is usually sufficiently large and carries enough features to be the primary TV set in most households. A 25-inch set generally costs less. See "The types," on page 30.

Decide on the features. Features that add to price include a comb filter, sound enhancements, picture-in-picture, and a universal remote control that can work the whole video setup. See "Key features," below.

The easiest brands to find. RCA, Magnavox, and Zenith are the biggest-selling brands by far in 27-inch and smaller sizes. In larger TV sets, the big names are those plus Toshiba, Sony, Mitsubishi, and Zenith.

Key features

Recommended, if available:

Active channel scan lets the tuner run through the channels, pausing at each for a few seconds, when you press a button on the remote.

Automatic volume control, also called Smart Sound, keeps the TV volume from jumping when a commercial comes on or when you change channels.

Beeping remote helps you find a misplaced remote on some Magnavox sets.

Comb-filter circuitry. It increases resolution, cleans up image outlines, and eliminates most extraneous colors. Most 27-inch and larger sets have it. We recommend this feature.

Flesh-tone correction automatically adjusts skin tones that are too green or red.

Multichannel TV stereo (MTS) is a built-in stereo decoder and amplifier that reproduces stereo broadcasts.

Remote control features channel selection and volume, with less emphasis on tape controls.

Video jacks are better than the coaxial antenna jack for plugging in a VCR or other video gear. For video games or a camcorder, a set with additional jacks on the front makes hooking up easy.

Video noise-reduction filter smooths out "noisy" images.

White-balance controls let you tint background whites toward red or blue.

Useful for particular needs:

Alarm and sleep timer is a built-in clock that turns the set on or off at a predetermined time.

Audio output jacks let you run the set's sound through a hi-fi system.

Ambience modes go by names like Sound Retrieval System (SRS) and Spatial

Equalization (SEq). They're electronically enhanced stereo that attempts to envelop the listener in sound.

Channel block-out renders certain channels unviewable—usually, to limit a child's viewing.

Channel labeling (or captioning) is helpful if you have lots of channels. This lets you program channel names—ABC, MTV, CNN, ESPN—to appear on screen with the channel number.

Commercial-skip timer lets you change channels during the commercial and then automatically returns to the original channel after the time period you've selected.

Dark screens enhance contrast, particularly in a brightly lit room.

Dolby Pro Logic is one type of ambience mode. See the discussion of home theater, page 24.

External-speaker amplifier allows the set to drive a pair of external speakers. That improves both the sound quality and the stereo effect, but it's unnecessary if your set is hooked up to an audio/video receiver.

Multilingual menus are in English, Spanish, or French.

Picture-in-picture (PIP) lets you see another channel or video source as a small picture superimposed on the picture you're watching. The best PIP design has its own tuner; otherwise, you must hook up to a VCR or other video source. A cable box requires more complex connections—possibly an extra box.

Programmable audio/video lets you customize picture and sound settings. On some sets, each input retains its own settings to compensate for signal differences from VCRs and camcorders.

S-video jack is the best way to plug in high-band components—S-VHS VCRs, Hi8 camcorders, and laser-disc players.

Separate audio program (SAP) lets a

viewer switch to another soundtrack—say, in Spanish—with certain broadcasts.

Not worth paying extra for:

Flat screens are supposed to reduce distortion at the picture's edges, but we saw little effect in our tests.

Horizontal resolution of more than 425 lines. It can't be seen. Horizontal resolution is a measure of the detail a set can display on its screen. The numbers manufacturers advertise are not a reliable guide since different measurement techniques are used. In addition, the numbers they claim are overstated. A set claiming 600-line-resolution may actually have 425 lines of video.

VCRs

Features make the black box easier and easier to use. Worth getting: VCR Plus+ or other programming aids and various features.

Last CR report: *November 1996*
Ratings: *page 66*
Brand Repair Histories: *page 12*
Price range: *$125 to $925*

The formats

Most VCRs are **VHS** models, in either hi-fi or monophonic versions. Monophonic VCRs record sound decently; hi-fi models record near-CD quality sound and can play surround-sound movies.

VCRs in other formats—**8mm** and the "high band" formats of **S-VHS** and **Hi8**—are scarce. High-band VCRs boast excellent picture quality, special effects, and editing features but require expensive tapes and a TV set good enough to show off their abilities.

What's new

Manufacturers have been producing new and improved designs and putting these conveniences on cheaper and cheaper machines. Auto clock set, now on many models updates the time automatically. A new breed of programming tool makes programming a VCR an intuitive experience. StarSight is built into some TV sets and VCRs and is sold as an add-on black box under the Magnavox name. Like the tabular listings provided by cable channels or in the newspaper, StarSight lays out programs by time a week in advance and is updated daily. Unlike those printed listings, it lets you view the listing by type of program (sports, science/nature, and so forth), choose a program, and set your VCR to record a show with a few button presses. The guide costs $15 to start up and then about $4 a month, about what TV Guide costs by subscription. Other on-screen guides such as TV Guide Plus and VCR Plus+ are also becoming more available.

VCR Plus+ is now available built-in as a step-up feature in just about all VCR lines for $20 to $50 extra. To tape a show, you enter the numeric code printed in TV listings. A feature called Commercial Advance, currently on a few GE, Hitachi, Panasonic, Proscan, RCA, and Samsung models, "eliminates all commercials during playback" by locating fades-to-black, changes in sound level, and other clues, and then fast-forwards past them. It was very accurate on the 30 hours of taped programs we tried it on.

New features on this year's crop of VCRs include Plug and Play and Index

Plus+. Plug and Play VCRs self-start an automatic clock set and channel set sequence when connected to a signal source and wall power. Index Plus+ is a videotape archive feature that provides indexed access to recorded programs.

Reliability

According to our 1995 Annual Questionnaire, 1 in 10 of the machines our readers bought from 1990 to 1995 ever needed repair. Magnavox, Panasonic, Emerson, Quasar, Sanyo, and Toshiba were among the least troublesome brands. Zenith, Optimus (Radio Shack), Series LXI (Sears), Fisher, and Goldstar VCRs were among the most troublesome. See the Brand Repair Histories on page 12.

Shopping strategy

Picture quality, although generally much improved in recent years, is still variable. The price tag is no clue—our tests show no clear correlation between price and picture quality. Spending more can get you a hi-fi model, but it won't show off its CD-quality sound unless you connect the VCR to a good sound system. More money also gets you more features. If you have trouble programming, VCR Plus, a programming aid keyed to codes in daily TV listings, is worthwhile; new aids such as StarSight show the program guide on the TV screen.

A two-head VCR or a basic four-head model is all you need for taping TV programs for viewing later. For movie-watching without special effects, choose a hi-fi model for more theater-like sound. See the report on home theater, page 24.

Decide on the format. The four choices include VHS and 8mm and their high-band versions, S-VHS and Hi8.

Decide on key features. Manufactur-

ers that offer models with VCR Plus+ typically sell a similar model without it. Other steps up the price ladder: hi-fi sound, four heads instead of two, and a jog-shuttle control.

The easiest brands to find. RCA and Magnavox are the biggest-selling brands. Emerson and General Electric, the best-selling low-end brands, are likely to be sold by mass merchandisers and price clubs. Sony tends to price its products on the high side, as do some smaller brands such as Mitsubishi. Other small brands—notably Samsung—may offer good value.

Key features

Recommended:

Auto channel set automatically programs the channel lineup to skip empty channels. Standard on most models.

Auto clock set eliminates the flashing 12:00 by using information in the broadcast signal to set the VCR's clock. Some models offer instead a Daylight Savings Control; it adds or subtracts one hour at the press of a button.

Auto tracking eliminates the need to adjust the tracking control for each tape viewed. It's standard on most models.

Auto speed-switching slows recording from SP to EP if too little tape is left to complete a recording.

Cable-channel capacity of 125 channels is plenty for most cable users, and a standard feature.

Go-to searches the tape by time to find the passage you want to watch.

Index search is similar to Go-to, but more helpful. It places an electronic "bookmark" on the tape each time you begin to record so the VCR can quickly skip to that segment on playback.

Power backup retains clock and program settings during brief power outages.

Programming via menus is almost

universal. A menu on the TV screen prompts you through a sequence of time and channel-selection steps involving the remote or controls on the console.

Quick-start transport cuts the time needed to shift from Stop to Play, Play to Rewind, or Play to Fast Forward. Standard on most VCRs.

Remote control is standard even in low-end models. A universal remote—one that works TV sets, VCRs, and cable boxes of various brands—is now common. A VCR universal remote features tape controls; channel selection is secondary. A well-designed remote is comfortable to hold and has clearly labeled buttons grouped by function and differentiated by size, shape, or color. Often-used buttons should stand out.

VCR Plus+ and other programming aids make programming even simpler than do on-screen menus. VCR Plus+ is sold as a separate product for $40, or as a built-in feature that adds about $20 to $50 to the price of a VCR. After setting up the channel map, you tap in a program code (found in the TV listings of newspapers), and the device automatically orders the VCR into action at the right time. Most versions can program a cable box's multiple channels. Some manual systems, such as Panasonic's Program Director, are almost as convenient to use. A variant of VCR Plus+ called C^3 (Cable Channel Changer) controls the cable box, too, allowing cable subscribers to tape on more than one channel.

Useful for particular needs:

Childproof lock disables the controls or locks the cassette door.

Dimming display turns down the console's display.

Extra heads don't improve the picture; they just produce better special effects. Most VCRs have four heads. Models with two heads (the cheapest models and the typical TV/VCR) can't do special effects such as clean-looking freeze-frames. Some models have six or more heads.

Front-mounted audio and video jacks allow quick and easy hookup of a camcorder or a second VCR.

LP speed is a medium speed, in between SP and EP in length and in picture quality.

Multilingual menus are shown in English, Spanish, or French.

One-button skip lets you fast-forward 30 seconds or a minute with each press of the button, to jump past commercials. Commercial Advance fast-forwards automatically.

Quasi S-VHS playback lets you play back higher-resolution S-VHS tapes in a regular VHS machine, though without S-VHS picture quality.

Useful for people who edit tapes:

Audio dub lets you add music or narration to existing recordings.

Flying erase head lets you insert segments without video glitches.

Title generator identifies scenes.

Jog-shuttle, on the remote or the console, is a two-part control—one part to let you shuttle quickly, the other to slowly jog frame by frame. It's easier to use than separate buttons, especially for editing. On many models, tape-motion controls are made to look like a shuttle wheel.

Not worth paying extra for:

Auto head-cleaning consists of a tiny felt-tipped arm that gently buffs the video heads whenever a tape is inserted. Machines without this feature have worked fine for thousands of hours.

Picture enhancements such as Mitsubishi's Tape Optimization and Sony's Automatic Picture Control are supposed to improve signal quality and thus enhance picture quality. They had little, if any, effect in our viewing tests.

Camcorders

Even inexpensive models produce fine video these days.

Last CR report: *October 1996*
Ratings: *page 63*
Brand Repair Histories: *page 15*
Price range: *$400 to $2100*

The formats

8mm models use cassettes about the size of an audio tape cassette. Most cassettes hold two hours. The tapes won't play in standard VHS VCRs; you must hook the camcorder to the TV set and use it as the playback device. The pictures produced by 8mm camcorders are of similar quality to those from VHS-C, but 8mm produces slightly better sound.

Compact VHS (VHS-C) models use cassettes about the size of a cigarette pack. Tapes typically hold 30 minutes on fast speed, 90 minutes on slow. VHS-C uses an adapter to play tapes in any VHS VCR.

Full-sized VHS camcorders use the same cassettes as a VHS VCR. Most tapes hold two hours at the recording speed typically used (SP). These camcorders are bulky and heavy—more than five pounds. Because you rest them on your shoulder, you'll get slightly steadier shots than you would from a model that's handheld. Camcorders in this format make up less than a quarter of the market.

'Hi-band' formats. There are highband versions, Hi8 and S-VHS-C, with enhanced video resolution. But you'll get the full benefit of that quality only if you watch the tape on a TV set with an S-video input and a Hi8 or SVHS-C tape (which carries a premium price).

Digital video cassette models use the newly-standardized DVC format. See "What's new," below.

What's new

Prices. A model with all the features you're likely to need is priced from $500 to $850. The most significant price drop has been for Hi8 models: The least expensive cost $1200 a few years ago; some now sell for about $850.

A new format: DVC (digital video cassette) models have been introduced by such companies as Sony, Panasonic, JVC, RCA, and Sharp. These models can record very high quality images. Prices are high for now, as is typical of new technology but are expected to drop as availability increases.

Future consumer-priced digital models will have the ability to download recorded images directly to a PC.

New features. Sony's 8mm long-play option provides twice the recording time of SP. At the slower speed, the models we tested provided inferior image quality: Colors tended to flicker noticeably in hue and intensity.

Canon's FlexiZone focusing feature lets you direct the focus to a particular region in the scene by positioning a small rectangle in the viewfinder image. Wherever you move the rectangle is where the camcorder focuses. FlexiZone can also lock the exposure setting to the lighting in that rectangle. FlexiZone works as described but camcorders with manual focus and exposure overrides can handle the same sorts of problems.

Unique designs too new for us to have tested yet: An "eye-control" feature from

Canon has eye-controlled focus and switches, supposedly enabling you to operate most camcorder functions with the movement of an eye. A feature touted by Panasonic lets you program the camcorder for one-touch recording with a desired stop time, thereby allowing the person doing the taping to be in the recording.

Reliability

According to reader surveys, about 1 in 10 compact camcorders bought since 1990 has needed repair. The average repair cost was about $125. Among compact formats, Panasonic VHS-C and Sony 8mm models have been among the more reliable; RCA 8mm and Canon Hi8 models have been among the least reliable. For full-sized VHS camcorders, there was little difference in reliability among the brands examined. See the Brand Repair Histories on page 15.

Shopping strategy

Any camcorder can do a decent job of recording family gatherings or a baby's first steps. While overall picture quality and color vary, picture quality is only loosely connected to price. In our last test, we found some models priced at $600 or so that could produce pictures as good as those costing $800.

Sound quality also separates the formats, with 8mm inherently superior to VHS-C. The built-in microphone on most camcorders, however, would not do justice to a performance of Beethoven's Fifth. All are adequate for speech, and the best would be fine for a grade-school musical or recital.

For general advice on shopping for electronic gear, see page 22.

Decide on the format. The format determines the size of the camcorder and the running-time of the tape. The small formats—8mm and VHS-C—are the biggest sellers. Stepping up to a"high-band" version—Hi8 or S-VHS-C—used to cost extra, but now Hi8 prices overlap with standard models. Such models produce slightly sharper images.

Decide on the features. Spending more than $600 for a non-high-band model buys extra features that may make shooting more convenient or fun but that have little effect on basic performance.

The easiest brands to find. The many various camcorder models are made by only a handful of manufacturers. The biggest sellers are Sony, Matsushita (which manufacturers Panasonic and Quasar), Hitachi, JVC, Thomson (which sells models made by other companies under the RCA and GE names), and Sharp. Sony is the major maker of 8mm camcorders, while Matsushita and JVC dominate the VHS world, including VHS-C.

Electronics stores have the widest selection. Discount stores usually have less selection but good prices. Department stores carry few camcorders.

Key features

Features you'll usually find:

Fade lets you add professional-looking fade-in and fade-out effects. Such transitions between scenes are nice if they're not overused.

Playback controls—Play, Stop, Fast-forward, Rewind—come on all camcorders. They're used when you leave the tape in the camcorder and play it back on the viewfinder or though a TV set or VCR. They also let you reposition the tape before recording.

Record start/stop is usually a red button placed where your thumb rests. Push once to start taping, again to stop.

Speed control on every camcorder includes standard-play, or SP. A few 8mm models have a slower LP speed, which doubles recording time. All VHS-C camcorders have an extended-play, or EP, speed, which triples recording time. The slower speeds almost always mean some loss of picture quality.

Zoom control is typically a rocker switch—press one end to zoom to telephoto, the other to return to normal. On most camcorders, the zoom ratio ranges from 8:1 to 16:1. And some offer a digital zoom to extend the range to about 24:1, but with some fall-off in picture quality. And some models let you vary the zoom speed by pressing harder or more lightly on the switch.

Extras you'll sometimes find:

Audio/video input lets you record material from another camcorder or from a VCR—useful in copying part of someone else's video onto your own.

Battery options let you install a bigger battery than the original. Extra-capacity batteries typically run about twice as long as the one supplied.

Color viewfinder is nice to have if you have to watch an event from behind the camcorder, or if color aids your narration, say, when you're taping a tour of your flower garden. But a color viewfinder isn't any better than a black-and-white one for composing and focusing.

Electronic image stabilization, an increasingly common feature, tries to iron the jitters out of hand-held shots. Effectiveness varies somewhat from brand to brand. Some can slightly mar picture clarity. At best, image stabilizers provide only a moderate improvement in image steadiness. A video tripod is still the best tool for steady shots.

Fast shutter speeds—faster than the "normal" $\frac{1}{60}$th of a second—are useful only to study, say, a golf swing in slow motion or frame by frame. The fastest speeds require bright daylight.

Focus selection lets you choose autofocus, which adjusts for maximum contrast, or manual, for creative effects or problem situations, such as use in low light. With motorized manual focus, you may have to tap buttons repeatedly to focus just right.

Manual controls in many high-end camcorders let you control exposure, shutter speed, white balance, and focus at your option.

Microphone jack lets you use an external microphone. Unlike the built-in microphone, it doesn't pick up noises from the camcorder itself, and your subject can speak right into it, if the cord is long enough.

Refresh charging lets you fully drain the battery before recharging, to help maintain full running time. A battery that's repeatedly recharged when not totally "empty" can lose the ability to "fill" itself.

Remote control can operate the camcorder from afar—useful, primarily indoors, for taping yourself, or for using the camcorder as a playback device. Some are as small as a business card.

Title generator lets you use a built-in character generator to superimpose printed titles and captions.

Receivers

Basic models now offer full video switching, surround-sound capabilities, and lots of power.

Last CR report: *February 1996*
Ratings: *page 52*
Price range: *$150 to $1100*

The types

Basic **stereo-only** receivers make up the low end of the market. They're fine for a conventional component-audio system. A power output of 60 watts or so per channel is the norm. Expect to spend $175 to $250. Some high-end brands offer basic models with more power, for a lot more money.

More than three-quarters of receivers on the market are **A/V "surround sound"** receivers. These have connections for hooking up video gear and audio-switching capability, and they can drive extra "surround sound" speakers.

Dolby Pro Logic is a form of sound processing that converts special coding found on most movie soundtracks and some network TV programs and directs it to three front speakers, for main movie sound, and to two rear speakers, for "ambience" sound. Entry-level Dolby Pro Logic models can be had for about $250.

Spending more—$400 or so—buys a receiver with more connections, more power, and features such as other surround modes. Models priced at more than $500 typically deliver lots of power and switching abilities.

THX receivers are another type of surround sound receiver. They use a patented design to simulate the acoustics heard in theaters. A THX receiver typically has six amplifiers to handle the six channels of sound including a subwoofer (for deep bass rumbles), decoder, and controller components. An entry-level THX receiver costs $1000 to $2000; a complete setup, $4000.

New five-channel surround receivers, (often referred to as a 5.1 format, indicating a sixth channel for the subwoofer output) are available in the Dolby Surround AC-3 format: See "What's new," below. Price: $1200 and up.

What's new

Dolby AC-3. At the high-end, a few new receivers are incorporating decoders for digital five-channel surround sound. (Dolby Pro Logic is a four-channel format even though it uses five speakers.) To take advantage of the format, special software and an AC-3-compatible laserdisc player are needed. However, the available selection of laserdiscs with AC-3 encoding is limited, but expected to increase.

Dolby Pro Logic. The price of Dolby Pro Logic has fallen so low that all but the cheapest component receivers come with it.

Power. Manufacturers have beefed up the power output to the center channel to equal that of the left and right main channels. That gives home theater a more dramatic impact and prevents the center channel from being "out-shouted" at loud volume.

Component receivers with front-channel power of 80/80/80 watts or more are common. Surround-channel power remains considerably lower, since those speakers aren't expected to reproduce power-hungry deep-bass frequencies. The typical power—20 to 50 watts per speaker —is more than adequate.

Remote controls. Controls such as Mute are migrating from the front panel of the receiver to the remote control. That means the receiver will be only partially functional if you misplace or lose the remote.

Reliability

Component receivers have been around for so long that few bugs are left in their design. They also have few moving parts, which adds to their reliability.

As a result, receivers are generally quite reliable products.

Shopping strategy

For some years now, very good and excellent performance has been the norm in our tests. Receivers typically deliver an accurate frequency response, essential for faithful reproduction of music. Radio reception is less of a problem, too, though the ability to capture a station in rural areas does vary. Even the lowest-powered models these days have ample power to fill an average-sized living room with sound.

How much power do you need?

Even inexpensive receivers have plenty of power. Here's how to figure how much power a system actually needs:

Determine the sound "liveness" of your listening room. A space with hard floors, scatter rugs, and plain wood furniture will be acoustically "live"; one with thick carpeting, heavy curtains, and upholstered furniture, relatively "dead." Locate the room size (in cubic feet) and type (live or dead) at right and note the multiplier. To determine the watts per channel needed, multiply that figure by the speaker's minimum power requirement, as stated by the manufacturer.

Let's say you have a 4000-cubic-foot room with average acoustics and speakers that require 12 watts of power. The multiplier from the chart, 1.5, times the watts needed, 12, equals 18. At minimum, you need an amplifier with 18 watts of power per channel to drive the speakers at moderately high volume. To be safe and to do justice to CDs or bass-heavy music, double or triple the figure.

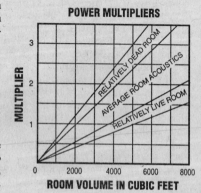

POWER MULTIPLIERS

RELATIVELY DEAD ROOM

AVERAGE ROOM ACOUSTICS

RELATIVELY LIVE ROOM

MULTIPLIER

ROOM VOLUME IN CUBIC FEET

For information on setting up a home theater system, loudspeaker compatibility, and power requirements, see pages 24 through 30.

Decide on the type. The choices include stereo-only models or a type of A/V surround-sound receiver, either Dolby Pro Logic, THX, or AC-3.

Decide on the features. A no-frills, stereo-only type is worth considering only if you never plan to incorporate video components in your system. For about $100 in most brand lines, you can step up to a Dolby Pro Logic a/v model. Once you've made that step, spending more buys power and features like a learning remote control, a graphical user interface, or more surround-sound modes. At the high end are models with THX or AC-3, enhanced home-theater systems.

The easiest brands to find. Receivers sell under more than 30 brand names. But five companies—Sony, Pioneer, Kenwood, Technics, and JVC—sell more than 80 percent of the models.

Key features

Recommended:

Bass boost is helpful for making small speakers sound fuller.

Digital radio-tuning is now standard, along with features such as seek (automatic searching for the next listenable station), direct-tuning buttons (to key in a station's numeric frequency), and 20 to 40 presets to call up your favorite station at the touch of a button. To catch stations too weak to pick up in the seek mode, most receivers also have a knob or buttons to let you step up and down manually. Manual stepping is convenient in one-channel increments. But most models creep in half or quarter steps, forcing a lot of unnecessary button tapping. Some Sony components lack manual stepping,

making it difficult to lock onto a weak station unless you know its frequency.

Direct frequency radio-tuning lets you enter a station's frequency on a keypad.

Digital signal processing is becoming common. DSP alters the sound signal by adding delays or reverb to simulate the acoustics of a nightclub, concert hall, or arena—a "soundfield," as it's called. Most Pro Logic receivers let you experience some surround-sound effects with fewer than five speakers. See the discussion of home theater, page 24.

Tone controls let you adjust bass and treble. Easiest to use are knobs—one for bass and one for treble. A graphic equalizer breaks the sound spectrum into more sections, a design that confers either greater control or greater confusion, depending on the design of the receiver and your mechanical aptitude. It's not much more effective than bass and treble controls unless it has at least seven frequency bands. Instead of tone controls, some receivers come with "tone styles" such as Jazz, Classical, or Rock, each accentuating a different frequency pattern; often you can craft your own styles, too. Since tone controls are most useful in correcting for room acoustics and listening preferences, not musical genre, the "tone style" approach seems needlessly indirect.

Tone-control bypass temporarily defeats any tone-control settings.

Remote control generally works only with the same brand of equipment and only if those components aren't too old. The design of audio remotes lags way behind that of video remotes. It's hard to find a receiver remote that feels comfortable in the hand, has easy-to-find primary-command keys, and buttons grouped and differentiated by size, shape, and color. More often, you'll see rows of small, crowded look-alike buttons.

Minisystems

These all-in-one packages can make decent instant-sound systems. But watch for confusing controls.

Last CR report: *February 1996*
Price range: *$200 to $1500*

A minisystem offers reasonably good overall performance without the cost, clutter, and wiring headaches of a component system—just the thing for casual listening in, say, a bedroom, dorm room, or family room.

The downside of minisystems is that they have components that are specifically designed to work with each other. You can't upgrade most minisystems with bigger speakers or other components, nor can you add a second pair of speakers to send music to another room.

The types

A minisystem's cabinet measures about 11 inches wide and 14 inches high, compared with standard-sized components, which are 17 inches wide.

A few are truly separate components; others can be divided in two, sitting side by side on a shelf. More compact "microsystem" models some as narrow as 6½ inches, are also available. Prices range from $200 to $1500.

What's new

The all-in-one minisystem usually has a molded facade that makes it look like many individual components in a stack. You'll find a receiver, speakers, CD player, and cassette deck (usually dual-well), all operated with a remote control.

Turntables have all but disappeared. The CD player is usually a changer rather than a single-play model.

While minisystems mimic the functions of a rack system or a component system, they add some capabilities of their own. The controls are more integrated than on a component system—but sometimes, confusingly so. Displays are often vivid, even hyperactive. Karaoke capabilities, using a microphone, are quite common.

Shopping strategy

Don't expect much from minisystems selling for less than $300. You won't get much more than a glorified boom box.

Systems in the $350-to-$500 price range include a CD changer, 20 to 50 watts of power per channel, and a good complement of features, but speakers and cassette decks can be problematic, our tests show.

Models that cost more than $500 are typically more powerful and more like component systems. Dolby Pro Logic systems start at about $700.

Decide on the type. Types vary by size—minisystem or even smaller microsystem. Some are separate components, others just look like a stack of separate components.

Decide on key features. Power is the most important consideration. For a large living room (15x25 feet or more), plan on 80 to 100 watts per channel. An average living room (10x25 feet) requires 65 to 80 watts per channel; a bedroom or dorm room (12x14 feet), 35 to 40 watts per channel.

The easiest brands to find. Sony,

Aiwa, and JVC are the biggest-selling brands of minisystems.

Key features

Many features are the same as those found in full-sized components; see the reports on the individual components. Features specific to minisystems:

Built-in clock function lets you program the system to turn on at a predetermined time, like a clock radio. You can also set the system's cassette deck to record from the radio later on, the same way you time-shift with a VCR.

Karaoke, or sing-along capability, is similar to that in full-sized components; some models come with a microphone.

Remote controls can be simpler on minisystems than a component-system of mixed brands because all the components are designed to work together. The downside: Buttons often perform two or more functions, sometimes confusingly.

Loudspeakers

They're the key to good sound. Buy the best you can afford.

Last CR report: *February 1996*
Ratings: *page 56*
Price range: *$30 to $10,000 or more*

The types

Mini. These speakers are smaller than a shoebox and cost under $100 per pair. They're useful as extension speakers in the kitchen or workshop. But their deficiency at producing bass rules them out for a larger sound system.

Bookshelf. These are sized to fit on a bookshelf and are appropriate for listening in a medium-sized room. Most lack the size to produce a rich, loud bass but can do a very good job over the rest of the sound spectrum. They cost $100 to more than $300 per pair.

Floor-standing. Large enough to command their own floor space, speakers of this type have a woofer of sufficient size to push the volume of air needed for full, loud bass. You'll find the best value—and sound to satisfy most listeners—among the less expensive models of

this type. Expect to pay at least $300 for a decent pair. You'll get speakers that can fill an average-sized living room with loud sound and a large living room with fairly loud sound.

As you go up in price, models are built more like furniture. Speakers at this level are intended for large rooms or serious listening. They cost anywhere from $600 to thousands and are often designed with unusual geometries and exotic-sounding technologies. But titanium or beryllium is not necessary to produce good frequency response, and "oxygen-free copper wiring" has no effect that we know of on sound that humans can hear.

Satellite/subwoofer systems. Comprising a bass module and two to five small, easy-to-place satellite speakers for mid-range and treble tones, these speaker sets can be an excellent solution to the sound/space problem. Volume controls are often found on satellite systems that use a powered bass module; they adjust the match between the bass module and the satellites. Satellite systems are priced at $250 or more.

Other types. Powered speakers have built-in amplifiers, so you can hook up a computer or a portable CD player, say, and have a sound system without the need for a receiver. Some are quite small and low-fi, others potentially on a par with bookshelf speakers. Price: $20 and up per pair. In-wall speakers solve the space problem by being built in. Price: $100 and up.

What's new

With the rise of home theater, you'll find speakers now marketed in two ways—as pairs or sets of "audio" speakers for traditional stereophonic listening, and singly or in sets of three or more "video" speakers for equipping a home theater. Video speakers typically have magnetic shielding so they can be close to a TV set without distorting its picture.

Reliability

Speakers are likely to be problem-free, although playing them too loud or with an underpowered receiver can damage them.

Shopping strategy

The extra money you spend on speakers will do more to improve your system's sound quality than an investment in any other component.

Our tests show that, except for the bass part of the sound spectrum, even cheap speakers can accurately reproduce sound. But equally accurate speakers are likely to sound different, so it's a good idea to listen before you buy. If you can audition them in a listening room at the store, compare only two pairs at a time and make sure they're equally loud; each time, judge the pair you prefer against the next pair. Take along a recording you know well that gives both the bass and treble ranges a good workout. Make sure you can return or exchange the speakers if they don't sound as good at home as in the showroom.

Check the speakers' impedance. Higher-impedance models (6 or 8 ohms) allow more freedom in choosing a receiver (see "System setup" on page 28). For information on choosing speakers for a home-theater system, see page 24.

Decide on the type. Smaller models, which typically cost less, are often fine except in their ability to produce low bass or play bass loudly without distortion. Larger speakers can evoke just about any sound you'd care to hear, but they cost more and take up more space.

The easiest brands to find. There are more than 300 brands, many made by small American companies. Bose and Radio Shack account for the biggest shares.

Compact-disc players —

Expect superb sound capability and look for the features you need.

Last CR reports: *February 1996, December 1995*
Ratings: *page 44*
Brand Repair Histories: *page 14*
Price range: *$100 to $600*

The types

Full-sized CD players are available as single-disc models and multiple-disc changers. Prices start at about $125 for a low-end single-disc player and $150 for a multiple-disc changer. Changers can play hours of music nonstop.

Magazine changers use a slide-in cartridge the size of a small, fat book. Each typically holds six discs—and each can double as a convenient disc storage box.

A carousel changer, with five or six discs around a platter, is easier to load and unload than the magazine type and usually lets you change any of the discs that aren't playing without disturbing the one that is. Carousel players that use a slide-out drawer can fit in a stack of components; those that load from the top must be on top.

CD jukeboxes store up to 200 discs. Prices reflect the newness of the category —$300 to $800. Size and stacking compatibility with other stereo components vary from model to model.

Portable CD players. Some are part of an overgrown boom box; others are scarcely bigger than the disc itself and weigh less than a pound.

All can be plugged in with an AC adapter. Most take two AA cells, but some require four. Battery use can be prodigious and varies considerably from model to model, according to our tests.

Over the long run, rechargeable batteries are the cheapest way to run free of power cords. No-name rechargeables are cheapest, but most portables require the use of their own, more expensive brand of rechargeable battery. Most CD portables come with a built-in charger, and many throw in a set of rechargeable batteries, usually of the nickel-cadmium type. Rechargeables last only about half as long as alkalines between charges.

Portable CD players sell from about $75 for a small, simple unit to more than $300 for a top-of-the-line model.

What's new

Prices for portables are dropping. According to our last tests, portables run longer on each set of batteries than they used to and better resist the bumps of a walk or a car ride (though not the jolts of jogging as yet).

Still, cassette walkabout stereos have some clear advantages over their CD counterparts, most notably in price. (See the report on walkabouts, page 50.) CD portables cost $75 and up; for about half that much, you can buy a fairly sophisticated walkabout tape player.

Don't expect a portable CD player to give you the kind of sound you'll get at home. The disappointing headphones supplied with personal stereos are the main culprit. You can address that problem by buying better 'phones; the box on page 47 gives some good choices.

Full-sized multidisc models offer long periods of uninterrupted play. Most accommodate 5 or 6 discs, but CD jukeboxes hold as many as 200.

Reliability

CD players hold up quite well, according to our survey. For most brands, 8 percent or fewer of those bought new by our readers between 1991 and 1995 needed repair. Denon carousel changers have been slightly more troublesome than most brands. Kenwood was the least reliable brand among magazine changers, but has since stopped offering models of that type.

For more information, see the Brand Repair Histories on page 14.

Shopping strategy

Virtually every CD player can produce superb hi-fi sound. The differences in sound reproduction we've uncovered are apparent only to a trained listener or a laboratory instrument. Differences boil down to how well the players handle ad-

46 COMPACT-DISC PLAYERS

verse conditions, like being bumped or playing a damaged disc, and what features they offer. If you need to save money in your system, do it with this component. By spending less, you give up niceties, not performance.

A full-sized model offers better value than a portable model. Multi-disc models are priced a little higher than single-play units but offer the convenience of hours of uninterrupted play. We prefer the carousel design. If uninterrupted play isn't crucial, consider a single-play model. You're likely to get more features for the money than you would with a changer. See "The types," above.

Decide on the features. Full-sized models are easier to use if they have a calender-type display, a favorite-track memory, and a numeric keypad. A remote control is another nicety. Portables should have a bass boost and important power aids such as battery-level indicator, auto power-off, and hold/lock. See "Key features," below.

The easiest brands to find. Five brands account for the most CD player sales: Pioneer, JVC, Sony, Technics, and Kenwood.

Key features

Recommended on full-sized models:

Calendar-type display shows a block of numbers representing the tracks on the active disc and highlights the track that's playing. Very easy to read.

Numeric keypad lets you punch in the numbers of the tracks you want; faster than Up and Down buttons.

Programming aids help you program the CD player to play tracks in a particular order. Favorite-track selection or Custom file lets the player remember programs you've encoded for specific discs. Some models have a Delete-track

function that skips over unwanted tracks.

Remote control allows armchair operation. CD remotes are typically fairly simple and work only the player.

Shuffle play mixes the playing order in a random sequence. Look for non-repeat shuffle.

Single-play drawer, found on some changers of the magazine type, lets you play a single disc without disturbing the ones already loaded in a magazine.

Useful if you tape a lot:

Auto-edit matches the tracks you plan on taping to the time available on the tape.

Digital output is a jack for a digital conduit—either a fiber-optic or coaxial cable. It lets you hook up the player to a digital recording device (a minidisc recorder or a digital tape deck).

Fade out/fade in performs the audio equivalent of a movie fade for less abrupt starts and endings on tapes you make.

Music-peak finder finds the loudest passage in a track you're going to record so you can adjust the tape deck's recording level in advance.

Running-time total lets you total the time of tracks you're recording so you can fit the maximum on a tape.

Synchronizing jack lets you connect a cable to a tape deck of the same brand so you can start and stop both machines simultaneously.

Useful features on portable models:

Auto power-off turns off the player when you press Stop, conserving power.

Bass boost compensates for poor bass in headphones. A switch with two positions is better than one.

Battery-level indicator shows when the batteries are running low.

Display light is useful in a car at night. On some models, the light turns off after you begin to play.

Electronic memory buffer (sometimes called ESP, for Electronic Shock or Skip Protection) holds the next few seconds of music in storage as protection against bumps. A buffer reduces battery life—usually by about 30 percent.

Hold/lock disables the controls so you don't accidentally activate the player.

Output jack and stereo cable are required for connections to a stereo system.

Resume makes the player pick up where it left off when you press Stop, then Play.

Useful features for particular needs:

DSP (digital signal processing) mimics the acoustics of a concert hall and various other spaces.

Fast scanning quickly finds a passage within a track.

Music sampling automatically plays the first few seconds of every track.

Optical digital output is useful only for those who record onto a minidisc, DCC, or DAT recorder.

Repeat track plays a track again and again, as long as you want.

Headphones for portables

■ **Sound quality.** Headphones are the weak link in personal stereos. Most give you much lower sound quality than the walkabout or CD player is capable of. These small headphones are especially poor at handling low bass and high treble. Replacing them can markedly improve the sound you hear.

We ran several sets of replacement headphones through the same accuracy tests as those that came with the portable CD players and walkabout stereos in our December 1995 report.

All the replacement models were more accurate than most of the headphones that came with the tested personal stereos. The top performer, the Sennheiser HD 580 Precision, was indeed very precise—as it should be, given its $300 price.

The other models were much less expensive—the Koss Porta-Pro Jr., $40; the Koss HV/PRO Digital, $60; the Sennheiser HD 36, $25; the Sennheiser HD 445, $70 (formerly HD 440 II); the Optimus (formerly Realistic) Pro-60, $50; and the Aiwa AP-A071, $10.

The least expensive sets, the Aiwa and the Sennheiser HD 36, are by far the best values of that bunch. Though a noticeable step below the pricey Sennheiser HD 580 set in accuracy, both headphone sets will improve the sound of almost any personal stereo. The Aiwa set is original equipment on some Aiwa personal stereos.

■ **Styles.** Of the four different style, the ones that are likely to give you the best sound are the muff style, which sit on the ear, or ball, ones that pivot to better contact the ear. But bud headphones, which sit inside the ear, are better at insulating you from outside noises. Buds tend to stay in place better when they're mounted on a band.

Cassette decks

After loudspeakers, the place to invest for good sound.

Last CR report: *February 1996*
Price range: *$100 to $1000*

The types

Dual-deck machines are the more common type. Also called "dubbing" decks, they lend themselves to copying tapes and playing cassettes in sequence. Dual decks come in two varieties: Single-record models allow playback from both cassette wells but can record from only one; dual-record decks allow playback and recording from both wells. Dual-deck models usually give up a little in audio performance. They tend to suffer slightly more from flutter (a wavy, watery sound defect), and their frequency response is slightly less accurate than that of single-decks.

Many **single-deck** machines are designed for serious audio buffs. The tape drive in a single-tape deck is often a cut above the drive in a comparably priced dual-deck machine.

What's new

Despite the minidisc's vaunted advantages over previous recording formats—sterling sound quality and speedy access to tracks—digital recorders and players have yet to catch on. One reason: They still cost too much. Component and portable minidisc recorders run $500 and up; portable minidisc players start at $300. And it's still not clear whether the medium, invented and propelled by Sony, will ever catch on. How many people are

eager to rebuild their entire music collection from scratch? Other types of digital recorders and players—digital compact cassette (DCC) and digital audio tape (DAT)—are also more expensive than their analog counterparts. They haven't caught on either.

Shopping strategy

Though the conventional cassette deck has probably reached the peak of its audio capability, it's still the medium of choice for recording and playing music at home. Today's best decks satisfy all but the most critical ear, despite their inherent limitations—slow access to individual tracks, background hiss, and a limited ability to capture the whole audible spectrum. A deck that has Dolby S, the most advanced noise-reduction circuitry, sounds nearly as clean as a CD player. And conventional decks are still priced far less than the new, rival digital-recording technologies.

Decide on the type. Prices of component tape decks start at $100 or so and run to more than $1000. Expect to pay anywhere from $200 to $500 for a deck that performs well. More money buys more convenience features but may not improve the sound.

Portable decks include boom boxes and —typically for playback only—walkabouts. You can hook up most personal tape players to a stereo system. Their basic playing performance can be quite acceptable, although the small controls may not be convenient. Boom boxes sell for about $40 and up; walkabouts, $20 and up.

Component decks hold either one tape or two. Tape changers that hold five or six cassettes are still a novelty.

Decide on the features. The features you'll need depend on the type of use. A deck that is used mainly for playback needs fast rewinding and autoplay, music search, intro scan, and headphone volume control (for use without a receiver). For recording, a deck should be equipped with adjustable bias (manual or automatic), real-time tape counter, tape monitoring (single-decks), and Dolby S noise-reduction circuitry. See "Key features," below.

The easiest brands to find. Sony, Pioneer, JVC, and Technics account for more than half of all cassette decks sold.

Key features

Recommended:

Adjustable bias control helps you adjust the deck to the type of tape you're using. Automatic bias control sets itself.

Autoplay will start playing tape when it's fully rewound.

Autoreturn/memory rewind lets you cancel a recording and return to the tape's starting point. Autoreturn is easier to use.

Autoreverse automatically plays the flip side of the tape when you reach the end of side one.

Dolby noise suppression is standard these days on most components. Dolby S, a step up from Dolby B and C, enhances the ability to reproduce noiseless loud and soft passages (dynamic range).

CD sync links the cassette deck to a CD player of the same brand to simplify recording.

Intro scan plays the first few seconds of a track to help you choose which selections you want to hear.

Music search lets you move the video-

Turntables

The turntable is not yet obsolete. Mindful of all the people who still treasure their collections of black-vinyl platters, major home-electronics manufacturers, including Sony, JVC, Technics, Kenwood, and Onkyo, make single-play turntables. Many models we've seen are priced at less than $200; a few sell for under $100—not too different from what they cost when we last tested turntables, in the early 1980s.

Many modern turntables come with the cartridge—the part that holds the needle, or stylus—already installed. The units work the same way they did years ago, turning the "table" via either direct drive or belt drive. Neither design holds an advantage, in our experience.

Receivers have changed over the last decade, however. The once-ubiquitous "phono" input on the back that sends the turntable's signal through the receiver's amplifier is now missing on some component receivers and on almost all minisystems. To compensate, many turntables are now designed with their own preamplifier. That allows you to connect them to the receiver via the "aux" line input, the same way you would an extra CD player or cassette deck. Be sure you get the right type for your system.

tape directly to a particular track.

Real-time tape counter is especially useful if it shows elapsed time in minutes and seconds and the tape time that remains. Some are electronic these days.

Record-mute inserts momentary silence between cuts when you record continuously. The silences then act as a

flag for search and scan features.

Features for tape monitoring

Three-head design found on many single-deck machines this lets you monitor the music off the tape as you record.

Two-button recording and dubbing helps avoid inadvertent taping by requiring two button presses instead of one.

Walkabouts

For music on the go, radio/tape players provide surprisingly good sound at relatively low prices.

Last CR report: *December 1995*
Price range: *$10 to $200*

The types

Radio/tape players are the most popular type. Some also can record. Price: $15 or so to more than $150.

Cassette-only models are priced at $10 to $25.

Radio-only models are the lightest; their prices range from $10 to $40.

What's new

Even though portable CD players have recently become less expensive and more popular (see the report on CD players, page 44), radio/tape walkabouts remain by far the most popular choice. And with good reason: Walkabouts cost about half as much as portable CD players.

And unlike CD players, walkabouts let you play your favorite music while jogging, although the music may sound "fluttery." And a built-in radio is virtually unavailable in a portable CD player.

Some walkabouts can make recordings, which CD players don't do, and walk-

abouts are more portable; they can fit where no CD player can go—on a belt clip or in a jeans pocket.

Shopping strategy

Most walkabouts produce surprisingly good sound, roughly equivalent to that of a low-priced home audio system. Spending more doesn't necessarily buy better sound quality or greater convenience. Our tests turned up $30 walkabouts that outperformed models priced between $60 and $100.

When you pay more than $50, you get such conveniences as digital tuning with station-presetting capability, Dolby noise suppression, and a bass booster.

Replacing the headphones can significantly improve sound quality. (See "Headphones for portables," page 47).

Decide on the type. Of the three types, radio/tape players, give you the most versatility. For sound-on-the-go, portable CD players are also worth considering (see page 45).

Decide on the features. The cheapest walkabouts have few features, save perhaps a switch that boosts bass performance. Far more popular are the $20-to-$50 models that combine a tape player and an AM/FM radio.

The typical radio/tape player has the

basics you need to play a cassette or tune a station. Slightly more expensive walkabouts add some worthwhile features: a digital radio tuner (for more convenient station changes), Dolby noise-reduction circuitry (to reduce tape "hiss"), or both.

The easiest brands to find. Sony is the biggest-selling brand, with General Electric a distant second.

Key features

Useful features include:

Autoreverse, found on most models. It lets you play a tape on both sides without flipping it.

Auto power off turns player off when you press Stop, conserving power.

Bass boost accentuates the bass but often results in "muddy" sounding music.

Battery-level indicator is most helpful with conventional alkaline batteries rather than rechargeable nickel-cadmium batteries.

Built-in mike. Desirable for recorders.

Digital radio-tuner makes for more convenient radio station changes.

Dolby noise-reduction circuitry. Reduces tape "hiss."

DC jacks let you plug into wall outlets at home or in the car's cigarette lighter.

Hold/lock prevents the machine from being turned on accidentally and batteries wasted. Lock ensures the machine won't be turned off by accident.

Tape-type switch brings out the best in higher-quality tapes. Any tape player is set up to play "normal" Type I tape. But not all walkabouts have the equalization circuitry needed to bring out the best in Type II (chrome) and Type IV (metal) tapes. You can play those tapes on a personal player without the circuitry, but they'll sound "bright" and trebly.

Water resistance means a more protective case, often recognizable by its bright color. Such models are geared toward outdoor sports and constructed to keep out water and sand, although manufacturers generally warn you not to use even water-resistant models on the beach or get them wet.

How to use the Ratings in the Buying Guide

■ **Read the Recommendations for information on specific models and general buying advice.**

■ **Note how the rated products are listed—in order of performance and convenience, price, or alphabetically.**

■ **The overall score graph gives the big picture in performance. Notes on features and performance for individual models are listed in the Comments column or "Model details."**

■ **Before going to press, we verify model availability for most products with manufacturers. Some tested models listed in the Ratings may no longer be available. Models that have been discontinued are marked Ⓓ; some may actually still be available in some stores for part of 1997. A model marked Ⓢ is a successor to the tested model, according to the manufacturer, and is noted in the Comments column or Model details. Features, though, may vary.**

Ratings *Receivers*
& Recommendations

The tests behind the Ratings

We test receivers using automated testing equipment. **FM** tuner tests include sensitivity, selectivity, and many other tests. **Power** is our measurement of watts per channel for left and right speakers. Center channels for all Dolby Pro Logic models are capable of delivering equivalent power. Rear surround channels are typically one-quarter to one-third of the front channel, sufficient for surround-sound effects. **Price** is approximate retail. Similar models to those we tested are noted in Details; features may vary. **Model availability:** Ⓓ means model is discontinued. Ⓢ means model is replaced, according to the manufacturer; successor model is noted in Details. New model was not tested; it may or may not perform similarly. Features may vary.

Standard features for these models

• Digital tuners with 20 to 40 presets. • Remote control that operates other components of the same brand. • AC outlet so receiver can control sound system.

Recommendations

Models differ mostly in features and controls. Very good and excellent performance is the norm.

See report, page 39. Last time rated in Consumer Reports: February 1996.

Overall Ratings *Listed in order of overall performance*

E ⊖ VG ⊖ G ○ F ◐ P ●

Brand and model	Price	Overall score 0 — 100	FM	Ease of use	Power 8/6 OHM
DOLBY PRO-LOGIC MODELS					
Technics SA-GX490, **A CR BEST BUY** Ⓢ	$290		⊖	⊖	97/125
Yamaha RX-V490	375		⊖	⊖	82/95
Technics SA-GX690 Ⓢ	385		⊖	⊖	114/127
JVC RX-717VTN Ⓓ	380		⊖	⊖	112/129
Yamaha RV-V390	300		⊖	⊖	71/82
Onyko TX-SV414PRO Ⓓ	370		⊖	⊖	75/92
JVC RX-517VTN Ⓓ	280		⊖	○	84/98
Sony STR-D865 Ⓢ	350		⊖	○	89/102
Sherwood RV-7050R	475		⊖	⊖	117/134

Brand and model	Price	Overall score 0 100	FM	Ease of use	Power 8/8 OHM
		P F G VG E			
Sony STR-D865 S	$350		⊖	○	89/102
Sherwood RV-7050R	475		⊖	⊖	117/134
Sony STR-D665	285		⊖	⊖	77/93
Sherwood RV-505 R	350		⊖	⊖	90/104
Kenwood KR-V5570 S	265		○	⊖	62/78
Sherwood RV-4050R	210		⊖	⊖	56/64
Kenwood KR-V7070 S	420		○	⊖	70/85
Fisher RS-737 S	320		⊖	○	92/112
Pioneer VSX-454 S	295		○	⊖	95/104
Optimus STAV-3370 D	350		◒	⊖	95/106
STEREO-ONLY MODELS					
Technics SA-GX190, A CR BEST BUY S	180		⊖	⊖	111/123
Kenwood KR-A5070	195		⊖	⊖	124/141
Sony STR-D365 S	190		⊖	⊖	108/118

Model details *Listed in order of overall score*

Dolby Pro Logic models

Technics SA-GX490 S $290

Accommodates: Turntable, CD player, tape deck (with monitoring), 2 VCRs (one with input only), TV monitor output, remote speakers in parallel. **Comments:** A superb tuner and one of the best control designs help make this the top-rated Pro Logic model. Keys are well labeled. The remote control is simple and easy to use. The tuner moves in one-channel increments for easy tuning. A Dolby 3 mode allows simulation of surround sound with only three speakers. But: There is no loudness switch for listening at low levels. **Successor:** SA-EX500. **Recommendation:** Excellent performance at a relatively low price makes this **A CR BEST BUY**.

Yamaha RX-V490 $375

Accommodates: Turntable, CD player, tape deck (with monitoring), 2 VCRs (one with input only), TV monitor output, remote speakers in parallel. **Comments:** This model has a fine tuner and a clear front panel. Excellent selectivity makes the Yamaha a good choice for those who live in an area crowded with stations. The tuner moves in one-channel increments for easy tuning. But: You can't enter station numbers directly. There's no Dolby 3 surround mode (although there are other modes) or loudness switch. Similar: RX-V590. **Recommendation:** Excellent performer.

Technics SA-GX690 S $385

Comments: Very similar to SA-GX490. A little more power, a more fully featured remote control, Dolby 3 and other surround modes, an output for a powered subwoofer for extra bass. It's one of the few receivers that allows 4-ohm speakers. **Successor:** SA-EX700. **Recommendation:** An excellent choice if you have 4-ohm speakers. Otherwise, the GX490 is a better value.

JVC RX-717VTN D $185

Accommodates: Turntable, CD player, 2 tape decks (one with monitoring), 2 VCRs (one with input only), TV monitor output, powered subwoofer.

Ratings continued ▶

Model details *Continued*

· ·

Comments: A chunky model with a superb tuner. Very good selectivity makes the JVC a good choice for those who live in an area crowded with stations. It has a graphic equalizer, though it was cumbersome to use. The display can be programmed to show a station's call letters. The JVC comes with a Dolby 3 mode and other surround modes. But: You can't enter station numbers directly. **Recommendation:** A very good performer, but the RX-517VTN (see below) is a better value.

Yamaha RX-V390 $300

Comments: Very similar to RX-V490, above, but rates lower due to differences in FM tuner, convenience features, and control layout. Unlike the 490, this model has Dolby 3 and other surround modes but delivers less power: 71 watts per channel with 8-ohm speakers and 9 watts per surround channel. **Recommendation:** A very good performer but not a good choice for home-theater setups.

Onkyo TX-SV414PRO Ⓓ $370

Accommodates: Turntable, CD player, 2 tape decks (one with monitoring), 2 VCRs (one with input only), TV monitor output, powered subwoofer, remote speakers in parallel. **Comments:** A simple model with a fine FM tuner. But: The display is hard to read from above, and there's no Dolby 3 mode. **Recommendation:** Expensive for what you get.

JVC RX-517VTN Ⓓ $280

Comments: Very similar to the RX-717VTN (above). This model has Dolby 3 and other surround modes. But: It has less power, an AM tuner a bit less sensitive, no graphic equalizer (no loss), no subwoofer connection. **Recommendation:** A better value than the RX-717VTN.

Sony STR-D865 Ⓢ $350

Accommodates: Turntable, CD player, 2 tape decks (one with monitoring), 4 VCRs (two with input only), TV monitor output, powered subwoofer, remote speakers in parallel. **Comments:** More video connectivity than with most models and a superb tuner whose selectivity makes it a good choice for those who live in an area crowded with stations. The display can be programmed to

show a station's call letters. But: This model is marred by a confusing control layout. The tuner is difficult to use—you must enter 0-9-2-0-3 to select FM 92.3, and there's no step tuning. A bass-boost switch instead of a loudness switch improves bass only, not treble. There's no Dolby 3 surround mode (although there are other modes). **Successor:** STR-DE605. **Recommendation:** Lots of features but limited.

Sherwood RV-7050R $475

Accommodates: Turntable, CD player, 2 tape decks (one with monitoring), 2 VCRs (one with input only), TV monitor output, powered subwoofer, auxiliary input. **Comments:** Along with a fine tuner, this model has many features that make it easy to use—the tuner moves in one-channel increments, a scan function previews stations, video inputs on the front panel allow easy camcorder connection. It has a Dolby 3 and other surround modes. But: You can't enter station numbers directly, and there's no loudness tone compensation. **Recommendation:** A very good but expensive model.

Sony STR-D665 Ⓢ $285

Comments: Although it's similar in performance and tuner design to the STR-D865, above, other aspects are quite different. This model has Dolby 3 and other surround modes. But: It has less power, no tape monitor function, and fewer inputs (for one less tape deck and two fewer VCRs). Remote speakers connect in series. **Successor:** STR-DE505. **Recommendation:** OK but limited.

Sherwood RV-5050R $350

Accommodates: Turntable, CD player, 2 tape decks (one with tape monitor), 2 VCRs (one with inputs only), and a TV monitor output. **Comments:** This model replaces the RV-5030R, **A CR BEST BUY** in the March '95 CR. This is the only Sherwood whose tuner allows direct frequency entry, an advantage. It also boasts an output for an external subwoofer, like the more expensive RV-7050R. **Recommendation:** A reasonable choice.

Kenwood KR-V5570 Ⓢ $265

Accommodates: Turntable, CD player, 2 tape decks (one with monitoring), 2 VCRs (one with input only), TV monitor output, remote speakers in parallel, **Comments:** A low-powered, low-featured model with Dolby 3 and other modes. **Successor:** KR-V5580. **Recommendation:** OK.

Sherwood RV-4050R $210

Comments: A couple of steps down the Sherwood line, this model is lower in power and has fewer features and inputs than the RV-7050R, above. Its only surround mode is Dolby 3. As with its brandmate, the tuner moves in one-channel increments. But: You can't enter station numbers directly. Nor can you connect a turntable, a second tape deck, or a remote pair of speakers. **Recommendation:** Decent, if limited, and the cheapest Pro Logic model tested.

Kenwood KR-V7070 Ⓢ $420

Comments: More power, features, and VCR connections than the KR-V5570 but rates lower partly because of slightly worse AM performance. It has Dolby 3 and other surround modes. This is one of the few receivers that allows 4-ohm speakers. But: A bass-boost switch instead of a loudness switch improves bass only, not treble. **Successor:** KR-V7080. **Recommendation:** An OK choice if you have 4-ohm speakers.

Fisher RS-737 Ⓢ $320

Accommodates: Turntable, CD player, 2 tape decks, 2 VCRs (one with input only), TV monitor output, powered subwoofer. **Comments:** Despite niceties like a front-panel camcorder connection, a graphic equalizer, and Dolby 3 and other surround modes, this oversized model isn't very easy to use. The tuner moves in one-channel increments for easy tuning and the remote layout is better than most. But: The front-panel controls are confusing, and there's no tape monitor. **Successor:** RS-939. **Recommendation:** There are better choices

Pioneer VSX-454 Ⓢ $295

Accommodates: Turntable, CD player, tape deck (with monitoring), 2 VCRs (one with input only), TV monitor output, powered subwoofer, remote

speakers in parallel. **Comments:** Excellent FM selectivity makes the Pioneer a good choice for those who live in an area crowded with stations. This model has Dolby 3 and other modes. But: AM performance was poor, the remote control is hard to use, and you can't enter station numbers directly. A bass boost switch instead of a loudness switch improves bass only, not treble. **Successor:** VSX-455. **Recommendation:** OK but limited.

Optimus STAV-3370 Ⓓ $350

Comments: Similar to the Pioneer VSX-454, above. (Pioneer makes equipment for Radio Shack, for which Optimus is a store brand.) **Recommendation:** OK but limited.

Stereo-only models

Technics SA-GX190 Ⓢ $180
Successor: SA-EX100.

Kenwood KR-A5070 $195

Sony STR-D365 Ⓢ $190
Successor: STR-DE305.

JVC RX-317TN Ⓓ $185

Pioneer SX-303R Ⓓ $195

All accommodate at least: Turntable, CD player, 2 tape decks, or tape deck and VCR or TV audio. **Comments:** These models, though less feature laden, resemble their Dolby Pro Logic brandmates, particularly in tuner and front-panel design. The Kenwood's and JVC's displays are hard to read from above, the Sony's tuner is irritating. Overall, the tuner performance of the Pioneer is a notch or two below the others. The Technics and Kenwood can connect a second pair of speakers in parallel. All but the JVC lack a loudness switch. The Technics' remote control is simple and easy to use. **Recommendation:** Excellent performance at a relatively low price makes the Technics the clear choice, a CR Best Buy for a stereo-only receiver. The other models are good or very good performers.

Ratings
& Recommendations
Budget loudspeakers

The tests behind the Ratings

We measure speaker performance in an echo-free chamber and then use a computer to simulate the effects of a room's walls and a receiver's tone controls. **Accuracy**, measured for tones ranging from deep bass to those a bit higher than most adults can hear, is given greatest weight in the overall score. For **bass handling**, we test bass to see how loudly you can play without much distortion (important for bass-heavy music). We measure **impedance** in ohms, a figure that affects the amount of current a speaker requires of a receiver. **Suggested minimum power** is what the receiver needs per channel to produce fairly loud sound in an average-sized room. Throughout, **price** is approximate retail. **Model availability:** Ⓓ means model is discontinued.

Standard features for these models

• Sold in pairs. • 8-ohm rating by the manufacturer. • Sound best if placed about 3½ feet from the side wall and 1 foot from the back wall.

Recommendations

Our tests show that, except for bass, even cheap speakers can accurately reproduce sound. Still, equally accurate speakers are likely to sound different. Listen before you buy. Reliability isn't usually a problem, but playing too loud or with an underpowered receiver can cause damage.

See report, page 43. Last time rated in Consumer Reports: February 1996.

Overall Ratings *Listed in order of performance*

Legend: E ⊖ VG ⊖ G ○ F ◑ P ●

Brand and model	Price	Overall score 0 — 100 (P F G VG E)	Accuracy	Bass handling	Impedance	Suggested min. power
Altec Lansing Model 85	$200		93/92	○	6 ohms	10 watts
B.I.C. V62si	200		92/92	⊖	7	10
DCM CX-07	190		94/87	⊖	6	6
Phase Technology 3T	260		92/89	⊖	6	13
RA Labs Mini Reference	224		91/91	○	4	11
Bose 201 Series III Ⓓ	200		93/87	⊖	8	12
Infinity RS-225 Ⓓ	200		90/90	○	5	15

Brand and model	Price	Overall score 0	100	Accuracy	Bass handling	Impedance	Suggested min. power
		P F G VG E					
Pinnacle AC 650	$240			91/88	○	4 ohms	14 watts
Polk S4 D	230			93/84	◒	4	13
Advent Baby III	170			91/84	◒	5	22
Yamaha NS-A636	120			91/85	◒	7	6
Optimus Pro LX5	300			63/74	●	6	16
Paradigm Titan	210			87/84	◒	5	23
Boston Acoustics CR7 D	260			86/73	○	5	38

Model details *Listed in order of overall score*

Altec Lansing 85 $200

17x9¾x9¼ in 15 lb.
The best accuracy makes this the top-rated model. Black cabinet. Tone correction for best accuracy: Set the bass to -1, the treble to -2. **Recommendation:** Excellent performance and a relatively low price make these a good value.

B.I.C. Venturi 62si $200

14½x9x8½ in 13 lb.
Compact size, very good bass handling, and magnetic shielding make this a good choice for home theater. Black cabinet. Tone correction: None. **Recommendation:** Excellent performance and a relatively low price make these a good value.

DCM CX-07 $190

15x8½x8¾ in 12 lb.
Magnetic shielding, very good bass handling, and built-in overload protection circuit to prevent speaker damage. Needs relatively little amp power. Black cabinet. Tone correction: Set the bass to +1, the treble to +3. **Recommendation:** Excellent performance and a relatively low price make these a good value.

Phase Technology 3T $260

15½x8x8½ in 11 lb.
The best model for handling loud bass. These speakers are also sold singly at half the pair price. Black cabinet. Tone correction: Set the bass to +1, the treble to +2. **Recommendation:** Excellent performance, but on the expensive side.

RA Labs Mini Reference $224

14x8½x8¼ in 10 lb.
If you play loud music for long periods, use these only with a receiver that can handle 4-ohm speakers. Black cabinet. Tone correction: None. **Recommendation:** Excellent performance and a relatively low price make these a good value.

Bose 201 Series III D $200

10x14¾x7¾ in 10 lb.
Especially smooth through the midrange. Speakers are designed to be a "left" and a "right." For better sound, try them closer than the usual 3½ feet from side wall. Light-wood-finish cabinet. Tone correction: Set the bass to -1, the treble to +3. **Recommendation:** Excellent performance and a relatively low price make these a good value.

Infinity RS-225 D $200

14½x9x8 in 12 lb.
Compact size makes placement easy. Light wood-finish cabinet. Tone correction: None. **Recommendation:** Excellent performance and a relatively low price make these a good value.

Ratings continued ▶

Model details *Continued*
••••••••••••••••••••••

Pinnacle AC 650 $240

16½x10x8¾ in 13 lb.
Only inaccuracy is a dip in the upper midrange.
For best sound, try these speakers farther than the
usual 3½ feet from the side wall. If you play
loud music for long periods, use these speakers
only with a receiver that can handle 4-ohm speakers. Dark wood-finish cabinet. Tone correction:
Set the treble to +2. **Recommendation:** Excellent
performance, but on the expensive side.

Polk S4 Ⓓ $230

15½x9½x7½ in 12 lb.
If you play loud music for long periods, use these
speakers only with a receiver that can handle 4-
ohm speakers. Light wood-finish cabinet. Tone
correction: Set the bass to +1, the treble to +4.
Recommendation: Expensive for what you get.

Advent Baby III $170

16¼x10x6¾ in 13 lb.
The drop in treble makes for a muted sound
(largely correctable). Black cabinet. Tone correction: Set the bass to +2, the treble to +5.
Recommendation: Very good performer.

Yamaha NS-A636 $120

16¼x10½x11½ in 14 lb.
Big for this class, these speakers may not fit on a
bookshelf. Magnetic shielding allows positioning near TV set. For better sound, try these speakers against the back wall. Black cabinet. Tone
correction: Set the bass to +2, the treble to +5.
Recommendation: Unusually low price and very
good performance make these a **CR BEST BUY**.

Optimus Pro LX5 $300

10½x6½x6 in 7 lb.
Comments: A large spike in mid-bass creates a
boomy sound quality. Since these speakers are
not magnetically shielded, putting them close to
a TV set can cause distortion. Black cabinet with
unusual dipole tweeters mounted on top. Tone
correction: None. **Recommendation:** There are
better choices.

Paradigm Titan $210

13x7¾x9½ in 10 lb.
Spike in mid-bass creates a boomy quality that
may sound disturbing. Black cabinet. Tone correction: Set the bass to -1, the treble to +1.
Recommendation: O.K.

Boston Acoustics CR7 Ⓓ $260

12¼x7¾x9¼ in 11 lb.
Uneven response creates a sound quality that
may be disturbing. This model requires more
amp power than others. Despite magnetic shielding and being sold singly and in pairs, this is
a poor choice for home theater. Black cabinet.
Tone correction: Set the treble to +6. **Recommendation:** There are better choices, especially at
this price.

Here are the best models still available from previous tests. All were judged good or better. Low-priced models below are a notch up from the budget models (see chart, page 56).

Ratings of other loudspeaker sizes *Listed alphabetically*

Brand and model	Price	Type	Recommendation
MID-PRICED MODELS (March 1995)			
Advent Heritage ☐	$300	Conventional	Good performer.
Allison AL 120 ☐	660	Conventional	Good performer, good value.
Bose Acoustimass 5 Series II	400	3-piece	Very good performer with excellent bass.
Boston Acoustics SubStat 7 ☐ ☐	725	3-piece	Good performer.
Cambridge Soundworks ☐	750	3-piece	Good performer.
Cerwin Vega DX-5	549	3-piece	Good performer with excellent bass.
DCM TF-400 Series Two ☐	500	Conventional	Good performer.
Infinity RS 525 ☐ ☐	500	Conventional	Good performer.
Miller & Kreisel SX-7/VX-7 ☐ ☐	575	3-piece	Very good performer.
NHT Super Zero/SW1P	745	3-piece	Good performer.
Paradigm 7seMk3 ☐	650	Conventional	Good performer.
Phase Technology 7T	575	Conventional	Very good performer with excellent bass.
Polk Audio S10 ☐ ☐	600	Conventional	Good performer.
RA Labs F-1 (formerly RDL F-1) ☐	600	Conventional	Very good performer.
Signet SL-280 B/U	580	Conventional	Very good performer.
Yamaha NS-A325/YST-SW120	700	3-piece	Very good performer, good value.
LOW-PRICED MODELS (March 1994)			
Allison AL-110 ☐	360	Conventional	Good performer.
Bose 301 Series III ☐	320	Conventional	Very good performer with excellent bass.
Cerwin-Vega L-7-B	345	Conventional	Very good performer.
DCM CX-17	365	Conventional	Very good performer.
Infinity RS 325 ☐ ☐	300	Conventional	Very good performer, good value.
Sony SS-U610 ☐	280	Conventional	Very good performer with excellent bass, good value.

☐ Needs receiver that can handle 4-ohm speakers.

Ratings
& Recommendations

Portable CD players

The tests behind the Ratings

Since sound quality of the players is excellent, we base the **overall score** mostly on headphone sound, performance on scratched discs, and resistance to bumping. Convenience, battery life, and weight are also considered. **Headphone sound** measures the ability to accurately reproduce frequencies from bass to treble. As a rule, the headphones overemphasized treble frequencies and were deficient in bass. **Scratched discs** is an indication of how a model dealt with a moderately scratched disc without interruption. **Bumps** measures how large a jolt the player could withstand without mistracking. The best machines withstood all but the very strongest jolts. **Price** is approximate retail. Models similar to those we tested are noted in Details; features may vary. **Model availability:** Ⓓ means model is discontinued. Ⓢ means model is replaced, according to the manufacturer; successor model is noted in Details. New model was not tested; it may or may not perform similarly. Features may vary.

Standard features for these models

• Excellent sound quality. • Headphones whose sound is weak on bass notes and somewhat uneven or harsh at treble frequencies. • AC adapter. • Weight, including batteries, of 11 to 17 ounces. • Digital, liquid-crystal display. • Play, Pause, Stop, Track-select, Resume, Hold, Shuffle-play, and Program functions. • Automatic power-off when Stop button is pressed. • A one-position (on-off) bass-boost switch. • Output jack for connection to a receiver.

Recommendations

All produced uniformly excellent sound, given the right set of headphones. Except for the models with the highest-scoring 'phones, any of the tested models would benefit from the Aiwa HP-A071 replacement headphone set, $10.

See report, page 44. Last time rated in Consumer Reports: December 1995.

Overall Ratings

E ⊖ VG ⊖ G ○ F ◖ P ●

Listed in order of headphone sound quality and player performance

Brand and model	Price	Overall score 0 ... 100	Headphone sound	Scratched discs	Bumps	Ease of use
		P F G VG E				
RCA RP-7913, **A CR BEST BUY**	$86	▓▓▓▓▓	⊖	⊖	⊖	⊖
Panasonic SL-S290 Ⓢ	134	▓▓▓▓	⊖	○	⊖	⊖

Brand and model	Price	Overall score 0–100 (P F G VG E)	Headphone sound	Scratched discs	Bumps	Ease of use
Panasonic SL-S160, A CR BEST BUY [S]	$92		⊖	⊖	⊖	⊖
RCA RP-7926A w/car kit	125		⊖	⊖	⊖	⊖
Panasonic SL-S490 [D]	195		⊖	○	⊖	⊖
Sony D-245	149		⊖	●	●	⊖
Sony D-141 [S]	89		○	○	○	⊖
Sony D-345	199		⊖	●	○	⊖
Sony D-335	283		○	●	●	⊖
Sony D-842K [D]	250		⊖	●	●	⊖
Sony D-143 [S]	110		○	●	●	⊖
Craig JC6111	68		○	⊖	●	⊖
JVC XL-P41 [D]	136		⊖	○	●	⊖
Fisher PCD-60 w/car kit [S]	183		⊖	●	⊖	○
Sony D-421SP [S]	258		○	●	●	⊖
Aiwa XP-559 w/car kit [D]	152		○	○	●	⊖
JVC XL-P61CR w/car kit [1] [S]	143		—	●	●	○
Aiwa XP-33 [S]	94		●	○	●	⊖
Onkyo DX-F71 w/car kit [D]	179		⊖	●	●	○
Kenwood DPC-151 [S]	94		⊖	●	⊖	⊖
Optimus CD-3450 [1] [S]	120		—	○	○	●
Kenwood DPC-951 w/car kit [S]	263		●	●	⊖	⊖
Magnavox AZ 6827C w/car kit [S]	149		○	○	⊖	⊖
Kenwood DPC-751 w/car kit [S]	213		●	●	●	⊖
Emerson HD6825 w/car kit	85		○	○	●	●
Koss CDP421CP w/car kit [S]	120		●	○	●	●

[1] Comes without headphones. Overall score and price calculated using the Aiwa HP-A071, an inexpensive and very good set of replacement headphones.

Model details *Listed in order of overall score*

RCA RP-7913, A CR BEST BUY $86

Panasonic SL-S290 [S] $134
Pluses: Has fast scanning, lighted display. Minuses: Buffer adds slight noise. Successor: SL-S240.

Panasonic SL-S160, A CR BEST BUY [S] $92
Pluses: Has fast scanning of tracks. Successor: SL-S140.

RCA RP-7926A w/car kit $125
Pluses: Has lighted display. Minuses: Can't show elapsed time of track. Similar: RP-7925A, RP-7923A.

Ratings continued ≫

Model details *Continued*

Panasonic SL-S490 D $195
Pluses: Has fast scanning of tracks, lighted display. **Minuses:** Buffer adds slight noise.

Sony D-245 $149
Pluses: Has music sampling, stereo cord, 2-position bass boost. **Minuses:** Buffer adds slight noise.

Sony D-141 S $89
Pluses: Has music sampling, stereo cord, 2-position bass boost. **Minuses:** No Resume. **Successor:** D-151.

Sony D-345 $199
Pluses: Has music sampling, stereo cord, 2-position bass boost. **Minuses:** Buffer adds slight noise.

Sony D-335 $283
Pluses: Has music sampling, jack for digital recording, stereo cord, 2-position bass boost, lighted display, remote on headphone.

Sony D-842K D w/car kit $250
Pluses: Has music sampling, 2-position bass boost, lighted display. **Minuses:** No headphones. Volume difficult to adjust. Buffer adds slight noise.

Sony D-143 S $110
Pluses: Has music sampling, stereo cord, 2-position bass boost. **Minuses:** No Resume. **Successor:** D-153.

Craig JC6111 $68
Pluses: Has music sampling, 2-position bass boost. **Minuses:** No Resume. **Similar:** JC6111A, JC6112.

JVC XL-P41 D $136
Pluses: Has music sampling. **Minuses:** No Resume. Can't display track and time together.

Fisher PCD-60 w/car kit S $183
Pluses: Has lighted display, 2-position bass boost. **Minuses:** No Resume, Hold, Shuffle play. Buffer adds slight noise. Can't show elapsed time of track. **Successor:** PCD-6600.

Sony D-421SP S $258
Pluses: Has music sampling, DSP (digital signal processing) for special effects, stereo cord, 2-position bass boost. Water resistant. **Minuses:** Heavier than most. **Successor:** D451SP.

Aiwa XP-559 w/car kit D $152
Pluses: Can display time remaining on track and disc. Has stereo cord, 2-position bass boost. **Minuses:** Volume hard to adjust. Heavier than most.

JVC XL-P61CR w/car kit S $143
Pluses: Has music sampling, lighted display. **Minuses:** No Resume, headphone. Can't display track and time together. **Successor:** XL-P6ZCR.

Aiwa XP-33 S $94
Pluses: Has stereo cord, 2-position bass boost. Can repeat part of track or disc, display time remaining on track and disc. Inserts silence between tracks for recordings. **Minuses:** Volume hard to adjust. Heavier than most. **Successor:** XP-220.

Onkyo DX-F71 w/car kit D $179
Pluses: Has stereo cord, 2-position bass boost, lighted display. **Minuses:** No Resume, Hold, Shuffle play. Buffer adds slight noise. Can't show elapsed time of track.

Kenwood DPC-151 S $94
Pluses: Has music sampling. **Minuses:** No Resume, line output jack for receivers. Can't display track and time together. **Successor:** DPC-361.

Optimus CD-3450 S $120
Pluses: Has music sampling, stereo cord. **Minuses:** No auto power off. No Resume, Hold, headphone. Can't display track and time together, AC adapter not included. **Successor:** CD-3540.

Kenwood DPC-951 w/car kit S $263
Pluses: Has music sampling, DSP (digital signal processing) for special effects, stereo cord, lighted display, separate remote with volume control and remote on headphone. **Minuses:**

Volume hard to adjust. No jack for receivers. **Successor:** DPC-861.

Magnavox AZ 6827C w/car kit ⑤ $149
Pluses: Has stereo cord, lighted display, fast scanning. **Minuses:** Volume hard to adjust. No repeat track. Heavier than most. **Successor:** AZ6832.

Kenwood DPC-751 w/car kit ⑤ $213
Pluses: Has music sampling, DSP (digital signal processing) for special effects, stereo cord, lighted

display, separate remote with volume control and remote on headphone. **Minuses:** Volume hard to adjust. No jack for receivers. **Successor:** DPC-761.

Emerson HD6825 w/car kit $85
Pluses: Has stereo cord. **Minuses:** No auto power off, Resume, Hold.

Koss CDP421CP w/car kit ⑤ $115
Pluses: Has stereo cord. **Minuses:** No auto power off, Resume, Hold. **Successor:** CDP600CP.

Ratings *Camcorders*
& Recommendations

The tests behind the Ratings

Picture clarity and **color** are based on judgments of a panel of trained viewers, who looked at footage shot at each model's available speeds. **Sound accuracy** is each model's frequency response with the built-in microphone. **Flutter** is a wavery distortion that's especially noticeable in music; the less flutter, the better the score. All the models were OK for recording speech. Models similar to those we tested are noted in Details; features may vary. **Model availability:** Ⓓ means model is discontinued. **Price** is the estimated average, based on a national survey.

Standard features for these models

• Automatic focusing. • Automatic adjustment for exposure, white balance, and sound level. • Power zoom. • Flying erase head for seamless transitions between scenes. • Single-button "quick review" of last few seconds of scene just recorded. • Fade control for picture and sound. • Ability to record date and time. • Automatic battery shutoff in camera mode. • Battery charger with "refresh" mode to drain battery before recharging to help it retain charge.

Recommendations

The Hitachi VM-H620A, a Hi8 model priced at $850, far surpassed the others, thanks to its high-band picture quality. But you need a TV set with an S-video input to take full advantage of it. Among 8mm models, consider the Hitachi VM-E220A, a plain 8mm machine priced at $600, and the Canon ES600, $675, whose "Spotlight" feature would be especially good for recording a lot of school plays. Among VHS-C machines, the clear choice is the Panasonic PV-A206, $600.

See report, page 36. Last time rated in Consumer Reports: October 1996.

Ratings continued ▶

Overall Ratings *Listed in order of overall score*

E ⊖ VG ⊖ G ○ F ◑ P ●

Brand and model	Format	Price	Overall score 0 — 100	Picture clarity Hi8 SP	SP	EP	Picture color	Sound ACCURACY	FLUTTER
			P F G VG E						
Hitachi VM-H620A	Hi8	$850		⊖	⊖	—	⊖	⊖	⊖
Hitachi VM-E220A	8mm	600		—	⊖	—	⊖	○	⊖
Sony CCD-TR84 Ⓓ	8mm	780		—	⊖	—	⊖	○	⊖
Canon ES600	8mm	675		—	⊖	—	⊖	○	⊖
Samsung SCH985	Hi8	850		⊖	⊖	—	⊖	○	⊖
Panasonic PV-A206	VHS-C	600		—	⊖	⊖	⊖	◑	○
Sharp VL-E34U	8mm	680		—	⊖	—	⊖	○	⊖
Sony CCD-TR44 Ⓓ	8mm	500		—	⊖	—	○	○	⊖
Panasonic PV-D406	VHS-C	800		—	⊖	○	○	◑	○
JVC GR-AX710	VHS-C	615		—	○	●	⊖	⊖	⊖
RCA CC617	VHS-C	550		—	○	●	⊖	◑	⊖

Model details *Listed in order of overall score*

Hitachi VM-H620A $850

• Hi8. • 2½ lb. • 12:1 optical zoom, digital zoom up to 24:1. • Battery: runs 60 min.; recharges in 40 min.; can also use 6 AA cells. Its Hi8 picture looked richer and more detailed than that of any other camcorder we've tested in this price range. Sound was superior, too—and in stereo. Features: Audio/video input (but optional cable required for use). Image stabilizer. Can be set to automatically record date in first scene shot each day. Remote control. Random assemble editing requires different, optional remote. Character generator for titles. Can record in wide "letterbox" format. Powered shoe for a small video light. Can run from AC adapter without removing battery. But: No exposure-compensation controls. Motorized manual focus hard to use. Lacks built-in lens cover (has a tethered cap instead). **Recommendation**: Excellent overall. Lives up to the promise of the Hi8 format at a very attractive price.

Hitachi VM-E220A $600

• 8mm. • 2½ lb. • 12:1 optical zoom, digital zoom up to 24:1. • Battery: runs 55 min.; recharges in 40 min.; can also use 6 AA cells.
Fine performance at an attractive price. Features: Can be set to automatically record date in first scene shot each day. Random assemble editing, with use of optional remote control. Character generator for titles. Powered shoe for a small video light. Can run from AC adapter without removing battery. But: No exposure-compensation controls. Motorized manual focus hard to use. Lacks fade control and built-in lens cover (has a tethered lens cap instead). **Recommendation**: Very good overall. Worth considering if you want an 8mm machine.

Sony CCD-TR84 Ⓓ $780

• 8mm. • 2 lb. • 12:1 optical zoom, digital zoom up to 24:1. • Battery: runs 80 min.; recharges in 55 min.; can also use 6 AA cells. One of two tested with an LP speed, for 4 hours' recording on a regular 8mm tape. Has a black-and-white viewfinder. Features: Remote control. High-shutter-speed modes. Image stabilizer. Unless you remove clock battery, unit always records date in first scene shot each day. Microphone jack. Beeper to confirm start and stop of taping, viewfinder warnings that tape heads are dirty or that something else requires service. But: Lacks fade control and manual focus. Has no "refresh" provision to drain the battery before recharging (and help maintain its ability to hold a charge). **Recommendation**: Very good overall.

Canon ES600 $675

• 8mm. • 2 lb. • 12:1 zoom. • Battery: runs for 70 min.; recharges in 60 min.
A good choice if you regularly tape school plays or other theatrical events. The Canon's "spotlight" setting was the only one that worked really well. Features: Audio/video input. Remote control. "FlexiZone" autofocus, which lets you select an area to be focused. "Sports" high-shutter-speed mode. Manual selection of shutter speeds. Very fast search speed. Character generator for composing titles. Microphone jack. But: Lacks manual focus, built-in lens cover (has a tethered lens cap instead). **Recommendation**: Very good overall. Worth considering for its "spotlight" setting.

Samsung SCH985 $850

• Hi8. • 2¼ lb. • 12:1 zoom. • Battery: runs for 50 min.; recharges in 60 min.
Overall, picture quality of this Hi8 model wasn't better than that of most regular 8mm camcorders. Features: Audio/video input. Remote control. Stereo sound. Manual override of automatic white-balance control. "Sports" high-shutter-speed mode. Rudimentary time-lapse capability. Self-timer. Powered shoe for a small video light. But: Lacks "quick review" for easy replay of the last few seconds of taping. "Spotlight" exposure mode had no effect. **Similar**: SCH996, $950, adds image stabilizer and digital zoom. **Recommendation**: Very good overall, but disappointing for a Hi8 model. There are better choices.

Panasonic PV-A206 $600

• VHS-C. • 2½ lb. • 14:1 zoom. • Battery: runs for 65 min.; recharges in 55 min.
Slightly better than its more expensive sibling, PV-D406. Features: Manual shutter-speed selection. Automatic shutoff to preserve battery works in all situations. But: Lacks tape counter, "quick review" for easy replay of the last few seconds of taping. **Similar**: PV-A306, $700, with 16:1 zoom,

video light. **Recommendation**: Very good overall; the best of the VHS-C models we tested.

Sharp VL-E34U $680

• 8mm. • 2 lb. • 8:1 zoom. • Battery: runs for 55 min.; recharges in 60 min.
Its basic performance was fine, but this camcorder was plagued with many disadvantages in our tests. Features: 3-in. color LCD panel for viewfinder. Warning that tape heads are dirty. But: Motorized manual focus hard to use; automatically zooms to wide-angle view if it can't find focus. Viewfinder panel easy to view when camcorder is mounted on a tripod, but awkward to orient in hand-held use. Lacks fade control, tape counter, clock/calendar for recording time and date, "quick review" for easy replay of the last few seconds of taping, "refresh" provision to drain battery before recharging, and built-in lens cover (has a tethered lens cap instead). **Recommendation**: Good overall, but there are better choices among the other tested 8mm camcorders.

Sony CCD-TR44 Ⓓ $500

• 8mm. • 2 lb. • 10:1 zoom. • Battery: runs for 80 min.; recharges in 55 min.; can use 6 AA cells.
One of two tested with an LP speed, for 4 hours' recording on a regular 8mm tape. Has a black-and-white viewfinder. Features: High-shutter-speed modes. Microphone jack. Beeper to confirm start and stop of taping, viewfinder warnings that tape heads are dirty or that something else requires service. Optional remote control. But: Lacks fade control, manual focus, "refresh" provision to drain battery before recharging. **Recommendation**: Good overall, but there are better choices.

Panasonic PV-D406 $800

• VHS-C. • 2¾ lb. • 16:1 optical zoom, digital zoom up to 22:1. • Battery: runs for 100 min.; recharges in 90 min.
Features: Image stabilizer. Manual shutter-speed selection. Automatic shutoff to conserve battery works in all situations. Powered shoe for a small video light. But: Lacks tape counter, "quick review" for easy replay of the last few seconds of taping. **Similar**: PV-D506, $850, with remote control and additional digital special effects. **Recommendation**: Good overall, but its brand-mate, PV-A206, is a better choice.

Ratings continued ⟫

Model details *Continued*

JVC GR-AX710 $615

• VHS-C. • 2¼ lb. • 14:1
zoom. • Battery: runs for 65 min.;
recharges in 55 min.
A feature-laden model marred by substandard
performance. Jittery picture at EP speed was un-
pleasant to watch. Features: Remote control.
Manual override of automatic white-balance control. High-shutter-speed modes. Can be set to
automatically record date in first scene shot each
day. Automatically records index-search mark
with first scene shot each day. Rudimentary time-
lapse and animation modes. Self-timer. Random
assemble editing. Character generator for titles.
Audio/video dubbing. Ability to record in wide
"letterbox" format. Viewfinder warning of problems requiring service. But: Automatically zooms
to wide-angle view if it can't focus. Motorized
manual focus hard to use. Lacks audio fade.
Similar: GR-AX510, $600, with optional remote

control and no video light; GR-AX910, $760, with
image stabilizer, digital zoom. **Recommendation:**
There are better choices.

RCA CC617 $550

• VHS-C. • 2 lb. • 12:1 zoom. • Battery:
runs for 65 min.; recharges in 55 min.
This model shares many characteristics with the
JVC, above, including jittery picture quality at EP
speed. Features: Manual override of automatic
white-balance control. "Theater" and high-shutter-
speed modes, with manual override of set exposure. Can be set to automatically record date in
first scene shot each day. Automatically records
index-search mark with first scene shot each day.
Character generator for titles. Ability to record
in wide "letterbox" format. But: Automatically
zooms to wide-angle view if it can't focus.
Motorized manual focus hard to use. Lacks audio
fade. **Recommendation:** There are better choices.

Ratings *VCRs*
& *Recommendations*

The tests behind the Ratings

Picture quality is given greatest weight. A viewing panel compared side-by-side
test images, judging clarity and freedom from video noise. Judgments are of
tapes made at standard (SP) and extended-play (EP) speeds; we give SP greatest
weight. **Tuner tests** tell us how well the VCR filtered unwanted channels next to
the one being watched and how well the tuner works in fringe-signal areas. **Price**
is an average, based on national surveys. Models similar to those we tested are noted in Details; features may vary. **Model availability:** Ⓓ means model is discontinued.

Standard features for these models

• Can receive at least 125 cable channels. • Records at SP and EP speeds and play
back at SP, LP, and EP speeds. • Can be programmed to record seven or eight
events 365 days in advance. • Comes with a universal remote. • Can be programmed from console as well as remote. • Has four video heads, VCR Plus+,
pause button on console, Index search, on-screen help for menu manipulation,
secondary audio program, multi-speed search, ability to record timed programs
after a power failure, and memory for VCR+ map.

Recommendations

If you're looking to watch tapes with stereo sound, the GE VG-4258 ($220) is our first pick because of its high-quality picture and sound and its favorable price. For a mono model, consider the RCA VR522 ($190) or the GE VG-4058 ($170). Both offer good value and very good performance. Features are sparse on mono models; refer to Model details for what each model has.

See report, page 33. Last time rated in Consumer Reports: November 1996.

Overall Ratings

Rating key: E ⊖ VG ⊖ G ○ F ⊖ P ●

Within types, listed in order of overall score

Brand and model	Price	Overall score 0—100	Picture quality SP	Picture quality EP	Tuner	Sound	User friendliness
STEREO HI-FI MODELS							
Sony SLV-760HF	$350		⊖	○	⊖	⊖	○
Panasonic PV-4661	300		⊖	○	○	⊖	○
Panasonic PV-4662	340		⊖	⊖	⊖	⊖	○
GE VG-4258, A CR BEST BUY	220		⊖	⊖	⊖	⊖	○
Hitachi VT-FX613A	320		⊖	⊖	○	⊖	○
Samsung VR8905	450		⊖	○	⊖	⊖	○
Sharp VC-H955U	270		⊖	○	○	⊖	○
Hitachi VT-FX611A	265		⊖	○	○	⊖	○
Quasar VHQ660	210		⊖	○	⊖	⊖	◐
RCA VR618 HF	250		⊖	○	⊖	⊖	◐
Symphonic SE436D	180		⊖	◐	⊖	⊖	◐
JVC HR-VP634U	300		⊖	●	◐	⊖	⊖
MONOPHONIC MODELS							
RCA VR522	190		⊖	⊖	○	⊖	○
GE VG-4058	170		⊖	⊖	⊖	○	◐
Quasar VHQ650	190		⊖	○	⊖	⊖	◐
RCA VR508	170		⊖	⊖	○	⊖	◐
Emerson VR4450	170		⊖	◐	⊖	⊖	◐
Panasonic PV-4611 A	200		⊖	○	⊖	○	○
Magnavox VRU342AT21	180		⊖	⊖	◐	⊖	◐
JVC HR-VP434U	220		⊖	●	◐	○	⊖
JVC HR-J430U	200		⊖	●	○	○	○
Goldstar GVR-E448 D	250		○	●	○	⊖	○

Ratings continued ▶

68 VCRs

Model details *Within types, listed in order of overall score*

Stereo hi-fi models

Sony SLV-760HF $350
• Auto clock set
Excellent picture quality in SP speed and standout audio performance in both hi-fi and mono. Best tuner performance of the tested models, and among the best choices for people who record programming from cable stations but who don't use a cable box. Jog and shuttle controls make this a good machine for editing. But: Lacks index search and doesn't offer on-screen help to make programming easy. It cannot be programmed for time-shift recording if remote is lost, and the remote cannot control a cable box. It can program recordings only one month in advance. **Recommendation:** Overall excellent performance makes this our top-rated model.

Panasonic PV-4661 $300
• Plug & play
Excellent picture quality in SP and standout audio performance in both hi-fi and mono. But: It lacks index search and can program recordings only one month in advance. Cannot pause tape if remote is lost. Similar model: PV-4664, average price $400. **Recommendation:** Good value and excellent overall performance from one of the more reliable brands.

Panasonic PV-4662 $340
• Cable channel changer • Plug & play
Excellent picture in SP and very good EP speed. Excellent hi-fi and good mono audio. Convenient for cable viewers using a cable box who want to "time shift, " or program for later recording. But: Lacks index search. Can program recordings only one month in advance. Cannot pause tape if remote is lost. **Recommendation:** Excellent overall performance from one of the more reliable brands.

GE VG-4258 $220
• Go-to search
Best picture quality in both SP and EP combined with standout audio performance in both hi-fi and mono at an attractive price make this model a CR Best Buy. Among the best choices for people who use cable without a cable box. Alerts you if you program it to record two shows in the same time slot. But: Lacks on-screen help for menu manipulation. Remote cannot control a cable box. Cannot be programmed for time-shift recording if remote is lost and will not record timed programs after a power failure. **Recommendation:** Excellent overall performance for an exceptional value. A CR Best Buy.

Hitachi VT-FX613A $320
• Cable channel changer • Auto clock set
This model has very good picture quality in both SP and EP, and we found it easy to use. Excellent hi-fi and good monophonic sound. Shuttle control assists in editing. But: Lacks on-screen help for menu manipulation. Cannot be programmed for time-shift recording if remote is lost. **Recommendation:** Very good overall performance.

Samsung VR8905 $450
• Cable channel changer • Auto clock set
Rich in features, it was the only model we tested with StarSight program guide and with closed caption decoder for the hearing impaired. Very good SP picture, good quality in EP. Standout audio performance in both hi-fi and mono. Alerts you if you program it to record two shows in the same time slot. Can automatically switch from SP to EP to complete timed recording. Jog and shuttle on console and remote make it good for tape editing. But: Lacks VCR Plus. Cannot be programmed for time-shift recording if remote is lost, and can program recordings only one month in advance. **Recommendation:** Very good overall performance, but expensive.

Sharp VC-H955U $270
• Cable channel changer • Auto clock set
Very good SP picture, good quality in EP. Excellent hi-fi and good mono audio, and we found it easy to use. Shuttle control assists in editing. But: Lacks on-screen help for menu manipulation. Cannot record tapes from a camcorder if remote is lost or record timed programs after a power failure. **Recommendation:** Very good overall performance, and a good value.

Hitachi VT-FX611A $265
• Auto clock set
Very good SP picture, good quality in EP. Excellent

hi-fi and good mono audio. But: Limited features. Lacks VCR Plus and on-screen help for menu manipulation. Cannot be programmed for time-shift recording or pause tape if remote is lost. **Recommendation:** Very good overall performance.

Quasar VHQ660 $210

Very good SP picture; good quality in EP. Standout audio performance in both hi-fi and mono. But: Very limited status information on front panel. Limited features. It lacks VCR Plus, and its remote cannot control cable box or TV from another manufacturer. It can program recordings only one month in advance. It cannot pause tape if remote is lost. Lacks index search. Will not record timed programs after power failure. **Recommendation:** Very good overall performer.

RCA VR618 HF $250

• Go-to search
Very good SP picture, good quality in EP. Excellent hi-fi and good mono audio. Alerts you if you program it to record two shows in the same time slot. But: Lacks on-screen help for menu manipulation. Cannot be programmed for time-shift recording if remote is lost, and the remote won't control the cable box. **Recommendation:** Good overall performance.

Symphonic SE436D $180

• Go-to search
Picture quality very good in SP; only fair in EP. Standout hi-fi and mono audio performance. Can switch automatically from SP to EP to complete timed recording. But: Very limited status information on front panel. Less convenient to use than other models we tested. Limited features. Lacks VCR Plus+ and on-screen help for menu manipulation. Remote cannot control cable box or TV from another manufacturer. Cannot be programmed for time-shift recording if remote is lost, and will not record timed programs after power failure. **Recommendation:** Priced lower than most monophonic models, but there are better selections.

JVC HR-VP634U $300

• Cable channel changer • Plug & play
Very good SP picture, but poor quality in EP. Full-featured and easy to use. Excellent hi-fi and good mono audio. Jog and shuttle controls make this a good machine for editing. But: A poor

choice for users receiving cable without a cable box. Recommendation: Has some performance shortcomings; there are better choices.

Monophonic models

RCA VR522 $190

• Auto clock set • Go-to search
Best picture quality in both SP and EP. Very good monophonic sound. Its limited features are easy to use. Alerts you if you program it to record two shows in the same time slot. But: Reception of cable without a cable box judged only fair. Lacks on-screen help for menu manipulation. Remote cannot control a cable box. Cannot be programmed for time-shift recording if remote is lost. Will not record timed programs after power failure. **Recommendation:** Good value and very good overall performance.

GE VG-4058 $170

• Go-to search
Very good picture in both SP and EP, and good monophonic sound. Alerts you if you program it to record two shows in the same time slot. But: Limited features. Lacks on-screen help for menu manipulation. Remote cannot control a cable box. Cannot be programmed for time-shift recording if remote is lost. After power failure recording timer will not function and VCR Plus channel map must be re-entered. **Recommendation:** Good value and very good overall performance.

Quasar VHQ650 $190

Very good SP picture, good EP. Very good mono sound. Among the best choices for people who use cable without a cable box. But: Limited features. Lacks index search. Remote cannot control cable box or TV from another manufacturer. Can program recordings only one month in advance. Cannot pause tape if remote is lost. Will not record timed programs after power failure. **Recommendation:** Very good overall performance; a good value.

RCA VR508 $170

• Go-To search
Very good picture in both SP and EP, and very good mono sound. Alerts you if you program it to record two shows in the same time slot. But: Very limited status information on front panel. Limited features. Lacks VCR Plus+. Remote can-

Ratings continued ⟩

70 VCRs

not control cable box or TV from another manu-facturer. Cannot be programmed for time-shift recording if remote is lost. Will not record timed programs after power failure. **Recommendation:** Very good overall performance.

Emerson VR4450 $170

Very good SP picture and mono sound, but only fair in EP. Shuttle control assists in editing. Among the best choices for people who use cable without a cable box. But: Limited features. Just 6-month warranty on video heads. Lacks VCR Plus+ and on-screen help for menu manipulation. Remote cannot control cable box or TV from another man-ufacturer. If remote is lost, it cannot be pro-grammed for time-shift recording, cannot pause tape, and cannot record tapes from a camcorder. Will not record timed programs after power failure. **Recommendation:** Good overall performance.

Panasonic PV-4611 A $200

Very good SP picture, good quality in EP. Good mono sound. But: Poor off-the-air reception of channels 14 and up. Lacks index search. It can program recordings only one month in advance. Cannot pause tape if remote is lost. Will not record timed programs after power failure. **Recommendation:** Good overall performance, but has some shortcomings.

Magnavox VRU342AT21 $180

Very good picture in both SP and EP. Very good monophonic sound. Alerts you if you program it to record two shows in the same time slot. But: Jog and shuttle controls make this a good machine for editing. A poor choice for receiving cable without a cable box. Lacks index search and on-screen

help for menu manipulation. Remote cannot con-trol a cable box. Cannot be programmed for time-shift recording if remote is lost. Will not record timed programs after power failure. **Recom-mendation:** Good picture and sound, but has some performance shortcomings.

JVC HR-VP434U $220

• Cable channel changer • Plug & play
Very good in SP. Poor picture quality in EP makes this unit better-suited to rental playback than to time-shift recording of long programs. Good mono, and easy to use. But: Reception of cable without a cable box judged only fair. **Recom-mendation:** There are better choices.

JVC HR-J430U $200

• Auto clock set
Very good SP picture, but poor quality in EP. Good monophonic sound. But: Limited features. Reception of cable without a cable box judged only fair. Lacks VCR Plus and on-screen help for menu manipulation. **Recommendation:** There are better choices.

Goldstar GVR-E448 $250

• Auto clock set • Go-to search
Very good sound, and easy to use. Can auto-matically switch from SP to EP to complete timed recording. But: Poorest picture quality in either tape speed of tested models. Poor off-the-air re-ception of VHF channels. Lacks on-screen help for menu manipulation. Cannot be programmed for time-shift recording if remote is lost. Cannot record tapes from a camcorder if remote is lost. Availability: Discontinued but still available. **Recommendation:** There are better choices.

APPLIANCES

Ranges, cooktops & ovens ──

Free-standing ranges offer the best value. Basic performance varies very little, but some models have inconveniences that are hard to live with.

Last CR report: *electric ranges, November 1996; gas ranges, March 1996; cooktops and wall ovens, July 1994*
Ratings: *pages 105 and 109*
Brand Repair Histories: *page 16*
Price range: *$200 to $2000*

The configurations

Cabinetry and floor plan will probably dictate the width and position of the range. Here are the choices:

Freestanding ranges. The old-standby, a freestanding range fits in the middle of a counter or at the end. Widths of this type range from 20 to 40 inches, but most are 30 inches. Price: $200 to $1500.

Built-in ranges. They come in two types: slide-ins, which fit into a space between cabinets, and drop-ins, which fit into cabinets connected below the oven. Drop-ins lack a storage drawer. Both types look built-in. Price: $450 to $1600.

Dual-oven ranges. The second oven—sometimes a microwave—is usually above the cooktop. Price: $1000.

Modular. A cooktop paired with a wall oven allows the most flexibility in layout. Most cooktops are 30 inches wide and are made of porcelain-coated steel or ceramic glass, with four elements or burners. Some are 36 inches wide, with space for an extra burner. Modular cooktops have pop-in grills, rotisseries, and other options.

Wall ovens come in 24-, 27-, and 30-inch widths (but some 30-inch ovens require a 33-inch cabinet). You can install an oven at eye level, nest the oven under a cooktop, or stack two ovens. Together, a cooktop and wall oven typically cost more than an all-in-one range. Price: $150 to $1100 for the cooktop, $375 to $2000 for the oven.

Element and burner types

Gas burners. Gas cooktops can be glass, porcelain-coated steel, or stainless steel. Gas burners—even so-called high-speed burners—tend to heat more slowly than electric elements. Burners that are sealed, with no space for spills to seep below the cooktop, are a bit easier to clean than conventional ones but, of the two types, the sealed ones have a slightly higher repair rate.

Electric elements. Electric elements heat quickly and can maintain low heat levels.

Coil elements are still the most common and least expensive type. Coils are fairly forgiving of warped and dented pots and, if they break, they're easy and cheap to replace. Spills burn off the coils and drip into bowls that are easily cleaned; heavy spills may go into wells under the prop-up cooktop. Ranges with coils usually have a porcelain cooktop.

Underneath the ceramic glass of a smoothtop may lie radiant, halogen, or induction elements.

Radiant elements are essentially very thin coils under a smoothtop.

Halogen burners are tungsten-halogen bulbs. Indicator lights on both types of cooktop signal when the surface is hot, even if the elements are off. A temperature limiter may guard against overheating. For efficient heating, radiant and halogen elements require flat-bottomed pots of about the same diameter. Halogen burners heat up slightly faster than radiant ones with the same wattage, but radiant elements come in higher wattages.

Induction elements use "magnetic induction" from a high-frequency electrical coil to heat the pot without heating the glass surface. Removing the pot from the surface turns off the heat. Heat goes on and off instantaneously. Pots must be iron or steel (magnetic metals) but don't have to have a flat bottom. Induction elements are the most expensive type of heating element.

A smoothtop's ceramic glass can be a black or patterned grayish-white ceramic glass. A patterned surface shows smudges and fingerprints less than a shiny black surface.

Spills are easy to clean, but sugary foods, which can pit the glass, should be wiped up promptly. To clean Ceran, according to the manufacturer, you should scape off any crust with a safety-razor in a holder and then apply Cook Top Cleaning Creme for Smooth Top Ranges, made by Elco Laboratories (708 534-3400). Though pricey, about $6 for a 10-ounce bottle, it works well on Ceran.

What's new

In addition to easier-to-clean smooth or sealed worktops, controls are becoming smooth, with electronic touchpads replacing traditional dials. There are more color choices, including faux marble patterns for cooktop surfaces, and brushed chrome for the professional look.

Modular units let you mix different

sizes of ovens and cooktops, different kinds of burners, and even different fuels.

Reliability

We collect repair data on ranges, but not on cooktops or wall ovens. According to our reader surveys, electric ranges have proven more reliable than gas models. Models of either type with conventional dial controls have been slightly more reliable than those with electronic controls on the oven.

Our 1995 survey of electric smooth-top and coil ranges purchased between 1989 and 1995 found that Whirlpool was one of the more reliable brands and Magic Chef, among the least reliable.

Among gas ranges bought between 1988 and 1995, Caloric had the worst record and Magic Chef, the second worst record. For more information, see the Brand Repair Histories on page 16.

Shopping strategy

For years, almost every range we've tested—gas or electric—has cooked, baked, and broiled just fine. Differences have centered around cooktop cleaning and other aspects of use.

Choose the type—gas or electric. The time-honored advantage of gas is fingertip control of the burner flame. But improvements in electric-burner technology have improved cooking with electricity. The conventional coil has been joined by radiant, halogen, and induction elements, which work in electric smoothtop models. Electric ovens have traditionally been more capacious and have heated more evenly than gas ones, but recent improvements have made gas ranges comparable in oven size and cooking performance. Many people don't have a choice of fuel, if they have no gas or propane. On average, a gas range costs $200 to $250 more than a comparable electric one.

Decide on the configuration. The freestanding electric range with coil elements remains the biggest-selling type. That's not surprising, since it's relatively inexpensive, dependable, and available in the widest selection of models. You'll pay a premium for stylish, specialized, and modular units such as built-in ranges, cooktop and wall ovens, and dual or combination ovens.

Decide on key features. Sealed gas burners make cleaning a bit easier. Smoothtop electric models are easier to clean than coil-burner models. Other aids to cleaning include: a self-cleaning oven, a porcelain or glass backguard.

Electronic oven controls use a keypad or buttons, rather than dials, to set time and temperature; any advantage is minor. See "Key features," below.

The easiest brands to find. General Electric, Whirlpool, and Sears, with its Kenmore brand, account for more than half the electric ranges sold. GE and Sears, with its Kenmore brand, sells the most gas ranges, with Tappan and Magic Chef following close behind. The big names in cooktops and wall ovens include GE, Jenn-Air, Maytag, Magic Chef, Kenmore (Sears), and Whirlpool.

Key features

Oven cleaning. Most ovens are lined with plain porcelain enamel, which must be cleaned with an oven cleaner. For $100 to $150 extra, you can opt for a self-cleaning oven. It uses a high-heat cycle (as high as 1000°) to turn accumulated spills and splatters into ash. When the cycle is complete, you wipe away the residue with a damp sponge. Another option is a "continuous clean" oven, whose special textured surface camouflages dirt and is supposed to dissipate grime.

Cooktop cleaning. Sealed burners on gas cooktops make cleaning a bit easier, especially those with removable parts. But ranges with these controls are more likely to need repair. They also add $75 to $100 to the price. Among electric cooktops, smoothtops are easy to clean but require special cleaners (see page 74).

Features that ease cleaning: porcelain drip pans; glass or porcelain backguard instead of a painted one; seamless corners and edges (especially where cooktop joins the backguard); a raised edge around the cooktop to contain spills; and no chrome edges. On a conventional, unsealed cooktop, look for deep wells to contain spills, minimal clutter under the cooktop, and a cooktop that props up for cleaning.

Oven capacity. Models with similar exterior dimensions may differ in capacity because of shelf supports and other protrusions. Some ovens are so small that you can't cook casseroles on two racks at the same time. Ovens that double as convection ovens typically lose space to the fan.

Oven controls. Dial controls and an analog clock/timer are generally less expensive than electronic controls. They also tend to be more reliable. Oven temperature is easy to set.

But electronic controls—digital timers with touchpads and light-emitting diode (LED) displays—are often easier to clean. They're more precise, too. The easiest designs to use have prompts and a phone-style keypad for entering time directly.

Cooktop controls. Dials are still the norm. Freestanding electric ranges have the controls laid out on the backguard; freestanding gas ranges, in front of the cooktop. On electric ranges, controls may be divided left and right, with the oven controls in between, giving you a quick sense of which control works which element. Controls clustered in the center of the backguard, however, are visible even when tall pots sit on back elements.

Downdraft vents. These eliminate the need for a range hood by venting the range from underneath the unit. Such an installation is useful for a cooktop in an island or peninsula.

Automatic-drip coffee makers

All automatic-drip machines make very good coffee. But some models are much easier to use than others.

Last CR report: *November 1996*
Price range: *$20 to $100*

The types

Size. Automatic-drip machines range from single-cup models to full-sized units that are supposed to brew 12 cups at a time. Ten and 12-cup machines are the biggest sellers.

Programmable or basic? It's nice to wake up to the smell of coffee, but a programmable coffee maker's built-in timer can add substantially to its price. Besides, you can brew your coffee in 15 minutes or less even with a no-frills coffee maker. Basic models start at about $20; programmables, at about $35.

What's new

Style. Color choices have expanded from the standard black or white to green or blue. The shape of the carafe can be sleek and globelike—like the carafe for the Krups Crystal Arome Time—or boxy, like most basic models. When it comes to replacing a carafe, note that stylish ones may cost more. The Krups' costs about $20, compared with $10 for a plain carafe.

Built-in water filters. These claim to reduce chlorine taste and odor. But, if you think your water is "chloriney," you'll probably want more than a coffee-maker filter.

Shopping strategy

Our tests over the years, including the ones for the most recent report, show that all automatic-drip coffee makers are capable of making very good coffee. It's safe then to choose a machine by price, convenience, and styling. See "Features," below.

In our last report, we found three CR Best Buys, all Mr. Coffees: two basic models, Accel PR15 ($22) and AD10 ($20), and the programmable Accel PRX20, $37.

Mass merchandisers, including Target and Wal-Mart, are good choices for low-priced brands such as Mr. Coffee. Department stores are the place to go for prestige brands. Coffee-maker sales are highest—and prices often lowest—in November and December.

Features

Time programming. Brews coffee at a preset time; you load water and ground coffee in advance. The grounds may lose some flavor from being exposed to air; whether you'll notice the loss in the brew itself depends on your palate and how long the grounds sit before the coffee's made.

Auto shut-off. Turns off the carafe's hotplate—usually after two hours. On some models, the shut-off time is adjustable up to 4 or 5 hours (though experts say coffee's all but ruined after about an hour). Standard on the programmables; sometimes also on basic models.

Espresso machines

Steam or pump? Steam machines make very good cappuccino and latte, and good espresso. Pump machines deliver excellent espresso, cappucino, and latte. Steam machines range from about $50 to $100; pump machines, about $140 to $200.

Recommendations. If you drink straight espresso and you're a purist about it, buy a pump machine. Only a pump will deliver coffee that's smooth, full-bodied, and crowned by rich crèma. If the machine will be used mostly to make milk-based drinks, or you don't mind settling for second-best espresso, there's no need to pay for a pump model. A steam espresso-maker will make cappuccinos and lattes that are almost as pleasing as those from a pump.

In our last report, November 1996, three pump models stood out: the Estro 410 ($190), available only at Starbucks coffee bars; Gaggia Espresso ($250); and DeLonghi Bar 19 FU ($170). Among steam machines, the top-rated Krups Il Primo 972 ($75) was top rated. Two models were almost as good, but a bit harder to clean—Mr. Coffee ECM8 ($45) and Betty Crocker BC-1724 ($40).

Clear markings. Marks on the carafe and inside the reservoir make it easier to add the amount of water you need. Instead of reservoir markings, some models have a narrow window or tube that shows the water level, sometimes with a floating ball to mark the cups as you load the water.

Easy loading. A big flip-top lid makes it easiest to pour in water.

Drip-stop. Prevents lingering drips after the pot is removed at the end of the brew cycle. It also allows you to sneak a cup before the whole pot is brewed (the stolen brew may be a bit weaker or a bit stronger than the batch as a whole).

Hotplate with nonstick coating. Helps with cleanup after a spill. Most models have it.

Small-batch setting. Some machines have a setting that adjusts the hotplate temperature for smaller quantities, to avoid overheating the coffee. Others have a setting that changes water flow, supposedly to saturate the smaller quantity of coffee grounds for a longer time. Neither feature is really necessary, in our view.

Brew-strength control. In past tests, we've found these have little effect. Our advice: Vary coffee strength by varying the grind and the amount of coffee you use.

Built-in water filter. Some of these claim to remove chlorine taste. But if you notice a chlorine taste in your coffee, it will probably bother you when you drink any water from the tap; you may want to use a tap-water filter. Braun also claims its filters remove the minerals that cause calcification. But even if they do, you'd only be trading the chore of descaling the machine with that of changing its filter cartridge (a necessary step with any built-in filter). And the cartridges can be pricey.

Cleanup. A Bunn model we tested has a descaling rod to physcially dislodge deposits, but we couldn't manipulate it successfully. For those with "hard" tap water, occasional "descaling" is required, but that's easily done by running white vinegar or a special solution through the coffee maker.

Microwave ovens ─────

Mid-sized models offer the best combination of price, cooking speed, and capacity.

Last CR report: *August 1996*
Ratings: *page 92*
Price range: *$100 to $250*

The sizes

A microwave oven's labeled size refers to the cooking cavity. The Association of Home Appliance Manufacturers defines microwave oven categories as follows:

subcompact, 0.59 cubic foot or less; *compact*, 0.60 to 0.79 cubic foot; *mid-sized*, 0.8 to 1.09 cubic feet; *family-sized*, 1.1 to 1.39 cubic feet; and *large-sized*, 1.4 or more. How that space translates into three dimensions depends on the design of the cabinet, which can use space more or less efficiently.

Most microwave ovens are designed to sit on a countertop. Small models can be mounted under cabinets. Some medium-sized models are specifically designed to be mounted over the range, under specially sized cabinets.

Size aside, the main difference between

large and small ovens is the power produced by the magnetron, which generates the high-energy microwaves that do the cooking. Family-sized models generally generate 900 to 1000 watts; mid-sized models, 800 to 900 watts; compact ovens, 600 to 700 watts. The more powerful the oven, the more quickly it heats food—a difference especially noticeable when you cook large quantities.

Large or family-sized ovens are the biggest selling sizes. They can hold lots of food, but they also take up lots of space on the counter—they're typically 22 to 24 inches wide and 16 to 19 inches deep. Price: $200 to $350.

Mid-sized ovens are much less bulky, and they sacrifice little in capacity, power, and versatility. It's the size we recommend. Price: $150 to $250.

The smallest ovens, somewhat larger than a toaster oven, may be too small for some frozen dinners or containers. But for basic chores like popping corn and warming beverages and leftovers, a small oven may be fine. Price: $100 to $150.

What's new

If you haven't bought a microwave oven lately, here are some of the ways these products have changed:

They cost less. In 1981, prices ranged from $400 to $500 or more for a large oven. Today, you can buy that size for anywhere from $120 to $290.

They're smaller and lighter. The last batch of ovens we tested are about two inches shorter and as much as four inches shallower than older models. One compact Sanyo uses a vertical format instead of the usual horizontal.

They deliver more power. Mid-sized and large ovens deliver 800 to 1050 watts at full power, so they cook faster than many older 750-watt models.

They're more styled. All-black or all-white, gray, almond, and faux stone cabinets are replacing the wood-grain look.

Reliability

Mid-sized microwave ovens have been slightly more reliable than full-sized models, our reader surveys show. Reliability by brand is not available this year.

Shopping strategy

Most of the ovens we've tested proved easy to use and quite capable of handling typical microwaving tasks.

Decide on size and power. Size and power usually go hand in hand. The larger the model, the more powerful its magnetron and the more quickly it cooks. Large models hold more, of course, but they also cost more and take up more space. See "The sizes," above.

Decide on the key features. If you want a microwave oven that's particularly easy to use, look for quick-setting and moisture-sensing features. See "Key features," below.

The easiest brands to find. Sharp dominates the microwave-oven market. Other prominent brands include General Electric, Kenmore (Sears), Panasonic, and Tappan.

People buy microwave ovens most often at discount stores like Wal-Mart and Kmart, followed by appliance/TV stores and Sears. New models are introduced spring through summer, with sales strongest from September to December.

Key features

Child lock-out. Nearly standard on mid- and full-sized models, this lets you punch in a code to disable the power.

Cooking-time entry. Most microwave ovens have 10 numbered electronic touchpads plus two or more special touchpads for reheating, popping popcorn, defrosting, and other tasks. Ordinarily, to set a heating time, you enter it directly: for example, 2, 3, 8 for 2 minutes and 38 seconds. A less convenient design requires you to enter that time by tapping a 1-minute pad twice, a 10-second pad 3 times, and a 1-second pad 8 times.

Instant-on. Controls with this feature cut down on button presses. You just press the cooking time and the oven starts. No need to touch Time or Start to get things going.

Interior light. Look for one that goes on when the door opens and whose light-bulb you can change without a service call.

Shortcut touchpads. With some ovens, you can tap in extra minutes to extend the time of a setting that's already on. With some, you can extend a setting by 30 seconds at a time.

Food programs. Many ovens have settings for cooking specific foods, such as potatoes or muffins. Typically, these settings time the cooking automatically.

Moisture sensor. Ovens with a moisture sensor reheated food especially well in our tests. The sensor is also helpful for other tasks, such as cooking vegetables.

Turntable. This improves cooking uniformity, but it also reduces usable space. One with a lip helps contain spills.

Window. Visibility varies, depending on the glass pattern and color.

Refrigerators

Except for some small models, they do a good job of keeping things cold. Energy-efficiency and convenience vary.

Last CR reports: *May 1996, February 1996*
Ratings: *page 97*
Brand Repair Histories: *pages 17 and 18*
Price range: *$450 to $6000*

The types and sizes

Top-freezer models. These are the most common type, and generally the least expensive to buy and run. They offer the widest choice of sizes, styles, and features. Width ranges from about 24 to 36 inches.

The eye-level freezer offers easy access. Fairly wide shelves in the refrigerator compartment make it easy to reach things at the back, but you have to bend or crouch to reach the bottom shelves. Nominal capacity ranges from about 10 to almost 26 cubic feet, but usable capacity is about 25 percent less, according to our tests. The apartment-sized top-freezer units (14 to 16 cubic feet) in our last test were noisier than any of the larger top-freezer models we've recently tested.

Typical 23-cubic-foot and larger models sell for $950 to $1500; 20- to 22-cubic-foot models, $700 to $1300; 18- to 19-cubic foot models, $550 to $900; 14- to 16-cubic foot models, $450 to $700.

Side-by-side models. These tend to be large—about 19 to 30 cubic feet of nominal capacity, 30 to 36 inches in width—and most expensive to buy and run. Advantages that may justify the expenditure: You can store food at eye level in both freezer and refrigerator compartments. The high, narrow compartments make it easy to find stray items (but hard to get at items in the back). The narrow doors require little clearance to open. The freezer is proportionally larger than in comparably sized top-freezer models. Side-by-side models come in a fairly wide selection of capacities and styles. Ice and water dispensers are most common in this configuration. Expect ice-makers to take up about a cubic foot of freezer space; ice-makers with ice and water dispensers, nearly two cubic feet.

Selling prices: large (24 to 30 cubic feet), $1050 to $2150; small (20 to 22 cubic feet), $800 to $1300.

Bottom-freezer models. These form a tiny part of the market and may be hard to find. Fairly wide eye-level shelves in the refrigerator compartment provide easy access to frequently used items. The freezer is low but often has a pull-out basket. In-door ice and water dispensers are unavailable. Nominal capacity: 20 to 22 cubic feet; width, about 33 inches. Price: about $1000.

Built-in models. Built-ins, sized from 10 to 33 cubic feet, are designed to fit flush with surrounding kitchen cabinets. Configured with the freezer on top or side-by-side, they're only 24 inches deep—a half-foot shallower than conventional models. They're also higher and wider. You can face them with custom door panels to match the cabinetry. Built-ins are expensive: $2000 to $6000. Installation can also be a major expense.

Built-in-style models. These can accept door panels to match cabinetry but aren't as shallow or wide as built-ins. They're available in bottom-freezer and side-by-side models types and have a typical capacity of 20, 21, and 24 cubic feet. Price: $1700 and up.

Compact models. With no more than six cubic feet of nominal capacity, this type is handy for a college dorm, office,

or small apartment. The models we've tested have been just rudimentary as refrigerators. Freezers, typically within the refrigerator compartment, get no colder than 15° or 20°; at those temperatures, ice cream turns soupy after only a few hours. If you adjust the control to make the freezer colder, items in the refrigerator compartment freeze. Compacts don't defrost automatically. This size generally isn't energy-efficient.

This segment of the market is dominated by familiar appliance names known better in electronics, such as Sanyo and Goldstar. General Electric and Whirlpool are also major players in this marketplace. Price: $150 to $400.

What's new

Models that use refrigerants known as hydrofluorocarbons (HFCs) are fast replacing those that use chlorofluorocarbons (CFCs). Since CFCs deplete the earth's ozone layer, a refrigerator that uses HFC refrigerant is a better choice. (Chemicals in the more recent models can also affect the ozone layer, but to a far lesser extent.) On the whole, the new refrigerators appear to be as competent and efficient as the older designs—and they cost no more.

Reliability

Refrigerators with ice-makers have been much more likely to need repairs, according to our surveys of CONSUMER REPORTS readers.

Among plain top-freezer models bought new between 1989 and 1995, Magic Chef, White-Westinghouse, Whirlpool, and Kenmore (Sears) were among the more reliable brands. Among the brands in our repair history, Amana had the worst repair record.

Among side-by-side refrigerators bought during the same period, General Electric has been among the least reliable brands. For more information, see the Brand Repair Histories on pages 17 and 18.

Shopping strategy

Even with improvements in energy efficiency, a refrigerator uses a lot of electricity over its life, which is typically about 15 years. Operating costs depend largely on how big the refrigerator is and whether it's a top-freezer, side-by-side, or bottom-freezer model. But design matters, too. Over the years, our tests have regularly shown that some manufacturers offer more efficient models than others. Be sure to check the bright-yellow energy-guide label on models in the store. Our findings show that the Energy Guide label can help you choose a more efficient model.

Decide on the size. Width is the key dimension in fitting a refrigerator, though you should also measure how much room you have overhead and for the door. Newer homes nearly always have room for a refrigerator that's at least 20 to 22 cubic feet—a medium-sized top-freezer refrigerator or a small side-by-side unit. The openings for refrigerators in some apartments and older homes are only 30 inches wide—and so can accommodate a top-freezer refrigerator of up to only 19 cubic feet.

Decide on the type. Top-freezer refrigerators are less expensive than other types, and they generally use space and electricity more efficiently. Next most popular are side-by-side designs; they put nonfrozen food at eye level, but their narrow compartments can make some items hard to reach. Many taller people prefer bottom-freezer models.

Decide on key features. These include shelf type (glass shelves are a step up from wire ones); temperature and humidity controls; and ice-makers and water dispensers. Generally, the larger the refrigerator, the more richly endowed—and, of course, the more expensive—it will be. A through-the-door ice-maker and dispenser, for example, may add $200 or so to the price; it will also eat up almost two cubic feet of freezer space.

The easiest brands to find. The top sellers are General Electric, Kenmore (Sears), Amana, and Whirlpool. Kenmore refrigerators are made by other manufacturers, including General Electric and Whirlpool. General Electric also makes Hotpoint models, and Whirlpool makes KitchenAid models. Such family ties often result in strong similarities between refrigerators that bear different nameplates.

Key features

Automatic ice-maker. These typically produce three or four pounds of ice a day—and use about a cubic foot of freezer space. Standard on some models; available as a kit ($70 to $100) on others. Installation takes a fairly handy person an hour or less. Today's ice-makers appear to be sturdier than the trouble-prone devices of old, but models with an ice-maker still have a higher repair rate than those without.

Door bins. These help contain items and (unlike door shelves) can be removed for cleaning. Some have covers to guard against spills and to protect smaller items.

Door-opening direction. Top- and bottom-freezer models have doors that can hinge either on the right or left, depending on the kitchen workspace.

Door-shelf adjustments. These help prevent items from tumbling or sliding when the door is opened. Shelf-height extenders support tall bottles. "Snuggers" hold articles in tight; some double as a bottle holder.

Freezer light. Handy for locating items.

Humidity-controlled crispers. Some refrigerators have controls that allow you to adjust humidity in their crisper drawers. The controls work, as our tests show, but crispers without them can retain moisture just as well.

No-frost operation. This is practically a given these days except on the smallest, cheapest models. Most self-defrosting models defrost about once a day, after their compressor has run for a certain number of hours. State-of-the-art defrost systems modify the defrost cycle as needed.

See-through compartments. Transparent crispers, dairy compartments, and meat drawers let you tell at a glance what's inside.

Separate temperature controls. A single control that governs the main compartment and freezer works fine, but separate controls make it easier to accommodate special preferences—say, to keep ice cream soft.

Spill-proof glass shelves. Much easier than wire shelves to clean and to adjust in height. Sealed, raised edges help contain spills. Some shelves slide out for better access, or fold or slide sideways, to make room for tall items below.

Temperature-controlled drawer for meat. Most refrigerators have a separate drawer for storing meat and fish. Some send chilled air directly into the drawer to make it reach 30° to 32°—the ideal temperature for storing fresh meat and fish. (The optimal temperature for the main compartment is 37°.)

Utility bins. These are useful for storing odds and ends on shelves. Some have covers. Some are made to hold eggs, but we think it's safer to keep eggs in their original carton.

Wine-bottle rack. Prevents bottles from cluttering the door or rolling about on shelves.

Dishwashers

Washing performance among mid-priced models is uniformly good. Avoid budget-priced models.

Last CR report: *October 1995*
Brand Repair Histories: *page 19*
Price range: *$250 to $1000*

The types

Built-in models. This type attaches permanently to a hot-water pipe, a drain, and electrical lines. It generally fits into a 24-inch-wide space under the countertop, between two base cabinets. Compact models fit in an 18-inch space. Price: $250 to $1000.

Portable models. Portable machines, for kitchens without the space for a built-in dishwasher, are a small but steady part of the market. They're identical to built-ins, except they come in a finished cabinet on rollers and hook up to the sink faucet for use. Portables can later be converted to an under-cabinet installation. Price: $400 to $500.

What's new

They use less energy. Prodded by Federal regulations that went into effect in 1994, manufacturers have found ways to use less energy while maintaining good cleaning performance. The newest models do it mainly by reducing hot water consumption—fewer wash and rinse cycles, with less water.

They're "smarter." A new generation of "smart" dishwashers use what's called "fuzzy logic" technology. This pricey feature adjusts wash and rinse times to the soil on the dishes.

Reliability

Whirlpool, Hotpoint, Amana, GE, and Magic Chef have been among the most reliable built-in dishwasher brands, according to our reader survey asking about dishwashers bought new from 1989 to 1995. White-Westinghouse and Frigidaire have been among the least reliable. For more information, see the Brand Repair Histories on page 19.

Shopping strategy

Our tests have usually turned up substantial performance differences among models of dishwashers, more than with other major appliances. But in our most recent test of mid-priced models, cleaning performance was uniformly good. You can find solid performers for less than $500. But avoid budget models—they're not likely to clean nearly as well as midline models. Quietness of operation did not correlate with price.

Energy efficiency varies. Models in our last test would cost $55 to $75 a year for electrically heated water and $30 to $45 for water heated with gas, at average national utility rates. You can compare energy efficiency by using the yellow Energy Guide stickers.

Decide on the type. Nearly all dishwashers these days are built-in, under-cabinet models. Sales of portables with faucet hookup are a small part of the market.

Decide on the key features. Features such as electronic controls, "fuzzy logic," specialized cycles, and decorator colors add to a dishwasher's price, and manufacturers generally make models with and without those elements.

Other aspects of a machine are more integral to the brand. For instance, one manufacturer's rack design may or may not suit your dishes and glassware better than another's. Or the rack design may offer more or less flexibility in loading. See "Key features," below.

The easiest brands to find. Kenmore (Sears), General Electric, Whirlpool, Maytag, and Kitchen Aid account for more than three-fourths of the dishwashers sold in the U.S. You'll also find European-made models such as Bosch, Miele, Asko, and GE's Monogram line.

Key features

Controls. Manual controls consist of simple push buttons and a dial, which let you reset cycles quickly. They do the job just fine and cost less than electronic controls. Electronic models couple touchpads with displays that show the time for various dishwasher operations or flash warnings about malfunctions.

Cycles. Three basic cycles—a light cycle for less-soiled loads, a normal one for typical soil, and a heavy cycle for tough or hardened soil—are all you need. Dishwashers clean best on their heaviest cycle, but a light cycle may be sufficient for lightly soiled dishes. Most people stick with the normal setting.

Many models have a *rinse-and-hold* cycle that rinses dishes until you have enough for a full load. That may be useful if it takes you more than a few days to accumulate a full load. Other cycles—

Pot Scrubber, Soak-and-Scrub, and *China-and-Crystal*—are mainly an excuse for a higher price tag.

Fuzzy logic. Found on top-of-the-line GE and Maytag models, this feature adjusts the wash and rinse cycles to the dirt on the dishes. In our tests, it worked well but not necessarily better than some machines without it.

Noise. Quiet operation is a major selling point—and claims and labels are a poor guide to choosing a quiet machine, according to our tests. European-made models have been the quietest in our tests.

Filter. Our tests have shown that machines with filters clean much better than those without them. Look for self-cleaning filters, which require no attention.

Racks and baskets. Most designs put cups and glasses on top and plates on the bottom. Rack variations include folding shelves to let you add extra cups and glasses; small spring-loaded arms to secure lightweight items, and an adjustable upper rack for tall glasses. Flatware baskets are typically in the main dish rack.

Water and energy-conserving features. Most of the energy a dishwasher uses is in the form of hot water from your water heater. The pump, motor, and heating element use relatively little electricity.

A *Delay-start* setting lets you program the dishwasher to start later, a useful feature if your utility has off-peak rates. All dishwashers let you choose between a heated dry cycle and the more energy-efficient no-heat dry.

Soft-food disposer. Models with this feature grind and dispose of soft food.

Tub. A porcelain-coated steel tub resists stains better than a plastic tub, but porcelain is vulnerable to chipping. The most durable tub material is stainless steel, but you may pay a premium for it.

Washing machines

They all get clothes clean. Differences are in capacity and energy efficiency.

Last CR report: *July 1996*
Ratings: *page 88*
Brand Repair Histories: *page 18*
Price range: *$250 to $2000 or more*

The types

Most people buy a **top-loader** because that's mainly what's available. Top-loaders have clear advantages over **front-loaders**. By opening from the top, they're easier to load and it's easy to add items mid-cycle. They're about twice as roomy as a front-loader, and their cycle time is faster. They're also as much as $500 cheaper, but that's offset by operating expenses. Price: $250 to $800.

While a front-loader costs more to buy, it takes less energy and much less water than a top-loader. In a regular-wash cycle, water used is about 16 to 25 gallons, versus 37 to 46. Front-loaders also handle unbalanced loads better. Capacity may improve with the new Frigidaire, whose tub is supposed to be almost as roomy as a top-loader's. The selection is limited to Frigidaire, Asko, and Miele. Amana and Maytag are expected to offer models in the next year. Price: $1000 to $2000.

What's new

Washers more efficient than the ones we tested may be on the horizon.

Although the U.S. Department of Energy is not likely to raise efficiency standards for at least several years, some manufacturers plan to offer more efficient washers by 1997 or 1998.

The yellow Energy Guide tag on all washers offers a rough idea of efficiency. But it doesn't take maximum load size into account, as we do, and it penalizes a washer that offers a warm rinse

Reliability

On the basis of our readers' experience with washing machines bought new between 1989 and 1995, we've found Whirlpool to be among the most reliable brands; Frigidaire, Magic Chef, and White-Westinghouse, among the least reliable. For more information, see the Brand Repair Histories on page 18.

Shopping strategy

All the washers we've tested in recent years cleaned clothes well when they were set for a hot wash and cold rinse and for the longest and strongest agitation. But even the gentler cycles cleaned well, especially if the load wasn't heavily soiled.

Differences come down to capacity, features, and energy efficiency. You can get a rough idea of energy use and operating costs for any washer by checking its yellow "Energy Guide" label.

Decide on the type. Top-loaders are the most practical choice for now, but Federal energy requirements are likely to change that in the next few years.

Decide on key features. Most are niceties, not necessities. See "Key features, below."

The easiest brands to find. A few manufacturers dominate the laundry market. Just four brands—Kenmore (Sears), Whirlpool, Maytag, and General Electric—account for most of the washers sold in the U.S.

Key features

Controls. Look for dials and buttons that are clearly labeled, logically arranged, and easy to push and turn. Also desirable: an illuminated control panel, a cycle-indicator light, and a buzzer to signal the end of a cycle.

Cycles. Regular, Permanent Press, and Delicate are all you usually need. The cycle you choose may determine the speed and water temperature, though on many models those choices are up to you. Extra speeds let you choose your own combinations, to tailor the washer's actions to the washload, if you want to bother.

Dispensers. Some machines have dispensers that release bleach and fabric softener at the appropriate time. The least convenient dispensers are small and let bleach splatter into the tub itself, where it can damage laundry.

Drain height. A washer must drain into a waste line, which may be quite a bit higher than the top of the machine. The maximum drain height ranges from four to eight feet.

Fill level. The most economical way to wash is with a full load. When that's not practical, you can lower the fill level to save water, detergent, and energy. Some models let you fine-tune the water level to the gallon. Machines that offer five fill levels are less versatile, but better than those with only three or four.

Finish of the top and lid. We recommend porcelain-coated steel, which, though prone to chip, withstands the inevitable scraping and scratching better than a painted finish.

Lid/door opening. Top-loaders have lids hinged at the back or to the right or left. Make sure the direction fits your installation. A lid hinged at the rear adapts to all locations. Doors to front-loader washers open down or to the side.

Noise. Models vary greatly in the noise they generate. Claims for quietness did not correlate with the results of our tests.

Serviceability. Accessibility is important if anything goes wrong. The GE models are the most service-friendly.

Temperature settings. You generally need only three wash temperatures: hot, warm, and cold, followed by a cold rinse.

Warm water doesn't rinse any better than cold water, and it wastes energy. Automatic temperature control, a feature found in Kenmore models, helps adjust the temperature of incoming water. It worked in our tests, although not perfectly. It might be useful if you have unusually cold or warm water piped to your house.

Tubs. Most are porcelain-coated steel. If the porcelain chips, the steel underneath is apt to rust. That won't happen with a stainless-steel or plastic tub.

Clothes dryers

Virtually any dryer will dry clothes adequately. You'll pay extra for convenience features.

Last CR report: *May 1995*
Brand Repair Histories: *page 19*
Price range: *$200 to $600*

Size and capacity

Full-sized models are 27 to 29 inches wide and have a drum capacity of 5 to 7 cubic feet. Some brands offer only one size of drum for all dryers in their line; other brands offer a larger drum in their top-of-the-line machines. The larger the drum, the more easily a dryer handles bulky items, and the less likely big loads will come out wrinkled. Price: $250 to $600.

Manufacturers also make compact models (mostly electrics) with capacities roughly half that of full-sized models, about 3½ cubic feet. Often, you can save space by stacking a compact atop a companion washer. And it can plug into a regular outlet instead of a heavy-duty, 240-volt line. But drying takes much longer with a compact model. Compacts generally sell for $300.

What's new

Like washing machines, dryers must meet Government energy standards that took effect in mid-1994. To do so, all dryers must have at least one automatic-drying cycle.

Reliability

Data from our reader survey show that Magic Chef and Frigidaire electric dryers purchased between 1989 and 1995 have been more trouble-prone than other brands of electric or gas dryers.

For gas dryers, Whirlpool and Sears have been among the more reliable brands. For more information, see the Brand Repair Histories on page 19.

Shopping strategy

Nearly all the dryers we've tested in the past five years dried ordinary laundry well. Spending more buys convenience such as drying racks and lighted drums. It can also buy more electronic controls for dryness and more temperatures.

If you have gas service, opt for a gas dryer. Although gas dryers are priced about $50 more than electrics, they are cheaper to run. The energy you save should offset the price difference within the first year of ownership.

Decide on the size and capacity. Machines vary in the size of their drum, which determines the size of the load and if you can dry bulky items like comforters. Dryers also come in compact versions that take up less space.

Decide on features. Even basic models now offer an auto-dry cycle, which automatically shuts off the dryer when the laundry is dry. A moisture sensor can further reduce wasteful overdrying, but that feature comes only in mid- and high-priced models. See "Key features," below.

The easiest brands to find. The biggest-selling brands are Kenmore (Sears), Whirlpool, GE, and Maytag.

Key features

Antiwrinkling. Most dryers let you extend cool tumbling from 15 minutes to a couple of hours after the end of the drying cycle. This useful feature, sometimes called Wrinkle Guard or Press Guard, helps prevent wrinkling if you can't empty the dryer right away. Less useful is Wrinkle Remove or a similarly named feature that puts wrinkled dry clothes through a short spell of tumbling at low or no heat followed by a cooldown. Any dryer with a temperature selector can do that.

Auto-dry systems. Most dryers use a thermostat to check dampness indirectly. As clothes dry, the air leaving the drum gets progressively hotter. When the temperature rises enough, the sensor signals

the thermostat to cycle off, and the timer advances until the heat goes on again. The process is repeated until the heating part of the cycle has ended. Top-of-the-line and some mid-priced models use a moisture sensor that actually gauges dryness. Such sensors are usually a bit more accurate than thermostats.

Controls. Electronic controls may prove slightly more convenient once you've mastered them. Our tests show that electronic controls tend to work more precisely than dials. Regular dial controls generally work well and are easy to use as long as too many choices aren't squeezed onto the dial.

Cycles. Basic dryers offer just one automatic-drying cycle. Pricier ones typically offer two or three—Regular, Permanent Press, and Knit/Delicate, for instance—plus unheated settings. A more-dry-to-less-dry range on the automatic settings lets you fine-tune drying to the load.

Door opening. A large opening makes loading and unloading easier. Some doors open down, some to the right, and a few are reversible.

End-of-cycle signal. Most models have a buzzer or other warning that sounds the end of the drying cycle. You can disarm the signal or adjust loudness in some models..

Finish. The cabinet top and drum on most dryers are coated with baked enamel. More expensive models have a porcelain top, which resists scratching better.

Lint filter. One type fits inside the drum opening. Another opens from the top of the dryer's cabinet. The top-mounted filters are generally easier to clean.

Two-way tumbling. This Frigidaire feature allows tumbling in one direction for about five minutes, then the other way for about half a minute. It's supposed to cut drying time by a third and reduce wrinkling, but we haven't seen the proof.

Breadmakers

They bake great-tasting bread, but some do it better than others and with less fuss.

Last CR report: *December 1995*
Ratings: *page 114*
Price range: *$90 to $300*

What's new

Prices are dropping. As more companies have begun to make them, breadmakers have become less expensive. You can buy a basic model for about $90, a full-featured model for about $300.

The size. The one-pound loaf has given way to larger loaves—$1\frac{1}{2}$ and 2 pounds.

The shape. Most machines now turn out a nearly square loaf, rather than the odd-looking round one of a few years ago.

Shopping strategy

All the breadmakers we've tested make good bread if you use fresh ingredients and measure them correctly. But a model with well-designed controls and simple loading and cleanup is easiest to live with.

Decide on capacity and features. Machines make loaves of various sizes: 1, $1\frac{1}{2}$, or 2 pounds, or 8 to 16 slices. Choose according to the size of your household and how often you'll be making bread. A small machine is the least expensive—$90 to $120. The larger breadmakers are priced at $120 to $270; they can make a small loaf as well.

Extra cycles and controls generally cost extra. See "Key features" below.

The easiest brands to find. A few years ago, there were nine major breadmaker brands; today there are about 20.

West Bend is the biggest brand, followed by Welbilt, Toastmaster, and Oster.

Key features

Controls. All models have a digital display indicating time left. Some also indicate the stage of preparation. Setting controls is usually easy.

Cycles. White, Whole wheat, and Dough cycles are standard. The Dough cycle shuts off the machine so you can remove the dough for shaping and baking in a conventional oven. Rapid cycle cuts an hour or so off the kneading and rising time, but bread made that way is not as high or fluffy as standard-cycle bread.

Delay-start timer. This lets you add the ingredients and select a time (up to 13 hours ahead) for the bread to be ready.

Door opening. Typically, the door is on top of the machine. The door on one West Bend model opens from the front. That makes for easier access, but we had trouble shutting it and it exposes you to the hot areas as you take out the bread.

Mix-in signal. A buzzer lets you know when to add raisins, caraway seeds, and so forth. If your machine has no mix-in signal, add such ingredients before the end of the second knead cycle.

Special cycles. They include French bread, sweet bread, cake, and "sandwich" bread. The Custom cycle on the Zojirushi lets you program kneading, rising, and baking times yourself, but you have to make the adjustments manually. The Zojirushi model also makes jam. And one Toastmaster model can churn fresh butter from cream in half an hour.

Viewing windows. Most models have a window to let you view the action.

Ratings *Washing machines*
& Recommendations

The tests behind the Ratings

Cleaning tells how well a machine cleaned an eight-pound load in its longest and most "aggressive" wash cycle when set for a hot wash, cold rinse, and maximum water fill. Under **capacity**, we determined the pounds of **wash** a machine could circulate effectively and how many gallons of **water** it used at that capacity. **Efficiency** is based on a machine's consumption of water (at the max. fill level) and energy (an average of electricity and gas costs) per pound of laundry. **Price** is the estimated average, based on a national survey. Models similar to those we tested are noted in Details; features may vary. **Model availability:** D means model is discontinued. S means model is replaced, according to me manufacturer; successor model is noted in Details. New model was not tested; it may or may not perform similarly. Features may vary.

Standard features for these models by brand

Whirlpool washers we tested: • Have an extra-long wash. • Lack a lip on top to contain spills. Also for Sears/Kenmore washers: • A lid that hampers access; it opens to the left and doesn't lie flat. General Electric washers (family includes Hotpoint): • Handle unbalanced loads better than most. • Are easier to service than others. • Have a small, shallow bleach dispenser. Maytag washers: • Have porcelain on top and lid; harder to scratch than paint. • Have a better bleach dispenser than most. • Lack self-leveling rear legs; hard to install washer in a niche. • Lack a lip on top to contain spills. Amana (family includes Speed Queen) washers: • Have a stainless-steel basket. • Can provide a warm rinse with a warm wash. • Are harder to service than most. Frigidaire (family includes White-Westinghouse, Kelvinator, Gibson, Tappan) washers: • Can provide a warm rinse with a warm wash. • Handle unbalanced loads better than most. • Have especially convenient controls. • Have only two wash/spin speed combinations.

Recommendations

All cleaned well. Base your choice on capacity, features, efficiency, and price. If your laundry is piled high on washday, consider one of the GE or Kenmore machines. They hold 14 or 15 pounds of laundry and are fairly efficient with energy and water. The best value is the General Electric WJSR2080T, $400.

See report, page 83. Last time rated in Consumer Reports: July 1996.

Overall Ratings

E VG G F P

Listed in order of washing ability, capacity, and efficiency

Brand and model	Price	Overall score 0 · · · 100	Cleaning	Capacity WASH	WATER	Efficiency
		P F G VG E				
Kenmore (Sears) 2598 Ⓓ	$600		⊖	15 lb.	43 gal.	⊖
Kenmore (Sears) 2588 Ⓢ	530		⊖	15	41	⊖
General Electric Profile WPSQ4160T	500		⊖	14	39	⊖
Kenmore (Sears) 2581 Ⓓ	480		⊖	15	42	⊖
Kenmore (Sears) 2575 Ⓓ	450		⊖	15	42	⊖
General Electric WJSR2080T	400		⊖	14	43	⊖
Amana LW8303 [W] 2 Ⓓ	440		⊖	14	42	⊖
Whirlpool LSL9355D Ⓓ	520		⊖	14	42	○
KitchenAid KAWE77B	510		⊖	14	42	⊖
Maytag LAT9824AA Ⓓ	620		⊖	11	37	○
Admiral LATA400AA	400		⊖	12	41	○
Whirlpool LSR7233D Ⓓ	400		⊖	14	42	○
Speed Queen AWM573 [W] 2 Ⓓ	430		⊖	12	42	○
Maytag LAT9605AA Ⓓ	540		⊖	11	37	○
Roper RAX7245B Ⓓ	380		⊖	13	43	○
Magic Chef W225L Ⓓ	390		⊖	12	39	○
Frigidaire FWS445RB Ⓓ	380		⊖	11	46	◐
White-Westinghouse WWS445RB Ⓢ	350		⊖	11	46	◐

Model details *Listed in order of overall score*

Kenmore (Sears) 2598 Ⓓ $600
• HxWxD: 42¼x27x27 in.
It lets you choose among four wash/spin speed combinations and has an extra rinse you can select at the start, a porcelain top and lid, and an automatic detergent dispenser. It can blend hot and cold water to a preset temperature and provide a warm rinse with both warm and hot washes. Its bleach dispenser is timed and works better than others. **Recommendation:** A very good performer that holds 15 pounds, has many desirable features, and is quieter than most. But other Sears models may be a better value.

Kenmore (Sears) 2588 Ⓢ $530
• HxWxD: 42¼x27x26¼ in.
Similar to the 2598, above, except it lacks an automatic detergent dispenser and timed bleach dispenser and is slightly noisier. **Successor:** 2684. **Recommendation:** Very good. A lot like the 2598 and less expensive.

Ratings continued ▶

Model details *Continued*

General Electric Profile WPSQ4160T $500

• HxWxD: 41x27x26 in.
It has an extra rinse and extra spin you can select at the start. It can provide a warm rinse with a warm wash. You can ask it to beep when it's finished. It has mechanical touchpad controls. **Recommendation:** Very good and has some desirable features.

Kenmore (Sears) 2581 Ⓓ $480

• HxWxD: 42¼x27x26¼ in.
It lets you choose among four wash/spin speed combinations. It has an extra rinse, but you must set it after the washer is finished. It can blend hot and cold water to a preset temperature and can provide a warm rinse with both warm and hot washes. But: It has only three water levels. **Recommendation:** Very good and holds 15 lbs.

Kenmore (Sears) 2575 Ⓓ $450

• HxWxD: 42¼x27x26¼ in.
It has an extra rinse, but you must set it after the washer is finished. It can provide a warm rinse with both warm and hot washes. Its controls are more convenient to use than most. **Recommendation:** Very good, but has few added features.

General Electric WJSR2080T $400

• HxWxD: 41x27x26 in.
Its controls are especially convenient. But: It has only two wash/spin speed combinations and only three water levels. **Recommendation:** Very good and is a good value.

Amana LW8303[W]2 Ⓓ $440

• HxWxD: 42½x25¾x28 in.
It lets you choose among four wash/spin speed combinations. **Recommendation:** Very good.

Whirlpool LSL9355D Ⓓ $520

• HxWxD: 41¾x27x26¼ in.
It has an extra rinse you can select at the start and can provide a warm rinse with a warm wash. It has mechanical touchpad controls. A dispenser for fabric softener is available from the manufacturer at no extra charge. **Recommendation:** Very good and is quieter than most.

KitchenAid KAWE77B $510

• HxWxD: 42x27x26¼ in.
It has an extra rinse you can select at the start and a porcelain top and lid. It buzzes when it's finished. It can provide a warm rinse with warm and hot washes. But: It lacks a lip on top to help contain spills. **Recommendation:** Good and quieter than most.

Maytag LAT9824AA Ⓓ $620

• HxWxD: 43x25½x26¾ in.
It lets you choose among four wash/spin speed combinations, has a porcelain top and lid, has an extra rinse you can select at the start, and can provide a warm rinse with a warm wash. **Similar:** LAT9804, $640. **Recommendation:** Good and quieter than most. But it's expensive, and holds only 11 lbs.

Admiral LATA400AA $400

• HxWxD: 43½x27x27 in.
It lets you choose among four wash/spin speed combinations and has an automatic dispenser that releases liquid detergent during Pre-wash. But: It's harder to service than most. The bleach dispenser is small and shallow, and it let bleach spatter into the basket. **Recommendation:** Good overall, but be careful if you use bleach.

Whirlpool LSR7233D Ⓓ $400

• HxWxD: 41¾x27x26¼ in.
The controls are especially convenient. But: It has only three water levels. **Recommendation:** Good, but it has few features.

Speed Queen AWM573[W]2 Ⓓ $430

• HxWxD: 42½x25¾x28 in.
It can provide a warm rinse with a warm wash. It has a stainless-steel inner tub, and its controls are especially convenient. But: It has only two wash/spin speed combinations, and it's harder to service than most. **Recommendation:** Good and quieter than most.

Maytag LAT9605AA Ⓓ $540

• HxWxD: 43x25½x26¾ in.
It has a porcelain top and lid and can provide a warm rinse with a warm wash. But: It has only

Ratings continued ▶

four water levels and two wash/spin speed combinations. **Recommendation:** Good and quieter than most. But it's fairly expensive, and holds only 11 lbs.

Roper RAX7245B Ⓓ $380

• HxWxD: 41¼x27x26¼ in.
It can provide a warm rinse with a hot wash. But: It has only two wash/spin speed combinations and a single spin speed, and it lacks a lip on top to help contain spills. **Recommendation:** Good overall, but it has few features.

Magic Chef W225L Ⓓ $390

• HxWxD: 43½x27x27 in.
It's harder to service than most. The bleach dispenser is small and shallow, and it let bleach spatter into the basket. It comes without a dispenser for fabric softener. **Recommendation:** Good overall, but it has few features. Be careful if you use bleach.

Frigidaire FWS445RB Ⓓ $380

• HxWxD: 41½x27x27 in.
Recommendation: Good enough overall, but it holds only 11 lbs. of laundry and is less energy-efficient than most.

White-Westinghouse WWS445RB Ⓢ $350

• HxWxD: 42½x27x27 in.
Successor: MWS445RE. **Recommendation:** See the Frigidaire, above.

How to use the Ratings in the Buying Guide

■ Read the Recommendations for information on specific models and general buying advice.

■ Note how the rated products are listed—in order of performance and convenience, price, or alphabetically.

■ The overall score graph gives the big picture in performance. Notes on features and performance for individual models are listed in the Comments column or "Model details."

■ Before going to press, we verify model availability for most products with manufacturers. Some tested models listed in the Ratings may no longer be available. Models that have been discontinued are marked Ⓓ; some may actually still be available in some stores for part of 1997. A model marked Ⓢ is a successor to the tested model, according to the manufacturer, and is noted in Comments or Model details. Features may vary.

■ Models similar to the tested models, when they exist, are indicated in Comments or Model details.

■ To find our last full report on a subject, check the reference above the Ratings chart or the eight-year index, page 342.

Ratings
& Recommendations
Microwave ovens

The tests behind the Ratings

Brand and model may have brackets around a number or letter; the bracketed part will change with the oven's color. **Overall score** is based on performance and convenience. We assessed **even heating** by cooking a large batch of whipped canned yams on High, without stirring. We tested **automatic defrost** by thawing one-pound packages of frozen ground chuck. The four models with no score had no Auto Defrost key. Models similar to those we tested are noted in Details; features may vary. **Price** is the estimated average, based on a survey. **Model availability:** Ⓓ means model is discontinued. Ⓢ means model is replaced, according to the manufacturer; successor model is noted in Details. New model was not tested; it may or may not perform similarly. Features may vary.

Standard features for these models

• A white body and white window screen, which may reduce visibility. • 6 to 10 power levels. • An Automatic Defrost setting and automatic settings for popcorn and other specific foods. • Electronic controls with numbered touchpads. • Settings you can program for up to almost 100 minutes. • A glass turntable that must be in place for the oven to operate. • An LED display. • A clock and kitchen timer. • An interior light with a bulb you can't replace yourself. • A child lock-out safety feature. • A push-panel door latch.

Recommendations

Best of the large was the Panasonic NN-77[5]5A, $220, or its successor, the NN-S776[ ]A, which sells for about $190. An excellent family-sized oven: the Sharp R-4H[1]7, $200. For a very good mid-sized oven: The GE JE940[W]W, $140. Best of the compacts: the Samsung MW4552[W], $115.

See report, page 76. Last time rated in Consumer Reports: August 1996.

Overall Ratings

	E	VG	G	F	P
	⊖	⊖	○	○	●

Listed by size; within size, listed in order of overall score

Brand and model	Price	Overall score 0 ... 100	Ease of use	Even heating	Auto defrost
		P F G VG E			
LARGE					
Panasonic NN-77[5]5A Ⓢ	$220	▬▬▬▬▬	⊖	○	⊖ [1]
Sharp R-5H[1]6 Ⓓ	240	▬▬▬▬	⊖	◐	⊖ [1]

Brand and model	Price	Overall score 0 — 100 (P F G VG E)	Ease of use	Even heating	Auto defrost
General Electric JE1550[G]V [S]	$240		⊖	○	◒
Kenmore (Sears) 8968[6] [S]	170		○	○	○
FAMILY-SIZED					
Sharp R-4H[1]7	200		⊖	○	⊖ [1]
Sharp R-4A[9]7 [D]	170		⊖	○	⊖ [1]
Samsung MW6552[W]	180		⊖	○	⊖
General Electric JE1240[W]V [S]	170		○	◒	⊖ [1]
Tappan TMT117U1[W]0 [D]	170		○	○	⊖
Whirlpool MT5111XD[Q] [D]	140		⊖	○	⊖
Kenmore (Sears) 8948[1] [S]	160		○	◒	⊖
Amana R[W]635T	230		○	◒	—
Magic Chef DM46K[W]-17T	180		○	◒	—
MID-SIZED					
Sharp R-3A[9]7 [D]	150		⊖	⊖	⊖
General Electric JE940[W]W	140		○	⊖	⊖ [1]
Tappan TMS083U1[S]0 [D]	130		○	○	○
Quasar MQS0853[H] [D]	140		⊖	◒	○
Goldstar MA-108[0]M [D]	130		⊖	◒	○
Magic Chef DM15K[W]-15T	125		○	◒	○
COMPACT					
Samsung MW4552[W]	115		⊖	○	⊖
Whirlpool MT1066XB[Q]	140		⊖	○	⊖
General Electric JE640[W]V [D]	135		○	◒	○
Emerson MW8675[W] [D]	100		○	⊖	⊖
Emerson MW8775[W] [D]	110		◒	○	⊖ [1]
Sharp R-2A[4]7 [S]	110		○	○	—
Kenmore (Sears) 8912[0]	100		○	◒	⊖
Sharp R-1A[5]6 [D]	90		◒	⊖	—
Goldstar MA-685M [D]	100		◒	○	○

[1] Defrosted especially fast—within 5 to 7 minutes, plus 5 minutes' standing time.

Model details *Within size, listed in Ratings order*

NOTES ON THE DETAILS Exterior size is rounded to the next higher inch. Capacity is two numbers: claimed and usable (as measured in our labs, with the turntable rotating and excluding corners).

Turntable diameter is rounded to the next lower quarter-inch and excludes the rim. An empty bracket in the names of similar and replacement models represents a space for the color code.

Ratings continued ▶

Model details *Continued*

• •

Large

Panasonic NN-77[5]5A Ⓢ $220
• 1000 watts. • HxWxD: 15x24x18 in.
• 1.5 cu. ft. claimed/1.1 usable. • 13¼-in. turntable.
It has word prompts, a moisture sensor, and a separate timer. **Successor:** NN-S776[ ]A. **Recommendation:** An excellent choice; defrosted fast and is especially easy to use.

Sharp R-5H[1]6 Ⓓ $240
• 1000 watts. • HxWxD: 14x25x19 in.
• 1.6 cu. ft. claimed/1.1 usable. • 15-in. turntable.
It has a moisture sensor, separate timer, and "Memory" pad you can program with a frequently used setting. You can turn off the beeps. A kit can make the oven a built-in. But: The view inside is poor in bright light, and for most auto cooking, you must consult codes inside the door. **Recommendation:** Very good, though it heated a bit less evenly than the other large ovens.

General Electric JE1550[G]V Ⓢ $240
• 1000 watts. • HxWxD: 14x24x16 in.
• 1.5 cu. ft. claimed/1.0 usable. • 12¾-in. turntable.
It has a moisture sensor, a separate timer, and a very good view inside. You can replace the light bulb and turn off the beeps. But: For most auto cooking, you must consult codes inside the door. **Successor:** JE1550[ ]W. **Recommendation:** Very good overall, but only fair at defrosting.

Kenmore (Sears) 8968[6] Ⓢ $170
• 1000 watts. • HxWxD: 14x24x18 in.
• 1.6 cu. ft. claimed/1.3 usable. • 13¼-in. turntable.
You press a touchpad for High power; other ovens choose High by default. It has a confusing child lock-out: The light, fan, and turntable (though not the microwaves) can still be turned on. **Successor:** 6640[ ]. **Recommendation:** Very good and spacious, but a notch less convenient than the top three.

Family-sized

Sharp R-4H[1]7 $200
• 1000 watts. • HxWxD: 13x22x18 in. • 1.2 cu. ft. claimed/0.9 usable. • 13¼-in. turntable.
It has word prompts, a moisture sensor, and a separate timer. You can turn off the beeps. A kit can make the oven a built-in. Instead of touchpads, it has buttons. But: For most auto cooking, you must consult codes inside the door. **Recommendation:** An excellent choice; it defrosted fast and proved especially easy to use.

Sharp R-4A[9]7 Ⓓ $170
• 900 watts. • HxWxD: 13x22x18 in.
• 1.2 cu. ft. claimed/0.9 usable. • 13¼-in. turntable.
Though it lacks the moisture sensor of the more powerful Sharp above, it does have word prompts and a separate timer, and you can turn off the beeps. A kit can make the oven a built-in. **Recommendation:** Nearly as good overall as the Sharp above, and cheaper.

Samsung MW6552[W] $180
• 900 watts. • HxWxD: 13x22x16 in.
• 1.1 cu. ft. claimed/0.8 usable. • 13-in. turntable.
It has a separate timer, and you can turn off the beep. Its Auto Defrost includes 10 minutes of standing time. **Recommendation:** Very good overall and an excellent defroster.

General Electric JE1240[W]V Ⓢ $170
• 900 watts. • HxWxD: 13x22x17 in.
• 1.2 cu. ft. claimed/0.8 usable. • 13-in. turntable.
It has a separate timer, and you can turn off the beeps. But: For most auto cooking, you must consult codes inside the door. **Successor:** JE1240[ ]W. **Recommendation:** Very good overall and an excellent defroster.

Tappan TMT117U1[W]0 Ⓓ $170
• 1000 watts. • HxWxD: 12x21x16 in.
• 1.1 cu. ft. claimed/0.7 usable. • 12-in. turntable.
The touchpad labels are especially small. **Similar:**

Frigidaire FMT117U1[ ]O. **Recommendation:** Very good overall and an excellent defroster. But perhaps not a good choice if eyesight is poor.

Whirlpool MT5111XD[Q] Ⓓ $140

• 1000 watts. • HxWxD: 12x21x16 in.
• 1.1 cu. ft. claimed/0.7 usable. • 12-in. turntable.
The view inside is poor in bright light. **Recommendation:** Very good overall and an excellent defroster.

Kenmore (Sears) 8948[1] Ⓢ $160

• 900 watts. • HxWxD: 13x22x18 in.
• 1.2 cu. ft. claimed/0.9 usable. • 13½-in. turntable.
It has a confusing child lock-out: The light, fan, and turntable (though not the microwaves) can still be turned on. **Successor:** 6630[ ]. **Recommendation:** Very good overall and an excellent defroster.

Amana R[W]635T $230

• 1000 watts. • HxWxD: 15x22x18 in.
• 1.2 cu ft. claimed/0.7 usable with turntable; 1.1 without turntable. • 12-in. turntable.
You can remove the turntable to accommodate large dishes. It has a separate timer. You can reprogram the times set for automatic cooking pads, replace the light bulb, and turn off the beeps. But: The lift-up handle is inconvenient. **Recommendation:** Good but pricey.

Magic Chef DM46K[W]-17T $180

• 1100 watts. • HxWxD: 15x23x17 in.
• 1.3 cu. ft. claimed/0.9 usable with turntable on; 1.2 with it off. • 12¾-in. turntable.
You can turn off the turntable to accommodate large dishes, and it has a separate timer. But: It has no automatic cooking pads, is noisy, and the view inside is poor in bright light. It has no child lock-out. Instructions say the plastic turntable may discolor and must be shielded from packaged popcorn. **Recommendation:** Especially powerful for its size, but very basic.

Mid-sized

Sharp R-3A[9]7 Ⓓ $150

• 850 watts. • HxWxD: 12x21x16 in. • 0.9 cu. ft. claimed/0.7 usable. • 12-in. turntable.
It has word prompts and a separate timer, and you can turn off the beep. But: The view inside is poor in bright light. **Recommendation:** An excellent choice and easier to use than the other mid-sized models.

General Electric JE940[W]W $140

• 850 watts. • HxWxD: 12x21x16 in.
• 0.9 cu. ft. claimed/0.6 usable. • 11¾-in. turntable.
It has a separate timer, and you can turn off the beeps. The window screen is black, not white, and the view inside is excellent. But: For most auto cooking, you must consult codes inside the door. **Recommendation:** Very good and defrosted fast.

Tappan TMS083U1[S]O Ⓓ $130

• 800 watts. • HxWxD: 11x20x14 in.
• 0.8 cu. ft. claimed/0.6 usable. • 11¼-in. turntable.
It has a very good view inside. But: The touchpad labels are especially small. It has few automatic cooking or reheating settings. **Similar:** Frigidaire FMS083U1[ ]O. **Recommendation:** Very good overall and an excellent defroster.

Quasar MQSO853[H] Ⓓ $140

• 800 watts. • HxWxD: 12x21x15 in.
• 0.8 cu. ft. claimed/0.6 usable. • 11½-in. turntable.
It has a separate timer and a "Memory" pad you can program with a frequently used setting. **Recommendation:** Very good overall.

Goldstar MA-108[O]M Ⓓ $130

• 850 watts. • HxWxD: 13x21x16 in.
• 1.0 cu. ft. claimed/0.8 usable. • 12-in. turntable.
It has "international food" touchpads, if you care. **Recommendation:** Good.

Magic Chef DM15K[W]-15T $125

• 900 watts. • HxWxD: 13x22x15 in. • 0.8 cu. ft. claimed/0.5 usable with turntable on; 0.8 with it off. • 11-in. turntable.
You can turn off the turntable to accommodate large dishes, and it has a separate timer. But: The view inside is poor in bright light. It has no child lock-out. Instructions say the plastic turntable may discolor and must be shielded

Ratings continued ▶

from packaged popcorn. It has few automatic cooking or reheating settings. **Recommendation**: A basic model. There are better choices.

Compact

Samsung MW4552[W] $115
- 700 watts. • HxWxD: 11x20x14 in.
- 0.7 cu. ft. claimed/0.5 usable. • 10½-in. turntable.

It has a separate timer, and you can turn off the beeps; its Auto Defrost includes 10 minutes of standing time. **Recommendation**: Very good overall and an excellent defroster. The best compact oven by far.

Whirlpool MT1066XB[Q] $140
- 625 watts. • HxWxD: 10x19x14 in.
- 0.6 cu. ft. claimed/0.4 usable. • 9½-in. turntable.

It has a separate timer. But: It has few automatic cooking or reheating settings and has a poor view inside in bright light. Under-the-cabinet mounting kit is available. **Recommendation**· A good oven overall and excellent defroster, but basic.

General Electric JE640[W]V ⓓ $135
- 700 watts. • HxWxD: 11x19x13 in.
- 0.6 cu. ft. claimed/0.5 usable. • 10¼-in. turntable.

It has a separate timer, and you can turn off the beeps. But: For most auto cooking, you must consult codes inside the door. An under-the-cabinet mounting kit is available. **Recommendation**: OK.

Emerson MW8675[W] ⓓ $100
- 600 watts. • HxWxD: 11x19x14 in.
- 0.6 cu. ft. claimed/0.5 usable. • 9¼-in. turntable.

It lacks a kitchen timer, and no light goes on when you open the door. **Recommendation**: An OK choice and an excellent defroster, but basic.

Emerson MW8775[W] ⓓ $110
- 700 watts. • HxWxD: 11x19x14 in.
- 0.7 cu. ft. claimed/0.5 usable. • 10¼-inch turntable.

See the Emerson, above. **Recommendation**: OK.

Sharp R-2A[4]7 Ⓢ $110
- 600 watts. • HxWxD: 12x18x15 in.
- 0.6 cu. ft. claimed/0.4 usable. • 10¼-in. turntable.

It lacks a kitchen timer, there's no child lock-out, and no light goes on when you open the door. It has an LCD display, dimmer than an LED. **Successor**: R-2A[ ]8. **Recommendation**: An OK choice but very basic.

Kenmore (Sears) 8912[0] $100
- 575 watts. • HxWxD: 10x19x14 in.
- 0.6 cu. ft. claimed/0.4 usable. • 9½-in. turntable.

It has few automatic cooking or reheating settings. It has an LCD display, dimmer than an LED, and it has a poor view inside in bright light. **Recommendation**: An OK choice and an excellent defroster, but basic.

Sharp R-1A[5]6 ⓓ $90
- 525 watts. • HxWxD: 14x14x14 in.
- 0.5 cu. ft. claimed/0.3 usable. • 10-in. turntable.

Unusual because of its shape (a cube), minimal power levels (only High and Defrost), lack of clock or timer, and maximum programmable time of 30 minutes. You have to press 5-min., 1-min., and 15-second pads to "count up" to the desired time. There's no child lock-out. It did a poor job with popcorn. **Recommendation**: Very basic and slow; there are better choices.

Goldstar MA-685M ⓓ $100
- 600 watts. • HxWxD: 10x19x14 in.
- 0.6 cu. ft. claimed/0.4 usable. • 9½-in. turntable.

It has few automatic cooking or reheating settings. It has an LCD display, dimmer than an LED. Its Popcorn key sometimes turned out a low yield of popcorn. **Recommendation**: There are better choices.

Ratings *Refrigerators*
& Recommendations

The tests behind the Ratings

We test refrigerators in our environmental chamber, where temperature and humidity can be varied. **Energy cost** per year assumes 37°F in the main compartment and 0° in the freezer, and is based on the national average electricity rate of 8.6 cents per kilowatt-hour. **Temperature** performance represents a composite judgment derived from tests for temperature balance, uniformity, and compensation. **Price** is approximate retail, without optional ice-maker. Models similar to those we tested are rated in Details; features may vary. **Model availability:** Ⓓ means model is discontinued. Ⓢ means model is replaced, according to the manufacturer; successor model is noted in Details. New model was not tested; it may or may not perform similarly. Features may vary.

Standard for these models

For most types (except apartment-sized top-freezers): • Should be able to maintain temperature of 37°F in the main compartment and 0° in the freezer. • Come with or can accept an ice-maker that produces 3 to 5 pounds a day; adding ice-maker uses about 1 cu. ft. of freezer space. Features: • Spill-proof glass shelves usually pull-out. • Door with at least 1 door shelf or bin to hold gallon containers. • See-through crisper, meat drawer, dairy compartment. (Meat drawer may have its own temp. control; crispers, humidity controls.) • Freezer compartment with light, and at least 1 wire shelf, 2 door shelves, ice-tray shelf, ice bin. • Controls conveniently located in front of main compartment. • Condensor located beneath cabinet and behind removable kickplate. **For apartment-sized top-freezer models:** • Full-width wire (not glass) shelves in main compartment. • No meat drawer. • Crispers without controls that are opaque. • Single wire shelf in freezer. • See-through dairy compartment. • CFC-free. • Dimensions: Height includes top hinge; depth excludes handles. • Clearances indicate the room you need to open the door fully. • Capacity is minus ice-maker, if present.

Recommendations

Top-freezer refrigerators are less expensive than other types, and generally use space and electricity more efficiently. Next most popular are side-by-side designs; they put nonfrozen food at eye level, but their narrow compartments can make it hard to reach items. Strongly consider energy-efficiency and features when you buy a refrigerator. Both affect overall cost—and features affect convenience.

See report, page 78. Last time rated in Consumer Reports: February & May 1996.

Ratings continued ▶

Overall Ratings

E VG G F P

Within types, listed in order of overall performance

Brand and model	Price	Overall score 0 — 100 P F G VG E	Energy COST EFFICIENCY	Temp.	Noise	Convenience
LARGE TOP-FREEZER MODELS (25 cu. ft.)						
Whirlpool ET25DKXD	$950		$78	⊖	⊖	⊖
Kenmore (Sears) 65571	1000		84	⊖	⊖	⊖
General Electric Profile TBX25PAX	950		84	⊖	⊖	⊖
MEDIUM-SIZED TOP-FREEZER MODELS (21 to 22 cu. ft.)						
Whirlpool ET21DKXD	800		57	⊖	⊖	⊖
Kenmore 65171	850		57	⊖	⊖	⊖
Amana TR22S4 [1]	850		55	⊖	⊖	○
Amana TR21S4 [1]	810		55	⊖	○	⊖
KitchenAid KTRS21KD	820		57	⊖	⊖	⊖
General Electric TBX21ZAX	760		72	⊖	○	○
Hotpoint CTX21GAX	660		72	⊖	○	○
Whirlpool ET22DKXD	930		71	○	⊖	⊖
General Electric TBX22PAX	900		79	○	○	○
Kenmore (Sears) 65271 [S]	790		79	⊖	○	○
SMALL TOP-FREEZER MODELS (18 to 19 cu. ft.)						
Kenmore (Sears) 65971	830		59	⊖	⊖	○
KitchenAid KTRP18KD	670		59	⊖	⊖	○
Whirlpool ET18HTXD	650		59	⊖	⊖	○
General Electric TBH18ZAX	650		59	⊖	⊖	○
General Electric TBX18ZAX	650		70	○	○	○
Frigidaire FRT18NRC	600		74	◑	○	○
APARTMENT-SIZED TOP-FREEZER MODELS (14 to 16 cu. ft.)						
General Electric TBH14DAX	520		49	⊖	◑	○
General Electric TBH16JAX	580		51	⊖	◑	○
Hotpoint CTH14CYX	480		49	⊖	◑	◑
Hotpoint CTH16CYX	550		51	⊖	◑	◑
Kenmore 65431	530		64	○	⊖	◑
BOTTOM-FREEZER MODEL (22 cu. ft.)						
Amana BR22S6	940		57	⊖	○	⊖
LARGE SIDE-BY-SIDE MODELS (24 to 30 cu. ft.)						
KitchenAid KSRS27QD	1570		69	⊖	⊖	⊖
Whirlpool ED27DSXD	1450		65	⊖	⊖	⊖

Brand and model	Price	Overall score 0 100 P F G VG E	Energy COST EFFICIENCY	Temp.	Noise	Convenience
LARGE SIDE-BY-SIDE MODELS (24 to 30 cu. ft.)						
Amana SRD25S5	$1375		$74	○	⊖	⊖	⊖
Kenmore (Sears) 55761	1700		77	○	⊖	⊖	⊖
General Electric Profile TFH30PRT	1820		95	○	⊖	⊖	⊖
Frigidaire FRS26WNC	1210		96	●	⊖	○	⊖
General Electric TFX24JWX	1310		87	⊖	○	○	⊖
SMALL SIDE-BY-SIDE MODELS (20 to 22 cu. ft.)						
Whirlpool ED22PSXD ⑤	1050		56	⊖	⊖	⊖	⊖
Kenmore (Sears) 55071	1150		77	⊖	○	⊖	⊖
Whirlpool ED20TWXD	940		77	⊖	○	⊖	○
General Electric TFX20NWX	970		83	●	○	○	⊖
'BUILT-IN' SIDE-BY-SIDE MODELS (20 to 21 cu. ft.)						
Amana SRD20S4	1590		69	○	⊖	⊖	⊖
General Electric Profile TPX21BRX	1570		130 ②	●	⊖	⊖	⊖

① For models of these Amanas equipped with new thermostats only—those with serial numbers that start with a number of 9602 or larger.

② Freezer needed to run at minus 10°F for refrigerator to reach 37°, thus increasing energy use.

Model details *Within types, listed in order of overall performance*

NOTES ON THE DETAILS Height includes top hinge; depth excludes handles. Clearances tell how much room you need to open the door fully. Capacity is manufacturer's claim/our measurement.

Large top-freezers (25 cu. ft.)

Whirlpool ET25DKXD $950

• HxWxD: 69½x35½x31¼ in. • Clearances: 34 in. front, 31 in. side. • Capacity: 25.1/18.5 cu. ft.

A roomy, well-lit model that's a little more efficient and quieter than the competition. Has slide-out shelves. 1 half-shelf slides sideways. 2 dairy compartments. Extra freezer shelf. Height extensions for door bins to keep tall items from falling out. Meat-keeper isn't separately controlled, but it worked very well. Crisper didn't work well. **Similar:** ET25DMXD, $1050. **Recommendation:** Well worth considering.

Kenmore (Sears) 65571 $1000

• HxWxD: 68x34¾x31¼ in. • Clearances: 32 in. front, 22 in. side. • Capacity: 24.7/19.2 cu. ft.

A very good performer on the whole. Only fair performance under hot conditions. Warm spots developed in the freezer during defrost. Tilt-out and slide-out storage bins in door. Crisper didn't work well. Controls located inconveniently in upper rear of main compartment. **Recommendation:** Worth considering.

General Electric Profile TBX25PAX $950

• HxWxD: 68x34¾x31¼ in. • Clearances: 32 in. front, 22 in. side. • Capacity: 24.7/19.1 cu.ft.

Has many of the same features, virtues, and vices of the Kenmore, preceding. Has bottle holder, 2 microwaveable containers for leftovers. **Similar:** TBX25PCX, $1300. **Recommendation:** Worth considering.

Ratings continued ▶

Model details *Continued*
••••••••••••••••••••••

Medium-sized top-freezers (21 to 22 cu.ft.)

Whirlpool ET21DKXD $800

• HxWxD: 66½x32¾ x30½ in. • Clearances: 31¾ in. front, 25 in. side. • Capacity: 20.8/15.5 cu. ft.

One of the quietest models. The shelves slide out, and the crispers—but not the meat drawer—have controls. Has covered utility bin, a movable door shelf, and height extenders on door bins. Dairy compartment can be mounted on either side of door. Automatic antisweat heater. Freezer floor pulls forward, and a half-shelf in the main compartment slides sideways. **Recommendation:** An excellent performer—very quiet and very energy-efficient.

Kenmore 65171 $850

• HxWxD: 66½x32¾x30½ in. • Clearances: 31¾ in. front, 25 in. side. • Capacity: 20.9/16.0 cu. ft.

Much the same as Whirlpool above, except slightly roomier and lacking some of its features—the sliding freezer floor, the bin-height extenders, and the sliding half-shelf. **Recommendation:** An excellent performer—very quiet and very energy-efficient.

Amana TR22S4 $850

• HxWxD: 68x32¾x32½ in. • Clearances: 31½ in. front, 30¼ in. side. • Capacity: 21.6/16.7 cu. ft.

Noisier than some models, but this Amana boasts an impressive array of features. The shelves slide out, and there are controls on the crispers and on the meat-keeper—which can be mounted on either side of the main compartment. (The dairy compartment is also movable). Has wine rack, door-bin height extenders, and a covered bin on the door. Movable bins on freezer door. A foot can be screwed down to prevent unit from rolling. **Recommendation:** An excellent performer, though Amana's repair record has been a concern.

Amana TR21S4 $810

• HxWxD: 68x32¾x31¼ in. • Clearances: 31½ in. front, 30¾ in. side. • Capacity: 20.7/16.2 cu. ft.

Much like Amana above, except a little less roomy

and lacking its freezer-door bins, covered door bin, and movable dairy compartment. **Recommendation:** An excellent performer, though Amana's repair record has been a concern.

KitchenAid KTRS21KD $820

• HxWxD: 66½x32¾x30½ in. • Clearances: 31¾ in. front, 25 in. side. • Capacity: 20.7/14.5 cu. ft.

One of the quietest refrigerators, but also the medium-sized model with the smallest usable capacity. Its fine performance is marred slightly by warm spots on the freezer door. Both the main-compartment shelves and the freezer floor slide out. The crispers have controls, but the meat drawer does not. Has wine rack, shelf for cans, and covered utility bin. Automatic antisweat heater. **Similar:** KTRS21MD, $890. **Recommendation:** A very good, very quiet performer.

General Electric TBX21ZAX $760

• HxWxD: 67¾x31¼x30 in. • Clearances: 30 in. front, 26¼ in. side. • Capacity: 20.6/16.4 cu. ft.

Among the best models for evenness of temperature, but noisier and less energy-efficient than some others. Crispers have controls, as does the excellent meat-keeper. The door has only shelves —no adjustable bins. The freezer shelf isn't very rigid; it bowed under a load. No ice bin or freezer light. Temperature controls inconveniently located. **Similar:** TBX21ZIX, TBX21JAX, TBX21JIX. **Recommendation:** A very good performer.

Hotpoint CTX21GAX $660

• HxWxD: 67¾x31¼x30 in. • Clearances: 30 in. front, 26¼ in. side. • Capacity: 20.6/17.4 cu. ft.

Very much like GE, above, but slightly roomier and with fewer features: The glass shelves aren't spill-proof, and the crisper and meat-keeper lack controls. **Similar:** CTX21EAX, CTX21BAX. **Recommendation:** A very good performer, but other models offer more conveniences.

Whirlpool ET22DKXD $930

• HxWxD: 67x32½x30½ in. • Clearances: 31½ in. front, 27¼ in. side. • Capacity: 21.8/15.5 cu. ft.

Quiet and convenient, but among the worst models for energy-efficiency. The crispers have controls, the shelves pull out, and one half-shelf moves sideways. Has covered utility bin, door bins with height extenders, and two dairy compartments. The freezer floor pulls forward. **Recommendation**: A very good performer, but there are much better values.

General Electric TBX22PAX $900

• HxWxD: 67¾x31¼x31¼ in. • Clearances: 28¾ in. front, 19¼ in. side. • Capacity: 21.6/16.8 cu. ft.
Noisier than some other models and among the least energy-efficient refrigerators we tested. Controls on crispers. Control on the excellent meat-keeper. Has wine rack, tilt-out storage bin and containers for leftovers on the main door, and bins on the freezer door. But shelves don't pull out, freezer shelf isn't very rigid (it bowed under a load) and temperature controls inconveniently located. **Similar**: TBX22PIX, $1000. **Recommendation**: A very good performer, but there are much better values.

Kenmore (Sears) 65271 Ⓢ $790

• HxWxD: 67¾x31¼x31¼ in. • Clearances: 28¾ in. front, 19¼ in. side. • Capacity: 21.6/17.6 cu. ft.
Much the same as GE above, except with a bit more usable capacity and without the GE's controls on crispers and meat-keeper, ice-tray shelf, ice bin, and freezer light. Also, its glass shelves aren't spill-proof. **Successor**: 66281. **Recommendation**: A very good performer, but other models offer more conveniences.

Small top-freezers (18 to 19 cu. ft.)

Kenmore (Sears) 65971 $830

• HxWxD: 66¾x29¾x30½ in. • Clearances: 29 in. front, 24 in. side. • Capacity: 18.8/14.6 cu. ft.
Quiet and efficient. Has slide-out shelves in main compartment. Height extensions for door bins, to keep tall items from falling out. Meat-keeper not temperature-controlled. Crispers aren't sealed, but they performed all right. **Similar**: 75971, $930. **Recommendation**: Best of this group—but not superior enough to justify its price.

KitchenAid KTRP18KD $670

• HxWxD: 66¾x29¾x29¼ in. • Clearances: 29 in. front, 24 in. side. • Capacity: 18.1/13.8 cu. ft.
Quiet outside, bright inside. Has bottle holder, fold-up section on door for tall items. Meat-keeper not temperature-controlled. **Recommendation**: Best value in this group.

Whirlpool ET18HTXD $650

• HxWxD: 66¾x29¾x29¼ in. • Clearances: 29 in. front, 24 in. side. • Capacity: 18.1/13.8 cu. ft.
Not as refined as others in this group. Shelves not sealed at edge to catch spills. No shelf dividers. Has shelves, not bins, on door; fold-up section on door. Meat-keeper not temperature-controlled. Crispers neither sealed nor separately controlled, but they performed all right. Tapered opening in handle can pinch fingers. **Recommendation**: A very good performer, but lacks some features.

General Electric TBH18ZAX $650

• HxWxD: 65½x29¾x30¼ in. • Clearances: 29 in. front, 26 in. side. • Capacity: 18.2/13.6 cu. ft.
More efficient and quieter than its sibling below. Otherwise comparable in performance. Controls inconveniently located in upper rear of main compartment. **Recommendation**: A very good performer.

General Electric TBX18ZAX $630

• HxWxD: 65½x29¾x30¼ in. • Clearances: 29 in. front, 26 in. side. • Capacity: 18.2/13.7 cu. ft.
Not very efficient and fairly noisy. Crispers didn't hold in moisture. Fair performance under heavy load. Freezer developed warm spots during defrost. No half-width bins on door. Controls inconveniently located in upper rear of main compartment. **Similar**: TBX18ZIX, $670; TBX18JAX, $620. **Recommendation**: A very good performer overall, with a few weaknesses.

Frigidaire FRT18NRC $600

• HxWxD: 65½x29¾x29¾ in. • Clearances: 29 in. front, 29 in. side. • Capacity: 18.0/13.7 cu. ft.
Another inefficient, noisy model. Shelves not

Ratings continued ▶

102 Refrigerators

Model details *Continued*

sealed at edge to catch spills. No shelf dividers, half-shelves, or storage bins on door. Meat-keeper not temperature-controlled. Crispers neither sealed nor separately controlled, but they worked better than most. Small freezer, which developed warm spots during defrost. Freezer control inconveniently located in rear of compartment. Condenser behind cabinet. **Similar:** FRT18JRC, $550; F44N18CE, $590; FRT18PRC, $600; FRT18NNC, $650; FRT18QRC, $650; FRT18TRC, $660; FRT18RRC, $690; FRT18TNC, $700. **Recommendation:** There are better choices.

Apartment-sized top-freezers (14 to 16 cu.ft.)

General Electric TBH14DAX $520
• HxWxD: 62x28¼x28½ in. • Clearances: 26½ in. front, 25 in. side. • Capacity: 14.4/11.7 cu. ft.
A solid performer with a few frills. Has a meat drawer. Glass bottom shelf provides view into crispers, which also are see-through. Has utility bin. **Recommendation:** A very good performer; among the most convenient of this group.

General Electric TBH16JAX $580
• HxWxD: 65x28¼x28½ in. • Clearances: 26½ in. front, 25 in. side. • Capacity 15.6/12.6 cu. ft.
The least austere model of a Spartan group, and among the most energy-efficient. Has glass shelves; the bottom shelf provides a view into the crispers, which also are see-through. Also has meat drawer and utility bin. **Recommendation:** A very good performer; among the most convenient of this group.

Hotpoint CTH14CYX $480
• HxWxD: 62x28¼x28½ in. • Clearances: 26½ in. front, 25 in. side. • Capacity: 14.4/11.5 cu. ft.
Much like GE TBH14DAX, above, but lacking most of its conveniences. Has no meat drawer, its dairy compartment and crispers are opaque, and it has only an ice-tray shelf in the freezer. Also, its "pocket" handles are harder to grasp than regular protruding handles. Despite lacking controls, its crispers actually maintained humidity better than any crispers we tested—with or without controls. **Recommendation:** A very good performer.

Hotpoint CTH16CYX $550
• HxWxD: 65x28¼x28½ in. • Clearances: 26½ in. front, 24¾ in. side. • Capacity: 15.6/12.3 cu. ft.
Much like Hotpoint, above, except a little roomier. **Recommendation:** A very good performer.

Kenmore 65431 $530
• HxWxD: 62x28¼x28½ in. • Clearances: 26½ in. front, 25 in. side. • Capacity: 14.4/11.8 cu. ft.
A small energy hog: Uses more electricity than many of the medium-sized refrigerators. No meat drawer. Bottom shelf is glass. **Similar:** 65461. **Recommendation:** A good performer, but the least energy-efficient of this group.

Bottom-freezer (22 cu.ft.)

Amana BR22S6 $940
• HxWxD: 69x32¾x32¾ in. • Clearances: 32 in. front, 32 in. side. • Capacity: 21.7 cu. ft./15.9 cu. ft.
Efficient, easy to use; our best overall performer. Slide-out shelves in main compartment, slide-out basket in freezer. Bottle holder. Door extensions for door bins, to keep tall items from falling out. Refrigerator control in upper rear of main compartment; freezer control in upper front of freezer. **Recommendation:** Well worth considering.

Large side-by-sides (24 to 30 cu.ft.)

KitchenAid KSRS27QD $1570
• HxWxD: 70x35½x32¼ in. • Clearances: 17 in. front, 15 in. side. • Capacity: 26.5/14.8 cu. ft.
Quiet, capable, and convenient. Slide-out shelves. Lazy Susan-type circular drawer, handy but space consuming. Bottle holder. Adjustable soda-can shelves on door. **Similar:** KSRB27QD, $1770. **Recommendation:** Best of the side-by-sides.

Whirlpool ED27DSXD $1450
• HxWxD: 70x35¼x32¼ in. • Clearances: 17 in. front, 15 in. side. • Capacity: 26.6/15.5 cu. ft.
Quiet, convenient, and efficient for a big side-

by-side. Snack drawer. 1 half-shelf slides sideways. Bottle holder. Height extensions for door bins, to keep tall items from falling out. **Recommendation**: Well worth considering.

Amana SRD25S5 $1375

• HxWxD: 68³/₄x35³/₄x32½ in. • Clearances: 20 in. front, 20 in. side. • Capacity: 24.6/15.4 cu. ft.
Very good performance, but noisier than others in this group. 2 crispers. Slide-out shelves. Half-shelves and beverage chiller. Height extensions for door bins, to keep tall items from falling out. 2 dairy compartments. Automatic night light on ice/water dispenser. Controls located inconveniently in rear of refrigerator compartment. "Knuckle buster" door handle. **Recommendation**: A very good choice.

Kenmore (Sears) 55761 $1700

• HxWxD: 70x35½x32¼ in. • Clearances: 17 in. front, 15 in. side. • Capacity: 26.7/15.8 cu. ft.
Quiet, convenient, but less efficient than other large side-by-sides. Slide-out shelves. Has height extensions for door bins, to keep tall items from falling out. Snack bin. **Recommendation**: Very good but pricey.

GE Profile TFH30PRT $1820

• HxWxD: 70½x36x32³/₄ in. • Clearances: 17 in. front, 16 in. side. • Capacity: 29.8/19.6 cu. ft.
The largest side-by-side available, but costly to run. Slide-out shelves; 1 shelf folds in half. Snack drawer and bottle holder. Crisper worked better than most. Coated-steel interior. Controls located inconveniently in upper rear of refrigerator compartment. Freezer developed warm spots during defrost. **Similar**: TFX30PRY, $1820. **Recommendation**: Big but expensive.

Frigidaire FRS26WNC $1310

• HxWxD: 68 x 35¼ x 34 in. • Clearances: 18 in. front, 19 in. side. • Capacity: 25.6/16.2 cu ft.
Short on useful features, expensive to run. Shelves not sealed at edge to catch spills. No shelf dividers. Only 1 slide-out bin in freezer. Unsealed crisper. Freezer control located in upper front. No crushed ice from ice dispenser. Freezer developed warm spots during defrost. Poor temperature uniformity. **Similar**: FRS26WRC, $1400; FRS26XGC, $1500. **Recommendation**: OK.

General Electric TFX24JWX $1200

• HxWxD: 68x35¼x30½ in. • Clearances: 20 in. front, 18 in. side. • Capacity: 23.6/15.8 cu. ft.
So-so performance, fairly expensive to run. Shelves not sealed at edge to catch spills. Only 1 slide-out bin in freezer. Snack drawer. Crisper worked better than most. Coated-steel interior. No crushed ice from ice dispenser. Poor compensation for room-temperature changes. **Similar**: TFX24ZRX, $1300; TRX24PRX, $1550. **Recommendation**: There are better choices.

Small side-by-sides (20 to 22 cu.ft.)

Whirlpool ED22PSXD Ⓢ $1050

• HxWxD: 66¾x32³/₄x32¼ in. • Clearances: 17 in. front, 18 in. side. • Capacity: 21.7/12.8 cu. ft.
Quiet, capable, very efficient, but flawed by a poor design that can crush fingers caught between door and cabinet at hinge side. Only 1 slide-out bin in smallish freezer. Snack drawer. Height extensions for door bins, to keep tall items from falling out. Crisper neither sealed nor separately controlled. No crushed ice from ice dispenser. **Successor**: ED22PSQD. **Recommendation**: Worth considering.

Kenmore (Sears) 55071 $1150

• HxWxD: 66¾x32³/₄x29 in. • Clearances: 19 in. front, 18 in. side. • Capacity: 19.8/13.0 cu. ft.
Quiet and small, otherwise undistinguished. Only 1 slide-out bin in smallish freezer. **Similar**: 55281, $1349. **Recommendation**: OK.

Whirlpool ED20TWXD $940

• HxWxD: 66¾x32³/₄x29 in. • Clearances: 19 in. front, 18 in. side. • Capacity: 19.8 /13.0 cu. ft.
Like the Kenmore, above, but less convenient. Shelves not sealed at edges to catch spills. 1 slide-out bin in smallish freezer. Door has shelves, not bins. Crisper neither sealed nor separately controlled. Dispenser can't deliver crushed ice. **Recommendation**: OK.

Ratings continued ▶

Model details *Continued*

General Electric TFX20NWX $970
• HxWxD: 67³/₄x31³/₄x30½ in. • Clearances:
17 in. front, 16 in. side. • Capacity: 19.7/13.7
cu. ft.
An undistinguished model, fairly inefficient.
Shelves not sealed at edges to catch spills. Lacks
shelf dividers. Drawers and dairy-compartment
cover not see-through. Only 1 slide-out bin in
smallish freezer. No utility bin in refrigerator.
Crisper and meat-keeper not separately controlled. Controls inconveniently located at upper
rear. Coated-steel interior. Unlighted dispenser
can't deliver crushed ice. **Similar:** TFX20JAX,
$820; TFX20JRX, $990. **Recommendation:** There
are better choices.

'Built-in' side-by-sides (20 to 21 cu.ft.)

Amana SRD20S4 $1590
• HxWxD: 69¼x36x26½ in. • Clearances: 20
in. front, 20 in. side. • Capacity: 19.6/12.0
cu. ft.

Very good, convenient choice if you want a custom look without breaking the budget. Slide-out
shelves. 2 dairy compartments, 2 half-shelves, 2
crispers. Beverage chiller on door, and height
extensions for door bins, to keep tall items from
falling out. Controls located inconveniently at
rear of compartment. Freezer developed warm
spots during defrost. "Knuckle buster" door handles. **Recommendation:** Worth considering.

GE Profile TPX21BRX $1570
• HxWxD: 70¼x36x26½ in. • Clearances: 20
in. front, 18 in. side. • Capacity: 20.7/13.6
cu. ft.
Mediocre temperature control makes this model
an energy hog. Slide-out shelves. Bottle holder,
snack drawer, 1 shelf that folds in half. Coated-
steel interior. Controls located inconveniently in
upper rear of refrigerator compartment. Freezer
developed warm spots during defrost. **Similar:**
TPX21PRX, $1600. **Recommendation:** Poor value.

How to use the Ratings in the Buying Guide

■ Read the Recommendations for information on specific models and general buying advice.

■ Note how the rated products are listed—in order of perfor-mance and convenience, price, or alphabetically.

■ The overall score graph gives the big picture in perfor-mance. Notes on features and performance for individual mod-els are listed in the Comments column or "Model details."

■ Before going to press, we verify model availability for most products with manufacturers. Some tested models listed in the Ratings may no longer be available. Models that have been discontinued are marked Ⓓ; some may actually still be available in some stores for part of 1997. A model marked Ⓢ is a succes-sor to the tested model, according to the manufacturer, and is noted in Comments or Model details. Features may vary.

■ Models similar to the tested models, when they exist, are in-dicated in Comments or Model details.

■ To find our last full report on a subject, check the reference above the Ratings chart or the eight-year index, page 342.

Ratings *Gas ranges*
& Recommendations

The tests behind the Ratings

We test ranges by baking cakes, broiling burgers, and melting chocolate to find out if the burners' lowest setting is low enough. We assess ease of **cleaning** the **cooktop** and we determine how well the **oven** self-cleaning cycle works by baking on and then removing our own gloppy mixture. We also measure usable **oven size. Price** is approximate retail. Models similar to those we tested are noted in Details; features may vary. **Model availability:** Ⓓ means model is discontinued. Ⓢ means model is replaced, according to the manufacturer; successor model is noted in Details. New model was not tested; it may or may not perform similarly. Features may vary.

Standard features for these models

• Have an ample oven that's excellent at baking, good or very good at broiling, and very good or excellent at self-cleaning its interior (less good at cleaning the window). • Have sealed burners so spilled food doesn't seep below cooktop. • Provide ample cooktop space for large pots and pans. • Have a cooktop surface that is fairly easy to keep clean.

Recommendations

The ranges we tested vary little in cooking performance; choose one primarily for how easy it is to use and clean, and for its brand's reliability record (see Brand Repair histories, page 16).

See report, page 71. Last time rated in Consumer Reports: March 1996.

Overall Ratings

E ⊖   VG ⊖   G ○   F ◒   P ●

Listed primarily in order of convenience and cleaning

Brand and model	Price	Overall score 0 — 100	Brand family	Cleaning COOKTOP	OVEN	Oven size
		P F G VG E				
GE JGBP79WEV Ⓢ	$850		GE	⊖	⊖	⊖
GE JGBP35WEV Ⓢ	750		GE	⊖	⊖	⊖
GE JGBP30WEV Ⓢ	700		GE	⊖	⊖	⊖
Sears 7586 Ⓢ	900		GE	○	⊖	⊖
Amana AGS781 Ⓓ	800		Caloric	○	⊖	⊖
Hotpoint RGB745WET	600		GE	○	⊖	⊖

Ratings continued ▶

Overall Ratings *Continued*

E VG G F P
⊖ ⊖ ○ ◐ ●

Brand and model	Price	Overall score 0—100	Brand family	Cleaning COOKTOP	OVEN	Oven size
Tappan TGF356BC	$650	P F G VG E	Tappan	⊖	⊖	⊖
Caloric RSK3700U Ⓓ	650		Caloric	○	⊖	⊖
Tappan (Ward) 28584 Ⓓ	630		Tappan	○	⊖	⊖
Whirlpool SF387PEY Ⓓ	800		Tappan	○	⊖	⊖
Maytag CRG9800BA Ⓢ	760		Maytag	○	⊖	⊖
Magic Chef 3468VV	650		Maytag	○	⊖	⊖
Caloric RSF3410U Ⓓ	610		Caloric	○	⊖	⊖
Tappan TGF362B	1000		Tappan	○	⊖	⊖
Whirlpool SF367PEY Ⓓ	650		Tappan	○	⊖	⊖

Model details *Within "families," listed in order of overall score*

The GE family • GE • Sears • Hotpoint

GE makes several lines under its own name; we tested models from two. It also makes lower-priced models under the Hotpoint name, as well as a line of ranges for Sears. Expect: Spacious oven, with six oven-rack positions, rather than the usual five. • Cooktop control panels and storage-drawer fronts are porcelain-clad. • A high-output burner (a plus) and a low-output one (a minus).

What distinguishes models: The Sears and the three GE models have the same burners. They differ in control design and oven-window size (and staining), and in whether the backguard is glass, porcelain (less chic), or painted (hardest to clean). Compared with those models, the Hotpoint's cooktop is more difficult to clean, and has less powerful burners and less hefty grates.

Recommendation: All very good or excellent overall. These ranges are all fine choices—even the Hotpoint, which has some limitations. However, the highest-priced models are somewhat expensive for what you get.

GE JGBP79WEV Ⓢ $850

• Electronic oven controls. • Porcelain drip pans. • Glass backguard. • Burners (Btu/hr.): 5000; 2@9500; 12,000.
The high-output burner (also on other GEs and the Sears) heats a large pot of water in about 19 minutes—versus 24 minutes for a standard-output burner. It's the only model that comes with three oven shelves, though other ranges in this family let you order a third shelf. The controls' large characters are very easy to read, and there's a cooktop light. **Successor:** JGBP79WEW.

GE JGBP35WEV Ⓢ $750

• Electronic oven controls. • Porcelain drip pans, backguard. • Burners: 5000; 2@9500; 12,000.
Compared with the JGBP79WEV, above, this model lacks a cooktop light and a third oven shelf, has a backguard that's porcelain instead of glass, and has controls that aren't as easy to read. **Successor:** JGBP35WEW.

GE JGBP30WEV Ⓢ $700

• Dial and electronic oven controls. • Chrome drip pans • Porcelain backguard. • Burners: 5000; 2@9500; 12,000.
Similar to the model above, except for its oven controls. But: No display shows when it's OK to unlock the oven after self-cleaning, a minor drawback. **Successor:** JGBP30WEW.

Sears 7586 Ⓢ $900

• Electronic oven controls. • Chrome drip pans. • Painted backguard. • Burners: 5000; 2@9500; 12,000.
Unlike the preceding models, this has a painted backguard. Also, the right-front burner blew out when we let the oven door slam shut. **Successor:** 7587.

Hotpoint RGB745WET $600

• Dial and electronic oven controls. • Chrome drip pans. • Painted backguard. • Burners: 4500; 2@9200; 10,000.
A bit less adept than its siblings at delicate cooking and a bit slower at heating a large pot of water. Hard-to-clean burners have porcelain caps that stained in testing.

The Caloric family • Caloric • Amana

Raytheon Corporation makes ranges for two brands—Caloric and Amana. The "Ultra-Ray" broiler radiates heat from the middle of the oven—and broiled more burgers than the other ranges. Amana and Caloric ranges lack drip pans, so spills have to be cleaned off each burner's surrounding cooktop surface. Burners have indexed steps, not continuously variable intensity.
What distinguishes models: The higher-rated pair better accommodate large pots and pans on the cooktop, and differ from one another mostly in oven cleaning. The lower-rated model has dial controls, rather than the all-electronic controls found on the Amana and the other Caloric.
Recommendation: Though the Amana/Caloric ranges are very good overall, Caloric gas ranges have been the most trouble-prone of the six brands whose reliability we've evaluated.

Amana AGS781 Ⓓ $800

• Electronic oven controls. • No drip pans • Glass backguard. • Burners: 7000; 3@9100.
The oven door locks automatically when self-cleaning starts, a safety plus. Oven controls are convenient and easy to use, and there's a cooktop light. But: During oven cleaning, the cooktop dials got very hot. Permanent stains may mar the light-gray porcelain grates and burner tops.

Caloric RSK3700U Ⓓ $650

• Electronic oven controls. • No drip pans. • Glass backguard. • Burners: 7000; 3@9000.
Compared with the Amana's, above, the Caloric's oven cleans better. But: The oven door gets hotter during self-cleaning and the oven window is smaller; the cooktop dials are harder to read.

Caloric RSF3410U Ⓓ $610

• Dial oven controls. • No drip pans. • Painted backguard. • Burners: 7000; 3@9100.
The oven window was the cleanest of all the models after self-cleaning, and provided an excellent view of the interior. But: The cooktop is cramped and the dials have only one marked setting ("Hi"); it's hard to adjust flame size on the burners, and there's no oven-on indicator.

The Frigidaire family • Tappan • Whirlpool • Frigidaire • White-Westinghouse

Frigidaire makes ranges for itself and the other brands in this family. We tested models from Tappan and Whirlpool, the best-selling of those brands. All shared the same burners, which change flame intensity in indexed steps—not continuously, as on some other ranges. On all models, the cooktop dials or the center of the cooktop (or both) got quite hot during oven self-cleaning.
What distinguishes models: Mostly differences in controls, backguards, drip pans, and burner grates.
Recommendation: Most members of the Frigidaire family offer value. The fancy "professional" Tappan TGF362 is expensive, but underneath its haute facade is a distinctly ordinary range.

Tappan TGF356BC $650

• Electronic oven controls. • Porcelain drip pans. • Glass backguard. • Burners: 4@ 9000.
The oven door latches automatically when the self-cleaning cycle starts (a safety plus), and its window provides an excellent view of the interior. **Similar:** Frigidaire FGF353.

Ratings continued ▶

Tappan 28584 Ⓓ $630

• Dial oven controls. • Porcelain drip pans.
• Glass backguard. • Burners: 4@ 9000.
This range is part of the "Designer Series by Tappan," sold only in Montgomery Ward stores. It differs from its sibling above in having a cooktop light, and in lacking an automatic door lock during self-cleaning.

Whirlpool SF387PEY Ⓓ $800

• Electronic oven controls. • Chrome drip pans. • Painted backguard. • Burners: 4@ 9000.
Whirlpool ranges are like Tappan's at heart. They differ in oven controls, and the Whirlpools' cooktop dials don't get hot during oven self-cleaning.

Tappan TGF362B $1000

• Electronic oven controls. • No drip pans.
• Stainless-steel backguard. • Burners: 4@ 9000.
This "professional" Tappan has a distinctive appearance—all-black with stainless-steel trim and grates that cover the entire cooktop. The back burners were better able to accommodate a large stockpot than the other ranges. The oven door latches automatically when self-cleaning starts (a safety plus), and its window provides an excellent view of the interior. But: It was slower than the other ranges at heating a pot of water, and all those grates have to be moved to wipe up spills.

Whirlpool SF367PEY Ⓓ $650

• Dial oven controls. • Chrome drip pans.
• Painted backguard. • Burners: 4@ 9000.
This is the dial-control version of the Whirlpool described above. The only other difference of note is a negative one: The oven-temperature dial has somewhat imprecise markings, making it hard to set the temperature you want.

The Maytag family • **Maytag** • **Magic Chef**

Maytag makes ranges for its own nameplate, as well as that of the less upscale Magic Chef brand. This family's spacious oven was one of the best at self-cleaning (though exterior parts get hot during the cleaning cycle). The two high-output burners are a plus if you often boil water in more than one large pot at a time. However, the burners are hard to clean because no parts are removable, and the front burners go out if the oven door is opened quickly when they're set to Low. The cooktop is cramped and the backguards stained badly during the oven's self-cleaning cycle.
Recommendation: Both tested ranges are less convenient than ranges in most families. Magic Chef models have one of the worst frequency-of-repair records of the six brands whose reliability we've evaluated.

Maytag CRG9800BA Ⓢ $760

• Electronic oven controls. • No drip pans.
• Painted backguard. • Burners: 2@ 9200; 2@ 12,000.
The Maytag has a cooktop light, a minor plus. The oven window provides an excellent view of the interior. The exterior didn't stain as badly as the Magic Chef, below. **Successor**: CRG9800CA.

Magic Chef 3468VV $650

• Electronic oven controls. • No drip pans.
• Painted backguard. • Burners: 2@ 9200; 2@ 12,000.
Aside from a greater range of color choices, the Magic Chef's main distinction from the Maytag is its cooktop controls. They're confusingly arranged—with the front and rear dials in the same left-right position on both sides, rather than in the usual left-right/right-left arrangement, which most people would find more intuitive. It also lacks a cooktop light. **Similar**: 3488VV.

Ratings *Electric ranges*
& Recommendations

The tests behind the Ratings

For **cooktop speed,** we measured the time needed to bring a pot of water to a near boil. We tested oven cooking by baking layer cakes. **Self cleaning** scores reflect how well self-cleaning models disposed of a baked-on mess of our own concoction, both within the oven and on the oven window. **Price** is the estimated average, based on a national survey, except where an * indicates the price we paid. A bracketed character in the model number varies with color. Models similar to those we tested are noted in Details; features may vary. **Model availability:** Ⅾ means model is discontinued. Ⓢ means model is replaced, according to the manufacturer; successor model is noted in Details. New model was not tested; it may or not not perform similarly. Features may vary.

Standard features for these models

• Controls on the backguard; cooktop controls are almost always dials, while oven controls may be dials, electronic keys, or a combination of dial and electronic. • At least 1 cooktop indicator light and a timer that can be used while the oven is on. (Smoothtops have heating elements outlined and 1 or more warning lights.) • At least 2 chromed-steel oven shelves with safety stops and 4 or 5 positions. • Removable storage drawer. • Front that gets hot during self-cleaning and broiling. • Very good low-heat cooking capability.

Recommendations

It's a safe bet that any new range will cook and bake well. Use reliability and features to narrow the choices. According to our surveys, the more reliable brands were Whirlpool, Hotpoint, GE, and Kenmore (Sears) models. Magic Chef and Frigidaire were among the worst. (See Brand Repair Histories, page 16.) Features for each model are noted in Model details.

Electric ranges, brand by brand

General Electric family: GE, Hotpoint. The tested self-clean models don't stain on the outside. Overall, ranges in this family are competent and sometimes outstanding performers, but they're usually priced higher than the competition, and their ovens lack height. **The Maytag family:** Maytag, Jenn-Air, Magic Chef. Ovens tend to be large; cooking speeds are excellent for coil burners, very good for smoothtops. **The Whirlpools:** Large ovens. Self-cleaning models were better at baking. One of the more reliable brands. **The Amanas:** Excellent cooking speed for coil-burner models, very good for smoothtops. Convenient touches include an easy-to-clean glass backguard. **The Frigidaire family:** Frigidaire, Tappan.

Ratings continued ▶

Frigidaire makes a number of different brands in addition to its own. They have large ovens. Coil-burner models offer good value. The **Kenmores (Sears):** The ovens, which tend to be small, performed competently. **The KitchenAids:** The one we tested has an abundance of features, but a smallish oven.

See report, page 71. Last time rated in Consumer Reports: October 1996.

Overall Ratings

Legend: E ◒ VG ◒ G ○ F ◗ P ●

Within types, listed in order of overall score

Brand and model	Price	Overall score	Cooktop SPEED	Cooktop CLEANING	Oven size	Self-cleaning OVEN	Self-cleaning WINDOW
SELF-CLEAN SMOOTHTOP MODELS							
General Electric JBP79WV[WW] ⑤	$860		◒	◒	○	◒	○
Magic Chef 3868XV[W]	660		◒	◒	◒	◒	○
Maytag CRE9600CC[E]	720		◒	◒	◒	◒	○
Whirlpool RFE76PXD[Q] ⑩, A CR BEST BUY	680		◒	◒	◒	◒	◒
Frigidaire FEF368CC[S]	750		◒	○	◒	◒	○
Amana ART6600[WW] ⑤	775		◒	◒	◒	◒	○
Kenmore (Sears) 9584[5] ⑩	800		◒	◒	○	◒	◗
Kenmore (Sears) 9545[5] ⑤	700*		○	◒	○	◒	○
SELF-CLEAN CONVECTION-OVEN SMOOTHTOP MODELS							
Jenn-Air FCE70610[W]	1120		◒	◒	◒	◒	◗
General Electric JBP90WV[WW] ⑤	1140		◒	◒	◗	◒	◗
KitchenAid KERC507Y[WH] ⑤	1100		◒	○	◗	◒	○
SELF-CLEAN COIL-BURNER MODELS							
Tappan TEF354BC[W]	430		◒	◒	◒	◒	○
Whirlpool RF365PXD[Q] ⑩	470		◒	◒	◒	◒	○
Amana ARR626[WW] ⑩	445		◒	◒	◒	◒	○
Frigidaire FEF350CA[S]	495		◒	○	◒	◒	○
General Electric JBP45GV[WH] ⑤	520		◒	◒	○	◒	◗
Maytag CRE9300CC[W]	480		◒	◒	◒	◒	○
Kenmore (Sears) 9354[5] ⑩	550		◒	○	○	◒	○
SELF-CLEAN MICROWAVE-OVEN/COIL-BURNER MODEL							
Magic Chef 3962VV[V]	675		◒	○	◒	◒	◒
MANUAL-CLEAN COIL-BURNER MODELS							
Tappan TEF324BC[W]	380		◒	○	◒	—	—
General Electric JBS27GV[WH]	385		◒	○	○	—	—

Brand and model	Price	Overall score 0 ... 100		Cooktop SPEED	Cooktop CLEANING	Oven size	Self-cleaning OVEN	Self-cleaning WINDOW
		P F G VG E						
MANUAL-CLEAN COIL-BURNER MODELS								
Frigidaire FEF322BA[W]	$360			⊖	○	⊖	—	—
Hotpoint RB536V[WH] [S]	410			⊖	○	○	—	—
Whirlpool RF310PXD[Q] [D]	400			⊖	○	⊖	—	—

Model details *Within type, listed in order of overall score*

Self-cleaning smoothtops

General Electric JBP79WV[WW] [S] $860
• Electronic oven controls. • Burners (watts): 2500/1000, 2000, 2 @ 1500. Cooktop features include a dual-element zone suitable for small pans or large pots, a raised frame to contain heavy spills, and 4 bright warning lights to show which zones remain hot. Oven automatically turns off after 12 hours, for safety. Self-cleaning left no exterior residue. **Successor**: JBP79WW, $900. **Recommendation**: Very good overall. One of the best in its class, but fairly expensive.

Magic Chef 3868XV[W] $660
• Electronic oven controls. • Burners (watts): 2 @2200, 2 @ 1200. Oven automatically turns off after 12 hours, for safety. Self-cleaning left no exterior residue. But: Brand has had high repair rate. **Similar**: 3888XV[ ], $720. **Recommendation**: Very good overall, but reliability may be a concern.

Maytag CRE9600CC[E] $720
• Electronic oven controls. • Burners (watts): 2 @ 2200, 2 @ 1200. Oven automatically turns off after 12 hours, for safety. The front of the cooktop stayed cooler than any other during broil. Storage drawer has a removable plastic liner. **Recommendation**: Very good overall.

Whirlpool RF376PXD[Q] $680
• Electronic oven controls. • Burners (watts): 2400, 2100, 1700, 1400. One of the few models with 4 different-sized heat zones. Has 4 bright warning lights to show which zones remain hot. The raised frame around the cooktop contains heavy spills. But: Cooktop area is cramped. You must press a "Start" pad to turn the oven on, but there's no prompt to do so. The only electronic model with no automatic cooking, no preset self-cleaning. **Recommendation**: Very good overall. **A CR BEST BUY.**

Frigidaire FEF368CC $750
• Electronic oven controls. • Burners (watts): 2100/700, 2100, 2 @ 1200. Dual-element zone is suitable for small pans or large pots. Back elements accommodate large pots without obstructing controls. Heat zones were quite cool by the time the warning light shut off. Oven door latches automatically for self-cleaning. But: Metal panel above door gets quite hot during broiling or baking at high temps. Stains were quite evident on the outside after self-cleaning. **Similar**: FEF367CA[ ], $700. **Recommendation**: Very good overall.

Amana ART6600[WW] [S] $775
• Electronic oven controls. • Burners (watts): 2500/1000, 2000, 1500, 1200. One of the few tested models with 4 different-sized heat zones. Dual-element zone suitable for small pans or large pots. Heat zones were quite cool by the time warning light shut off. Fast-set dial for oven temperature and timing. The oven automatically turns itself off after 12 hours, for safety; the oven door latches automatically for self-cleaning. But: Markings are easily scratched off cooktop dials. **Successor**: ART6610[ ], $950. **Recommendation**: Very good overall.

Ratings continued ▶

Model details *Continued*

Kenmore (Sears) 9584[5] Ⓓ $800

• Electronic oven controls. • Burners (watts): 2400/1000, 1900, 2 @ 1400.
Dual-element zone is suitable for small pans or large pots, and 4 bright warning lights show which zones remain hot. Oven automatically turns off after 12 hours, for safety. But: Minimal lip around the cooktop to contain spills. Obvious exterior stains after self-cleaning. **Recommendation**: Very good overall.

Kenmore (Sears) 9545[5] Ⓢ $700*

• Dial/electronic oven controls. • Burners (watts): 2 @ 1900, 2 @ 1400.
Heat zones were quite cool by the time the warning light shut off. Oven automatically turns off after 12 hours, for safety. The front of the range stayed cooler than most during self-cleaning. But: Lacks automatic cooking. Minimal lip around the cooktop to contain spills. Obvious exterior stains after self-cleaning. Has a fixed self-cleaning length. **Successor**: 9546[ ], $750. **Recommendation**: There are better choices.

Self-cleaning convection-oven smoothtops

Jenn-Air FCE70610[W] $1120

• Electronic oven controls. • Burners (watts): 2200/700, 2200, 2 @ 1200.
The only tested model with electronic cooktop controls for heat zones. Dual-element zone suitable for small pans or large pots. Oven automatically turns off after 12 hours, for safety. Convection fan worked well in our tests and didn't deprive the large oven of space. Oven has 3 shelves. **Recommendation**: Excellent overall.

General Electric JBP90WV[WW] Ⓢ $1140

• Electronic oven controls. • Burners (watts): 2500/1000, 2000, 2 @ 1500.
Cooktop has a dual-element zone suitable for small pans or large pots, a raised frame to contain heavy spills, and 4 bright warning lights to show which zones remain hot. Convection fan worked well in our tests. There are 3 oven shelves, plus a small rack for convection roasting. Self-cleaning left no exterior residue. But: Convection fan robs oven of cooking space. **Successor**: JBP90WW[ ],

$1300. **Recommendation**: Very good overall, but the small oven is a drawback.

KitchenAid KERC507Y[WH] Ⓢ $1100

• Electronic oven controls. • Burners (watts): 2400, 2100, 1700, 1400.
One of the few models with 4 different-sized heat zones. Has 4 bright warning lights to show which zones remain hot. Oven controls utilize a telephone-like touchpad, very easy to use. Convection fan worked well in our tests. Oven automatically turns itself off after 12 hours, for safety. Oven door latches automatically for self-cleaning. Front of the range stays cooler than most during self-cleaning. Has 3 oven shelves, small convection rack. But: Scarcely any lip around the cooktop to contain heavy spills. Convection feature robs oven of cooking space. **Successor**: KERC507E[ ], $1200. **Recommendation**: Very good overall.

Self-cleaning models with coil-burners

Tappan TEF354BC[W] $430

• Dial oven controls. • Burners (watts): 2 @ 2600, 2 @ 1500.
Easy-to-clean porcelain drip bowls. Back burners accommodate large pots without obstructing controls. Oven door latches automatically for self-cleaning. But: Panel above door gets hot during broiling or baking at high temps. **Similar**: TEF352SC[ ], $410. **Recommendation**: Very good overall.

Whirlpool RF365PXD[Q] Ⓓ $470

• Dial oven controls. • Burners (watts): 2 @ 2600, 2 @ 1500.
Cooktop stayed cooler than most after hot cooktop test. But: There's no light to indicate when oven door will open after self-cleaning. **Recommendation**: Very good overall.

Amana ARR626[WW] Ⓓ $445

• Dial oven controls. • Burners (watts): 2 @ 2600, 2 @ 1500.
Easy-to-clean porcelain drip bowls. But: There's no light to indicate when oven door will open after self-cleaning. **Recommendation**: Very good overall.

Frigidaire FEF350CA[S] $495
• Dial oven controls. • Burners (watts): 2 @ 2600, 2 @ 1500.
Easy-to-clean porcelain drip bowls. Oven door latches automatically for self-cleaning. But: Metal panel above door gets hot during broiling or baking at high temps. **Similar**: FEF350SA[ ], $420, FO4B350E[ ], $450. **Recommendation**: Very good overall.

General Electric JBP45GV[WH] Ⓢ $520
• Dial/electronic oven controls. • Burners (watts): 2 @ 2350, 2 @ 1325.
Easy-to-clean porcelain drip bowls. Oven automatically turns off after 12 hours, for safety. Self-cleaning left no exterior residue. **Successor**: JBP45WW[ ], $570. **Recommendation**: Very good overall.

Maytag CRE9300CC[W] $480
• Dial oven controls. • Burners (watts): 2600, 3 @ 1500.
Left no residue after self-cleaning. But: Only one 8-inch burner, located in front of cooktop; a large pot won't fit on either small rear burner. Three drip bowls have no hole in the bottom, allowing grease build-up. There's no light to indicate when oven door will open after self-cleaning. **Recommendation**: OK.

Kenmore (Sears) 9354[5] Ⓓ $550
• Dial/electronic oven controls. • Burners (watts): 2 @ 2600, 2 @ 1500.
Cooktop stayed cooler than most after hot cooktop test. The front of the range stayed cooler than most during self-cleaning. Oven automatically shuts off after 12 hours, for safety. **Recommendation**: OK.

Self-cleaning coil-burner model with microwave

Magic Chef 3962VV[V] $675
• Electronic oven controls. • Burners (watts): 2 @ 2600, 2 @ 1500.
Microwaving capability sets this model apart. It did save roasting and defrosting time for large items in our tests. The cooktop stayed cooler than most after hot cooktop test. Fast-set dial for oven temperature and timing. Oven automatically shuts off after 12 hours, for safety. Self-

cleaning left no exterior residue. But: Drip bowls have no hole in the bottom, allowing grease build-up. The oven door sticks a bit. Fan is fairly loud during microwave cooking and self-cleaning. **Recommendation**: Very good overall, but can't be used as a regular microwave oven.

Manual-clean coil-burner models

Tappan TEF324BC[W] $380
• Dial/electronic oven controls. • Burners (watts): 2 @ 2600, 2 @ 1500.
Easy-to-clean porcelain drip bowls. Back burners accommodate large pots without obstructing controls. But: Lacks automatic cooking. Metal panel above door gets hot during broiling or baking at high temps. **Recommendation**: The model of choice if you don't want a self-cleaning range.

General Electric JBS27GV[WH] $385
• Dial/electronic oven controls. • Burners (watts): 2 @ 2350, 2 @ 1325.
Cooktop stayed cooler than most after hot cooktop test. But: Lacks automatic cooking. **Recommendation**: Good but Spartan.

Frigidaire FEF322BA[W] $360
• Dial/electronic oven controls. • Burners (watts): 2 @ 2100, 2 @ 1250.
Easy-to-clean porcelain drip bowls. But: Lacks automatic cooking. Metal panel above oven door gets hot during broiling or baking at high temps. **Recommendation**: Good but Spartan.

Hotpoint RB536V[WH] Ⓢ $410
• Dial/electronic oven controls. • Burners (watts): 2 @ 2350, 2 @ 1325.
Somewhat like GE JBS27GV, but with a painted oven door that may show scratches. But: Lacks automatic cooking. **Successor**: RB536GW[ ], $410. **Recommendation**: Good but Spartan.

Whirlpool RF310PXD[Q] Ⓓ $400
• Dial/electronic oven controls. • Burners (watts): 2 @ 2100, 2 @ 1250.
Lowest oven temperature is just under 100°F, good for bread dough or warming plates. Cooktop stayed cooler than most after hot cooktop test. But: Front of range gets hot at high oven settings. No auto cooking. **Recommendation**: There are better choices.

Ratings *Breadmakers*
& Recommendations

The tests behind the Ratings

We test breadmakers using bread recipes and a packaged mix, observing how well they bake basic loaves and loaves with ingredients like whole-wheat flour and raisins. All the tested models bake very good bread. The **overall score** includes how easy models are to use and clean, and how noisy they are. **Loaf weight** is approximate for largest white loaf model can make. **Price** is approximate retail. Models similar to those we tested are noted in Comments; features may vary. **Model availability:** Ⓓ means model is discontinued. Ⓢ means model is replaced, according to the manufacturer; successor model is noted in Comments. New model was not tested; it may or may not perform similarly. Features may vary.

Standard features for these models

• Digital cycle-time display, delay-start timer. • White, whole-wheat, and dough cycles. • Adjustment to vary crust color. • Viewing window, mix-in signal. • Cool-down or keep-warm phase after bread bakes.

Recommendations

All breadmakers bake very good bread, but some are more convenient than others. The top three machines in our Ratings are easier to use and clean than most.

See report, page 87. Last time rated in Consumer Reports: December 1995.

Overall Ratings

E VG G F P
⊖ ⊖ ○ ◐ ●

Listed in order of performance and convenience

Brand and model	Price	Loaf weight	Overall score 0 — 100					Ease of use	Cleaning	Comments
			P	F	G	VG	E			
Regal Kitchen Pro K6743	$165	2 lb.						⊖	⊖	French-bread, sweet-bread cycles. No cool-down. Cycle time: 3:20. Resumes cycle after power interruption of up to 10 min. Display shows stage of cycle. **Similar:** K6742, no window.
Hitachi HB-E303 Bread Master II	250	2						⊖	⊖	Rapid cake, jam, pizza dough cycles. Cycle time: 4:10. Bread is airier than most. Resumes cycle after power interruption of up to 10 min. Display shows stage of cycle.

Brand and model	Price	Loaf weight	Overall score 0 ⎯⎯⎯ 100 P F G VG E	Ease of use	Cleaning	Comments
Breadman Plus TR-600	$195	2 lb.		⊖	⊖	French-bread, rapid cycles. Cycle time: 2:50. **Similar:** TR-710LEB; TR-600MAY, May Co. Stores; TR-710FED, Federated Stores; TR-710PNY, J.C. Penney; TR-710LE, Macy's; TR-710LEC, Sears.
Pillsbury Bread & Dough Maker 1016 ⑤	160	1.5		⊖	⊖	French-bread, sweet-bread cycles. No mix-in signal. Cycle time: 3:40. Resumes cycle after power interruption of up to 10 min. Display shows stage of cycle. **Successor:** 1021.
Breadman TR-500	145	1.5		⊖	⊖	"Basic wheat" cycle for white and whole-wheat bread. French-bread cycle. Cycle time: 2:30.
Black & Decker All-In-One-Plus B1800 Ⓓ	175	2		○	⊖	French-bread, sweet-bread cycles. Cycle time: 2:50.
Mr. Coffee The Breadmaker BMR200	110	2		○	⊖	French-bread, sweet-bread cycles. Cycle time: 2:50.
West Bend Bread & Dough Maker 41040X ⑤	150	1.5		○	⊖	French-bread, sweet-bread, rapid cycles. Cycle time: 3:40. Bread is denser than most. Display shows stage of cycle. **Successor:** 41044.
Zojirushi Home Bakery BBCC-S15A	270	1.5		○	◑	One cycle for white and whole-grain bread. French-bread, cake, jam, rapid, custom cycles. Has clock. Cycle time: 3:50. Bread is airier than most. Resumes cycle after power interruption of up to 10 min. Display shows stage of cycle. Delay-start timer is more complicated than most.
Oster Deluxe Designer 4812	145	1.5		○	○	French-bread, sweet-bread, rapid cycles. Cycle time: 3:30. Display shows stage of cycle. **Similar:** 4811.
Panasonic Bread Bakery SD-YD200 ⑤	220	2		○	⊖	Sandwich-bake, rapid cycles. Loaf is rectangular. Has yeast dispenser. No viewing window, crust-color adjustment. Cycle time: 4:00. Bread is airier than most. Resumes cycle after power interruption of up to 10 min. **Successor:** SD-YD205.
Hitachi HB-D102	130	1.5		⊖	⊖	Rapid cake, pizza dough cycles. Cycle time: 4:10.
Welbilt The Bread Machine ABM4100T	150	2		○	○	"Normal" cycle for white and whole-wheat bread. Sweet-bread, rapid cycles. Cycle time: 3:20. Bread is airier than most. Resumes cycle after power interruption of 1 sec. Display shows stage of cycle.

Ratings continued ▶

Overall Ratings *Continued*

E VG G F P
⊖ ⊖ ○ ◐ ●

Brand and model	Price	Loaf weight	Overall score 0-100						Ease of use	Cleaning	Comments
			P	F	G	VG	E			
Sanyo The Bread Factory Plus SBM-15 Ⓓ	$150	1.5 lb.	▬▬▬					○	⊖	French-bread, sweet-bread, rapid cycles. No mix-in signal. Pan volume smaller than others. Cycle time: 3:20. Crust color is uneven. Resumes cycle after power interruption of up to 10 min. Display shows stage of cycle.
Goldstar HB-026E Ⓓ	120	1.5	▬▬▬					◐	⊖	French-bread, sweet-bread, rapid cycles. Cycle time: 3:40.
Toastmaster Bread Box 1195	145	2	▬▬▬					○①	○①	Noisy. French-bread, sweet-bread, rapid, butter-churn cycles. Cycle time: 2:50.
West Bend 41080	300	2	▬▬▬					○	◐	Rapid cycles for French bread, sweet bread. Rectangular loaf. Extend rise option. Bread is denser than most. Resumes cycle after power interruption of up to 10 min. Display shows stage of cycle. Door hard to close. Heating element more exposed. Noisy. Cycle time: 3:30.

① Original pan was defective; score is for replacement pan.

How to use the Buying Guide

■ Read the article for general guidance about types, features, and how to buy. There you'll find a discussion of the choices you'll face in the marketplace, what's new, and key buying advice.

■ The Ratings graph the overall score so you can quickly understand the big picture in performance. Details on features or performance are also noted. For many products, we also have information on how reliable a brand is likely to be. See page 11.

■ To find our last full report on a subject, refer to the article or the Ratings for the listing, or check the eight-year index, page 342.

HOME CARE

Vacuum cleaners

You don't have to pay big bucks to get a machine that cleans well. Uprights are generally cheaper and more convenient, but a canister cleans more nimbly.

Last CR reports: *shop vacs, July 1996; uprights & canisters, March 1996; handheld, July 1992*
Ratings: *pages 132, 139*
Price range: *$20 to $1200*

The types

Uprights. Uprights outsell canisters by more than five to one. Most are easier to handle than a canister vacuum, require less storage space, and cost less. Uprights come in two basic designs: a soft, outer bag or a bag enclosed in a stiff housing. Pushing an upright is usually easy, since most weigh only 13 to 18 pounds. Some of the heavier models propel themselves with motorized rear wheels.

Uprights have a rotating beater brush, which beats the dust and dirt out of pile carpet. They're less effective on hard surfaces; their brushes may disperse debris rather than vacuum it up. Most come with a long hose and an assortment of attachments for vacuuming stairs, under furniture, upholstery, and such.
Price: $70 to $400.

Canisters. Superior suction makes canister vacuums good at vacuuming bare floors. Most full-sized canisters now include a power-nozzle attachment whose rotating brush, like those found on uprights, helps to deep-clean carpets. Even with that rather bulky attachment, canisters are still easier to maneuver around furniture than uprights are.

Full-sized canister vacuums weigh more than uprights (most weigh more than 20 pounds). The canister's hose and numerous detachable wands can be cumbersome to store. A canister's bag is often smaller than an upright's, but it's usually easier to change.

Price: anywhere from $75 to $1100; most sell for less than $300.

Compact canister vacs are easier to carry than full-sized canisters, but their cleaning performance in our tests has been disappointing.

Wet/dry vacuums. Also known as "shop vacs," these specialty machines are for a garage or workshop. They tackle chores that are beyond the typical household vacuum, such as gobbling up nails or bailing out a wet basement. But they're also noisy, exhaust much of the dust back into the room, and lack various amenities.

In basic design, these cleaners are little more than a hose and nozzle attached to a plastic tank with a motor on top. Tank size varies from 6 to 20 gallons. Small shop vacs store easily and hold enough for most chores, but larger models are generally quieter and more stable.

Price: $50 to $150.

Electric brooms. Also called "stick vacs," these are lightweight versions of an upright. Electric brooms with a built-in power nozzle are usually strong enough to remove crumbs from the surface of a carpet, but not ground-in grit. Their light weight (typically six pounds or so) and small head make them very portable and easy to maneuver—ideal for

quick cleanup in small areas. Some electric brooms have a removable plastic dirt holder; others require disposable bags. All have limited capacity.

Price: less than $25 to $80.

Handheld vacuums. Cordless models can do their job anywhere, but they can work for only about 10 minutes before needing a battery recharge. Wet/dry models can deal with one spilled box of cereal or a spilled bowl of cereal and milk. Plug-in hand vacuums can't roam as freely as cordless units. Plug-in models generally provide more suction than rechargeables, and some have a built-in revolving brush. Car vacs have a 15- or 20-foot cord that plugs into the car's cigarette-lighter socket. They can run for extended periods without draining the car battery much.

Price: $20 to $75.

What's new

More kinds of cleaners. Cleaning appliances are undergoing what's known as "niche marketing," in which manufacturers "position" specialized products to appeal to various groups of special users. If people aren't happy with an upright or canister vacuum cleaner, then manufacturers can hope to entice them with special machines—shop vacs, hand vacs, car vacs, stick vacs, battery-powered stick vacs, deep-cleaning vacs, rug shampooers, and so on—that do things regular cleaners can't. There's a certain amount of sense in this approach—sometimes a specialized appliance can perform a specialized task better than an all-purpose appliance can. But there's also a great deal of marketing hype.

Fewer canister vacuums. At the same time, traditional canister vacuum cleaners are becoming harder to find. One reason: wall-to-wall carpeting, a surface for which upright models were designed. Another reason: Uprights seem to have appropriated the functions of canisters more successfully than canisters have mimicked uprights. Many upright vacuums now include an on-board extension hose, which makes tools easy to connect. A power-nozzle attachment can give a canister the carpet-cleaning power of an upright, but canisters so equipped remain gawky machines, heavy and bulky to store.

Two-in-one models. One line of uprights actually lets you detach the module containing the motor and hose and use it separately as a hand-held canister vacuum. Our tests showed that the machines, from Bissell, cleaned surface dirt better than they did deep dirt.

Vacuum cleaners as air cleaners. For decades, vacuum-cleaner vendors have sold very expensive machines by playing on Americans' fear of dirt. The modern version of this sales pitch draws on a real problem for some people: Most vacuum cleaners emit some dust and, with it, allergens such as dust-mite particles. To solve this problem, many manufacturers offer special filtration, sometimes involving $100 filters or other complex dirt-collection methods.

Our tests show that some machines indeed emit more dirt than others, but some fairly ordinary models, not just the ones with the special filters, were among the cleanest. Premium-priced microfiltration dust bags, which are supposed to limit dust dispersion, are an option with some machines. But in our tests over the years, most of these have proven no more effective than standard bags.

Truth is, once you stop vacuuming and the dust settles, allergens that exist in your household environment will still be there. Vacuum cleaners are not air cleaners. Still, if you are allergic, it makes sense to avoid the machines that pick up dust from the floor and disperse it in the air.

Dirt sensor. It's easy to tell when you've vacuumed up surface debris, but how can you tell when you've cleaned deep down? In our labs, we dose carpets with a measured amount of "dirt"; after vacuuming, we can pick up the carpet and weigh it to find out. At home, you can't really tell. Some models (from Panasonic and Hoover) offer a "dirt sensor." But this device merely tells you when the machine has stopped picking up dirt, not if all the dirt has been picked up.

Shopping strategy

Decide on the type. The layout of your house may help you choose. If you have carpets of medium or deeper pile, an upright with tools at the ready is the best choice. If you have a lot of bare floor or if you have low-pile carpets or flat-weave rugs, choose a model that excels at surface cleaning. A canister might be a better choice than most uprights, which don't come with a floor tool.

Stairs present a problem for any type. On an upright, look for a long hose or a "stair handle" on the body. A canister, with its smaller and lighter tool head, might be easier to handle.

Electric brooms can be handy to give carpets and floors a once over, lightly. Their weight and compact size also make them handy for people with limited mobility or hand strength.

Hand vacs are versatile picker-uppers when they're stored accessibly. The plug-in variety lacks the mobility but is more powerful than a rechargeable.

Rather than relying on one machine, you might decide to have two: one for upstairs and one for downstairs or a carpet machine and a bare floor machine.

Decide on key features. Manufacturers often make several lines, each with five or six variants priced in $10 to $30 steps, according to features. You'll pay $100 or so extra for self-propulsion in an upright or for a power nozzle in a canister line. A high-efficiency filter is another premium feature. On an upright, make sure the beater brush can be turned off and that it has a variable-speed motor or a control to moderate suction. See "Key features," below.

The easiest brands to find. Four brands—Hoover, Eureka, Royal, and Sears Kenmore account for 70 percent of all upright vacuums sold. Sears dominates the canister market. Black & Decker and Royal Dirt Devil account for three-fourths of all handheld vacs. One of every three vacuum cleaners is sold at discount stores like Wal-Mart, Kmart, and Target, which advertise heavily and often run promotions. Sears is the single largest vacuum seller, but selection is largely limited to its own Kenmore label and a couple of other popular brands. Speciality stores may offer more choices, including fancy European imports (Nilfisk, Miele, etc.), but prices are apt to be high. You'll find the most sales in August, November, and December.

Two brands—Shop Vac and Sears Craftsman—account for 8 out of 10 wet/dry vacs sold.

Key features

Amps and horsepower. Regardless of type, all vacuums are labeled with claims of amperage, peak hp, or "cleaning effectiveness per amp." We've found no correlation between claims and performance in our tests.

Controls. An On/off switch that's high on an upright's handle is easy to use. On/off switches on most canisters are designed to be triggered by a foot. Most canisters have a separate foot switch to turn off the power nozzle. That's helpful when, say, a scatter rug gets stuck and you need to free it quickly to avoid overheating the power-nozzle motor.

Cord. In most cases, the longer the cord, the better. A built-in winder that rewinds the power cord is convenient. You'll find that design most often on canister models. Uprights generally have two hooks around which you wind the cord. If one or both hooks swivel, you can release the cord quickly.

Dirt bags. Most full-sized cleaners collect dirt in a disposable paper bag. Some models signal when the bag is full or airflow is blocked. Soft-body uprights have the largest bags (about a four-quart capacity), but bigger isn't necessarily better: Clogged pores in the bags decrease suction, so bags often have to be changed before they're full.

Installing a bag is easiest if its cardboard collar drops into a slot. Sliding the bag's sleeve over a tube and securing it with a spring band isn't as easy. And removing the bag from a soft-body upright without dumping the contents is a challenge. The plastic dust collectors on most electric brooms and hand vacs are easy enough to remove and empty.

Drain. On a wet/dry vac, this eliminates the need to lift the unit to dump out wet waste. You can roll the vac to a suitable spot and open the spout.

Dust control. Despite what ads may say, even the best vacuum won't capture all dust and debris. Uprights with the fan in front of the vacuum bag tend to capture the most. Canisters generally emit the most dust in their exhaust, though they are far cleaner than shop vacs. As a rule, machines that use paper dust bags are cleaner than models with a bagless dust collector or an elaborate water-filtration system.

Microfiltration dust bags that supposedly minimize dirt dispersion are an option on some vacuums. Our tests have shown that most are no more effective than standard, cheaper bags. The best way to control dust and allergens is to limit carpeting.

On wet/dry vacs, a cartridge filter is easier to install and remove than paper-over-foam or cloth-over-foam "bag type" filters. Cartridge filters don't have to come off—as bags do—when you switch from dry to wet pickup.

Hoses. The most convenient ones swivel. Nonswiveling ones can kink annoyingly as you vacuum. On a shop vac, a 2½-inch hose can pick up more and bigger debris than the standard 1¼-inch hose.

Noise. No vacuum cleaner can be called quiet, but the canisters we tested were slightly less noisy than the uprights. Among uprights, hard-body models were less noisy than soft-bodies. Electric brooms and handheld vacs tend to whine at a higher pitch than full-sized vacs. Wet/dry vacs are the noisiest.

Power nozzle. Look for a vacuum cleaner that allows raising or lowering the motorized beater brush with a dial, sliding lever, or pedal. Some models claim to adjust height automatically, but they usually aren't as effective as those you adjust. With some uprights, you can switch off the beater brush to avoid scattering dirt on hard floors.

In a hand vac, a revolving brush improves carpet cleaning, but it also competes with suction, flinging coarser soil about instead of sucking it in. A few battery-powered models come with a brush.

Pushing and carrying features. Big wheels or rollers make uprights easier to push than canisters, especially when the beater brush is set to the proper height. Self-propelled vacs require very little effort.

Stair-climbing features. The longer the hose, the better the reach. Uprights usually have too large a "footprint" to fit securely on a stair; canisters tend to be more cooperative. Some vacuum cleaners come with a small power nozzle for vacuuming carpet on stairs. On any power nozzle, the less space between the brush and the outer edge of its housing, the closer you can get to the back of the stair and to baseboards.

Suction adjustment. When you vacuum loose or billowy objects, excessive suction can cause the vacuum to inhale the fabric. Most canisters and some uprights let you reduce suction by uncovering a hole or valve near the handle. Some models have more than one speed to let you vary suction.

How to use the Buying Guide

■ Read the article for general guidance about types, features, and how to buy. There you'll find a discussion of the choices you'll face in the marketplace, what's new, and key buying advice.

■ The Ratings graph the overall score so you can quickly understand the big picture in performance. Details on features or performance are also noted. For many products, we also have information on how reliable a brand is likely to be. See page 11.

■ To find our last full report on a subject, refer to the article or the Ratings for the listing, or check the eight-year index, page 342.

Air-conditioners

Most room models do a good job of cooling and dehumidifying. Features and noise levels vary.

Last CR reports: *large models, June 1996; small and mid-sized, June 1995*
Ratings: *page 143*
Price range: *$200 to $850*

The types

All window air-conditioners contain pretty much the same components. The part facing outdoors contains a compressor and condenser; the part facing indoors, a fan and an evaporator. The main things that distinguish one air-conditioner from another are cooling capacity, energy efficiency, and comfort control—how well it maintains the desired temperature.

Cooling capacity. How much you need depends mainly on the size of the room, the number of windows, and the local climate. Use the chart opposite to determine how much you need. An air-conditioner with too little capacity won't cool adequately. Too much capacity can make you feel clammy, since the air-conditioner will tend to cycle off before it can dehumidify the room.

The smallest models, suitable for a small bedroom, are rated at about 5000 Btu of cooling per hour. Medium-sized models, about 8000 to 10,000 Btu/hour, can cool a living room or master suite. Large models, those rated at 11,000 to 12,000 Btu/hour, can cool about 500 square feet—a large room, or areas that run together, such as a living room/dining room. Models larger than that usually require a 240-volt line.

Small units are generally priced $200 to $500; mid-sized models, $400 to $700; and large units, about $500 to $850.

Comfort control. Ideally, an air-conditioner should allow temperature swings of no more than 1½ degrees above or below the set point and should keep relative humidity fairly constant.

What's new

Better energy-efficiency. A model's Energy Efficiency Rating (EER), the guide to its energy consumption, is figured by dividing the Btu per hour by the power used, in watts. All else being equal, the higher the EER, the lower the energy consumption. We recommend models with EERs of 9 or higher.

Lighter units. The newest models may have shed some pounds, but they're still back-breakers. The large models we recently tested ranged from 67 to 115 pounds; small models, about half that. Installing or removing them remains a two-person job.

Shopping strategy

Expect most air-conditioners today to do a good job of cooling and dehumidifying. Comfort performance, however, varies dramatically from one model to another. Some cope better than others with low voltage, or with awkward placement in a room. Some are more efficient than others, ranging from 9 to 11.7. And some are much noisier.

Decide on the cooling capacity. This depends on the size of the room, the windows, and the local climate. See the box at right.

Decide on key features. A digital readout of the set temperature is convenient; so is a built-in time that can set the unit cooling before you return home. See "Key features," below.

The easiest brands to find. Even though there are more than two dozen brands of air-conditioners, many come from the same makers. Fedders, for instance, makes Emerson Quiet Kool and Airtemp models. Frigidaire makes Gibson and White-Westinghouse. Matsushita Electric makes Panasonic and Quasar.

Fedders is the leading brand. It, along with Sears Kenmore, GE, Whirlpool,

How much cooling?

Use the chart below to determine how much cooling you'll need for a space with an eight-foot ceiling.

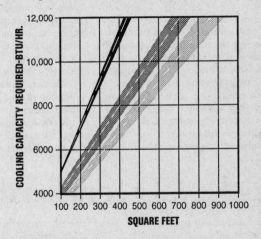

1. At the bottom of the chart, find the square footage you need to cool.

2. From there, move to a band, based on what's above your room: The thin band for an occupied area above; medium-width for an insulated attic above; thick for a noninsulated attic.

3. Within the band, move down for rooms facing mostly north or east, up for mostly south or west.

4. Read across to the appropriate Btu/hour.

5. From that Btu/hour, subtract up to 15 percent if you live in a cool, northern climate; add up to 10 percent for a hot, southern climate. Subtract 30 percent if the unit will be used only at night. If more than two people regularly occupy the area, add 600 Btu/hour of cooling capacity for every additional person. Add 4000 Btu/hour if the area includes the kitchen.

and White-Westinghouse account for almost half of all sales in the U.S.

Key features

Controls. Look for a thermostat with clear markings. Controls should be logically arranged and easy to operate. Some models have a digital readout; it shows the temperature you've set and that the power is on. The latter is helpful in the Energy-Saver mode, when fan and compressor cycle on and off together.

Energy-saving options. A timer can turn an air-conditioner on before you get home, saving the need for it to run all day. An Energy-Saver setting, included on many models, is less useful. It cycles the fan on and off with the compressor instead of letting the fan run continuously. It doesn't save much energy, and the change in noise levels can be jarring as the fan and compressor cycle on and off together, especially at night.

Installation features. Most room air-conditioners are designed to fit in a double-hung window. A limited selection of models is sized for casement windows. Some models are made for through-the-wall installation.

Some models come fully assembled; others require you to add their side panels —usually an easy job. A slide-out chassis greatly simplifies installation: You secure the empty cabinet in the window, then slide in the machine's innards.

Louvers. Many room models can't direct the air effectively—important if the unit is in a corner or if you want spot-cooling. Models that let you close some louvers can redirect air more forcefully through the ones that remain open. A vent setting blows some room air outdoors. Some models also draw in fresh air, although not effectively.

'Power thrust.' Also called "Super Thrust" and the like, this fan control sends the cooled air farther into the room. It's useful if you must mount the unit at the narrow end of a long room.

Smoke, CO & radon detectors

These inexpensive sensors can make your home safer.

Last CR report: *smoke detectors,
May 1994; radon detectors, July 1995;
CO detectors, November 1996*
Price range: *less than $10 to $100*

Shopping strategy

Every home should have a smoke detector—it cuts the risk of dying in a fire by half, according to some studies. Homes would be safer still if more people took care of their smoke detectors. Though they're now in most homes, many cannot properly warn of fire because of dead or missing batteries.

There are two types: One handles smoky fires best; another, blazing fires. See "Smoke detector types," below.

Carbon monoxide detectors should be in any home with a fuel-fired furnace or space heater, wood stove, fireplace, or attached garage—all common sources of carbon monoxide. If the home is tightly weather-sealed, the risk is even greater. We recommend the AC-powered plug-in type that digitally displays the CO level.

Radon is easy to detect and get rid of, but most people don't bother to test their homes for this health hazard until it's time to sell the property. A short-term kit gives feedback usually within two weeks but a long-term kit gives more reliable results. See "Radon-detector types."

Smoke detector types

Smoke detectors are widely sold in home centers and in discount and hardware stores. They range in price from less than $10 to $30. One company, BRK Electronics, makes most of the smoke detectors you'll come across; its First Alert and Family Guard brands account for three of every four units sold. Brands sold through electrical suppliers include BRK, Firex, Fyrnetics, and Dicon.

Most smoke detectors use a nine-volt battery. Those that are AC-powered (with a battery for backup power) are more suitable to renovations and new construction. Models designed for the hearing impaired or that use AC-power generally cost a premium.

Detectors vary in how they work:

Ionization. This is by far the easiest type of detector to find. Ionization detectors use radioactive material (an amount so small it poses no significant hazard) to make the air in the detector chamber conduct electricity. Smoke interferes with that electric current and triggers the alarm. Ionization detectors are the most effective way to sense blazes that give off little smoke.

Photoelectric. These smoke detectors shine a small beam of light past a sensor. Smoke disperses the light, tripping the alarm. Photoelectric models are best at sensing a smoldering, smoky fire—the kind that might start in upholstery, say.

Combination. Some models use both ionization and photoelectric sensors, thereby minimizing the disadvantages of each type.

For the hearing-impaired. Smoke detectors for the hearing-impaired rouse sleepers with a flashing strobe.

Smoke detector features

Alarm loudness. An industry standard specifies a minimum loudness of 85 decibels. Many alarms are far more raucous, a consideration if you're hard of hearing or sleep soundly.

Alarm testing. Most smoke detectors have a small LED (light-emitting diode) that flashes every minute or so to indicate a state of readiness.

All detectors have a button that lets you test the unit's circuitry, battery, and horn. Flat buttons are easier to press with a broom handle than rounded ones. Some models respond to a flashlight beam. Units with automatic testing sound the alarm briefly every week at the same time.

Auxiliary lights. When some models sound the alarm, they also turn on built-in reflector lights to help guide you through the smoke. But the lights are usually too small and weak to be of much use in a smoky fire. Consider keeping a large halogen-bulb flashlight handy.

Hush button. Detectors will sound as long as there's smoke, even if the cause is burnt toast. Most are hard to silence once they go off. As a result, many people detach the battery and forget to reconnect it. A Hush button solves the problem.

Missing-battery indicator. Almost all smoke detectors signal the absence of a battery, as the safety standard requires.

Weak-battery warning. All models chirp or beep periodically for at least 30 days or until the battery is replaced.

CO detector types

If you have a fuel-burning appliance or fireplace, you should have at least one CO detector, ideally in a hallway or sleeping area. Most CO detectors come from hardware stores and home centers. First Alert dominates the market, but other brands are readily available and, in our tests, worked better. Price can range from $30 to $100, but good models with digital display can be had for $55 or less.

CO detectors come in two main types:

Plug-in. Most models are the AC-powered plug-in type; a few can be hardwired. They work by heating a metal-oxide sensor that reacts with CO to sound the alarm. A six-foot power cord is typical. Only a few offer battery backup.

Battery-powered. A new type has a fuel-cell detector that works well. An older type has a translucent disk that darkens upon prolonged exposure to CO, a change that is detected by an infrared sensor. In our tests, this type tended to take hours rather than minutes to recover after the air was cleared. Its sensor also tends to accumulate CO over time, so the alarm could end up reacting to a prolonged spell of air pollution.

CO detector features

Most are designed to show blinking lights and chirp intermittently as preliminary warnings. Then all of them sound the full alarm with a shrill, shrieking horn. Once you've ventilated the area, a detector should reset itself and go silent when the danger is past.

Digital display. An even safer method of letting you know the danger is past is used by models that digitally display the CO level of the surroundings. We strongly recommend this safety feature. At low CO levels, it can tip you off to a potential problem before it becomes severe.

Recall. Models with this feature show, on demand, the highest CO level sensed since the last resetting of the unit's memory. That might prove handy for checking on conditions after you've been away from home.

Hush/reset button. The "hush" button is supposed to silence the horn yet leave the CO censor active.

From our most recent test, we recommended AC-powered plug-in detectors with digital displays from Nighthawk (900-0046, 900-0014, 900-0056, 900-0057). They were most impressive. Their digital displays were extremely accurate, and although they lack early-warning lights and shrieks, they sounded full alarms well within the time limits. The Lifesaver FYCO-6N ($53) and S-Tech STCO-500LC ($55) also deserve serious consideration, even though their displays are dimmer and not quite as accurate as the Nighthawks.

Radon-detector types

Radon-detection kits are widely available at hardware stores, home centers, and other retail outlets. Key Technology, First Alert, and Air Check are the most widely distributed brands. Kits cost from $10 to $30, including lab analysis and a written report.

There are two main types:

Short-term. This type uses a charcoal-containing canister, envelope, or tray to track radon levels for up to seven days.

Long-term. A piece of plastic picks up an imprint from the radon gas to give the average exposure for 90 days or more.

Both types of kit work in much the same way. You place the open kit in the lowest occupied living area. If you have and use a finished basement playroom, that's the place. If you visit your basement only a few times a week to load and unload the washer, test the first-floor living space instead. After the specified period of time, you seal the kit and promptly send it to the lab for analysis.

Fire extinguishers

Every home should be equipped with the right types. Fire-fighting ability is a given, but some are easier to use than others.

Last CR report: *May 1994*
Price range: *less than $10 to $100*

The types and sizes

Fire extinguishers are labeled according to the type of fire they're meant to fight and the size of fire they can fight, based on tests by Underwriters Laboratories, an independent testing organization.

Fire type. Letter codes define the fire types: **"A"** fires involve combustibles like paper, wood, cloth, and upholstery, and they can be put out with water. **"B"** fires involve flammable liquids—cooking grease, paint solvents, gasoline. **"C"** fires involve electrical equipment like a computer, a TV set, or a fuse box.

Fire size. Numbers preceding the A:B:Cs denote the size of the fire a unit can fight. You'll see labels that read 2-A:10-B:C or 5-B:C (no size is assigned to "C" fires). Other things being equal, an extinguisher rated at 10-B will put out twice as much flaming grease as a 5-B unit. Those numbers also give a rough idea of how long each extinguisher can spray. A longer spray time buys critical extra seconds to fight a fire. But the higher the numbers, the bigger the unit, and large models are clumsy to store and heavy to use.

What's new

Fire extinguishers use water, carbon dioxide gas, or dry chemicals to kill fires.

Models with halon gas, once sold for electrical fires, have all but disappeared because halon vapor damages the earth's ozone layer. The most common fire-fighting material is a dry-chemical mix.

Shopping strategy

Decide on the type and size. Every home should have at least one extinguisher on every floor level. An A:B:C extinguisher is the most versatile, capable of handling fires of all common burning materials. Such units are the best choice for rooms that have a wood-burning stove or fireplace. Models labeled B:C are particularly useful in kitchens, because the sodium bicarbonate powder typically used is better for smothering grease fires. In the store, try a large model—say, one rated at 3-A:40-B:C—to see if you can manage it. If it's too cumbersome, choose a medium-sized unit (rated at 2-A:10-B:C).

Decide on key features. Any aspect of an extinguisher that's inconvenient could waste critical seconds in an emergency. A hooklike hanging bracket is the easiest to operate. See "Key features," below.

The easiest brands to find. Two brands—Walter Kidde and First Alert—dominate the selection in home centers, discount stores, and hardware stores.

Key features

Mountings. A simple hooklike hanging bracket is easier to use in a hurry than a marine bracket. With a marine bracket, you must unsnap the ring that holds the unit to the bracket. (The ring prevents an extinguisher from being knocked off the wall accidentally.)

Pressure indicators. Models with a dial-type gauge show at a glance whether they have sufficient pressure. Instead of a dial, some use a pressure-check pin. You check it by pushing down on the pin; if it pops back, the pressure is adequate.

Recharging. Once an extinguisher is discharged, even partially, it must be either recharged or replaced. Most models can be recharged after a fire or a drop in pressure (look under "fire extinguishers" in the Yellow Pages). Recharging is less wasteful than disposal, but it may cost as much as buying a new one. Models that aren't rechargeable should be replaced if the pressure has ebbed, or as the manufacturer recommends—at least every 12 years.

Weight. The multipurpose units we've tested range in weight from 4 to 10 pounds; B:C models, 1 to 10 pounds. Try hefting a model before you buy.

Lawn mowers

Buying the right type can save you hundreds of dollars. So can accepting good, instead of superior, cutting performance.

Last CR reports: *manual & electric, June 1994; gasoline push-type, June 1995; self-propelled, June 1996; riding, June 1993*
Ratings: *page 149*
Brand Repair Histories: *pages 20 & 21*
Price range: *$65 to $5000*

The types

Manual reel mowers. The reel mower has been brought up-to-date with lightweight alloys and plastic parts, but the way it works hasn't changed. A series of blades linked to wheels slice the grass.

Reel mowers are quiet, inexpensive, and relatively safe to operate. They require no maintenance aside from occasional sharpening or blade adjustment. Most can't be set to cut higher than $1\frac{1}{2}$ inches, and those we tested had a hard time plowing through thick, high grass. Reel mowers can mow no closer than three inches around obstacles. The cutting swath ranges from 14 to 18 inches. Reel mowers are best suited to small, flat lawns. Price: $65 to $200.

Electric mowers. These use an electric motor to spin the blades, generally while you push. The motors are less powerful than the engines on gasoline-powered mowers, but that may not correlate with performance. In our tests, some electrics have cut tall grass better than some gas models did.

Electric mowers are quiet and require little maintenance. They tackle tall and thick grass or weeds as well as most gasoline-powered mowers do. Many models mulch—chop grass up extra fine so clippings can decompose naturally in the lawn. They run on standard house current. Such models are suitable for lawns of about one-quarter-acre—typically, what can be reached by the 100-foot cord. Price: $150 to $250.

Gasoline-powered mowers. *Push-type* gasoline-powered mowers are free to roam as long as there's fuel in the tank. Many can gobble up tall and thick grass or weeds. Handling for most ranges from easy to very easy. Most models can mulch. But gasoline-powered mowers are noisy, and they require regular maintenance, including blade sharpening. Gasoline-powered push-type mowers are best suited for lawns of up to one-half acre and for trimming larger lawns. The engine is typically a one-cylinder, four-stroke design that spins a 20- to 22-inch blade; power ranges from 3.5 to 5.5 hp. (A few models use a two-stroke engine, which uses a gasoline/oil fuel mixture and emits more pollutants.) Price: $100 to $650.

The *self-propelled* feature adds anywhere from $155 to $225 to the selling price. The premium is worthwhile if your lawn is a half-acre or larger, or if it's hilly. The engines, typically the same size as those in push-type models, power either the front or rear wheels. Rear-drive models are better at climbing hills, but some can be a bit harder to maneuver through U-turns. Price: $100 to $800.

Riding mowers and tractors. Riding mowers and small tractors are best suited for lawns about one-half acre and larger. In addition to saving you the effort of walking, they have wider cutting swaths than walk-behind mowers, so a lawn requires fewer passes to mow. Price: $900 to $4000 for a riding mower or a lawn tractor; $2000 to $5000 for a garden tractor.

What's new

New Federal standards that aim to reduce the overall hydrocarbon emissions from gasoline-powered mowers and other outdoor power equipment by about 30 percent took effect September 1996. California has already started certifying engines that meet its similar standard. By 1997, all approved engines should be wearing an EPA certification sticker, although such mowers will be a small part

Mower safety

As a safety precaution, all walk-behind power mowers have a "deadman" control that stops the blade when you let go of the handle. That and other safety features seem to have made mowing safer. Injuries due to walk-behind mowers have dropped to about half what they were 10 years ago. Still, thousands of people head to hospital emergency rooms every year because of an injury caused by a lawn mower or tractor.

When you mow, keep safety in mind:

■ Mow only when and where it's safe. Don't mow when the grass is wet; your foot could slip under the mower. Push a mower across a slope, not up and down. If you have a riding mower or tractor, travel up and down, not across. If the slope is more than about 15 degrees, don't mow at all; on slopes that steep, a push-mower can get away from you, and a ride-on mower can tip over.

■ Wear sturdy shoes and close-fitting clothes. Consider wearing ear protection for a noisy mower.

■ Before mowing, pick up toys, hoses, rocks, and twigs. Make sure no people or pets are nearby; a mower can hurl objects.

■ Keep hands and feet away from moving parts.

■ Don't defeat safety devices.

■ Don't let children use or ride a mower.

of what's available for some time. If you choose a mower with a certified engine, you'll be doing the environment a favor.

Even stricter standards are on the horizon. As of 1999, California will require that engines reduce emissions an additional 70 percent. An upgraded EPA standard is expected to take effect shortly thereafter. Note that the two-stroke engines still found on a few gas mowers have their own requirements, which currently allow for more pollution. A four-stroke engine is likely to pollute much less than a similar-sized two-stroke.

Battery-powered mowers offer much promise as an environment-friendly choice. But the models we've seen are expensive and limited in power. The models we tested in 1995 mowed up to .4 acre per charge and cut well but were heavy. In 1996, the battery-powered *Ryobi Mulchinator BMP2418*, $450, was a competent cutter with nice controls but it quit after only about .15 acre.

Reliability

The more complex the mower, the more likely it will need repair, according to our readers' experience. Overall, readers report that about 14 percent of push-type gasoline mowers bought since 1989 needed repairs. About 25 percent of self-propelled models needed repair during the same period. The repair rates for Honda models were generally low for both types. For more information, see the Brand Repair Histories on pages 20 and 21.

Shopping strategy

Decide on the type. Let the size and the terrain of the lawn determine the type of mower you buy. If you mow a quarter-acre or less of flat lawn, consider a manual reel mower; for a half-acre or less, a gas or electric mower that you push; for a half-acre to an acre, especially if the land is hilly, a self-propelled model; and for an acre or more, a riding mower.

How you handle clippings is almost as important as your choice of a mower. Mowers come with a bag at the back or the side. You can simply discharge the clippings (and then rake) or, with many models, mulch the clippings. If you bag clippings, choose a mower with a bag at the back; rear bags are generally bigger than side bags and make a mower more maneuverable. A side-bagging model is apt to be less expensive, however. Good mulchers come in both designs, rear- and side-bagging.

Decide on the key features. Desirable features that add to the price include a blade-brake/clutch safety system, self-propulsion, a rear bag, and an electric start. See "Key features," below.

The easiest brands to find. Sears Craftsman and Murray are the biggest-selling brands.

You'll find low-priced models from brands like Murray, Rally, Lawnflite, and private labels at discount stores like Kmart, Wal-Mart, and Target. Medium-priced models from Craftsman, Lawn-Boy, Lawn Chief, MTD, Murray, Snapper, Yard-Man, and White are sold at home centers, hardware chains, and Sears. Independent dealers often sell the more expensive brands: Ariens, Cub Cadet, Honda, John Deere, and Troy-Bilt.

New models appear by March or April. May is the most active month for sales. You'll find sale prices anytime from August through October, but your selection of models is likely to be limited.

Key features

Amps, horsepower. You can't predict performance by motor or engine size alone. Electric motors range from 6.5 to 12 amps. Engines in gasoline-powered mowers typically range from 3.5 to 6 hp. Riders have 8- to 10-hp engines; lawn tractors and garden tractors, up to 20 hp.

Choke. The most convenient design is set simply by adjusting the throttle control. Most mowers use a simpler device to help start the engine—a primer, a little rubber bulb located on the engine. You press the bulb before you pull the cord.

Changing mowing modes. The most convenient let you change from bagging to mulching mode by removing the bag and inserting a plate or plug, and change from bagging to discharging by letting a chute fall into place. Other mowers make you wrestle them onto their side and use a wrench to change their blade.

Clutch. The control should be within easy reach of your fingers as you mow.

Cord handling. An electric extension cord is a nuisance, but the inconvenience can be minimized with a sliding clip that lets the cord flip from side to side. The clip is better than a handle you flip over every time you reverse direction.

Cutting-height adjustment. Most mowers have spring-loaded adjusters on each wheel. They're easy enough to use, but easier yet is a single lever or crank handle that adjusts all four wheels at once.

Deck. On most mowers, the deck is made of stamped steel. Higher-priced models usually have a deck of cast aluminum or plastic, which resist corrosion.

Electric start. This makes starting a gasoline-powered mower much easier than tugging on a rope. It adds about $100 to the price of the mower.

Engine type. Of the three types of engine—the four-stroke, overhead-valve engine; the four-stroke, side-valve; and the two-stroke—the overhead-valve engine tends to be least polluting, and the two-stroke engine, the dirtiest, partly

because it burns oil along with gasoline. As of September 1996, new small-engine lawn and garden tools must meet new emissions standards.

Grass bags. You can install or remove the best designs without tricky manipulations, carry them easily with one hand whether empty or full, and dump their contents with little shaking. A sewn-on handle at the back of a rear bag is an extra help.

Noise. Manual reel and electric mowers are the most civilized. Gasoline-powered mowers are quite noisy, but not dangerously so.

Safety systems. Of the two types, *engine-kill* is the one you'll see most often. It uses a deadman control, usually in the form of a "bail"—a metal loop you keep pressed against the mower handle. Releasing the deadman, even for an instant, kills the engine. That system can mean a lot of annoying restarts, and some people may be tempted to override it.

A better but more expensive system is the *blade-brake/clutch*. It adds about $100 to the price of the mower. When you release the deadman control, the clutch releases the blade and a brake halts it, but the engine keeps running. To get the blade turning again, you press the control against the handle. This system cuts down on restarts, say, for emptying the bag, and lets the engine help power the mower back to the garage without the blade trying to "mow" the driveway.

Speeds. Some mowers have one engine speed, usually about 2½ mph; others have several; still others have a continuous range, typically from 1 to 3 mph. One speed is fine, but two speeds let you adjust to the terrain and the grass. Extra speeds are nice, but note that some six-speed mowers aren't as versatile as they seem—two or three of their low speeds are virtually the same.

Ratings
& Recommendations
Vacuum cleaners

The tests behind the Ratings

Cleaning is given the greatest weight. **Deep** cleaning reflects how much embedded sand and talcum powder the cleaner could extract from a medium-pile carpet. The best removed around four times as much as the worst. **Surface** cleaning measures how much air flows through the hose. Machines that created fewer breathable dust particles were rated better in **emissions**. Even the least raucous cleaner makes plenty of **noise**. The models ranged from a slightly annoying hum to whines, whistles, and rattles loud enough to drown out conversation. **Price** is approximate retail. **Model availability:** Ⓓ means model is discontinued.

Standard features for these models

• A 4- to 10-foot hose and a 15- to 30-foot power cord. • On-board tool storage.

Recommendations

Among uprights, the top-rated Sharp Twin Energy, $200, is noteworthy if performance is the only consideration. Less expensive, and almost as good is the Eureka Powerline Plus for $140, but it lost points for noise and dirt disposal and showed signs of durability problems. Among canisters, the top-rated models sell in the $800 range. The best performer at the most reasonable price is Eureka World Vac 6865B, $210.

See report, page 117. Last time rated in Consumer Reports: March 1996.

Overall Ratings *Listed in order of overall score*

Legend: E ⊖ VG ⊖ G ○ F ◓ P ●

Brand and model	Price	Overall score (0–100)		Cleaning DEEP	Cleaning SURFACE	Emissions	Noise
			P F G VG E				
UPRIGHTS							
Sharp Twin Energy EC-12TWT4	$200			⊖	⊖	⊖	⊖
Hoover Power Drive Supreme U6323-930	320			⊖	○	⊖	◓
Kirby G4	1350			⊖	⊖	⊖	◓
Eureka Bravo! The Boss 9334DT	80			⊖	○	⊖	◓
Eureka Powerline Plus 9741AT	140			⊖	⊖	⊖	◓
Hoover Power Drive U6311-930	270			⊖	○	◓	◓
Royal Dirt Devil Lite Plus 085300	95			⊖	○	⊖	●
Kenmore (Sears) Whispertone 3511290 Ⓓ	200			◓	⊖	⊖	○

Brand and model	Price	Overall score	Cleaning DEEP	Cleaning SURFACE	Emissions	Noise
		P F G VG E				
Hoover Dimension Supreme U5221-930 Ⓓ	$200	▬▬▬▬	⊖	⊖	⊖	⊖
Eureka Bravo! SureValu 9205DT Ⓓ	80	▬▬▬▬	○	○	⊖	●
Hoover Encore Supreme U4261-930 Ⓓ	90	▬▬▬▬	⊖	○	⊖	⊖
Royal Dirt Devil MVP 088305 Ⓓ	135	▬▬▬▬	○	⊖	⊖	⊖
Hoover Dimension U5209-930	180	▬▬▬▬	⊖	○	⊖	⊖
Fantom F11051	300	▬▬▬▬	○	○	⊖	○
Sanyo Performax SC-U11MA Ⓓ	400	▬▬▬▬	⊖	⊖	⊖	○
Royal Dirt Devil Classic 086600 Ⓓ	100	▬▬▬▬	⊖	○	⊖	⊖
Panasonic Quickdraw MC-V5315 Ⓓ	120	▬▬▬▬	⊖	⊖	⊖	○
Bissell Plus 3550A	260	▬▬▬▬	⊖	⊖	⊖	⊖
Kenmore (Sears) Power Path 3581090 Ⓓ	100	▬▬▬▬	⊖	⊖	⊖	○
Electrolux Epic Series 3500 SR	650	▬▬▬▬	⊖	⊖	⊖	⊖
Panasonic Quickdraw MC-5190-1 Ⓓ	100	▬▬▬▬	⊖	○	⊖	⊖
Panasonic Dirt Sensor Quickdraw MC-V5375 Ⓓ	200	▬▬▬▬	⊖	⊖	⊖	⊖
Hoover Preferred U4655-930	150	▬▬▬	⊖	⊖	○	●
Hoover Encore Supreme Soft & Light U4293-930	100	▬▬▬	○	○	○	⊖
Miele Powerhouse Plus S174i	320	▬▬▬	⊖	○	⊖	○
Eureka Powerline Plus Victory 4441AT	150	▬▬▬	⊖	○	⊖	⊖
Royal Dirt Devil Impulse 085400	90	▬▬▬	○	⊖	⊖	●
Eureka The Boss Victory 4335BT	100	▬▬▬	⊖	⊖	●	○
Singer SB12720	80	▬▬▬	⊖	●	⊖	●
White-Westinghouse Millenium WWU2020	100	▬▬▬	⊖	⊖	⊖	●
Regina Plus HO6505 Ⓓ	110	▬▬	⊖	⊖	⊖	⊖
Eureka Excalibur 6425AT Ⓓ	200	▬▬	⊖	●	⊖	○
Regina Ultra HO6508 Ⓓ	150	▬▬	●	○	●	⊖
Singer Poweramp HB1412	180	▬▬	○	●	●	●
CANISTERS						
Nilfisk GS90	800	▬▬▬▬	⊖	⊖	⊖	⊖
Miele White Pearl S434i	850	▬▬▬▬	○	⊖	⊖	⊖
Eureka Excalibur 6975A	300	▬▬▬▬	⊖	⊖	⊖	⊖
Eureka World Vac 6865B	210	▬▬▬	⊖	⊖	●	○
Hoover PowerMAX Supreme S3611	300	▬▬▬	⊖	○	●	○
Oreck Super Celoc XL1500 Ⓓ	500	▬▬▬	○	⊖	⊖	⊖
Panasonic Dirt Sensor MC-V9635	320	▬▬▬	⊖	⊖	⊖	○
Kenmore (Sears) Power-Mate 2521190 Ⓓ	200	▬▬▬	○	⊖	●	○

Ratings continued ▶

Overall Ratings *Continued*

	E	VG	G	F	P
	⊖	⊖	○	●	●

Brand and model	Price	Overall score 0—100	Cleaning DEEP	Cleaning SURFACE	Emissions	Noise
Hoover Futura S3567	$200	▇▇ (P F G VG E)	⊖	○	●	○
Kenmore (Sears) Whispertone 25212 Ⓓ	300	▇▇	⊖	⊖	○	○
Electrolux Epic Series 6500 SR	700	▇▇	⊖	⊖	⊖	○
Rainbow Performance Edition SE	1400	▇▇	⊖	⊖	●	○
White-Westinghouse V.I.P. WWP9500	200	▇▇	⊖	○	⊖	○
Royal M4600 Ⓓ	550	▇▇	○	○	○	⊖
Electrolux Renaissance C104A	900	▇▇	○	○	○	⊖
Hoover Encore Supreme S3395-040	150	▇▇	○	⊖	●	⊖
COMPACT CANISTERS						
Sharp EC-7311	135	▇▇	⊖	○	⊖	⊖
Sanyo SC-585	80	▇	⊖	⊖	⊖	⊖
Royal Dirt Devil Can Vac 082023 Ⓓ	160	▇	⊖	●	●	⊖
Hoover Portapower II Supreme S1353	150	▇	⊖	●	●	⊖
Eureka Worldvac Mighty Mite II 3661A	120	▇	●	⊖	●	○
Eureka The Boss Mighty Mite II 3621A	75	▇	●	●	●	○
Hoover Portapower II S1337	90	▇	●	●	⊖	○

Model details *Listed in order of overall score*

Uprights

Sharp Twin Energy Twin Energy EC-12TWT4 $200

Hard-body upright with stair handle; fan pulls dirt into bag. Hose ready for use with on-board tools. **Recommendation:** Convenient and relatively quiet, this is a superior performer at a moderate price, though the sturdiness of the power-head housing is a worry.

Hoover Power Drive Supreme U6323-930 $320

Self-propelled hard-body upright with stair handle; fan pushes dirt into bag. Good side edge cleaner. Tools on board are covered. Easy-to-maneuver hose. Manual carpet-height adjustment. **Recommendation:** Superior cleaner, but heavy and bulky.

Self-propelled feature is expensive and takes some getting used to.

Kirby G4 $1350

Self-propelled, soft-body upright with stair handle; fan pushes dirt into bag. Good side edge cleaner. No tools or hose on board; hard to convert for use with tools. Easy-to-maneuver hose. Suction control. Manual carpet-height adjustment. Low emissions. **Recommendation:** Inconvenience, heft, and astronomical price more than counter this model's fine performance.

Eureka Bravo! The Boss 9334DT $80

Soft-body upright with stair handle; fan pushes dirt into bag. Good side edge cleaner. Tools on board, but hose is flimsy. Awkward cord handling. Manual carpet-height adjustment. Low emissions.

Recommendation: Low price and fine performance. But inconvenient, and durability is a worry.

Eureka Powerline Plus 9741AT $140

Hard-body upright with stair handle; fan pushes dirt into bag. Good side edge cleaner. Tools on board. Easy-to-maneuver but flimsy hose. Manual carpet-height adjustment. **Recommendation:** Low price and fine performance, but durability is a worry.

Hoover Power Drive U6311-930 $270

Very similar to the Hoover Power Drive Supreme, except for minor features. **Recommendation:** Good value for a self-propelled model.

Royal Dirt Devil Lite Plus 085300 $95

Soft-body upright with stair handle; fan pushes dirt into bag. Tools on board. Low emissions. **Recommendation:** Low price and fine, if noisy, performance. Durability is a worry.

Kenmore (Sears) Whispertone 3511290 ⅅ $200

Hard-body upright with stair handle; fan pulls dirt into bag. Hose ready for use with on-board tools. Suction control. Manual carpet-height adjustment. On/off switch for beater brush. **Recommendation:** A good choice if you don't have deep carpets.

Hoover Dimension Supreme U5221-930 ⅅ $200

Hard-body upright with stair handle; fan pushes dirt into bag. Good side edge cleaner. Tools on board are covered. Easy-to-maneuver hose ready for use with tools. Manual carpet-height adjustment. Low emissions. **Recommendation:** Good performance and convenient design at a moderate price. Models in this line offer good value.

Eureka Bravo! SureValu 9205DT ⅅ $80

Very similar to Eureka Bravo! The Boss, except for hose length and minor features. Low emissions. **Recommendation:** Low price and fine performance, but noisy and inconvenient. Durability is a worry.

Hoover Encore Supreme U4261-930 ⅅ $90

Soft-body upright; fan pushes dirt into bag. Good side edge cleaner. Tools on board. Manual carpet-height adjustment. Low emissions. **Recommendation:** Low price and fine performance, but inconvenient.

Royal Dirt Devil MVP 088305 ⅅ $135

Hard-body upright with stair handle; fan pulls dirt into bag. Hose ready for use with on-board tools. Manual carpet-height adjustment. **Recommendation:** Good performer but not very convenient.

Hoover Dimension U5209-930 $180

Very similar to Hoover Dimension Supreme, except for minor features. **Recommendation:** Good performance and convenient design at a moderate price. Models in this line offer good value.

Fantom F11051 $300

Hard-body upright; fan pulls dirt into plastic dirt container. Good side edge cleaner. Suction control. Easy-to-maneuver hose ready for use with on-board tools. Manual carpet-height adjustment. Low emissions. **Recommendation:** A good choice.

Sanyo Performax SC-U11MA ⅅ $400

Hard-body upright with stair handle; fan pulls dirt into bag. Hose ready for use with tools. Suction control. **Recommendation:** A good, if expensive, choice if you don't have deep carpets.

Royal Dirt Devil Classic 086600 ⅅ $100

Hard-body upright with stair handle; fan pushes dirt into bag. Hose ready for use with tools. Manual carpet-height adjustment. Low emissions. **Recommendation:** Good performer but not very convenient.

Panasonic Quickdraw MC-V5315 ⅅ $120

Hard-body upright; fan pulls dirt into bag. Good side edge cleaner. Easy-to-maneuver hose ready for use with tools. **Recommendation:** A good choice if you don't have deep carpets.

Bissell Plus 3550A $260

Hard-body upright with detachable hand-held canister unit and stair handle; fan pulls dirt into bag. Hose ready for use with on-board tools. On/off switch for beater brush. **Recommendation:** A good choice if you have stairs or low-pile or flat-weave rugs.

Kenmore (Sears) Power Path 3581090 ⅅ $100

Similar to Panasonic Quickdraw, above, but easier to service. **Recommendation:** A good, inexpensive choice if you don't have deep carpets.

Ratings continued ≫

Model details *Continued*

Electrolux Epic Series 3500 SR $650

Hard-body upright with stair handle; fan pulls dirt into bag. Easy-to-maneuver hose, but hose and tools are not on board; hard to convert for use with tools. Suction control. Special power nozzle for stairs. On/off switch for beater brush. **Recommendation:** Expensive for what you get.

Panasonic Quickdraw MC-5190-1 Ⓓ $100

Hard-body upright; fan pulls dirt into bag. Hose ready for use with on-board tools. **Recommendation:** Relatively quiet, convenient; a good choice if you don't have deep carpets.

Panasonic Dirt Sensor Quickdraw MC-V5375 Ⓓ $200

Similar to Panasonic above. Has additional features, including Dirt Sensor. **Recommendation:** A good choice if you don't have deep carpets.

Hoover Preferred U4655-930 $150

Soft-body upright with stair handle; fan pushes dirt into bag. Good side edge cleaner. Tools on board. Manual carpet-height adjustment. **Recommendation:** Good performer but noisy.

Hoover Encore Supreme Soft & Light U4293-930 $100

Soft-body upright with stair handle; fan pushes dirt into bag. Good side edge cleaner. Manual carpet-height adjustment. **Recommendation:** Good performer but not very convenient.

Miele Powerhouse Plus S174i $320

Hard-body upright with stair handle; fan pulls dirt into bag. Tools on board are covered; hose ready for use with tools. Suction control. On/off switch for beater brush. Retractable cord. **Recommendation:** A good, if expensive, choice if you don't have deep carpets.

Eureka Powerline Plus Victory 4441AT $150

Hard-body upright with comfortable, contoured handle and stair handle; fan pulls dirt into bag. Hose ready for use with tools. Manual carpet-height adjustment. Easy to service. **Recommendation:** A good choice if you don't have deep carpets.

Royal Dirt Devil Impulse 085400 $90

Hard-body upright; fan pushes dirt into bag. **Recommendation:** Good, inexpensive performer but noisy and not very convenient.

Eureka The Boss Victory 4335BT $100

Hard-body upright with comfortable, contoured handle and stair handle; fan pulls dirt into bag. Good side edge cleaner. Hose ready for tools. Awkward cord handling. Manual carpet-height adjustment. Easy to service. But: high emissions. **Recommendation:** Good, inexpensive performer but not very convenient.

Singer SB12720 $80

Soft-body upright with stair handle; fan pushes dirt into bag. Good side edge cleaner. Hose ready for use with tools. Awkward cord handling. Manual carpet-height adjustment. **Recommendation:** There are better choices.

White-Westinghouse Millenium WWU2020 $100

Soft-body upright with stair handle; fan pushes dirt into bag. Hose ready for use with tools. Awkward cord handling. Manual carpet-height adjustment. **Recommendation:** There are better choices.

Regina Plus HO6505 Ⓓ $110

Hard-body upright with stair handle; fan pulls dirt into bag. Hose ready for use with on-board tools. Awkward cord handling. Manual carpet-height adjustment. **Recommendation:** There are better choices.

Eureka Excalibur 6425AT Ⓓ $200

Hard-body upright with stair handle; fan pulls dirt into bag. Hose ready for use with on-board tools. Easy-to-maneuver hose. Suction control. On/off switch for beater brush. Manual carpet-height adjustment. Easy to service. But: bulky and heavy. **Recommendation:** There are better choices, especially at this price.

Regina Ultra HO6508 Ⓓ $150

Hard-body upright with stair handle; fan pulls dirt into bag. Hose ready for use with on-board tools. Awkward cord handling. Manual carpet-height adjustment. But: high emissions. **Recommendation:** There are better choices, especially at this price.

Singer Poweramp HB1412 $180

Hard-body upright with stair handle; fan pushes dirt into bag. Good side edge cleaner. Hose ready for use with on-board tools. Manual carpet-height adjustment. But: bulky, heavy, and high emissions. **Recommendation:** There are better choices.

Canisters

Nilfisk GS90 $800

Good side edge cleaner. No tools on board or provision for cord storage. Suction control. On/off switch for beater brush. High-efficiency filter. Price includes optional power nozzle and special filter. **Recommendation:** Superior cleaner with low emissions but inconvenient and extremely expensive.

Miele White Pearl S433i $850

Good side edge cleaner. Tools on board are covered. Easy-to-maneuver hose and retractable cord. Suction control. On/off switch for beater brush. Manual carpet-height adjustment. High-efficiency filter. Price includes optional power nozzle and special filter. **Recommendation:** Superior cleaner with low emissions but extremely expensive.

Eureka Excalibur 6975A $300

Good side edge cleaner. Tools on board are covered. Retractable cord. Suction control. On/off switch for beater brush. **Recommendation:** More features than the Eureka World Vac, but motor and wiring may not be as sturdy.

Eureka World Vac 6865B $210

Good side edge cleaner. Tools on board. Easy-to-maneuver hose and retractable cord. Suction control. But: high emissions. **Recommendation:** Low price and very good performance make this a good value if emissions are not a problem.

Hoover PowerMax Supreme S3611 $300

Tools on board are covered. Easy-to-maneuver hose and retractable cord. Suction control. On/off switch for beater brush. But: high emissions. **Recommendation:** Good performer if emissions are not a problem.

Oreck Super Celoc XL1500 Ⓓ $500

Tools on board. Retractable cord. Suction control. On/off switch for beater brush. But: heavy and bulky. **Recommendation:** Good performer but expensive and not very convenient.

Panasonic Eagle Eye Dirt Senor MC-V9635 $320

Dirt Sensor. Tools on board are covered. Easy-to-maneuver hose and retractable cord. Suction control. On/off switch for beater brush. Manual carpet-height adjustment. **Recommendation:** A good choice if you don't have deep carpets.

Kenmore (Sears) Power-Mate 2521190 Ⓓ $200

Tools on board. Easy-to-maneuver hose and retractable cord. Suction control. Special power nozzle for stairs. Manual carpet-height adjustment. But: high emissions. **Recommendation:** Good, inexpensive performer but not very convenient.

Hoover Futura S3567 $200

Tools on board. Easy-to-maneuver hose and retractable cord. Suction control. But: high emissions. **Recommendation:** Good value if emissions are not a problem.

Kenmore (Sears) Whispertone 25212 Ⓓ $300

Tools on board are covered. Easy-to-maneuver hose and retractable cord. Suction control. On/off switch for beater brush. Manual carpet-height adjustment. **Recommendation:** A good choice if you don't have deep carpets.

Electrolux Epic Series 6500 SR $700

Tools on board. Retractable cord. Suction control. On/off switch for brush. Special power nozzle for stairs. **Recommendation:** Expensive for what you get.

Rainbow Performance Edition SE $1400

Dirt collected in water instead of disposable bag. Suction control. On/off switch for beater brush. Manual carpet-height adjustment. Easy to service. But: high emissions and heavy, water-filled tank to lug around. **Recommendation:** Emissions, inconvenience, and astronomical expense outweigh its cleaning ability.

Ratings continued ▶

White-Westinghouse V.I.P. WWP9500 $200

Tools on board. Awkward cord handling. Suction control. **Recommendation:** Good, inexpensive performer but not very convenient.

Royal M4600 Ⓓ $550

Tools on board. Awkward cord handling. Suction control. On/off switch for beater brush. Manual carpet-height adjustment. **Recommendation:** Expensive for what you get.

Electrolux Renaissance C104A $900

Good side edge cleaner. Tools on board are covered. Retractable cord. Suction control. On/off switch for beater brush. Special power nozzle for stairs. **Recommendation:** Very expensive for what you get.

Hoover Encore Supreme S3395-040 $150

Tools on board. No cord storage provision. Suction control. But: High emissions. **Recommendation:** A good, inexpensive choice if you don't have deep carpets and emissions are not a problem.

Compact canisters

Sharp EC-7311 $135

Tools on board. No power nozzle. Retractable cord. **Recommendation:** Quietness and good surface cleaning make this compact model top-rated.

Sanyo SC-585 $80

Tools on board, but they fall off easily. No power nozzle. Dirt collected in plastic compartment, very messy to dump out. Retractable cord. **Recommendation:** Inconvenient and messy.

Royal Dirt Devil Can Vac 082023 Ⓓ $160

Tools on board. Carrying strap. Awkward cord handling. Power nozzle with on/off switch. Suction control. But: High emissions. Price includes optional power nozzle, available directly from manufacturer only. **Recommendation:** Fair performer.

Hoover Portapower II Supreme S1353 $150

Awkward cord handling. Power nozzle. Suction control. **Recommendation:** Fair performer.

Eureka Worldvac Mighty Mite II 3651A $120

Good side edge cleaner. No power nozzle. Awkward cord handling. Suction control. But: High emissions. **Recommendation:** There are better choices.

Eureka The Boss Mighty Mite II 3621A $75

Very similar to Eureka 3651A, above, but with less powerful motor. **Recommendation:** There are better choices.

Hoover Portapower II S1337 $190

Similar to Hoover Portapower, above, but with less powerful motor, no power nozzle, and no suction control. **Recommendation:** There are better choices.

Ratings & Recommendations *Wet/dry vacuums*

The tests behind the Ratings

Overall score is based mostly on performance, stability, and convenience. **Dry performance** was tested using dense items—nails, bolts, and the like. **Wet performance** is how quickly and thoroughly each model could pick up measured amounts of water. **Stability** is based mainly on results from tests in which the vacs were pulled across an uneven floor and a carpet, and placed on a board that was progressively inclined until the machine tipped over. **Ease of use** is based mostly on maintenance (including cleaning the filter and emptying the tank), maneuverability, and ease of storage. **Price** is a national average, based on price surveys. Models similar to those we tested are noted in Details; features may vary. **Model availability:** Ⓢ means model is replaced, according to the manufacturer; successor model is noted in Details. New model was not tested; it may or may not perform similarly. Features may vary.

Recommendations

The highest-rated vacs in both size groups are very good machines, but they're pricey. A step down from the top are less-expensive models that perform nearly as well: the small Craftsman (Sears) 17744, $40; and the large Shop Vac QSP QM30A/925-59, $80, and Hoover S6631, $90—both relatively quiet machines with a capacity of about 12 gallons.

See report, page 117. Last time rated in Consumer Reports: July 1996.

Overall Ratings

Rating key: E ⊖ VG ⊖ G ○ F ◐ P ●

Listed by group; within groups, listed in order of overall score

Brand and model	Price	Overall score 0 (P F G VG E) 100	Performance DRY	Performance WET	Noise	Stability	Ease of use
LARGE MODELS							
Craftsman (Sears) 17706	$140	▇▇▇▇▇	⊖	⊖	◐	⊖	⊖
Royal Dirt Devil 081600	150	▇▇▇▇	⊖	○	●	⊖	⊖
Shop Vac QSP QM30A/ 925-59, **A CR BEST BUY**	80	▇▇▇	⊖	⊖	○	○	○
Hoover S6631	90	▇▇▇	○	⊖	○	○	○
Hoover S6755	130	▇▇▇	⊖	⊖	◐	◐	○
Genie PRO20-4031	95	▇▇▇	⊖	⊖	●	◐	○

Ratings continued ≫

Overall Ratings Continued

	E	VG	G	F	P
	⊖	⊖	○	⊖	●

Brand and model	Price	Overall score (0–100)	Performance DRY	WET	Noise	Stability	Ease of use
LARGE MODELS							
Shop Vac 8040/870-64-2	$130		⊖	○	⊖	⊖	○
Eureka Shop Boss Quiet Kleen 2832A	110		⊖	⊖	○	⊖	○
Eureka Corvette Convertible 2829A [S]	150		⊖	⊖	●	⊖	○
Genie SV12-200-20	75		○	⊖	●	●	⊖
Shop Vac 800M/808-32-9	100		⊖	○	●	●	⊖
SMALL MODELS							
Craftsman (Sears) 17701	70		⊖	⊖	●	⊖	⊖
Royal Dirt Devil 08900	85		⊖	○	●	⊖	○
Craftsman (Sears) 17744	40		⊖	⊖	⊖	●	⊖
Eureka Shop Boss 2812A	75		⊖	⊖	⊖	⊖	⊖
Shop Vac 3332.0E/333-32-8	65		○	○	○	⊖	⊖
Genie RV6-150-22	50		○	⊖	⊖	⊖	⊖
Shop Vac 700M/707-02-6	40		○	○	○	●	⊖
Shop Vac 700E/707-21-6	50		⊖	○	⊖	●	⊖
Hoover S6529	55		⊖	⊖	○	●	⊖

Model details *Within size groups, listed in order of overall score*

Large models

Craftsman (Sears) 17706 $140

• 16 gal. • Detachable blower. • Cartridge filter. • Wide hose. • On-board tools. • 20-ft. cord. • 26 lb. • 6 hp.

This vac can pick up just about anything; the best model for fine dust and among the best for water. Very stable. Tank drain. Easy-on, easy-off lid. Utility and squeegee nozzles. But: Fairly noisy. High in dust emissions. **Recommendation:** An excellent performer.

Royal Dirt Devil 081600 $150

• 16 gal. • Detachable blower. • Cartridge filter. • Wide hose. • On-board tools. • 20-ft. cord • 23 lb. • 5 hp.

Picks up just about anything well—except fine debris. Among the most stable machines. Tank drain. Floor, utility, and squeegee nozzles. But: Very noisy. **Recommendation:** An excellent performer.

Shop Vac QSP QM30A/925-59 $80

• 12 gal. • Bag filter. • Wide hose. • On-board tools. • 18-ft. cord. • 18 lb. • 3 hp.

No other model better combines solid performance with respectable scores for noise, stability, and convenience. Tank drain. Floor, utility, and squeegee nozzles. Crevice tool. But: Only fair for fine dust. Can't be used as a blower. **Similar:** 925-60, $90, 16 gal.; 925-58, $70, 10 gal., no tank drain; 925-57, $60, 8 gal., no tank drain. **Recommendation:** A very good performer; excellent value. **A CR BEST BUY.**

Hoover S6631 $90

• 12.5 gal. • Cartridge filter. • On-board tools
• 6-ft. cord. • 20 lb. • 27,500 rpm.
Though a little less adept at dry debris than the
Shop Vac, above, this Hoover similarly combines
solid performance with respectable scores for
noise, stability, and convenience. Tank drain.
Unique dual-tank system. Floor, utility, and
squeegee nozzles. Crevice tool. But: Only fair for
fine dust. **Recommendation**: A good performer;
very good value.

Hoover S6755 $130

• 16 gal. • Detachable blower. • Cartridge filter. • Wide and narrow hoses. • 12-ft. cord.
• On-board tools. • 26 lb. • 28,000 rpm.
Larger in capacity than its brandmate, above, a little better for dry pickup, and (as you'd expect at
this price) with additional accessories. Floor, utility, and squeegee nozzles. Crevice tool. But: Also
a bit noisier and a bit less stable than its mate.
Recommendation: A good performer.

Genie PRO20-4031 $95

• 20 gal. • Wide and narrow hoses. • Cartridge
filter. • 10-ft. cord. • 21 lb. • 4 hp.
An outstanding performer, especially on dry debris. Easy-on, easy-off lid. Floor, utility, and
squeegee nozzles. Crevice tool. But: Emits a noisy
screech. Quite unstable. High in dust emissions.
Recommendation: A good performer.

Shop Vac 8040/870-64-2 $130

• 20 gal. • Wide hose. • Bag filter. • 12-ft.
cord. • 19 lb. • 4 hp.
A solid performer. Utility nozzle. But: Fairly noisy.
Quite unstable. **Recommendation**: There are better choices.

Eureka Shop Boss Quiet Kleen 2832A $110

• 13 gal. • Wide and narrow hoses. • Bag filter.
• On-board tools. • 6-ft. cord. • 17 lb. • 5 hp.
True to its name, one of the quietest machines.
Easy-on, easy-off lid. Floor, utility, and squeegee
nozzles. But: Otherwise undistinguished, at best.
Recommendation: There are better choices.

Eureka Corvette Convertible 2829A Ⓢ $150

• 13 gal. • Detachable blower. • Bag filter
• On-board tools. • 6-ft. cord. • 18 lb. • 5 hp.
A solid performer on water. Easy-on, easy-off
lid. Floor and squeegee nozzles. But: Otherwise
undistinguished, at best. **Successor**: Convert-a-
Vac 2829A, $150. **Recommendation**: There are
better choices.

Genie SV12-200-20 $75

• 12 gal. • Bag filter. • 6-ft. cord. • 15 lb. • 2 hp.
Picked up debris competently. Easy-on, easy-off
lid. Floor and squeegee nozzles. But: Among the
noisiest and most unstable models. **Similar**:
SV10-200-20R, $50, 10 gal. **Recommendation**:
There are better choices.

Shop Vac 800M/808-32-9 $100

• 12 gal. • Bag filter. • 6-ft.cord. • 13 lb. • 3 hp.
Picked up competently. Floor and squeegee nozzles. But: Among the noisiest and most unstable
models. High in dust emissions. **Recommendation**: There are better choices.

Small models

Craftsman (Sears) 17701 $70

• 8 gal. • Wide hose. • Cartridge filter. • On-
board tools. • 6-ft. cord. • 13 lb. • 3 hp.
This vac can pick up just about anything—among
the best models for water, and better than most at
fine dust pickup. Utility and squeegee nozzles.
Crevice tool. But: Fairly noisy and fairly unstable.
Can't be used as a blower. **Recommendation**:
Very good in performance and value.

Royal Dirt Devil 08900 $85

• 8 gal. • Detachable blower. • Wide hose.
• Cartridge filter. • 14-ft. cord. • On-board
tools. • 22 lb. • 3.5 hp.
Among the best for dry, large debris, and among
the most stable. Floor, utility, and squeegee nozzles. But: Very noisy. Heavy for its size. **Recommendation**: A very good performer.

Craftsman (Sears) 17744 $40

• 6 gal. • Wide hose. • Cartridge filter. • On-
board tools. • 6-ft. cord. • 12 lb. • 2 hp.
Though competent and inexpensive, this Sears
can't match the overall performance of its larger
brandmates. Better than most for fine dust. Utility
nozzle. But: Very unstable. Fairly noisy. Among the
worst for water. Can't be used as a blower.
Recommendation: A good—if limited—
performer.

Ratings continued ▶

Model details *Continued*
••••••••••••••••••••••

Eureka Shop Boss 2812A $75

• 9 gal. • Bag filter. • On-board tools. • 6-in. cord. • 14 lb. • 1.5 hp.
A solid performer on water, and among the most stable. Easy-on, easy-off lid. Floor and squeegee nozzles. But: Among the worst for dry debris. Very noisy. **Recommendation**: A good—if limited —performer.

Shop Vac 3332.0E/333-32-8 $65

• 6 gal. • Detachable blower. • Bag filter. • 6-ft. cord. • 10 lb. • 2 hp.
Among the quietest machines. Floor and squeegee nozzles. But: Very unstable and quite inconvenient. **Similar**: 333-33-6, $75, 10 gal.; 333-34-4, $85, 12 gal. **Recommendation**: There are better choices.

Genie BV6-150-22 $50

• 6 gal. • Detachable blower. • Bag filter. • 6-ft. cord. • 13 lb. • 1.5 hp.
A solid performer. Easy-on, easy-off lid. Floor and squeegee nozzles. But: Very unstable, fairly noisy, and inconvenient. **Similar**: BV8-150-22, $60, 8 gal. **Recommendation**: There are better choices.

Shop Vac 700M/707-02-6 $40

• 6 gal. • Bag filter. • 6-ft. cord. • 9 lb. • 1.5 hp.
Much like the Shop Vac, above, but with a smaller motor, no blower, fewer tools—and a much lower price. **Similar**: 707-03-4, $45, 8 gal.; 707-01-8, $35, 5 gal. **Recommendation**: There are better choices.

Shop Vac 700E/707-21-6 $50

• 8 gal. • Bag filter. • 6-ft. cord. • 10 lb. • 2 hp.
Much like its brandmate above, but with a larger capacity, no blower, and fewer tools. **Similar**: 707-22-4, $60,10 gal. **Recommendation**: There are better choices.

Hoover S6529 $55

• 6 gal. • Bag filter. • On-board tools. • 6-ft. cord. • 10 lb. • 23,500 rpm.
The quietest vac tested, and very good for water. Floor nozzle. But: The worst for picking up dry debris and for dust emissions. **Recommendation**: There are better choices.

How to use the Ratings in the Buying Guide

▨ Read the Recommendations for information on specific models and general buying advice.

▨ Note how the rated products are listed—in order of performance and convenience, price, or alphabetically.

▨ The overall score graph gives the big picture in performance. Notes on features and performance for individual models are listed in the Comments column or "Model details."

▨ Before going to press, we verify model availability for most products with manufacturers. Some tested models listed in the Ratings may no longer be available. Models that have been discontinued are marked Ⓓ; some may actually still be available in some stores for part of 1997. A model marked Ⓢ is a successor to the tested model, according to the manufacturer, and is noted in Comments or Model details. Features may vary.

▨ Models similar to the tested models, when they exist, are indicated in Comments or Model details.

▨ To find our last full report on a subject, check the reference above the Ratings chart or the eight-year index, page 342.

Ratings *Large air-conditioners*
& Recommendations

The tests behind the Ratings

Comfort is how well unit kept room to desired temperature and humidity. Some directed **airflow** well only in one direction. Some did poorly in a **brownout**. **Indoor noise** on low is important for sleeping. **Price** is approximate retail. If you live in a humid area, look in Details for a unit with high moisture removal and/or an outside drain hole for condensation. Models similar to those we tested are noted in Details; features may vary.

Standard features for these models

• Were fairly easy to install. • Have adjustable louvers. • Have expandable side panels. • Have a 5-ft. cord.

Recommendations

If the size of your room and its exposure to the sun send you to the bigger models, consider the high-rated General Electrics or Sharp models. Or consider the Carrier Electronic. Among 8900-to-9200-Btu/hr. models, the inexpensive Amana Quiet Zone would be a good choice. If you want a slightly smaller model, look first to the 7800 Btu/hr. Panasonic in the chart on page 148; we top-rated it in 1995. Another choice from that chart would be the inexpensive 5450 Btu/hr. Kenmore, which is smaller and a very good, efficient performer.

See report, page 122. Last time rated in Consumer Reports: June 1996.

Overall Ratings

E ⊖ VG ⊖ G ○ F ◑ P ●

Within capacity, listed primarily in order of comfort performance

Brand and model	Price	Overall score 0 — 100	Comfort	Airflow LEFT	Airflow RIGHT	Brownout	Noise ON LOW
11,500-12,000 BTU/HR. MODELS							
Friedrich SS12J10A [1]	$770	P F G VG E	⊖	○	◑	⊖	⊖
General Electric AMH12AB	550		⊖	⊖	◑	⊖	⊖
Carrier Electronic XCB121E	520		⊖	⊖	◑	○	⊖
Sharp AF-T1206X	520		⊖	●	⊖	⊖	○
Gibson GAX128Y1A	600		⊖	◑	○	○	⊖
White-Westinghouse WAL126Y1A	480		⊖	⊖	◑	⊖	⊖
Quasar HQ2121KH	520		⊖	⊖	◑	○	⊖

Ratings continued ▷

Overall Ratings *Continued*

Legend: E ⊜ VG ⊖ G ○ F ◒ P ●

Brand and model	Price	Overall score (0–100) P F G VG E	Comfort	Airflow LEFT	Airflow RIGHT	Brownout	Noise ON LOW
11,500-12,000 BTU/HR. MODELS							
Amana 12QZ22RC	$580		⊖	○	⊖	●	⊖
Fedders A3J12E2AG	450		⊖	⊖	●	⊖	⊖
Emerson Quiet Kool 12HT13	440		⊖	⊖	●	⊖	○
Whirlpool ACQ122XD	530		⊖	⊖	⊖	○	○
Kenmore (Sears) 72129	530		○	◒	●	◒	○
Goldstar LW-L1210CL	500		◒	○	●	◒	⊖
10,000-10,500 BTU/HR. MODELS							
General Electric AMD10AB	500		⊖	⊖	○	⊖	⊖
Friedrich SS10J10A [1]	770		⊖	○	◒	⊖	⊖
Sharp AF-T1106X	520		⊖	●	⊖	⊖	○
Amana 10QZ22RC	520		⊖	⊖	⊖	○	○
Quasar HQ2101KH	470		⊜	⊖	○	⊖	○
Whirlpool ACQ102XD	480		⊖	⊖	○	○	○
Kenmore (Sears) 76109	500		⊖	○	◒	○	○
White-Westinghouse WAL103Y1A	440		⊖	⊖	○	◒	⊖
Fedders A2Q10F2BG	380		○	⊖	●	⊖	⊖
Carrier TCA101D	480		⊖	○	⊖	●	○
8900-9200 BTU/HR. MODELS							
Amana 9QZ22RC	480		⊖	⊖	⊖	◒	○
Friedrich SS09J10A [1]	700		⊖	⊖	○	●	⊖
Gibson GAX098Y1A	510		⊖	◒	○	●	⊖

[1] Friedrich models may need to have thermostat sensor repositioned, a free fix. See story, page 122.

Model details *Within capacity, listed in Ratings order*

11,500-12,000 Btu/hr.

Friedrich Quietmaster Electronic SS12J10A $770

• 12,000 Btu/hr. • 10.5 EER. • 3.5 pints/hr. moisture-removal. • 111 lb. • Fits 28-to-42-in. window.
Very efficient—but bulky and expensive. Has a slide-out chassis, exterior support bracket with leveling provision, 4 fan speeds on cool, 24-hr. timer, digital readout. But: Hard to install; no upper-sash lock; no expandable side panels, no slide-out filter. **Recommendation:** Very good, but expensive—and may need the free fix Friedrich is offering. See story, page 00.

GE Premium AMH12AB $550

• 11,500 Btu/hr. • 10.0 EER. • 3.6 pints/hr. moisture-removal. • 96 lb. • Fits 27-to-43-in. window.

A very good, efficient air-conditioner—and quieter than others. Features a slide-out chassis and such niceties as power louvers, a 12-hour timer, and an outside drain hole for condensation. But: No upper-sash lock. **Similar**: Panasonic Deluxe CW-1206FU, $600. **Recommendation**: A very good unit—quiet, too.

Carrier Electronic XCB121E $520

• 12,000 Btu/hr. • 10.0 EER. • 4.4 pints/hr. moisture-removal. • 115 lb. • Fits 31-to-47-in. window.
A very good, efficient unit—tops at removing moisture. Among its niceties: a slide-out chassis, power louvers, 24-hr. timer, digital readout, outside drain hole. But: Heavier than most; no upper-sash lock; filter pulls out from bottom and may hit sill. **Recommendation**: A very good choice, especially for a large window.

Sharp Comfort Touch AF-T1206X $520

• 12,000 Btu/hr. • 9.2 EER. • 3.6 pints/hr. moisture-removal. • 80 lb. • Fits 26-to-37-in. window.
Relatively lightweight to handle and install—but smaller and less efficient than others in this group. Niceties: slide-out chassis, 12-hr. timer, digital readout. But: No upper-sash lock; has short power cord. **Recommendation**: Very good for a small window—unless you want airflow to the left.

Gibson Air Sweep GAX128Y1A $600

• 12,000 Btu/hr. • 9.5 EER. • 3.5 pints/hr. moisture-removal. • 93 lb. • Fits 29-to-45-in. window.
A good, efficient performer, despite mediocre directional control. Quiet indoors on High. Slide-out chassis, exterior support bracket with leveling provision, power louvers, outside drain hole. But: Expensive; short cord; filter pulls out from bottom and may hit sill. **Recommendation**: A good choice, unless you will mount the unit in a corner.

White-Westinghouse Custom WAL126Y1A $480

• 12,000 Btu/hr. • 9.5 EER. • 3.4 pints/hr. moisture-removal. • 89 lb. • Fits 29-to-40-in. window.
A good, efficient performer overall—and fairly low in price. Slide-out chassis, exterior support bracket with leveling provision, outside drain hole. But: Lacks energy-saver mode; has short cord. **Similar**: White-Westinghouse Continental WAL123Y1A, $480; Frigidaire Custom FAL123Y1A, $510. **Recommendation**: A good value.

Quasar HQ2121KH $520

• 12,000 Btu/hr. • 9.1 EER. • 3.6 pints/hr. moisture-removal. • 96 lb. • Fits 27-to-44-in. window.
Good overall performance—but less efficient than others in this group. Slide-out chassis, power louvers, outside drain hole. But: No upper sash lock. **Similar**: Panasonic Standard CW-1205FU, $550. **Recommendation**: A good choice.

Amana Quiet Zone 12QZ22RC $580

• 11,800 Btu/hr. • 10.0 EER. • 3.3 pints/hr. moisture-removal. • 104 lb. • Fits 30-to-45-in. window.
A very efficient model, good for large windows. Slide-out chassis, exterior support bracket with leveling provision, outside drain hole. But: Very noisy outdoors; no slide-out filter. **Recommendation**: A good choice unless your area often has brownouts.

Fedders Regency A3J12E2AG $450

• 12,000 Btu/hr. • 9.5 EER. • 3.9 pints/hr. moisture-removal. • 102 lb. • Fits 26-to-39-in. window.
Good, efficient performance; inexpensive. Slide-out chassis, exterior support bracket with leveling provision. But: Hard to install; lacks energy-saver mode; very noisy outdoors; no upper-sash lock; no expandable side panels. **Similar**: Emerson Quiet Kool Modulaire 12GJ14, $470. **Recommendation**: A good choice unless you need to direct airflow to the right.

Emerson Quiet Kool Modulaire 12HT13 $440

• 12,000 Btu/hr. • 9.5 EER. • 3.9 pints/hr. moisture-removal. • 95 lb. • Fits 29-to-45-in. window.
Good, efficient performance; inexpensive. Slide-out chassis; exterior support bracket with leveling provision. But: Hard to install; lacks energy-saver mode; very noisy outdoors; no upper-sash lock;

Ratings continued ❯

Model details *Continued*
••••••••••••••••••••••••

no expandable side panels. **Similar**: Fedders Whisperer A3T12F2AG, $400. **Recommendation**: A good choice unless you need to direct airflow to the right.

Whirlpool DesignerStyle ACQ122XD $530

• 12,000 Btu/hr. • 9.0 EER. • 4.0 pints/hr. moisture-removal. • 99 lb. • Fits 28- to-46 in. window.
Very good at dehumidifying, though less efficient than others. Slide-out chassis; outside drain hole. But: Very noisy outdoors; short cord; thermostat settings have no numbers. **Recommendation**: A good choice, but less efficient than others—and may cost more to operate.

Kenmore (Sears) 72129 $530

• 12,000 Btu/hr. • 9.0 EER. • 3.9 pints/hr. moisture-removal. • 90 lb. • Fits 26-to-44-in. window.
A mediocre performer and less efficient than others. Didn't keep room comfortable in energy-saver mode. Hard to install; very noisy outdoors. **Recommendation**: There are better choices.

Goldstar LW-L1210CL $500

• 12,000 Btu/hr. • 9.0 EER. • 3.2 pints/hr. moisture-removal. • 92 lb. • Fits 26-to-40-in. window.
Mediocre at dehumidifying, and less efficient than others. Slide-out chassis, exterior support bracket with leveling provision, outside drain hole. But: Lacks energy-saver mode; no upper sash lock. **Recommendation**: There are better choices.

10,000-10,500 Btu/hr.

GE Premium AMD10AB $500

• 10,000 Btu/hr. • 10.0 EER. • 3.2 pints/hr. moisture-removal. • 96 lb. • Fits 27-to-43-in. window.
A very good, efficient performer—quiet indoors on High and quieter outdoors than most. Slide-out chassis, power louvers, 12-hr. timer, outside drain hole. But: No upper sash lock. **Similar**: Panasonic Deluxe CW-1006FU, $550. **Recommendation**: A very good choice, especially if you have nearby neighbors.

Friedrich Quietmaster Electronic SS10J10A $839

• 10,200 Btu/hr. • 11.7 EER. • 2.6 pints/hr. moisture-removal. • 112 lb. • Fits 28-to-42-in. window.
Very efficient—but bulky and expensive. Has a slide-out chassis, exterior support bracket with leveling provision, 4 fan speeds on cool, 24-hr. timer, digital readout. But: Hard to install; no upper-sash lock; no expandable side panels, no slide-out filter. **Recommendation**: Very good, but expensive—and may need the free fix Friedrich is offering. See story, page 122.

Sharp Comfort Touch AF-T1106X $520

• 10,500 Btu/hr. • 9.5 EER. • 3.2 pints/hr. moisture-removal. • 78 lb. • Fits 26-to-37-in. window.
A very good, efficient unit that's easy to install in a small window. Slide-out chassis, 12-hr. timer, digital readout. But: Short cord; no upper-sash lock. **Recommendation**: A very good choice unless you need to direct airflow to the left.

Amana Quiet Zone 10QZ22RC $520

• 10,200 Btu/hr. • 10.1 EER. • 3.0 pints/hr. moisture-removal. • 102 lb. • Fits 30-to-45-in. window.
A very good, highly efficient performer. Slide-out chassis; exterior support bracket with leveling provision, outside drain hole. But: No slide-out filter. **Recommendation**: A very good choice.

Quasar HQ2101KH $470

• 10,000 Btu/hr. • 9.1 EER. • 3.2 pints/hr. moisture-removal. • 94 lb. • Fits 27-to-44-in. window.
A very good performer, but not very efficient. Slide-out chassis, outside drain hole. But: No upper-sash lock. **Similar**: Panasonic Standard CW-1005FU, $530. **Recommendation**: A good performer, though not as efficient as others.

Whirlpool DesignerStyle ACQ102XD $480

• 10,000 Btu/hr. • 9.0 EER. • 2.6 pints/hr. moisture-removal. • 96 lb. • Fits 28-to-46 in. window.

A good performer, but not very efficient. Slide-out chassis and an outside drain hole. But: Thermostat settings have no numbers; short power cord. **Recommendation:** An OK—and low-priced—choice, but may cost more to operate than others.

Kenmore (Sears) 76109 $500

• 10,000 Btu/hr. • 9.0 EER. • 2.9 pints/hr. moisture-removal. • 88 lb. • Fits 26-to-44-in. window.
A good performer, but not very efficient. Hard to install; thermostat settings have no numbers. **Recommendation:** An OK choice, but less efficient—may cost more to operate than others.

White-Westinghouse Continental WAL103Y1A $440

• 10,000 Btu/hr. • 9.5 EER. • 2.5 pints/hr. moisture-removal. • 84 lb. • Fits 29-to-40-in. window.
A good, efficient unit—but it doesn't dehumidify as well as others. Slide-out chassis, exterior support bracket with leveling provision. But: Lacks energy-saver mode; very noisy outdoors; short cord. **Similar**: White-Westinghouse Custom WAL106Y1A, $460; Frigidaire Custom FAL103Y1A, $480; Frigidaire Deluxe FAL106Y1A, $490. **Recommendation:** An OK choice in an area that doesn't get too humid.

Fedders Portable A2Q10F2BG $380

• 10,000 Btu/hr. • 9.2 EER. • 3.3 pints/hr. moisture-removal. • 74 lb. • Fits 25-to-39-in. window.
Low-priced, relatively lightweight, suited for small windows. Exterior support bracket with leveling provision. But: Hard to install; lacks energy-saver mode; very noisy outdoors; no upper-sash lock; no slide-out filter. **Similar**: Emerson Quiet Kool Compact Q 10GC13, $410. **Recommendation:** OK unless you need to direct airflow to the right.

Carrier Siesta TCA101D $480

• 10,000 Btu/hr. • 9.0 EER. • 3.2 pints/hr. moisture removal. • 67 lb. • Fits 27-to-36-in. window.

Lightweight, ideal for small windows—but less efficient than others. Outside drain hole. But: Lacks energy-saver mode; very noisy outdoors. **Recommendation:** An OK choice unless your area often has brownouts.

8900-9200 Btu/hr.

Amana Quiet Zone 9QZ22RC $480

• 9100 Btu/hr. • 10.8 EER. • 2.5 pints/hr. moisture-removal. • 94 lb. • Fits 30-to-45-in. window
A very good, efficient performer. Slide-out chassis; exterior support bracket with leveling provision; outside drain hole. But: No slide-out filter. **Recommendation:** A very good choice.

Friedrich Quietmaster Electronic SS09J10A $789

• 9,200 Btu/hr. • 11.5 EER. • 1.7 pints/hr. moisture-removal. • 108 lb. • Fits 28-to-42-in. window.
Very efficient—but bulky and expensive. Has a slide-out chassis, exterior support bracket with leveling provision, 4 fan speeds on cool, 24-hr. timer, digital readout. But: Hard to install; no upper-sash lock; no expandable side panels, no slide-out filter. **Recommendation:** Very good unless your area often has brownouts, but expensive—and may need the free fix Friedrich is offering. See story, page 122.

Gibson Air Sweep GAX098Y1A $510

• 8900 Btu/hr. • 9.5 EER. • 2.3 pints/hr. moisture-removal. • 88 lb. • Fits 29-to-45-in. window.
A good, quiet unit—but mediocre directional control. Fairly quiet outdoors and at High indoors. Slide-out chassis, exterior support bracket with leveling provision, power louvers, outside drain hole. But: Short cord; filter pulls out from bottom and may hit sill. **Recommendation:** A good choice unless your area often has brownouts.

If you need a smaller air-conditioner . . .

These models, high-rated in 1995, are still on the market. Price is approximate retail.

Overall Ratings

Listed in order of performance of small and medium sizes

Brand and model	Size	Price	Overall score 0 — 100
			P F G VG E
5100-5800 BTU/HR. MODELS			
Panasonic CW-606TU	5800 Btu/hr.	$400	
Sharp AF-505M6B	5100	290	
Kenmore (Sears) 75055	5450	300	
Carrier UCA051B	5200	340	
7800-8300 BTU/HR. MODELS			
Panasonic CW-806TU	7800	490	
Sharp AF-802M6	8300	450	
Kenmore (Sears) 75089	8000	450	

How to use the Ratings in the Buying Guide

■ Read the Recommendations for information on specific models and general buying advice.

■ Note how the rated products are listed—in order of performance and convenience, price, or alphabetically.

■ The overall score graph gives the big picture in performance. Notes on features and performance for individual models are listed in the Comments column or "Model details."

■ Before going to press, we verify model availability for most products with manufacturers. Some tested models listed in the Ratings may no longer be available. Models that have been discontinued are marked Ⓓ; some may actually still be available in some stores for part of 1997. A model marked Ⓢ is a successor to the tested model, according to the manufacturer, and is noted in Comments or Model details. Features may vary.

■ Models similar to the tested models, when they exist, are indicated in Comments or Model details.

■ To find our last full report on a subject, check the reference above the Ratings chart or the eight-year index, page 342.

Ratings
& Recommendations

Self-propelled lawn mowers

The tests behind the Ratings

For most tests, we cut grass that was about 4 inches high, with the mower set as close as possible to a cutting height of 2½ inches and driven at about 2½ mph. For mulching tests, we set the cutting height at about three inches. For **tall-grass** tests, grass was 8 to 12 inches high, and we ran mowers at their lowest speed and highest cutting height. **Bagging, discharging, mulching** scores show how mowers did in those modes. Under each heading, cutting shows how evenly mowers cut. Under bagging, the vacuuming score represents how completely a mower sucks up clippings. Mowers that mulch cut and recut clippings into small bits that fall back into the grass, eventually to decompose. All models have a provision for mulching, either supplied with the mower or, in a few cases, as an extra-cost kit; with most, you needn't change the blade. **Price** is approximate retail, including catcher, mulching kit, and discharge chute. Usually those are sold separately; you may be able to save about $20 to $80 by eliminating one or more of those options. An * indicates that the mower comes loaded with all three accessories. **Model availability:** Ⓓ means model is discontinued. Ⓢ means model is replaced, according to the manufacturer; successor model is noted in Details. New model was not tested; it may or may not perform similarly. Features may vary.

Standard features for these models

• Four-stroke, side-valve engine. • Primer bulb instead of a choke. • Throttle on the handle. • Rear-wheel drive. • Swath of 21 or 22 inches. • Deck of stamped steel. • Handle that can be adjusted for height (although that may require tools or disassembly) and folded for storage.

Recommendations

If you're on a limited budget and usually bag clippings, consider the Murray Ultra 3nOne 21865x8, $350, or the White LC-899, $420. If you want to mulch, many mid-priced mowers will fill the bill—look for those with high scores in mulching. If you want to discharge clippings, any of the top four side-baggers might do. All cost less than $450. If you demand the very best, consider the top three in the rear-bagging groups.

See report, page 128. Last time rated in Consumer Reports: June 1996.

Ratings continued ≫

Overall Ratings

Legend: E ⊖ VG ⊖ G ○ F ◒ P ●

Within types, listed in order of cutting, handling, and convenience

Brand and model	Price	Overall score (P F G VG E)	Bagging CUT	Bagging VACUUM	Mulching CUT	Mulching DISPERSAL	Discharging CUT	Discharging DISPERSAL	Discharging TALL GRASS
REAR-BAGGERS WITH BLADE-BRAKE/CLUTCH SAFETY SYSTEM									
John Deere Silver Series 14SB	$757		⊖	⊖	⊖	⊖	⊖	⊖	⊖
Honda Harmony HRM215KHXA	793		⊖	⊖	⊖	⊖	○	○	○
Honda Masters HR215K1SXA	838		⊖	⊖	⊖	○	○	○	⊖
Kubota W5021SC Ⓓ	845		⊖	⊖	○	⊖	⊖	⊖	⊖
Toro Super Recycler 20475	800		⊖	⊖	⊖	⊖	○	◒	●
Lawn-Boy Medallion 10533	500		⊖	⊖	⊖	○	○	◒	⊖
REAR-BAGGERS WITH ENGINE-KILL SAFETY SYSTEM									
Husqvarna Royal 53S Ⓓ	665		⊖	⊖	⊖	⊖	⊖	◒	⊖
Ariens Swivel System LM226SP	710		○	⊖	⊖	⊖	⊖	⊖	⊖
Ariens Mowing System LM225SP	*690		○	⊖	⊖	⊖	⊖	⊖	⊖
Toro Super Recycler 20472	630		⊖	⊖	⊖	⊖	○	◒	◒
Lawn-Boy Gold Series 10522 Ⓓ	530		⊖	⊖	⊖	⊖	○	⊖	◒
Yard-Man 126-E849E-401 Ⓓ	550		⊖	⊖	⊖	⊖	○	○	⊖
Murray Ultra 3nONE 21865x8	350		⊖	○	⊖	◒	⊖	○	◒
Lawn-Boy Gold Series 10518	540		⊖	⊖	○	⊖	○	⊖	●
Cub Cadet 899R Ⓓ	510		⊖	○	⊖	⊖	○	○	⊖
White LC-899	420		⊖	○	⊖	⊖	○	○	⊖
Yard-Man 126-849C-401 Ⓓ	400		⊖	○	⊖	⊖	○	○	○
Murray 2nONE 21785x7	300		⊖	◒	⊖	◒	○	○	⊖
Snapper RP21600	610		○	⊖	⊖	○	○	○	⊖
Lawn-Boy Silver Series 10305 Ⓓ	410		⊖	○	⊖	⊖	○	○	●
Lawn Chief 126-478L-022	360		⊖	○	⊖	⊖	○	○	⊖
MTD 126-478N-000 Ⓓ	330		⊖	○	⊖	⊖	○	○	⊖
Snapper FRP21600TV	680		○	◒	⊖	⊖	○	○	⊖
Toro Recycler 20454	500		○	○	⊖	○	⊖	○	●
Husqvarna 56SF	*370		○	○	○	⊖	○	⊖	⊖
Sears Craftsman 37628 Ⓓ	330		○	⊖	○	⊖	○	○	⊖
Sears Craftsman 37634 Ⓓ	*400		○	⊖	○	⊖	○	○	⊖
Husqvarna 56HS	*400		○	○	○	⊖	○	○	⊖
MTD 126-458B-000	330		○	○	⊖	○	○	⊖	○
Murray Ultra 3nONE 22859X8	420		⊖	○	●	●	⊖	○	⊖

Brand and model	Price	Overall score	Bagging		Mulching		Discharging		
		P F G VG E	CUT	VACUUM	CUT	DISPERSAL	CUT	DISPERSAL	TALL GRASS
SIDE-BAGGERS WITH ENGINE-KILL SAFETY SYSTEM									
Yard-Man 126-149C-401 [D]	$400		⊖	⊖	○	⊖	○	⊖	⊜
White LC-149	439		○	⊖	○	⊖	○	⊖	⊜
Lawn Chief 126-138L-022	360		⊖	⊖	○	⊖	○	⊖	⊜
MTD 126-138C-000	350		⊖	⊖	○	⊖	○	⊖	⊜
Troy-Bilt 34021 [S]	541		○	○	○	⊖	[1]	[1]	○
MTD 126-528N-000	440		⊖	○	[2]	[2]	○	○	○
Lawn Chief 126-262C-022	260		○	○	[2]	[2]	○	○	●

[1] Model has no discharge mode.   [2] Mulching not tested; samples looked at or bought lacked necessary part.

Model details *Within types, listed in order of overall score*

NOTES ON THE DETAILS Weight includes grass catcher. **Horsepower** is as rated by the manufacturer.

Rear-baggers, blade-brake/clutch

John Deere Silver Series 14SB $757

• 5.5-hp Kawasaki overhead-valve engine.
• 5 speeds, from 1.2 to 3.8 mph. • 99 lb.
It's slightly less noisy than others and has an easy-to-use pull starter, a convenient choke, and a cast-aluminum deck. The bag is very easy to remove, empty, and reinstall. But: Drive engages abruptly; the gear lever has vague stops; and to mulch, you must change the blade. **Similar:** 14SE, $877, electric start. **Recommendation:** Excellent in all cutting modes. The pick of the lot.

Honda Harmony HRM215KHXA $793

• 5-hp Honda overhead-valve engine.
• Hydrostatic drive gives nearly continuous speed adjustment from 0.7 to 3.2 mph.
• 93 lb.
A nice-handling machine sold as a mulcher but no slouch as a bagger. It's slightly less noisy than others. It has an easy-to-use pull starter and a convenient choke. Drive engages smoothly; the gear shift and throttle control are easy to use. It has a molded-plastic deck. The bag is very easy to remove, empty, and reinstall. But: The mower cut well in tall grass only at a very slow speed. When used without a bag, in four-inch grass, the discharge chute tended to clog. The deadman control is hard to engage and hold down. And to mulch, you must change the blade. **Recommendation:** Excellent bagger, very good mulcher.

Honda Masters HR215K1SXA $838

• 5-hp Honda overhead-valve engine. • 3 speeds, from 1.9 to 3.3 mph. • 105 lb.
It has an easy-to-use pull starter and a convenient choke. Its deadman control is convenient; its gear shift and throttle control are easy to use. It has a cast-aluminum deck. The bag is very easy to remove, empty, and reinstall. The handle vibrates slightly less than most. But: Drive engages abruptly. When used without a bag, in four-inch grass, the discharge chute tended to clog. And to mulch, you must change the blade. **Recommendation:** Very good but pricey.

Kubota W5021SC [D] $845

5-hp Kubota overhead-valve engine.
• 2 speeds, 1.8 and 2.6 mph. • 102 lb.
It's slightly less noisy than others. It has an easy-to-use pull starter and a convenient choke. It has a comfortable handle and a convenient deadman control, and the throttle control is easy to use. It has a cast-aluminum deck. The bag is very easy to remove and reinstall. But: It's hard to maneuver. Drive engages abruptly, and the gear lever is awkwardly placed on the deck. To mulch, you

Ratings continued ❯

Model details *Continued*
••••••••••••••••••••••••

must change the blade and install a special deck shield. **Recommendation:** Very good but pricey.

Toro Super Recycler 20475 $800

• 6-hp Briggs & Stratton overhead-valve engine. • 3 speeds, from 1.7 to 3.3 mph. • 99 lb.

It's slightly less noisy than others and has an easy-to-use pull starter and throttle control, a convenient choke, and a cast-aluminum deck. But: Don't put off mowing for too long; it was poor in tall grass. Drive/deadman and shift controls are inconvenient to operate, and the handle vibrates slightly more than most. **Similar:** 20465, $760 without optional bag; 20476, $870 with electric start. **Recommendation:** Very good, especially for bagging and mulching, but it has some annoying faults.

Lawn-Boy Medallion 10533 $500

• 6-hp Briggs & Stratton overhead-valve engine. • 3 speeds, from 1.8 to 2.7 mph. • 100 lb.

Mower has convenient choke and a cast-aluminum deck. The bag is easy to empty, remove, and install. Throttle control is easy-to-use. Easy to adjust cutting height. But: Drive/deadman and shift controls are inconvenient to operate. It's hard to change cutting height. **Recommendation:** Very good. It doesn't approach the performance of the better blade-brake clutch models—but it costs a lot less.

Rear-baggers, engine kill

Husqvarna Royal 53S Ⓓ $665

• 4.5-hp overhead-valve Kawasaki engine. • Continuous speed adjustment from 1.5 to 2.7 mph. • 113 lb.

It's slightly less noisy than others. It has a convenient choke. It has a comfortable handle that vibrates less than most. It has a molded-plastic deck. A single lever adjusts cutting height on all four wheels. But: When the bag is full, the front wheels may lift off the ground when you put it in Drive. The bag is hard to empty and lacks a rear handle. **Recommendation:** Very good. It handles nicely, is convenient to operate, and excels at bagging.

Ariens Swivel System LM226SP $710*

• 5.5-hp Briggs & Stratton engine. • Continuous speed adjustment from 1.1 to 3.6 mph. • 104 lb.

Front swivel wheels make it more maneuverable. It has a large, easy-to-grab starter handle. The bag is very easy to remove and reinstall. But: There's no throttle control. The handle vibrates slightly more than most. It's hard to change cutting height, and you'll need tools to put on the discharge chute or mulching cover. **Recommendation:** Very good, especially in discharge mode.

Ariens Mowing System LM225SP $690*

• 5.5-hp Briggs & Stratton engine. • Continuous speed adjustment from 1 to 3.9 mph. • 100 lb.

Much like the Ariens Swivel, above, except that its front wheels don't swivel, so it's less maneuverable. **Recommendation:** See Ariens Swivel.

Toro Super Recycler 20472 $630

• 5.5-hp Briggs & Stratton engine. • 3 speeds, 1.8 to 3.6 mph. • 87 lb.

It has a cast-aluminum deck. It's slightly less noisy than others. The throttle control is easy to use. But: Drive/deadman and shift controls are inconvenient to operate. **Similar:** 20473, $740, with electric start; 20462, $620 without optional bag; 20463, $700, with electric start, without optional bag. **Recommendation:** A very good performer in most areas, and priced favorably, though you'll put up with some annoyances.

Lawn-Boy Gold Series 10522 Ⓓ $530*

• 5.5-hp Briggs & Stratton engine. • 3 speeds, from 1.8 to 3.7 mph. • 87 lb.

It's easy to push and maneuver. Drive engages smoothly, and the throttle control is easy to use. It has a cast-aluminum deck. The bag is very easy to empty. But: Shifting control is inconvenient to operate. The bag chute has no cover and points at the operator. Start the mower with the bag off by mistake, and the chute can spit clippings in your face. **Recommendation:** Very good except in tall grass, and priced favorably.

Yard-Man 126-E849E-401 Ⓓ $550*

• 6-hp Briggs & Stratton engine. • 6 speeds from 2.1 to 3.4 mph (2 lowest speeds are about the same). • 95 lb.
An easy-to-use electric starter helps compensate for the inherent disadvantage of an engine-kill safety system. A single lever adjusts cutting height on all four wheels. But: It's slightly noisier than others, the bag lacks a rear handle, and the mower handle can't be fully folded for storage. **Recommendation**: Very good, and an all-around good value, with a few foibles.

Murray Ultra 3nONE 21865x8 $350*

• 6-hp Briggs & Stratton engine. • 1 speed, 2.6 mph. • 91 lb.
The grass bag is very easy to remove, empty, and reinstall. A single lever adjusts cutting height on all four wheels. But: It struggled in tall grass and didn't disperse clippings well when mulching. You can't adjust its handle height. **Recommendation**: Very good. It cut evenly and bagged clippings well.

Lawn-Boy Gold Series 10518 $540

• 5-hp Lawn-Boy engine. • 3 speeds, from 1.7 to 3.5 mph. • 82 lb.
Similar to the Lawn-Boy Gold Series 10522, above, but it has a two-stroke engine, which pollutes more. It also cut less evenly when mulching and was weaker in tall grass. **Similar**: 10523, $520. **Recommendation**: The other, four-stroke, Gold Series is a better choice.

Cub Cadet 899R Ⓓ $510*

• 6-hp Briggs & Stratton engine. • 6 speeds, from 2.1 to 3.3 mph (2 lowest speeds are about the same). • 86 lb.
A single lever adjusts the cutting height on all four wheels. But: It's slightly noisier than most; the bag lacks a rear handle; and the mower handle can't be fully folded for storage. **Recommendation**: Very good, and an all-around good value, with a few foibles.

White LC-899 $420*

• 6-hp Briggs & Stratton engine. • 6 speeds, from 2.2 to 2.9 mph (3 lowest speeds are about the same). • 86 lb.

Much like the Cub Cadet 899R, above. **Similar**: 899E, electric start, $570. **Recommendation**: Very good. Similar to the Cub Cadet, but cheaper.

Yard-Man 126-849C-401 Ⓓ $400*

• 6-hp Briggs & Stratton engine. • 6 speeds, from 2.1 to 3.2 mph (2 lowest speeds are about the same). • 88 lb.
Much like the Yard-Man 126-E849E-401, above, except that it lacks an electric starter and was less effective in tall grass. **Recommendation**: Very good. Like its electric-start brandmate, a good buy with a few foibles.

Murray 2nONE 21785x7 $300

• 4.5-hp Briggs & Stratton engine. • 1 speed, 2.5 mph. • 87 lb.
Its bag is very easy to remove, empty, and reinstall. But: The mower didn't disperse clippings well when mulching, and the handle height can't be adjusted. **Similar**: 21785x8, $300. **Recommendation**: Very good, though it leaves some clippings behind.

Snapper RP21600 $610

• 6-hp Briggs & Stratton engine. • 6 speeds, from 1.3 mph to 3.5 mph. • 90 lb.
It has an easy-to-use shifter and is easy to maneuver. The bag is easy to empty. But: The bag chute has no cover and points at the operator. Start the mower with the bag off by mistake, and the chute can spit clippings in your face. Hard to adjust cutting height. Starting position less secure than most. **Recommendation**: Very good, but you can buy equal performance for much less money.

Lawn-Boy Silver Series 10305 Ⓓ $410

• 5.5-hp Tecumseh engine. • 1 speed, 2.6 mph. • 75 lb.
It's easy to push and maneuver, and it's slightly less noisy than others. Drive engages smoothly, and the bag is very easy to empty. But: It was poor in tall grass. The bag chute has no cover and points at the operator. Start the mower with the bag off by mistake, and the chute can spit clippings in your face. **Recommendation**: A very good buy for mulching and bagging.

Ratings continued ⟩⟩

Model details *Continued*
••••••••••••••••••••••••

Lawn Chief 126-478L-022 $360

• 5.5-hp Briggs & Stratton engine. • 1 speed, 2 mph. • 88 lb.

The bag is very easy to empty. But: The rear flap's plastic hinge broke on the mower we tested. **Similar**: Tradesman (Sam's Club) 126-478L-118, $300. **Recommendation**: A good performer for the money, but that hinge shouldn't break.

MTD 126-478N-000 Ⓓ $330

• 5.5-hp Briggs & Stratton engine. • 1 speed, 2.7 mph. • 87 lb.

Much like the Lawn Chief 126-478L-022, above. **Recommendation**: See the Lawn Chief above.

Snapper FRP21600TV $680

• 6-hp Tecumseh overhead-valve engine.
• 6 speeds, from 1.8 to 4.3 mph. • 89 lb.

It has an easy-to-use shifter and is easy to maneuver. The bag is easy to empty. But: The handle vibrates slightly more than most and the mower is slightly noisier than others. The bag chute has no cover and points at the operator. Start the mower with the bag off by mistake, and the chute can spit clippings in your face. Hard to adjust cutting height. **Recommendation**: Good, but vastly overpriced.

Toro Recycler 20454 $500

• 4.5-hp Briggs and Stratton engine.
• 1 speed, 2.6 mph. • 79 lb.

Easy to maneuver and push and slightly less noisy than others. But: The bag chute clogs easily, and the bag holds little grass. The drive/deadman control is inconvenient to operate. **Similar**: 20444, $450 without optional bag. **Recommendation**: A good cutter, but try another.

Husqvarna 56SF $370*

• 5.5-hp Briggs & Stratton engine. • 1 speed, 2.5 mph. • 86 lb.

It has a comfortable handle. But: Its front-wheel drive makes for weak traction and poor handling. The drive control is inconvenient. The bag lacks a rear handle and is hard to empty. **Similar**: 56SFE, electric start, $500. **Recommendation**: A good cutter, but try another.

Sears Craftsman 37628 Ⓓ $330

• 6-hp Tecumseh engine. • 1 speed, 2.6 mph. • 81 lb.

A front-wheel-drive mower that has weak traction and handles poorly. The drive control is inconvenient, and the throttle control is awkwardly placed on the engine. The bag lacks a rear handle. **Recommendation**: A good cutter, and excellent in tall grass, but there are better choices.

Sears Craftsman 37634 Ⓓ $400*

• 6.5-hp Tecumseh engine. • 3 speeds from 1.9 to 3 mph. • 93 lb.

It's hard to maneuver, the throttle control is awkwardly placed on the engine, and the bag lacks a rear handle. When used without a bag, in four-inch grass, the discharge chute tended to clog. **Recommendation**: A good cutter, but try another.

Husqvarna 56HS $400*

• 5.5-hp Briggs & Stratton engine. • 1 speed, 2.6 mph. • 93 lb.

Much like Husqvarna 56SF, above, except for rear "high wheels"; sharp turns are difficult. **Recommendation**: A good cutter, but try another.

MTD 126-458B-000 $330

• 5-hp Briggs & Stratton engine. • 1 speed, 2.8 mph. • 78 lb.

A poor-handling front-wheel-drive mower whose greatest grace is that it's slightly less noisy than most. The bag is hard to remove and reinstall, and lacks a rear handle. To mulch, you must change the blade and add a baffle. **Recommendation**: A good cutter, but try another.

Murray Ultra 3nOne 22859X7 $429

• 5.5-hp Kawasaki overhead-valve engine.
• 3 speeds, from 1.8 to 2.9 mph. • 108 lb.

It has a convenient choke. A single lever adjusts cutting height on all four wheels. The bag is easy to empty, remove, and install. But: The mower labored and stalled during our mulching tests. It's hard to maneuver. The gear lever and throttle lever have vague stops. The starter cord blocks the gas cap. **Recommendation**: If you mulch at all, don't buy this mower.

Side-baggers, engine kill

Yard-Man 126-149C-401 Ⓓ $400

• 6-hp Briggs & Stratton engine. • 6 speeds, from 1.9 to 2.5 mph (3 lowest speeds are about the same). • 84 lb.
The bag is conveniently close to the mower but holds little grass. **Recommendation:** Very good for discharge and mulching.

White LC-149 $439

• 6-hp Briggs & Stratton engine. • 6 speeds, from 1.9 to 2.7 mph (2 lowest speeds are about the same). • 84 lb.
The bag is conveniently close to the mower but holds little grass. **Recommendation:** Very good for discharge and mulching.

Lawn Chief 126-138L-022 $360

• 5.5-hp Briggs & Stratton engine. • 1 speed, 2.5 mph. • 79 lb.
The bag holds little grass. **Recommendation:** Very good for discharge and mulching.

MTD 126-138C-000 $350

• 5-hp Briggs & Stratton engine. • 1 speed, 2.6 mph. • 79 lb.
Much like the Lawn Chief, above. **Recommendation:** Very good for discharge and mulching.

Troy-Bilt 34021 Ⓢ $541

• 4-hp Briggs & Stratton engine. • 1 speed, 3.1 mph. • 82 lb.

It has a cast-aluminum deck, a convenient choke, an easy-to-use throttle control, a comfortable handle, and a single crank to adjust cutting height on all four wheels. It won't start without the bag or mulching cover in place. But: Its front-wheel drive makes for weak traction and poor handling. The bag holds little grass, and there is no discharge mode. The drive control is inconvenient to operate. **Successor:** 34321. **Recommendation:** An interesting specimen, particularly for mulching, but with too many drawbacks.

MTD 126-528N-000 $440

• 5.5-hp Briggs & Stratton engine. • 1 speed, 2.5 mph. • 91 lb.
Rear "high wheels"; sharp turns are difficult. **Recommendation:** A good cutter, but try another.

Lawn Chief 126-262C-022 $260

• 3.75-hp Briggs & Stratton engine. • 1 speed, 2.3 mph. • 73 lb.
Its front-wheel drive makes for weak traction. The bag holds little grass. Its discharge chute tended to clog in tall grass and when the bag was attached. Fueling and adding oil are inconvenient, and the spark plug is hard to get at. **Similar:** MTD 126-262C-054 (Coast to Coast Hardware, ServiStar), $260. **Recommendation:** A good cutter, but try another.

How to use the Buying Guide

▓ Read the article for general guidance about types, features, and how to buy. There you'll find a discussion of the choices you'll face in the marketplace, what's new, and key buying advice.

▓ The Ratings graph the overall score so you can quickly understand the big picture in performance. Details on features or performance are also noted. For many products, we also have information on how reliable a brand is likely to be. See page 11.

▓ To find our last full report on a subject, refer to the article or the Ratings for the listing, or check the eight-year index, page 342.

HOME OFFICE

Computers

Buy with an eye to the future, so you can easily upgrade the computer with a faster processor, more memory, and the like.

Last CR report: *September 1996*
Price range: *$1000 to $4000*

The choices

Family PC or office PC? Family computers come with educational, financial, and entertainment software, a sound system, and a modem. Many manufacturers also offer computers for the home office virtually identical to family machines but with business software and a more modest sound system. If you intend to use the computer primarily for work, a package like this is the better choice.

Macintosh or Windows? Objectively, Windows and Mac OS machines are comparable. It's OK to make a choice based on your experiences or your preferences. And you need not worry if you use Windows at the office and a Mac at home; most files and documents can be translated from one system to the other.

Desktop or notebook? A desktop computer gives you the most capability for the money. But it takes up precious space and is hard to move from place to place. If space or portability is important to you, a notebook computer may be your best choice. If you do consider a notebook, you'll need to either spend $2500 to $4000 to get the speed and memory that a $2000 desktop model offers, or settle for less power and storage capacity—and less upgradability.

Big name or custom clone? A number of lesser-known manufacturers sell computers through mail-order ads in computer magazines. But unless you know that the company offers good service, the few dollars you'll save won't be worth the trouble you may face if the computer breaks down.

Some computer stores and repair shops assemble customized computers. Such clones may cost more than a major brand and probably won't include much software besides Windows 95, but they can give you a broad choice of components.

Wherever you buy, use a credit card; that gives you some protection.

What's new

All Windows machines (those also known as IBM-compatibles) come with Windows 95, the operating platform that Microsoft introduced in August 1995.

Apple has rechristened the Macintosh operating system Mac OS and licensed it to manufacturers who produce Macintosh clones. The Mac OS machines we tested use a 100- or 120-MHz PowerPC processor; much faster Macs for the consumer market have been introduced since. Otherwise, Mac OS machines are configured very much like Windows-based ones: at least 16MB of RAM, a 1- or 2-gigabyte (GB) hard drive, a 8X CD-ROM drive, and an 28.8 kbps fax-modem.

Shopping strategy

Know the choices. Notebook computers let you work on the go (or work at home if space is very limited), but they may not have the combination of speed, memory, and hard-drive capacity of comparably priced desktop units. Desktop computers usually come with lots of software pre-installed and detailed set-up instructions. See "The choices," above.

Decide what to spend. A well-equipped desktop computer—one with at least a 100-MHz processor, 16 MB of RAM, and a 1-GB hard drive—starts at around $1500, but prices are constantly falling. Increased speed, memory, and hard-drive capacity add to the price. Costly extras include a 17-inch monitor (about $400 more than a 15-inch) or enhanced video and sound hardware. Lesser desktop units can cost $1000 or less; laptops, $1400 to $5000. Some retailers may sell the keyboard or other necessities separately, or include a cheap monitor in an attractively priced package.

Know where to shop. Many brands are sold through mail-order catalogs; brands like Dell and Gateway 2000 are sold only by mail. A local computer store has knowledgeable staff and specializes in personal service. Superstores like CompUSA or Computer City carry a wide range of computers and will upgrade components. Consumer electronics stores carry a somewhat narrower selection and may not handle repairs or upgrades on site. Office-supply and department stores offer few brands, and those only in standard configurations. Warehouse clubs offer low prices, period. There's no best time to buy; prices fall throughout the year.

Key features

Processor. The standard processor for Windows machines now is the Pentium, for Mac, it's the Power PC. Both chips are designed to handle multiple software applications simultaneously or to process full-screen, full-motion video. Last year, the typical computer's processor ran at a speed of 75 to 100 megahertz (MHz). This year, the typical processor runs at 133 to 200 MHz for Windows, 120 to 225 for Mac.

Memory. To meet the increased demands of software running under Windows 95, PCs now provide at least 16 megabytes of memory (or, in the lingo, 16 MB of RAM). To run Windows applications at their best, a PC needs at least 8 MB of RAM. Macs come standard with 8 MB of RAM, but 12 or more MB RAM is recommended.

Hard drive. The typical storage capacity now exceeds one gigabyte (GB), or about 1000 megabytes. Many models offer a 2-GB or even a 3-GB hard drive.

Multimedia. Once an amenity but now a necessity to run all manner of software, the majority of machines include an 8x CD-ROM drive, the ability to play sound, speakers, and a microphone. Those components let machines play multimedia software, and record sound from a microphone or audio component. Sound quality is restricted by the small size of the speakers, but speakers built into the monitor are generally worse.

Most Windows-based systems include software to play full-screen, full-motion video CDs encoded in a format called MPEG-1. Mac OS machines have their own video playback system called Quicktime. Neither system can match the picture quality you'd get on a TV set playing a videotape or a cable-TV signal. Images had obvious blotches or telltale jerkiness. Still, the ability to play back video discs will become more important over the next year or two, as high-capacity digital versatile disc drives, or DVD-ROMs, begin to appear on computers. These discs can hold a full-

length feature film or many hours of lower-quality video, plus CD-quality soundtracks. See the report on CD-ROM drives, page 167.

Fax-modem. Most new computers have a built-in fax-modem that sends and receives data at a rate of 28.8 or 33.6 kilobits per second (kbps), significantly faster than older 14.4 kbps modems. See the report on modems, page 164.

Monitors. These are usually optional, not sold as part of the computer bundle. Expect to pay about $400 for a 15-inch monitor—the minimum recommended size for a new computer—or around $800 for a 17-inch version. See the report on monitors, opposite.

Features for upgradability

Expansion bays. The APC case should have at least two empty spaces for hard drives and the like, so you can add more drives or newer ones. At least one empty bay should be accessible from the outside and designed for a standard drive. External hard drives can easily be added to a Mac.

Processor As a rule, the faster the better. If the fastest processors available exceed your budget, drop down a notch or two in speed, but make sure the computer can take a faster processor.

Expansion slots. These are space for plug-in cards and most other add-ons. The more empty slots, the more expandable the computer, although some crowded motherboards make it impossible to use all the slots. On PCs, look for a combination of PCI and ISA slots, so you can use current and future plug-in cards.

Graphics adapter. This determines the resolution, color range, and speed with which images display on the monitor. It typically includes at least 1 MB of its own memory (DRAM or the faster and costlier VRAM), which will display 65,000 colors at a resolution of 800 by 600 pixels. To allow for higher resolution in the future, look for a board that accepts at least 2 MB of video memory. A plug-in graphics card is better than one built into the motherboard, because you can eventually replace it with a better one.

Parallel and serial ports. These are sockets for connecting an external device such as a printer or modem. An enhanced parallel port will communicate with external devices at higher speeds than a conventional parallel port on a Windows machine. Serial ports now include a communication chip called a 16550 UART, which provides the maximum communication speed for an external modem.

Cache memory. A type of memory that can speed up the computer. If the computer can accept external cache memory, be sure it has at least 256K installed.

Motherboard. The design of this main circuit board largely determines how fast your computer can run and what types of components you can plug in. All the computers we tested are designed around the manufacturer's own motherboard, limiting how much they can be upgraded. Clone machines can use any universal motherboard.

Mac buyers need not fret about this component. On PCs, the motherboard should have a zero insertion force (ZIF) processor socket to easily change processors. It should also have a flash BIOS that supports such industry standards as Plug and Play and power management. A motherboard that has two IDE (integrated drive electronics) sockets lets you plug in an additional hard drive, CD-ROM drive, and the like.

Memory sockets. Part of the motherboard, these determine how much memory (RAM) you can add to speed up your computer and enhance its performance. Machines have memory chips mounted on small plug-in boards called SIMMs, usually in denominations of 8 or 16 MB. The motherboard should have enough empty memory sockets to let you add 16 or 32 MB without removing existing memory.

Computer monitors

Fifteen-inch models are a lot cheaper than 17-inch models, and their basic performance is the same.

Last CR report: *July 1996*
Ratings: *page 181*
Price range: *$250 to $2000*

Screen sizes

Desktop monitors, like TV sets, come in sizes based on the diagonal measurement of the tube; 14, 15, and 17 inches are the most common. The nominal size may be substantially larger than the actual size of the image, depending on how much tube the housing reveals and how the electronics "size" the image. There is no Federal rule governing monitor screen size, as there is for TV screen size. The only sure way you'll know the active screen size is to measure it in the store.

A 14-inch model is large enough for common needs. A 15-inch monitor offers a 15 percent larger image, making higher resolution text easier to read. A 17-inch model offers about 30 percent more area than a 15-inch monitor. Fifteen and 17-inch monitors can typically handle multiple resolutions—that is, they can display different numbers of the small square boxes (or elements) that make up the images, vertically and horizontally. Depending on the resolution mode you select, such monitors can display larger images or more information on the screen.

* You can pay less than $300 for a 14-inch monitor, or more than $2000 for a 21-inch model. Fifteen-inch models typically sell for $300 to $500; 17-inch models, for $650 to $1000.

What's new

Color monitors and big screens were once the exclusive domain of the professional. While they're still not cheap, prices have dropped somewhat and should continue to drop.

Shopping strategy

Decide on the size. Try improving your existing display by using the monitor's controls to increase the image size. Or try software that lets you magnify text or zoom in on images. But if your 14-inch monitor is on the blink or seems too small to display the software you use, it's worth upgrading to a 15-inch monitor. Bigger monitors—17 inches or larger—don't give as much bang for the buck, but they do present larger images or can show more of the image you're working with. When shopping, don't go by the manufacturer's claimed screen size; measure the largest usable screen size yourself.

Decide on key features. Spending more gets you a bigger picture, higher resolution modes, and advanced display features useful to high-end and professionals users.

Don't overbuy. Don't pay extra for features that aren't supported by the video card or monitor driver in your computer. A card more than two years old may not support high-resolution modes or some combinations of plug and play and power management. (See "Key features," below.) Check with the monitor manufacturer to be sure you have the latest version of its software specific to your monitor.

To render color images accurately, a computer running a 17-inch monitor at a resolution of 1024 by 768 pixels needs at least 2 megabytes of memory on the video card to get 65,536 colors. A computer running a 15-inch monitor at 800 by 600 pixels needs 1 megabyte for that many colors. If you want more colors (useful if you work with photos), you'll need more video memory or, for $100 to $250, a new video card.

Some discounters and mail-order dealers keep prices down by bundling computers with inferior monitors. Don't buy if the dealer won't let you compare monitors in the store, won't allow a reasonable time to try the monitor at home, or won't provide dot pitch, resolution, or refresh rate. See "Key features," below.

The easiest brands to find. Major computer makers—Apple, Compaq, IBM, Packard Bell—all market their own brand of monitors. Other leading brands include NEC, Samsung, Sony, and ViewSonic. Superstores like CompUSA offer a wide selection and return privileges.

Key features

Standard features on monitors include vertical and horizontal control and adjustments for screen height and width, brightness, and contrast.

Dot pitch. This describes the spacing between the color phosphor patches on the inside of the tube, which should be .28 mm or smaller.

Color temperature control. This

allows users to adjust how white is rendered. It affects how photo and video images will be rendered, on the basis of the lighting that was used when the image was captured.

On-screen menu. Seventeen-inch screens typically allow you to use on-screen menus or some sort of on-screen display to execute controls that are accessed via the control panel.

Plug and play. A feature intended to make it easier to connect the parts of a computer system.

Power management. A feature that allows the computer to reduce the power the monitor and other components use.

Refresh rate. Tells you how many times the full image is redrawn on the screen in one second. Look for a vertical refresh rate of no less than 72 hertz in 15- and 17-inch models.

Resolution rate. The number of rows and columns of pixels on the screen. To display more information on the screen, you need to switch to a higher resolution. A monitor running at a resolution of 1024 by 768 pixels displays 64 percent more information on the screen than one running at 800 by 600 pixels. The size of the type or pictures may be smaller, however, depending on the monitor size.

Speakers. Built-in speakers are convenient and space-saving, but they're not worth paying extra for. In monitors we've tested, built-in speakers offered sound no better than that of a small clock radio.

Computer printers

Consider a laser printer only if speed of printing is very important to you. A color ink-jet costs as little as $200, but color-printing costs can be high.

Last CR report: *October 1996*
Ratings: *page 188*
Price range: *$200 to $1000*

The types

Ink-jet printers. Two of every three computer printers sold in 1995 were ink-jet machines, which print by firing ink from tiny nozzles into a moving printhead. Sales of ink-jets are expected to go still higher in 1997, since prices have dropped and print quality at reproducing both color graphics and black-and-white text is high.

The best ink-jets now print black-and-white text nearly as well as a laser printer and are much more adept than a laser (or the laser's close relative, the LED printer) at graphics. Overall, our tests show that print quality varies anywhere from good to excellent for both text and graphics.

You can expect two to three pages of text per minute from the typical ink-jet model, and more at the low-resolution setting. Printing graphics can take much longer, up to several minutes per page. Color photos are typically the slowest.

Trueness of the colors is usually better from "CMYK" models (whose color cartridge includes black), than from CMY models, which blend cyan (C), magenta (M), and yellow (Y) inks to make black. CMY models also require you to change the cartridge when switching from plain text to color printing and back.

Paper and ink costs, while low for printing plain text, can be quite high if you print a lot of densely colored pages.

Ink-jet printers range in price from $200 to $500.

Ink for text typically costs two to seven cents per page; ink for graphics, five cents to several dollars. Paper costs can range from a penny or so per page for copier paper—which is usually fine for text—to a dime or even a dollar for a page of premium stock, which is best for graphics.

Ink-jet printers have the advantage of being virtually maintenance-free.

Laser and LED printers. These printers produce images with a scanning laser or an array of LEDs (light-emitting diodes). Using technology like that in photocopiers, they create images using toner, quickly reproducing an almost limitless variety of type forms and sizes. Laser printers for home use print just in black; color capability is still available only on high-priced professional machines

Text pages printed by home laser printers are consistently excellent in quality. They're not so good at grays, so graphics and photos are rendered less well. Print quality for graphics in our tests ranged from fair to good. Text pages typically print at a rate of four to five pages per minute; graphics about three to five pages per minute.

Laser and LED printers are priced from $350 to $500. Color lasers prices are still high; they start at $3000.

Toner and paper costs are less than they are for ink-jet models. Toner costs range from two to four cents per page. Paper costs about a penny or so a page for copier stock, which should be fine for printing all but the fanciest documents.

Unlike ink-jets, laser printers require periodic attention, such as cleaning the paper rollers, shaking the toner cartridge, and cleaning the print mechanism occasionally. Laser and LED models typically require less space than ink-jet models and older laser printers.

What's new

Color is more affordable. Until a year or so ago, if you were shopping for an inexpensive computer printer, you had to choose between machines that offered letter-quality printing and those that could print in color. No low-priced machine could do both unless it used special, expensive paper. But text pages printed on plain copier paper by the best new color ink-jet printers are as crisp as those from black-and-white laser printers.

Prices for ink-jet models have plummeted. Our recent tests of printers turned up some very good ink-jets priced as low as $230, at least $100 less than low-end ink-jets from a year ago. Lasers are dropping in price, too.

Shopping strategy

Decide on the type. Unless you need blazing speed, give first consideration to an ink-jet model. They're versatile and inexpensive, but slow. You'll have to spend $300 or so to get a CMYK model, with its better color quality.

If text is all you print, you might want to consider a laser printer, typically twice as fast as the ink-jet models. Entry-level lasers are now less than $400.

If work space is at a premium, and you're also shopping for a fax machine, you might consider buying a fax-combo —a fax machine and a printer in one (see fax machines, page 165).

Decide on the features. Printers aren't feature-laden. Spending more for a laser or LED printer usually brings a bit of extra speed and better graphics performance; higher-priced ink-jets sometimes offer better color quality. See "Key considerations," below.

The easiest brands to find. Hewlett-Packard leads the market, followed by Canon, Epson, and Apple (whose models are for Macintosh computers only). Printers are most often bought at electronics and computer stores, office supply chains like Staples, or discount outlets like Wal-Mart. Printers are discounted heavily, especially when new models are about to be introduced. Also, manufacturers' rebates are sometimes offered.

Key considerations

Compatibility with your computer operating system. Only a few models work with both a PC and a Mac computer. Some machines—such as Texas Instruments and Canon lasers—can be used only with a PC that operates in Windows. Most PC-compatible printers will run in both Windows and DOS, though you lose some features in DOS, including two-way communication with the printer via on-screen menus to alert you to such problems as a paper jam or low toner level. DOS users should pay attention to the number of fonts that reside in the printer, since you may be limited to using only those. Windows and Macintosh models let you use any fonts stored on the hard drive.

Memory. It's less important that a printer have the memory to download an entire print order, now that many PCs run in Windows, which allows users to regain control of their computer soon

after sending a document to print. The Macintosh operating system has long had such a "background" arrangement. A large memory can allow a printer to handle a very large file (a complex graphic, say) in fewer "bites," which serves to speed up printing.

Speed of printing. When printing text, speed varied by more than two pages a minute among the ink-jets (graphics are generally slower to print). No ink-jet achieved laser-printer pace—though the speediest ink-jets were nearly as fast (three pages a minute) as the slowest lasers.

Two-sided printing. Most printers can't print satisfactorily on both sides of the paper; either ink shows through the page (ink-jets) or toner from the page dirties the paper rollers, causing streaking (lasers). However, most computer software lets you do two-sided printing by printing the odd-numbered pages of a document, after which you retrieve the printed sheets, turn them over, and print the even-numbered ones on the other side, on a second pass through the printer.

Label printing. All lasers can do this. Some ink-jet printers cannot.

Printer languages. If you're buying a printer for desktop publishing and expect to work with another printer at a service bureau, you'll want a more sophisticated model than any we tested, one that "talks" in a printer language known as PostScript. A number of printers (including all the Hewlett-Packard models) speak a less complex lingo, Hewlett-Packard's Printer Control Language. PCL helps assure a document printed on one PCL-compatible printer will look very similar when printed on any machine that also converses in PCL.

Computer modems

The fastest ones cost more, but it's money well spent.

Last CR report: *May 1996*
Ratings: *page 184*
Price range: *$100 to $250*

The types

Transmission speeds. To enter cyberspace, you need a modem to translate digital data from the computer into an analog signal for the phone line, and vice versa. Modems can do that at various speeds: 14.4, 28.8, and 33.6. The fastest modems on the market operate at 28.8 or 33.6 and cost $120 to $400. Slower ones (known as V.32bis) operate at speeds up to 14.4 kbps and cost about $50 to $100. Modems any slower than that may be unsatisfactory for surfing the net. Even 14.4 kbps modems may be too slow except for sending or receiving e-mail messages or signing onto computer bulletin boards—less graphical than the World Wide Web and thus less demanding.

Under ideal conditions, a 28.8 modem communicates twice as fast as a 14.4. But ideal conditions rarely happen over real telephone lines. The best-performing modems we've tested had to lower their receiving speed a little to overcome line interference.

Internal/external. Add-on modems can be bought as a separate box or can be added to the inside of the computer. Modems for notebook computers are in the form of a PC-card, which is often easy to install. An internal modem usually costs less than a comparable external one, but internal modems can be difficult to install. Instructions are often poor.

Plug and play is supposed to make it easier to install an internal modem in an IBM-compatible. But the system doesn't always work well, particularly in computers not running Windows 95.

What's new

New computers now typically come with a 28.8-kbps modem built in. Prices for 28.8 modems are still about twice those of 14.4 models. Prices of both are likely to decline.

Shopping strategy

Decide on the type. If you have no modem, it's worth the extra money to start with a 28.8 model. On the basis of our experience in recent tests, we think you should consider buying an internal modem for an IBM-compatible PC only if your computer has no spare high-speed serial port or you're willing to pay extra for installation.

Decide on key features. A legible display, the presence of a power switch, and software that supports the functions you need can make a modem easier to live with. See "Key features," below.

The easiest brands to find. Robotics is the biggest-selling brand. Zoom Telephonics and Motorola are major manufacturers.

Modems are sold mostly by computer stores, but mail-order sources and electronics stores are also places to look.

Key features

Card length. Internal modems come in the form of "cards." Half-length cards take up less space and connections in your PC than full-length ones.

Display (external modems). Look for LEDs that are clear and easy to read.

Manual jumpers (internal modems). These small bars let you move from one pair of pins to another to set things like the modem's address in computers running DOS or Windows 3.1.

Power switch (external modems). Without this, you have to plug and unplug the modem to turn it on and off.

Serial-port cable (external modems). Most modems don't come with their own.

For an IBM-compatible, make sure you buy a cable that fits your machine's particular serial port. For a Macintosh, be sure to use a high-speed cable.

Software support. Terminal and fax support is basic. Some models also support voice mail, file sharing, speakerphone, and caller ID.

Voice/data communication. Modems with this feature allow voice/data exchange in addition to sending data and faxes. Such models usually include a speakerphone, voice mail, and features associated with telephone answerers.

Fax machines

There are basic fax machines, and there are machines that combine the fax function with a computer printer and a scanner.

Last CR report: *September 1996*
Ratings: *page 193*
Price range: *$200 to $500*

The types

Thermal-paper fax machines. They're the least expensive type (about $200 to $400) and the simplest: Images are seared onto special heat-sensitive paper, so there's no toner, ink, or ribbons to replace. The print from all the thermal-paper models we tested was sharp and crisp. The paper, however, is thin and shiny, and it typically feels waxy to the touch. It's also apt to curl (since it's unreeled from a roll). What's more, thermal paper may turn brown over time, making its text progressively harder to read. And thermal-paper faxes may cost a few cents more per page than do plain-paper faxes.

Certain machines address at least some

of those drawbacks. Paper curling wasn't much of a problem on about half the models we tested, since they flatten out paper after printing. Brother, Sharp, and Panasonic sell special thermal paper that looks and feels more like plain paper (it's still prone to turn brown, however, and sometimes costs a bit more than regular thermal paper).

Plain-paper fax machines. Like computer printers, these machines—which include five of the stand-alone models and all of the fax-combos we tested—use regular plain paper, eliminating the main problems of thermal-paper faxes. However, unlike the thermal models we tested, the plain-paper machines were far from uniformly good in print quality.

The best plain-paper units in our tests produced pages that looked as good as thermal-paper faxes; pages from a fax-combo even looked a little better. Those better performers use ink-jet or laser printing (see the report on printers, page 161). But plain-paper machines that employ thermal-transfer printing—a variant on the technology used in thermal-paper units—produced disappointing results. The images were sometimes marred by incomplete and broken letters. What's more, thanks to their pricey ribbons, pages printed by thermal-transfer can cost as much as 12 cents apiece. That's about twice the typical cost for thermal paper or for paper and ink (or toner) for other plain-paper fax machines. Price: $400 to $550.

What's new

Stand-alone units now compete with fax-combos, and computer accessories such as fax-modems.

A fax-combo is a very versatile and space-efficient alternative to a fax machine. It faxes, copies, prints, and scans—all for as little as $500. You'd have to spend at least $1000 to buy separate machines to do all those functions.

However, once you did, you'd own a higher-quality, more versatile home-office set-up than a fax-combo provides—you'd probably own a color printer and scanner, for example. Like the minisystems and boomboxes of the audio world, fax-combos are compact compromises that may not meet everyone's needs. They do many things, but not all of them as well as stand-alone machines.

A fax-modem, the data-handling machine that allows computers to communicate via telephone lines, might be a better choice than a stand-alone device if most of the faxes you send are generated as files in your computer. It may be ideal, too, if you'd rather accept faxes as computer files than as pages on paper.

Shopping strategy

Decide on type. For sending and receiving faxes informally, a simple thermal-paper machine suffices—and demands the least space (reserve a space 10 inches high by 14 inches wide by 20 inches deep). For business use, a good plain-paper machine may be a better choice because of its paper (though it's a bit bulkier—to be safe, reserve 14 inches by 16 inches by 20 inches).

Consider a fax-combo if you're short on space and need to integrate faxing with computer functions. (Fax-combos demand only a little more space than stand-alone plain-paper models—reserve about 16 inches by 19 inches by 24 inches.)

For a basic thermal-paper machine, plan on $200 to $400. For a plain-paper model, $500 should be close to your upper limit. You can spend $500 to $1000 for a fax-combo, but look first to see what separate machines (copier, scanner, fax-modem plus software, and printer) can do for you. If all you're after is computer compatibility, a fax-modem can supply that for around $200 and put you on the World Wide Web besides.

Decide on key features. Some features expand the capabilities of the machine, others merely make it easier to use. See "Key features," below.

Know where to shop. Office discount outlets often have broad selections at low prices. Retail office-supply dealers may provide better service. Prices at mail-order outlets can be low, but you can't look goods over before you buy.

Key features

Answering machine. An answerer built into a fax machine is usually all-digital. Typical features: automatic message count, selective erase, personal mailboxes, and remote retrieval of messages. Memory is often shared between faxes and voice calls—so if voice messages use up the machine's entire memory, none will be left to store faxes should the paper supply run out.

Shortcut calling aids. One-touch keys and speed-dial numbers allow connection to frequently called numbers with a button press or two. The more keys and numbers a fax machine has the better, if you repeatedly fax a lot of numbers.

Distinctive-ring detection. Allows the machine to take advantage of a phone-company service (called "Ring Mate," "Custom Ring," or the like) that gives you a second number for your existing phone line.

Overseas calling features. These help handle noise on the phone line during foreign calls. Most useful is Error Correction, a feature which helps the fax maintain a high transmission speed despite noise. Less useful is Overseas Mode, which automatically slows down transmission over a noisy line.

Delayed sending. Delays transmitting a document until a programmed time when phone rates are lower.

LCD display. This can show phone numbers being reached, error messages, and brief instructions. Some display only 15 or 16 characters; more useful ones show 40 or even 80 characters.

Document feeder. Holds pages for copying or feeding. Large capacity is a godsend for long documents.

Memory features. A machine with a memory can, if its paper supply runs out, store 5 to 25 pages of text until the supply is replenished.

Memory can also enable machines to:

• Broadcast, or disseminate the same fax (as long as memory permits) to many destinations without having to scan it over and over. (Sets of phone numbers you fax often—a committee, for example—can be assigned in a group to a single one-touch key.)

• Scan and send, or scan a document and let you have it back before it's sent (no need to re-scan should the phone line be busy).

• Retrieve remotely—use any fax machine to retrieve faxes received by your machine.

• Forward faxes, or automatically send transmissions from your machine to another, at a different phone number.

Pager notification. For pager users—the machine pages you when a fax arrives.

CD-ROM drives

A quad-speed (4x) CD-ROM drive is the best overall choice; you can find excellent models for as low as $130.

Last CR report: *June 1996*
Ratings: *page 186*
Price range: *$100 to $400*

The CD-ROM itself is fast supplanting the diskette for much software. That's because a single CD-ROM disc can store 650 megabytes of information—the equivalent of more than 450 diskettes.

Older computers may not have a CD-ROM drive or may have one that's too slow. It pays to upgrade an IBM-compatible computer with a CD-ROM drive only if it has at least a 66-MHz 486DX/2 processor and 8 megabytes of RAM; a Macintosh, if it has a 20-MHz 68030 processor and 8 megabytes of RAM.

Drive speed

What passed for fast a couple of years ago is now considered slow. The first

CD-ROM drives ferried data from disc to computer at 153 kilobytes per second.

That so-called transfer rating category, commonly expressed as 1x, is still the basis for measuring CD-ROM speed. Double-speed (2x) drives, which spin the disc twice as fast, were the norm for a time. They've been supplanted by 4x (quad-speed), 6x and 8x drives, which now are being challenged in turn by 10x and 12x drives.

Expect to pay from $100 for a basic 4x unit to $200 or more for a 6x or 8x drive.

Internal or external?

Internal IDE (Integrated Device Electronics). This type is generally the easiest to install in newer IBM-compatibles and costs about $100 less than an external drive. If your computer has only one hard drive, an IDE should plug directly into existing circuitry.

SCSI (Small Computer System Interface). This type covers both internal and external drives. An external SCSI drive is your only choice if the computer can't accommodate an internal drive.

Installing an SCSI drive in a Macintosh is easy. But putting a drive in an IBM-compatible may be more problematic.

For an IDE drive, you'll need an IDE-controller adapter card. For an SCSI drive, the computer needs an SCSI adapter card.

If you're reluctant to open the computer, have someone experienced handle the installation. Retailers will often do the work free if you buy the drive from them.

If you do opt to install a drive yourself, choose one designed for Plug and Play, which is supposed to simplify the installation of hardware on IBM-compatibles.

What's new

Drives that read the new Digital Versatile Disc (DVD) format should arrive early in 1997. These drives are supposed to be at least 9x speed and read both new high-density discs and conventional CD-ROMs.

Shopping strategy

Decide on the speed. Some software will perform better on a 4x drive than on a 2x. But high-speed drives like the 6x and up ones we tested may not improve software performance much—unless the CD has been specifically optimized, or organized, for rapid retrieval.

So if the 1x or 2x drive you now have seems too slow, upgrading to 4x makes the most sense. It will take some time for software publishers to issue large numbers of titles optimized for faster drives. See "Drive speed," above.

Decide on internal or external. An external drive connects to the computer with a cable. An internal drive fits into the computer case like a diskette drive. See "Internal or external," above.

The easiest brands to find. The big names in this market include Creative Labs, NEC, and Sony.

Companies selling CD-ROM drives buy their hardware from other manufacturers, sometimes intermingling parts from different suppliers. The most important part is the drive mechanism.

Computer and electronic stores account for half of the retail sales; mail-order is another source.

Key features

Disc drawer. Easy-to-use drives hold discs in a slide-out drawer, so you don't need a separate caddy or holder.

Front-panel controls. Volume, Eject, and other frequently used controls are handiest on the front of the drive rather than buried in the software.

Multidisc changer. This is useful if you expect to use a lot of discs and don't want the inconvenience of frequently swapping. Neither of the units we tested could switch most current multidisc applications without your having to intervene in some way.

Multimedia kits. For software like games, cookbooks, and encyclopedias that demand sound capability and speakers, you'll need a multimedia kit: a CD-ROM packaged with a sound card and speakers. Macintoshes come with multimedia ca-

pability, but it often has to be added to an IBM-compatible. The simplest strategy, if your computer has at least a 66-MHz 486 processor: Buy the CD-ROM drive as part of a multimedia upgrade kit, which starts at about $150. When comparing kits, look for one with a sound card that's compatible with Sound Blaster and that includes AC-powered speakers with volume and tone controls.

Plug-and-Play-compatible. Drives designed to this standard make hardware installation easier on IBM-compatibles.

Pagers

Shop first for service—that's where most key decisions lie—and then for the pager.

Last CR report: *August 1996*
Ratings: *page 197*
Price range: *$50 to $350*

Pager service

The main considerations:

Message volume. The average user gets paged seven times a day—more than 200 times a month. Some contracts offer unlimited pages; most others include only 100 to 300 calls a month, after which you're billed a dime, a quarter, or more for every additional page you receive. Alphanumeric pagers, which display text along with call-back numbers, generally come with two phone numbers assigned: one for numeric service; the other for written messages, which require callers to talk to an operator. Text messages are counted separately; there's usually a far smaller quota for them, and overages can be costly—sometimes 25 or 50 cents a piece.

Coverage area. The cheapest plans are for local-area coverage. Such coverage—which can take in a few states—is all that most consumers probably need. Comparing the local coverage maps companies provide is worthwhile, since claimed service areas do vary. Many companies also offer regional and nationwide paging—for considerably more money than local service. Nationwide numeric paging, for instance, runs about $25 or $35 a month, compared with the $6 to $12 a month typical for local coverage. (Local service is sometimes available for far less; for example, an outfit called SmartBeep advertises a $2-a-month deal in several cities, although we can't vouch for the quality of the company's service.)

Contract fine print

Activation fee. Though this is sometimes waived—included in the price of pager and service, in effect—services usually charge a $10 or $20 fee for setting up the pager. After you sign up, you call a central number. You're then paged back in an hour or so with the new phone number that's been assigned for your pager.

170 Pagers

Buying vs leasing. Leasing a pager ($3 or $4 a month for a basic model) is a little cheaper in the first year. If you plan to keep a pager longer, it probably pays to buy.

Pager number. Consider where your callers will be dialing from—you may be offered a choice of area codes. Some providers don't assign local numbers; instead, they have your callers dial a toll-free line, followed by a PIN for your pager. The call is free, but it demands that your callers key in more digits.

Insurance. For about $2 or $3 extra a month, you can buy insurance that covers about half the beeper's purchase price. It's probably not worth it for most people.

Cancellation fee. It may cost $20 or more to break a one-year contract—and you may have to give a month's notice.

Exchanges. A decent pager is sometimes bundled with poor service—the coverage area isn't what was claimed. In such a case, you can sometimes bring your pager to a new provider and exchange it for one that works on their new system.

Types of pagers

Once you've decided on the service you want, you're ready to consider which pager might be best for you.

There are two types: *Numeric* pagers alert you with your caller's phone number. *Alphanu-meric* pagers, which also display brief written messages, are more costly to buy and to use.

Either type can employ one of two technologies. *POCSAG*, known by its industry acronym, is the older transmission system and is quite adequate. The newer *Flex* system offers longer battery life but is offered by only some providers. Also, Flex technology is more versatile, so a Flex pager is more likely than a POCSAG model to be able to carry new types of paging service.

However, Flex pagers often cost a little more than POCSAG models and may be harder to find (not all providers offer Flex service yet).

What's new

From computer to pager. You can now send text messages directly to an alphanumeric pager if you have a computer and modem. Several methods involve the Internet. If you subscribe to SkyTel paging, for example, people can send messages to your pager via regular e-mail. If you're a Sprint paging customer, anyone who has your pager PIN can send messages from the company's World Wide Web site. Some paging companies offer software (free or for about $30) that allows you to receive messages via phone lines from almost any computer equipped with a modem. Callers dial directly into the paging system's computer, and the words then appear on your pager's display.

A pager that replies. SkyTel is the first service provider to let you respond to messages by pressing buttons on the pager itself—no need to find a phone to get back to the caller. Via an operator, callers can send you questions in multiple-choice format. You then push one of the labeled buttons to respond. Your choice is carried back to the paging operator, with whom the caller can later check. Such two-way paging requires an alphanumeric pager, which costs about $400.

A pager that talks. As of this writing, PageNet, the nation's largest paging provider, plans to roll out its VoiceNow service in late 1996. The system relies on a fancy pager that has a built-in speaker. When callers phone in, they can record a voice-mail message to be transmitted directly to the pager for listening.

A pager/watch. Swatch, the Swiss designer watch company, crossed a numeric pager with a wristwatch to get the Swatch The Beep, $100. This hybrid demonstrated poor reception in our tests, in part because of the unit's size, which is small for a pager but large for a watch. Also, The Beep uses the older POCSAG technology and operates on the 150-MHz band. It offers 20 message slots. Overall, the Beep is convenient to use, but short on features.

Shopping strategy

The best way to buy paging is to start locally—compare stores and providers in your area for the packages of pager and service they're offering. Among those deals, chances are good that you'll find many of the pagers we tested—although you may need to check the manual to verify the model name, since retailers often relabel pagers with their company name.

As you shop around, you'll probably find offers that combine the pager, the activation fee, and service contracts. To limit confusion, try to recalculate the price offers—or have the store do it—to yield a bottom-line annual cost that makes it easier to compare deals.

Decide on key features. Some models are more convenient than others. And some have an edge in sensitivity—making it less likely that you'll miss a message in an area where signals are weak. See "Key features," below.

Decide on the type. When choosing the type of pager, keep in mind that alphanumeric models, though more informative than numeric pagers, are more costly to buy and to operate. Compare leasing costs with buying.

Consider a pager with Flex technology, especially if you're buying; it will use fewer batteries and is unlikely to become obsolete any time soon.

Ask about trial use. Some providers let you try out a pager before signing up. That gives you the chance to dial in from the locations you're likely to be in.

The easiest brands to find. Most of the pagers you'll find in stores and display rooms are made by Motorola. When you buy or lease a pager, however, you may not know the manufacturer or model name. Paging providers generally put their own stickers and logos on the case. Check the pager's accompanying manual for the name of the manufacturer.

Pagers are available from two sources: retail stores (which are allied with service providers) and the service providers themselves. The retailers that sell pagers include electronics, department, and office-supply stores, as well as mass merchandisers and even some drugstores.

More than a thousand paging providers dot the U.S. They range from mom-and-pop operations whose antennas cover very limited areas to large companies—including PageNet, SkyTel, and Mobile-Comm—that broadcast in most states.

Key features

Auto on/off. Allows you to program the unit to power on and off at set times daily. This is a handy battery saver in case you forget to turn off your pager at night or at other times when it's not needed.

Readable display. Some LCDs show letters half the size of others and are much harder to read. Some alphanumeric models show a four-line, 80-character display, good for longer messages; others display only one 15-character line—you must scroll along the message. A lighted display is a must for dark places.

Display style. Numeric pagers usually display messages at the top, where they're easy to read even when clipped to a belt. Side-mounted pagers, which show messages on their broad side, are worn in belt holsters. They usually display more information, but you may have to take the pager out to read the message.

Out-of-range indicator. "Listens" for signals your service provider sends to other pagers on similar frequencies. If there's no activity for a while, you've probably moved beyond the company's effective paging area—and the indicator displays a symbol to warn you.

Time stamp, date stamp. Tells when a message came in. Some pagers can also serve as a watch—or as a timer to remind you about parking meters or the like.

Battery back-up. This is a very desirable feature. Retains clock settings and messages stored in memory as you insert new batteries.

Low-battery warning. A must. Without it, a pager gives no notice when batteries are about to quit.

Message storage. Current pagers can retain eight or more messages until you

erase them. A Message Lock feature prevents new messages bumping old ones out of memory. A Duplicate Message feature tells you when you've been beeped twice by the same number.

Message alert. Beyond beeping, some pagers chirp or vibrate when a message arrives. A few flash an LED message-alert light. Some chirp persistently to remind you to look at an unread message.

Easy-to-use controls. Some pagers use a single button to set all features, retrieve messages, erase them, and turn the beeper on and off. If you never mastered setting a multifunction digital watch—button presses in proper sequence and timing—look for a pager with more than one button. Too many buttons, though, can be just as intimidating, especially on a pager that's glutted with features and set-up menus that you must step through. A compromise is two big buttons and a separate On/off switch.

Telephones

Corded models offer the best sound quality and the best value.

Last CR report: *corded, November 1995; cordless, November 1996; cellular, January 1993*
Ratings: *page 199*
Price range: *$10 to $500*

Shopping strategy

Decide on the type. Corded phones still offer better sound quality than most cordless or cellular models. Although we've found variations in sound quality among the corded models we've tested, they're likely to matter only in very noisy environments. Corded phones come in a cou-

ple of designs. We still recommend that every home have at least one corded phone, which will keep working in power outages (cordless phones require household current to work). See the "Corded phone types," below.

Problems with portable phones have steadily decreased, and those phones' usefulness has made them the fastest selling. The sound quality of cordless models we've tested lately suffers from less background noise than in older models. Types and styles are changing rapidly. See "Cordless phone types" and "Cellular phone types," below.

Decide on key features. Standard phone features include memory functions and automatic redial. Features that cost extra include speakerphone, ability to handle more than one telephone line, and a built-in answering machine. In our tests, we've noted wide variation in how well such features are designed. See "Features," below.

The easiest brands to find. AT&T is still the dominant brand of corded and cordless models. Sony, General Electric, Panasonic, Bell South, and Uniden share the rest of the cordless-phone market; GE, Conair, Bell South, and Radio Shack, the corded-phone business. Motorola is the leading brand of cell phones.

What's new

Prices are dropping. As cordless and cellular models soar in popularity, prices for some corded models have taken a nose dive, with lots of bargains to be found. The basic, bottom-of-the-line cordless model has become the 10-channel phone. You'll find the most features on 25-channel models. Prices of 900-megahertz (MHz) cordless phones, with extra range, have dropped as more models have been introduced. Cell phones are sometimes even given away—the money is made on the service, not the hardware.

User-friendly designs. Manufacturers have responded to peeves with innovative solutions: LCDs to keep track of numbers in memory; easy-to-pocket cordless handsets akin to cellular phones; extra battery chargers so there's always a fresh charged spare; headphones that plug into the handset for hands-free use.

Corded phone types

Most conventional, corded phones have two components: a handset and a base that plugs into a telephone jack.

Corded phones run on low-voltage power from the telephone line.

Console models. These are updated versions of the traditional Bell desk phone. Console models range in price from $50 to more than $200.

Trim-style models. These are space-savers; the push buttons are on the handset itself, and the base is about half as wide as a console's. They range in price from about $20 to $75.

Features of corded phones

Caller ID compatibility. This can be built into a phone or bought as a stand-alone device. With it, subscribers to the phone company's service can see the phone number and, in some locations, the name of the person calling.

Easy-to-see keys. Keys that are lighted let you dial in the dark. Big keys make dialing easy for kids or for those with poor eyesight or poor coordination.

Flash. This feature makes it easier to use call-waiting. It briefly disconnects a call so you can take another call on the same line.

LCD display. This shows information such as the number dialed, time of day, and perhaps the time you've spent talking.

Memory features. Most phones with memory can store from 3 to 15 numbers of 16 digits or more, generally sufficient even for international dialing. The redial feature recalls the last number dialed. A few models can redial a busy number several times automatically. One-touch speed-dialing stores a number that you can then call by touching a single key. A Save feature lets you store a number you've just dialed.

Pulse/tone dialing. Most phones have a switch that lets you go back and forth between pulse and tone dialing. That lets you use computer or voice-mail systems even if you don't have tone service.

Ring sound. Most chirp; some warble.

Speakerphone. This feature lets you have a conversation without the handset. Sound quality usually isn't as good as with the handset.

Two-line capability. This allows you to handle a second phone line and to "conference" two callers in a three-way conversation.

Volume controls. Typically, one control raises or lowers the volume at the handset; another, the phone's ringer. Speakerphones also have a volume control for the speaker in the base. Mute disconnects the microphone so a caller can't hear sounds from your end. Hold cuts the mike and earpiece.

Cordless-phone types

Besides standard phone features, cordless phones have several features unique to cordless transmission. Cordless phones come in varying configurations: with dual keypads (which allow the base to function as speakerphone); dual handset (where a corded and a cordless handset are integrated into the base); extra charging base (for charging the handset in a second room); and multi-handset base (which supports more than one cordless handset). They come with built-in answerers and with two lines.

Cordless phones vary in how they transmit their signals:

25- and 10-channel 43/49-MHz models. Ten channels are sufficient for a neighborhood that's not densely populated. Models with 25 channels offer more protection against neighbors' phones, garage-door openers, and the like. Prices for 43/49 MHz models: $50 to $100.

Two-channel models. These basic models, are disappearing as 10-channel models are becoming bottom-of-the-line models. Two-channel phones are vulnerable to interference from nearby phones operating on the same radio channel.

900-MHz models. These have anywhere from 25 to 100 channels and a range of about 900 feet, so they're capable of letting you roam around acres. They also less vulnerable to interference and static. Digital versions cost an extra $50 or so; they're static-free and virtually impossible to eavesdrop on without exotic equipment. Basic 900 MHZ models cost $150 to $250.

Features of cordless phones

Cordless phones have many of the usual phone features—flash, speed-dialing, and such. Other features include:

Antenna. Short and flexible ones are now standard.

Autoscan. This automatically finds the clearest channel.

Batteries. All cordless handsets use replaceable batteries. A typical 43/49-MHz phone's fully charged battery will last about eight hours in continuous use, according to our tests; a 900-MHz phone's battery may not last as long.

Keypad on base. When the handset is in another room, you can use the base to answer or make calls.

LCD display. A display on the handset or the base; shows the number being dialed, the channel being used, and sometimes a low-battery condition, as well as answering machine information if there's one incorporated.

Low-battery indicator. It lets you know when to recharge the battery.

Out-of-range warning. This gives an audible alert when the handset is too far from the base.

Paging/intercom. One-way paging lets you send a signal from the base to the handset. Two-way lets you send the signal either way, which can help find a lost handset. On models with an intercom, you can talk as well.

Power-off switch. Located on the handset, it can lengthen battery time.

Ringer in base. When you're near the base, this alerts you to an incoming call, no matter where the handset may be.

Voice scrambling. This feature reduces the possibility of eavesdropping by inverting audio frequencies.

Volume control. Look for one that lets you adjust the earpiece's sound level, as well as the ringer. Mute/hold lets you talk to someone nearby without letting the person on the other end of the phone hear.

Cellular service and phones

The use of a cellular phone involves the purchase of the phone and a service contract with a company operating in your area. If you travel out of that area, you must generally pay another carrier to "roam." Most carriers offer plans tailored to common calling patterns, with a fixed fee for a monthly time allotment, something the sales brochures persist in describing as "free." If you exceed the allotment, you pay a certain amount for each extra minute used during "peak" hours (usually daytime weekdays) and a lower amount for "off peak" use.

If you're not sure which plan is best for you, or if you plan to use the phone only for emergencies, start with the plan with the lowest monthly fee. You should have no problem switching to a higher-volume plan before the contract is up. If you call mostly at night, look for the lowest "off-peak" rates. The fine print can sometimes hide major differences between carriers, such as the number of "peak" hours in a day.

If you are concerned about call security, look for a carrier that has taken measures to thwart eavesdroppers and phone-number thieves. A phone and carrier that operate digitally provide the best security, but digital service is still not available widely.

Some carriers make you dial extra numbers to reach a long-distance company other than the one with which they're affiliated; others let you select your own company when you sign up.

There are three kinds of phones:

Portable and microportable phones. The lightweight, handheld cell phone is the best-selling type. Price: $50 to $300, without a service contract.

Mobile phones. This type, the original cellular phone, is permanently installed in a vehicle, usually by a professional. It transmits at three watts and requires an external antenna. Price: $100 to $300, without a service contract.

Transportable phones. A mobile phone you can remove from the car. These phones draw power from a rechargeable battery pack or a car's cigarette-lighter plug. Though technically portable, such a phone can weigh more than you might care to tote—five pounds or so. Price: $30 to $100, without a service contract.

Features of cellular phones

Common features on cellular phones:

Built-in help. With many phones, hitting a key or two displays instructions for features you don't use often.

Call timer. Cellular calls are expensive, so keeping track of air time is important. Besides displaying elapsed time, some models have a second timer to tally all your calls over a given period. You can also set most phones to beep at fixed intervals for time keeping.

Fast recharge. This cuts recharging

time from more than eight hours to one or two. If your phone doesn't come with this, you can probably buy a separate product that does the same thing.

Low-battery indicator. Cellular-phone batteries, typically the nickel-cadmium type, sustain conversation for at least an hour and standby status for eight hours. A visual or audible indicator warns when the battery is running low. If you're home, you can recharge the battery; on the road, insert a fresh battery.

Memory and speed dialing. Most models can store at least 30 numbers. You can usually speed-dial a number by pressing two or three buttons.

Own-number display. Every cellular carrier assigns its own phone number. If you forget the number you're calling from, the phone's display can summon it up.

Roaming features. In cellular parlance, "roaming" is the term for leaving the area covered by your carrier. Calls made outside your area are charged at a higher rate. Most models can be assigned more than one phone number, allowing you to register with more than one carrier to reduce roaming charges. All models can be programmed to halt roaming temporarily so you don't inadvertently run up extra charges.

Features particularly useful for automobile use include:

Answering features. These ease phone use while driving. Any-key answer lets you pick up incoming calls by pressing any key—not a specific key, as with many models—so you can keep your eyes on the road. Automatic-answer picks up for you after a couple of rings.

Automatic number selection. If you have numbers for more than one carrier, this feature switches them automatically.

One-touch dial. Keys have preset numbers to shorten dialing time.

Speakerphone. This feature lets you talk with both hands on the wheel.

Voice activation. Mostly found on mobile phones, this lets you verbally send and receive calls and access memory.

Telephone answerers ⸻

Sound quality and user friendliness vary a lot, and price is no guide.

Last CR report: *December 1994*
Price range: *$50 to $300*

The types

A phone answerer can be a separate machine you attach to a phone, or it can come integrated with a corded or cordless phone, or even with a fax machine or computer. An answerer with a built-in phone saves space and may be less expensive than buying a phone and answerer separately. But if either part of an integrated unit fails, everything must go to the repair shop. Integrated phone/answering machines are typically priced between $75 and $300; answer-only units, between $50 and $160.

Answerers, with or without phones, use various recording designs:

Digital/microcassette or all-digital. Digital machines have become the biggest-selling type. Memory chips like those found in computers store the greeting; on hybrid models, a cassette records the message. All-digital machines store both greeting and messages on memory chips. In theory, digital models are less likely to break down than cassette models, since circuits replace moving parts. They let you skip through messages more quickly and delete individual messages with the press of a button. Memory chips used to limit recording time, but that's changed with data compression, which has increased the incoming message capability from an average of 5 minutes to 10 to 15 minutes, according to an industry trade group. Chips are also more expensive than tape. They can lose messages if they are without power. In past tests, voice quality on machines with chips was clear, but less natural than with taped messages. These answerers tend to be smaller than the other types. Prices of digital machines have fallen to below $100 in some lines.

Single or dual cassette. These use a single tape cassette for both the outgoing and incoming messages, or one cassette for each. Single-cassette machines, the cheaper type, can be compact, but messages are often limited to a minute or two apiece, and callers must wait for the tape to shuttle forward before they can begin their message. On a dual-cassette machine, callers can leave a message without that delay, and the greeting can be longer.

What's new

Machines are smarter. Voice-actuated circuits reduce annoying empty messages by hanging up automatically if no one speaks. Machines with "mailbox" capabilities can record messages specifically for different members of the family, or for a home business.

They're getting smaller. As digital technology has eliminated cassette tapes, answering machines have shrunk to the size of a VHS video cassette.

Prices are dropping. The price of digital models has dropped as more brands and models have become available. Cassette models have become markdown items.

Shopping strategy

Decide on the type. If your needs are simple—or if you're away from home for extended periods and need maximum space for messages—look for an answerer with dual tape cassettes or for a digital/microcassette machine.

If you don't need a new phone, buy just an answerer. But an integrated phone/answering machine makes the desk or side table tidier, and it can be a good value as well.

Decide on key features. Call screening, remote access, and many other features have become standard. Features you'll pay extra for include such things as audible message indicator, voice mailboxes, and two-line capability. See "Key features," below.

The easiest brands to find. AT&T accounts for about a third of all answering machines sold in the U.S. Other major brands include General Electric, Bell South, Phonemate, and Panasonic.

Key features

Features you'll likely find on higher-priced answerers:

Announce only. This lets you post a greeting without recording incoming calls.

Audible message indicator. Machines with this feature beep when a message has been received so you know without looking that there's a new message.

Greeting bypass. Callers who don't want to hear your outgoing message can bypass it by pressing a touch-tone key, usually the "star."

Message transfer. This automatically dials a preprogrammed telephone number when a message comes in.

Multi-outgoing greetings. This lets you use two greetings and switch between them, which could be useful for a home-based business.

Room monitor. This lets you call in and listen to the room sound—useful for checking on children.

Selective save and delete. Some digital answering machines let you save or delete individual messages at will and free up the memory for new messages.

Time and date. The machine notes the time and date of each incoming message and announces them when you play back the message.

Two-line capability. This lets the machine take messages for two separate phone numbers.

Two-way record. Records your conversation at the press of a button.

Voice mailboxes. This digital feature allows people to share an answering machine while retaining their privacy. Callers are instructed on how to leave a message for the specific person they want to reach.

Voice prompt. A synthesized voice instructs you on how to program for time, date, remote operation, and the like.

Standard features on answering-machine include.

Call counter. Some machines use a light to signal that at least one message is waiting. Better are units whose light blinks to tell you how many messages there are. The best machines provide a digital read-out of the number of calls. Most counters ignore hang-ups occurring before the beep.

Call screening. This lets you listen to a message as it is coming in, so you can avoid nuisance calls and not miss important ones. Extras worth having:

Auto-disconnect, which automatically stops recording as soon as you pick up any phone in the house; and Auto-reset, which stops the recording and resets the machine.

Number of rings. You can set the number of rings the machine will allow before it answers the call. When you're out, you can set it to answer after fewer rings.

One-touch. This single button rewinds, plays messages, and sets the machine for new calls.

Pause and Skip. These help control playback of recorded messages. Pause temporarily stops a message so you can jot down a name or number. Skip moves the tape back or forward one message.

Power backup. Most answerers keep their memory for at least a short time during a power failure, but some reset the call counter to zero. The best designs have a battery backup that holds the settings for hours—critical for an all-digital machine, which will otherwise lose the contents of its chips. A battery-strength indicator warns you when to replace the battery.

Remote access. All machines let you use a touch-tone phone to hear messages when you're away from home. Some prompt you with synthesized voice messages. Some have a programmed security code; others let you set the code yourself. Codes with at least three digits offer the most security.

Remote activation. If you've left the unit off, this allows you to turn it on from another phone.

Toll-saver. This lets you avoid a charge for calling your machine long-distance to check for possible messages. You set the machine to answer the first call after, say, four rings and later calls after only two. You save money because if the machine hasn't picked up by ring number three, you know there are no messages.

Ergonomic chairs

Well-designed chairs cost upward of $400. But a less-expensive model may fit you fine, as it did many of our chair-testing panelists.

Last CR report: *September 1996*
Price range: *$100 to $900*

The choices

Although you can find office-type chairs for as little as $25, you'll have to spend more to get what we consider a basic ergonomic chair—one with a lever to adjust seat height pneumatically, a contoured backrest, armrests, and a five-wheel base that swivels. Some come with or without arms and in different sizes or with different back heights. Fabric and colors can vary, affecting price.

What's new

Scientifically speaking, ergonomics is design that takes into account how the human body interacts with the object. In the late 1950s, industrial designer Henry Dreyfuss pioneered the application of ergonomics to chairs and other office equipment, but there is still no official definition for what makes an ergonomic piece of furniture. The American National Standards Institute, along with the Human Factors and Ergonomics Society (the latter is a professional association of ergonomists), is in the process of rewriting a voluntary standard for VDT workstations that manufacturers can use to identify products for basic "ergonomic" criteria. Meanwhile, marketers have latched onto the term, turning it into a buzz-word; you should check to see if the furniture claims to meet ANSI/HFES standards.

Shopping strategy

Before you choose an ergonomic chair, decide how adjustable you'll need it to be. Will you be sharing the chair with someone who has a different height and build? If so, you'll want one whose seat height and backrest easily adjust up and down. Will you be spending long hours at the computer? Then it's worth spending more, if needed, to buy a well-designed chair. Adjustable armrests are a worthwhile extra, too. The most important thing: The chair should fit *your* body.

Decide what to spend. In our tests, well-designed chairs cost upward of $400 and came from the furniture manufacturers that supply corporate offices. But you may be able to find something acceptable for half that at an office-supply store or at a used-office-furniture store. You may also find a less-expensive model to be just fine, as many of the test panelists did.

What's in the stores. Contract furniture makers—Steelcase, Herman Miller, HON, Knoll, BodyBilt, Girsberger—which usually sell to corporate accounts, increasingly sell to consumers, either through their own dealers or at home-furniture stores. Brands such as Global and Acco/Vogel Peterson are at office superstores like Office Depot, Office Max, and Staples.

Key features

Backrest angle. An adjustment on some chairs. The chairs easiest to use just let you lean back while keeping your feet flat on the floor. Others require you to press a lever.

Cushioning. It should be soft enough that you don't feel pressure at points where your body hits the chair, but not so soft that you sink into the chair and can't move around freely.

Seat height. If at the seat's lowest setting your feet aren't flat on the floor, the chair doesn't go low enough; if at the highest setting your knees angle up, it doesn't go high enough. Use a footrest if a chair's too high. A large, stable footrest allows you to move around in your seat without knocking the footrest out of place. For a chair that's too low, try a chair cushion.

Wheel base. Generally, five wheels roll more stably than four, important for larger and heavier users and for people who are accustomed to scooting around their work area. Even with five wheels, some chairs still wobble noticeably. Try sitting far forward and back in a chair; reject any chairs that seem to be tippy.

Backrest height and lumbar sup- port. Match the contours in the back of the chair to the natural curve of your spine by adjusting the backrest height or moving the lumbar support. If you have a chair with too little curve, attach a special lumbar pillow or a rolled-up towel to its back. A pillow might help if the chair curves more than your back does, but it won't offer much support.

Armrests. A worthwhile option, armrests should support your arms naturally. If you have to drop your shoulders to use them, the armrests are too far apart or too low. If you must hunch your shoulders, they're too high.

Seat depth. When you sit back there should be a few fingers to a fist's worth of space between the edge of the chair and the back of your knees so the seat doesn't cut off circulation to your lower legs.

Forward tilt. A lever on some chairs angles the seat and backrest forward. Designed for typing, this tilt lets you lean into your work without losing the support of the backrest.

How to use the Ratings in the Buying Guide

■ Read the Recommendations for information on specific models and general buying advice.

■ Note how the rated products are listed—in order of performance and convenience, price, or alphabetically.

■ The overall score graph gives the big picture in performance. Notes on features and performance for individual models are listed in the Comments column or "Model details."

■ Before going to press, we verify model availability for most products with manufacturers. Some tested models listed in the Ratings may no longer be available. Models that have been discontinued are marked Ⓓ; some may actually still be available in some stores for part of 1997. A model marked Ⓢ is a successor to the tested model, according to the manufacturer, and is noted in Comments or Model details. Features may vary.

■ Models similar to the tested models, when they exist, are indicated in Comments or Model details.

Ratings
Computer monitors
& Recommendations

The tests behind the Ratings

We used laboratory instruments and the judgments of a trained viewing panel. **Contrast** measures how well the monitor renders lightness and darkness under typical home conditions: the full range between its whitest whites and darkest blacks; differences between dark and light in average pictures; and how evenly it renders uniform shades. **Clarity** reflects the ability to reproduce fine details without unnatural borders at edges. **Color** indicates the ability to render realistic colors without unwanted effects such as fringes of color around the edges of objects. **Distortion** measures how faithfully the monitor reproduces the shape, size, and position of objects in the image. **Price** is the national average, based on a price survey. Models similar to those we tested are noted in Details; features may vary.

Standard features for most models

• Vertical and horizontal position controls. • Screen height and width controls. • Brightness and contrast controls. • On-screen display (control-level indicator), on-screen menu (control options), or both, on 17-inch models. • Power management, to control the monitor's electricity use. • Compliance with the Government's Energy Star power-conservation program. • Plug-and-play capability. • Compliance with both MPR II and the extremely-low-frequency portion of the more stringent TCO 95 electromagnetic-field emissions standards.

Recommendations

You can safely choose among the monitors we tested according to price and image size. The Samsung monitors offer the best combination of high picture quality and moderate price. We've judged both the 15- and 17-inch versions A CR Best Buy. If a large screen is a priority, consider the MAG InnoVisions; they had the largest image size and attractive prices.

See report, page 159. Last time rated in Consumer Reports: July 1996.

Overall Ratings

E VG G F P

Within types, listed in order of picture quality

Brand and model	Price	Picture quality 0 — 100 (P F G VG E)	Contrast	Clarity	Color	Distortion
15-INCH MODELS						
NEC MultiSync XV15+	$480		⊖	⊖	⊖	⊖

Ratings continued ▷

Overall Ratings *Continued*

Legend: E ⊖ VG ⊖ G ○ F ◑ P ●

Brand and model	Price	Picture quality 0—100 (P F G VG E)	Contrast	Clarity	Color	Distortion
15-INCH MODELS						
Samsung SyncMaster 15GLe, A CR BEST BUY	$430		⊖	⊖	⊖	⊖
Sony Multiscan 15sx	430		○	⊖	⊖	⊖
ViewSonic 15ES	380		○	⊖	○	○
MAG InnoVision DX1595	380		◑	⊖	○	⊖
17-INCH MODELS						
Samsung SyncMaster 6Ne, A CR BEST BUY	700		⊖	⊖	⊖	⊖
NEC MultiSync XV17+	850		⊖	⊖	⊖	⊖
Nanao FlexScan F2-17	870		⊖	⊖	○	⊖
ViewSonic 17EA	660		⊖	⊖	⊖	⊖
Nokia Valuegraph #447L	680		○	⊖	⊖	⊖
Sony Multiscan 17sfII	900		○	⊖	⊖	⊖
MAG InnoVision DX1795	680		○	○	⊖	⊖

Model details *Within types, listed in order of picture quality*

15-inch models

NEC MultiSync XV15+ $480
- Image size: 13.7 in. • Dot pitch: 0.28 mm.
- Free color-matching software for printer.

A warm image; reddish tint in gray images. Smallest 15-inch model tested, but consistent performance makes it a top performer. Front panel controls easy to use. But: Hard-to-read labels. Limited ability to tilt face upward. **Similar:** 500. **Recommendation:** Excellent performance.

Samsung SyncMaster 15GLe $430
- Image size: 13.8 in. • Dot pitch: 0.28 mm.

Consistent, strong performance in all tests. A cool image with greenish tint in gray images. Controls easy to access and operate. But: Labels hard to read. **Similar:** 15GLi. **Recommendation:** Very good overall. **A CR Best Buy.**

Sony Multiscan 15sx $430
- Image size: 13.9 in. • Dot Pitch: 0.26 mm.
- Free color-matching software for printer.

Gives a noticeable wintry blue-gray cast to photo images. Push-button controls easy to use. But: A faint horizontal line can be distracting under some viewing conditions. Screen has slightly darker areas. Labels hard to read. **Recommendation:** Very good overall, but there are better choices.

ViewSonic 15ES $380
- Image size: 14 in. • Dot pitch: 0.28 mm.

Cool image with slight green tint in gray images. Only the essential controls. But: Images have less contrast than with other monitors and are noticeably unstable when they change rapidly between white and black. People with large hands may have trouble accessing the controls. Control labels hard to read. Lacks Plug and Play. **Recommendation:** A few slight shortcomings, but very good overall.

MAG InnoVision DX1595 $380
- Image size: 14.3 in. • Dot pitch: 0.28 mm.

A very cool image with green tint that can be seen in gray images. Largest 15-inch model tested. Front-panel control buttons easy to access and operate. But: Images have less contrast than with other monitors. Only limited ability to tilt face upward. Lacks Energy Star. **Recommendation**: A good value overall.

17-inch models

Samsung SyncMaster 6Ne $700
• Image size: 15.9 in. • Dot pitch: 0.28 mm.
• On-screen display, color-temperature controls.
A generally cool image with occasional faint reddish-brown tint that can be seen in gray images. Well-regulated power supply keeps image stable. Controls easy to access, on-screen display easy to use, and control labels easy to read. **Similar**: 17GLi. **Recommendation**: The best combination of performance, features, and price among the 17-inch monitors. **A CR Best Buy.**

NEC MultiSync XV17+ $850
• Image size: 15.3 in. • Dot pitch: 0.28 mm.
• On-screen menu, color-temperature controls. • Color-matching software for printer; tutorial.
Normally has a very cool image, but controls let you adjust images. Yellow-green tint can be seen in gray images. Smallest 17-incher tested, but strong performance makes it a top performer. Controls and on-screen menu easy to use. **Recommendation**: An excellent performer.

Nanao FlexScan F2-17 $870
• Image size: 15.8 in. • Dot pitch: 0.28 mm.
• On-screen menu, color-temperature and color-level controls. • Color-matching software for printer.
Generally a very cool image, but controls let you compensate. Well-regulated power supply keeps image very stable. Abundant controls useful for doing specialized color image work. But: Controls can be complicated to use. Front-panel controls can be very difficult to access. **Similar**: F2-17ex. **Recommendation**: Very good overall, but expensive. Consider if you have special needs.

ViewSonic 17EA $660
• Image size: 16 in. • Dot pitch: 0.28 mm.
• On-screen menu, color-temperature

and color-level controls. • Built-in speakers.
• Extra-cost color-matching software.
Image can be very cool, but controls let you compensate. Red tint can be seen in gray images. Controls easy to access. But: On-screen menu system not as easy to learn as others. Control labels hard to read. Speakers have sound like that of a clock radio. **Recommendation**: Very good overall; a good value.

Nokia Valuegraph #447L $680
• Image size: 15.7 in. • Dot pitch: 0.28 mm.
• Built-in speakers. • Color-matching software for printer.
A warm image. Yellow-brown tint can be seen in gray images. Well-regulated power supply keeps image very stable. Front-panel controls very easy to use and labels easy to read. But: Lacks Plug and Play. No color-temperature control. Speakers have sound like that of a clock radio. **Similar**: 447W. **Recommendation**: Very good performance.

Sony Multiscan 17sfII $900
• Image size: 16 in. • Dot pitch: 0.25 mm.
• On-screen display, color-temperature controls. • Color-matching software for printer.
Image is free from color tinting in gray areas. Generally cool image, with continuous color-temperature control that can be used to produce warm flesh tones or wintry cool photo images. Front-panel controls easy to use, labels easy to read. But: Two faint horizontal lines in display can be distracting under some conditions. **Recommendation**: Very good performance, but there are better values.

MAG InnoVision DX1795 $680
• Image size: 16.3 in. • Dot pitch: 0.26 mm.
• On-screen display, color-temperature and color-level controls.
A generally cool image; controls let you compensate. The largest image of the 17-inch models we tested. Front-panel control buttons easy to access, and on-screen display very easy to operate. But: Images are less sharp and have less contrast than with other monitors. Labels are hard to read. **Recommendation**: A good performer overall.

Ratings *Computer modems*
& Recommendations

The tests behind the Ratings

We tested all the models by having them communicate with a reference modem. **Data mode** reflects performance relative to a 14.4 modem under the same conditions; a score of 100 means the modem was twice as fast as the 14.4. **Data-mode speed** (receiving/2-way): Receiving tests measure how fast the modem can receive the kind of data that's typically transmitted over the phone under various phone-line conditions. Two-way tests measure how quickly the modem can both send and receive, as well as process compressed data under the best of conditions. **Faxing:** ⊜ means test should be clear and readable under all phone-line conditions; ○ means test should be clear and readable on a good phone line, but may miss pages, blur text, or transmit slowly on a poor line; ◐ means consistently missed pages when sending on a noisy line. **Comments:** Surge test mimics a nearby lightning strike. **Price** is the approximate selling price. **Model availability:** Ⓢ means model is replaced, according to the manufacturer; successor model is noted in Comments. New model was not tested; it may or may not perform similarly. Features may vary.

Recommendations

In general, we recommend external modems over internal ones because they are easier to install. U.S. Robotics Sportsters were best as data modems, especially in the two-way test. However, if you often use your modem for faxing or if you experience equipment failure due to lightning strikes, we recommend the Boca Bocamodem MV.34ED or Zoom V.34X model 470, or for Macs, the Global Village Teleport Platinum.

See report, page 164. Last time rated in Consumer Reports, May 1996.

Overall Ratings

	E	VG	G	F	P
	⊜	⊜	○	◐	●

Listed in order of performance in speed tests in data mode

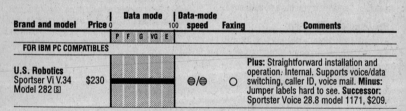

Brand and model	Price	Data mode 0——100	Data-mode speed	Faxing	Comments
		P F G VG E			
FOR IBM PC COMPATIBLES					
U.S. Robotics Sportser Vi V.34 Model 282 Ⓢ	$230		⊜/⊜	○	**Plus:** Straightforward installation and operation. Internal. Supports voice/data switching, caller ID, voice mail. **Minus:** Jumper labels hard to see. **Successor:** Sportster Voice 28.8 model 1171, $209.

Brand and model	Price	Data mode P F G VG E	Data-mode speed	Faxing	Comments
FOR IBM PC COMPATIBLES					
U.S. Robotics Sportster V.34	$220		⊖/⊖	○	External. **Plus:** LEDs easy to see, has power switch. **Minus:** No serial cable.
Zoom V.34X Model 470	170		⊖/⊖	⊖	External. Passed surge test. **Plus:** LEDs easy to see and informative. Power light and switch. **Minus:** No serial cable.
Boca Office Communicator V.34 FDVSP34I	215		⊖/⊖	○	Internal. Passed surge test. **Plus:** Supports voice/data switching, voice mail, file sharing. **Minus:** Not compatible with some PCs, installation can crash PC. Over sized card.
Boca Bocamodem MV.34ED	190		⊖/○	⊖	External. Passed surge test. **Plus:** LEDs easy to see. Power switch and all cables. Can connect to 9- and 25-pin ports.
Zoom Comstar 28.8 Model 620	200		⊖/⊖	⊖	Internal. **Plus:** Has microphone and speaker, supports voice/data, speakerphone, voice mail, caller ID. **Minus:** Very hard to install. Inadequate documentation.
Hayes Accura 288B V.34 ⓢ	200		⊖/⊖	⊖	Internal. **Plus:** Straightforward to install and operate. **Successor:** 288B + Fax.
Supra Express 288i PnP	150		○/○	⊖	Internal. **Plus:** Straightforward Plug and Play installation, even on older PCs. **Minus:** Wouldn't communicate on certain phone lines.
Supra Express 288 PnP	170		⊖/○	⊖	External. **Minus:** LEDs difficult to see and not informative. No power switch. Wouldn't communicate on certain phone lines.
FOR MACINTOSH					
U. S. Robotics Sportster for Macintosh V.34	220		⊖/⊖	○	External. **Plus:** LEDs easy to see. Power light and switch; high speed serial cable.
Global Village Teleport Platinum	220		⊖/○	○	External. Passed surge test. **Plus:** Robust surge protection. Power light and switch, high speed serial cable. **Minus:** LEDs hard to see and not informative.

Ratings *CD-ROM drives*
& Recommendations

The tests behind the Ratings

We tested the drives by running many types of software available on CD-ROM. Drives for IBM compatibles were tested under DOS, Windows 3.1, and Windows 95; drives for Macintosh under System 7.5. **Overall score** reflects effective speed on all types of applications. **Performance** scores indicate speed in specific applications. Models with higher scores will be noticeably faster in the respective area: **multi** refers to multimedia software, which relies heavily on sound and video; **access** indicates how quickly the drive located data on a CD, and was a major factor in differentiating the performance among the 4x drives. In Comments, the **Speed rating** is shorthand for the nominal "transfer rating," the speed at which the drive spins the CD-ROM disc. **Price** is approximate retail.

Standard features for these models

- Eject control. • Headphone jack and volume control for audio CDs.
- Internal adapter card. • Data cable. • No-caddy design. • IBM-compatible.

Recommendations

At $130, the Sony CSD-760E is the best value among the tested models for IBM-compatibles; the Creative Blaster CD 4x MK4013, $160, and Diamond Multimedia Kit 500, $200, also performed well, though the Creative Blaster was hard to install. If you have a Macintosh, the Apple drive is a fine, though somewhat expensive, choice.

See report, page 167. Last time rated in Consumer Reports: June 1996.

Overall Ratings

E VG G F P

Within types, listed in order of overall score

Brand and model (drive brand)	Price	Overall score 0 ___ 100	Performance MULTI ACCESS		Instal- lation	Comments
		P F G VG E				
SINGLE-PLAY						
NEC MultiSpin 6Xi CDR-502 (NEC CDR-502)	$400		⊖	⊖	⊖	SCSI type. Internal. 6x speed rating. **Pluses:** Plug and Play compatible. **Minuses:** Lacks adapter card. Requires caddy.
Sony CSD-760S (Sony CDU76S)	300		○	○	⊖	SCSI type. Internal. 4x speed rating. **Pluses:** Can be used vertically.
Sony CSD-760E (Sony CDU76E)	130		⊖	⊖	○	IDE type. 4x speed rating. **Pluses:** Can be used vertically.

Brand and model (drive brand)	Price	Overall score 0 100	Performance MULTI	ACCESS	Instal-lation	Comments
		P F G VG E				
SINGLE-PLAY						
Diamond 8x (OTI D2 Stingray 8422IDE)	$360	▬▬▬▬▬	⊖	⊖	⊖	IDE type. 8x speed rating. **Minuses:** Lacks manual eject.
Diamond Multimedia Kit 500 (Toshiba XM-5302B)	200	▬▬▬▬▬	⊖	⊖	○	IDE type. 4x speed rating. **Pluses:** Can be used vertically.
Creative Blaster CD 4X MK4013 (Goldstar GCD-R540B)	160	▬▬▬▬	⊖	⊖	◓	IDE type. 4x speed rating.
AppleCD 600e (AppleCD 600e)	340	▬▬▬▬	⊖	⊖	⊖	SCSI type. Mac compatible. External. 4x speed rating. **Minuses:** Lacks data cable.
Reveal CDQ-100 (Mitsumi CRMC-FX400D)	160	▬▬▬▬	⊖	○	○	IDE type. 4x speed rating.
Creative Blaster CD 6X MK4014 (Creative CD620E)	230	▬▬▬▬	○	○	⊖	IDE type. 6x speed rating. **Pluses:** Plug and Play compatible.
Goldstar GCD-R542B (Goldstar GCD-R542B)	120	▬▬▬▬	⊖	⊖	○	IDE type. 4x speed rating. **Minuses:** Lacks data cable and adapter card.
MULTIDISC CHANGERS						
NEC MultiSpin 4Xc CDR-C302 (NEC CDR-C302)	400	▬▬▬▬	○	○	◓	SCSI type. IBM/Mac compatible. External. Can hold 7 discs. 4x speed rating. **Minuses:** Lacks manual eject and adapter card.
NEC MultiSpin 4x4 CDR-C251 (NEC CDR-C251)	280	▬▬▬▬	⊖	⊖	○	IDE type. Can hold 4 discs. 4x speed rating. **Minuses:** Lacks manual eject.

How to use the Buying Guide

██ Read the article for general guidance about types, features, and how to buy. There you'll find a discussion of the choices you'll face in the marketplace, what's new, and key buying advice.

██ The Ratings graph the overall score so you can quickly understand the big picture in performance. Details on features or performance are also noted. For many products, we also have information on how reliable a brand is likely to be. See page 11.

██ To find our last full report on a subject, refer to the article or the Ratings for the listing, or check the eight-year index, page 342.

Ratings *Computer printers*
& Recommendations

The tests behind the Ratings

Overall score is based mainly on print quality and speed. Models can be used with an **IBM-compatible PC, Macintosh** computer, or **both. Black-and-white** performance includes staff panel's quality judgments of samples with identical **text, graphics** (pie and bar charts), and photos; on copier paper (results similar on other papers). For most, speed ranged from 2 to 4 pages-per-minute output for double-spaced black text with standard margins; outlyers are noted in Details. Cost averaged 2 to 4 cents per page; it includes ink or toner, wear to printhead (for inkjets) or drum (for laser and LEDs), but not paper. **Color** performance (see "color-printing" chart) is based on a staff panel's judgments of print-outs of graphics and photo. **Printing** was judged on copier and glossy paper, as recommended by manufacturer. **Color accuracy** is compared to original reference hue. Color **cost** is for ink only. Graphics or photos might cost up to eight times less to print on a printer that scored excellent for cost than on one that scored poor. Models similar to those we tested are noted in Details; features may vary. **Model availability:** Ⅾ means model is discontinued. **Price** is the manufacturer's estimate for October 1996.

Standard features for these models

• Capability for two-way communication with Mac computer or PC with Windows. • Paper output tray. • Feeder that holds 100 or 150 sheets of paper, or 10, 15, or 20 envelopes. • Modes: energy-saving (when not in use); economy printing (saves ink). • Ability to print on only one side of paper. • Toner/ink cartridges included. • No computer cable provided. • Technical support by toll-free phone call, fax, and computer/modem.

Recommendations

The top-rated Hewlett-Packard DeskJet 855Cse, $500, was a clear standout among the dozen ink-jets we tested; it's the machine of choice if you demand optimum performance, regardless of price. For much less money, however, the high-rated Hewlett-Packard 682C ink-jet, $300, performed nearly as capably and qualifies as **A CR Best Buy.** If speed of printing is your top priority, the NEC SuperScript 860, a laser printer, $500, should get first consideration; nearly as good were the Panasonic KX-P6500 laser, $450, and HP LaserJet SL, $480.

See report, page 161. Last time rated in Consumer Reports: October 1996.

Overall Ratings

	E	VG	G	F	P
	⊖	⊖	○	◓	●

Within types, listed in order of overall score

Brand and model	Price	PC/MAC	Overall score 0 — 100	Black-and-white performance TEXT	GRAPHICS	PHOTOS
			P F G VG E			
INK-JET MODELS (COLOR)						
Hewlett-Packard DeskJet 855Cse	$500	Both		⊖	⊖	⊖
Hewlett-Packard DeskJet 682C, **A CR BEST BUY**	300	PC		⊖	⊖	○
Hewlett-Packard DeskJet 600C	250	PC		⊖	○	◓
Epson Stylus Color II Ⓓ	230	Both		⊖	○	○
Hewlett-Packard DeskWriter 600	250	Mac		⊖	⊖	○
Canon BJC-610 Ⓓ	430	PC		○	⊖	⊖
Canon BJC-210 Ⓓ	150	PC		⊖	◓	⊖
Apple Color StyleWriter 1500	280	Mac		⊖	○	●
Canon BJC-4100 Ⓓ	230	PC		○	⊖	○
Apple Color StyleWriter 2500	380	Mac		○	◓	●
Epson Stylus Color IIs Ⓓ	190	PC		⊖	◓	◓
Lexmark 2070 Jetprinter Ⓓ	350	PC		○	◓	◓
Lexmark 1020 Jetprinter Ⓓ	150	PC		○	◓	◓
LASER AND LED MODELS (BLACK-AND-WHITE)						
NEC SuperScript 860 (laser)	500	PC		⊖	⊖	◓
Panasonic KX-P6500 (laser)	450	PC		⊖	⊖	◓
Hewlett-Packard LaserJet 5L	480	PC		⊖	⊖	○
Texas Instruments MicroLaser Win/4	380	PC		⊖	◓	○
Canon LBP-460 (laser) Ⓓ	350	PC		⊖	○	◓
Okidata OL600e (LED)	400	PC		⊖	◓	◓

Ratings continued ▷

Color printing of ink-jet models

Legend: E ◒ VG ◒ G ○ F ◒ P ●

Brand and model	PC/MAC	Graphics COPIER	Graphics GLOSSY	Photos COPIER	Photos GLOSSY	Accuracy	Cost
Hewlett-Packard DeskJet 855Cse	Both	◒	◒	○	◒	◒	◒
Hewlett-Packard DeskJet 682C, **A CR BEST BUY**	PC	◒	◒	○	◒	◒	◒
Hewlett-Packard DeskJet 600C	PC	◓	◓	◓	◒	◒	◒
Epson Stylus Color II	Both	◓	◓	◓	◒	○	○
Hewlett-Packard DeskWriter 600	Mac	◓	◒	◓	○	◒	◒
Canon BJC-610	PC	○	◒	○	○	◒	◒
Canon BJC-210	PC	◓	◓	◓	◓	○	○
Apple Color StyleWriter 1500	Mac	◓	○	●	○	◓	◓
Canon BJC-4100	PC	○	◒	◓	◓	◒	○
Apple Color StyleWriter 2500	Mac	◓	○	◓	○	○	●
Epson Stylus Color IIs	PC	◓	◒	●	◒	○	◒
Lexmark 2070 Jetprinter	PC	◓	◒	●	◓	○	○
Lexmark 1020 Jetprinter	PC	◓	○	●	◒	○	○

Model details *Within types, listed in order of overall score*

Ink-jet models

HP DeskJet 855Cse $500
• DxWxH: 19x18x9 in. • 600x600 dpi b&w, 600x300 color. • Memory: 1MB. • CMYK cartridge.
Laser-quality text at low cost and exceptional color performance. Ink cartridge accepted for recycling. Comes with software to create letterhead, business cards, etc. But: Phone support isn't toll-free. **Recommendation**: Premium-priced, but an excellent printer.

HP DeskJet 682C $300
• DxWxH: 17x17x8 in. • 600x600 dpi b&w, 600x300 color. • Memory: 512K. • CMYK cartridge.
Color performance identical to HP, above, and text pages nearly as good (if markedly more expensive to print). Can print on both sides of paper. Comes with software for cards, letterhead, etc. Only ink-jet tested that can print banners. But:

Poor instruction manual. Phone support isn't toll-free. **Recommendation**: A very good printer and an excellent value. A CR Best Buy.

HP DeskJet 600C $250
• DxWxH: 20x17x8 in. • 600x600 dpi b&w, 600x300 color. • Memory: 544K. • CMY cartridge.
On a par with HP, above, in text quality, but a notch below it in b&w graphics and photos, and several notches below it in color. Glossy paper improves color-photo performance, though images can take days to dry (compared to an hour or so for most machines). Ink cartridge accepted for recycling. **Recommendation**: A very good printer; excellent value if you seldom require top-quality color printing.

Epson Stylus Color II Ⓓ $230
• DxWxH 22x17x15. • 720x720 dpi.
• Memory: 56K. • CMYK cartridge.
From a PC, this Epson printed our color photo

more swiftly than most. Glossy paper improves graphics and photos. But: Listed text speed is for PC only; printing from a Mac is twice as slow. **Recommendation**: A very good, economical printer.

HP DeskWriter 600 $250

• DxWxH: 21x18x8 in. • 600x600 dpi b&w, 600x300 color. • Memory: 544K. • CMY cartridge.
The Mac version of HP DeskJet 600C; performed similarly, but had better b&w graphics and photos on plain paper. Ink cartridge accepted for recycling. But: Phone support isn't toll-free. **Recommendation**: A very good, economical printer.

Canon BJC-610 Ⓓ $430

• DxWxH: 20x17x11 in. • 720x720 dpi. • Memory: 96K. • CMYK cartridge.
Unique design makes color printing relatively inexpensive. Printed our color graphics faster than most. Excellent instructions. Comes with software to create letterhead, cards, etc. Only ink-jet text not smudged by highlighter. But: Text pages print very slowly (1.3 ppm), look less attractive, and are more costly to print than others (13¢/page). Lacks energy-save mode. **Recommendation**: A very good printer, but pricey.

Canon BJC-210 Ⓓ $150

• DxWxH: 7x14x11 in. • 720x360 dpi b&w, 360x360 color. • Memory: 62K. • CMY cartridge.
A bit better at printing text (and much cheaper) than its brandmate BJC-610, though it's less adept at graphics and photos. Automatically recommends best settings for particular tasks. Excellent instructions. Comes with software for cards, letterhead, etc. But: No output tray. Manufacturer does not recommend printing labels. Comes with color cartridge only (black cartridge extra). No energy-save mode. **Recommendation**: A good printer and a fine choice for tight budgets.

Apple Color StyleWriter 1500 $280

• DxWxH: 11x14x11 in. • 720x360 dpi b&w, 360x360 color. • Memory: 512K. • CMY cartridge.
Performance good at best, although text was printed very quickly and quite competently. Comes with printer cable, software for cards, letterhead,

etc. Excellent instructions. But: Among the worst machines for color accuracy and b&w photos. No output tray. **Recommendation**: A good printer, but there are better choices at this price.

Canon BJC-4100 Ⓓ $230

• DxWxH: 22x15x11 in. • 720x360 dpi. • Memory: 64K. • CMYK cartridge.
Performs very much like its brandmate BJC-610, and much more cheaply. Automatically recommends best settings for particular tasks. Excellent instructions. But: Prints slowly (1.7 ppm). Manufacturer does not recommend printing labels. **Recommendation**: A good printer, but there are better choices at this price.

Apple Color StyleWriter 2500 $380

• DxWxH: 23x15x11 in. • 720x360 dpi. • Memory: 512K. • CMYK cartridge.
Its strong suit (and only distinction) is text speed—the highest of the ink-jets. Excellent instructions. Comes with printer cable, software for cards, letterhead, etc. But: Highest cost per color page of any printer. Glossy paper a must for even passable color work. Among the worst machines for b&w graphics and photos. **Recommendation**: A good printer, but there are much better choices at this price.

Epson Stylus Color IIs Ⓓ $190

• DxWxH: 21x16x11 in. • 720x720 dpi. • Memory: .5K to 15K. • CMY cartridge.
A fine but very slow (.7 ppm) machine for printing text. But: No memory. Special paper a must for even passable color work. Manufacturer does not recommend printing labels. Among the worst machines for b&w graphics and photos. **Recommendation**: A good printer and an OK, budget choice if you print little except plain text.

Lexmark 2070 Jetprinter Ⓓ $350

• DxWxH: 21x17x17 in. • 600x600 dpi. • No memory. • CMYK cartridge.
Printed color graphics faster than most and special paper improved the quality of those graphics substantially. But: Among the worst machines for b&w graphics and photos. Difficult to replace ink cartridge. Phone support isn't toll-free. **Recommendation**: A good printer, but there are much better choices at the price.

Ratings continued ▶

Model details *Continued*
....

Lexmark 1020 Jetprinter Ⓓ $150
• DxWxH: 8x14x12 in. • 300x300 dpi.
• CMY cartridge.
Performed similarly to Lexmark, above, only slower (though with better color performance on glossy paper). But: No memory. Comes with color cartridge only (black cartridge is extra). Poor instructions. No output tray. Phone support isn't toll-free. **Recommendation**: A good printer and an OK, budget choice if you print little except plain text.

Laser and LED models

NEC SuperScript 860 $500
• DxWxH: 19x15x10 in. • 600x600 dpi.
• Memory: 1MB standard, 5MB max.
Top-notch text at unequalled speed (7.9 ppm). Can print on both sides of paper. Excellent instructions. Comes with extra fonts for Windows. **Recommendation**: An excellent printer.

Panasonic KX-P6500 $450
• DxWxH: 15x12x17 in. • 600x600 dpi.
• Memory: 512K standard, 4.5MB max.
A bit slower (5.5 ppm) than NEC, above, but otherwise just as competent. Can print on both sides of paper. Excellent instructions. **Recommendation**: An excellent printer and a good value.

HP LaserJet 5L $480
• DxWxH: 12x14x15 in. • 600x600 dpi.
• Memory: 1MB standard, 9MB max.
Slower (4.2 ppm) than NEC 860 and Panasonic, above, and a bit better at photos; otherwise not much different. Can print on both sides of paper. Toner cartridge accepted for recycling. **Similar**: LaserJet 5L Xtra, $480, adds business software. **Recommendation**: An excellent printer.

Texas Instruments MicroLaser Win/4 $380
• DxWxH: 12x12x11 in. • 600x600 dpi.
• No memory.
Slightly more compact and lightweight than other machines. Print speed: 4.2 ppm. But: Among the worst models for graphics. Lacks energy-save mode, fax and online support. **Recommendation**: A very good printer, but a poor choice if graphics is a priority.

Canon LBP-460 $350
• DxWxH: 14x14x14 in. • 300x300 dpi.
• No memory.
Competent enough. Toner cartridge accepted for recycling. Comes with extra fonts for Windows. Excellent instructions. But: Lacks output tray. Holds only 7 envelopes. **Recommendation**: A very good printer.

Okidata OL600e $400
• DxWxH: 19x13x7. • 600x600 dpi.
• Memory: 1MB standard, 18MB max.
LED model, produces text of the same high standard as the lasers. Optional paper trays available. But: Among the worst models for graphics. Holds only 1 envelope. **Recommendation**: A very good printer, but a poor choice if graphics is a priority.

Ratings
& Recommendations

Fax machines & fax-combos

The tests behind the Ratings

Overall score is based primarily on appearance of received faxes, and how well they resist fading and curling. **Faxes: Speed in** is based on time to print an incoming 3-page, single-spaced fax sent in "standard" mode. **Speed out** is based on time to send a 20-page, triple-spaced fax in "standard" mode. **Copies: Looks** and **speed** are compared to a good home-office copier. **Ease of use** reflects unit's particular advantages and disadvantages. **Fax-combos only: Scanned photos** compares clarity to a scan from a good stand-alone scanner. Because the **looks** of a machine's copies, faxes, and computer printouts are each judged against a different standard, judgments for each cannot be directly compared. **Price** is an average, based on national surveys. Models similar to those we tested are noted in Details; fratures may vary. **Model availability:** Ⓓ means model is discontinued. Ⓢ means model is replaced, according to the manufacturer; successor model model is noted in Details. New model was not tested; it may or may not perform similarly. Features may vary.

Standard features for these models

- Copier capability. • Data-transfer rate of at least 9.6 kilobits per second (kbps). • Fax/tel switch, enabling operation on a phone line used for voice calls. • Interface to enable use with an answering machine. • Speaker (to hear transmissions). • Digital clock, to schedule delayed-send feature. • Transmission-resolution switch (fine, for the most detail; photo; or standard). Most also have:
- Overseas mode. • Way to initiate reception from extension phones.
- Capability to use "distinctive ring detection."

Recommendations

For sending and receiving faxes informally, a simple thermal-paper machine like the Brother 625 ($240) or the Sharp UX-176 ($250) or its successor, UX-177, should suffice. The Sharp was better with photos and the Brother, faster at transmitting. For business use, consider the plain-paper HP Fax 700 ($500) or, if transmitting and copier speed aren't critical, the Canon B540 ($420). Among fax-combos, the Brother MFC-4500ML ($1000) or its successor, MFC-4550, was by far the best performer, but keep in mind that no fax-combo is likely to be as good as stand-alone machines.

See report, page 165. Last time rated in Consumer Reports: September 1996.

Ratings continued ▶

Overall Ratings Fax machines

Legend: E ⊖ VG ⊖ G ○ F ◕ P ●

Listed by type; within type, listed in Ratings order

Brand and model	Price	Overall score (0–100)	Faxes SPEED IN	SPEED OUT	Copies LOOKS	SPEED	Ease of use
THERMAL-PAPER MODELS							
Brother 825MC [S]	$300		⊖	⊖	○	⊖	⊖
Panasonic KX-F750 [D]	350		⊖	○	○	⊖	○
Brother 625	240		⊖	⊖	○	⊖	○
Radio Shack TFX-1032	380		⊖	◕	○	○	◕
Sharp UX-176 [S]	250		⊖	◕	○	⊖	○
Muratec M800	210		⊖	○	○	○	◕
Sharp NX-2	190		⊖	◕	○	○	◕
PLAIN-PAPER MODELS							
HP Fax 700	500		○	⊖	◕	○	⊖
Canon B540	420		○	○	◕	◕	⊖
Muratec M4500	430		○	◕	●	⊖	◕
Brother PPF-1350UM [S]	440		○	⊖	○	⊖	⊖
Panasonic KX-F1000 [D]	440		○	⊖	◕	⊖	○

Overall Ratings Fax-combos

Legend: E ⊖ VG ⊖ G ○ F ◕ P ●

Brand and model	Price	Overall score (0–100)	Faxes SPEED IN	SPEED OUT	Computer printing	Scanned photos	Copier LOOKS	SPEED	Ease of use
FAX-COMBOS									
Brother MFC-4500ML [S]	$1000		○	⊖	⊖	⊖	◕	⊖	⊖
Xerox Work Center 250 [D]	600		○	⊖	◕	○	◕	○	○
HP Office Jet 350	600		⊖	⊖	○	○	◕	⊖	⊖
Brother MFC-1950MC [S]	500		⊖	⊖	◕	◕	○	⊖	⊖

Model details *Listed by type; within type, listed in order of overall score*

NOTES ON THE DETAILS: includes cost per page (ink or toner, thermal- or (at a penny a page) plain paper; memory, in single-spaced typed pages; one-touch keys and speed-dial numbers; LCD characters; document-feeder capacity; paper supply, in pages or feet of paper roll.

Thermal-paper models

Brother 825MC S $300

• 7¢/pg. • 25-pg. memory. • 20 one-touch, 40 speed-dial nos. • 16-char. LCD. • 15-pg. feeder. • Paper: 164-ft. roll.
At about a page per minute, one of the fastest receivers in our tests. The most convenient thermal-paper machine, and the only one with memory —lots of it. Broadcast, scan/send, fax-forward, paging-number, and remote-retrieve capabilities. Error-correction mode. Faxes barely curled. Premium paper available. **Successor:** MFC-890MC, $300. **Recommendation:** A very good, richly featured machine; excellent value.

Panasonic KX-F750 D $350

• 7¢/pg. • 12 one-touch, 28 speed-dial nos. • 15-char. LCD. • 15-pg. feeder. • Paper: 164-ft. roll.
This model excels at sending photos. No jack for separate answering machine. Average curling of faxes. Premium paper available. Speakerphone. **Recommendation:** A good but pricey machine.

Brother 625 $240

• 7¢/pg. • 20 one-touch, 20 speed-dial nos. • 16-char. LCD. • 15-pg. feeder. • Paper: 164-ft. roll.
Much like the Brother, above, but lacking its memory features and a little slower at receiving. Similars: MFC-670, MFC-690, both $270 and both with Missing Link. **Recommendation:** Excellent value in a good, basic machine.

Radio Shack TFX-1032 $380

• 6¢/pg. • 8 one-touch, 20 speed-dial nos. • 16-char. LCD. • 10-pg. feeder. • Paper: 98-ft. roll.
A very basic model; it can't even delay sending or recognize "distinctive rings." Can enlarge and reduce copies. Faxes barely curled. **Recom-** mendation: A good machine; a poor value.

Sharp UX-176 S $250

• 7¢/pg. • 20 one-touch, 30 speed-dial nos. • 16-char. LCD. • 20-pg. feeder. • Paper: 164-ft. roll.
Another Spartan model. Faxes come out very curly. Lacks overseas mode. **Successor:** UX-177, $250. **Recommendation:** A good, basic machine; worth considering for its price.

Muratec M800 $210

• 6¢/pg. • 5 one-touch, 20 speed-dial nos. • 16-char. LCD. • 10-pg. feeder. • Paper: 98-ft. roll.
A competent performer. Can't be started from all extension phones. Yields curly faxes. Premium paper available. Lacks overseas mode. **Recommendation:** An OK machine; worth considering for rock-bottom budgets.

Sharp NX-2 $190

• 6¢/pg. • 5 one-touch, 15 speed-dial nos. • 16-char. LCD. • 5-pg. feeder. • 98-ft. paper roll.
A competent performer, but cuts many corners on convenience—the smallest page feeder, no cutter (you'll have to cut apart faxes page by page), no delayed sending. Lacks overseas mode. **Recommendation:** Cheap, but no bargain.

Plain-paper models

HP Fax 700 $500

• Ink-jet printing. • 4¢/pg. • 13-pg. memory. • 10 one-touch, 40 speed-dial nos. • 40-char. LCD. • 20-pg. feeder. • Paper: 100 sheets.
Fax pages are crisp, clear, and very inexpensive. Fairly large memory, and has broadcast and scan-send capabilities. Error-correction mode, but lacks overseas mode. Lacks phone handset, but has jack for extension phone. **Recommendation:** A very good machine; good value if you receive a lot of faxes.

Canon B540 $420

• Ink-jet printing. • 5¢/pg. • 6-pg. memory. • 20 one-touch, 50 speed-dial nos. • 16-char.

Ratings continued ❯

Model details *Continued*

••••••••••••••••••••••

LCD. • 20-pg. feeder. • Paper: 100 sheets.
A bit slower than the HP 700, above, and with slightly fewer conveniences. Broadcast and scan-send capabilities. Error-correction mode. Lacks handset, and can't be started from all extension phones. **Similar:** B550, $435. **Recommendation:** A good machine.

Muratec M4500 $430

• Thermal-transfer printing. • 7¢ /pg. • 6-pg. memory. • 20 one-touch, 60 speed-dial nos. • 40-char. LCD. • 20-pg. feeder. • Paper: 250 sheets.
Copier pages look the best of any machine, but fax pages are middling. A somewhat slow performer. Beeps when a fax is complete. Can't be started from all extension phones. **Recommendation:** A good machine.

Brother PPF-1350M Ⓢ $440

• Thermal-transfer printing. • 12¢ /pg.
• 5-pg. memory. • 30 one-touch, 60 speed-dial nos. • 16-char. LCD. • 20-pg. feeder.
• Paper: 200 sheets.
Fax pages are only fair—and are very expensive. Copies, though, are good and fast, and can be enlarged or reduced. Broadcast, scan-send, fax-forward, paging-number, and remote-retrieve capabilities. Error-correction mode. **Successors:** PPF-1250, $380; MFC-1750, $450, includes Missing Link. **Recommendation:** OK, but poor value, given its per-page cost.

Panasonic KX-F1000 Ⓓ $440

• Thermal-transfer printing. • 8.5¢ /pg. • 14 one-touch, 60 speed-dial nos. • 15-char. LCD. • 15-pg. feeder. • Paper: 250 sheets.
Lacks memory and its faxes, while readable, lack crispness. Superior at faxing photos, however. Speakerphone. **Recommendation:** OK but limited.

Fax-combo models

Brother MFC-4500ML Ⓢ $1000

• Laser printing. • 3.5¢/pg. • 17-pg. memory.
• 24 one-touch, 100 speed-dial nos. • 32-char. LCD. • 30-pg. feeder. • Paper: 200 sheets.
The sole laser-printing model tested, its faxes (unsurprisingly) look the best of all machines.

It was far from the best at copies, however (though it can enlarge or reduce them), and pages from a computer file would likely look better from a stand-alone laser printer. Broadcast, scan-send, fax-forward, and paging number capabilities. Error-correction mode. **Successor:** MFC-4550, $800. **Recommendation:** A very good machine.

Xerox Work Center 250 Ⓓ $600

• Ink-jet printing. • 5¢ /pg.• 12-pg. memory.
• 10 one-touch, 90 speed-dial nos. • 80-char. LCD. • 20-pg. feeder. • Paper: 100 sheets.
Pages in all formats look much like those from the Brother, above, though fax pages are a notch lower in quality. Can enlarge or reduce copier pages. Excellent as a scanner; TWAIN-compatible and comes with a fine optical character-recognition (OCR) program. Broadcast and scan-send capabilities. Error-correction mode. Can't utilize phone company "distinctive-ring" services. **Recommendation:** A good machine. Worth considering, especially if you often scan documents.

HP Office Jet 350 $600

• Ink-jet printing. • 4¢ /pg.• 12-pg. memory.
• 10 one-touch, 65 speed-dial nos. • 40-char. LCD. • 20-pg. feeder. • Paper: 100 sheets.
A notch below Brother MFC-4500ML and Xerox Work Center in many respects. Beeps when fax reception is completed. No phone handset, but has jack for extension phone. TWAIN-compatible scanner. Omnipage LTD. Optical character-recognition (OCR) software provided. **Recommendation:** A good machine.

Brother MFC-1950MC Ⓢ $500

• Thermal-transfer printing. • 12¢ /pg.
• 12-pg. memory. • 30 one-touch, 100 speed-dial nos. • 16-char. LCD. • 20-pg. feeder. • Paper: 200 sheets.
Pages are expensive and below par in looks, except for copies (which can also be enlarged or reduced). Broadcast, scan-send, fax-forward, and paging-number capabilities. Error-correction mode. **Successor:** MFC-1950MC+, $500. **Recommendation:** No bargain, despite a price that's low for a fax-combo.

Ratings *Pagers*
& Recommendations

The tests behind the Ratings

Overall score is based equally on: **Sensitivity**, which reflects how faint a signal the pager could respond to; **convenience**; and **features**, our judgment of the usefulness of the pager's array of features. **Price** is approximate retail for the pager alone. Though service is not included, price assumes purchase of some—usually three months' worth. **Model availability:** Ⓓ means model is discontinued.

Standard features for these models

• Have low-battery indicator. • Use 1 or 2 AA or AAA batteries. Most models we tested • Will chirp or vibrate, and sound a reminder if you overlook a message.

Recommendations

Compare stores and providers in your area for the packages of pagers and services. Chances are good that you'll find many of the pagers we tested—although you may need to check the manual to verify the model name, since retailers often rebadge pagers with their own company name. Choose among the rated pagers by the sensitivity and convenience needed.

See report, page 169. Last time rated in Consumer Reports: August 1996.

Overall Ratings

E ⊖   VG ⊖   G ○   F ◑   P ●

Listed by type; within type, listed in order of overall score

Brand and model	Price	Overall score 0 — 100	Sensitivity	Convenience	Features
		P F G VG E			
NUMERIC MODELS					
Motorola Ultra Express	$85		⊖	○	⊖
Motorola Ultra Express FLX	100		⊖	○	⊖
NEC Message Maker Executive Ⓓ	75		⊖	⊖	⊖
Motorola Renegade	65		⊖	○	○
Motorola Lifestyle Plus	75		○	⊖	○
NEC Facts Sports II	75		○	◑	○
ALPHANUMERIC MODELS					
Motorola Memo Express	125		⊖	○	⊖
Motorola Advisor Gold FLX	175		⊖	◑	⊖
NEC Message Maker Companion	165		○	◑	⊖

Ratings continued ≫

Model details *Listed by types; within types, listed in order of overall score*

Numeric models

Motorola Ultra Express $85

• POCSAG technology. • Auto On/off.
• Battery back-up. • 16-message memory.
Among the most sensitive pagers tested, with a
fine array of features. Alarm clock. **Recommendation**: An excellent pager; good value.

Motorola Ultra Express FLX $100

• Flex technology. • Battery back-up.
• 16-message memory.
The Flex version of the Motorola, above; performs (and looks) very much like it, but lacks
Auto On/off feature. Alarm clock. **Recommendation**: An excellent pager.

NEC Message Maker Executive Ⓓ

• Flex technology. • 32-message memory.
Another fine performer. Among the most convenient models, despite its complex menu system.
Upward-facing display. Alarm clock. **Recommendation**: An excellent pager; very good value.

Motorola Renegade $65

• POCSAG technology. • 10-message memory.
A no-frills model. Upward-facing display. But:
No message protection or time stamp. Single-button control—hard to set pager to vibrate
rather than beep. Requires two batteries. **Recommendation**: A very good pager.

Motorola Lifestyle Plus $75

• POCSAG technology. • 16-message memory.
Another basic model. Sliding switch—easy to
silence or turn off pager. Upward-facing display.
But: No chirper or out-of-range indicator.
Recommendation: A very good pager.

NEC Facts Sports II $75

• POCSAG technology. • 8-message memory.
Upward-facing display. Among the least convenient models. Single button must be pressed at
just the right time to turn off or to set clock.
Battery must be removed to delete a message
(battery was briefly displaced during drop tests;
one message was lost). No date stamp or
Message Lock. **Recommendation**: A good pager.

Alphanumeric models

Motorola Advisor Gold FLX $175

• Flex technology. • Multiline display. • Auto
On/off. • Battery backup. • 19-message
memory.
A fine performer, despite its complex menu system. Electronic notepad for memos and the like.
Alarm clock. Date stamp. **Recommendation**: An
excellent pager.

Motorola Memo Express $125

• POCSAG technology. • Auto On/off. • Battery
back-up. • 15-message memory.
Among the most sensitive pagers. Lighter on
features and lower in price than other alphanumerics. Alarm clock. **Recommendation**: An
excellent pager. Good value for an alphanumeric.

NEC Message Maker Companion

• Flex technology. • Multiline display.
• Battery back-up. • 16-message memory.
"Reversed" (white on black) display is hard to
read. Notepad for memos and the like.
Countdown timer. Alarm clock. Date stamp.
Recommendation: A very good pager.

Ratings Cordless phones
& Recommendations & answerers

The tests behind the Ratings

Overall score is based primarily on speech clarity and handset convenience. Models with answerers are rated primarily on their performance as telephones. More channels didn't increase a model's score, nor did ranges beyond 400 feet. **Clarity** reflects the accuracy with which a phone reproduced speech and its freedom from noise, as judged by a panel of testers using a corded phone for comparison. **Ease of use** includes such factors as how comfortable the handset felt at the ear, its weight, battery time, and how easy the buttons are to use in normal and low lighting. **Range** is the approximate distance at which the connection started to get noisy, measured outdoors without any obstructions between base and handset. Ranges will be shorter inside a building. **Talk time** is approximately how long a fully charged battery lets you talk before you must recharge it. Some phones, noted in Details, failed our lightning surge test; you may want to disconnect them during a storm.

For answerers, **message quality** judges how natural messages sounded when played back through the answerer's loudspeaker. Details on the models notes recording capacity, which is the maximum recording time for all greetings and messages combined, usually 15 min. Longest greeting/message indicates about how long voices can be recorded for each. Counter limit and voice mailboxes enumerate those features. Unless otherwise noted, **price** is the estimated average, based on a national survey. Models similar to the tested models are noted in Details; features may vary.

Recommendations

Our top-performer, the AT&T 4336 ($50) is a very good basic phone at a very attractive price. And at $50, it's A CR BEST BUY. The next three models—the AT&T 5830 ($100), the Cobra CP-2500 ($75), and the Toshiba FT-7505 ($90)—are also very good but pricier. If you need a two-line phone, the AT&T 5552 ($180) is the clear choice. All of the 900-MHz models were very good performers; differences were a matter of convenience. Among answerers, the Sharp CL-505 ($150) offers the best value.

See report, page 172. Last time rated in Consumer Reports: November 1996.

Ratings continued ▶

Overall Ratings Cordless phones

E VG G F P
⊖ ⊖ ○ ◐ ●

Listed by type; within type, listed by overall score

Brand and model	Price	Overall score P F G VG E	Clarity	Convenience	Range	Channels	Talk time
43/49-MHZ MODELS							
AT&T 4336, A CR BEST BUY	$50		⊖	⊖	255 ft.	10	12¾ hr.
AT&T 5830	100		⊖	⊖	190	25	12
Cobra CP-2500	75		⊖	○	140	25	11¾
Toshiba FT-7505	90		⊖	⊖	165	25	9¼
Uniden XC3510	60		⊖	○	100	25	10
Panasonic KX-TC100	80		⊖	○	275	25	11½
Sony SP-Q300	130		○	⊖	125	25	13
Motorola 210	115		⊖	◐	150	10	5¾
Radio Shack ET-531	90		⊖	○	135	10	15¼
GE 2-9535	45		⊖	○	40	10	8
BellSouth 39030	80		○	◐	175	25	9½
GE 2-9782	80		○	○	90	25	6½
TWO-LINE, 43/49-MHZ MODELS							
AT&T 5552	180		⊖	⊖	190	10	12
Sony SPP-M100	140		○	⊖	200	25	14¼
900-MHZ MODELS							
Sony SPP-ER101	150		⊖	○	765	40	10
AT&T 9100 (digital)	170		⊖	◐	800	10	9¾
Panasonic KX-TC905	240		⊖	○	825	30	8¼
Uniden EXP901	150		⊖	⊖	700	40	5½
Southwestern Bell SST900 (digital)	220		⊖	◐	905	100	4½

Overall Ratings Cordless phones with answerers

E ⊖ VG ⊖ G ○ F ⊖ P ●

Brand and model	Price	Overall score 0 ... 100	CLARITY	EASE OF USE	Phone RANGE	CHANNELS	TALK TIME	Message quality
		P F G VG E						
Panasonic KX-T4500	$180		⊖	○	165 ft.	10	10¼ hr.	⊖
AT&T 5635	160		⊖	⊖	110	10	12½	⊖
Sharp CL-505	150		⊖	○	240	25	10½	○
Sony SPP-A5000	220		⊖	⊖	145	10	13¼	●
BellSouth 3892Z	150		⊖	●	175	25	19½	●
GE 2-9785	140		○	●	95	25	17¾	○

Model details *Within types, listed in order of overall score*

43/49-MHz models

AT&T 4336 $50
• 9-oz. handset • 9 speed-dial numbers
Excellent sound quality and comfortable handset with easy-to-use buttons make this a top performer. But: Handset lacks voice volume control. **Similar:** 4337, $55. **Recommendation:** Good value in a very good, basic phone—if 10 channels are enough in your area. A CR Best Buy.

AT&T 5830 $100
• 11-oz. handset • 20 speed-dial numbers
• Pager
Comfortable handset has lighted keypad, mute function. Voice volume higher than most when other extensions are also used. **Similar:** 5860, $125. **Recommendation:** A very good phone, but expensive.

Cobra CP-2500 $75
• 9-oz. handset • 10 speed-dial numbers
Comfortable handset with easy-to-use buttons and antenna hidden inside. Handset rings more loudly than most. But: Handset lacks voice volume control. No modular phone jack on base; damaged cord hard to replace. **Recommendation:** A very good phone.

Toshiba FT-7505 $90
• 8-oz. handset • 12 speed-dial numbers
• Pager/intercom • Speakerphone, second keypad on base
Handset can stand up. Ringer volume control. **Similar:** FT-7515, $100. **Recommendation:** A very good, full-featured phone.

Uniden XC3510 $60
• 9-oz. handset • 10 speed-dial numbers
• Pager • One-touch dialing buttons on handset
Handset rings more loudly than most. Handset has battery-save switch and can stand up. **Recommendation:** Very good over short range.

Panasonic KX-TC100 $80
• 8-oz. handset • 10 speed-dial numbers
• Pager
Handset has easy-to-use buttons, ringer volume control. But: Handset lacks voice volume control. **Recommendation:** A very good, basic phone with a long range.

Sony SSP-Q300 $130
• 11-oz. handset • 10 speed-dial numbers
• Pager/intercom • Speakerphone, second keypad on base • One-touch buttons on base

Ratings continued ▶

Model details *Continued*

Comfortable handset with easy-to-use buttons power-off switch and ringer volume control. Also has ringer in base. But: Incoming calls sounded a bit unnatural and muffled. Failed voltage surge test. **Recommendation**: Full-featured, but pricey.

Motorola 210 $115

• 7-oz. handset • 9 speed-dial numbers
• Voice scrambling • Pager • One-touch dialing buttons on handset.

A small, cramped handset modeled after Motorola's cell phones and a relatively short talk time dragged down this phone's overall score. Keys are flush with the handset and somewhat hard to hit positively. Handset rings more loudly than most, has mute function and battery-save switch. Has a belt clip. Handset has ringer volume control. But: Failed voltage surge test. **Recommendation**: A good performer, but there are more convenient choices.

Radio Shack ET-531 $90

• 10-oz. handset • 10 speed-dial numbers
• Pager

Uncomfortable handset rings more loudly than most. Handset can stand up. Also has ringer in base. But: Handset lacks voice volume control. Failed voltage surge test. **Recommendation**: Good, but overpriced.

GE 2-9535 $45

• 9-oz. handset• 10 speed-dial numbers
Comfortable handset with easy-to-use buttons. Very short range makes this model suitable only for use not far from the base. Voice volume higher than most when other extensions are also used. But: No modular phone jack on base; damaged cord hard to replace. Handset lacks voice volume control. Failed voltage surge test. **Recommendation**: Inexpensive, good, but limited phone.

BellSouth 39030 $80

• 8-oz. handset• 10 speed-dial numbers
• Pager.

Comes with extra recharger cradle. Handset has mute, stands up. But: Outgoing calls sounded a bit unnatural and muffled. Handset lacks voice volume control and isn't very comfortable against the face. **Similar**: 39000 and 39010, $80; 3901, 3902, 3903, 3904, $70. **Recommendation**: A good performer but not a good value.

GE 2-9782 $80

• 10-oz. handset• 10 speed-dial numbers
• Pager • LCD display on handset
Handset displays dialed number or stored speed dial numbers. Must stand up to charge. But: Relatively short talk time. Can't be wall-mounted. Failed voltage surge test. **Recommendation**: There are better choices.

2-line 43/49-MHz models

AT&T 5552 $180

• Allows three-way conferencing. • 10-oz. handset • 9 speed-dial numbers • Pager/ intercom • Speakerphone, second keypad on base

Excellent sound quality and conveniences like a comfortable handset with lighted keypad made this a top performer. Voice volume higher than most when other extensions are also used. Large base unit has mute and ringer. Handset has mute, too. But: Can't be wall-mounted. **Recommendation**: An excellent, full-featured phone.

Sony SPP-M100 $140

• Allows three-way conferencing • 11-oz. handset • 10 speed-dial numbers • Pager
Comfortable handset has mute, battery-save switch and battery-level indicator. But: Outgoing calls sounded a bit unnatural and muffled. Handset lacks voice volume control. Failed voltage surge test. **Recommendation**: A good, basic two-line phone.

900-MHz models

Sony SPP-ER101 $150

• 10-oz. handset • 10 speed-dial numbers
• Pager

Excellent sound pushed this Sony to the top spot among 900-MHz models, though its handset isn't as comfortable as the other Sonys'. Handset has power-off switch and must stand up in base to charge. **Recommendation**: A very good, basic phone.

Uniden EXP901 $150

• 11-oz. handset • 10 speed-dial numbers • Pager/intercom • One-touch dialing buttons on handset

Has two phone jacks on base for use with a stand-alone answerer. Base can charge a second, optional battery. Swapping base and handset batteries not convenient. Handset has mute, battery-save switch, and ringer volume control; can stand up. Has a belt clip. But: Speakerphone on base never quite shuts off; conversations can be overheard. **Recommendation**: A very good performer.

AT&T 9100 $170

• Digital • 11-oz. handset • 10 speed-dial numbers • Pager

The digital technology thwarts eavesdroppers and rejects interference, but the flat handset was uncomfortable against the face. Keys are flush with the handset and somewhat hard to hit positively. Handset has mute, ringer volume control. **Recommendation**: A good choice, particularly if privacy is critical.

Panasonic KX-TC905 $240

• Headset • 8-oz. handset • 12 speed-dial numbers • Pager • One-touch dialing buttons on handset

Small handset uncomfortable at the face but easily pocketed. It rings more loudly than most and has a backlit keypad that's easy to read, even in dark. But you don't need to hold it to use it—with headset and belt clip, it's designed for hands-free roaming. But: Handset lacks voice volume control. Can't be wall-mounted. **Recommendation**: A very good, though expensive, performer.

Southwestern Bell SST900 $220

• Digital • 11-oz. handset • 10 speed-dial numbers • Pager

Though spread-spectrum digital technology makes conversation completely secure over long ranges, short talk time held this model back. Handset has mute function and ringer volume control. Rings more loudly than most. But: Interfered with some other cordless phones. **Recommendation**: A very good performer, but expensive.

Models with answerers

Panasonic KX-T4500B $180

• 8-oz. handset • 10 speed-dial numbers • Pager/intercom • Longest greeting/message: 15/15 min. • Counter limit: 64 • 3 mailboxes

Offered the best sound quality for both the telephone and answerer. Handset has easy-to-use buttons, ringer volume control. LCD display on base shows call count and status of other functions. Can record a different greeting in each voice mailbox. Can record a telephone conversation. Activates remote beeper when incoming message is recorded. Remote caller can monitor room sounds. But: Failed voltage surge test. **Recommendation**: A very good, all-round performer.

AT&T 5635 $160

• 11-oz. handset • 10 speed-dial numbers • Pager • Recording capacity: 12 min. • Longest greeting/message: 2/12 min. • Counter limit: 9 • 2 mailboxes

A short recording capacity makes this a light-duty answerer. Voice volume higher than most when other extensions are also used. Comfortable handset has lighted keypad, mute, ringer volume control. Digital readout of calls and a periodic beep when messages are waiting. Can record telephone conversations. Remote caller can monitor room sounds. **Similar**: 5630, $165; 5631, $180. **Recommendation**: A very good performer if you don't get many messages.

Sharp CL-505 $150

• 9-oz. handset • 10 speed-dial numbers • Pager • Recording capacity: 24 min. • Longest greeting/message: 1/24 min. • Counter limit: 59 • 2 mailboxes

A long range and a large recording capacity make this model stand out. Voice volume higher than most when other extensions are also used. Backlit keypad is easy to read, even in dark. Handset has mute, battery-save switch, and ringer volume control. Handset rings more loudly than most. Digital readout of calls. Can record tele-

Ratings continued ▶

Model details *Continued*

phone conversation. Battery can be quick-charged in three hours. But: Message counter increases even when no message is left. Failed voltage surge test. **Recommendation**: A good performer and a good value.

Sony SPP-A5000 $220
• 11-oz. handset • 10 speed-dial numbers • Pager • Longest greeting/message: 4/15 min. • Counter limit: 19 • 1 mailbox
An excellent phone, but just so-so sound on the messages. Comfortable handset has mute, battery-save switch. Also has ringer in base. Includes a second, easy-to-change battery that can be charged while other battery is in use. Digital readout of calls and periodic beep when messages are waiting. A rotating knob allows versatile control of message playback speed and selection. Can record telephone conversation and answer calls without taking messages. But: Call counter resets after playback even when messages are saved. Handset lacks voice volume control. Failed voltage surge test. **Recommendation**: A very good performer with many useful features but expensive.

BellSouth 3892Z $150
• 10-oz. handset • 10 speed-dial numbers • Pager • Longest greeting/message: ½/3 min. • Counter limit: 63 • 5 mailboxes
An uncomfortable handset and the answerer's so-so message quality marred this model. Handset has battery-save switch and can stand up. Also has ringer in base. Digital readout of calls with periodic beep when messages are waiting. Can record a different greeting in each mailbox. But: Handset lacks voice volume control. **Similar**: 3980Z, 3891Z, $3893Z, $140. **Recommendation**: A good performer.

GE 2-9785 $140
• 9-oz. handset • 10 speed-dial numbers • Pager • Longest greeting/message: 15/15 min. • Counter limit: 39 • 1 mailbox
Weaknesses in sound quality, range, talk time, and handset design dragged this model down. Handset, with ringer volume control, must stand up in base to charge. Digital readout of calls. But: Can't be wall-mounted. Failed voltage surge test. **Recommendation**: There are better choices.

How to use the Ratings in the Buying Guide

■ Read the Recommendations for information on specific models and general buying advice.

■ Note how the rated products are listed—in order of performance and convenience, price, or alphabetically.

■ The overall score graph gives the big picture in performance. Notes on features and performance for individual models are listed in the Comments column or "Model details."

■ Before going to press, we verify model availability for most products with manufacturers. Some tested models listed in the Ratings may no longer be available. Models that have been discontinued are marked Ⓓ; some may actually still be available in some stores for part of 1997. A model marked Ⓢ is a successor to the tested model, according to the manufacturer, and is noted in Comments or Model details. Features may vary.

■ Models similar to the tested models, when they exist, are indicated in Comments or Model details.

■ To find our last full report on a subject, check the reference above the Ratings chart or the eight-year index, page 342.

HEALTH & RECREATION

Bicycles

A bike that's safe and satisfying to ride costs at least $200 to $400.

Last CR reports: *Kids' bikes, November 1996; mountain, June 1995; hybrid, August 1994*
Ratings: *page 235*
Price range: *$50 to $3000*

The types

Mountain bike. Certain features characterize this type and allow it to handle unpaved terrain: fat, knobby tires, 26-inch-diameter wheels, upright handlebars, wide seat, sturdy frame, multiple fears, and perhaps a shock-absorbing sus-

pension. Those features also make for a comfortable ride on any surface, though a mountain bike can feel a bit sluggish on pavement. Mountain bikes sell for $100 to $3000 or more. Our tests show you'll probably have to spend at least $200 to get a bike that's safe and satisfying to ride on pavement and dirt roads. For rougher terrain, figure on at least $450. Bikes for less than $200 may be unsafe; those with steel wheel rims have performed poorly in our wet-braking tests.

Road bike. This lightweight bike, designed for recreation or touring, comes with thin tires and "drop" handlebars. The design is fast and efficient, but casual riders may find it's not particularly comfortable, nor suited for rough surfaces. Although road bikes are the best choice for riding fast or far, they've declined in popularity. Price: $400 to $3000 or more.

Hybrid bike. Introduced in the late 1980s, the hybrid marked the return of the casual recreational bike. This type typically uses a medium-weight frame, upright handlebars, and moderately knobby tires, marrying a mountain bike's strength and comfort with a road bike's efficiency. A hybrid is a good choice for commuters or for those who occasionally travel a dirt road. Low-end hybrids start at about $250 and can go up to $700 for lighter-weight models.

Kids' bikes. These range from models with training wheels to down-sized mountain bikes. If your child is younger than about age seven, you'll mostly likely be choosing from various sizes of single-speed, coaster-brake BMX-style bikes, a type suited to short hops around the neighborhood. For children about age seven and up, you can also choose a kids' mountain bike, which has multiple speeds, hand brakes, and other features more suitable for going-somewhere riding.

What's new

New bike features include full-suspension frames on mountain bikes; exotic, lightweight frame-designs; wheels with three or four spokes for better aero-dynamics; and road bikes with triple cranksets for easier pedaling.

The vast majority of all bicycles sold now are mountain bikes and mountain bikes have given rise to the "hybrid," a bike designed for both on- and off-road riding, and to the "cruiser," a retro-50s style bike with single speed, cushiony seat, and wide tires.

Mountain bikes have also influenced kids' bikes, giving rise to a kids' version that sports multi-speed gearing, flat handlebars, wide tires with aggressive tread, and front and rear cantilever brakes.

Shopping strategy

Bicycle models and components change every year, but the basics of a good bike remain the same. The previous year's model may prove a good buy, with no compromise in performance or features.

Decide on the type of bike. The choices include mountain, with straight handlebars and fat, knobby tires; road, with down-turned handlebars and skinny tires; a hybrid, a combination of the two; or a strictly short-ride cruiser.

Decide on the key features. Concentrate on the frame and wheels; the dealer can easily change many other bike parts free or for a small service charge plus the difference in the prices of the components. See "Key features," below.

Adult bicycles that are safe and satisfying to ride cost at least $200 to $400, according to our tests. Spending more may translate into a lighter frame and higher-quality components, which make it easier to climb hills and ride long distances.

To find the right size, straddle the top tube with both feet flat on the floor. Allow three inches of clearance between the top tube and crotch for mountain bikes, two inches for hybrids, and one inch for road bikes. If a woman intends to ride more than just casually, we recommend a "men's" frame, which is sturdier than a step-through "women's" frame.

A specialty bike store that's close to home will be convenient for after-sales service, since a bike, like a car, needs regular tuneups and repairs. Better bike shops will fit the bike correctly to your size or will change a shifter or saddle, or make other initial adjustments to the bike. If the store allows, try before you buy. Ride over varying terrain, check the handling, and make sure that your posture and the saddle feel comfortable, and that the brakes respond evenly, without grabbing, as you increase pressure.

The easiest brands to find. In the moderate-price range, you can spend $200 to $400 on an adult's or kid's bicycle with a name like Schwinn, Trek, Diamondback, and Specialized, which are typically sold at specialty bike stores or chains. Huffy, Murray, and Roadmaster are lower-priced brands available at discount stores, warehouse clubs, and mass merchandisers like Wal-Mart, Kmart, and Toys 'R' Us. General sporting goods stores like Sports Authority and outdoor-equipment stores like REI also sell bikes.

Key features

Frame. The chassis determines a bike's fit and performance. Frames are made from a variety of materials: heavy steel on the cheapest bikes; lightweight aluminum, carbon fiber, or exotic metals like titanium or super-high-strength steel on the most expensive. Various grades of "chromoly," a steel alloy, are common on mid- to high-priced bikes. A heavier bike is less responsive, as is a bike whose frame flexes a lot. A low-priced steel mountain bike can weigh 30 pounds or more; a stiff, expensive carbon-fiber road bike can weigh less than 18 pounds.

Handlebars. Their size and shape influence riding efficiency and comfort. The bent-over posture required by the drop handlebars on road bikes and the low, flat handlebars of some performance-oriented mountain bikes reduces wind resistance and shocks from bumps and improves handling. That posture also lets muscles work efficiently. For casual rides on pavement, however, an upright posi-tion is likely to be more comfortable.

For off-road use, where you use your arms to navigate bumps and lumps, a flat handlebar is best. "Antler" handlebars on some mountain bikes and hybrids allow the most erect riding posture.

Gears. These let you pedal comfortably despite changes in road slope. With three sprocket wheels in front and six to eight in the rear, most mountain bikes and hybrids have 18 to 24 speeds. Off-road, we consider 18 the minimum needed. On pavement, 12 or 14 speeds may be enough. Road bikes usually have 12 to 16 speeds (two sprocket wheels in front, six to eight in the rear).

Shifters. Old-fashioned "friction" shifters were difficult to master until you developed a feel for them. "Indexed" shifters make changing gears far easier. There are at least three main types: a twist shift, which is a collar encircling each end of the handlebar; a lever underneath each end of the handlebar; and a thumb shifter, which is a lever above each end of the handlebar. Some above-the-bar levers offer a friction mode as well, in case the derailleurs are thrown out of alignment by a fall. Shifters for road bikes include frame-mounted levers and, for more expensive bikes, handlebar-mounted brake/shift levers.

Brakes. Road bikes typically use "caliper" brakes, which pinch the wheel from above. Most mountain and hybrid bikes have "cantilever" brakes mounted directly on the front wheel fork and the seat stay. According to our tests, both types can stop a bike quickly and controllably. If you ride in wet weather, avoid wheels with steel rims. In our wet-braking tests, they took much farther to stop than did bikes equipped with aluminum rims.

Tires. How the bike handles depends greatly on the tires, which can easily be changed to suit the terrain. For rough trails, a mountain bike's tires should have big, widely spaced knobs for traction. Such tires produce a sluggish, "buzzy" ride on pavement, though. Hybrid-bike tires have smaller and closer-spaced knobs and sometimes a ridge down the middle. That reduces off-road traction but improves rolling resistance on pavement. Road-bike tires, smooth or with a fine tread, are designed for low rolling resistance.

Saddle. Look for one that's comfortable. Saddles are easy to change—don't let a torturous one stop you from buying an otherwise good bike. Men's saddles are long and narrow; women's, short and wide.

Some manufacturers claim that seats filled with gel reduce shock and vibration. But in our tests with seats of all kinds, riders of both sexes found that the shape of the seat was the most important criterion for comfortable riding.

In-line skates

Good skates don't have to cost $300. You can find a good pair for half that.

Last CR report: *July 1996*
Price range: *$30 to $500*

In-line skates have been around in one form or another since the 1700s, but didn't begin replacing old-style roller skates until about 1980. The modern version has light plastic boots (for ankle support), polyurethane wheels (to absorb bumps), and dual bearings (for less friction). In 1986, a young company called Roller-blade broadened the sport's appeal: It gave away its product to roller-skate rental shops in Venice Beach, Calif. Joggers left their sneakers behind; bicyclists traded big wheels for small. Suddenly, in-line skating (by now, called blading) was more popular than tennis and nearly as popular as golf.

The types

Recreational/fitness. These skates typically strike a balance between maneuverability and stability. They have four wheels (sometimes three, on smaller skates) attached to a frame on a boot—

usually a hard-plastic shell over a cushioned liner. Price: $30 to $500.

Hockey. These skates are built to be quick and mobile and to withstand impact from sticks, pucks, and collisions. We tried two hockey skates and found that their short frame made them easy to turn, though less stable than recreational skates. And their cuffs didn't offer ankles much support.

Speed. These skates are all wheels: A short-cuffed boot sits on a long frame that supports five large wheels. They're stable and fast but don't support ankles well and are hard to turn quickly.

Aggressive. They look a lot like recreational skates—until you see them in action. Their smaller wheels and reinforced frame are designed for stair bashing (riding down steps), grinding (sliding down a rail), and doing an alley-oop (don't ask).

What's new

The standard heel brake tends to intimidate beginners because it takes balance and practice. The skater must lift the front wheels of one skate off the ground and press the heel to the pavement, an awkward position at first. Variations of the standard heel-stop include: The Oxygens' rear wheel slows as you press the heel. And Ultra-Wheels' variation is a cylinder brake. The two were no better or worse than a regular heel-stop.

Several new braking systems offer alternatives. They include:

Cuff-activated systems. These include Rollerblade's Active Brake Technology (ABT), California Pro's Ground Engaging Moveable System (GEM), and Bauer's Force Multiplier. This brake works as follows: Slide your braking foot forward, and the boot's cuff tilts back, applying the brake. It's easy, but the brake can drag during routine turns. You can raise the brake so it doesn't drag and use it like a standard heel brake.

Rear-wheel system. This brake, called the Dual Brake System, is used on several Roces skates. With it, you push down on the back of the braking boot and the two rear wheels contact brake shoes in the frame. Because you have to weight your heel just so, this brake isn't for beginners.

Toe-stop system. You stop by dragging the toe of the brake foot. The toe-stop got in the way of some routine maneuvers. And although it worked fine on a flat skating area, it was ineffective on steep hills.

Shopping strategy

You can get skates for as little as $30 or as much as $500, but our tests show that a good pair will cost at least $130 for an adult's pair and $65 for a kid's. Good fit is crucial, as are features like rated bearings and brakes that are easy to use.

Decide on the type of in-line skate. The most common type, which we tested, is called recreational/fitness, but other types include hockey, speed, and aggressive.

Decide on the key features. Your choice of bearings determines how freely and smoothly the wheels spin. Our tests showed that ABEC-rated bearings spin better than

non-rated ones. (ABEC is a designation from the American Bearing Manufacturer's Association.) Braking systems may vary from the standard heel brake that requires practice and balance to more beginner-friendly ones.

The easiest brands to find. Rollerblade is the big name in skates, followed by a low-end brand, Variflex. Other big sellers include Bauer, Ultra-Wheels, Roller Derby, and CCM. Sporting-goods stores and discount stores account for about 70 percent of skates sold. Other significant sources include department stores, speciality sports stores, and mail-order.

Key features

Liner. It's removable and made of padded nylon mesh. Make sure its insole, which may also be removable, is thick enough to cushion your foot from the hard bottom of the boot shell. Some insoles were too thin for comfort.

Shell. To many manufacturers, a change in skate size means only a change in the size of the liner—the outer shell of the boot may be the same for, say, sizes 8 and 9. Depending on the manufacturer, one shell may fit two to four full sizes. You'll get a more precise fit when the shell size changes with each skate size.

Cuff. If it's hinged, it lets you bend your knees adequately; if not, it may make maneuvering harder.

Boot. It consists of the shell and the liner. Boots should snugly cradle your instep, lower ankle, and heel. They shouldn't let your ankles wobble from side to side, but they should let you flex forward so you can keep your balance. Boots that don't let you flex backward are good for powerful turns but bad for turns that require finesse. Boots with buckles are easy to close, but laces give a better fit. The most convenient buckles retain their setting after you take off the skates.

Frame. The frame, attached to the bottom of the boot, is the chassis on which the wheels are mounted. A strong frame is especially important for stunt skating. Some frames let you "rocker" the wheels: Rather than have all four on the same level, you can make the middle two lower than the others. This position makes the skate less stable, but it makes turning easier.

Wheels. Large wheels roll faster, but small wheels are more stable and easier to maneuver. Wheels of 72 mm or less are best for beginners. Hubs are important for keeping bearings aligned; some cheap skates don't have them. Wheels vary in hardness, and many manufacturers make that a selling point by listing a "durometer" number—

two or three digits followed by "A." The higher the number, the harder the wheel. Hard wheels generally last longer than softer wheels and are faster on hard, smooth surfaces, but they don't damp vibration as well or grip as well on rough pavement. Most of the tested wheels are 78A or 82A, a medium hardness that works well on a variety of surfaces.

Bearings. Buy those with an ABEC rating. They let the wheels spin more freely and smoothly than nonrated bearings, and they last longer. Lower-quality bearings are only partly shielded against the elements so are more prone to damage.

Cameras & lenses

The better compacts can match the quality, but not the flexibility, of an SLR.

Last CR reports: *Compacts, December 1996; single-use, May 1996; SLRs, December 1993*
Price range: *$5 to $1200 or more*

Shopping strategy

If your interest in photography is casual, you'll probably be satisfied with an inexpensive compact camera or even a single-use camera. But if you have the time and interest to invest in photography as a hobby, consider a single-lens reflex (SLR) camera, which has interchangeable lenses and special accessories that can adapt to all photo situations.

One big advantage of compact 35mm cameras is that they're, well, compact. Picture quality varies, but most compact models deliver acceptable photos. Some even match the quality of an SLR. Zoom models can handle distant subjects and

wide-angle group shots. Medium-range zoom models offer a good compromise between flexibility in composing photos and size and weight.

Single-use cameras are good in a pinch, or for special capabilities, such as underwater or panoramic photography. In picture quality, they are comparable to simple low-end compact cameras.

A big advantage of an SLR is that what you see is exactly what the camera sees—the view is through the camera's lens. Our tests through the years have shown the optical quality of all the major brands of SLRs to be consistently high. Look for the features you want, then shop for price. These days, SLRs are generally sold without a lens, or are bundled with a zoom lens—a good, versatile choice.

Compacts and single-use cameras are by far the most popular types of camera. SLRs account for just 5 percent of sales, and the number of brands available is half what it was a decade ago. Manufacturers such as Canon, Minolta, Nikon, Olympus,

Pentax, and Yashica are among the leading makers of SLRs and high-end compacts. Kodak and Vivitar are the biggest-selling brands of inexpensive compact cameras.

Whichever camera you're interested in, hold it to your eye and check its viewfinder, controls, grip, and balance. Some camera stores rent cameras, an even better way to tell whether you'll be comfortable using it.

Before buying a camera, consider the weight of the camera and the lens—lugging extra ounces around your neck or in your camera bag quickly takes a toll.

If you like to shoot close-ups, find out how close the lens can focus. Some lenses let you come to within a foot; others make you stand well back.

Nearly all cameras these days run on batteries—either alkaline AA cells or expensive but long-lasting lithium cells. Battery life depends on the size and type and on the flash's range. In our tests, some batteries have been able to shoot five times as many pictures as others.

Prices. Few people pay list price for camera equipment. The discount you get depends mainly on local competition, but also on the customer service and convenience a store provides. For the best prices, especially on expensive gear, check mail-order ads in newspapers and photography magazines. Mail-order houses in large cities sometimes charge as little as half of the manufacturer's suggested retail price for some brands.

Selling tactics. Cutthroat competition, though, leads to some questionable selling tactics. The classic bait-and-switch: "We're all out of that, but we have something better." Don't accept substitutes. The "outfit" angle: An unusually low advertised price for a brand-name SLR camera might include a cheap, off-brand lens. The tie-in: You

can buy an item at its advertised price only if you buy something else—a camera case, say. Stripping: The store removes standard equipment and then sells it back to you. Ask the dealer whether the price includes all manufacturer-supplied accessories.

'Gray market' goods. These products are imported to this country outside the manufacturer's regular authorized distribution channel, so you may not get the manufacturer's U.S. warranty. An "international" warranty or a camera-store warranty may require you to send the camera abroad or to deal with the retailer for repairs. If a store says your sales slip is your warranty, the store, not the manufacturer, assumes responsibility for the warranty.

Shipping fees and returns. A mail-order company may try to offset a good deal with outrageous shipping fees. Ask about fees before ordering. Note that mail-order companies may impose a "restocking" fee of 5 to 15 percent for returned merchandise.

Extended warranties. Dealers may try to sell you an extended service contract. See page 10.

What's new

APS. A new, "smart" film and camera format, called APS, for Advanced Photo System, was introduced in 1996. This new system attempts to change everything about the film and processing part of photography. The format promises to make better quality pictures by recording data for the processor. To take advantage of it, though, you'll need a new camera to handle the slightly smaller film. (For more information, see the December 1996 issue of CONSUMER REPORTS.

Digital cameras. This new type of camera needs no film. Its images can be easily printed, modified, or E-mailed just about anywhere. Kodak's digital *DC20*, priced at about $300, connects with cables to Windows computers and Macintoshes so you can download the images to save them. It also comes with Pictureworks Technology's *PhotoEnhancer*, easy-to-use software that lets you retouch photos and print them.

The quality of the *DC20's* images is fine for most routine computer applications. But don't expect these photos, reproduced on a color printer, to come close to matching a conventional color print. For that, you'll need a much more expensive digital camera.

High-tech features. "Eye control focus," uses five small focusing frames in the viewfinder to let you focus the picture with your eye. The camera senses which frame you're looking at from the position of your eyeball, and automatically brings the portion of the scene in that frame into sharp focus. Another such feature, "predictive focus," determines when a subject is moving and automatically predicts the proper focus for the subject at the moment of exposure. So far, such features are found only on expensive SLRs, but they may eventually trickle down to mass-market models.

Compact camera types

Cameras with long-range zoom lens. Price: $180 to $500. A zoom range of around 35 to 115 mm or more offers a lot of flexibility in composition. Cameras with a zoom like this tend to be loaded with other features.

Cameras with medium-range zoom lens. Price: $140 to $200. These cameras also have autoexposure and autofocus. But, with a range of around 35 to 70 mm, they can't zoom in as tightly. Generally, the less powerful the telepho-

to end of the zoom, the more compact the camera.

Nonzoom cameras with autoexposure. Price: $50 to $165. A nonzoom lens is good enough for snapshots.

Basic and single-use cameras. Price: $5 to $50. They're for people who want to aim and shoot and who aren't fussy about results. A fixed-focus lens rules out intimate close-ups. It can keep objects beyond four feet or so reasonably sharp—adequate for travel scenes and group shots. Such cameras have no adjustment for exposure. Those without a flash restrict you to shooting outdoors in bright light.

SLR types

Auto-focus SLRs. Price: body only, $230 to more than $1200. Expect to add another $100 to $150 for a moderate-range zoom lens.

Manual-focus SLRs. These are still available in some brand lines. Price: body only, starting at less than $200 to more than $500. Manual lenses are priced similarly to autofocus ones, but the selection may be more limited.

SLRs with non-interchangeable lenses. These highly automated hybrids offer less creative control than an SLR but more versatility than a compact. This type, promoted mainly by Olympus, has an SLR viewfinder and a built-in zoom lens. The zoom range goes from about 28 to 35 mm at the wide angle end to 110 to 180 mm at the telephoto end.

Key features

Aside from the new APS cameras, traditional 35 mm compact cameras have built-in electronic flash and motorized film-handling. To load the film, you drop it in, pull out the leader, and close the camera. The camera automatically advances the film and rewinds it at the end of the roll.

Other features can greatly increase a camera's versatility and capability—but often at the cost of increased complexity and weight. Here are some of the more noteworthy ones.

Autofocus. Most compact-camera autofocus systems bounce an infrared beam off what's centered in the viewfinder to estimate distance. With some, you can temporarily center an off-center subject, hold the focus, and reframe with the subject off to the side. Models with "multi-beam" autofocus can handle slightly off-center subjects automatically. SLRs have more complex autofocus systems.

Automatic film-handling. Like compact cameras, most SLRs use a tiny motor to advance and rewind the film. Cameras with an auto-winder generally let you fire off two, three, even four shots per second. That's handy for following fast-paced action, but you can go through a roll of film in no time. Automatic DX-code readers set the film speed.

Backlighting compensation. Bright light behind a darker subject poses a tricky exposure problem. Some cameras can compensate to prevent underexposure.

Exposure controls. A built-in light sensor determines the proper exposure. Center-weighted metering monitors the entire frame but emphasizes the center. Spot metering reads only the light near the center of the frame. Multipattern metering divides the frame into several segments and selects an exposure setting based on an evaluation of the readings. Some SLR cameras allow you to choose from several modes. On most compact models, exposure is either automated or fixed. SLRs give more choices—typically four ways to control exposure: program, aperture priority, shutter priority, and manual. Program mode selects both the size of the lens opening (the aperture or f/stop) and shutter speed (how long the shutter remains open to expose the film to light). Aperture-priority mode lets you manipulate the f/stop while the camera automatically chooses the shutter speed. In shutter-priority mode, the opposite happens. Manual exposure mode is useful for special effects—when you want to silhouette the subject, say, or shoot a city skyline at night. Typically, an LED indicator in the viewfinder confirms when you've set a suitable f/stop/shutter-speed combination for a given lighting situation and film speed.

Flash. Flashes cover different distances, from only 4 or 5 feet to 20 feet or more. The smartest ones work with the zoom to broaden or narrow the beam according to what the camera is seeing. Some units turn themselves on when they're required; others merely signal you to do so. Ideally, a camera shouldn't let you shoot until the flash is charged, but some do. Flash on demand let's you fill in harsh shadows in bright, sunlit portraits.

The closer the flash is to the camera lens, the more prone it is to giving subjects looking directly at the camera "red-eye." Cameras, compacts and SLRs, typically have some provision for reducing red-eye, such as a light that comes on before the picture is taken to constrict the subject's pupils.

Built-in flashes are generally less powerful than separate flash units, available for any SLR. Add-on flash units range from small models with limited features that sell for about $50 to high-powered "potato mashers"—side-mounted, hand-held units popular among wedding photographers—that are loaded with features and sell for more than $400.

Focusing. Autofocusing isn't foolproof, especially in scenes with repetitive graphic patterns or low contrast or in very dim light. In some versions, a red beam shines on the subject to help the autofocus work in low light. Autofocus SLRs can also be focused manually, usually by judging when the image on the ground-glass screen looks sharpest.

Lenses. SLR lenses range from 180-degree-view fish-eyes to 1000mm telephotos, providing perspective and magnification possible with any compact.

About 85 percent of SLR buyers fit their camera body with a zoom lens, rather than the old standard 50mm lens. A moderate zoom—28 to 105mm—should cover most situations.

SLR zoom lenses have improved markedly in recent years, according to

our tests. Although image quality is still apt to drop off slightly at either extreme of the zoom range, imperfections aren't likely to be noticeable.

Most SLR bodies can accept either a lens of the same brand or one of an independent lens brand, such as Tamron, Sigma, or Vivitar. Independent brands sell for considerably less than the camera brand models. If you're considering such a lens, check whether it's fully compatible with your camera's exposure control program and buy it with the proper mount for your camera.

Panorama mode. It provides wide vistas by blocking off the top and bottom of the film's frame. A panoramic print is twice as wide as a conventional print.

Exercise equipment

Well-designed exercise equipment isn't cheap. Expect to pay at least several hundred dollars.

Last CR reports: *Home gyms, November 1993; treadmills, January 1996; exercise bikes, January 1996; stair climbers, May 1992; ski machines, September 1994; exercise riders, January 1996*
Ratings: *page 231*
Price: *$100 to $5000*

Shopping strategy

Decide on the type. Most exercise machines—from exercise bikes to rowing machines—are designed primarily to boost cardiovascular fitness. Home gyms aim to help you strengthen and tone specific muscles. To see what kind of machine you like best, try some out at a health club or a friend's house. And before you buy a piece of exercise equip-

ment, try it to make sure it fits your body.

The very cheapest equipment is neither durable nor very effective, as a rule. If you shop carefully—and if you're willing to spend several hundred dollars or more—you can find well-designed home exercise equipment that will give you a good workout. But don't expect home equipment to give you the kind of workout you get in a gym. Health-club machines are much more expensive and higher quality than home equipment. Treadmills and home gyms tend to be more expensive than other equipment. Prices are often lowest in the fall, during holiday sales.

The easiest brands to find. Companies that specialize in exercise equipment include: DP, Roadmaster (Vitamaster), Tunturi, and Proform. Life Fitness, Nordic Track, Precor, and Trotter make high-end home machines and health-club models. Bicycle companies such as Schwinn and Roadmaster make exercise bikes.

What's new

Exercise equipment goes in and out of vogue. Cross-country ski machines were hot when they were first introduced. Then stair-climbers. Now, treadmills—particularly ones that you can fold when not in use. Exercise riders like the Health Riders are being pushed hard in television infomercials. These machines are non-motorized affairs that look a bit like a cross between a stationary bike and a teeter-totter.

Home gym types

Gyms, widely sold through infomercials, range in price from $200 to $4500. Spending more generally buys a gym that's more durable and offers a wider selection of exercise levels. Some models even allow two people to work out simultaneously. Look for models that make switching from one exercise to another easy. Assembly can be difficult; consider paying the store to do the job.

No one system is inherently better than any other at toning or building muscles, but each has a distinctive feel that may or may not appeal to you. We've found that changing resistance is easiest on gyms with weight stacks, flexible rods, and elastic bands.

Here's how they work:

Weights. You lift a stack of heavy metal plates via a cable-and-pulley system. The more plates you engage with a pin, the higher the resistance—which remains essentially constant throughout the range of your motion.

Rubber bands. Thick rubber bands are attached at one end to the lever you push or pull and at the other end to the gym's frame. You vary resistance, which increases as the bands stretch, by using bands of different thickness or by using more or fewer bands.

Flexible rods. You pull a cable that's attached to one or more springy plastic rods mounted to the gym's frame. As with bands, you vary resistance by the number and thickness of rods. Resistance increases as the rods bend.

Shock absorbers. Hydraulic or pneumatic cylinders that look and work like a car's shock absorbers resist your pushing or pulling. Changing the point at which the shocks are attached to the lever you push and pull changes the resistance.

Centrifugal brakes. Brake shoes mounted on a spring-loaded pulley in a case lined with friction pads generate friction when you move a lever connected to the pulley. You can increase the amount of resistance by pulling harder on the lever and by rerouting the cable that connects the lever to the pulley.

Key features for gyms

Padding. A gym with plenty of padding keeps hard plastic and metal parts from hurting you while you exercise.

Resistance settings. A wide range of resistance settings keeps you from outgrowing the gym.

Treadmill types

Treadmills can cost as little as $100 or as much as $7000 to $10,000.

The best value is a mid-priced, motorized model—one that costs $500 to $1500. Low-priced machines can be dreary to use and unsuitable for anything much faster than a brisk walk. Very expensive treadmills feel sturdy and allow you to set your own programs to vary speed or incline. They also tend to be of better quality.

Motorized. These keep you moving along steadily at a pace you select. On some models, you can program in "hills" or a series of sprints and walks. Most models have a tethered key that brings the belt to a rapid halt if it's yanked out, a safety feature in case you slip or fall. (Removing the key prevents tampering by children.) Even though most machines accelerate the belt slowly from a standing start, you should straddle the belt when you turn on the treadmill to avoid being thrown off when the belt starts to move.

The motor in some treadmills draws so much current that you may not be able to plug anything else into the same electrical circuit. Those motors may boast a lot of horsepower, but we found manufacturers' horsepower ratings to be a poor predictor of performance in our tests. Price: $300 to $2200.

Nonmotorized. The belt is driven by the user's walking motion. With no motor, these machines are less expensive. They force you to walk with an unnatural gait, however. To gain the leverage you need to move the belt, you're forced always to walk on an incline and to push off against the hand rails. Things get more awkward as you increase the incline. A jog is almost impossible because of the small size of the belt and this position. Price: $100 to $600.

Some models of both types are dual-action: As you walk along, you can push and pull pivoting handlebars to get something of a full-body workout.

Key features for treadmills

Walking surface. Generally, the larger the belt, the more freedom of movement. Make sure the treadmill has a belt long enough and wide enough to accommodate a full stride of the largest user.

Speed controls. A variable speed accommodates slow or brisk walking or running. Maximum speeds ranged from 6 mph to 12 mph in our tests. Look for push-button controls for adjusting speed.

Incline adjustment. This allows the user to increase the grade of the walking

Exercise riders

The exercise machine that's dominating television infomercials lately is the exercise rider, a non motorized affair that looks a bit like a hybrid of a stationary bike and a teeter-totter. Priced between $150 and $550, riders promise to give you a "total body workout" as you push and pull your way to toned muscles and a fitter heart.

We tested six riders: ExerHealth's HealthRider, $544 (including shipping and handling, by mail-order) and the aeROBICRider, a lower-cost version of the HealthRider, $299; Weslo's CardioGlide, $199; and CardioGlide Plus, $249 (also sold by Sears as the Lifestyler Cardiofit and Cardiofit Plus). Of the six, only the CardioGlide, A CR Best Buy at $199, will provide a good workout for most people. Note that this model was also the hardest to assemble; some stores will do the assembling for a fee.

surface for a more difficult workout. Motorized adjustments are much more convenient than manual ones.

Monitor. The most useful displays to have are time, speed, and distance. Look for easy-to-reach controls and large easy-to-see displays.

Folding models. These save space by folding into an upright position for storage. The mid-priced model we looked at was a real space-saver. While we judged it adequately sturdy for walking or running (on par with the good quality nonfolding models in our January 1996 report), the handrails and monitor swayed quite a bit during use.

Handrails. Partial handrails are a worthwhile safety feature for those who need them. And on dual-action models, they allow you to exercise your upper body while you walk. They're likely to get in the way of jogging, however.

Exercise-bike types

Some bikes cost less than $200 and some more than $1500. Differences, according to our tests, lie not so much in basic performance as in features, particularly the programs of roller-coaster "hills" that add variety to a workout.

Dual-action upright bikes. Most dual-action bikes are inexpensive. They are supposed to provide a whole-body workout; as you pedal, you pump the handlebars, which move back and forth automatically (and usually rather jerkily) with each turn of the pedals. On many of these bikes, pedaling turns a fan (enclosed in a wire cage or plastic cover for safety); the faster you pedal or pump, the more air resistance—and the more noise—the fan produces. On many dual-action models, pedaling faster or slower is the only way to vary the intensity of the workout—a major drawback. All dual-action bikes allow you to use only the handlebars, and some, only the pedals.

Regular upright bikes. These usually use the least floor space of all exercise bikes. They look and feel like regular bikes—except you stay in one place and turn a heavy flywheel. On most, you can adjust for a light warm-up to a heavy workout. To work harder, you increase drag on the flywheel, either by tightening a strap or brake pads to boost friction, or by stepping up magnetic resistance. Some models let you replace the seat with a regular bike saddle.

Recumbent bikes. Here, the seat is like a sports car's low bucket seat; you sit in it rather than perch on it, and your legs extend forward to the pedals. For many people, including those who are overweight or have a back problem, the recumbent position may be more comfortable than pedaling upright. Seats are usually well cushioned. You adjust the level of your workout by changing the resistance offered by a fan or a flywheel that uses magnetic or friction resistance. Recumbents generally require more floor space than do the other types.

Key features for bikes

Exercise-intensity adjustment. Regular upright bikes and recumbents have a control to make the pedals easier or harder to turn. Some models have electronic programs that automatically vary resistance during the workout—a useful but costly feature.

Seat. The height of the seat is usually adjustable; one that's continuously adjustable is best. A seat tilt adjustment is helpful, although most bikes don't offer it. Make sure it's comfortably shaped.

Monitor. Most bikes have an easy-to-use monitor that electronically displays distance, time, and calories expended.

Information is displayed all at the same time or in a sequence.

Toe straps. They give your legs power on the upstroke.

Stair-climber types

These machines range in price from $200 to $2500. Less expensive models typically have steps that are linked—as one step goes down, the other goes up. The steps on more expensive models move independently. Independent steps are harder to use than dependent ones, but they give you a better workout and allow a more natural movement. Some high-end models let you use either mode. Dual-action steppers exercise the arms and legs. "Ladder" models are dual-action machines that mimic climbing a ladder.

Key features for climbers

Programs. On some machines, electronic programming changes resistance automatically at preset intervals. Also helpful is an indexed resistance knob you can adjust while exercising.

Monitor. Some high-end machines come with heart-rate monitors. Some measure your aerobic capacity: You step for a few minutes and take your pulse, then punch in the reading, your age, weight, and sex, and the machine tells you how fit you are.

Ski-machine types

Ski machines come in two types: dependent and independent leg-motion. Price: $200 to $2000.

Dependent leg-motion. The foot platforms are linked—when the right leg slides forward, the left leg slides backward and vice versa. That keeps a beginner's legs from sliding too far, but it forces the user into a stiff shuffle. Friction pads or straps in some stair climbers provide resistance but don't mimic the feel of snow; most other designs provide no leg resistance.

Independent leg-motion. This design, which uses unlinked skis or foot platforms, is difficult to master initially. But once you learn the technique, this type of machine can give you a more vigorous workout than a dependent model. It also allows you to use a more natural leg motion, more akin to actual cross-country skiing.

Typically, independent models are more expensive than those with dependent leg-motion.

Key features for ski machines

Incline. A machine with a variable incline increases the workout for the muscles in the front of the leg.

Monitor. It may show one function—distance, say, or time or speed—or scan through the displays. A readout of your heart rate helps you maintain an effective level of exertion.

Indexed resistance settings. These settings let you repeat the difficulty level from one workout to the next; they also lets you increasing difficulty gradually. That's especially helpful if others are using the machine exercise at a different level.

Storage. Most ski machines fold up compactly for storage in a closet. Wheels make them relatively easy to move about.

Medical test kits

Many home test kits are compact, smart, and quick. But our tests of the kits turned up several that are unreliable.

Last CR report: *October 1996*
Ratings: *pages 223 to 227*
Price range: *$5 to $160*

Home medical tests of all kinds have become simple and quick; many provide results in minutes. Many involve just a single step, such as holding a stick in the urine stream to test for pregnancy or ovulation. Some, like blood-pressure monitors, are so highly automated that they seem to act of their own volition.

Many of the tests can save you money. A positive result may send you to a doctor, but the test itself usually costs less than a professional lab test—less than $15 for a home pregnancy test versus $35 to $45 for a lab test.

There's a public-health benefit as well: Home tests may be used by people who wouldn't otherwise get themselves tested. For example, a recent Government survey found that only 20 percent of people at increased risk for HIV infection planned to be tested by a health professional within a year, but 42 percent said they were likely to use a home test kit.

The four most common types of home medical tests are blood-pressure monitors, blood-glucose meters, ovulation detectors, and pregnancy detectors. We evaluated the test kits for accuracy, consistency, and convenience. We found good, reliable products in each category—but we also found some that are best avoided.

Many drugstores and mass merchandisers prominently display medical kits.

Some mail-order businesses, such as The Sharper Image and Fingerhut, stock electronic blood-pressure monitors.

Pregnancy tests

Today's pregnancy test kits have been greatly simplified and are quite easy to use. They work by detecting the presence of human chorionic gonadotropin (hCG), a hormone that builds up quickly in early pregnancy, doubling every two to three days. All the test kits we looked at proved to be sensitive enough to detect a hormone level likely to be present in urine by the first day of a missed menstrual period.

Although the kits say you can test any time of the day, the first morning urine sample has the highest concentration of hCG. Pregnancy kits should be read as soon as possible after the stated waiting period. Allowing as little as 10 to 20 additional minutes to pass can make a negative result turn positive.

The types. One basic type has an absorbent tip or a small well. A woman holds it briefly in her urine stream, then waits five minutes or less for an answer.

A second design also claims to be one-step, though it requires first collecting urine in a cup. Depending on the model, several drops are then placed in the well of a plastic testing device, or the device is immersed in the cup of urine. Testing time for both types is about the same. Price range for both types: $8 to $13.

Regardless of type, most kits indicate pregnancy with the appearance of a line in the test window; others display symbols. Some are easier to interpret than others; the design of the Answer positive indicator is especially clear. Less user-friendly are kits with a faint indicator line against a background of the same color.

Buying advice. A pregnancy test that's highly sensitive to hCG and easy to interpret will be the best choice for most women. Three of the tested products deserve first consideration: Answer, Clearblue Easy One-step, and e.p.t.

Less sensitive kits, such as Conceive One-step and Confirm One-Step, may be a better choice for women who have recently given birth, miscarried, or used fertility drugs (Pregnyl or Profasi).

Most brands offer kits with one and two tests. The double package is usually only a few dollars more than the single kit, a good deal if you think you'll need to test more than once.

Ovulation tests

Ovulation prediction kits promise to detect a hormonal change that occurs a day or two before ovulation—the interval when intercourse is most likely to result in pregnancy.

They work by looking for the spike in the level of luteinizing hormone (LH) that occurs in the middle of a woman's menstrual cycle. The LH surge, which can last for just hours or for as long as two days, triggers the ovary to release a mature egg for its journey into the Fallopian tube, where fertilization can occur. Identifying the start of the surge requires testing urine samples for several days in mid-cycle.

The devices indicate the presence of LH with a colored line, dot, or test area whose intensity has to be compared against a reference.

The types. Some test kits require mixing chemicals and carefully timing steps. Others are simpler, requiring just one or two easy steps.

All of the models in our test contained either five or six ovulation tests, enough for women whose cycles vary three days or less. Women with longer or very irregular cycles may want to use kits with nine tests or buy two five-test kits. Price: $20 to $45.

Buying advice. Women vary widely in how much LH they produce at the time of the surge, so it's important to pick a product that's as sensitive as possible. The most sensitive kits were Clearplan Easy One-step and Ovukit Self-Test—they should work reliably for about 85 percent of women.

If a woman doesn't get a positive result using these tests, it may be that she didn't ovulate that month or that her LH surge was too low to be detected by a home ovulation test. In such cases, daily sonograms and occasional blood tests may be required to plot her ovulation cycle. Another possibility is that her LH surge is short—less than 10 hours—and she's missing it with a single daily test. If ovulation is indeed occurring, two tests per day may catch the surge.

Blood-pressure monitors

A blood-pressure monitor measures two levels of pressure: the increased force exerted on your arteries when your heart contracts, known as systolic pressure; and the lesser force as your heart rests between beats, the diastolic pressure. The reading is given as systolic over diastolic pressure—for example, 120/80.

The types. Mechanical models resemble the blood-pressure monitors used by health professionals, with an arm cuff, a squeeze bulb for inflation, a stethoscope, and a mechanical gauge.

This type is the least expensive, and it can be quite accurate—if it's properly used. But therein lies the drawback: You must don the cuff, pump it up, and listen carefully to the artery as you turn a valve to slowly deflate the cuff while keeping an eye on the gauge's needle. As bloodflow starts to resume, you'll hear a hollow thumping sound through the stethoscope. The first of these sounds marks the systolic pressure. As the cuff continues to deflate, the thumping increases, then suddenly decreases. At this point, disatolic pressure is measured. The procedure for this kind of monitor takes practice. It also demands good eyesight and hearing and the dexterity to do things with one hand. Price: $20 to $25.

Taking your pressure with an electronic monitor can be as easy as wrapping your arm or wrist with an inflatable cuff—or slipping your finger into one—and pressing a button. In most electronic units the machine does the rest, providing the result within minutes in a clear, digital display. (A few models make you inflate the cuff manually by squeezing a rubber bulb, which can be difficult for a person with weak hands.)

But while all electronic monitors are easier than mechanical ones to use, they cost a lot more—$40 to $160. The lowest-priced electronic monitors (about $40) require you to pump up the cuff, but deflation is automatic. More expensive models ($50 to $200) inflate and deflate the cuff automatically.

Electronic monitors are usually quick, easy, and intuitive to use. Those with an arm cuff are harder to use; the cuff must be placed on the upper arm so that it lies over the brachial artery, located on the "pinky" side of the crook of the elbow. Several models have a tab or diagram on the cuff to aid in proper placement. By comparison, models with wrist cuffs are typically stiffer and shaped to fit the wrist, making them easy to slip on properly.

Several self-inflating electronic monitors have a switch that lets you choose an inflation level, which should be about 30 mmHg (millimeters of mercury) above your usual systolic pressure. This feature is helpful and worked well in the models we tested. Other models try to sense the inflation pressure needed. All self-inflating monitors are smart enough to reinflate to a higher pressure if the first level seems too low.

Buying advice. Mechanical monitors offer the best value if you're comfortable using them. If correctly used, they generally proved more accurate in our tests than electronic models. With practice, most people with good eyesight and hearing and the dexterity to do things with one hand should have little trouble using them.

Generally, models with an arm cuff were the most accurate of the electronic monitors. They also tended to score higher in consistency, a measure of how closely successive readings agree. Overall, wrist-cuff models earned lower but respectable scores. They'd be a good choice if you have difficulty adjusting an arm cuff.

We judged the two finger-cuff models tested Not Acceptable. They were significantly worse in accuracy and consistency, most likely because the finger is farther from the heart than the arm or wrist, allowing more factors to interfere with an accurate reading.

Blood-glucose meters

New models are smaller, faster, and easier to use than the devices introduced in the early 1980s. Most meters now are about the size and heft of a pack of cards, and give a readout in less than a minute. Based on the results, a person with diabetes can quickly adjust insulin, exercise, or diet to keep blood glucose within acceptable levels. Typically blood glucose is checked four times a day—before meals and bedtime.

Blood-glucose meters typically come with a small supply of blood-glucose test strips, disposable lancets and a lancing device, a check strip to be sure the meter is working properly, and a control solution to check that the meter and test strips are working together as a system. A carrying case and a log to record results are also included.

Each meter requires essentially the same steps: pricking a finger with the lancet and depositing a drop of blood on the test strip, which the meter reads to determine the blood-glucose level.

The types. While the steps are the same, designs differences affect convenience. Some meters require more blood than others or make it hard to place the blood correctly on the strip. Kits in which blood is placed on the portion of the strip that is outside the meter don't require regular cleaning, a distinct advantage. Much less convenient is an older type that requires careful timing and wiping blood from the strip with a cotton ball, extra steps that take longer and can introduce error.

Another variable is memory. Some contain enough memory for several hundred test results. The fanciest models link each result with a time, date, and code that specifies a relevant event, such as a meal, exercise, or illness. A few meters also average the data. None of these features is necessary to gain good control over diabetes—recording the information in a logbook will work as well. But a memory feature can be helpful in identifying patterns, especially for someone who doesn't jot down test results.

Several models with memory contain a data port that allows the meter to be hooked up to a computer so that stored glucose readings can be graphed and analyzed at home. If your doctor has such a data management system, be sure the meter you're considering is compatible. If your physician doesn't have a system, check with local pharmacies. Some will download your data and provide reports to your doctor at no cost.

Meters range in price from $50 to $100. But if you shop carefully, you can get one at a fraction of the list price or even free, since the major manufacturers offer large rebates and trade-ins on older or competitive models.

Buying advice. All meters in our test provided results that were accurate enough to be used with confidence by most people with diabetes. And all the meters also scored acceptably well in consistency. The simplest meters display your glucose level and store the last reading.

How to use the Buying Guide

■ Read the article for general guidance about types, features, and how to buy. There you'll find a discussion of the choices you'll face in the marketplace, what's new, and key buying advice.
■ The Ratings graph the overall score so you can quickly understand the big picture in performance. Details on features or performance are also noted. For many products, we also have information on how reliable a brand is likely to be. See page 11.
■ To find our last full report on a subject, refer to the article or the Ratings for the listing, or check the eight-year index, page 342.

Ratings *Pregnancy kits*
& Recommendations

The tests behind the Ratings

Sensitivity is a measure of how well a test kit could detect low levels of pregnancy hormone. **Type of test** refers to whether urine is placed on the test stick in-stream or is collected in a cup and then tested, a process we refer to as "two-step." **Model availability:** D means model is discontinued. **Price** is an average, based on national surveys, rounded to the nearest dollar.

Standard features for these models

• Can detect pregnancy on the first day of a missed period. • Take 2 to 5 minutes. • Control line or window shows if test is valid.

Recommendations

The three top-rated tests—Answer, Clearblue Easy One-step, and Advance—were highly sensitive and easy to interpret. (Advance is supposed to be discontinued December 1996.) Less sensitive kits like Conceive 1-Step or Confirm 1-Step may be preferable for women who have recently given birth, miscarried, or used certain fertility drugs (their urine may contain low levels of HCG, which can cause false positives with the more sensitive products).

See report, page 219. Last time rated in Consumer Reports: October 1996.

Overall Ratings *Listed in order of overall score*

E ⊖ VG ⊖ G ○ F ◐ P ●

Brand and model	Price/kit 1-TEST	Price/kit 2-TEST	Overall score	Sensitivity	Ease of interpretation	Type of test
Answer [1]	$9	—		⊖	⊖	Two-step
Clearblue Easy One-step	13	$18		⊖	⊖	In-stream
Advance D	11	15		⊖	⊖	In-stream
e.p.t.	13	18		⊖	⊖	In-stream
Conceive 1-Step	9	12		○	⊖	Two-step
Confirm 1-Step	9	14		○	⊖	In-stream
Fact Plus [2] D	13	18		⊖	○	Two-step
Walgreens Pregnancy Test Stick	8	—		○	○	In-stream
Precise One-Step	11	15		○	○	Two-step
Be Sure Plus Pregnancy Test Stick	9	—		○	◐	In-stream

[1] Not the same as Answer Quick and Simple, which was not tested. [2] Not the same as Fact Plus 1-Step, which was not tested.

Ratings *Ovulation tests*
& Recommendations

The tests behind the Ratings

Lab tests were done to determine **sensitivity**, a measure of how well a kit could detect low levels of luteinizing hormone, which surges prior to ovulation. Volunteers scored the kits for **ease of use**, and noted the **testing time**, how long it took to get a reading. **Type of test** refers to whether urine is placed on the test stick in-stream; collected in a cup and added to a test cassette (a two-step process); or mixed with chemicals in a multi-step process. **Cost/test** is the price divided by the **number of tests** in a kit. **Price** is the national average, rounded to the nearest dollar, based on a price survey.

Standard features for these models

• Provide a chart to indicate when to start testing. • Except for Ovukit Self-Test, have a control line or spot to indicate the test is valid.

Recommendations

Only one model—the top-rated Clearplan Easy One-step (27)—delivered excellent sensitivity and ease of use. Ovukit Self-Test, which was also highly sensitive, came in a distant second because it was more difficult to use.

See report, page 220. Last time rated in Consumer Reports: October 1996.

Overall Ratings *Listed in order of overall score*

E ⊖ VG ⊖ G ○ F ◐ P ●

Brand and model	Price	No. of tests	Cost/ test	Overall score 0 100					Sensi- tivity	Ease of use	Type of test	Test time
				P	F	G	VG	E				
Clearplan Easy One-step	$27	5	$5.40						⊖	⊖	In-stream	6 min.
Ovukit Self-Test	42	6	7.00						⊖	◐	Multi-step	74 [1]
OvuQuick Self-Test	45	6	7.50						⊖	○	Multi-step	9 [2]
OvuQuick One-Step	35	6	5.83						○	⊖	Two-step	39
Conceive 1-Step	20	5	4.00						●	⊖	Two-step	59

[1] Preparation of a control stick requires an hour before first use.

[2] Preparation of solution requires 10 min. before first use.

Ratings *Blood-glucose meters*
& Recommendations

The tests behind the Ratings

Six panelists with diabetes used each of the meters for a week to evaluate **convenience**, which included how easy it was to place blood on the test strip, to operate the device, and to understand the meter's messages. Lab tests were done to determine **consistency**, which reflects how well a meter agrees with itself over several readings of the same sample, and **accuracy**, how closely a meter reading corresponds to professional lab results. **Price** is the national average rounded to the nearest dollar, based on a price survey, but does not include rebates.

Standard features for these models

• Offer satisfactory toll-free technical support. • Provide error messages to warn of improper test conditions.

Recommendations

Unless you need very precise readings, such as during pregnancy, any of the tested meters will do. Choose one with high marks in convenience. Further narrow the choice by shopping for price: Ask the store and your doctor about special purchase offers or call the manufacturer about rebates (see Manufacturers' phone numbers, page 339).

See report, page 221. Last time rated in Consumer Reports: October 1996.

Overall Ratings *Listed in order of overall score*

E ⊖   VG ⊖   G ○   F ◔   P ●

Brand and model	Price	Overall score 0 — 100 (P F G VG E)	Ease of use	Consistency	Accuracy
Glucometer Elite	$ 90	▬▬▬▬▬▬	⊖	⊖	⊖
Lifescan One Touch Profile	100/	▬▬▬▬▬	⊖	⊖	○
Accu-Chek Advantage	54	▬▬▬▬▬	⊖	○	○
Lifescan One Touch Basic	50	▬▬▬▬▬	⊖	⊖	○
Accu-Chek Easy	78	▬▬▬▬	⊖	○	⊖
MediSense Precision Q.I.D.	70	▬▬▬▬	⊖	○	○
Glucometer Encore	52	▬▬▬▬	○	○	⊖
Accu-Chek III	89	▬▬▬	◔	⊖	⊖

Ratings continued ▶

Model details *Listed in order of overall score*

NOTES ON THE DETAILS: How test strips are packaged, either in bulk vials or individually wrapped in foil; the cost per strip, based on a package of 100 strips and derived from a national price survey; the minimum analysis time, as claimed by the manufacturer; which models have especially wide or narrow temperature ranges; and the power source.

Glucometer Elite $90

• Individually wrapped strips. • 72¢/strip (50-strip pkg.). • 60 sec. • Replaceable batteries.
Excellent consistency and very good accuracy. Very easy to master and to get a reading. Model tested stores the last result. Manufacturer says model now stores last 10 results. The strip draws in just the right amount of blood. No cleaning required. Operates over a wide range of temperatures: 50° to 104° F. But: Strip is small and can be hard to insert into the meter unless you use the foil package as a handling aid. Lancing device judged less desirable than most. **Recommendation:** An excellent meter.

Lifescan One Touch Profile $100

• Bulk vial. • 58¢/strip. • 45 sec. • Replaceable batteries.
Excellent consistency and good accuracy. Can store 250 readings and can link the time and date, insulin type and dose, carbohydrates consumed, and 15 events to each test result. Provides a 30-day average of test results and a 14-day average of readings linked to specific events. Contains data port for computer. But: Features may make it more complicated to use. Must be cleaned regularly. **Recommendation:** An excellent choice if you want lots of features.

Accu-Chek Advantage $54

• Bulk vial. • 61¢/strip. • 40 sec. • Replaceable batteries.
Accuracy and consistency are good. Stores the results, time, and date of 100 tests. Contains a data port for computer. Easy to learn to use, and doesn't require frequent cleaning. But: Operates only between 64° and 90°F. **Recommendation:** Very good overall; excellent convenience.

Lifescan One Touch Basic $50

• Bulk vial. • 58¢/strip. • 45 sec. • Replaceable batteries.

Excellent consistency and good accuracy. A no-frills meter that's easy to learn to use. Stores the last reading. But: Must be cleaned regularly. **Recommendation:** A very good, basic meter.

Accu-Chek Easy $78

• Bulk vial. • 55¢/strip. • 15-60 sec.
• Replaceable batteries.
Excellent accuracy and good consistency. Memory stores 350 test results, and can link the time, date, and one of 14 event codes to each reading. Displays average, minimum, and maximum test results for the previous week. But: Requires regular cleaning and is harder to clean than other meters. Operates only between 64° and 90°. **Recommendation:** A very good meter with many features.

MediSense Precision Q.I.D. $70

• Individually wrapped strips. • 50¢/strip.
• 20 sec. • Replaceable batteries.
Accuracy and consistency are good, although we found lot-to-lot differences in the consistency of test strips. Stores last 10 readings. Doesn't require cleaning. But: Operates only between 64° and 86°. **Recommendation:** Very good overall, and fast.

Glucometer Encore $52

• Individually wrapped strips. • 70¢/strip (50-strip pkg.). • 30 sec. • Non-replaceable battery.
Excellent accuracy, consistency is good, although we found lot-to-lot test strip differences. Stores 10 most recent tests and averages results. But: Placing blood correctly is harder than with others. Meter must be cleaned regularly. Operates only between 63° and 86°. Lancing device judged less desirable than most. **Recommendation:** Consider it primarily if you need a high degree of accuracy.

Accu-Chek III $89

• Bulk vial. • 65¢/strip. • 120 sec. • Replaceable battery.
Excellent accuracy and consistency. Stores 20 test values with date and time. Contains data port for computer. But: It's difficult and takes longer to use. **Recommendation:** There are better choices.

Ratings
& Recommendations

Electronic blood-pressure monitors

The tests behind the Ratings

A registered nurse tested two samples of each model on 41 staffers, with and without high blood pressure, over the course of 14 weeks. At the same time, he took readings with a medical-quality blood-pressure monitor to determine each model's accuracy and its consistency, the ability to provide consistent measurements from reading to reading. **Accuracy** and **consistency** were calculated for both **systolic (S)** pressure, the force exerted when the heart pumps, and **diastolic (D)** pressure, the lower pressure between beats, which is medically more important. Models similar to those we tested are noted in Details. **Price** is the approximate retail price. **Model availability:** Ⓓ means model is discontinued.

Standard features for these models

• Have very clear liquid-crystal digital display, ⁵⁄₁₆ to ¼ inch high. • Have automatic power shutoff. • Have low-battery indicator. • Provide error messages. • Measure pulse rate to within 2 beats per minute. • Allow rapid deflation of cuff. • Weigh approximately one pound or less.

Recommendations

The AND UA-767, $80, delivered top-notch accuracy and consistency. Its only fault was that it's somewhat noisy. The Omron HEM-711, $90, had excellent accuracy and very good consistency. Two monitors were judged CR Best Buys: the AND UA-702, ($45), a manual inflation unit, was very good, though basic, and the Omron HEM-712C ($60), a fully automatic model. Wrist models, which were less accurate than the better arm models, had two noteworthy units: Omrons HEM-605 and HEM-601, both about $100. Mechanical models are also worth considering. The five top-rated models from our report in 1992 are still on the market, and are relatively inexpensive: the Omron HEM-18, $20; Lumiscope 100-021, $20; Walgreens 2001, $20; Marshall 104, $25; Sunmark 100, $25. With practice, they give accurate and consistent readings, although they require coordination and good hearing. The finger models were judged Not Acceptable (see report, page 220).

See report, page 220. Last time rated in Consumer Reports: October 1996.

Ratings continued ▶

Overall Ratings *Within types, listed by overall score*

Legend: E ⊖ VG ⊖ G ○ F ◑ P ●

Brand and model	Price	Self-inflating	Overall score (0–100)	Accuracy S/D	Consistency S/D	Ease of use	Instructions
ARM MODELS							
AND UA-767	$80	✓		⊖/⊖	⊖/⊖	⊖	⊖
Omron HEM-711	90	✓		⊖/⊖	⊖/⊖	⊖	⊖
AND UA-702, A CR BEST BUY	45	—		⊖/⊖	⊖/⊖	○	⊖
Omron HEM-712C, A CR BEST BUY	60	✓		⊖/⊖	⊖/⊖	⊖	⊖
Lumiscope 1085M	90	✓		⊖/⊖	⊖/○	⊖	○
Sunbeam 7652	65	✓		⊖/⊖	⊖/○	⊖	⊖
Walgreens 91 ⒹⒹ	65	✓		○/⊖	⊖/○	⊖	⊖
Omron HEM-412C	40	—		○/⊖	⊖/○	○	⊖
Lumiscope 1065	50	—		○/○	⊖/◑	○	○
Sunmark 144	54	—		◑/○	○/○	○	○
Sunbeam 7622	40	—		○/◑	○/◑	○	⊖
WRIST MODELS							
Omron HEM-605	110	✓		○/⊖	⊖/○	⊖	⊖
Omron HEM-601	100	✓		○/○	○/○	⊖	⊖
Lumiscope 1090	110	✓		○/○	○/○	⊖	⊖
AND UB-325	125	✓		○/◑	○/○	⊖	⊖
FINGER MODELS							
NOT ACCEPTABLE: The following models gave inaccurate and inconsistent readings.							
Omron HEM-806F	160	✓		◑/○	◑/●	⊖	⊖
AND UB-211	110	✓		●/◑	●/●	⊖	○

Model details *Within types, listed in order of overall score*

NOTES ON THE DETAILS: Power source and inflation method are indicated.

Arm models

AND UA-767 $80
• 4 AA batteries. • Self-inflating.
Top-notch in accuracy and consistency. Easy to use, with a large display and clear, large-print instruction booklet. A switch lets you preset the inflation level, and you can adjust the rate of deflation. A different cuff size can be ordered for an additional charge. But: It's noisier than most, and lacks a storage case. **Recommendation:** Excellent, if somewhat noisy.

Omron HEM-711 $90
• 4 AA batteries. • Self-inflating.
Excellent accuracy and very good consistency. Cuff has a marker to help you place it properly on

your arm. Different cuff sizes are available at additional cost. Has an AC adapter jack; adapter must be bought separately from the company. But: It has no storage case. **Recommendation**: Very good overall but pricey.

AND UA-702 $45

• 4 AA batteries. • Manual inflation.
Excellent accuracy and very good consistency. Instruction booklet is thorough and has large print. Rate of cuff deflation can be adjusted. Different cuff sizes are available at additional cost. But: It lacks a storage case. **Recommendation**: Very good. Though basic, it has the essentials—accuracy, consistency, and good value. **A CR Best Buy.**

Omron HEM-712C $60

• 4 AA batteries. • Self-inflating.
Excellent accuracy and very good consistency. Has memory recall of the last pressure reading. Has switch for preset inflation levels; for higher levels, press the Start button until it reaches the pressure you want. A tab on the cuff helps with proper placement on your arm. Different cuff sizes are available at additional cost. Equipped with an AC adapter jack; adapter must be purchased separately from the company. But: Lacks a storage case. **Similar**: Sunmark 175, Marshall 92. **Recommendation**: Very good; fully automatic, high marks on performance, and a reasonable price tag. **A CR Best Buy.**

Lumiscope 1085M $90

• 4 AA batteries. • Self-inflating.
Excellent accuracy and good consistency. The display is the largest of all tested models. You can preset the inflation level electronically by pressing a button. Provides reading of last pressure taken. Comes with storage pouch. **Recommendation**: A very good performer, but pricey.

Sunbeam 7652 $65

• 4 AA batteries. • Self-inflating.
Accuracy is very good; consistency is good. Displays the last pressure reading. Inflation level can be preset electronically. Comes with a hard, protective case. But: Rigid material at the edges of the cuff may pinch skin. Some samples had a slow deflation rate, which can cause discomfort. **Recommendation**: Performs well, but may cause some discomfort.

Walgreens 91 Ⓓ $65

• 4 AA batteries. • Self-inflating.
Very good accuracy and good consistency. A tab on the cuff helps you place it properly on your arm. Different cuff sizes are available at additional cost. Equipped with an AC adapter jack; adapter must be purchased from the company. But: Lacks a storage case. **Recommendation**: Monitor works well.

Omron HEM-412C $40

• 4 AA batteries. • Manual inflation.
Very good accuracy and good consistency. A tab on the arm cuff helps with proper placement. Different cuff sizes available at additional cost. But: Lacks a storage case. **Similar**: Marshall 82. **Recommendation**: Works well, but lacks the convenience of self-inflating cuff.

Lumiscope 1065 $50

• 9-volt battery. • Manual inflation.
Accuracy is good and consistency is fairly good. Memory holds last pressure reading. But: Lacks a storage case. Warranty: One year for materials, workmanship, and accuracy. **Recommendation**: Lacks the quality and convenience of other monitors. There are better choices.

Sunmark 144 $54

• 9-volt battery, included. • Manual inflation.
Accuracy is good and consistency is fair. A tab on the arm cuff helps with proper placement. Different cuff sizes can be purchased. Monitor kit comes with a digital thermometer. But: Lacks a storage case. **Recommendation**: There are better choices.

Sunbeam 7622 $40

• 4 AA batteries. • Manual inflation.
Accuracy and consistency are fair. Memory provides last pressure reading. Comes with a hard, protective case. But: Rigid material at edges of cuff may pinch skin. Some samples had a slow deflation rate, which can cause discomfort. **Recommendation**: There are better choices.

Ratings continued ▶

Model details *Continued*

Wrist models

Omron HEM-605 $110

• 2 AAA batteries, included. • Self-inflating.
Very good accuracy and good consistency. Easy
to use. It's uniquely lightweight and compact:
Processor sits atop the cuff like a large wristwatch. Comes with hard, protective case. **Recommendation**: Very good, the best of the wrist-cuff
models.

Omron HEM-601 $100

• 4 AA batteries, included. • Self-inflating.
Very good accuracy and good consistency. Easy
to use and read, with a large, clear display. Has
switch to select preset inflation level; pressing
Start button lets you choose a higher pressure.
Comes with a hard, protective case for cuff and
tubing. **Similar**: Sunmark 161. **Recommendation**:
Performs well; easy to use.

Lumiscope 1090 $110

• 4 AA batteries. • Self-inflating.
Fair accuracy and fair consistency. Diagram on
wrist cuff helps with proper placement. Easy-to-
follow instructions are printed on the lid of the
monitor housing. Memory can store 28 blood
pressure and pulse readings for one person, or 14
readings for two; time and date are also recorded.
Comes with inflatable pad to help position wrist at
heart level. A protective shell encases the monitor. **Recommendation**: Acceptable performance

and lots of features, but there are better wrist
monitors.

AND UB-325 $125

• 4 AA batteries. • Self-inflating.
Accuracy and consistency are fair. Diagram on
wrist cuff helps with proper placement. Booklet
instructions are in large print; instructions are also
provided on the lid of the monitor housing. Memory can store time, date, and 28 pressure and
pulse readings, or 14 readings for two people.
Provides inflatable arm rest to position wrist at
heart level. A protective shell encases the monitor.
Recommendation: Offers many features and acceptable performance, but there are better monitors.

Finger models

Omron HEM-806F $160

• 2 AA batteries, included. • Self-inflating.
Performance was never better than fair, and
sometimes worse. Often gave wrong measurement without providing an error message.
Recommendation: Not Acceptable. Did not give
reliable results.

AND UB-211 $110

• 2 AA batteries. • Self-inflating.
Accuracy and consistency are poor. Monitor often
gave wrong reading without providing an error
message. **Recommendation**: Not Acceptable. Did
not give reliable results.

How to use the Buying Guide

■ Read the article for general guidance about types, features, and
how to buy. There you'll find a discussion of the choices you'll
face in the marketplace, what's new, and key buying advice.

■ The Ratings graph the overall score so you can quickly understand the big picture in performance. Details on features or
performance are also noted. For many products, we also have information on how reliable a brand is likely to be. See page 11.

■ To find our last full report on a subject, refer to the article or the
Ratings for the listing, or check the eight-year index, page 342.

Ratings *Exercise bikes*
& Recommendations

The tests behind the Ratings

Overall score is based mainly on the range of exercise levels, ergonomics, and ease of use. **Ergonomics** reflects how well each model lets users of various sizes exercise effectively. **Rigidity** is how sturdy the bike feels during exercise. **Adjustment** of **exercise intensity** reflects how easy it is to change resistance; a dash means intensity can be varied only by changing pedaling speed. **Price** is the approximate retail. **Model availability:** Ⓓ means model is discontinued. Ⓢ means model is replaced, according to the manufacturer; successor model is noted in Details. New model was not tested; it may or may not perform similarly. Features may vary.

Standard features for these models

• A challenging workout, even for fit users. • Resistance that's adjustable during exercise. • Adjustable seat height, but no seat-tilt. • Poorly shaped saddle on an upright bike, well-cushioned bucket seat on a recumbent bike. • An easy-to-use, easy-to-read monitor that electronically displays distance, time, and calories, and that shows displays simultaneously or automatically scans displays in sequence. • Toe straps to give you power on the upstroke (but no toe straps on dual-action models). • Wheels for easy transport.

Recommendations

Within types, the bikes we tested differ mostly in price and features—most notably the programs of roller-coaster "hills." If you have the floor space, consider the Tunturi F505, $325, a recumbent bike that's a successor to the F510, A CR Best Buy. The F510 performed similarly to the top-rated Tunturi F570, $650, which has programs. Among upright bikes, consider the Bodyguard 955, $350, which performs very similarly to the discontinued Tunturi Executive Ergometer TEE-S, our first choice. The Schwinn Airdyne, $500, offered the best combination of price, and sturdiness of any of the dual-action bikes.

See report, page 217. Last time rated in Consumer Reports: January 1996.

Ratings continued ▶

Overall Ratings

Legend: E ⊖ VG ⊖ G ○ F ⊖ P ●

Within type, listed primarily in order of ergonomics

Brand & model (length x width)	Price	Overall score (0–100)	Ergonomics	Rigidity	Intensity	Adjustment EXERCISE	Adjustment SEAT HEIGHT
RECUMBENT MODELS							
Tunturi Motivational Recumbent F570 (75x30 in.)	$650		○	⊖	⊖	⊖	⊖
Tunturi Recumbent F510 [S], **A CR BEST BUY** (71x32 in.)	400		○	⊖	⊖	⊖	⊖
Precor 855e (71x24 in.)	900		⊖	⊖	○	⊖	●
Schwinn Professional 230 (60x24 in.)	965		○	⊖	○	⊖	●
Ross Aerocumbent Pro 977 (82x23 in.)	945		○	⊖	○	○	●
Schwinn Personal Trainer 205 (71x25 in.)	350		○	○	○	○	○
Precor 817e (66x24 in.)	400		⊖	⊖	⊖	○	●
UPRIGHT, SINGLE-ACTION MODELS							
Precor M8.2E/L (41x23 in.) [D]	1130		○	○	○	⊖	⊖
Lifecycle 3500 (40x25 in.) [D]	695		○	⊖	⊖	○	○
Tunturi Motivational Electronic F460 (39x24 in.)	900		○	○	⊖	⊖	○
Tunturi Executive Ergometer TEE-S [D] (39x19 in.)	220		○	⊖	⊖	⊖	⊖
Bodyguard 955 (38x18 in.)	350		○	⊖	⊖	⊖	⊖
UPRIGHT, DUAL-ACTION MODELS							
Schwinn Airdyne (48x24 in.)	500		○	⊖	●	—	○
Ross Futura 950 (50x24 in.)	630		○	⊖	●	—	○
DP Prime Fit 14-5300 (51x25 in.)	180		●	●	●	—	○
DP Airgometer Sprint 14-5400 [D] (52x25 in.)	170		●	●	○	—	⊖
DP Airgometer Silent Rider 14-5390 [D] (53x25 in.)	145		●	●	○	—	⊖
Vitamaster Whisper Air 9906 [D] (51x27 in.)	185		●	○	○	—	●
Vitamaster Air Maximum 9848 [D] (47x26 in.)	140		●	○	●	—	●

Model details *Within types, listed in order of overall score*

Recumbent models

Tunturi Motivational Recumbent F570 $650

Pluses: Has programs that automatically vary exercise level. Seat position continuously adjustable. Easy to mount and dismount. **Minuses:** Seat is tilted down. Monitor vulnerable to damage because of its position. Seat position may aggravate a knee injury, or strain knee during heavy exercise. One sample had unbalanced flywheel. **Comment:** Operates on house current.

Tunturi Recumbent F510, A CR BEST BUY ⓢ $400

Pluses: Seat position continuously adjustable. Easy to mount and dismount. **Minuses:** Resistance levels not indexed. Seat is tilted down. Monitor vulnerable to damage because of its position. Seat position may aggravate a knee injury, or strain knee during heavy exercise. **Successor:** F505, $325.

Precor 855e $900

Pluses: Has programs that automatically vary exercise level. Seat position continuously adjustable. Easy to mount and dismount. **Minuses:** Seat adjustment jams. Toe straps not suited to men's feet larger than size 9½. Can pinch user's fingers. **Comment:** Operates on house current.

Schwinn Professional 230 $965

Pluses: Has programs that automatically vary exercise level. Seat position continuously adjustable. Has base levelers. Good pinch protection. **Minuses:** Poor seat shape. Not suited to short users. Seat causes user to slouch. Toe straps not suited to men's feet larger than size 9½. **Comment:** Must be assembled by dealer. Operates on house current.

Ross Aerocumbent Pro 977 $945

Pluses: Has programs that automatically vary exercise level, and user can design own programs. Seat position continuously adjustable. Easy to mount and dismount. Very stable. **Minuses:** Unfit users have to pedal slowly. Monitor harder to use than others. Seat adjustment jams. Toe straps

not suited to men's feet larger than size 9½. Monitor hard to reach. Seat position may aggravate a knee injury, or strain knee during heavy exercise. No exercise manual. **Comment:** Operates on house current.

Schwinn Personal Trainer 205 $350

Pluses: Seat position continuously adjustable. Easy to mount and dismount. Very stable. **Minuses:** Resistance levels not indexed. Poor seat shape. Toe straps not suited to men's feet larger than size 9½. Monitor hard to reach. Seat position may aggravate a knee injury, or strain knee during heavy exercise. **Comment:** Must be assembled by dealer.

Precor 817e $400

Pluses: Seat position continuously adjustable. Easy to mount and dismount. Easy to assemble. **Minuses:** Resistance levels not indexed. Monitor harder to use than others. Seat adjustment jams. Toe straps not suited to men's feet larger than size 9½. Monitor hard to reach.

Upright, single-action models

Precor M8.2E/L $1130

Pluses: Optional chest strap for pulse. Has programs that automatically vary exercise level, and user can design own programs. Good seat shape. Good pinch protection. Easy to assemble. **Minuses:** Seat is tilted down. Seat position may aggravate a knee injury, or strain knee during heavy exercise. **Comment:** Operates on house current.

Lifecycle 3500 $695

Pluses: Optional chest strap for pulse. Has programs that automatically vary exercise level. Stores max. target pulse. Interactive video game extra-cost option. Good pinch protection. Can be set to maintain selected heart rate. **Minuses:** Poor seat cushioning. Seat is tilted up. Toe straps not suited to men's feet larger than size 9½. Has base levelers. **Comment:** Operates on house current.

Tunturi Motivational Electronic F460 $900

Pluses: Has programs that automatically vary exercise level. Good seat shape. Seat tilt can be

Ratings continued ▶

adjusted. Good pinch protection. **Minuses:** Handlebars don't clamp securely. Poor seat cushioning. Seat position may aggravate a knee injury, or strain knee during heavy exercise. **Comment:** Operates on house current.

Tunturi Executive Ergometer TEE-S ☐ $220

Pluses: Easy to assemble. Seat position continuously adjustable. Good seat shape. **Minuses:** Poor seat cushioning. Seat is tilted down. Toe straps come loose. Monitor hard to reach. **Comment:** Analog displays.

Bodyguard 955 $350

Pluses: Good seat shape. Seat tilt can be adjusted. Seat can be replaced with standard bicycle saddle. **Minuses:** Handlebars don't clamp securely. Poor seat cushioning. Toe straps not suited to men's feet larger than size 9½. **Comment:** Analog displays.

Upright, dual-action models

Schwinn Airdyne $500

Pluses: Has footrests for exercising arms only. Seat tilt can be adjusted. Seat can be replaced with standard bicycle saddle. Fan cools user. Has base levelers. **Minuses:** Poor seat cushioning. Not suited to short users. Doesn't coast; pedals (and handlebars) move when fan or flywheel is turning. **Comment:** Must be assembled by dealer.

Ross Futura 950 $630

Pluses: Has footrests for exercising arms only. Seat tilt can be adjusted. Seat can be replaced with standard bicycle saddle. Has base levelers. Has toe straps. **Minuses:** Handlebars move jerkily. Not suited to short users. Toe straps not suited to men's feet larger than size 9½. Doesn't coast; handlebars move when fan is turning. Inertia makes handlebars hard to stop.

DP Prime Fit 14-5300 $180

Pluses: Converts to single-action. Has footrests for exercising arms only. **Minuses:** Seat is tilted

up. Not suited to short users. Seat-adjustment increments too large. Can pinch user's feet. Doesn't coast; pedals (and handlebars) move when fan is turning. Seat position may aggravate a knee injury, or strain knee during heavy exercise.

DP Airgometer Sprint 14-5400 $170

Pluses: Converts to single-action. Has footrests for exercising arms only. **Minuses:** Handlebars move jerkily. Seat is tilted up. Not suited to short users. Seat-adjustment increments too large. Can pinch user's feet. Sharp edges. Doesn't coast; pedals (and handlebars) move when fan is turning. Seat position may aggravate a knee injury, or strain knee during heavy exercise.

DP Airgometer Silent Rider 14-5390 $145

Pluses: Has footrests for exercising arms only. Stores max./min. target pulses. **Minuses:** Handlebars move jerkily. Seat is tilted up. Not suited to short users. Seat-adjustment increments too large. Can pinch user's feet. Doesn't coast; pedals (and handlebars) move when fan is turning. Seat position may aggravate a knee injury, or strain knee during heavy exercise.

Vitamaster Whisper Air 9906 $185

Pluses: Converts to single-action. Has footrests for exercising arms only. **Minuses:** Handlebars move jerkily. Seat is tilted up. Not suited to users taller than about 5'7". Seat-adjustment increments too large. Doesn't coast; pedals (and handlebars) move when fan is turning. Seat position may aggravate a knee injury, or strain knee during heavy exercise.

Vitamaster Air Maximum 9848 $140

Pluses: Converts to single-action. Has footrests for exercising arms only. **Minuses:** Handlebars move jerkily. Seat is tilted up. Not suited to users taller than about 5'7". Seat-adjustment increments too large. Sharp edges. Doesn't coast; pedals (and handlebars) move when fan is turning. No wheels for transport.

Ratings *Kids' bikes*
& Recommendations

The tests behind the Ratings
Overall score for the small bikes is based primarily on durability, bearing quality, and fit range. For the larger bikes, scores are based primarily on durability, handling, and braking performance, with shifting also considered for mountain bikes. **Handling** (large BMX-style bikes) is how easily the bikes could be maneuvered through a slalom course and how stable they felt in wide, high-speed turns. **Bearings** measures smoothness of turning and ease of adjustment. **Fit range** is how wide a range of rider sizes the bike will fit, based mainly on its seat-height adjustment and frame height. **Price** is approximate retail. Models similar to the tested models are noted in Comments or Model details; features may vary. **Model availability:** Ⓢ means model is replaced, according to the manufacturer; successor model is noted in Comments. New model was not tested; it may or may not perform similarly. Feaures may vary.

Standard features for these models
BMX bikes: • A rear coaster brake. • Excellent durability. • Training wheels (not on 20-inch models). • Steel ball bearings. • Wide fore and aft adjustability of the handlebars. • A padded crossbar on the handlebars. • A fairly hard seat. • A padded top tube. **Mountain bikes:** • 20-inch wheels. • Excellent durability. • Very good handling. • Six gear speeds. • Cantilever-style hand brakes, front and rear. • Aluminum-alloy wheel rims. • Steel ball bearings. • Very smooth gear shifting. • Flat-style handlebars. • Grip shift. • Handlebar adjustment that doesn't affect the front brake. • Brake levers that adjust to the child's hand size. • Rear derailleur guard.

Recommendations
Among mountain bikes, consider first two CR Best Buys at $130: the Pacific Jubilee (boys) and Wolverine (girls). If you're buying a girl's first two-wheeler, two 12-inch-wheel BMX models should meet your needs well: the Schwinn Tigress, $110, and the Magna Walla Koala, $55—the better buy of the two. Since the boys' 12-inch models are all poor for fit, the best strategy is probably to buy one of the better inexpensive models. In 16-inch models, the standout Trek Mountain Cubs, both $140, are worth buying if your budget allows. In 20-inch wheel models, consider the boy's Roadmaster Tech Racer 1330TRB, $80, and the girl's Roadmaster Mystic 1331TRB, $80, or the Huffy Double Take, $90.

See report, page 205. Last time rated in Consumer Reports: November 1996.

Ratings continued ▶

Overall Ratings

E ⊖	VG ⊖	G ○ F ◑ P ●

Within types, listed in order of overall score

Mountain bikes

Brand and model (Boys or Girls)	Price	Overall score 0 — 100 (P F G VG E)	Braking WET	DRY	Fit range	Comments
20-INCH WHEEL MODELS						
Specialized Hardrock (G)	$210		⊖	⊖	⊖	27 lbs. Antler handlebar.
Trek Mountain Lion 60 (G&B)	220		⊖	⊖	⊖	27¼ lbs. **Minuses:** No water-bottle fittings. Other: Antler handlebar.
Specialized Hardrock (B)	210		⊖	⊖	⊖	26¾ lbs.
Pacific Jubilee (G) Ⓢ, **A CR BEST BUY**	140		⊖	⊖	⊖	28 lbs. Thumb shift. Seatpost quick-release, fittings for luggage rack. **Minuses:** Rear wheel may lift off ground in hard stops. Brake levers not adjustable for hand size. **Other:** Water bottle and handlebar-mounted bag. Onyx has grip shift, upgraded derailleur. **Successor:** Onyx, $140.
Pacific Wolverine (B), **A CR BEST BUY**	140		⊖	⊖	⊖	30 lbs. Thumb shift. Seatpost quick-release, fittings for luggage rack. **Minuses:** Rear wheel may lift off ground in hard stops. **Other:** Water bottle and seat-mounted bag. Tiger shark has grip shift, upgraded derailleur. **Similar:** Tiger Shark, $140.
GT Little Timber (G)	190		⊖	⊖	⊖	27 lbs. **Minuses:** Handlebar adjustments affect front brake operation. No derailleur guard.
Schwinn Thrasher 2.0 (B, G)	200		⊖	⊖	⊖	27 lbs. (B), 27¼ LBS. (G). **Minuses:** Shifts a bit less smoothly than others.
GT Outbound (B)	190		⊖	⊖	○	27¾ lbs. **Minuses:** Rear wheel may lift off ground in hard stops. Handlebar adjustments affect front brake operation. No derailleur guard.

Small BMX-style bikes

Brand and model (Boys or Girls)	Price	Overall score 0 — 100 (P F G VG E)	Bearings	Fit range	Comments
12-INCH WHEEL MODELS					
Schwinn Tigress (G)	$110		○	⊖	18½ lbs. Padded handlebar stem.
Schwinn Tiger (B)	110		○	●	18¾ lbs. Padded handlebar stem.
Magna Walla Koala (G)	55		◑	○	17l lbs. **Minuses:** Handlebar not adjustable. Top tube not padded.
Ross Bitsy Lady (G)	100		◑	⊖	17¼ lbs. Padded handlebar stem.
Ross Pronto (B)	100		◑	●	18 lbs. Padded handlebar stem.

Small BMX-style bikes *(cont'd)*

Brand and model (Boys or Girls)	Price	Overall score 0–100 (P F G VG E)	Bearings	Fit range	Comments
Magna Mud Shark 8521-03 (B)	$55		⊖	●	17 lbs. **Minuses:** Handlebar not adjustable.
Kent Rock On (G)	50		●	●	16 lbs. Padded handlebar stem. **Minuses:** Handlebar not adjustable.
Kent Micro Force (B)	50		●	●	16 lbs. Padded handlebar stem. **Minuses:** Handlebar not adjustable.
Roadmaster Joy Ride 7357 (G)	60		●	●	17¾ lbs. **Minuses:** No top-tube padding. Training wheels prone to falling off. Similar: 7253KMC, $60.
Roadmaster Racing Pro 7202WMB (B)	60		●	●	17½ lbs. Minuses: No top-tube padding. Training wheels prone to falling off. Similar: 7302KMC, $60.
16-INCH WHEEL MODELS					
Trek Mountain Cub (G)	140		○	⊖	24½ lbs. Seat tilts, is softer than most, can be easily replaced. Padded handlebar stem.
Trek Mountain Cub (B)	140		○	⊖	24¼ lbs. Seat tilts, is softer than most, can be easily replaced. Padded handlebar stem.
Murray Fancy Free (G)	55		⊖	●	21¼ lbs. **Minuses:** No top-tube padding. **Similar:** Girl Power 7-6961
Murray Comp 1 (B)	55		⊖	●	21½ lbs. **Minuses:** No top-tube padding. **Similar:** Team 7-6960, $55.
Huffy Blue Racer (B)	65		●	●	19½ lbs. Padded handlebar stem. **Minuses:** Jittery handling. Handlebar not adjustable.

Large BMX-style bikes

Brand and model (Boys or Girls)	Price	Overall score 0–100 (P F G VG E)	Braking DRY	Braking WET	Handling	Bearings	Fit range
18-INCH WHEEL MODELS							
Kent New Image (G)	$70		●	○	○	⊖	⊖
Kent Fire Power (B)	70		●	○	○	⊖	●
20-INCH WHEEL MODELS							
Roadmaster Tech Racer 1330TRB (B)	80		●	○	○	⊖	⊖
Roadmaster Mystic 1331TRB (G)	80		●	⊖	○	⊖	○
Huffy Double Take (G)	90		●	○	○	⊖	⊖
Magna Mud Shark 8531-65 (B)	65		●	○	⊖	⊖	●
Huffy Caliber 2000 (B)	90		●	○	○	⊖	○
Ross Young Lady (G)	145		●	⊖	○	○	⊖
Ross Boomerang (B)	145		●	○	○	○	●

Ratings continued ▶

Overall Ratings *Continued*
••••••••••••••••••••••••••

			E	VG	G	F	P
			⊖	⊖	○	⊖	●

Large BMX-style bikes *(cont'd)*

Brand and model (Boys or Girls)	Price	Overall score	Braking		Handling	Bearings	Fit range
	0 100	P F G VG E	DRY	WET			
20-INCH WHEEL MODELS							
Murray Blackfoot (B)	$55	▬▬▬▬	●	○	⊖	⊖	●
Murray Girl Magic (G)	55	▬▬▬	●	⊖	⊖	⊖	●

Model details *Within types, listed in order of overall score*

18-inch wheel BMX-style models

Kent New Image $70

26 lbs. Seat softer than most. Accepts front and rear hand brakes. **Minuses**: Top tube not padded. **Other**: Water bottle, handlebar-mounted bag, training wheels. **Similar**: Rock On, $70.

Kent Fire Power $70

27 lbs. Seat safer than most. Rear hand brake. Accepts front hand brake. **Minuses**: Top tube not padded. **Other**: Water bottle, training wheels. **Similar**: F-14 Tomcat, $70.

20-inch wheel BMX-style models

Roadmaster Tech Racer 1330TRB $70

28¾ lbs. Accepts front and rear hand brake. Seat softer than most; adjusts fore/aft and for tilt. Padded handlebar stem. **Minuses**: No top tube padding. **Other**: Water bottle. **Similar**: 1430, $80.

Roadmaster Mystic 1331TRB $70

28¼ lbs. Accept front and rear hand brakes. Seat adjusts for tilt. Padded handlebar stem. **Minuses**: No top tube padding. **Other**: Water bottle. Handlebar bag.

Huffy Double Take $90

28 lbs. Rear hand brake. Seat softer than most, adjusts for tilt. **Minuses**: No top tube padding. Hand brake makes rear-wheel removal more difficult.

Magna Mud Shark 8531-65 $65

28 lbs. Rear hand brake. Seat softer than most.

Seat adjusts for tilt. **Minuses**: Hand brake makes rear-wheel removal more difficult. **Other**: Water bottle.

Huffy Caliber 2000 $90

29 lbs. Rear hand brake. Seat adjusts for tilt. **Minuses**: Hand brake makes rear-wheel removal more difficult. No top tube padding. **Other**: Water bottle.

Ross Young Lady $145

28½ lbs. Rear hand brake (not on Little Lady). Seat adjusts for tilt. Padded handlebar stem. Accepts front hand brake. **Minuses**: Fork damaged in low-speed crash test. Hand brake makes rear-wheel removal more difficult. **Similar**: Little Lady, $140.

Ross Boomerang $145

28½ lbs. Rear hand brake (not on Radical). Seat adjusts for tilt. Padded handlebar stem. Accepts front hand brake. **Minuses**: Fork damaged in low-speed crash test. Hand brake makes rear-wheel removal more difficult. **Similar**: Radical, $140.

Murray Blackfoot $55

26¼ lbs. Accepts rear hand brake. Seat adjusts for tilt. **Minuses**: No top tube padding. **Similar**: Team 7-5350, $55.

Murray Girl Magic $55

25¼ lbs. Accepts rear hand brake. **Minuses**: No top tube padding. **Similar**: Girl Power 7-5231, $55.

AUTOS

New cars

The 1996 autos and light trucks are mostly competent and sophisticated—and, ar-
guably, the safest ever. But several models
deserve special mention. Here are our
picks of the very best in five categories:

Best family sedan. For excellent family transportation at a moderate price,
you need look no further than the *Toyota
Camry*. In overall performance, it ranks
with cars costing thousands more. And it's
been exceptionally reliable for years.

Best inexpensive car. That has to be
the new *Honda Civic*, a far more polished
design than you'd expect for the price.
The *Civic* matches the very best small cars
in ride, seating comfort, and fuel economy.
And it, too, has been very reliable.

Best sport-utility vehicle. The *Ford*
Explorer outscores its competition mainly
because it's the least trucklike. Its interi-
or is roomy and versatile, and it offers
full-time selectable four-wheel drive as
an option.

Highest-mileage car. Among cars
with a gasoline engine, the 1996 *Toyota
Tercel* with a manual four-speed transmission recorded the best fuel economy
in our recent tests: about 39 mpg, overall.
If the highest possible mileage is your
ultimate goal, then the *Volkswagen Golf*
with the new direct-injection TDi diesel
engine is the car of choice. But diesels
aren't for everyone. They're noisy, idle
roughly, and are none too peppy.

Most fun to drive. If you enjoy driving a car that's small and nimble, with
quick and accurate steering, a responsive
and throaty engine, and a precise manual

shifter, you could fall in love with the two-seater *Mazda MX-5 Miata*. Some of our test-drivers thought the new *BMW 318ti* hatchback was also fun to drive.

Best regardless of price. The luxurious and meticulously finished *Mercedes-Benz E-Class*, now represented by the redesigned *E320*, wins out. It scored highest of any car in our tests—mainly because of its ability to balance several often-conflicting demands. It accelerated splendidly without using too much fuel. And it combined responsive handling with a quiet and composed ride. Its base price has been lowered to $43,500. But even so, with many fine cars available for half as much, few people will find the *E320* worth its high cost.

This year, we profile more vehicles than ever. In the world of cars, as in other arenas of commerce, "niche" marketing (selling based on specialized need) and "line extensions" (applying a brand name successful in one niche to new types of products) are the name of the game. And, as with other products, there's less diversity than the profusion of models might indicate. Many models have a "twin" or "cousin"—an essentially similar model or a somewhat similar model sold under another nameplate (the *Ford Taurus* and *Mercury Sable*, for example). Sometimes, models use another model's chassis or engine or share other key parts (the *Geo Prizm* and *Toyota Corolla*, for example, share most components).

As a quick reference, here's how nameplates are related: General Motors sells Buick, Cadillac, Chevrolet, Geo, GMC, Oldsmobile, Pontiac, and Saturn. Ford sells Lincoln and Mercury. Chrysler sells Dodge, Plymouth, Eagle, and Jeep. Toyota makes Lexus. Honda makes Acura. And Nissan makes Infiniti.

Profiles of the 1996 models start on page 242. Ratings of recently tested models start on page 255. For easy reference, we note in each profile the issue of CONSUMER REPORTS in which a full report appeared. For recently tested models, a report by fax is available (see right).

Used cars

As new-car prices go up, used-car sales also go up. Now that the average selling price of a new car is more than $20,000, used cars are looking more attractive to many prospective car owners.

Demand for used cars may be driving up their prices. Last year, according to our calculations, the average new car had depreciated 33 percent over three years. According to our price data this year, new cars have depreciated only 26 percent over three years. Models that are in great demand, such as sport-utility vehicles, depreciate the least.

A used car is more car than it used to be. Air bags, antilock brakes, and other desirable features have been available long enough to be common in used cars, too. And cars are becoming more reliable.

CONSUMER REPORTS readers can help you here. Their experiences recounting problems over the years, which we collect via our Annual Questionnaire, give us unique information on how troublesome various models are likely to be. On page 270, you'll find our list of reliable used cars, categorized by price. You'll also find a list of used cars to avoid—those likely to be particularly troublesome. We derived both lists from our Frequency-of-Repair data. Those records, for 224 models, start on page 275.

Shopping strategy

Decide new or used. New cars have an understandable appeal; but in some ways, a used car is a smarter buy. New cars can depreciate as much as 50 percent in value over their first 3 years. People looking to spend less than $10,000 can find many choices among our reliable used cars (see page 270), only a few basic models among new ones. Our guide to buying a used car, page 267, can help you avoid the major pitfalls of buying a previously owned vehicle.

Decide on how to buy. As new car prices move up and up, lease deals look more attractive. See "How to lease a new car," page 263. "How to buy a new car," page 261, can help you negotiate a good deal.

Decide on how to equip the car. New cars often come with a huge array of standard and optional features. Our "Key auto features," page 264, can help you choose what you need.

More on Autos From Consumer Reports

Cars: The Essential Guide on CD-ROM
This interactive CD-ROM covers new and used cars, minivans, pickups, and sport-utility vehicles from 1988 through 1997 in an easy-to-use database. It includes 30 minutes of interactive video for practicie negotiating with dealers, and for inspecting and buying a used car. You'll also find Ratings and buying advice on auto products and accessories. For more information, see page 356.

New Car Price Service
This service provides the latest price information for cars, minivans, sport-utility vehicles, and light trucks. Sticker prices and dealer-invoice costs for the vehicle and factory options show you how much room you have to negotiate, plus you get the latest information on rebates along with advice on getting the best price. To order, see page 357.

Used Car Price Service
With a touch-tone phone, you can get purchase and trade-in prices for cars, minivans, sport-utility vehicles, and light trucks, from 1988 to 1996 models. Prices for used 1996 models are available as of January 1997. Prices take into account the vehicle's age, mileage, major options, and condition, and the region you live in. A Trouble Index, based on Consumer Reports Frequency-of-Repair data, is available for many models. To order, see page 358.

Auto Insurance Price Service
This service provides a personalized report for your region and coverage needs that lets you compare prices and coverage of as many as 25 of the lowest-priced policies. It also includes Ratings scores and tips. To order, see page 359.

Profiles of the 1996 cars

Here, listed alphabetically by make and model, you'll find descriptions of nearly all the 1996 models of cars, minivans, sport-utility vehicles, and pickups. For most of these models, our comments are based on a recent test, if not of the '96 model itself, then of its very similar '95 or '94 predecessor (most models don't change significantly from year to year).

At the end of each entry, you'll find the date of the last full road test published in CONSUMER REPORTS. These detailed reports are available at libraries or by fax or mail from our Consumer Reports by Request 24-hour service. To use the service, note the four-digit fax number at the end of the model's entry and call 800 896 7788 from a touch-tone phone. The cost is $7.75 per report.

Predicted reliability is a judgment based on our Frequency-of-Repair data for past models (see page 275). If a vehi-

cle has been recently redesigned, only data for models relevant to the 1996 models are considered. **Depreciation** predicts how well a new model will keep its value, based on the difference between a model's original sticker price and its resale value over the past three years. The average depreciation for all cars was 26 percent. As a group, sport-utility vehicles had the best rate (17 percent). Minivans and sports/sporty cars also tend to hold their value. Large cars have a relatively high depreciation (38 percent, on average).

Throughout, ✔ indicates a model recommended by CONSUMER REPORTS; **NA** means data not available; **New** means there's no data because the car is new or has been redesigned.

⊖	⊖	○	◑	●
Much better than average				Much worse than average

Model	Predicted reliability	Depre-ciation	Comments
Acura CL	⊖	NA	The CL is a fairly upscale coupe based on the Honda Accord. Expect good handling and a refined, quiet ride. The "VTEC" Four and the V6 are both good engine choices. **Last report/fax: —/—**
✔ Acura Integra	⊖	⊖	This reliable but expensive little car accelerates well and handles nimbly. The cabin feels a little cramped and is a little noisy. **Last report/fax: November 94/9923**
✔ Acura RL	⊖	NA	**Last report/fax: November 96/9513**
Acura SLX	⊖	NA	A rebadged Isuzu Trooper that we rate Not Acceptable because of its tendency to roll over. It's big and boxy, and a handful to maneuver. It is well built, but has a bouncy ride with excessive body lean. **Last report/fax: October 96/9508**
✔ Acura TL	⊖	NA	Handles competently, with a firm yet supple ride. Good ergonomics and room for four, but not five. Nice but not outstanding all around. **Last report/fax: February 96/9456**
Audi A4	New	NA	A European sports sedan with quick, precise handling and a firm ride. The interior is well laid out but a little cramped, especially in the rear. **Last report/fax: February 96/9456**
Audi A6	NA	●	Audi claims to have fixed several shortcomings—including a mediocre ride and sluggish acceleration—that plagued this car's predecessor, the Audi 100. We haven't tested the A6 yet. **Last report/fax: August 92/7736**

Model	Predicted reliability	Depreciation	Comments
✔ BMW 3-Series	◓	○	Precise sports-car handling and tenacious tire grip make the driver feel fully in control. A firm but comfortable ride and good noise insulation give a sense of quality. **Last report/fax: August 94/9792**
BMW 318ti	New	NA	The 318Ti is the newest addition to BMW's 3-series cars. It is a hatchback coupe, similar to the regular 318 but shorter. Expect precise sports-car handling and tenacious tire grip, plus a firm but comfortable ride. **Last report/fax: —/—**
✔ BMW 5-Series	◓	◒	The new 5-Series offers pure, functional precision. It handles precisely and gives you a good feel of the road, making it a joy to drive. The ride is firm but quiet and comfortable. **Last report/fax: November 96/7732**
BMW 740i	NA	◒	A luxury V8 that competes with the world's finest and costliest cars. It delivers exceptional power, smoothness, quietness, and comfort, and comes loaded with accessory gadgets. **Last report/fax: —/—**
BMW Z3	New	NA	A sleek new roadster built in South Carolina. It's based on components from the 3-Series sedans. Unlike a Mazda Miata, it's big enough for six-footers. **Last report/fax: —/—**
Buick Century	○	○	Never an inspired design, the Century is dated and badly outclassed. It's big on the outside but cramped inside. Reliability is its one strong point. **Last report/fax: January 95/9981**
Buick Le Sabre	◓	◒	A large, softly-sprung freeway cruiser with slow, vague steering and so-so handling. Still, a quiet car with a smooth power train. **Last report/fax: January 96/9447**
Buick Park Avenue	○	●	This high-line freeway cruiser is a longer, more luxurious version of the Buick Le Sabre. It emphasizes a soft ride, and it comes with every imaginable electronic accessory. **Last report/fax: —/—**
✔ Buick Regal	○	◒	A mainstream sedan that delivers a comfortable, quiet ride on good roads, but rather sloppy handling. Moderate price and decent reliability are this car's main selling points. **Last report/fax: February 94/7771**
Buick Riviera	○	NA	This large, heavy coupe was completely redesigned for 1995. It accelerates well and comes fully equipped. Tall drivers need more head room, and short drivers must sit too close to the wheel. The controls and displays are awkward. **Last report/fax: July 95/9423**
Buick Roadmaster	◒	◒	An old-fashioned freeway cruiser with a big V8, full-frame construction, and rear-wheel drive. Handling is clumsy, but there's plenty of room inside. 1996 was its last model year. **Last report/fax: January 92/7307**
Buick Skylark	○	◒	This basically unimpressive car responds slowly to its steering, and the body leans sharply in turns. The V6 is a better choice than the Four. **Last report/fax: June 92/7704**
Cadillac De Ville	○	●	The De Ville is a big, plush, roomy land yacht. The upscale Concours version comes with GM's sophisticated aluminum V8 called the Northstar. **Last report/fax: —/—**
Cadillac Eldorado	●	●	A plush coupe with a powerful aluminum engine and smooth-shifting automatic transmission. This car is cumbersome to maneuver in sharp turns. The ride isn't as smooth as you'd expect in this type of car. **Last report/fax: July 93/9325**
Cadillac Fleetwood	●	●	This big, plush freeway cruiser delivers a soft, quiet ride. It can tow a heavy tailer with ease, thanks to its powerful V8 and its rear-wheel drive. 1996 was its last model year. **Last report/fax: —/—**
Cadillac Seville	●	●	A sophisticated aluminum V8 helps this luxury sedan accelerate very quickly. The ride is smooth except on poor roads. The rear seat is not very comfortable. **Last report/fax: November 93/7351**

Model	Predicted reliability	Depreciation	Comments
Chevrolet Astro	●	○	Though the Astro has an enormous cargo area, the design is dated. It can haul a lot of cargo or a trailer, but drawbacks include ponderous handling and an uncomfortable ride. All-wheel drive is available. Similar: GMC Safari. **Last report/fax: July 96/7766**
Chevrolet Beretta	○	◐	It's supposed to be a sporty version of the Chevy Corsica. The steering feels vague, and the ride is busy on all but the smoothest roads. Low seats make it hard to see over the hood. The back seat is cramped. **Last report/fax: June 92/7704**
Chevrolet Blazer	◐	⊖	The Blazer (and similar GMC Jimmy) are roomy and quiet. Still, they have mediocre brakes, a so-so ride, and a cramped rear seat. Full-time all-wheel-drive (without low range) is available on high-trim versions. **Last report/fax: August 95/9421**
Chevrolet C/K 1500	○	⊖	The Chevy (and similar GMC Sierra) offers a commanding view, a smooth powertrain, and a quiet cabin. The third (rear) door on extended-cab versions is a worthwhile option. But the handling is trucklike and the ride is stiff and boundy. **Last report/fax: September 96/9499**
Chevrolet Camaro	◐	○	One of the last of the rear-wheel-drive muscle cars. Seating is decent for two, but the driver can't see out well. The optional V8 is the engine of choice. **Last report/fax: October 93/7341**
Chevrolet Caprice	◐	◐	Best points are a smooth ride and, with the optional 5.7-liter V8, powerful drivetrain. The optional firmer suspension helps tame the wallowing in corners. 1996 was its last model year. **Last report/fax: March 94/9714**
✓Chevrolet Cavalier	◑	NA	Its 1995 redesign made the Cavalier a competitive, pleasant to drive economy car. Ergonomics are good and seating is comfortable for four. **Last report/fax: June 95/9416**
Chevrolet Corsica	○	◐	A humdrum econobox with vague steering and a busy ride. Low seats make it hard to see over the hood. The back seat is cramped as well. Superseded in late 1996 by the new Malibu. **Last report/fax: June 92/7704**
Chevrolet Corvette	●	◐	Sophisticated electronics blend with brute muscle-car force in this legendary sports car. The suspension is stiff, but the car feels bulky, and the body flexes too much on rough roads. **Last report/fax: September 92/7758**
✓Chevrolet Lumina	○	◐	The Lumina comes nicely equipped and performs competently but not outstandingly. The interior is well laid out and very quiet, but the seats are thinly padded and not so comfortable. **Last report/fax: January 95/9981**
Chevrolet Lumina van	●	○	Expect uninspired overall performance from this and GM's other front-drive minivans. Faults include numerous blind spots and mediocre ride and handling. A redesign called Venture is due for 1997. **Last report/fax: July 94/7789**
Chevrolet Monte Carlo	◐	NA	This coupe version of the Lumina sedan offers good ergonomics but an unimpressive combination of sloppy handling and boundy ride. The LS rides better than the sporty Z34 model. **Last report/fax: July 95/9423**
Chevrolet S-Series	●	⊖	The "S" pickup is a fairly new design, with a quiet cabin and good powertrain. Ride and handling are unexceptional. Reliability has been poor, and this truck didn't do well in Government crash tests. **Last report/fax: November 95/9434**
Chevrolet Suburban	○	⊖	This huge truck-based station wagon emphasizes utility. It can carry nine people and tow a heavy trailer. Poor reliability has dogged this vehicle. **Last report/fax: —/—**

Model	Predicted reliability	Depreciation	Comments
Chevrolet Tahoe	◒	⊖	The spacious Tahoe nestles between the elephantine Suburban and compact Blazer. The ride is quiet and not bad for a truck. It lends itself well to hauling and towing, but fuel economy is poor and the brakes mediocre. **Last report/fax: October 96/9508**
Chrysler Cirrus	●	NA	A roomy compact with spirited acceleration, the Cirrus handles well and has a taut, well-controlled ride, comfortable seating, and a nicely designed interior. **Last report/fax: March 95/9995**
✓ Chrysler Concorde	○	○	This large sedan handles as nimbly as a much smaller car, yet it seats five adults comfortably. Reliability has improved of late. **Last report/fax: March 93/7948**
Chrysler LHS	○	NA	A stretched version of the Chrysler Concorde, the LHS handles well and boasts a limousine-like rear seat. **Last report/fax: March 94/9714**
Chrysler Sebring	○	NA	This sporty coupe is based on the Mitsubishi Galant platform. The Sebring is similar to its Dodge Avenger cousin. Both are stylish but a little humdrum. **Last report/fax: July 95/9423**
Chrysler Sebring Convertible	New	NA	Despite the name, this car is closer to the Cirrus, a good, up-to-date mid-sized sedan, than to the Sebring coupe. Expect nicely laid-out controls and an interior that's roomy for a convertible. **Last report/fax: —/—**
Chrysler Town & Country	New		This is a loaded version of the Dodge Grand Caravan and Plymouth Grand Voyager. A well-designed package with good ride and handling and useful details. **Last report/fax: October 95/7766**
Dodge Avenger	○	NA	This sporty coupe performs adequately in most ways. It's fairly nimble and quick. We'd choose the 2.5-liter Mitsubishi V6 over the noisy Chrysler 2.0-liter Four. **Last report/fax: July 95/9423**
Dodge Caravan	New	○	The Dodge Caravan/Plymouth Voyager twins, redesigned for 1996, perform exceptionally well, overall. The second, left-side, sliding door is very handy. Reliability is unknown. **Last report/fax: July 96/7789**
Dodge Dakota	●	⊖	The Dakota has a roomy bed but a dated interior, ponderous handling, and a mediocre ride. A redesign is due for 1997. **Last report/fax: November 95/9434**
Dodge Grand Caravan	New	○	The Grand Caravan is a longer-bodied version of the Dodge Caravan. Overall, it's a well-designed package—comfortable, quiet, roomy, and nice to drive. **Last report/fax: October 95/9431**
Dodge Intrepid	◒	○	This large sedan handles as nimbly as a much smaller car, yet it seats five adults comfortably. Reliability problems cloud the fine overall performance. **Last report/fax: January 95/9981**
Dodge Neon	●	NA	This small car has a roomy interior and a fairly large though noisy engine. The ride is choppy. Handling is predictable and safe, but not exactly sporty. **Last report/fax: March & May 96/9471**
Dodge Ram	◒	○	All new in 1994 and refined since then, the Ram still won't let you forget you're driving a truck. Handling is ponderous but steady. Extended-cab versions lack a third (rear) door for the present. (The new Ford F-150 is far more up-to-date.) **Last report/fax: September 96/9499**
Dodge Stratus	●	NA	The Stratus is a roomy compact that handles fairly well; the ride is so-so. The V6 accelerates well, better than the Four, the controls and displays are first rate. The seats are a little lumpy but not uncomfortable. **Last report/fax: December 95/9443**
Eagle Summit	⊖	NA	This entry-level subcompact, now discontinued, rides uncomfortably and stops poorly. The optional antilock brakes are a must. The Summit's one saving grace was a zesty powertrain. **Last report/fax: August 93/7302**

Model	Predicted reliability	Depreciation	Comments
✓ Eagle Summit Wagon	⊖	○	Made by Mitsubishi, this cross between a small station wagon and an even smaller van delivers peppy acceleration, a quiet ride, and lots of cargo space. Handling is a little clumsy. **Last report/fax: September 93/7331**
Eagle Talon	●	○	The redesigned Talon comes from a joint venture of Chrysler and Mitsubishi. Turbocharging and all-wheel drive are available for extra performance and traction. **Last report/fax: —/—**
Eagle Vision	⊖	⊖	This large sedan handles as nimbly as a much smaller car, yet it seats five adults comfortably. Reliability problems cloud the fine overall performance. **Last report/fax: March 93/7771**
Ford Aerostar	○	○	An old-fashioned rear-wheel-drive minivan that hangs on because it remains a sound choice for heavy-duty work such as pulling a trailer. All-wheel-drive is available and preferred. **Last report/fax: September 92/7766**
Ford Aspire	NA	NA	This little commuter car is a chore to drive. Good fuel economy, head room, and luggage space don't make up for poor acceleration, handling, and ride. **Last report/fax: October 94/9921**
Ford Bronco	●	⊖	A big, utilitarian truck on frame, but with various levels of convenience appointments. It carries a long history of worse-than-average reliability. **Last report/fax: —/—**
✓ Ford Contour	○	NA	A good, solid family sedan. It handles nimbly and has roomy and comfortable front seats, but the rear is cramped and the four-cylinder engine is noisy. Choose the V6 if you can. **Last report/fax: August 96/9493**
✓ Ford Crown Victoria	○	⊖	An old-fashioned V8 freeway cruiser. It handles decently, especially with the upgraded handling package, and it offers a serene ride and a huge trunk. **Last report/fax: March 94/9714**
Ford Escort	○	○	An uninteresting little econobox except in the highest trim-line GT version. The standard 1.9-liter engine is anemic, the steering is slow and sloppy, and the handling is clumsy. The 1997 model is much improved. **Last report/fax: September 93/7331**
✓ Ford Explorer	○	⊖	Lots of cargo space for a compact SUV. Ride and handling are both pretty good, and the V6 accelerates adequately. Full-time all-wheel drive, a major plus, is optional. The XLT is a better value than the higher trim lines. **Last report/fax: August 95/9421**
Ford F-150	New	NA	The 1997 redesign set new standards for comfort, handling, and overall refinement in a full-sized pickup. **Last report/fax: September 96/9499**
Ford Mustang	⊖	⊖	A 1994 redesign gave this old-fashioned muscle car a new, more rigid body and a new interior. Unfortunately, the Mustang doesn't feel sporty to drive. The V6 version falls particularly short. **Last report/fax: June 94/9742**
Ford Probe	⊖	○	A nicely balanced sporty hatchback made by a Mazda/Ford joint venture. In GT trim, it accelerates powerfully and handles well, though its ride is stiff and jittery. The Mazda MX-6 is a coupe version. **Last report/fax: January 93/7936**
✓ Ford Ranger	○	⊖	Our top-rated compact pickup. It rides and handles quite well. The interior is quiet, comfortable, and well-laid-out. Similar: Mazda B-Series. **Last report/fax: November 95/9434**
Ford Taurus	New	NA	Redesigned for 1996, the Taurus is a good, well-rounded family sedan. It corners responsively and offers a firm ride. The front is roomy and comfortable; head room is scarce in the rear. Similar: Mercury Sable. **Last report/fax: January 96/9447**

Model	Predicted reliability	Depreciation	Comments
Ford Thunderbird	◒	◒	Expect a decent ride, particularly for front-seat occupants, but fairly clumsy handling. Standard equipment includes a wealth of power accessories. The 4.6-liter V8 is the better engine choice. **Last report/fax: July 95/9423**
Ford Windstar	●	NA	A commendable performer, but first-year reliability was much worse than average. The ride is comfortable, and the interior is very roomy and quiet. Like many minivans, this one feels clumsy in hard turns. **Last report/fax: December 94/9927**
GMC Jimmy	◒	⊖	The Jimmy (and similar Chevy Blazer) are roomy and quiet. Still, they have mediocre brakes, a so-so ride, and a cramped rear seat. Full-time all-wheel-drive (without low range) is available on high-trim versions. **Last report/fax: August 95/9421**
GMC Safari	●	⊖	Though the Safari has an enormous cargo area, the design is dated. It can haul a lot of cargo or a trailer, but drawbacks include ponderous handling and an uncomfortable ride. All-wheel drive is available. Similar: Chevy Astro. **Last report/fax: July 96/7766**
GMC Sierra C/K 1500	○	⊖	The Sierra (and similar Chevy C/K pickup) offers a commanding view, a smooth powertrain, and a quiet cabin. The third (rear) door on extended-cab versions is a worthwhile option. But the handling is trucklike and the ride is stiff and boundy. **Last report/fax: September 96/9499**
GMC Sonoma	●	●	The Sonoma and similar Chevy "S" pickup is fairly new but not especially carlike. The ride is quiet but stiff, and handling is unexceptional. Reliability and crash-worthiness remain concerns. **Last report/fax: November 95/9434**
GMC Suburban	○	⊖	This huge truck-based station wagon emphasizes utility. It can carry nine people and tow a heavy trailer. Poor reliability has dogged this vehicle. **Last report/fax: —/—**
GMC Yukon	◒	⊖	The Yukon nestles between the huge GMC Suburban and the compact GMC Jimmy. The cabin is quiet and exceptionally roomy. Yukon lends itself well to hauling cargo or a heavy trailer. **Last report/fax: October 96/9508**
Geo Metro	○	●	The Metro was redesigned for 1995. It's still a very small car—one that's happier zipping around town than cruising down the highway. Fuel economy is about as good as it gets. **Last report/fax: September 95/9429**
✔ Geo Prizm	⊖	⊖	A very good, reliable small car. Ride and handling are both decent, and the interior layout is close to ideal. The rear seats are cramped. **Last report/fax: August 93/7302**
Geo Tracker	⊖	○	This noisy, slow, and ungainly little Jeeplike runabout is better suited to running errands around town than cruising long distances. Four-wheel drive is optional. **Last report/fax: June 96/9478**
✔ Honda Accord	⊖	○	One of the best family sedans. Expect peppy acceleration, decent handling, a good ride, comfortable seats, and high reliability. The EX version handles better than the DX or LX. **Last report/fax: January 96/9447**
✔ Honda Civic	⊖	○	A very good small car. The 1.6-liter Four is very well matched to the optional automatic transmission. The interior is thoughtfully designed, and the ride is exceptionally good for a small car. **Last report/fax: March & May 96/9471**
Honda Civic del Sol	○	⊖	It should drive like a sports car—but it doesn't. Instead, the driving characteristics are more like those of a small sedan. The ride is busy, and the body flexes too much. **Last report/fax: October 93/7341**

Model	Predicted reliability	Depre-ciation	Comments
✔ Honda Odyssey	⊜	NA	Honda's first-ever minivan has four doors, like a wagon. It's lower and narrower than most vans. The only engine choice is a Four. Ride and handling are very carlike, and visibility and maneuverability are both good, too. **Last report/fax: October 95/9431**
Honda Passport	○	NA	It's really an Isuzu Rodeo with a Honda badge. It leans sharply in turns, steers slowly, and delivers a mediocre ride. The Rodeo has had shaky reliability as well. **Last report/fax: July 94/7789**
✔ Honda Prelude	⊜	⊜	This well-rounded coupe blends lively acceleration with nimble handling. It's easy and fun to drive, but the cabin is cramped even for a coupe. **Last report/fax: January 93/7936**
Hyundai Accent	NA	NA	This fairly new entry-level Hyundai is a small, basic runabout with a well-equipped, modern interior and so-so ride. Reliability is unknown—but previous Hyundai models have been very troublesome. **Last report/fax: September 95/9429**
Hyundai Elantra	New	NA	Redesigned for 1996, the Elantra fits between the small Accent and mid-sized Sonata. Neither the ride, handling, or engine performance are very impressive. **Last report/fax: May 92/7397**
Hyundai Sonata	NA	NA	The Sonata tries to imitate the Japanese compacts, but with limited success. If you equip it decently, it's not competitive in price. Reliability is unknown—but previous Hyundai models have been very troublesome. **Last report/fax: February 95/9992**
✔ Infiniti G20	⊜	◖	An overlooked gem, discontinued after 1996. It feels like a good European sports sedan. Handles nimbly, rides well, and offers comfortable seats, plus a good balance of acceleration and fuel economy. **Last report/fax: November 94/9923**
✔ Infiniti I30	⊜	NA	The new Infiniti is an upscale version of the Nissan Maxima that came out in 1996. The I30 is competent all around but the ride could be better. **Last report/fax: February 96/9456**
✔ Infiniti J30	⊜	●	This pleasant model emphasizes near-absolute road isolation over sporty handling. The small back seat and trunk make it functionally a luxury coupe despite its four doors. **Last report/fax: May 93/7914**
✔ Infiniti Q45	⊜	●	A fine but expensive luxury car. The latest generation has sacrificed cutting-edge acceleration to create a quieter, more refined ride. The rear seat is cramped for a such a large and supposedly luxurious car. **Last report/fax: November 93/7351**
Isuzu Hombre	New	NA	A basic Chevy compact pickup with slightly different sheet metal. Expect a stiff but quiet ride, unremarkable handling, and a weak and rough engine. **Last report/fax: —/—**
✔ Isuzu Oasis	⊜	NA	A rebadged Honda Odyssey, it's a smallish minivan that rides and drives like a Honda Accord. **Last report/fax: October 95/9431**
Isuzu Rodeo	○	⊜	A compact sport-utility vehicle that accelerates modestly and leans heavily during cornering. It offers little more cargo space than does a standard station wagon. **Last report/fax: July 94/7789**
Isuzu Trooper	⊜	○	We have rated the Trooper Not Acceptable because of its rollover propensity in our tests. Even without that it was a tall, expensive box with unganily handling and a so-so ride. **Last report/fax: October 96/9507**
Jaguar XJ6	NA	●	A very refined sedan with a few quirks, it has powerful acceleration and a well-mannered ride. The control layout has been improved, though the cockpit remains a little cramped. **Last report/fax: November 93/7351**
Jeep Cherokee	◖	⊜	More a tall wagon than a real sport-utility vehicle. Lots of cargo room but a noisy, harsh ride. The narrow seats are comfortable only for slender people. **Last report/fax: September 91/7976**

Model	Predicted reliability	Depreciation	Comments
✔ Jeep Grand Cherokee	○	⊖	One of the most civilized sport-utility vehicles made, with an almost carlike ride and a sophisticated driveline. All-wheel drive is available. Its spotty reliability has improved of late. **Last report/fax: August 95/9421**
Jeep Wrangler	New	NA	Extensively redesigned for 1997, this unique small Jeep was greatly improved but remains tedious to drive on long trips. The ride is choppy and with the soft-top very noisy. It should be a good off-roader. **Last report/fax: —/—**
Land Rover Discovery	NA	NA	Land Rover's Discovery is a smaller and a lot cheaper than the Range Rover, but is still roomy and comes well equipped. It feels slow and heavy, and gets miserable fuel economy. **Last report/fax: August 95/9421**
✔ Lexus ES300	⊖	○	An upscale version of the Toyota Camry, it does everything well—but it's no bargain. Expect sound handling, strong and quiet performance, and lots of standard equipment. **Last report/fax: May 95/9401**
✔ Lexus GS300	⊖	○	Among luxury sports sedans, the GS300 emphasizes the luxury end of the spectrum. Exceptionally quiet ride, but the steering feels too light. Displays and controls are exceptional. **Last report/fax: May 94/7732**
✔ Lexus LS400	⊖	○	This is Toyota's flagship luxury car. Redesigned for '95, it's a little roomier now. Expect an extremely quiet, comfortable ride, and plush accommodations. **Last report/fax: November 93/7351**
Lexus LX450	⊖	NA	This is a Toyota Land Cruiser with a slightly softer suspension. Leisurely acceleration and a busy ride detract a little from this imposing luxury-truck's driving pleasure. **Last report/fax: —/—**
✔ Lexus SC400/SC300	⊖	⊖	This two-door luxury coupe gets fine performance from its aluminum V8 in SC400 trim, but the much-cheaper SC300's Six accelerates well too. Quality and refinement are top-notch. **Last report/fax: July 93/9325**
Lincoln Continental	○	●	Redesigned for '95, the well-equipped Continental picked up a fine-performing aluminum V8. A so-so ride and ordinary interior mars the driving experience. **Last report/fax: November 96/9513**
✔ Lincoln Mark VIII	○	●	A sophisticated, rear-drive luxury two-door with a spirited aluminum V8. Handling is agile for such a large car. The cockpit is modern and the front seats are comfortable. **Last report/fax: July 93/9325**
Lincoln Town Car	⊖	●	A big, old-fashioned, rear-wheel-drive highway cruiser with a modern V8 and lots of luxury appointments. Expect a quiet, soft ride and seating for six. **Last report/fax: —/—**
✔ Mazda 626	○	○	A well-rounded and high-rated family sedan. The pricey V6 runs particularly smoothly and powerfully, but the Four is a better value. **Last report/fax: January 94/9392**
✔ Mazda B-Series	○	⊖	This is a Ford Ranger compact pickup under the nameplate. Quiet and comfortable, it's probably the best in the class, but these trucks all suffer from vague steering, and so-so ride and handling. **Last report/fax: November 95/9434**
Mazda MPV	○	○	This minivan rides badly, handles awkwardly, and is a chore to convert from people-carrying to cargo hauling. The rear seat is cramped, and the engine must struggle to overcome this truck's weight problem. **Last report/fax: July 96/7766**
✔ Mazda MX-5 Miata	⊖	⊖	A rear-wheel-drive two-seater that's as fun to drive as any sports car on the road, despite a noisy, stiff ride and pathetically small trunk. Excellent handling, steering, and brakes and a smooth-running engine add to the enjoyment. **Last report/fax: October 93/7341**

Model	Predicted reliability	Depreciation	Comments
Mazda MX-6	◓	○	Similar to the Ford Probe, but with a coupe body instead of a hatchback. We prefer the V6 to the Four. Handling is smooth and predictable, the ride is decent. **Last report/fax: January 93/7936**
✔ Mazda Millenia	◓	NA	A refined and high-rated luxury sedan that's quiet and comfortable, pleasant to drive, and well put together. The high-line "S" model offers both high power and relatively good fuel economy. **Last report/fax: May 95/9401**
✔ Mazda Protegé	◓	○	One of the best in the crowded small-car market, though a little pricey. A roomy car in a small package, it rides decently and handles well. **Last report/fax: June 95/9416**
Mazda RX-7	NA	◓	Comfort and practicality take a back seat to pure, uncompromising performance. Handling is top-notch but the ride is terribly stiff. Fun to drive for people who fit, but the cockpit is too small for tall people. 1996 is its last year. **Last report/fax: September 92/7758**
Mercedes-Benz C-Class	◓	NA	A strong engine, responsive handling, a supple ride, and quiet interior are strong points. The seats may be too firm for some, and it's pricey for its size. **Last report/fax: August 94/9792**
✔ Mercedes-Benz E-Class	◓	◓	One of the world's finest cars, this model is a joy to drive. It's a fine balance of spirited acceleration, precise handling, and a luxurious ride. **Last report/fax: November 96/7732**
Mercury Cougar	◓	○	A slightly up-market version of the Ford Thunderbird. Expect roomy front seats, and fairly quick steering. The optional V8 is the engine of choice. **Last report/fax: July 95/9423**
✔ Mercury Grand Marquis	○	◓	A big, old-fashioned V8 freeway cruiser, similar to the Ford Crown Victoria, with a serene ride, a huge trunk, and good towing capability. The Handling and Performance package is a worthwhile option. **Last report/fax: March 94/9714**
✔ Mercury Mystique	○	NA	This compact handles exceptionally well and is sensibly appointed, but the rear seat is cramped. The V6 is a better choice than the noisy four-cylinder that comes standard. **Last report/fax: March 95/9995**
Mercury Sable	New	NA	Redesigned for 1996, the Sable and its Ford Taurus cousin are improved in nearly every way from their predecessors. Both offer good handling and decent comfort. The Sable offers a little more head room in the rear but still not enough. **Last report/fax: January 96/7948**
Mercury Tracer	○	◓	In top-level LTS trim, this is a peppy little car. Lower trim lines are disappointing. But the annoying motorized shoulder belts are intrusive in any trim line. The 1997 model offers many improvements. **Last report/fax: October 94/9921**
✔ Mercury Villager	○	◓	The Villager and its twin the Nissan Quest are among the best minivans, very carlike and pleasant to drive. The worst drawbacks: a relatively modest cargo area compared to the competition, and the lack of a left-side sliding door option. **Last report/fax: July 96/7943**
Mitsubishi 3000 GT	○	○	With all-wheel drive and twin turbochargers, this technological showpiece is fast and furious. But it's pricey—and somehow not as much fun to drive as, say, a Mazda Miata. The more basic versions are nothing special. **Last report/fax: April 92/9377**
Mitsubishi Diamante	◓	◓	Mitsubishi's flagship luxury car never stood out in the fast company it competes with. It is redesigned for 1997. **Last report/fax: February 92/7345**
Mitsubishi Eclipse	●	○	This sporty coupe, a sibling of the Eagle Talon, was redesigned for 1995. The turbocharged versions are the ones to choose. **Last report/fax: —/—**
✔ Mitsubishi Galant	○	○	A competent, good-performing family sedan. The Four delivers lively acceleration. Reliability has not been as good as it might have been. **Last report/fax: January 94/9392**

Model	Predicted reliability	Depreciation	Comments
Mitsubishi Mirage	⊖	○	A small econobox with poor brakes and a rather uncomfortable ride. A zesty powertrain is its sole good point, and it carries over into a redesigned 1997 model. **Last report/fax: August 93/7302**
Mitsubishi Montero	NA	⊖	The best things about the high, boxy Montero are its sophisticated all-wheel-drive system and seven-passenger seating option. The worst is its cumbersome emergency handling. **Last report/fax: November 92/—**
✔ **Nissan 200SX**	⊖	NA	This coupe version of the Nissan Sentra was new for 1995. Lower trimlines are inexpensive but a little dowdy. The SE-R trimline makes the transition to a nimble, good-performing sporty coupe. **Last report/fax: May 96/9471**
Nissan 240SX	NA	○	A rear-wheel-drive sporty coupe. Expect sound handling and a fairly comfortable ride. As in other sporty coupes, the rear seat is best left uninhabited. **Last report/fax: —/—**
✔ **Nissan 300ZX**	○	⊖	A two-seater that's everything a sports car should be—fast and fun, and remarkably smooth and easy to drive. One of the best sports cars available, but very pricey. **Last report/fax: September 92/7758**
✔ **Nissan Altima**	⊖	○	This model is advertised as an "affordable luxury car." It performs decently overall, but it falls short of luxury. The sports-oriented SE version handles better than the top-line GLE, but the best value is the mid-level GXE. **Last report/fax: November 94/9923**
✔ **Nissan Maxima**	⊖	○	We'd put the Maxima a notch below the Toyota Camry. The powertrain is first rate, but the ride, seat comfort, and handling are only good, not great. **Last report/fax: February 95/9992**
✔ **Nissan Pathfinder**	⊖	⊖	A 1996 redesign gave the Pathfinder unit-body construction, and carlike ride and handling, as well as a full complement of safety features. Modest interior size compromises rear-seat comfort and cargo space. **Last report/fax: October 96/9508**
✔ **Nissan Quest**	○	⊖	The Quest and its twin, the Mercury Villager, are among the best minivans, very carlike and pleasant to drive. The worst drawbacks: a relatively modest cargo area compared to the competition, and the lack of a left-side sliding door option. **Last report/fax: July 96/7943**
✔ **Nissan Sentra**	⊖	◒	The Sentra falls just a notch or two below the best here, the Mazda Protegé, Chevy Cavalier, and Honda Civic. Adequate in most respects, but the steering is a little sluggish, and the cockpit is a little cramped for tall people. **Last report/fax: June 95/9416**
Nissan Truck	○	○	A basic compact pickup made in Tennessee. The only engine is a four-cylinder, and four-wheel ABS is unavailable. **Last report/fax: —/—**
Oldsmobile 88	○	●	A big, quiet, softly sprung freeway cruiser with a responsive V6. We'd choose the optional touring suspension, which improves handling markedly. **Last report/fax: January 92/7307**
Oldsmobile 98	○	◒	A big freeway cruiser, now out of production. Cars like this emphasize a soft ride and a wealth of power accessories. Handling can be quite sloppy, though the optional Touring Suspension package helps somewhat. **Last report/fax: —/—**
Oldsmobile Achieva	◒	◒	Expect a quite interior and adequate power, but an unsettled ride and mediocre handling and braking. The interior looks bigger than it is. Not a bad car—just not a very good one. **Last report/fax: August 96/7704**
Oldsmobile Aurora	◒	NA	Overstyled and overweight. The V8 powertrain is top-notch, but its heavy steering, poor visibility, lack of roominess, and middling ride quality put it behind the luxury competition. **Last report/fax: May 95/9401**

Model	Predicted reliability	Depreciation	Comments
Oldsmobile Bravada	◒	NA	A loaded version of the Chevy Blazer. All-wheel drive is standard. Expect powerful acceleration and smooth shifting but considerable body lean, and vague steering. Cargo space is generous. **Last report/fax: —/—**
Oldsmobile Ciera	○	●	An aging and unsinspired design, due for replacement in winter, 1997. It's large outside but cramped inside. Reliability is this car's sole strong point. **Last report/fax: January 95/9981**
Oldsmobile Cutlass Supreme	◒	◒	Perhaps the least appealing of GM's family sedans. Sloppy handling, a poor ride, and uncomfortable seats head its list of faults. Due to be replaced by the new Intrigue in mid-1997. **Last report/fax: February 94/7771**
Oldsmobile Silhouette	●	○	Expect uninspired overall performance from this and GM's other front-drive minivans. Faults include numerous blind spots and mediocre ride and handling. A redesign comes for 1997. **Last report/fax: July 94/7789**
Plymouth Breeze	New	NA	This cousin of the Dodge Stratus has a roomy rear seat and well designed controls and displays. Handling is sound; ride, braking, and acceleration about average. **Last report/fax: August 96/9493**
Plymouth Grand Voyager	New	○	The Grand Voyager is a longer-bodied Voyager. It rides quietly, handles nimbly, and easily converts between people- and cargo-hauling duties. The optional left-side sliding door is very handy. **Last report/fax: October 95/7766**
Plymouth Neon	●	NA	This small car has a roomy interior and a relatively large though noisy engine. The ride is choppy. Handling is predictable and safe, but not sporty. **Last report/fax: March & May 96/9471**
Plymouth Voyager	New	○	Redesigned for 1996. Nimble handling and a quiet ride lead the list of plaudits. Abundant cargo space and easy conversion between cargo and people-moving add to its appeal. Best engine choice is probably the 3.3-liter V6. Reliability remains the big unknown. **Last report/fax: July 96/7789**
✔ Pontiac Bonneville	○	○	Properly equipped, the Bonneville is one of the best large sedans. The optional firm suspension and touring tires markedly improve handling. Pass up the supercharged V6; the standard V6 does just fine. **Last report/fax: March 94/9714**
Pontiac Firebird	●	⊖	An old-fashioned rear-wheel-drive muscle car, like its cousin, the Chevrolet Camaro. The optional V8 provides effortless acceleration and makes the standard V6 seem sluggish by comparison. **Last report/fax: October 93/7341**
Pontiac Grand Am	○	⊖	The interior is quiet, the shifting is smooth, and the control layout is improved, but the ride remains mediocre, handling is imprecise, and the seating feels claustrophobic. **Last report/fax: August 96/9317**
Pontiac Grand Prix	◒	○	This mid-sized sedan is a decent though unexceptional design. It has quick steering with minimal body roll. An all-new 1997 model has replaced it. **Last report/fax: February 94/7771**
✔ Pontiac Sunfire	○	NA	The Sunfire, new in 1995, aims to be a sporty and inexpensive small car, with some success. It's pleasant enough to drive, and comes with many useful amenities. **Last report/fax: May 96/9471**
Pontiac Trans Sport	●	○	Expect uninspired overall performance from this and GM's other front-drive minivans. Faults include numerous blind spots and mediocre ride and handling. A new 1997 redesign should improve matters. **Last report/fax: July 94/7789**
Range Rover	New	NA	Power everything and leather galore festoon this luxurious large sport-utility. It rides comfortably for an SUV and handles adequately, but it doesn't accelerate briskly. **Last report/fax: —/—**

Model	Predicted reliability	Depreciation	Comments
Saab 900	◒	○	This is an able if slightly quirky sports sedan. Handling, performance, and accommodations are all quite good. Several controls are oddly placed on the floor between the front seats. **Last report/fax: August 94/9792**
✔ Saab 9000	◒	◓	A well-designed and pleasant-to-drive European-style sports sedan. The control layout is a little inconvenient. The hatchback is roomy, and turbo versions are very quick. **Last report/fax: May 94/7732**
Saturn	◒	◒	A 1996 freshening improved the car somewhat but failed to hush the noisy engine and fix the transmission's annoying shift characteristics. The SL1 compromises handling for ride comfort; the SL2 does the opposite. **Last report/fax: March 96/9457**
✔ Saturn SC	◒	◒	Among the coupe versions of the Saturn, the SC2 is the one to choose. It provides quick acceleration and nimble handling. The ride is stiff, even jarring at times. Reliability has been good. **Last report/fax: July 92/7734**
✔ Subaru Impreza	◒	◓	Properly equipped, the Impreza is a very nice small car with good handling and comfortable if slightly tight accommodations. It's the only all-wheel-drive small sedan on the market. **Last report/fax: August 93/7302**
✔ Subaru Legacy	◒	◓	A competent, well-rounded sedan, and one of the few that offer all-wheel drive. Much improved in 1995, it's one of our top-rated cars. The regular wagon versions are a good bet too—better than the Outback, which is a faux SUV. **Last report/fax: June 96/9478**
✔ Subaru SVX	NA	●	Think of the SVX as more of a touring coupe than a true sports car. It rides comfortably and quietly. Handling is good but not great. All-wheel-drive is standard. **Last report/fax: September 92/7758**
Suzuki Esteem	New	NA	The Esteem offers good accommodations and reasonable performance and fuel economy. But it's slightly behind in interior noise and ride comfort. **Last report/fax: March 96/9457**
Suzuki Sidekick	◒	◒	A small Jeeplike runabout, noisy, slow, and uncomfortable. The four-door is a foot longer and commensurately roomier than the two-door. **Last report/fax: June 96/9478**
Suzuki Swift	○	○	One of the smallest cars on the road, the Swift and similar Geo Metro get good fuel economy but are neither peppy nor nimble. They may be fine for tooling around town, but no fun for long-distance cruising. **Last report/fax: September 95/9429**
Suzuki X90	New	NA	More of a conversation piece than a real car. To the basic impracticality of a two-seater add awkward handling and a harsh, noisy ride. Not a good bet. **Last report/fax: June 96/9478**
✔ Toyota 4Runner	◒	NA	The 1996 redesign endowed the 4Runner with good performance and relatively good fuel economy. The ride could be better, but it handles soundly, it's quiet inside, and it holds lots of cargo. Altogether, a good package. **Last report/fax: October 96/9508**
✔ Toyota Avalon	◒	NA	Think of the Avalon as an extended-length Camry. It's comfortable, quiet, refined, and easy to drive. Though not sporty, the Avalon offers great utility because of its roominess and attention to detail. **Last report/fax: May 95/9401**
✔ Toyota Camry	◒	○	One of the best sedans on the market—quiet, refined, and easy to drive, with comfortable seating. It feels like a luxury car, and it has been exceptionally reliable. **Last report/fax: January 96/9447**
✔ Toyota Celica	◒	○	A well-rounded sporty coupe, though not as fast as competitors like the Ford Probe. It rides and handles well, gives good fuel economy, and has been very reliable. As in most coupes, the rear seat is very cramped. **Last report/fax: June 94/9742**

Model	Predicted reliability	Depre- ciation	Comments
✔ Toyota Corolla	⊖	◓	An able overall performer with good reliability. The car handles predictably, though it's not nimble. Front seating is fine, but the rear is a little cramped. **Last report/fax: August 93/7302**
✔ Toyota Land Cruiser	⊖	⊖	Big and imposing, the Land Cruiser competes at the expensive end of the sport-utility-vehicle market. Expect leisurely acceleration and subpar fuel economy. You get a high, commanding view but a slightly busy, rubbery ride. **Last report/fax: July 94/7789**
Toyota Paseo	⊖	○	A sporty version of the Tercel. Acceleration is peppy but the handling is not nimble. A soft suspension and numb steering rob it of true sportiness. **Last report/fax: July 92/7734**
✔ Toyota Previa	⊖	⊖	A good though expensive minivan, with responsive steering and a good, quiet ride. The Previa has been the most reliable of any mini-van. **Last report/fax: October 92/7766**
Toyota RAV4	New	NA	The only small SUV that rides and handles well. It steers quickly and nimbly, and offers full-time all-wheel-drive. The front seats are firm and supportive. Cargo space is good for such a small vehicle as well. **Last report/fax: June 96/9478**
✔ Toyota Supra	⊖	○	Lots of flash for lots of cash. In its highest trim, the Supra is a muscular speedster with a bone-jarring ride. We think the Mazda Miata is more fun to drive—and at half the price. **Last report/fax: June 94/9742**
Toyota T100	⊖	○	A full-sized pickup, designed for hauling and towing. If you plan to do much of either, take the V6 instead of the standard Four. A reliable truck, but pricey. **Last report/fax: —/—**
Toyota Tacoma	New	NA	Unimpressive, overall. This compact pickup has a responsive powertrain (with the V6) and a quiet cabin, but slow steering and an awful ride. The non-antilock brakes perform poorly. The cargo box is rimmed with flimsy sheet metal, easily dented. **Last report/fax: November 95/9434**
Toyota Tercel	⊖	○	First and foremost an economy car. Long suits are a peppy power-train, and excellent fuel economy and reliability. Unfortunately, it also delivers a rough, noisy ride in a cramped cabin, and, without ABS, mediocre braking. **Last report/fax: September 95/9429**
Volkswagen Golf	◓	○	A sporty, zippy little hatchback that's fun to drive. Expect a fairly quiet ride. Handling is nimble, although the body leans a lot in turns. **Last report/fax: May 96/9471**
Volkswagen Jetta	◓	○	Think of the Jetta as a Golf with a very large trunk instead of a hatchback. It's a practical, relatively inexpensive car. Expect fine handling, a good ride, and comfortable seats. **Last report/fax: November 94/9923**
✔ Volkswagen Passat	○	NA	VW's costliest car rides and handles very well. It has a roomy rear seat and big trunk. The automatic transmission blunts the engine's performance; we recommend the manual instead. **Last report/fax: February 95/9992**
✔ Volvo 850	⊖	◓	Volvo's only front-wheel-drive car. It's nimble for a Volvo, and turbo versions are fast. Large, comfortable front seats only partly make up for a stiff, jiggly ride. **Last report/fax: August 94/9792**
✔ Volvo 960	○	◓	This is the most expensive model in Volvo's 900 Series. Expect good seating for four and a huge trunk. The car rides and handles well, and the Six accelerates enthusiastically. **Last report/fax: August 92/7746**

Ratings of the 1996 cars

The following cars include those for which we have recent test data. To earn our recommendation—marked by a ✔—a model has to perform well in our tests and must have been at least average in reliability. In some cases, our tests apply to more than one model. These models, called "siblings," are essentially similar models that are sold under different nameplates. They're grouped and marked with square bullets. **Fuel usage** is overall mpg and is based on our tests on and off the track. **Tested model** notes the trim line, engine, drivetrain, and braking system of the model tested—items that can affect test results.

Model	Overall score	Fuel usage	Tested model
	P F G VG E		
SMALL CAR WITH MANUAL TRANSMISSION			
Volkswagen Jetta		23 mpg	GLX 2.8 V6; man 5
✔ Acura Integra		30	LS 1.8 Four; man 5
Volkswagen Golf		30	GL 2.0 Four; man 5
✔ Geo Prizm		33	LSi 1.8 Four; man 5
Mercury Tracer		28	LTS 1.8 Four; man 5
✔ Subaru Impreza		29	L 1.8 Four; man 5
Dodge/Plymouth Neon		26	Sport 2.0 Four; man 5
Hyundai Accent		35	L 1.5 Four; man 5
Toyota Tercel		39	Base 1.5 Four; man 5
Ford Aspire		36	Base 1.3 Four; man 5
Geo Metro		35	LSi 2-door 1.0 Three; man 5
SMALL CAR WITH AUTO TRANMISSION			
✔ Mazda Protegé		26	ES 1.8 Four; auto 4
✔ Honda Civic		31	LX 1.6 Four; auto 4
✔ ▪Chevrolet Cavalier		26	LS 2.2 Four; auto 3
✔ ▪Pontiac Sunfire		26	Chevrolet Cavalier LS 2.2 Four; auto 3
✔ Toyota Corolla		30	LE 1.8 Four; auto 4
✔ Nissan Sentra		28	GXE 1.6 Four; auto 4
Suzuki Esteem		29	GLX 1.6 Four; auto 4
Saturn		29	SL1 1.9 Four; auto 4
Toyota Tercel		32	DX 1.5 Four; auto 4
Dodge/Plymouth Neon		26	Highline 2.0 Four; auto 3
Hyundai Accent		28	Base 1.5 Four; auto 4
Geo Metro		29	LSi 4-door 1.3 Four; auto 3

Model	Overall score					Fuel usage	Tested model
	P	F	G	VG	E		
SMALL COUPE							
✔ Honda Civic Coupe						34 mpg	EX 1.6 Four; man 5
Volkswagen Golf GTI						27	2.0 Four; man 5
✔ ▪ Chevrolet Cavalier Coupe						25	Pontiac Sunfire GT 2.4 Four; man 5
✔ ▪ Pontiac Sunfire Coupe						25	GT 2.4 Four; man 5
Dodge/Plymouth Neon Coupe						30	Sport 2.0 Four; man 5
COUPE							
✔ Lexus SC400						19	4.0 V8; auto 4
✔ Lincoln Mark VIII						19	4.6 V8; auto 4
▪ Chrysler Sebring						22	Dodge Avenger ES 2.5 V6; auto 4
▪ Dodge Avenger						22	ES 2.5 V6; auto 4
▪ Ford Thunderbird						20	LX 4.6 V8; auto 4
▪ Mercury Cougar						20	Ford Thunderbird LX 4.6 V8; auto 4
Cadillac Eldorado						15	4.6 V8; auto 4
Buick Riviera						17	3.8 V6; auto 4
Chevrolet Monte Carlo						18	Z34 3.4 V6; auto 4
SPORTS/SPORTY CAR UNDER $25,000							
✔ Nissan 200SX						28	SE-R 2.0 Four; man 5
✔ Acura Integra Coupe						30	GS-R 1.8 Four; man 5
Ford Probe						24	GT 2.5 V6; man 5
Pontiac Trans Am						17	5.7 V8; auto 4
✔ Toyota Celica						28	GT 2.2 Four; man 5
✔ Mazda MX-5 Miata						29	Base 1.6 Four; man 5
Mazda MX-6						24	LS 2.5 V6; auto 4
✔ Saturn SC						29	SC2 1.9 Four; man 5
✔ Honda Prelude						26	Si 2.3 Four; man 5
Ford Mustang						18	GT 5.0 V8; auto 4
Chevrolet Camaro						19	Base 3.4 V6; auto 4
Honda Civic del Sol						32	Si 1.6 Four; man 5
SPORTS/SPORTY CAR OVER $25,000							
✔ Toyota Supra						22	Turbo 3.0 Six; man 6
✔ Nissan 300ZX						21	Turbo 3.0 V6; man 5
Chevrolet Corvette						17	5.7 V8; man 6
Mazda RX-7						19	Touring 1.3 rotary; man 5
✔ Subaru SVX						19	LS 3.3 Six; auto 4

Model	Overall score					Fuel usage	Tested model
	P	F	G	VG	E		
MEDIUM CAR UNDER $25,000							
✔ Toyota Camry V6						23 mpg	LE V6 3.0 V6; auto 4
✔ Toyota Camry 4						24	LE 4 2.2 Four; auto 4
✔ Subaru Legacy						23	LS 2.2 Four; auto 4
✔ Infiniti G20						29	2.0 Four; man 5
✔ Nissan Maxima						24	GXE 3.0 V6; auto 4
Chrysler Cirrus						22	LXi 2.5 V6; auto 4
✔ Honda Accord V6						21	EX V6 2.7 V6; auto 4
✔ Volkswagen Passat						20	GLX 2.8 V6; auto 4
✔ Mercury Mystique						23	LS 2.5 V6; auto 4
✔ Honda Accord 4						26	EX 4 2.2 Four; auto 4
✔ Mazda 626						25	LX 2.0 Four; auto 4
▪ Ford Taurus						21	LX 3.0 V6; auto 4
▪ Mercury Sable						21	Ford Taurus LX 3.0 V6; auto 4
✔ Ford Contour						24	GL 2.0 Four; auto 4
✔ Mitsubishi Galant						24	LS 2.4 Four; auto 4
✔ Buick Regal						20	Gran Sport 3.8 V6; auto 4
Pontiac Grand Prix						19	GT 3.4 V6; auto 4
✔ Chevrolet Lumina						21	LS 3.1 V6; auto 4
✔ Nissan Altima						23	SE 2.4 Four; man 5
Plymouth Breeze						23	Base 2.0 Four; auto 4
Hyundai Sonata						21	GLS 3.0 V6; auto 4
Dodge Stratus						20	Base 2.4 Four; auto 4
Oldsmobile Cutlass Supreme						20	SL 3.1 V6; auto 4
Pontiac Grand Am						24	SE 2.4 Four; auto 4
Oldsmobile Achieva						24	SL Series III 2.4 Four; auto 4
Chevrolet Corsica						25	LT 2.2 Four; auto 3
▪ Buick Century						22	Special 3.1 V6; auto 4
▪ Oldsmobile Ciera						22	Buick Century Special 3.1 V6; auto 4

Model	Overall score					Fuel usage	Tested model
	P	F	G	VG	E		
MEDIUM CAR OVER $25,000							
✔ Volvo 850						22 mpg	Turbo 2.3 Five; auto 4
✔ Toyota Avalon						22	XLS 3.0 V6; auto 4
✔ BMW 325i						24	2.5 Six; auto 4
✔ Mazda Millenia						22	S 2.3 V6; auto 4
✔ Lexus ES300						22	3.0 V6; auto 4
✔ Saab 9000						21	CSE 2.3 Four; auto 4
✔ Infiniti I30						23	Base 3.0 V6; auto 4
✔ Infiniti J30						20	3.0 V6; auto 4
Audi A4						22	2.8 V6; auto 5
✔ Acura 2.5TL						23	2.5TL Premium 2.5 Five; auto 4
Mercedes-Benz C280						20	2.8 Six; auto 4
Saab 900						22	SE 2.5 V6; auto 4
Mitsubishi Diamante						20	LS 3.0 V6; auto 4
Oldsmobile Aurora						17	4.0 V8; auto 4
LARGE CAR							
Chrysler LHS						20	3.5 V6; auto 4
✔ Chrysler Concorde						21	3.5 V6; auto 4
Dodge Intrepid						20	Base 3.3 V6; auto 4
Eagle Vision						21	TSi 3.5 V6; auto 4
✔ Pontiac Bonneville						18	SSEi 3.8 V6; auto 4
Chevrolet Caprice						17	Classic LS 5.7 V8; auto 4
✔ ▪ Ford Crown Victoria						19	LX 4.6 V8; auto 4
✔ ▪ Mercury Grand Marquis						19	Ford Crown Victoria LX 4.6 V8; auto 4
Buick LeSabre						20	Custom 3.8 V6; auto 4
LUXURY CAR							
✔ Mercedes-Benz E320						22	3.2 Six; auto 4
✔ Lexus GS300						21	3.0 Six; auto 4
✔ BMW 528i (1997)						20	2.8 Six; auto 4
✔ Acura 3.5 RL						20	3.5 V6; auto 4
✔ Infiniti Q45						17	Q45a 4.5 V8; auto 4
Lincoln Continental						18	4.6 V8; auto 4
Cadillac Seville						17	STS Touring 4.6 V8; auto 4

Model	Overall score	Fuel usage	Tested model
	P F G VG E		
WAGON			
✔ Toyota Camry Wagon		21 mpg	LE 3.0 V6; auto 4
✔ Honda Accord Wagon		25	EX 2.2 Four; auto 4
✔ Subaru Legacy Wagon		21	Outback 2.5 Four; auto 4
✔ Toyota Corolla Wagon		28	DX 1.8 Four; auto 4
Ford Escort Wagon		27	LX 1.9 Four; auto 4
SMALL SPORT-UTILITY VEHICLE			
Toyota RAV4		25	2.0 Four; man 5
Suzuki Sidekick		23	JLX Sport 1.8 Four; man 5
Geo Tracker		24	LSi 1.6 Four; man 5
Suzuki X90		27	1.6 Four; man 5
SPORT-UTILITY VEHICLE			
✔ Toyota 4Runner		22	SR5 4WD 3.4 V6; auto 4
✔ Ford Explorer		17	Limited 4.0 V6; auto 4
✔ Nissan Pathfinder		19	LE 4WD 3.3 V6; auto 4
✔ Jeep Grand Cherokee		15	Limited 5.2 V8; auto 4
✔ Toyota Land Cruiser		14	4.5 Six; auto 4
▪ Chevrolet Tahoe		13	LS 4-door 4WD 5.7 V8; auto 4
▪ GMC Yukon		13	Chevrolet Tahoe LS 4-door 4WD 5.7 V8; auto 4
▪ Chevrolet Blazer		17	LT 4.3 V6; auto 4
▪ GMC Jimmy		17	Chevrolet Blazer LT 4.3 V6; auto 4
▪ Honda Passport		16	EX 3.2 V6; auto 4
▪ Isuzu Rodeo		16	Honda Passport EX 3.2 V6; auto 4
Land Rover Discovery		13	3.9 V8; auto 4
MINIVAN			
▪ Chrysler Town & Country		18	Dodge Grand Caravan SE 3.3 V6; auto 4
▪ Dodge Grand Caravan		18	SE 3.3 V6; auto 4
▪ Plymouth Grand Voyager		18	Dodge Grand Caravan SE 3.3 V6; auto 4
Ford Windstar		20	LX 3.8 V6; auto 4
▪ Chrysler Town & Country LX		19	Dodge Caravan LE 3.3 V6; auto 4
▪ Dodge Caravan		19	LE 3.3 V6; auto 4
▪ Plymouth Voyager		19	Dodge Caravan LE 3.3 V6; auto 4
✔ ▪ Honda Odyssey		21	EX 2.2 Four; auto 4
✔ ▪ Isuzu Oasis		21	Honda Odyssey EX 2.2 Four; auto 4

Model	Overall score					Fuel usage	Tested model
	P	F	G	VG	E		
MINIVAN *continued*							
✔ ▪ Mercury Villager						19 mpg	GS 3.0 V6; auto 4
✔ ▪ Nissan Quest						19	Mercury Villager GS 3.0 V6; auto 4
✔ Toyota Previa						18	LE 2.4 Four; auto 4
▪ Chevrolet Lumina van						18	Pontiac Trans Sport SE 3.8 V6; auto 4
▪ Oldsmobile Silhouette						18	Pontiac Trans Sport SE 3.8 V6; auto 4
▪ Pontiac Trans Sport						18	SE 3.8 V6; auto 4
▪ Chevrolet Astro						15	GMC Safari SLE 4.3 V6; auto 4
▪ GMC Safari						15	SLE 4.3 V6; auto 4
Mazda MPV						16	LX AWD 3.0 V6; auto 4
COMPACT PICKUP (EXTENDED CAB)							
✔ ▪ Ford Ranger						18	XLT 4.0 V6; auto 4
✔ ▪ Mazda B-Series						18	Ford Ranger XLT 4.0 V6; auto 4
▪ Chevrolet S-Series						17	GMC Sonoma SLE 4.3 V6; auto 4
▪ GMC Sonoma						17	SLE 4.3 V6; auto 4
Dodge Dakota						17	SLT 3.9 V6; auto 4
Toyota Tacoma						21	LX 3.4 V6; auto 4
FULL-SIZED PICKUP (EXTENDED CAB)							
Ford F-150 (1997)						16	XLT 4.6 V8; auto 4
▪ Chevrolet C1500						15	Silverado 5.0 V8; auto 4
▪ GMC Sierra C 1500						15	Chevrolet C 1500 Silverado 5.0 V8; auto 4
Dodge Ram 1500						13	Laramie SLT 5.2 V8; auto 4

How to buy a new car

The steps to a good deal

Narrow the choices. Decide what size and type of vehicle suits your needs. Don't fall in love with any one car: Consider at least two or three makes and models. The new-car profiles beginning on page 242 will help you select models that meet your criteria. Sometimes a car's sibling—an essentially similar model sold under a different nameplate—may cost less.

Learn the dealer's cost. By finding out what the dealer paid for the car—the wholesale, or "invoice," price—you know how much room you have to negotiate a price. On average, the dealer cost is 90 percent of the manufacturer's suggested retail price (MSRP), also known as the sticker price, but it can be as little as 80 percent or as much as 96 percent.

You can get information on dealer costs, in different levels of detail, from various sources: Printed price guides are available at bookstores, newstands, and libraries, and information is also available from auto clubs and on the Internet. The Consumer Reports New Car Price Service offers detailed information, sent to you by fax or mail, on the dealer's cost for a car with specific options in the form of a worksheet; see page 357. That call can also give you the trade-in value of your current car, or you can call our Used Car Price Service directly (page 358).

If you want to make your own worksheet for each vehicle:

■ Write down the make, model, and trim line. List each option or options package you want, by name and manufacturer's code number (you'll find that information on the price printouts).

■ Note in two columns the wholesale and retail prices for the basic car and each extra-cost option. Add the destination charge to both columns (it's a fixed charge, and dealers take no markup on it). Total your columns, and subtract any factory-to-dealer rebate from the wholesale column. The difference between the final wholesale and retail prices represents the room you have to bargain.

Start to bargain. Bring your worksheet to the dealership. Present your figures to the salesperson and ask for the lowest markup over dealer cost the dealership will accept. If your figures are challenged, ask to see documentation that they are wrong.

The dealership may include a "conveyance" or "documentation" fee in the final price. This largely arbitrary charge, purportedly to cover the cost of preparing the paperwork, can range from $50 to $300 or more. You probably won't be able to negotiate the fee away, so consider it part of the price—and a reason to choose one dealer over another.

Throughout the negotiations, always bargain up from the invoice price, not down from the sticker price. Keep the negotiations simple: Don't discuss trade-ins, leases, or financing until you reach a firm price for the new car.

Play the endgame. You will probably be made to wait for lengthy periods while the salesperson ferries the deal to the dealership's sales manager. Sometimes the long waits are a tactic designed to wear you down. Stay calm. You can't negotiate well if you are angry or anxious.

You don't have to say how much you're willing to pay, and you should never say, "I want to pay X-dollars a month"—that only gives the salesperson reason to structure a loan over a longer period to make it seem more reasonable. (In fact, you'll wind up paying more for the car because the longer loan term increases the amount of interest you'll pay.) As a rule, it's best to take the shortest-term loan you can afford, to hold down the interest cost and thus reduce the overall cost of ownership.

Don't be rushed into making a decision immediately. A deal that's good today should be good tomorrow as well. Be frank about your willingness to shop elsewhere. If you feel you're getting a runaround, get up and leave.

After you've agreed on a price, you may be passed on to a "business manager," ostensibly to close the deal. Be wary. This individual may try to sell you undercoating, rustproofing, fabric protection, etching of the vehicle identification number on the windows, or a costly extended warranty. Such dealer add-ons, in our experience, are worthless, overpriced, or both.

What's the bottom line? For a brand-new model in tight supply, you may have to pay the full sticker price or close to it. Otherwise, paying $300 to $500 over invoice is reasonable for most models.

Only after you have a firm price should you talk about leasing or financing. If you have a car to trade in, find out how much it's worth. You can check a printed guide, such as the "N.A.D.A. Official Used Car Guide" or the "Kelley Blue Book"—libraries and bank loan officers generally have copies—or call the Consumers Reports Used Car Price Service. See page 358.

Dealers and manufacturers sometimes offer low loan rates as a sales incentive. Calculate the final cost of such loans carefully. For instance, does a low "teaser" rate apply only if you pay the full sticker price, or is it offered even after you've negotiated a lower price? Don't jump at the dealer's terms without checking local bank or credit-union rates.

Read the fine print. Read the sales contract carefully. If you see something you don't like—or if you think something should be included—ask for changes. Also, be sure the contract really is a sales contract, if you're buying the car. People sometimes believe they're buying a car, only to find that the dealership has maneuvered them into a lease agreement instead. Be sure, too, that an officer at the dealership signs the contract.

Alternatives to haggling

If you're uncomfortable bargaining over price here are some alternatives:

No-haggle dealers. GM's Saturn Corp. popularized the practice of selling cars for a fixed, take-it-or-leave-it price. Some dealers for other car makes have also adopted a no-haggle pricing policy; many others have a "no-haggle" price on a few specific models.

The policy does make it easy to come to terms with the dealer. However, our experience in buying cars for our testing program has shown that a no-haggle price isn't always lower than one a shrewd bargainer can obtain.

Auto-buying services. These firms do all or part of the negotiating for you. You explain exactly what you're looking for, and the service contacts one or more dealers in your area and negotiates a price. Sometimes you pay the service a flat fee ($50 is typical); other times the service gets its fee or commission from the dealer.

Unfortunately, you can't be sure how good a deal a buying service is unless you research prices on your own. For that reason, we would be wary of using a service as the sole source of price information.

Local buying services are listed in the Yellow Pages under "Automobile Brokers." Few services operate at a national level. One, Auto Insider, is essentially a free referral service. It provides the names of local dealers who have said that they will provide discounts. But the service doesn't give you the factory-invoice prices—you still need to find those out for yourself so you can be sure you're getting a good deal.

Another service, Car Bargains, run by the Center for the Study of Services in Washington, D.C., charges a $150 fee for quote sheets from local dealers who agree to sell a car for a certain amount over the factory-invoice price.

Online shopping. It's now possible to shop for a car using a computer, with various services accessible through one of the major online services or the Internet. Those sources can give you information about car models, car pricing, and option availability for new and used cars. You can find directories of dealers and dealer home pages.

Some services have set up networks of dealers who have agreed to give discounts and claim that they will make buying a car as easy as picking up the phone. Again, you need to do your homework first, to find out how good a deal you're getting.

How to lease a new car

The least expensive way to buy a car is to pay cash. Financing is more costly because of the interest you pay. Leasing, whether a new or used car, is often costlier still, but it can make sense in certain circumstances.

Leasing requires little or no cash up front. And monthly payments are lower than those for a car loan because, in essence, you're borrowing to cover only the car's depreciation while you have it. But after the typical 36-month lease ends, the lease customer owns nothing, while the buyer still has a car worth thousands of dollars. Even if the monthly loan payments for a car run substantially more than the monthly lease payments, the owner will normally come out several hundred dollars ahead of the lease customer.

If you're still tempted to lease, keep the following basics in mind:

■ Read the advertising fine print. The most attractive terms are often available only if you pay a "capitalized cost reduc-tion"—the money you must put down to qualify for the low payments touted in the ad. Further, those payments are sometimes available only on stripped-down models. Expect to pay more if you want a car with extra features or a larger-than-standard engine.

■ Be sure you can live within the lease restrictions. Most dealers limit you to between 12,000 and 15,000 miles of driving a year. Clock any more and you could be charged as much as 25 cents a mile.

■ Ask what protections you'll have to cover repairs or damage. Make sure the manufacturer's warranty covers the entire term of the lease and the number of miles you're likely to drive.

A standard lease contract requires you to pay for "excess wear and tear"; ask the dealer to spell out what that means. If you don't, you risk paying steep repair bills when the lease is up.

Make sure, too, that the lease includes "GAP" insurance. If the car is stolen or totaled, that insurance will pay the difference between what you owe on the lease and what the car is worth—a difference that can amount to thousands of dollars.

■ Know what the car's residual value will be. Leasing companies base the monthly payments on an estimate of the car's "residual," or ultimate resale, value. You can often buy the car at that price when the lease is up (although lately, an increasing number of the contracts we've seen do not give this option). If you want to end the lease early, you'll have to pay the difference between the car's estimated value and the total monthly payments you've made to that point. That often amounts to all the remaining payments you'd owe to the lease's expiration.

■ Take your time before you sign. Ask to take home a copy of the lease contract and scrutinize it closely. Sizing up a leasing deal is complicated because contract terms vary widely from state to state and even dealer by dealer.

Watch out for extra charges, such as fees for conveyance, disposition, and preparation. Those are pure dealer profit and can be negotiated.

New national rules, due from the Federal Reserve Board in late 1996 but probably at least a year away, will require all car leases to use standardized terminology. That should make comparison-shopping for auto leases much simpler. Until then—and probably after, too—buckle up. You're on your own.

Key auto features

Options are sold two ways: individually or as part of a package (such as a "Preferred Equipment Group"). Packages can be good deals if you want most of the items. On some imported cars, desirable options like antilock brakes are available only on cars equipped with expensive frills such as leather seats.

Here's a guide to options available today. A check (✔) indicates a recommended option—one that we think adds significantly to safety or comfort and convenience.

Air bags • cruise control • seating

Air bags. Dual air bags are standard in almost all cars and many other passenger vehicles. Single air bags are standard or optional (about 400) in some trucks. Markedly reduce chances of serious injury or death in frontal crash, though safety belts are still needed for full protection. Recommendation: A must for both front seats.

Adjustable steering column. $130 to $235. Lets you position steering wheel comfortably; eases access to driver's seat. Some have power tilt and telescoping and a memory feature. Recommendation: Especially useful for cars with more than one driver.

Cruise control. $175 to $395. Helps you stay within speed limit; may reduce driver fatigue and improve fuel economy. But can lull the driver into inattention. Practical only where traffic is light. Recommendation: Best for those who do a lot of long-distance driving.

Power seat. $175 to $955. Adjustable for comfort and driver visibility. Convenience of controls varies. Some cars also have power for the front passenger seat. Memory feature remembers settings for several drivers. Recommendation: A big help in cars with otherwise low front seats.

Leather upholstery. $490 to $1675. Looks and feels luxurious, but is often slippery and clammy. Without a seat heater ($225 to $580 additional), leather feels cold in winter. Recommendation: Durable and easier to clean than cloth, but an indulgence.

Air-conditioning • phone • sound system

Air-conditioning. $520 to $1950, but standard on many vehicles. Add $100 to $200 for automatic temperature control. Improves comfort, reduces outside noise, and prevents window fogging year-round. Reduces fuel economy, particularly in stop-and-go traffic. Costly to repair. Recommendation: A must in the South and Southwest, and very nice anywhere. Just try to sell a used car without it.

Theft-deterrent system. $100 to $585 gets you some combination of alarms, flashing lights, honking horns, and autosound systems that become useless if yanked loose. May deter theft and reduce your insurance rates, but false alarms disturb the neighbors. Alarms are widely ignored in most cities. Recommendation: Worthwhile, but cheaper ones are available as aftermarket devices.

Autosound system. $25 to $2075, depending on components and features. CD or tape player lets you listen to what you like. The best systems approach room acoustics. But the costlier the system, the more tempting to thieves. Recommendation: A matter of personal preference.

Cellular phone. $650 to $950. Lets you call police, ambulance, or tow truck— or just tell someone you'll be late. Hands-free operation is preferable while driv-

ing. Monthly and per-call charges are dropping. Recommendation: Regular cellular phones will work, but those designed specially for cars allow hands-free use. Some cars come prewired for a phone.

Electronic instrument-panel display. $245 to $490. Large digital speedometer may be easy to read. But often, these designs are more confusing than analog versions. Recommendation: A fix for something that's not broken.

Trip computer/vehicle monitor. $200 to $440; often packaged with electronic instrument-panel display. This gadget displays fuel use, miles to empty, and such. The monitor may provide warnings of a burned-out taillight, needed engine service, etc. Recommendation: Expensive replacement for pencil and paper. When a bulb burns out, display goes blank.

Brakes • drivetrain • suspension

Antilock brakes. Standard in many vehicles, $500 to $1160 if an option. Rapid on-off pulsing of the brakes lets you maintain control during hard stops and stop shorter on slippery roads. To use, don't pump the brakes, just stomp and steer. Recommendation: Highly recommended safety item.

Traction control. Standard on some cars, $175 to $1950 as an option. Improves traction and directional stability on slippery roads, though not as effectively as all-wheel drive. Sophisticated systems work at all speeds; others, typically, below 25 mph. Recommendation: Worthwhile, especially in rear-wheel-drive cars.

All-wheel drive. Costs $1000 to $3890 where it's not standard. Greatly improves traction and directional stability in snow and mud. Full-time all-wheel drive, which requires no driver action to engage, also improves handling on dry roads. Selectable all-wheel drive is almost as easy to use. Part-time four-wheel drive can't be used on dry roads. Recommendation: Makes a vehicle more sure-footed but reduces fuel economy, and it's costly to repair.

Limited-slip differential. $95 to $505. Improves traction on slippery roads, but can cause the driving wheels to slip to the side. Recommendation: Traction control or all-wheel drive does the job better than this feature.

Adjustable ride control. $100 to $2200. Theoretically lets you tailor the ride and handling to conditions. Recommendation: More gimmick than benefit.

Automatic level control. $175 to $910. Adjusts height of rear suspension to keep car level regardless of load. Recommendation: Useful if you often carry a full load or tow a trailer.

Child seat • sun roof • spare

Integrated child seat. $100 to $250. More expensive than many seats sold separately, but no fumbling or difficulty installing it correctly. When not deployed, it may reduce comfort for passenger in its place. Recommendation: Worthwhile for families with small children.

Sun roof/moon roof. $350 to $1700. Generally, a sun roof lets in light only when open; a moon roof is like a window (with tint) in the roof. Improves ventilation, brightens the interior. Usually reduces head room. Noisy when open. Recommendation: Go ahead, but check head room.

Conventional spare. $80 to $260. Adds a fifth (full-sized) tire to the rotation. Harder to handle than limited-service spare, but no speed or distance restriction. Recommendation: Worthwhile

if there's room in the trunk, but not very common anymore.

Transmission • engine

Automatic transmission. Standard in most vehicles; costs up to $1450 as an option. Reduces driver fatigue in traffic. Overdrive gear and lock-up torque converter improve fuel economy. Today's automatics are practical even with a small engine. Some models now have a five-speed automatic. Recommendation: Manual transmissions usually deliver better fuel economy, but automatics are much easier to drive, particularly in bumper-to-bumper traffic.

Optional engine. Getting more horsepower adds $110 to $1425. A larger engine gives you more power and better acceleration, of course, and usually less noise at highway speeds, but typically worsens fuel economy. May be available only with other equipment upgrades. Recommendation: Most base engines are adequate in passenger cars. Light trucks, minivans, and SUVs may benefit, especially for trailer-towing.

Windows • locks • mirrors

Rear-window defroster. $70 to $330, but standard in most cars. Keeps the rear window clear of fog, frost, and snow. Recommendation: Worth getting.

Rear-window wiper/washer. $120 to $280, but standard in many vehicles. Clears grime from rear window of wagons, hatchbacks, sport-utility vehicles, and vans. Recommendation: Worthwhile for those vehicles.

Central locking system. $25 to $440. Lets you lock and unlock all doors at once, inside or out, with a remote control. Variations abound. The best design depends on your comfort level where you travel. Possible nuisances: automatic systems that don't let you open your door from inside; systems that automatically unlock all the doors when the car is put in Park (as in many GM cars). Recommendation: A feature that soon can seem an indispensible convenience; especially worthwhile where security is a concern.

Power mirrors. $70 to $140. More than a convenience, they contribute to safety by making the mirrors easy to adjust. Recommendation: Especially useful for cars with more than one driver.

Power windows. $250 to $330. Some give you one-touch lowering of driver's window and driver's control of all windows. Lock-out feature reduces hazard to children. Switches can be confusing and hard to find at night. Recommendation: An indulgence, perhaps, but after you've lived with power, turning a window crank can seem burdensome.

Not worth the money

Extended-service contract. Cost varies. Extends manufacturer's warranty, which typically runs for three years. Recommendation: May be worthwhile for an unreliable model—but you wouldn't want to buy one of those anyway.

Dealer "packs," or add-ons. Cost varies. Packs include dealer-installed rustproofing, pinstripes, paint and upholstery preservatives, etc. At best, they're unnecessary or no better than aftermarket products you apply yourself. Improperly applied rustproofing can hasten corrosion. Recommendation: A waste of money.

How to buy a used car ———

Look for a reliable model

You can minimize the risk of buying a used-car lemon if you buy a model with a good reliability record. Our Frequency-of-Repair records, based on readers' experiences with more than 630,000 cars, trucks, sport-utility vehicles, and vans, describe the reliability history of 1988 through 1995 models. From those records, we have derived a list of reliable used cars (see page 270) and another list of models to avoid (page 273). However, the older the car, the less important our records and the more important the condition of the individual car.

Where to buy

Superstores and new-car dealers. They're usually the safest source, with the best-quality cars, many of them coming off lease deals short enough that the original manufacturer's warranty is still in effect. Many such dealers offer their own warranty as well. It's typically just long enough to let you make sure the car's not a lemon, but it's longer on some high-end models. You may be able to negotiate an extension to the manufacturer's warranty, too. New-car dealers have repair facilities. Some also lease used cars. But: Prices at both superstores and new-car dealers tend to be high.

Independent used-car dealers. Prices are apt to be lower than those at a superstore or a new-car dealer. But: The stock may be lower in quality. A car may have come from a dealer who rejected it, a wholesale auction, a police department, or a taxi fleet. Most dealers who sell only used cars lack repair facilities, so their cars may have had only cosmetic repairs before being put on sale.

Service stations and independent garages. If they've serviced the car, they can recount its history, a big advantage—if they're truthful. Choose an established station with a good reputation. But: Selling cars is just a sideline, so selection will be limited.

Banks and other lenders. They sell repossessed cars. But: You have no assurance of the car's condition.

Private owners. They tend to charge the lowest prices. But: You'll have little recourse if problems develop.

Checking it out

If you're buying a car from a private owner, ask to see service and repair receipts, or the warranty booklet. A car sold by a dealer must have a "Buyer's Guide" sticker with warranty information. Read it carefully. In most states, the words "as is" mean you have no warranty coverage. Walk away if you don't see convincing evidence that the car has been serviced regularly and treated well.

These are the most important areas to check:

Fluid levels and leaks. Automatic-transmission fluid should be transparent or pinkish and shouldn't smell burnt. Coolant shouldn't look rusty, and there should be no green stains on the radiator (evidence of leaks). Low engine oil or transmission fluid is a sign of neglect.

Body integrity. Look for rust, especially in the trunk, wheel wells, and rocker panels (under the doors). Bring along a small magnet and apply it to those areas. If it doesn't stick, suspect a hasty (and nonpermanent) patch-up job with body putty. Look for signs of an accident—new welds, discolored surfaces, rippled body work, panels whose

color doesn't quite match, doors that don't fit properly. A fresh paint job or fresh undercoating may be hiding some serious sins.

Tires. If the car has less than 25,000 miles on the odometer, it should have its original tires, still with some useful tread. Bald or new tires could mean that the odometer has been turned back. Uneven tire wear could signal accident damage or poor wheel alignment. Make sure there's a usable spare tire and a jack.

Suspension. Pull and push on the top of each front tire: Any play or clunks could mean bad wheel bearings or suspension joints. Push down and quickly release each corner of the car: More than one or two bounces could mean worn shocks or struts. Look at the car from the rear and side: A lopsided stance could mean sagging springs.

Interior. Seats shouldn't sag like an old chair, smell musty, or have ripped upholstery. Pedal wear should jibe with the odometer's reading. See that safety belts and controls work. Check the trunk for mildew or moisture.

You'll need about a half hour for a thorough test drive; pick a clear, dry day. First, be sure the driving position is comfortable and that the controls are easy to see and reach. Then, check these points:

Steering. With the engine off but the ignition on, there should be no more than two inches of play when you jiggle the steering wheel. Steering should be smooth and precise, with a minimum of vibration. A car that pulls to one side may need a simple alignment or proper tire inflation—or it may have been in an accident. "Crabbing," a sideways drift as the car moves forward, may mean the car was in an accident that twisted the body.

Engine. Look for smooth acceleration and ample power on hills and when passing. Pinging or knocking is a sign of an out-of-tune engine, and blue smoke is a sign the car's burning oil. A bit of puffy white smoke on a cold day is all right, but a lot of smoke could mean a bad head gasket or worse.

Transmission. Shifting should be smooth. Signs of wear: in an automatic, a hesitation between the engine's acceleration and the car's; in a manual, a clutch that slips or doesn't engage smoothly.

Brakes. On a straight, traffic-free road, try a series of stops from about 45 mph. Warning signs: strong pulling to one side, pedal vibration (except with antilock brakes), an abnormally long stopping distance. With the engine idling, step firmly on the brake pedal for 30 seconds. If it feels spongy or sinks, the brake system may have a leak.

Exhaust system. Sputtering or rumbling could mean a leak that could be costly to fix.

Comfort and quiet. Drive at 30 to 40 mph over a bumpy road. Excessive bouncing may point to suspension problems. Rattles and squeaks are hard to trace; you may have to live with them.

Have a mechanic inspect the car (approximate cost: $60 to $100). Make sure the mechanic performs a compression test and assesses any flaws you've found. Ask the mechanic to give you a written estimate of repairs; you can use it in negotiating.

What to pay?

Typical prices for used cars can be found in printed guides available in most libraries. Sometimes, however, the prices in those guides represent only a starting point for dealers. Also, a printed guide may not be up-to-date. Consumer Reports' Used Car Price Service provides current prices at which cars in varying condition are actually selling in various parts of the country. See page 358.

The National Highway Traffic Safety Administration (800 424-9393) can tell you whether a model has been recalled. Also, the Buying Guide lists all auto recalls published in CONSUMER REPORTS during the last year. See page 320.

How to use the Buying Guide

- Read the article for general guidance about types, features, and how to buy. There you'll find a discussion of the choices you'll face in the marketplace, what's new, and key buying advice.
- The Ratings graph the overall score so you can quickly understand the big picture in performance. Details on features or performance are also noted. For many products, we also have information on how reliable a brand is likely to be. See page 11.
- To find our last full report on a subject, refer to the article or the Ratings for the listing, or check the eight-year index, page 342.

Used cars—good & bad

The list of reliable used cars includes 1988 to 1994 models whose overall reliability has been better than average for their model year, according to our Frequency-of-Repair data (see page 275).

The reliable cars are grouped by price, as reported in the April issue of consumer reports. Most are likely to have dropped to a lower price by 1997. Prices are averages in the Midwest for cars with average mileage (10,000 to 15,000 miles a year) and with air-conditioning, AM/FM cassette stereo, and automatic transmission. (Prices for sporty cars are with manual transmission.) Luxury cars are priced with leather seats, sun roof, and CD player.

The list of used cars to avoid—see page 273—includes models whose overall records have been considerably worse than their model-year average.

In both lists, problems with the engine, engine cooling, transmission, clutch, and body rust—troubles likely to be serious and costly to repair—have been weighted more heavily than other problems.

Within groups, models are listed alphabetically. Except as noted, a listing covers all body styles, engines, and drive types. Throughout, 2WD is two-wheel drive, 4WD is front-wheel drive.

Reliable used cars

Less than $4000

DODGE
Colt, '89

EAGLE
Summit (except Wagon), '89

FORD
Festiva, '88-90

MAZDA
323, '88

MITSUBISHI
Mirage, '89
Pickup 4, '88

PLYMOUTH
Colt, '89

$4000-$6000

DODGE
Colt, '91
Colt Wagon, '89
Dakota Pickup 2WD, '88

EAGLE
Summit (except Wagon), '91

HONDA
Accord, '88
CRX, '89
Civic, '88

MAZDA
323, '90-91
626, '89 [1]
929, '88
MX-6, '88-89 [1]
Pickup 2WD, '89-90
Protegé, '90

MITSUBISHI
Mirage, '91

NISSAN
Pickup 2WD, '88-89

PLYMOUTH
Colt, '91
Colt Wagon, '89, '91

TOYOTA
Camry, '88

Corolla, '88-90
MR2, '88

$6000-$8000

AUDI
80/90, '88

BUICK
Century, '90
Riviera, '89

CADILLAC
Eldorado, '88

DODGE
Colt, '92
Colt Wagon, '91

EAGLE
Summit (except Wagon), '92

GEO
Prizm, '91-92

HONDA
Accord, '89
CRX, '90-91
Civic, '89-90

$6000-$8000 (cont.)

MAZDA
323, '92
626, '90
929, '89
MX-6, '90
Pickup 2WD, '91
Protege, '91

MITSUBISHI
Galant 4, '89, '90 ☑

NISSAN
Maxima, '88 ☑
Sentra, '91-92
Stanza, '90 ☑

PLYMOUTH
Colt, '92

SUBARU
Legacy, '90

TOYOTA
Camry, '89
Celica, '89
Corolla, '91
Pickup, '89
Tercel, '91

VOLVO
240 Series, '88
740 Series, '88

$8000-$10,000

ACURA
Integra, '90-91
Legend, '88 ▫

BMW
3-Series, '88
5-Series, '88

BUICK
Century, '93

CADILLAC
Eldorado, '89

FORD
Ranger Pickup 2WD, '93

GEO
Prizm, '93

Tracker, '92

HONDA
Accord, '90
Civic, '91-92
Prelude, '89-90

ISUZU
Pickup 4, '91

MAZDA
626, '91
MPV 4, '89
MX-5 Miata, '90
MX-6, '91
Pickup 2WD, '92
Protege, '93

MITSUBISHI
Galant 4, '91
Mirage, '92

NISSAN
Maxima, '89 ☑
Pathfinder, '88
Pickup 2WD, '91-92
Stanza, '91-92

PLYMOUTH
Colt Wagon, '92

SUBARU
Impreza, '93

SUZUKI
Sidekick, '92

TOYOTA
4Runner, '88
Camry, '90-91
Celica, '90
Corolla, '92
Cressida, '89-90
Paseo, '92
Pickup, '90-91
Tercel, '92-93

VOLVO
240 Series, '89

$10,000-$12,000

ACURA
Integra, '92
Legend, '89 ☑

BMW
3-Series, '89

CADILLAC
Fleetwood, '89

GEO
Prizm, '94
Tracker, '93-94

HONDA
Accord, '91
Civic, '93-94
Prelude, '91

LEXUS
ES 250, '90

MAZDA
MX-5
Miata, '91
Protegé, '94

MITSUBISHI
Galant 4, '92
Montero, '90-91

NISSAN
240SX, '91
Altima, '93
Maxima, '90 ☑
Pathfinder, '89
Pickup 2WD, '93
Sentra, '94

OLDSMOBILE
Cutlass Ciera, '93

PLYMOUTH
Colt Vista Wagon, '94

SATURN
SC Coupe, '93
SL, SW, '93

SUBARU
Impreza, '94
Legacy, '91

SUZUKI
Sidekick, '93

TOYOTA
Celica, '91-92
Corolla, '93
Pickup, '92
Tercel, '94

☐ Manual transmission only. ☑ Automatic transmission only.

Continued ≫

$10,000-$12,000 (cont.)

VOLVO
240 Series, '90
740 Series, '89-90

$12,000-$15,000

ACURA
Integra, '93-94
Legend, '90 ▢
Vigor, '92

BUICK
Regal, '93

CADILLAC
Fleetwood, '90

EAGLE
Summit Wagon, '94

HONDA
Accord, '92-93
Prelude, '92-93

INFINITI
G20, '91-92

LEXUS
ES 250, '91

MAZDA
MX-5 Miata, '92-93

NISSAN
240SX, '92-93
Altima, '94
Maxima, '91-92
Pathfinder, '90-91 [1]

SATURN
SC Coupe, '94 [1]
SL, SW, '94

SUBARU
Legacy, '92-93

SUZUKI
Sidekick, '94

TOYOTA
4Runner, '89-90
Camry, '92-93
Celica, '93
Corolla, '94

Cressida, '91
Land Cruiser, '89
Pickup, '93-94
Previa Van, '91
T100 Pickup, '93

VOLVO
940 Series, '91

$15,000-$20,000

ACURA
Legend, '91 [2] , '92
Vigor, '93

FORD
Explorer, '94

HONDA
Accord, '94
Prelude, '94

INFINITI
G20, '93-94
Q45, '90-91

ISUZU
Trooper, '93

MAZDA
MX-5 Miata, '94

MITSUBISHI
Diamante, '92
Expo LRV, '94

NISSAN
Maxima, '93-94
Pathfinder, '92, '93

SUBARU
Legacy, '94

TOYOTA
4Runner, '91 [2] , '92
Camry, '94
Celica, '94
Previa Van, '92-93
VOLVO 740 Series, '92

$20,000-$25,000

ACURA
Legend, '93

Vigor, '94

BUICK
Park Avenue, '94

INFINITI
J30, '93

ISUZU
Trooper, '94

LEXUS
ES 300, '92-93
LS 400, '90-91

MERCEDES-BENZ
300, '89
S-Class, '88-89

MITSUBISHI
Diamante, '94

NISSAN
Pathfinder, '94

TOYOTA
4Runner, '93-94
Land Cruiser, '91
Previa Van, '94

VOLVO
850 Series, '93
940 Series, '94
960 Series, '94

$25,000 and up

ACURA
Legend, '94

INFINITI
J30, '94
Q45, '94

LEXUS
ES 300, '94
GS 300, '93-94
LS 400, '92-93
SC 300/400, '92-93

MERCEDES-BENZ
300, '91

TOYOTA
Land Cruiser, '94

[1] Manual transmission only. [2] Automatic transmission only.

Used cars to avoid

ACURA
SLX, '96

BMW
3-Series, '91

BUICK
Roadmaster, '94
Skylark, '88-91, '94

CADILLAC
Eldorado, '93-94
Fleetwood RWD, '93-94
Seville, '93-94

CHEVROLET
Astro Van, '92-94
Blazer, '88-93
Camaro, '88-94
Caprice, '94
Cavalier, '88-93
Celebrity, '88, '90
Corsica, Beretta, '90, '92-93
Corvette, '89-90, '92-94
K-Blazer, '94
K1500-2500 Pickup, '93
Lumina, '94
Lumina APV Van, '90, '93-94
S-10 Blazer V6 2WD, '91,
   '93-94 & 4WD, '88-94
S-10 Pickup 2WD, '91, '94 &
   4WD, '89-92, '94
Sportvan, '89-94
Suburban, '88-93

CHRYSLER
Le Baron Coupe/Conv., '88-
   94
New Yorker, '89-93
New Yorker LHS, '94
Town & Country Van 2WD,
   '90-94 & 4WD, '92-94

DODGE
Aries, '89
Caravan V6 2WD, '88-92

Dakota Pickup 2WD, '94 &
   4WD, '92, '94
Daytona, '88-90
Dynasty, '92-93
Grand Caravan V6 2WD, '88-
   94 & 4WD, '91-94
Intrepid, '93-94
Monaco, '90-91
Omni, '88-90
Ram Pickup, '94
Ram Van/Wagon B150-250,
   '89-94
Shadow, '89, '94
Stealth 2WD, '93

EAGLE
Premier V6, '88-91
Vision, '93-94

FORD
Aerostar Van, '88-92
Bronco, '88-94
Bronco II, '88-90
Club Wagon, Van, '88-94
Escort, '88-89
Explorer, '91-92
F150-250 Pickup 2WD,
   '88-93 & 4WD, '88-94
Mustang 4, '88-89
Mustang V8, '92-94
Probe, '91, '93
Ranger Pickup 4WD, '92
Taurus 4, '88-90
Taurus SHO, '89-94
Taurus V6, '88-89, '91
Tempo, '88-94
Thunderbird V6, '93
Thunderbird V8, '94

GMC
Jimmy, Yukon, '89, '92-94
S-15 Jimmy V6 2WD, '91,
   '93-94 & 4WD, '88-94

S-15 Sonoma Pickup 2WD,
   '91, '94 & 4WD,
   '89-92, '94
Safari Van, '92-94
Sierra K1500-2500
   Pickup, '93
Suburban, '88-93

GEO
Storm, '90, '92

HYUNDAI
Excel, '88-94
Sonata, '89-94

ISUZU
Rodeo, '91-93
Trooper, '91, '95-96
Trooper II, '88

JAGUAR
XJ6, XJS, '89-90

JEEP
Cherokee/Wagoneer, '90, '94
Wrangler, '88-94

LINCOLN
Continental, '88-91

MAZDA
MX-6, '93
Navajo, '91-92

MERCURY
Cougar V6, '93
Cougar V8, '94
Sable, '88-89, '91
Topaz, '88-94

MITSUBISHI
3000GT 2WD, '93
Galant 4, '94

NISSAN
300ZX, '93

Continued ❯

Continued

OLDSMOBILE
Bravada, '91-94
Cutlass Calais, '88-91
Cutlass Supreme, '89-90,
    '93-94
Silhouette Van, '90, '93-94

PLYMOUTH
Grand Voyager V6 2WD, '88-
    94 & 4WD, '91-94
Horizon, '88-90
Reliant, '89

Sundance, '89, '94
Voyager V6 2WD, '88-92

PONTIAC
Firebird, '88-94
Grand Am, '88-94
Grand Prix V6, '89-91, '94
Sunbird, '88-94
Trans Sport Van, '90,
    '93-94

SAAB
900 Series 4, '94

9000 Series, '89-90

SUBARU
Coupe, Sedan & Wagon,
    '88-89
Loyale, '90

VW
Golf, '89
Jetta, '92
Passat, '90-93

Auto batteries

Battery basics

Types. *Low-maintenance batteries* have caps or covers over their cells to permit periodic checking and refilling. *Maintenance-free batteries*, the type most new cars come with, are designed to reduce water loss further; indeed, some have no refill caps. They may not endure a deep discharge as well as low-maintenance batteries.

Size. Manufacturers categorize batteries by group size—24, 26, 34, and so forth—which denotes the size of the case (but has no direct bearing on the power output). You can find the size that fits your car on the case of the old battery or in the battery dealer's handbook.

Cold-cranking amps. Manufacturers rate the cold-cranking amperage (CCA) of their models. The CCA is the amount of current a battery should be able to deliver at 0°F without dropping below a certain cutoff voltage for 30 seconds. That translates into the battery's ability to supply power long enough to start a car in below-freezing weather.

Reserve capacity. This describes the battery's ability to continue supplying power to the engine and headlights if the charging system fails.

Shopping strategy

Many car owners don't need a battery with a CCA level of more than 500 to 550. For them, good buys include the *Exide Mega Cell Classic 24-60*, *NAPA Power 6024*, and *Omega 48-24* (Wal-Mart), all about $40. In the 600-to-700-CCA group, the standouts are the *Sears DieHard Weatherhandler 36524* (sold in warm-weather regions) and *36424;* both are $60 and have a large reserve capacity and a fairly long warranty.

Auto reliability

Frequency-of-repair records, 1988-1995

With the help of its readers, CONSUMER REPORTS has been reporting on automobile reliability for some 40 years. Each year, we ask readers to report on a year's worth of car troubles by answering our Annual Questionnaire. This year, we report on cars going back eight years, instead of six.

From all the reports—on more than 630,000 cars, minivans, pickups, and sport-utility vehicles this year—we develop:

■ The Frequency-of-Repair charts, which detail the reliability history of 277 models.

■ The lists of reliable used cars and used cars to avoid on page 270.

■ The predicted reliability of new models in the auto profiles, starting on page 242.

■ Trends and patterns. Cars continue to get more reliable. The reliability of American cars has improved dramatically over the last thirty years. GM's Saturn and Geo models have the lowest problem rate—fewer than 20 per 100 cars. In contrast, GM's Cadillac division has a relatively high problem rate.

Japanese models continue to reduce their problem rate, too, averaging 17 problems per 100 cars. European makes as a group are now about as reliable as American cars. Sport-utility vehicles have improved dramatically—as a group they're comparable with American passenger cars.

How to read the charts

The symbols in the charts show the proportion of owners who have reported serious problems for each trouble spot. The data we used to create the charts are standardized to minimize differences due to varied mileage, and the symbols are on an absolute scale, so a ⊖ means the same for any trouble spot, any year, and any car. A ⊖ means that 2 percent or fewer of our readers' cars of that make, model, and year reported problems during the 12 month survey period. A ● in one or more trouble spots should raise doubt in your mind about the car and point to areas that merit careful inspection.

At the time of the survey, the 1995 models were less than six months old, with an average of 3000 miles. On a 1995 car, regard any score of ○ or worse as a warning sign.

Of course, as cars grow older, they become more trouble-prone. While some older models still earn a ⊖ in many areas, scores of ⊖ or ○ are not uncommon—and are generally not cause for concern. For most trouble spots, scores of ⊖ or ● reflect too many problems, we believe—especially if those low scores are in areas like transmission and body rust, which are costly and difficult to repair. 2WD = 2-wheel drive; 4WD = 4-wheel drive; — = model not made that year; 4, 6,V6 or V8 = 4-, 6-, or 8-cylinder engine.

KEY TO PROBLEM RATES	
⊖	2.0% or less
⊖	2.0% - 5.0%
○	5.0% - 9.3%
◑	9.3% - 14.8%
●	More than 14.8%
✱	Insufficient data
☐	Not applicable

Trouble Spots Explained

Turn to the Frequency-of-Repair chart for any car you're considering and compare its scores with the average for the same year. That gives you a sense of whether a car's problems are the ones to be expected with age, or something more serious. As the average chart shows, many cars have brake problems by the time they're three or four years old. But if

What they include

Pistons, rings, valves, block, heads, bearings, camshafts, gaskets, turbocharger, cam belts & chains, oil pump, leaks, overhaul.

Radiator, heater core, water pump, thermostat, hoses, intercooler & plumbing, overheating.

Choke, fuel injection, computer & sensors, fuel pump, tank, emissions controls, carburetion setting, leaks, stalling.

Spark or glow plugs, coil, distributor, electronic ignition, sensors & modules, timing, too-frequent tune-ups, knock or ping.

Transaxle, gear selector, linkage, coolers & lines, leaks, malfunction or failure.

Gearbox, transaxle, shifter, linkage, leaks, malfunction or failure.

Lining, pressure plate, release bearing, linkage & hydraulics.

Starter, alternator, battery, horn, switches, controls, instruments, lights, radio & sound system, accessory motors, electronics, wiring.

Compressor, condenser, evaporator, expansion valves, hoses, dryer, fans, electronics, leakage.

Linkage, power-steering gear, pump, coolers & lines, alignment & balance, springs & torsion bars, ball joints, bushings, shocks & struts, electronic or air suspension.

Hydraulic system, linings, discs & drums, power boost, antilock system; parking brake & linkage, malfunction.

Manifold, muffler, catalytic converter, pipes, leaks.

Corrosion, pitting, perforation.

Fading, discoloring, chalking, peeling, cracking; loose trim, moldings, outside mirrors.

Seals, weather stripping, air & water leaks, wind noise, rattles & squeaks.

Window, door, seat mechanisms; locks, safety belts, sun roof, glass, wipers.

TROUBLE SPOTS	The Average Model							
	88	89	90	91	92	93	94	95
Engine	◐	○	○	⊖	⊖	⊖	⊖	⊖
Cooling	◐	◐	○	⊖	⊖	⊖	⊖	⊖
Fuel	○	○	○	⊖	⊖	⊖	⊖	⊖
Ignition	○	⊖	⊖	⊖	⊖	⊖	⊖	⊖
Auto. trans.	○	○	○	○	⊖	⊖	⊖	⊖
Man. trans.	⊖	⊖	⊖	⊖	⊖	⊖	⊖	⊖
Clutch	◐	◐	○	○	⊖	⊖	⊖	⊖
Electrical	●	●	●	◐	○	○	○	⊖
A/C	⊖	◐	○	○	○	⊖	⊖	⊖
Suspension	○	○	○	○	⊖	⊖	⊖	⊖
Brakes	●	●	●	◐	◐	○	⊖	⊖
Exhaust	⊖	◐	○	○	⊖	⊖	⊖	⊖
Body rust	○	○	⊖	⊖	⊖	⊖	⊖	⊖
Paint/trim	⊖	◐	○	○	⊖	⊖	⊖	⊖
Integrity	⊖	◐	○	○	○	○	◐	○
Hardware	⊖	◐	○	○	○	○	○	⊖

you compare the Ford Bronco or Taurus SHO against this chart, you'll see that they have had more than their share of brake problems.

Electrical problems and hardware failures (windows, locks, seat mechanisms) are fairly common in newer cars. But some late-model GM vehicles—Chevrolet Camaro, the Astro van and some sport-utility vehicles—are especially prone to hardware problems, as well as to leaks, rattles, and squeaks.

Reliability Records

TROUBLE SPOTS	Acura Integra 88 89 90 91 92 93 94 95	Acura Legend 88 89 90 91 92 93 94 95	Acura Vigor 88 89 90 91 92 93 94 95	BMW 3-Series 88 89 90 91 92 93 94 95
Engine				
Cooling				
Fuel				
Ignition				
Auto. trans.				
Man. trans.				
Clutch				
Electrical				
A/C				
Suspension				
Brakes				
Exhaust				
Body rust				
Paint/trim				
Integrity				
Hardware				

(Acura Vigor: data present for 92 93 94 95; Man. trans. and Clutch marked ★. BMW 3-Series Auto. trans., Man. trans. and Clutch rows marked ★ = insufficient data.)

TROUBLE SPOTS	BMW 5-Series 88 89 90 91 92 93 94 95	Buick Century 88 89 90 91 92 93 94 95	Buick Electra, Park Avenue & Ultra 88 89 90 91 92 93 94 95	Buick LeSabre 88 89 90 91 92 93 94 95
Engine				
Cooling				
Fuel				
Ignition				
Auto. trans.				
Man. trans.				
Clutch				
Electrical				
A/C				
Suspension				
Brakes				
Exhaust				
Body rust				
Paint/trim				
Integrity				
Hardware				

(BMW 5-Series: Man. trans. and Clutch rows marked ★ / "Insufficient data" for 90–93; Buick Century, Buick Electra/Park Avenue & Ultra, and Buick LeSabre have no Man. trans. or Clutch data.)

Buick models

TROUBLE SPOTS	Buick Regal 88 89 90 91 92 93 94 95	Buick Riviera 88 89 90 91 92 93 94 95	Buick Roadmaster 88 89 90 91 92 93 94 95	Buick Skylark 88 89 90 91 92 93 94 95
Engine				
Cooling				
Fuel				
Ignition				
Auto. trans.				
Man. trans.				
Clutch				
Electrical				
A/C				
Suspension				
Brakes				
Exhaust				
Body rust				
Paint/trim				
Integrity				
Hardware				

(Buick Riviera columns 92–94 marked *Insufficient data*; Buick Roadmaster columns 88–90 and 94–95 marked *Insufficient data*; Buick Skylark column 95 marked *Insufficient data*)

Cadillac models

TROUBLE SPOTS	Cadillac Brougham, Fleetwood (RWD) 88 89 90 91 92 93 94 95	Cadillac De Ville, Fleetwood (FWD) 88 89 90 91 92 93 94 95	Cadillac Eldorado 88 89 90 91 92 93 94 95	Cadillac Seville 88 89 90 91 92 93 94 95
Engine				
Cooling				
Fuel				
Ignition				
Auto. trans.				
Man. trans.				
Clutch				
Electrical				
A/C				
Suspension				
Brakes				
Exhaust				
Body rust				
Paint/trim				
Integrity				
Hardware				

(Cadillac Brougham/Fleetwood RWD columns 92 and 95 marked *Insufficient data*; Cadillac Eldorado columns 92–94 marked *Insufficient data*)

Legend: ⊖ ⊖ ○ ⊝ ● — Few ← Problems → Many • ★ Insufficient data

Chevrolet Astro Van

TROUBLE SPOTS	88	89	90	91	92	93	94	95
Engine	⊖	○	○	⊖	⊖	○	⊖	⊖
Cooling	⊖	○	○	⊖	⊖	⊖	⊖	⊖
Fuel	○	○	⊖	⊖	○	○	⊖	⊖
Ignition	○	○	⊖	⊖	⊖	⊖	⊖	⊖
Auto. trans.	○	○	⊖	⊖	⊖	○	⊖	⊖
Man. trans.	★	★						
Clutch	★	★						
Electrical	●	●	●	●	●	●	●	○
A/C	●	○	○	○	○	○	⊖	⊖
Suspension	⊖	○	⊖	⊖	⊖	⊖	⊖	⊖
Brakes	⊖	○	⊖	⊖	⊖	⊖	⊖	⊖
Exhaust	⊖	○	⊖	⊖	⊖	⊖	⊖	⊖
Body rust	⊖	○	⊖	⊖	⊖	⊖	⊖	⊖
Paint/trim	●	●	●	●	●	⊖	○	○
Integrity	⊖	⊖	⊖	⊖	●	●	⊖	●
Hardware	●	●	●	●	●	●	●	●

Chevrolet Blazer, K-Blazer, Tahoe

TROUBLE SPOTS	88	89	90	91	92	93	94	95
Engine	○	○	⊖	⊖	⊖	○	⊖	⊖
Cooling	●	○	○	⊖	⊖	⊖	⊖	⊖
Fuel	○	○	⊖	⊖	○	⊖	⊖	⊖
Ignition	○	○	⊖	○	⊖	⊖	⊖	⊖
Auto. trans.	○	○	⊖	⊖	○	○	⊖	⊖
Man. trans.	★	★	★	★	★	★	★	★
Clutch	★	★	★	★	★	★	★	★
Electrical	●	●	●	●	●	⊖	○	○
A/C	⊖	⊖	⊖	⊖	⊖	⊖	⊖	⊖
Suspension	○	⊖	○	⊖	⊖	⊖	⊖	⊖
Brakes	⊖	⊖	●	●	⊖	⊖	○	⊖
Exhaust	⊖	⊖	⊖	⊖	⊖	⊖	⊖	⊖
Body rust	●	⊖	⊖	⊖	⊖	⊖	⊖	⊖
Paint/trim	●	●	⊖	○	○	⊖	⊖	⊖
Integrity	●	●	⊖	⊖	⊖	○	○	○
Hardware	●	●	●	●	⊖	⊖	○	○

Chevrolet C1500-2500 Pickup

TROUBLE SPOTS	88	89	90	91	92	93	94	95
Engine	⊖	○	○	○	⊖	⊖	⊖	⊖
Cooling	●	○	○	⊖	⊖	⊖	⊖	⊖
Fuel	⊖	○	⊖	⊖	⊖	⊖	⊖	⊖
Ignition	○	○	○	○	⊖	⊖	⊖	⊖
Auto. trans.	○	⊖	○	○	⊖	⊖	⊖	⊖
Man. trans.	○	⊖	⊖	○	○	★	★	★
Clutch	⊖	●	●	○	○	★	★	★
Electrical	●	●	●	●	⊖	○	○	○
A/C	○	○	○	⊖	⊖	⊖	⊖	⊖
Suspension	●	○	○	⊖	⊖	⊖	⊖	⊖
Brakes	●	⊖	○	○	⊖	⊖	⊖	⊖
Exhaust	●	⊖	⊖	⊖	⊖	⊖	⊖	⊖
Body rust	○	⊖	⊖	⊖	⊖	⊖	⊖	⊖
Paint/trim	●	●	●	○	○	○	⊖	⊖
Integrity	⊖	○	○	○	○	○	○	○
Hardware	⊖	○	○	○	○	○	○	○

Chevrolet Camaro

TROUBLE SPOTS	88	89	90	91	92	93	94	95
Engine	○	○		○		⊖	⊖	⊖
Cooling	●	●		○			⊖	⊖
Fuel	●	●		○			⊖	⊖
Ignition	⊖	●		⊖			⊖	⊖
Auto. trans.	⊖	○		⊖			⊖	⊖
Man. trans.	★	★	Insufficient data	★	Insufficient data	★	⊖	★
Clutch	★	⊖	★	★	★	★	⊖	★
Electrical	○	○		⊖			○	○
A/C	⊖	○		⊖			⊖	⊖
Suspension	⊖	⊖		⊖			⊖	⊖
Brakes	⊖	○		○			○	⊖
Exhaust	⊖	○		○			⊖	⊖
Body rust	⊖	○		⊖			⊖	⊖
Paint/trim							○	○
Integrity	●	●		⊖			●	⊖
Hardware	●	●		⊖			●	⊖

Chevrolet Caprice

TROUBLE SPOTS	88	89	90	91	92	93	94	95
Engine	○	○	○	⊖	⊖	⊖	⊖	⊖
Cooling	●	⊖	⊖	⊖	⊖	⊖	⊖	⊖
Fuel	⊖	○	⊖	○	⊖	⊖	⊖	⊖
Ignition	⊖	○	⊖	⊖	⊖	⊖	⊖	⊖
Auto. trans.	⊖	○	⊖	⊖	⊖	⊖	⊖	⊖
Man. trans.	★		★	⊖	★	★	★	★
Clutch	★		★	⊖	★	★	★	★
Electrical	●	●	●	●	●	●	●	○
A/C	⊖	○	○	○	○	⊖	⊖	⊖
Suspension	⊖	⊖	⊖	⊖	⊖	⊖	⊖	⊖
Brakes	●	⊖	⊖	⊖	⊖	⊖	○	○
Exhaust	●	●	⊖	⊖	⊖	○	○	○
Body rust	⊖	⊖	⊖	○	○	⊖	⊖	⊖
Paint/trim	●	●	⊖	⊖	○	○	○	○
Integrity	⊖	○	○	○	○	○	○	○
Hardware	●	●	●	●	⊖	○	⊖	○

Chevrolet Cavalier

TROUBLE SPOTS	88	89	90	91	92	93	94	95
Engine	⊖	⊖	○	○	○	⊖	⊖	⊖
Cooling	⊖	⊖	⊖	○	○	⊖	⊖	⊖
Fuel	⊖	⊖	⊖	○	⊖	⊖	⊖	⊖
Ignition	⊖	⊖	⊖	⊖	⊖	⊖	⊖	⊖
Auto. trans.	○	○	⊖	⊖	⊖	⊖	⊖	⊖
Man. trans.	★	⊖	★	⊖	★	★	★	★
Clutch	★	⊖	★	⊖	★	★	★	★
Electrical	●	●	●	●	●	⊖	○	⊖
A/C	⊖	○	○	○	○	⊖	⊖	⊖
Suspension	⊖	○	○	⊖	⊖	⊖	⊖	⊖
Brakes	⊖	⊖	⊖	⊖	●	○	○	⊖
Exhaust	●	⊖	⊖	⊖	⊖	○	○	○
Body rust	⊖	⊖	⊖	○	○	⊖	⊖	⊖
Paint/trim	●	⊖	○	○	○	⊖	⊖	⊖
Integrity	●	●	●	⊖	⊖	⊖	⊖	⊖
Hardware	⊖	⊖	⊖	⊖	⊖	⊖	⊖	⊖

Chevrolet Celebrity

TROUBLE SPOTS	88	89	90	91	92	93	94	95
Engine	○	○	⊖					
Cooling	⊖	⊖	●					
Fuel	⊖	○						
Ignition	⊖	○						
Auto. trans.	○	○	○					
Man. trans.	★							
Clutch	★							
Electrical	●	●	●					
A/C	○	○	○					
Suspension	●	○	○					
Brakes	●	●	●					
Exhaust	●	●	●					
Body rust	●	●	○					
Paint/trim	●	●	●					
Integrity	⊖	⊖	⊖					
Hardware	⊖	⊖	⊖					

Chevrolet Corsica, Beretta

TROUBLE SPOTS	88	89	90	91	92	93	94	95
Engine	○	○	○	○	⊖	⊖	⊖	⊖
Cooling	⊖	⊖	⊖	⊖	⊖	⊖	⊖	⊖
Fuel	●	●	○	○	⊖	⊖	⊖	⊖
Ignition	●	●	⊖	⊖	⊖	⊖	⊖	⊖
Auto. trans.	○	⊖	⊖	⊖	⊖	⊖	⊖	⊖
Man. trans.	⊖	⊖	★	★	★	★	★	Insufficient data
Clutch	●	⊖	★	★	★	★	★	
Electrical	●	●	●	●	●	●	⊖	○
A/C	⊖	○	○	○	○	⊖	⊖	⊖
Suspension	●	●	●	●	●	⊖	⊖	⊖
Brakes	●	●	●	●	●	⊖	●	●
Exhaust	●	●	●	●	⊖	⊖	⊖	⊖
Body rust	○	⊖	⊖	⊖	⊖	⊖	⊖	⊖
Paint/trim	●	●	●	⊖	○	⊖	⊖	⊖
Integrity	●	●	●	●	●	●	⊖	○
Hardware	●	●	○	○	○	⊖	⊖	⊖

Chevrolet Corvette / Chevrolet K1500-2500 Pickup / Chevrolet Lumina / Chevrolet Lumina APV Van

TROUBLE SPOTS	Corvette 88	89	90	91	92	93	94	95	K1500-2500 88	89	90	91	92	93	94	95	Lumina 88	89	90	91	92	93	94	95	APV Van 88	89	90	91	92	93	94	95
Engine							○	⊖	⊖	⊖	○	⊖	⊖	⊖	⊖	⊖			⊖	○	○	⊖	⊖	⊖			○	⊖	⊖	⊖	⊖	⊖
Cooling							⊖	⊖	●	⊖	⊖	⊖	⊖	⊖	⊖	⊖			○	⊖	⊖	⊖	⊖	⊖			●	○	⊖	⊖	⊖	⊖
Fuel							⊖	⊖	⊖	⊖	⊖	○	⊖	⊖	⊖	⊖			○	○	⊖	⊖	⊖	⊖			⊖	⊖	⊖	○	⊖	⊖
Ignition							⊖		○	○	○	○	⊖	⊖	⊖	⊖			○	⊖	○	⊖	⊖	⊖			⊖	⊖	○	⊖	⊖	⊖
Auto. trans.							★	★	○	○	○	○	⊖	⊖	⊖	⊖			○	⊖	⊖	⊖	⊖	⊖			⊖	⊖	○	○	⊖	⊖
Man. trans.	Insufficient data	Insufficient data	Insufficient data	Insufficient data	Insufficient data	★	★	Insufficient data	★	★	○	★	○	★	○	★			★	★	★											
Clutch						★	★		★	★	●	★	○	★	○	★			★	★	★											
Electrical							●	⊖	●	●	○	○	○	○	○	⊖			●	●	●	○	○	○	⊖		●	●	●	●	○	○
A/C							○	⊖	○	○	○	○	⊖	⊖	⊖	⊖			⊖	⊖	⊖	⊖	⊖	⊖			○	○	○	⊖	⊖	⊖
Suspension							⊖	⊖	⊖	○	○	○	⊖	⊖	⊖	⊖			○	○	⊖	⊖	⊖	⊖			○	○	⊖	⊖	⊖	⊖
Brakes							⊖	⊖	●	●	○	○	○	⊖	⊖	⊖			●	●	●	○	○	⊖			●	●	○	⊖	⊖	⊖
Exhaust							⊖	⊖	●	●	○	○	○	⊖	⊖	⊖			⊖	⊖	⊖	⊖	⊖	⊖			⊖	⊖	⊖	⊖	⊖	⊖
Body rust							⊖	⊖	○	⊖	○	○	○	⊖	⊖	⊖			⊖	⊖	⊖	⊖	⊖	⊖			⊖	⊖	⊖	⊖	⊖	⊖
Paint/trim							○	○	○	○	○	○	⊖	⊖	⊖	⊖			○	○	○	⊖	⊖	⊖			●	○	○	○	⊖	⊖
Integrity							●	●	⊖	○	○	○	○	⊖	○	○			⊖	○	○	○	○	●			⊖	⊖	⊖	○	○	○
Hardware							●	●	⊖	○	○	○	○	○	⊖	○			●	⊖	○	○	○	○			●	⊖	○	○	○	○

Chevrolet Monte Carlo / Chevrolet S-10 Blazer, Blazer (2WD) / Chevrolet S-10 Blazer, Blazer (4WD) / Chevrolet S-10 Pickup (2WD)

TROUBLE SPOTS	Monte Carlo 88	89	90	91	92	93	94	95	S-10 Blazer (2WD) 88	89	90	91	92	93	94	95	S-10 Blazer (4WD) 88	89	90	91	92	93	94	95	S-10 Pickup (2WD) 88	89	90	91	92	93	94	95
Engine								⊖	⊖	○		⊖	○	○	○	⊖	⊖	○	⊖	⊖	○	○	⊖	⊖	○	○	⊖	⊖	○	⊖	⊖	⊖
Cooling								⊖	⊖	○		○	⊖	⊖	⊖	⊖	●	○	⊖	⊖	⊖	⊖	⊖	⊖	⊖	○	⊖	⊖	⊖	⊖	⊖	⊖
Fuel								⊖	○	⊖		⊖	⊖	⊖	⊖	⊖	○	○	⊖	⊖	⊖	⊖	⊖	⊖	⊖	○	⊖	⊖	⊖	⊖	⊖	⊖
Ignition								⊖	⊖	○		⊖	⊖	⊖	⊖	⊖	○	○	⊖	⊖	⊖	⊖	⊖	⊖	○	⊖	⊖	⊖	⊖	⊖	⊖	⊖
Auto. trans.								⊖	○	⊖	Insufficient data	⊖	★	⊖	⊖	⊖	⊖	○	⊖	○	⊖	⊖	⊖	⊖	⊖	⊖	⊖	⊖	⊖	⊖	⊖	⊖
Man. trans.								★	★	★		★	★	★	★	★	★	★	★	★	★	★	★	★	⊖	⊖	★	○	○	⊖	⊖	⊖
Clutch								★	★	★		★	★	★	★	★	★	★	★	★	★	★	★	★	⊖	○	★	○	○	○	○	⊖
Electrical								⊖	●	●		○	○	⊖	●	⊖	●	●	●	●	○	⊖	⊖	○	●	●	●	⊖	○	○	⊖	⊖
A/C								⊖	○	⊖		○	⊖	⊖	⊖	⊖	⊖	○	○	⊖	⊖	⊖	⊖	⊖	⊖	○	⊖	⊖	⊖	⊖	⊖	⊖
Suspension								⊖	○	⊖		⊖	○	○	⊖	⊖	⊖	○	○	○	○	⊖	⊖	⊖	⊖	⊖	⊖	⊖	○	⊖	⊖	⊖
Brakes								⊖	●	⊖		⊖	●	●	●	⊖	●	●	●	●	●	○	⊖	⊖	●	●	●	⊖	⊖	○	⊖	⊖
Exhaust								⊖	○	⊖		⊖	⊖	⊖	⊖	⊖	●	○	○	⊖	⊖	⊖	⊖	⊖	●	○	○	○	⊖	⊖	⊖	⊖
Body rust								⊖	○	⊖		○	⊖	⊖	⊖	⊖	⊖	●	●	○	⊖	⊖	⊖	⊖	●	●	○	○	⊖	⊖	⊖	⊖
Paint/trim								○	●	⊖		⊖	○	○	⊖	⊖	●	●	●	○	○	⊖	⊖	⊖	●	●	●	○	○	○	⊖	⊖
Integrity								⊖	●	⊖		●	○	⊖	⊖	⊖	●	●	●	●	○	○	○	○	●	●	●	○	○	○	○	○
Hardware								⊖	●	○		●	○	⊖	⊖	⊖	●	●	●	●	○	○	○	○	●	●	○	○	○	○	○	⊖

⊖ ⊖ ○ ◓ ●
Few ← Problems → Many

★ Insufficient data

Top table

Chevrolet S-10 Pickup (4WD) 88 89 90 91 92 93 94 95	Chevrolet Sportvan 88 89 90 91 92 93 94 95	TROUBLE SPOTS	Chevrolet Suburban 88 89 90 91 92 93 94 95	Chrysler Cirrus 88 89 90 91 92 93 94 95
● ⊖ · ⊖ ○ · · ⊖ ⊖	⊖ ⊖ ⊖ ⊖ ⊖ ⊖ ⊖	Engine	⊖ ⊖ ● ⊖ ⊖ ⊖ ⊖ ⊖	⊖
⊖ ⊖ · ⊖ ⊖ · · ⊖ ⊖	● ⊖ ⊖ ⊖ ○ ⊖ ⊖	Cooling	● ● ● ⊖ ○ ○ ⊖ ⊖	⊖
○ ○ · ○ ⊖ · · ⊖ ⊖	○ ⊖ ⊖ ⊖ ⊖ ⊖ ⊖	Fuel	○ ○ ⊖ ○ ⊖ ⊖ ⊖ ⊖	⊖
⊖ ⊖ · ○ ⊖ · · ⊖ ⊖	⊖ ⊖ ⊖ ⊖ ⊖ ⊖ ⊖	Ignition	⊖ ○ ○ ⊖ ⊖ ⊖ ⊖ ⊖	⊖
⊖ ○ · ⊖ ⊖ · · ○ ⊖	○ ○ ○ ○ ⊖ ○ ⊖	Auto. trans.	○ ⊖ ○ ⊖ ⊖ ⊖ ⊖ ⊖	⊖
★ ★ · ★ ★ · · ★ ★	★ ★	Man. trans.	★ ★ ★	
★ ★ · ★ ★ · · ★ ★	★ ★	Clutch	★ ★ ★	
● ● · ● ○ · · ● ○	● ● ⊖ ⊖ ● ●	Electrical	● ● ● ⊖ ● ● ○ ⊖	○
○ ⊖ · ⊖ ⊖ · · ⊖ ⊖	⊖ ● ⊖ ⊖ ○ ○	A/C	⊖ ⊖ ○ ○ ○ ⊖ ⊖	⊖
● ⊖ · ⊖ ⊖ · · ⊖ ○	⊖ ⊖ ○ ○ ⊖ ⊖	Suspension	⊖ ○ ○ ⊖ ⊖ ⊖ ⊖	⊖
● ⊖ · ⊖ ⊖ · · ○ ⊖	○ ⊖ ⊖ ● ⊖ ●	Brakes	● ● ● ⊖ ⊖ ○ ○ ⊖	⊖
⊖ ● · ⊖ ⊖ · · ⊖ ⊖	○ ⊖ ○ ⊖ ⊖ ⊖	Exhaust	● ⊖ ○ ○ ○ ⊖ ⊖ ⊖	⊖
● ● · ⊖ ⊖ · · ○ ⊖	● ⊖ ● ⊖ ⊖ ⊖ ⊖	Body rust	● ○ ⊖ ⊖ ⊖ ⊖ ⊖ ⊖	⊖
● ● · ⊖ ⊖ · · ○ ⊖	● ● ● ● ● ●	Paint/trim	● ● ⊖ ⊖ ○ ○ ⊖ ⊖	○
⊖ ● · ○ ⊖ · · ⊖ ○	● ● ● ● ● ●	Integrity	● ● ● ⊖ ⊖ ○ ○ ⊖	⊖
⊖ ● · ● ⊖ · · ⊖ ⊖	● ● ⊖ ● ● ●	Hardware	● ● ● ● ⊖ ⊖ ○ ○	⊖

Vertical note in Chevrolet S-10 Pickup columns (90, 93): *Insufficient data*

Vertical note in TROUBLE SPOTS / Sportvan area: *Insufficient data*

Bottom table

Chrysler Concorde 88 89 90 91 92 93 94 95	Chrysler Le Baron Coupe & Convertible 88 89 90 91 92 93 94 95	TROUBLE SPOTS	Chrysler Le Baron Sedan 88 89 90 91 92 93 94 95	Chrysler New Yorker, LHS 88 89 90 91 92 93 94 95
⊖ ⊖ ⊖	● ● ○ ○ ○ ⊖ ⊖	Engine	● ○ ○ ○ ⊖ ⊖	● ● ○ ⊖ ⊖ ⊖ ⊖
⊖ ⊖ ⊖	● ● ⊖ ⊖ ⊖ ⊖	Cooling	○ ⊖ ⊖ ⊖ ⊖	● ○ ○ ○ ⊖ ⊖ ⊖
⊖ ⊖ ⊖	⊖ ⊖ ⊖ ⊖ ⊖ ⊖	Fuel	⊖ ○ ○ ⊖ ⊖ ⊖	● ○ ○ ○ ⊖ ⊖ ⊖
⊖ ⊖ ⊖	○ ⊖ ⊖ ⊖ ⊖ ⊖	Ignition	○ ⊖ ⊖ ⊖ ⊖ ⊖	○ ⊖ ○ ⊖ ⊖ ⊖ ⊖
⊖ ⊖ ⊖	⊖ ⊖ ⊖ ● ⊖ ○	Auto. trans.	○ ⊖ ⊖ ⊖ ⊖ ○	○ ● ● ● ○ ○ ⊖
	★ ★ ★ ★ ★ ★	Man. trans.		
	★ ★ ★ ★ ★ ★	Clutch		
○ ○ ⊖	● ● ● ● ○ ○	Electrical	● ⊖ ⊖ ○ ○	● ● ● ● ⊖ ○ ⊖
○ ○ ⊖	● ● ○ ⊖ ○ ⊖	A/C	● ○ ○ ⊖ ⊖	● ● ○ ○ ○ ⊖ ⊖
⊖ ⊖ ⊖	● ● ● ⊖ ⊖ ⊖	Suspension	⊖ ⊖ ⊖ ⊖ ⊖	⊖ ⊖ ⊖ ⊖ ⊖ ⊖ ⊖
○ ○ ⊖	● ● ● ○ ○ ○	Brakes	● ● ○ ○ ⊖	● ● ● ● ⊖ ⊖ ⊖
⊖ ⊖ ⊖	○ ⊖ ○ ⊖ ⊖ ⊖	Exhaust	○ ⊖ ● ● ⊖	⊖ ⊖ ⊖ ⊖ ⊖ ⊖ ⊖
⊖ ⊖ ⊖	○ ○ ⊖ ⊖ ⊖ ⊖	Body rust	○ ⊖ ⊖ ⊖ ⊖	⊖ ⊖ ⊖ ⊖ ⊖ ⊖ ⊖
○ ○ ⊖	● ● ○ ○ ● ⊖	Paint/trim	○ ⊖ ⊖ ⊖ ⊖	● ○ ○ ○ ⊖ ⊖ ⊖
○ ⊖ ⊖	● ● ● ● ● ●	Integrity	○ ⊖ ⊖ ⊖ ⊖	● ● ○ ⊖ ○ ● ⊖
○ ⊖ ⊖	● ● ● ● ● ⊖	Hardware	⊖ ○ ⊖ ○ ⊖	● ⊖ ○ ⊖ ⊖ ● ⊖

Vertical note in TROUBLE SPOTS / Le Baron Sedan area: *Insufficient data*

Chrysler Sebring / Chrysler Town & Country Van (2WD) / Chrysler Town & Country Van (4WD) / Dodge Avenger

TROUBLE SPOTS	Chrysler Sebring (88–95)	Chrysler Town & Country Van (2WD) (88–95)	Chrysler Town & Country Van (4WD) (88–95)	Dodge Avenger (88–95)
Engine	95: ⊖	90:○ 91:○ 92:○ 93:○ 94:⊖ 95:⊖	92:○ 93:○ 94:○	95: ⊖
Cooling	95: ⊖	90:○ 91:⊖ 92:⊖ 93:⊖ 94:⊖ 95:⊖	92:○ 93:⊖ 94:⊖	95: ⊖
Fuel	95: ⊖	90:○ 91:○ 92:⊖ 93:⊖ 94:⊖ 95:⊖	92:○ 93:○ 94:⊖	95: ⊖
Ignition	95: ⊖	90:⊖ 91:⊖ 92:⊖ 93:⊖ 94:⊖ 95:⊖	92:⊖ 93:⊖ 94:⊖	95: ⊖
Auto. trans.	95: ⊖	90:● 91:● 92:◑ 93:○ 94:○ 95:⊖	92:● 93:◑ 94:○	95: ⊖
Man. trans.	95: ★			95: ★
Clutch	95: ★			95: ★
Electrical	95: ⊖	90:● 91:● 92:● 93:◑ 94:○ 95:⊖	92:● 93:○ 94:○	95: ⊖
A/C	95: ⊖	90:⊖ 91:⊖ 92:⊖ 93:○ 94:○ 95:⊖	92:⊖ 93:⊖ 94:⊖	95: ⊖
Suspension	95: ○	90:○ 91:○ 92:○ 93:○ 94:⊖ 95:⊖	92:○ 93:⊖ 94:⊖	95: ○
Brakes	95: ⊖	90:● 91:● 92:◑ 93:○ 94:⊖ 95:⊖	92:● 93:○ 94:⊖	95: ⊖
Exhaust	95: ⊖	90:⊖ 91:⊖ 92:⊖ 93:⊖ 94:⊖ 95:⊖	92:● 93:⊖ 94:⊖	95: ⊖
Body rust	95: ⊖	90:⊖ 91:⊖ 92:⊖ 93:⊖ 94:⊖ 95:⊖	92:● 93:⊖ 94:⊖	95: ⊖
Paint/trim	95: ⊖	90:○ 91:⊖ 92:⊖ 93:⊖ 94:⊖ 95:⊖	92:⊖ 93:⊖ 94:⊖	95: ⊖
Integrity	95: ○	90:⊖ 91:⊖ 92:⊖ 93:⊖ 94:○ 95:○	92:● 93:⊖ 94:○	95: ○
Hardware	95: ○	90:● 91:⊖ 92:⊖ 93:⊖ 94:○ 95:⊖	92:○ 93:○ 94:⊖	95: ○

(Chrysler Town & Country Van 4WD: "Insufficient data" for years 88–91 and 95.)

Dodge Caravan V6 (2WD) / Dodge Colt, Colt Wagon / Dodge Dakota Pickup (2WD) / Dodge Dakota Pickup (4WD)

TROUBLE SPOTS	Dodge Caravan V6 (2WD) (88–95)	Dodge Colt, Colt Wagon (88–95)	Dodge Dakota Pickup (2WD) (88–95)	Dodge Dakota Pickup (4WD) (88–95)
Engine	●:88 ●:89 ○:90 ○:91 ○:92 ⊖:93 ⊖:94 ⊖:95	●:88 ○:89 ⊖:90 ⊖:91 ⊖:92 ⊖:93	○:88 ○:89 ○:90 ◑:91 ⊖:92 ⊖:93 ⊖:94 ⊖:95	⊖:88 ○:89 ○:92 ⊖:93 ⊖:94 ⊖:95
Cooling	●:88 ●:89 ○:90 ⊖:91 ⊖:92 ⊖:93 ⊖:94 ⊖:95	○:88 ⊖:89 ⊖:90 ⊖:91 ⊖:92 ⊖:93	○:88 ○:89 ○:90 ○:91 ⊖:92 ⊖:93 ⊖:94 ⊖:95	⊖:88 ⊖:89 ○:92 ⊖:93 ⊖:94 ⊖:95
Fuel	●:88 ○:89 ○:90 ○:91 ⊖:92 ⊖:93 ⊖:94 ⊖:95	⊖:88 ⊖:89 ⊖:90 ⊖:91 ⊖:92 ⊖:93	○:88 ○:89 ○:90 ○:91 ⊖:92 ⊖:93 ⊖:94 ⊖:95	○:88 ○:89 ○:92 ○:93 ⊖:94 ⊖:95
Ignition	○:88 ⊖:89 ⊖:90 ⊖:91 ⊖:92 ⊖:93 ⊖:94 ⊖:95	○:88 ⊖:89 ⊖:90 ⊖:91 ⊖:92 ⊖:93	○:88 ○:89 ○:90 ○:91 ○:92 ⊖:93 ⊖:94 ⊖:95	⊖:88 ○:89 ○:92 ⊖:93 ⊖:94 ⊖:95
Auto. trans.	⊖:88 ⊖:89 ◑:90 ●:91 ◑:92 ○:93 ⊖:94 ⊖:95	○:88 ⊖:89 ⊖:90 ○:91 ○:92 ●:93	○:88 ●:89 ○:90 ◑:91 ○:92 ○:93 ○:94 ○:95	★:88 ★:89 ●:92 ○:93 ⊖:94 ⊖:95
Man. trans.		⊖:88 ⊖:89 ⊖:90 ⊖:91 ⊖:92 ⊖:93	★:88 ★:89 ★:90 ★:91 ★:92 ⊖:93 ★:94 ★:95	★:88 ★:89 ★:92 ★:93 ★:94 ★:95
Clutch		○:88 ⊖:89 ⊖:90 ⊖:91 ⊖:92 ⊖:93	★:88 ★:89 ★:90 ★:91 ★:92 ⊖:93 ★:94 ★:95	★:88 ★:89 ★:92 ★:93 ★:94 ★:95
Electrical	●:88 ●:89 ○:90 ⊖:91 ○:92 ○:93 ○:94 ⊖:95	○:88 ○:89 ○:90 ○:91 ○:92 ⊖:93	⊖:88 ⊖:89 ⊖:90 ○:91 ○:92 ⊖:93 ⊖:94 ○:95	⊖:88 ⊖:89 ○:92 ○:93 ○:94 ⊖:95
A/C	●:88 ○:89 ○:90 ⊖:91 ⊖:92 ⊖:93 ⊖:94 ⊖:95	○:88 ○:89 ⊖:90 ⊖:91 ⊖:92 ⊖:93	⊖:88 ⊖:89 ○:90 ○:91 ⊖:92 ⊖:93 ⊖:94 ⊖:95	★:88 ★:89 ⊖:92 ⊖:93 ⊖:94 ⊖:95
Suspension	○:88 ○:89 ○:90 ⊖:91 ⊖:92 ⊖:93 ⊖:94 ⊖:95	⊖:88 ⊖:89 ⊖:90 ⊖:91 ⊖:92 ⊖:93	○:88 ○:89 ○:90 ○:91 ○:92 ○:93 ⊖:94 ⊖:95	⊖:88 ⊖:89 ○:92 ○:93 ⊖:94 ⊖:95
Brakes	●:88 ●:89 ○:90 ●:91 ◑:92 ○:93 ○:94 ⊖:95	⊖:88 ●:89 ●:90 ◑:91 ○:92 ⊖:93	●:88 ●:89 ●:90 ◑:91 ○:92 ○:93 ○:94 ⊖:95	●:88 ●:89 ○:92 ○:93 ⊖:94 ⊖:95
Exhaust	⊖:88 ⊖:89 ⊖:90 ●:91 ⊖:92 ⊖:93 ⊖:94 ⊖:95	⊖:88 ⊖:89 ⊖:90 ⊖:91 ⊖:92 ⊖:93	⊖:88 ○:89 ○:90 ⊖:91 ⊖:92 ⊖:93 ⊖:94 ⊖:95	○:88 ○:89 ⊖:93 ⊖:94 ⊖:95
Body rust	○:88 ⊖:89 ⊖:90 ⊖:91 ⊖:92 ⊖:93 ⊖:94 ⊖:95	⊖:88 ⊖:89 ⊖:90 ⊖:91 ⊖:92 ⊖:93	⊖:88 ⊖:89 ⊖:90 ⊖:91 ⊖:92 ⊖:93 ⊖:94 ⊖:95	○:88 ○:89 ⊖:93 ⊖:94 ⊖:95
Paint/trim	○:88 ○:89 ⊖:90 ⊖:91 ○:92 ⊖:93 ⊖:94 ⊖:95	⊖:88 ⊖:89 ⊖:90 ⊖:91 ⊖:92 ⊖:93	⊖:88 ○:89 ○:90 ⊖:91 ⊖:92 ⊖:93 ⊖:94 ⊖:95	⊖:88 ○:89 ⊖:92 ⊖:93 ⊖:94 ⊖:95
Integrity	⊖:88 ⊖:89 ⊖:90 ⊖:91 ⊖:92 ⊖:93 ○:94 ○:95	⊖:88 ⊖:89 ⊖:90 ⊖:91 ⊖:92 ⊖:93	○:88 ○:89 ○:90 ○:91 ○:92 ○:93 ⊖:94 ⊖:95	⊖:88 ⊖:89 ○:92 ○:93 ○:94 ⊖:95
Hardware	●:88 ●:89 ●:90 ◑:91 ○:92 ○:93 ○:94 ⊖:95	○:88 ⊖:89 ⊖:90 ○:91 ○:92 ○:93	○:88 ⊖:89 ⊖:90 ⊖:91 ⊖:92 ⊖:93 ⊖:94 ○:95	○:88 ⊖:89 ○:92 ○:93 ○:94 ⊖:95

(Dodge Colt, Colt Wagon: "Insufficient data" for years 94–95. Dodge Dakota Pickup 4WD: "Insufficient data" for years 90–91.)

Legend: ⊖ ⊖ ○ ◑ ● — Few ← Problems → Many   ★ Insufficient data

Top chart

Dodge Daytona								TROUBLE SPOTS	Dodge Dynasty								Dodge Grand Caravan V6 (2WD)								Dodge Grand Caravan V6 (4WD)							
88	89	90	91	92	93	94	95		88	89	90	91	92	93	94	95	88	89	90	91	92	93	94	95	88	89	90	91	92	93	94	95
								Engine																								
								Cooling																								
								Fuel																								
								Ignition																								
								Auto. trans.																								
								Man. trans.																								
								Clutch																								
								Electrical																								
								A/C																								
								Suspension																								
								Brakes																								
								Exhaust																								
								Body rust																								
								Paint/trim																								
								Integrity																								
								Hardware																								

Dodge Daytona columns 91, 92, 93: Insufficient data

Dodge Grand Caravan V6 (4WD) column 95: Insufficient data

Bottom chart

Dodge Intrepid								TROUBLE SPOTS	Dodge Neon								Dodge Omni, America								Dodge Ram Van B150-250							
88	89	90	91	92	93	94	95		88	89	90	91	92	93	94	95	88	89	90	91	92	93	94	95	88	89	90	91	92	93	94	95
								Engine																								
								Cooling																								
								Fuel																								
								Ignition																								
								Auto. trans.																								
								Man. trans.																								
								Clutch																								
								Electrical																								
								A/C																								
								Suspension																								
								Brakes																								
								Exhaust																								
								Body rust																								
								Paint/trim																								
								Integrity																								
								Hardware																								

Dodge Ram Van B150-250 column 95: Insufficient data

Legend: ⊖ ⊜ ○ ◒ ● — Few ← Problems → Many; ★ = Insufficient data

Dodge Ram Pickup

Trouble Spot	88	89	90	91	92	93	94	95
Engine	⊖	○	⊖				⊖	⊖
Cooling	◒	⊖		Insufficient data			⊖	⊖
Fuel	⊖	○	⊖				⊖	⊖
Ignition	⊖	◒	⊖				⊖	⊖
Auto. trans.	○	○	★				○	⊖
Man. trans.	★	★	★				★	★
Clutch	★	★	★				★	★
Electrical	⊖	○	○				○	○
A/C	★	★	★				⊖	⊖
Suspension	⊖	○	⊖				○	⊖
Brakes	●	●	●				○	⊖
Exhaust	○	○	○				⊖	⊖
Body rust	○	○	○				⊖	⊖
Paint/trim	●	●	●				○	⊖
Integrity	⊖	○	⊖				⊖	⊖
Hardware	○	○	⊖				⊖	⊖

Dodge Shadow

Trouble Spot	88	89	90	91	92	93	94	95
Engine	●	●	◒	○	○	○	⊖	⊖
Cooling	●	●	○	○	⊖	⊖	⊖	
Fuel	○	⊖	○	○	⊖	⊖	⊖	
Ignition	○	○	⊖	⊖	⊖	⊖	⊖	
Auto. trans.	○	○	⊖	⊖	⊖	◒	○	
Man. trans.	★	★	★	★	⊖	⊖	★	
Clutch	★	★	★	★	⊖	⊖	★	
Electrical	●	●	●	◒	⊖	○	○	
A/C	●	●	●	○	⊖	⊖	⊖	
Suspension	●	●	○	⊖	⊖	⊖	⊖	
Brakes	●	●	○	○	⊖	⊖	⊖	
Exhaust	○	⊖	⊖	●	⊖	⊖	⊖	
Body rust	○	○	⊖	⊖	⊖	⊖	⊖	
Paint/trim	●	●	◒	○	⊖	⊖	⊖	
Integrity	⊖	○	○	○	○	○	○	
Hardware	●	●	○	○	○	○	○	

Dodge Spirit

Trouble Spot	88	89	90	91	92	93	94	95
Engine		○	○	○	○	⊖	⊖	⊖
Cooling		●	○	○	⊖	⊖	⊖	⊖
Fuel		○	○	○	⊖	⊖	⊖	⊖
Ignition		○	○	⊖	⊖	⊖	⊖	⊖
Auto. trans.		○	◒	⊖	⊖	⊖	○	⊖
Man. trans.		★	★	★	★	⊖		
Clutch		★	★	★	★	⊖		
Electrical		●	◒	◒	○	○	○	○
A/C		●	○	○	⊖	⊖	⊖	⊖
Suspension		○	○	⊖	⊖	⊖	⊖	⊖
Brakes		●	●	○	○	⊖	⊖	⊖
Exhaust		⊖	⊖	●	◒	⊖	⊖	⊖
Body rust		○	⊖	⊖	⊖	⊖	⊖	⊖
Paint/trim		○	○	⊖	⊖	⊖	⊖	⊖
Integrity		○	○	○	○	○	○	○
Hardware		○	○	○	○	○	○	○

Dodge Stealth (2WD)

Trouble Spot	88	89	90	91	92	93	94	95
Engine				⊖	⊖	⊖	⊖	
Cooling				⊖	⊖	⊖	⊖	
Fuel				⊖	⊖	⊖	⊖	
Ignition				⊖	⊖	⊖	⊖	
Auto. trans.				★	★	★	★	
Man. trans.				★	○	○	★	Insufficient data
Clutch				★	○	◒	★	
Electrical				○	⊖	◒	⊖	
A/C				⊖	⊖	⊖	⊖	
Suspension				⊖	⊖	⊖	⊖	
Brakes				○	⊖	⊖	⊖	
Exhaust				⊖	⊖	⊖	⊖	
Body rust				⊖	⊖	⊖	⊖	
Paint/trim				○	⊖	◒	⊖	
Integrity				○	⊖	◒	⊖	
Hardware				○	⊖	◒	⊖	

Dodge Stratus

Trouble Spot	88	89	90	91	92	93	94	95
Engine								⊖
Cooling								⊖
Fuel								⊖
Ignition								⊖
Auto. trans.								⊖
Man. trans.								★
Clutch								★
Electrical								○
A/C								⊖
Suspension								⊖
Brakes								⊖
Exhaust								⊖
Body rust								⊖
Paint/trim								○
Integrity								⊖
Hardware								○

Eagle Premier V6

Trouble Spot	88	89	90	91	92	93	94	95
Engine	⊖	○	○	⊖				
Cooling	●	●	●	◒				
Fuel	○	○	○	⊖				
Ignition	●	◒	○	⊖				
Auto. trans.	●	◒	○	⊖				
Man. trans.					Insufficient data			
Clutch								
Electrical	●	●	●	◒				
A/C	●	●	◒	○				
Suspension	●	○	○	⊖				
Brakes	●	●	◒	○				
Exhaust	●	●	◒	○				
Body rust	⊖	⊖	⊖	⊖				
Paint/trim	●	⊖	○	○				
Integrity	⊖	○	◒	○				
Hardware	●	●	◒	○				

Eagle Summit (except Wagon)

Trouble Spot	88	89	90	91	92	93	94	95
Engine	⊖	◒	⊖	⊖	⊖			
Cooling	⊖	⊖	⊖	⊖	⊖			
Fuel	⊖	⊖	⊖	⊖	⊖			
Ignition	⊖	⊖	⊖	⊖	⊖			
Auto. trans.	⊖	⊖	○	○	●			
Man. trans.	⊖	⊖	⊖	⊖	⊖	Insufficient data	Insufficient data	
Clutch	⊖	⊖	⊖	⊖	⊖			
Electrical	○	○	○	○	○			
A/C	○	○	○	⊖	⊖			
Suspension	○	○	○	⊖	⊖			
Brakes	●	◒	○	○	○			
Exhaust	○	○	⊖	⊖	⊖			
Body rust	⊖	⊖	⊖	⊖	⊖			
Paint/trim	○	○	○	○	○			
Integrity	⊖	○	○	○	○			
Hardware	⊖	○	○	○	○			

Eagle Summit Wagon

Trouble Spot	88	89	90	91	92	93	94	95
Engine					⊖	⊖	⊖	
Cooling					⊖	⊖	⊖	
Fuel					⊖	⊖	⊖	
Ignition					⊖	⊖	⊖	
Auto. trans.					○	⊖	⊖	
Man. trans.					★	★	★	Insufficient data
Clutch					★	★	★	
Electrical					○	○	○	
A/C					⊖	⊖	⊖	
Suspension					○	⊖	⊖	
Brakes					○	⊖	⊖	
Exhaust					⊖	⊖	⊖	
Body rust					⊖	⊖	⊖	
Paint/trim					○	⊖	⊖	
Integrity					○	⊖	⊖	
Hardware					○	⊖	⊖	

Legend: ⊖ ⊜ ○ ◒ ● — Few ← Problems → Many | ★ Insufficient data

Legend: ● = solid circle ○ = open circle ◐ = half circle ★ = insufficient data / not applicable

Eagle Talon (2WD)

Trouble Spot	88	89	90	91	92	93	94	95
Engine			◐	○	○	◐	◐	○
Cooling			◐	◐	◐	◐	◐	○
Fuel			◐	◐	◐	◐	◐	◐
Ignition			◐	◐	◐	◐	◐	○
Auto. trans.			○	○	◐	★	★	★
Man. trans.			○	○	◐	★		★
Clutch			○	◐	◐	★		★
Electrical			◐	◐	◐	◐	◐	○
A/C			◐	◐	○	◐	◐	◐
Suspension			◐	◐	○	◐	◐	◐
Brakes			◐	○	○	◐	◐	◐
Exhaust			○	○	◐	◐	◐	◐
Body rust			◐	◐	◐	◐	◐	◐
Paint/trim			○	○	○	◐	◐	◐
Integrity			○	○	○	○	○	○
Hardware			○	◐	●	◐	○	○

Eagle Vision

Trouble Spot	88	89	90	91	92	93	94	95
Engine						◐	◐	◐
Cooling						◐	◐	◐
Fuel						◐	◐	◐
Ignition						◐	◐	◐
Auto. trans.						◐	○	◐
Man. trans.								
Clutch								
Electrical						●	○	○
A/C						◐	○	◐
Suspension						◐	◐	◐
Brakes						◐	◐	◐
Exhaust						◐	◐	◐
Body rust						◐	◐	◐
Paint/trim						◐	◐	◐
Integrity						◐	◐	○
Hardware						◐	○	◐

Ford Aerostar Van

Trouble Spot	88	89	90	91	92	93	94	95
Engine	○	○	○	◐	○	◐	◐	◐
Cooling	●	●	◐	○	○	◐	◐	◐
Fuel	○	○	◐	◐	◐	◐	◐	◐
Ignition	○	○	◐	◐	◐	◐	◐	◐
Auto. trans.	●	○	○	○	◐	◐	◐	◐
Man. trans.	★	★	★	★	★	★	★	★
Clutch	★	★	★	★	★	★	★	★
Electrical	●	●	●	●	○	○	◐	○
A/C	●	●	●	◐	○	◐	◐	◐
Suspension	●	●	○	○	○	◐	◐	◐
Brakes	●	●	●	◐	◐	◐	◐	●
Exhaust	○	○	◐	◐	◐	◐	◐	◐
Body rust	●	●	○	○	◐	◐	◐	◐
Paint/trim	●	○	○	◐	◐	◐	◐	◐
Integrity	●	◐	○	○	○	○	○	○
Hardware	●	●	◐	○	◐	◐	○	○

Ford Bronco

Trouble Spot	88	89	90	91	92	93	94	95
Engine	◐	◐	◐	◐	◐	○	◐	
Cooling	◐	◐	◐	○	○	◐	◐	
Fuel	●	●	○	○	○	○	◐	
Ignition	○	○	◐	◐	◐	◐	◐	
Auto. trans.	○	◐	◐	○	◐	◐	◐	
Man. trans.	★	★	★	★	★	★	★	
Clutch	★	★	★	★	★	★	★	
Electrical	●	●	●	●	●	○	○	
A/C	●	◐	◐	◐	◐	◐	◐	
Suspension	●	●	●	●	●	●	●	
Brakes	●	●	●	●	●	●	●	
Exhaust	●	●	●	●	●	●	●	
Body rust	●	●	●	●	●	●	●	
Paint/trim	●	●	●	●	●	●	○	
Integrity	●	●	●	●	●	●	●	
Hardware	●	●	●	●	●	●	●	

Ford Bronco 95: Insufficient data

Ford Bronco II

Trouble Spot	88	89	90	91	92	93	94	95
Engine	◐	●	◐					
Cooling	●	●	○					
Fuel	○	○	◐					
Ignition	◐	○	◐					
Auto. trans.	◐	○	★					
Man. trans.	◐	◐	★					
Clutch	◐	◐	★					
Electrical	●	●	●					
A/C	●	●	●					
Suspension	○	○	◐					
Brakes	●	◐	◐					
Exhaust	●	●	◐					
Body rust	●	◐	○					
Paint/trim	●	●	◐					
Integrity	○	◐	◐					
Hardware	◐	●	◐					

Ford Club Wagon, Van

Trouble Spot	88	89	90	91	92	93	94	95
Engine	◐	○	◐	○	◐	○	◐	◐
Cooling	●	●	◐	○	◐	○	◐	
Fuel	●	◐	○	○	◐	◐	◐	
Ignition	◐	○	○	◐	◐	◐	◐	
Auto. trans.	○	○	○	○	○	◐	◐	
Man. trans.								
Clutch								
Electrical	●	●	●	◐	○	○	○	
A/C	●	●	●	●	◐	○	○	
Suspension	●	◐	◐	◐	◐	◐	◐	
Brakes	●	◐	◐	○	◐	◐	◐	
Exhaust	●	◐	◐	○	○	◐	◐	
Body rust	●	◐	◐	○	◐	◐	◐	
Paint/trim	●	◐	◐	◐	○	○	◐	
Integrity	●	●	●	●	○	○	○	
Hardware	●	◐	○	○	◐	○	○	

Ford Club Wagon, Van: Insufficient data (later years)

Ford Contour

Trouble Spot	88	89	90	91	92	93	94	95
Engine								◐
Cooling								◐
Fuel								○
Ignition								◐
Auto. trans.								◐
Man. trans.								◐
Clutch								◐
Electrical								◐
A/C								◐
Suspension								◐
Brakes								◐
Exhaust								◐
Body rust								◐
Paint/trim								◐
Integrity								◐
Hardware								○

Ford Crown Victoria, LTD Crown Victoria

Trouble Spot	88	89	90	91	92	93	94	95
Engine	○	○	◐	◐	◐	◐	◐	◐
Cooling	○	○	○	○	◐	◐	◐	◐
Fuel	○	○	○	◐	◐	◐	◐	◐
Ignition	◐	◐	◐	◐	◐	○	◐	◐
Auto. trans.	○	○	◐	◐	◐	◐	◐	◐
Man. trans.								
Clutch								
Electrical	●	●	●	◐	◐	○	○	○
A/C	○	○	○	○	◐	◐	◐	◐
Suspension	○	○	○	◐	◐	◐	◐	◐
Brakes	◐	●	●	●	●	◐	◐	◐
Exhaust	●	○	○	○	●	◐	◐	◐
Body rust	○	◐	◐	◐	◐	◐	◐	◐
Paint/trim	○	◐	◐	○	◐	◐	◐	◐
Integrity	○	◐	◐	○	◐	◐	◐	◐
Hardware	○	◐	◐	○	◐	◐	◐	◐

Ford Escort · Ford Explorer · Ford F150-250 Pickup (2WD) · Ford F150-250 Pickup (4WD)

TROUBLE SPOTS	Ford Escort 88 89 90 91 92 93 94 95	Ford Explorer 88 89 90 91 92 93 94 95	Ford F150-250 Pickup (2WD) 88 89 90 91 92 93 94 95	Ford F150-250 Pickup (4WD) 88 89 90 91 92 93 94 95
Engine	● ● ○ ⊖ ⊖ ⊖ ⊖ ⊖	○ ⊖ ○ ⊖ ⊖ ⊖	○ ○ ○ ⊖ ⊖ ⊖ ⊖ ⊖	⊖ ⊖ ○ ○ ○ ○ ○ ⊖
Cooling	● ● ○ ○ ⊖ ⊖ ⊖ ⊖	○ ○ ○ ⊖ ⊖ ⊖	⊖ ⊖ ○ ⊖ ⊖ ⊖ ⊖ ⊖	● ○ ○ ○ ○ ○ ⊖ ⊖
Fuel	● ● ● ○ ○ ⊖ ⊖ ⊖	⊖ ⊖ ⊖ ⊖ ⊖ ⊖	⊖ ⊖ ● ● ○ ○ ○ ⊖	⊖ ⊖ ○ ○ ○ ○ ○ ⊖
Ignition	⊖ ○ ○ ⊖ ⊖ ⊖ ⊖ ⊖	⊖ ⊖ ⊖ ⊖ ⊖ ⊖	○ ○ ○ ○ ⊖ ○ ○ ⊖	○ ○ ○ ○ ○ ○ ○ ⊖
Auto. trans.	● ● ○ ○ ⊖ ⊖ ⊖ ⊖	○ ⊖ ⊖ ⊖ ⊖ ⊖	○ ○ ○ ⊖ ○ ○ ⊖ ⊖	○ ○ ○ ○ ○ ○ ⊖ ⊖
Man. trans.	⊖ ⊖ ○ ○ ⊖ ⊖ ⊖ ⊖	⊖ ⊖ ⊖ ⊖ ✱	○ ○ ○ ○ ○ ⊖ ⊖ ⊖	○ ○ ○ ○ ○ ○ ⊖ ⊖
Clutch	○ ○ ○ ⊖ ⊖ ⊖ ⊖ ⊖	○ ○ ⊖ ⊖ ✱	⊖ ⊖ ⊖ ○ ○ ⊖ ⊖ ⊖	○ ○ ○ ○ ○ ○ ⊖ ⊖
Electrical	● ● ● ● ○ ○ ○ ⊖	⊖ ⊖ ⊖ ○ ○ ○	● ● ● ○ ○ ○ ○ ⊖	● ● ● ○ ○ ○ ○ ⊖
A/C	● ● ● ○ ○ ○ ⊖ ⊖	● ○ ⊖ ⊖ ⊖ ⊖	● ○ ○ ○ ○ ○ ○ ⊖	● ○ ○ ○ ○ ○ ○ ⊖
Suspension	● ● ● ○ ○ ○ ⊖ ⊖	⊖ ○ ⊖ ⊖ ⊖ ○	● ○ ○ ○ ○ ○ ○ ○	● ○ ○ ○ ○ ○ ○ ○
Brakes	● ● ● ○ ○ ○ ○ ⊖	● ● ○ ○ ○ ⊖	● ● ● ● ● ● ○ ○	● ● ● ● ● ● ○ ○
Exhaust	⊖ ○ ○ ○ ⊖ ⊖ ⊖ ⊖	⊖ ○ ⊖ ⊖ ⊖ ⊖	● ○ ○ ○ ⊖ ⊖ ⊖ ⊖	● ○ ○ ○ ⊖ ⊖ ⊖ ⊖
Body rust	⊖ ○ ○ ○ ⊖ ⊖ ⊖ ⊖	⊖ ⊖ ⊖ ⊖ ⊖ ⊖	⊖ ○ ⊖ ○ ⊖ ⊖ ⊖ ⊖	● ○ ○ ⊖ ⊖ ⊖ ⊖ ⊖
Paint/trim	● ● ● ○ ○ ○ ○ ○	○ ○ ⊖ ⊖ ⊖ ⊖	● ● ○ ○ ○ ○ ○ ⊖	● ● ○ ○ ○ ○ ○ ⊖
Integrity	● ● ● ○ ○ ○ ○ ○	○ ○ ○ ⊖ ⊖ ⊖	⊖ ○ ○ ○ ○ ○ ○ ⊖	○ ○ ○ ○ ○ ○ ○ ⊖
Hardware	⊖ ○ ○ ○ ○ ○ ○ ⊖	○ ○ ○ ⊖ ⊖ ⊖	⊖ ○ ○ ○ ○ ○ ⊖ ⊖	⊖ ○ ○ ○ ○ ○ ○ ⊖

Ford Festiva · Ford Mustang 4 & V6 · Ford Mustang V8 · Ford Probe

TROUBLE SPOTS	Ford Festiva 88 89 90 91 92 93 94 95	Ford Mustang 4 & V6 88 89 90 91 92 93 94 95	Ford Mustang V8 88 89 90 91 92 93 94 95	Ford Probe 88 89 90 91 92 93 94 95
Engine	⊖ ○ ⊖ ⊖ ⊖ ⊖	⊖ ○ · · · · · ⊖	○ ○ ⊖ ⊖ ⊖ ⊖ ⊖	○ ⊖ ⊖ ⊖ ⊖ ⊖ ⊖
Cooling	⊖ ⊖ ⊖ ⊖ ○ ○	● ○ · · · · · ⊖	⊖ ○ ○ ⊖ ⊖ ⊖ ⊖	⊖ ○ ⊖ ⊖ ⊖ ⊖ ⊖
Fuel	○ ○ ⊖ ⊖ ⊖ ⊖	● ○ · · · · · ⊖	○ ○ ○ ⊖ ⊖ ⊖ ⊖	⊖ ⊖ ⊖ ⊖ ⊖ ⊖ ⊖
Ignition	⊖ ⊖ ⊖ ⊖ ⊖ ⊖	○ ○ · · · · · ⊖	○ ○ ⊖ ⊖ ⊖ ⊖ ⊖	⊖ ⊖ ⊖ ⊖ ⊖ ⊖ ⊖
Auto. trans.	⊖ ✱ ✱ ✱ ✱	● ○ · · · · · ⊖	✱ ○ ⊖ ✱ ✱ ✱ ○ ✱	○ ○ ○ ⊖ ○ ⊖ ✱
Man. trans.	⊖ ⊖ ⊖ ⊖ ✱ ⊖	✱ ✱ · · · · · ✱	○ ○ ⊖ ✱ ✱ ✱ ⊖ ✱	⊖ ⊖ ⊖ ✱ ⊖ ⊖ ✱
Clutch	⊖ ⊖ ⊖ ⊖ ✱ ⊖	✱ ✱ · · · · · ✱	⊖ ⊖ ○ ✱ ✱ ✱ ⊖ ✱	⊖ ⊖ ⊖ ✱ ⊖ ⊖ ✱
Electrical	⊖ ○ ○ ○ ○ ○	● ● · · · · · ○	● ● ● ○ ○ ⊖ ○ ⊖	● ● ○ ○ ○ ⊖ ⊖
A/C	○ ○ ✱ ✱ ✱ ✱	● ● · · · · · ⊖	● ● ● ○ ○ ⊖ ⊖	● ● ○ ○ ⊖ ⊖ ⊖
Suspension	⊖ ⊖ ○ ○ ⊖ ⊖	○ ○ · · · · · ⊖	○ ○ ⊖ ○ ⊖ ⊖ ⊖	⊖ ⊖ ⊖ ⊖ ⊖ ⊖ ⊖
Brakes	● ● ● ● ○ ○	○ ○ · · · · · ⊖	○ ○ ⊖ ○ ⊖ ⊖ ⊖	⊖ ● ○ ○ ○ ⊖ ⊖
Exhaust	● ● ● ● ● ●	● ○ · · · · · ⊖	● ○ ⊖ ○ ⊖ ⊖ ⊖	⊖ ⊖ ⊖ ⊖ ⊖ ⊖ ⊖
Body rust	○ ⊖ ⊖ ⊖ ⊖ ⊖	● ○ · · · · · ⊖	⊖ ○ ⊖ ⊖ ⊖ ⊖ ⊖	⊖ ⊖ ⊖ ⊖ ⊖ ⊖ ⊖
Paint/trim	○ ⊖ ⊖ ⊖ ⊖ ⊖	● ○ · · · · · ○	● ○ ⊖ ⊖ ⊖ ⊖ ○	⊖ ⊖ ⊖ ⊖ ⊖ ● ○
Integrity	○ ○ ○ ⊖ ⊖ ⊖	● ○ · · · · · ⊖	● ● ● ● ○ ○ ○	⊖ ⊖ ⊖ ⊖ ● ● ○
Hardware	⊖ ○ ○ ⊖ ⊖ ⊖	● ⊖ · · · · · ○	● ● ● ● ○ ○ ⊖	● ● ● ○ ○ ○ ○

Columns 90–93 for Ford Mustang 4 & V6 marked "Insufficient data."

⊖ ⊖ ○ ⊖ ●
Few ← Problems → Many   ✱ Insufficient data

Ford Ranger Pickup (2WD) / Ford Ranger Pickup (4WD)

TROUBLE SPOTS	Ranger 2WD 88	89	90	91	92	93	94	95	Ranger 4WD 88	89	90	91	92	93	94	95
Engine	⊖	⊖	○	○	○	○	⊖	⊖	⊖	⊖	⊖	○	○	⊖	⊖	⊖
Cooling	⊖	⊖	○	⊖	⊖	⊖	⊖	⊖	⊖	⊖	○	⊖	⊖	⊖	⊖	⊖
Fuel	○	○	○	⊖	⊖	⊖	⊖	⊖	○	⊖	⊖	⊖	⊖	⊖	⊖	⊖
Ignition	○	○	⊖	⊖	⊖	⊖	⊖	⊖	⊖	⊖	⊖	⊖	⊖	⊖	⊖	⊖
Auto. trans.	●	○	○	⊖	⊖	⊖	⊖	★	○	★	○	★	★	⊖	⊖	⊖
Man. trans.	⊖	⊖	⊖	⊖	⊖	⊖	⊖	⊖	⊖	⊖	○	○	★	⊖	⊖	⊖
Clutch	○	○	⊖	⊖	⊖	⊖	⊖	⊖	⊖	○	○	○	★	⊖	⊖	⊖
Electrical	●	●	○	○	○	○	⊖	⊖	⊖	●	○	○	○	○	⊖	⊖
A/C	●	●	●	○	●	○	⊖	⊖	●	●	●	○	○	○	⊖	⊖
Suspension	○	○	⊖	⊖	⊖	⊖	⊖	⊖	○	○	⊖	⊖	⊖	⊖	⊖	⊖
Brakes	⊖	⊖	○	○	○	⊖	⊖	⊖	●	⊖	⊖	⊖	⊖	⊖	⊖	⊖
Exhaust	●	⊖	⊖	⊖	⊖	⊖	⊖	⊖	●	⊖	⊖	⊖	⊖	⊖	⊖	⊖
Body rust	●	●	○	⊖	⊖	⊖	⊖	⊖	●	●	○	○	⊖	⊖	⊖	⊖
Paint/trim	●	●	⊖	○	○	⊖	⊖	⊖	●	●	○	○	⊖	⊖	⊖	⊖
Integrity	○	○	○	○	○	⊖	⊖	○	○	○	○	○	○	⊖	⊖	○
Hardware	○	○	○	○	⊖	⊖	⊖	○	○	○	○	○	○	⊖	⊖	○

(Ford Taurus 4: Insufficient data 91–95; Ford Taurus SHO: Insufficient data 88–90)

Ford Taurus 4 / Ford Taurus SHO

TROUBLE SPOTS	Taurus 4 88	89	90	91	92	93	94	95	SHO 88	89	90	91	92	93	94	95
Engine	●	○	○								⊖	⊖	⊖	⊖	⊖	⊖
Cooling	●	●	○								⊖	⊖	⊖	○	○	○
Fuel	●	○	⊖								○	○	⊖	⊖	⊖	⊖
Ignition	⊖	⊖	○								⊖	○	○	⊖	⊖	⊖
Auto. trans.	●	⊖	⊖												○	⊖
Man. trans.	★										○	○	○	⊖	★	★
Clutch	★										●	●	●	○	★	★
Electrical	●	●	○								●	●	○	⊖	⊖	○
A/C	●	●	●								●	⊖	⊖	⊖	⊖	⊖
Suspension	●	●	●								⊖	⊖	⊖	⊖	⊖	⊖
Brakes	●	●	●								●	⊖	⊖	⊖	⊖	⊖
Exhaust	●	⊖	○								⊖	⊖	○	○	⊖	⊖
Body rust	●	⊖	⊖								⊖	⊖	○	⊖	⊖	⊖
Paint/trim	●	⊖	⊖								⊖	○	○	⊖	⊖	⊖
Integrity	⊖	●	○								⊖	⊖	○	⊖	●	●
Hardware	●	●	○								⊖	○	○	⊖	●	⊖

Ford Taurus V6 / Ford Tempo

TROUBLE SPOTS	Taurus V6 88	89	90	91	92	93	94	95	Tempo 88	89	90	91	92	93	94	95
Engine	⊖	○	○	⊖	⊖	⊖	⊖	⊖	⊖	⊖	⊖	○	○	○	○	⊖
Cooling	●	●	⊖	○	○	⊖	⊖	⊖	●	●	⊖	○	○	⊖	⊖	⊖
Fuel	⊖	○	○	○	○	⊖	⊖	⊖	●	●	⊖	○	○	⊖	⊖	⊖
Ignition	○	○	⊖	⊖	⊖	⊖	⊖	⊖	○	○	○	○	⊖	⊖	⊖	⊖
Auto. trans.	⊖	○	○	●	⊖	⊖	⊖	⊖	○	○	○	○	○	⊖	⊖	⊖
Man. trans.									⊖	⊖	★	★	★	★	★	★
Clutch									⊖	⊖	★	★	★	★	★	★
Electrical	●	●	●	○	○	⊖	⊖	⊖	●	●	●	○	○	○	⊖	⊖
A/C	●	●	●	○	○	⊖	⊖	⊖	●	●	●	○	○	○	⊖	⊖
Suspension	●	●	●	⊖	○	○	⊖	⊖	●	●	●	⊖	○	○	⊖	⊖
Brakes	●	●	●	⊖	○	○	⊖	⊖	●	●	●	⊖	○	○	⊖	○
Exhaust	⊖	⊖	⊖	⊖	⊖	⊖	⊖	⊖	●	⊖	⊖	⊖	⊖	○	⊖	⊖
Body rust	⊖	⊖	⊖	⊖	⊖	⊖	⊖	⊖	○	○	⊖	⊖	⊖	⊖	⊖	⊖
Paint/trim	●	●	●	⊖	○	○	⊖	⊖	●	●	●	○	○	○	⊖	○
Integrity	⊖	⊖	⊖	○	●	●	⊖	○	●	⊖	⊖	⊖	○	○	⊖	○
Hardware	⊖	⊖	⊖	⊖	⊖	●	⊖	○	⊖	⊖	⊖	⊖	⊖	⊖	●	○

Ford Thunderbird V6 / Ford Thunderbird V8

TROUBLE SPOTS	T-Bird V6 88	89	90	91	92	93	94	95	T-Bird V8 88	89	90	91	92	93	94	95
Engine	⊖	○	⊖	⊖	⊖	⊖	⊖	⊖	○			⊖	⊖	⊖	⊖	⊖
Cooling	⊖	○	⊖	⊖	⊖	⊖	⊖	⊖	⊖			⊖	⊖	⊖	⊖	⊖
Fuel	⊖	○	○	⊖	⊖	⊖	⊖	⊖	⊖			⊖	⊖	⊖	⊖	⊖
Ignition	○	⊖	⊖	⊖	⊖	⊖	⊖	⊖	⊖			⊖	⊖	⊖	⊖	⊖
Auto. trans.	○	○	⊖	⊖	⊖	⊖	⊖	⊖	○			○	⊖	⊖	○	⊖
Man. trans.	★	★	★	★	★	★										
Clutch	★	★	★	★	★	★										
Electrical	●	●	●	●	○	○	⊖	⊖	●			●	●	○	○	⊖
A/C	●	●	●	●	○	○	⊖	⊖	●			○	⊖	⊖	⊖	⊖
Suspension	⊖	⊖	○	○	○	⊖	⊖	⊖	●			○	⊖	⊖	⊖	⊖
Brakes	●	●	●	○	○	⊖	⊖	⊖	●			○	⊖	⊖	⊖	⊖
Exhaust	●	⊖	⊖	⊖	⊖	⊖	⊖	⊖	●			⊖	⊖	⊖	⊖	⊖
Body rust	○	⊖	⊖	⊖	⊖	⊖	⊖	⊖	○			⊖	⊖	⊖	⊖	⊖
Paint/trim	⊖	⊖	⊖	○	⊖	●	⊖	⊖	○			⊖	○	⊖	⊖	⊖
Integrity	○	⊖	⊖	○	○	○	⊖	○	○			○	⊖	○	⊖	○
Hardware	●	●	⊖	⊖	○	⊖	⊖	⊖				⊖	●	●	⊖	○

(Ford Thunderbird V6: Insufficient data 94–95 for man. trans. and clutch; Ford Thunderbird V8: Insufficient data 89–90)

Ford Windstar

TROUBLE SPOTS	88	89	90	91	92	93	94	95
Engine								⊖
Cooling								⊖
Fuel								⊖
Ignition								⊖
Auto. trans.								⊖
Man. trans.								*insufficient data*
Clutch								*insufficient data*
Electrical								◑
A/C								⊖
Suspension								⊖
Brakes								◑
Exhaust								⊖
Body rust								⊖
Paint/trim								⊖
Integrity								⊖
Hardware								○

Geo Metro

TROUBLE SPOTS	88	89	90	91	92	93	94	95
Engine	○	⊖	⊖	⊖	⊖	⊖	⊖	
Cooling	⊖	⊖	⊖	⊖	⊖	⊖	⊖	
Fuel	○	○	○	⊖	⊖	⊖	⊖	
Ignition	⊖	⊖	⊖	⊖	⊖	⊖	⊖	
Auto. trans.	★	★	⊖	○	★	★		
Man. trans.	⊖	⊖	⊖	⊖	⊖	⊖	⊖	
Clutch	○	⊖	⊖	⊖	⊖	⊖	⊖	
Electrical	◑	◑	○	○	○	○	⊖	
A/C	★	●	○	⊖	○	⊖		
Suspension	○	◑	⊖	⊖	⊖	⊖	⊖	
Brakes	●	○	○	○	○	⊖	⊖	
Exhaust	●	●	●	◑	◑	◑	⊖	
Body rust	○	⊖	⊖	⊖	⊖	⊖	⊖	
Paint/trim	○	○	○	○	⊖	⊖		
Integrity	●	●	●	◑	◑	◑	○	
Hardware	●	●	●	●	◑	○	○	

Geo Prizm

TROUBLE SPOTS	88	89	90	91	92	93	94	95
Engine			⊖	⊖	⊖	⊖	⊖	⊖
Cooling			○	⊖	⊖	⊖	⊖	⊖
Fuel			⊖	⊖	⊖	⊖	⊖	⊖
Ignition			⊖	⊖	⊖	⊖	⊖	⊖
Auto. trans.			⊖	⊖	⊖	⊖	⊖	⊖
Man. trans.			⊖	⊖	★	⊖	⊖	⊖
Clutch			⊖	○	★	⊖	⊖	⊖
Electrical			○	○	○	○	○	⊖
A/C			⊖	⊖	⊖	⊖	⊖	⊖
Suspension			⊖	⊖	⊖	⊖	⊖	⊖
Brakes			○	○	○	⊖	⊖	⊖
Exhaust			●	◑	○	⊖	⊖	⊖
Body rust			⊖	○	⊖	⊖	⊖	⊖
Paint/trim			○	○	○	○	○	⊖
Integrity			●	○	○	○	⊖	⊖
Hardware			●	◑	●	○	○	⊖

Geo Storm

TROUBLE SPOTS	88	89	90	91	92	93	94	95
Engine			○	○	⊖			
Cooling			○	○	◑			
Fuel			○	⊖	⊖			
Ignition			○	⊖	⊖			
Auto. trans.			★	★	★			
Man. trans.			★	⊖	★			
Clutch			★	⊖	★		*insufficient data*	
Electrical			●	○	⊖			
A/C			○	⊖	★			
Suspension			○	●	⊖			
Brakes			●	●	◑			
Exhaust			●	●	◑			
Body rust			⊖	○	⊖			
Paint/trim			○	○	○			
Integrity			●	○	○			
Hardware			●	◑	○			

Geo Tracker

TROUBLE SPOTS	88	89	90	91	92	93	94	95
Engine	●	○	○	⊖	⊖	⊖	⊖	⊖
Cooling	⊖	⊖	⊖	⊖	⊖	⊖	⊖	⊖
Fuel	⊖	⊖	⊖	⊖	⊖	⊖	⊖	⊖
Ignition	⊖	⊖	⊖	⊖	⊖	⊖	⊖	⊖
Auto. trans.	★	★	★	★	★	★	⊖	★
Man. trans.	★	★	★	⊖	⊖	⊖	⊖	★
Clutch	★	★	★	○	⊖	⊖	⊖	★
Electrical	○	○	○	○	○	○	⊖	⊖
A/C	★	★	★	○	⊖	⊖	⊖	★
Suspension	⊖	⊖	⊖	⊖	⊖	⊖	⊖	⊖
Brakes	●	●	●	●	◑	○	○	⊖
Exhaust	●	●	●	●	●	◑	○	⊖
Body rust	○	○	○	○	⊖	⊖	⊖	⊖
Paint/trim	○	○	○	○	○	⊖	⊖	⊖
Integrity	○	●	●	●	◑	◑	○	○
Hardware	●	●	●	●	◑	◑	○	○

GMC Jimmy, Yukon

TROUBLE SPOTS	88	89	90	91	92	93	94	95
Engine	○	○	⊖	⊖	○	⊖	⊖	⊖
Cooling	●	○	○	⊖	○	⊖	⊖	⊖
Fuel	○	○	⊖	⊖	○	⊖	⊖	⊖
Ignition	○	○	⊖	⊖	○	⊖	⊖	⊖
Auto. trans.	○	○	⊖	⊖	○	○	⊖	⊖
Man. trans.	★	★	★	★	★	★	★	★
Clutch	★	★	★	★	★	★	★	★
Electrical	⊖	⊖	⊖	⊖	○	●	◑	○
A/C	⊖	⊖	⊖	⊖	⊖	⊖	⊖	⊖
Suspension	○	○	⊖	⊖	⊖	⊖	⊖	⊖
Brakes	●	●	●	●	●	●	◑	○
Exhaust	●	●	●	◑	◑	○	⊖	⊖
Body rust	○	○	⊖	⊖	⊖	⊖	⊖	⊖
Paint/trim	●	●	●	●	◑	○	○	⊖
Integrity	●	●	●	●	●	◑	◑	○
Hardware	●	●	●	●	●	◑	◑	○

GMC S-15 Jimmy, Jimmy (2WD)

TROUBLE SPOTS	88	89	90	91	92	93	94	95
Engine	⊖	○		⊖	○	○	○	⊖
Cooling	⊖	○		○	⊖	⊖	⊖	⊖
Fuel	⊖	○		⊖	○	⊖	⊖	⊖
Ignition	⊖	○		⊖	○	○	⊖	⊖
Auto. trans.	⊖	⊖		⊖	★	⊖	⊖	⊖
Man. trans.	★	★	*insufficient data*	★	★	★	★	★
Clutch	★	★		★	★	★	★	★
Electrical	●	●		○	○	○	⊖	⊖
A/C	⊖	⊖		○	⊖	⊖	⊖	⊖
Suspension	○	⊖		⊖	⊖	⊖	⊖	⊖
Brakes	●	○		●	●	◑	○	⊖
Exhaust	⊖	○		●	◑	○	⊖	⊖
Body rust	⊖	○		○	⊖	⊖	⊖	⊖
Paint/trim	●	●		●	◑	○	○	⊖
Integrity	●	●		●	●	◑	●	○
Hardware	●	●		●	◑	○	◑	○

GMC S-15 Jimmy, Jimmy (4WD)

TROUBLE SPOTS	88	89	90	91	92	93	94	95
Engine	○	○	⊖	⊖	○	○	⊖	⊖
Cooling	●	○	⊖	⊖	○	⊖	⊖	⊖
Fuel	○	○	⊖	⊖	○	⊖	⊖	⊖
Ignition	○	○	○	⊖	○	⊖	⊖	⊖
Auto. trans.	○	⊖	○	⊖	○	⊖	⊖	⊖
Man. trans.	★	★	★	★	★	★	★	★
Clutch	★	★	★	★	★	★	★	★
Electrical	●	●	○	○	○	○	⊖	⊖
A/C	⊖	⊖	⊖	⊖	⊖	⊖	⊖	⊖
Suspension	⊖	○	⊖	⊖	⊖	⊖	⊖	⊖
Brakes	●	●	●	●	●	◑	○	⊖
Exhaust	●	●	●	◑	◑	○	⊖	⊖
Body rust	●	○	⊖	⊖	⊖	⊖	⊖	⊖
Paint/trim	●	●	●	●	◑	○	○	⊖
Integrity	●	●	●	●	●	◑	○	○
Hardware	●	●	●	●	●	◑	○	○

Few ← Problems → Many

★ Insufficient data

TROUBLE SPOTS	GMC S-15 Sonoma Pickup (2WD) 88 89 90 91 92 93 94 95	GMC S-15 Sonoma Pickup (4WD) 88 89 90 91 92 93 94 95	GMC Safari Van 88 89 90 91 92 93 94 95	GMC Sierra C1500-2500 Pickup (2WD) 88 89 90 91 92 93 94 95
Engine				
Cooling				
Fuel				
Ignition				
Auto. trans.				
Man. trans.				
Clutch				
Electrical				
A/C				
Suspension				
Brakes				
Exhaust				
Body rust				
Paint/trim				
Integrity				
Hardware				

Note: GMC S-15 Sonoma Pickup (4WD) columns marked "Insufficient data" for certain years.

TROUBLE SPOTS	GMC Sierra K1500-2500 Pickup (4WD) 88 89 90 91 92 93 94 95	GMC Suburban 88 89 90 91 92 93 94 95	Honda Accord 88 89 90 91 92 93 94 95	Honda Civic 88 89 90 91 92 93 94 95
Engine				
Cooling				
Fuel				
Ignition				
Auto. trans.				
Man. trans.				
Clutch				
Electrical				
A/C				
Suspension				
Brakes				
Exhaust				
Body rust				
Paint/trim				
Integrity				
Hardware				

Honda Civic del Sol / Honda CRX / Honda Odyssey / Honda Passport

Trouble Spots	del Sol 88	89	90	91	92	93	94	95	CRX 88	89	90	91	92	93	94	95	Odyssey 88	89	90	91	92	93	94	95	Passport 88	89	90	91	92	93	94	95
Engine						⊖	⊖		⊖	⊖	⊖	⊖												⊖							⊖	⊖
Cooling						⊖	⊖		⊖	⊖	⊖	⊖												⊖							⊖	⊖
Fuel						⊖	⊖		⊖	⊖	⊖	⊖												⊖							⊖	⊖
Ignition						⊖	⊖		○	⊖	○	⊖												⊖							⊖	⊖
Auto. trans.						⊖	★		★	★	★	★												⊖							⊖	★
Man. trans.						⊖	⊖		⊖	⊖	⊖	⊖																			⊖	★
Clutch						⊖	⊖		○	○	⊖	⊖																			⊖	★
Electrical						⊖	⊖		○	⊖	○	⊖												⊖							○	⊖
A/C						⊖	⊖		○	○	○	○												⊖							⊖	⊖
Suspension						⊖	⊖		⊖	⊖	⊖	⊖												⊖							⊖	⊖
Brakes						⊖	⊖		●	○	○	⊖												⊖							⊖	⊖
Exhaust						⊖	⊖		●	●	●	○												⊖							⊖	⊖
Body rust						⊖	⊖		●	○	⊖	⊖												⊖								⊖
Paint/trim						⊖	○		○	⊖	⊖	⊖												⊖							⊖	⊖
Integrity						●	●		○	○	○	⊖												⊖							○	⊖
Hardware						●	○		○	○	◐	⊖												⊖							○	⊖

Honda Civic del Sol: Insufficient data (88–92). Honda Odyssey: Insufficient data (88–94).

Honda Prelude / Hyundai Excel / Infiniti G20 / Infiniti J30

Trouble Spots	Prelude 88	89	90	91	92	93	94	95	Excel 88	89	90	91	92	93	94	95	G20 88	89	90	91	92	93	94	95	J30 88	89	90	91	92	93	94	95
Engine	⊖	⊖	⊖	⊖	⊖	⊖	⊖		●	●	◐	⊖								⊖	⊖	⊖	⊖	⊖						⊖	⊖	⊖
Cooling	⊖	⊖	⊖	⊖	⊖	⊖	⊖		●	●	○	⊖								⊖	⊖	⊖	⊖	⊖						⊖	⊖	⊖
Fuel	⊖	⊖	⊖	⊖	⊖	⊖	⊖		○	○	○	○								⊖	⊖	⊖	⊖	⊖						⊖	⊖	⊖
Ignition	⊖	⊖	⊖	⊖	⊖	⊖	⊖		○	○	○	○								⊖	⊖	⊖	⊖	⊖						⊖	⊖	⊖
Auto. trans.	○	★	★	⊖	★	★			●	○	★	★								⊖	⊖	⊖	⊖	⊖						⊖	⊖	⊖
Man. trans.	⊖	⊖	⊖	⊖	⊖	⊖	★		⊖	○	★	★								★	★	⊖	★	★								
Clutch	●	⊖	⊖	○	⊖	⊖	★		●	●	★	★								★	★	⊖	★	★								
Electrical	⊖	⊖	⊖	⊖	⊖	○	○		●	●	●	●								○	○	⊖	⊖	⊖						○	⊖	⊖
A/C	●	○	⊖	⊖	⊖	⊖	⊖		●	●	●	★								⊖	⊖	⊖	⊖	⊖						⊖	⊖	⊖
Suspension	○	⊖	○	○	⊖	⊖	⊖		○	○	○	○								⊖	⊖	⊖	⊖	⊖						⊖	⊖	⊖
Brakes	●	●	⊖	○	○	○	○		●	●	○	○								⊖	⊖	⊖	⊖	⊖						⊖	⊖	⊖
Exhaust	⊖	⊖	⊖	⊖	○	⊖	⊖		●	●	●	○								⊖	⊖	⊖	⊖	⊖						⊖	⊖	⊖
Body rust	●	⊖	⊖	⊖	⊖	⊖	⊖		○	○	○									⊖	⊖	⊖	⊖	⊖						⊖	⊖	⊖
Paint/trim	○	⊖	○	○	○	⊖	⊖		●	●	●	○								⊖	⊖	⊖	⊖	⊖						○	⊖	⊖
Integrity	○	○	○	○	○	○	○		●	●	●	○								⊖	⊖	⊖	⊖	⊖						○	⊖	⊖
Hardware	○	○	○	○	○	○	○		●	●	●	●								○	◐	○	⊖	⊖						○	⊖	⊖

Honda Prelude: Insufficient data (95). Hyundai Excel: Insufficient data (92–95). Infiniti G20: Insufficient data (88–90). Infiniti J30: Insufficient data (88–92).

Few ← Problems → Many: ⊖ ⊖ ○ ◒ ●
★ Insufficient data

Infiniti Q45 / Isuzu Pickup 4 / Isuzu Rodeo / Isuzu Trooper II, Trooper

TROUBLE SPOTS	Infiniti Q45 88–95	Isuzu Pickup 4 88–95	Isuzu Rodeo 88–95	Isuzu Trooper II, Trooper 88–95
Engine	⊖⊖⊖ ⊖ (90 91 92, 94)	○○⊖⊖○ (88–92)	○⊖●⊖⊖ (91–95)	●●○○⊖⊖⊖ (88–95)
Cooling	⊖⊖⊖ ⊖	○○●○⊖	○○⊖⊖⊖	●○⊖○⊖⊖⊖
Fuel	○⊖○ ⊖	○○○○○	⊖⊖⊖⊖⊖	○○⊖⊖⊖⊖⊖
Ignition	⊖⊖⊖	⊖⊖⊖⊖⊖	⊖⊖⊖⊖⊖	⊖⊖⊖⊖⊖⊖⊖
Auto. trans.	○○○ ⊖	★★★★★	★★★⊖★	⊖★★★★★⊖
Man. trans.	*Insufficient data*	★⊖⊖★⊖	★⊖★⊖★	●⊖⊖○★★★
Clutch	*Insufficient data*	★○⊖★⊖	★○★⊖★	●○○○★★★
Electrical	○○● ○	○⊖⊖○⊖	●○⊖○⊖	●●⊖⊖⊖○○
A/C	○○○ ⊖	★★⊖★★	○○○⊖⊖	○○⊖⊖⊖⊖⊖
Suspension	○○○ ⊖	○○○⊖○	⊖○⊖⊖⊖	⊖○⊖⊖⊖⊖⊖
Brakes	●●● ⊖	●●●●○	●○⊖⊖⊖	●●●⊖⊖⊖⊖
Exhaust	○○○ ⊖	●●○○⊖	⊖○⊖⊖⊖	⊖○⊖⊖⊖⊖⊖
Body rust	⊖⊖○ ⊖	⊖⊖○○○	⊖○⊖⊖⊖	⊖○⊖○⊖⊖⊖
Paint/trim	⊖⊖○ ⊖	⊖○○⊖○	●○⊖⊖⊖	○○⊖⊖⊖⊖⊖
Integrity	○⊖○ ⊖	○○○⊖○	⊖○○○⊖	○○○○○○○
Hardware	○⊖● ⊖	○○○⊖○	●○⊖⊖⊖	○○○○○⊖⊖

Jaguar XJ6, XJS / Jeep Cherokee, Wagoneer / Jeep Grand Cherokee 4WD / Jeep Wrangler

TROUBLE SPOTS	Jaguar XJ6, XJS 88–95	Jeep Cherokee, Wagoneer 88–95	Jeep Grand Cherokee 4WD 88–95	Jeep Wrangler 88–95
Engine	⊖⊖○	○○○⊖⊖⊖⊖○⊖	⊖⊖⊖ (93 94 95)	○●○⊖⊖⊖⊖
Cooling	⊖●○	⊖○⊖⊖⊖⊖⊖⊖	⊖⊖⊖	○⊖⊖⊖⊖⊖⊖
Fuel	○○○	⊖○⊖⊖⊖⊖⊖⊖	⊖⊖⊖	●●○○●⊖○
Ignition	○○○	○○⊖⊖⊖⊖⊖⊖	⊖⊖⊖	○○⊖⊖⊖⊖⊖
Auto. trans.	⊖○○	○○○⊖⊖⊖⊖⊖	○⊖⊖	★★★★★★★
Man. trans.	*Insufficient data*	⊖○○★★★⊖★	★★	○★★★⊖○⊖
Clutch	*Insufficient data*	●○●★★★○★	★★	⊖★★★○⊖⊖
Electrical	●●●	●●●●○○○⊖	⊖○○	●●●●⊖⊖⊖
A/C	●●●	○○○⊖⊖⊖⊖⊖	⊖○○	★★★★★★★
Suspension	●●●	○○⊖⊖⊖⊖⊖⊖	⊖○○	⊖○○○⊖⊖⊖
Brakes	●●●	●●●●○○○⊖	⊖○○	●○○○⊖⊖⊖
Exhaust	⊖●○	●●●○○○○⊖	⊖⊖⊖	⊖○○○⊖⊖⊖
Body rust	●○○	○●○⊖⊖⊖⊖⊖	⊖⊖⊖	⊖○○●⊖⊖⊖
Paint/trim	○○⊖	●●○○⊖⊖⊖⊖	⊖⊖⊖	⊖○⊖⊖●⊖⊖
Integrity	○⊖⊖	⊖●●●●●⊖⊖	○○⊖	○⊖⊖●●●⊖
Hardware	●●●	●●○○○○○○	○○⊖	⊖⊖⊖○○⊖⊖

Note: Jaguar XJ6, XJS shows "Insufficient data" for years 88–95 across several rows. Jeep Grand Cherokee 4WD and Jeep Wrangler show "Insufficient data" for earlier model years.

Top section

TROUBLE SPOTS	Lexus ES250 88	89	90	91	92	93	94	95	Lexus ES300 88	89	90	91	92	93	94	95	Lexus GS300 88	89	90	91	92	93	94	95	Lexus LS400 88	89	90	91	92	93	94	95
Engine			⊖	⊖									⊖	⊖	⊖	⊖					⊖	⊖					⊖	⊖	⊖	⊖	⊖	⊖
Cooling			⊖	⊖									⊖	⊖	⊖	⊖					⊖	⊖					⊖	⊖	⊖	⊖	⊖	⊖
Fuel			⊖	⊖									⊖	⊖	⊖	⊖					⊖	⊖					⊖	⊖	⊖	⊖	⊖	○
Ignition			⊖	⊖									⊖	⊖	⊖	⊖					⊖	⊖					⊖	⊖	⊖	⊖	⊖	⊖
Auto. trans.			⊖	⊖									⊖	⊖	⊖	⊖					⊖	⊖					⊖	⊖	⊖	⊖	⊖	○
Man. trans.			★	★									★	★																		
Clutch			★	★									★	★																		
Electrical			○	○									○	⊖	⊖	⊖					⊖	⊖					○	○	○	○	⊖	○
A/C			⊖	⊖									⊖	⊖	⊖	⊖					⊖	⊖					⊖	⊖	⊖	⊖	⊖	⊖
Suspension			⊖	⊖									⊖	⊖	⊖	⊖					⊖	⊖					○	⊖	○	⊖	⊖	⊖
Brakes			○	○									○	⊖	⊖	⊖					⊖	⊖					○	⊖	○	⊖	⊖	⊖
Exhaust			⊖	⊖									⊖	⊖	⊖	⊖					⊖	⊖					⊖	⊖	⊖	⊖	⊖	⊖
Body rust			⊖	⊖									⊖	⊖	⊖	⊖					⊖	⊖					⊖	⊖	⊖	⊖	⊖	⊖
Paint/trim			⊖	⊖									⊖	⊖	⊖	⊖					⊖	⊖					⊖	⊖	⊖	⊖	⊖	⊖
Integrity			○	○									○	⊖	⊖	○					⊖	⊖					⊖	⊖	⊖	⊖	⊖	⊖
Hardware			◒	○									○	⊖	⊖	⊖					⊖	⊖					⊖	⊖	⊖	⊖	⊖	⊖

(Lexus GS300: "Insufficient data" shown for 1995; Lexus ES250: "Insufficient data" for later years.)

Bottom section

TROUBLE SPOTS	Lexus SC300/400 88	89	90	91	92	93	94	95	Lincoln Continental 88	89	90	91	92	93	94	95	Lincoln Mark VII 88	89	90	91	92	93	94	95	Lincoln Mark VIII 88	89	90	91	92	93	94	95
Engine				⊖	⊖			⊖		●	●	◒	○	⊖	⊖	⊖	⊖	⊖	○											⊖	⊖	
Cooling				⊖	⊖			⊖		●	○	○	○	⊖	⊖	⊖	○	○	⊖											⊖	⊖	
Fuel				⊖	⊖			⊖		●	⊖	○	○	⊖	⊖	⊖	○	○	○											⊖	⊖	
Ignition				⊖	⊖			⊖		●	○	○	○	⊖	⊖	⊖	⊖	⊖	⊖											⊖	⊖	
Auto. trans.				⊖	⊖			⊖		●	●	◒	●	⊖	⊖	⊖	○	○	○											○	⊖	
Man. trans.				★	★		★																									
Clutch				★	★		★																									
Electrical				○	⊖		⊖			●	●	●	●	○	○	○	●	●	●											●	○	
A/C				⊖	⊖		⊖			●	●	●	●	○	⊖	⊖	●	●	●											⊖	⊖	
Suspension				⊖	⊖		⊖			●	●	●	○	⊖	⊖	⊖	●	●	⊖											○	⊖	
Brakes				⊖	⊖		⊖			●	●	●	●	○	⊖	⊖	●	●	●											⊖	⊖	
Exhaust				⊖	⊖		⊖			○	⊖	⊖	○	⊖	⊖	⊖	●	○	⊖											⊖	⊖	
Body rust				⊖	⊖		⊖			⊖	⊖	⊖	⊖	⊖	⊖	⊖	○	○	⊖											⊖	⊖	
Paint/trim				⊖	⊖		⊖			○	⊖	○	○	⊖	⊖	○	●	○	⊖											○	⊖	
Integrity				⊖	⊖		⊖			⊖	⊖	○	○	○	○	⊖	○	⊖	⊖											○	⊖	
Hardware				○	⊖		⊖			●	●	●	○	○	⊖	○	○	○	●											○	○	

(Lincoln Mark VII: "Insufficient data" for 1991–1995; Lincoln Mark VIII: "Insufficient data" for 1988–1992 and 1995; Lincoln Continental: "Insufficient data" for 1995; Lexus SC300/400: "Insufficient data" for 1994.)

Legend: ⊖ — ⊖ — ○ — ◒ — ● Few ← Problems → Many ★ Insufficient data

	Lincoln Town Car								Mazda 323								TROUBLE SPOTS	Mazda 626 4								Mazda 626 V6							
	88	89	90	91	92	93	94	95	88	89	90	91	92	93	94	95		88	89	90	91	92	93	94	95	88	89	90	91	92	93	94	95
Engine																																	
Cooling																																	
Fuel																																	
Ignition																																	
Auto. trans.													★																				★
Man. trans.													★																				★
Clutch													★																				★
Electrical													Insufficient data																				
A/C																																	
Suspension																																	
Brakes																																	
Exhaust																																	
Body rust																																	
Paint/trim																																	
Integrity																																	
Hardware																																	

	Mazda 929								Mazda Millenia								TROUBLE SPOTS	Mazda MPV Van V6 (2WD)								Mazda MPV Van V6 (4WD)							
	88	89	90	91	92	93	94	95	88	89	90	91	92	93	94	95		88	89	90	91	92	93	94	95	88	89	90	91	92	93	94	95
Engine																																	
Cooling																																	
Fuel																																	
Ignition																																	
Auto. trans.																																	
Man. trans.	★																	★								★							
Clutch	★																	★								★							
Electrical																																	
A/C																																	
Suspension																																	
Brakes																																	
Exhaust																																	
Body rust																																	
Paint/trim																																	
Integrity																																	
Hardware																																	

Mazda MX-3 / Mazda MX-5 Miata / Mazda MX-6 / Mazda Pickup (2WD)

TROUBLE SPOTS	MX-3 88	89	90	91	92	93	94	95	Miata 88	89	90	91	92	93	94	95	MX-6 88	89	90	91	92	93	94	95	Pickup 88	89	90	91	92	93	94	95
Engine					⊖	⊖					⊖	⊖	⊖	⊖	⊖		○	○	⊖	⊖		⊖	⊖		●	○	⊖	⊖	⊖	⊖	○	⊖
Cooling					⊖	⊖					⊖	⊖	⊖	⊖	⊖		○	⊖	⊖	⊖		⊖	⊖		○	⊖	⊖	⊖	⊖	⊖	⊖	⊖
Fuel					⊖	⊖					⊖	⊖	⊖	⊖	⊖		⊖	⊖	⊖	⊖		⊖	⊖		○	⊖	⊖	⊖	⊖	⊖	⊖	⊖
Ignition					⊖	⊖					○	⊖	○	⊖	⊖		⊖	⊖	⊖	⊖		⊖	⊖		⊖	⊖	⊖	⊖	⊖	⊖	⊖	⊖
Auto. trans.					*	*					*	*	*	*			●	●	○	*		⊖	*		*	*	⊖	⊖	*	⊖	*	⊖
Man. trans.					⊖	*					⊖	⊖	⊖	⊖	⊖		⊖	⊖	⊖	⊖		⊖	*		⊖	⊖	⊖	⊖	⊖	⊖	⊖	⊖
Clutch					○	*					⊖	⊖	⊖	⊖	⊖		⊖	⊖	⊖	⊖		⊖	*		○	⊖	⊖	⊖	⊖	⊖	⊖	⊖
Electrical					⊖	⊖					⊖	●	○	○	⊖		○	⊖	○	○		⊖	○		○	○	⊖	⊖	⊖	⊖	⊖	⊖
A/C					○	○					⊖	⊖	⊖	⊖	⊖		○	○	⊖	⊖		○	⊖		●	⊖	⊖	⊖	○	⊖	⊖	⊖
Suspension					⊖	⊖					○	○	○	⊖	⊖		○	○	⊖	○		⊖	⊖		⊖	⊖	⊖	⊖	⊖	⊖	⊖	⊖
Brakes					⊖	⊖					⊖	⊖	○	●	⊖		⊖	○	⊖	●		⊖	⊖		●	●	●	⊖	⊖	⊖	⊖	○
Exhaust					⊖	⊖					⊖	⊖	⊖	⊖	⊖		●	●	⊖	⊖		○	⊖		●	⊖	⊖	○	○	○	⊖	⊖
Body rust					○	⊖					⊖	⊖	⊖	⊖	⊖		⊖	⊖	⊖	⊖		⊖	⊖		○	○	○	⊖	⊖	⊖	⊖	⊖
Paint/trim					◑	◑					○	⊖	○	⊖	○		○	⊖	○	⊖		⊖	○		○	⊖	⊖	⊖	⊖	⊖	⊖	⊖
Integrity					●	●					○	○	○	○	○		○	⊖	⊖	⊖		●	●		○	⊖	⊖	⊖	⊖	⊖	⊖	⊖
Hardware					◑	⊖					○	○	○	⊖	○		●	⊖	⊖	⊖		◑	◑		○	⊖	⊖	⊖	⊖	⊖	⊖	⊖

Note: MX-3 columns 94 and 95 marked "Insufficient data"; Miata column 95 marked "Insufficient data"; MX-6 columns 92, 94 and 95 marked "Insufficient data" in part.

Mazda Protegé / Mercedes-Benz C-Class / Mercedes-Benz E-Class / Mercedes-Benz S-Class

TROUBLE SPOTS	Protegé 88	89	90	91	92	93	94	95	C-Class 88	89	90	91	92	93	94	95	E-Class 88	89	90	91	92	93	94	95	S-Class 88	89	90	91	92	93	94	95
Engine			⊖	⊖	⊖	⊖	⊖	⊖							⊖	⊖	○	⊖	○	○	○	○	⊖	⊖	⊖	○			○			⊖
Cooling			⊖	⊖	⊖	⊖	⊖	⊖							⊖	⊖	●	⊖	○	⊖	○	⊖	⊖	⊖	⊖	○						⊖
Fuel			⊖	⊖	⊖	⊖	⊖	⊖							⊖	⊖	○	⊖	○	⊖	⊖	⊖	⊖	⊖	○	○						⊖
Ignition			⊖	⊖	⊖	⊖	⊖	⊖							⊖	⊖	⊖	⊖	⊖	⊖	⊖	⊖	⊖	⊖	○	⊖						⊖
Auto. trans.			○	⊖	⊖	⊖	⊖	*							⊖	⊖	○	⊖	⊖	⊖	⊖	○	○		○	○			○			⊖
Man. trans.			⊖	⊖	⊖	⊖	⊖	*								*																
Clutch			⊖	⊖	⊖	⊖	⊖	*								*																
Electrical			◑	○	○	○	○	⊖							●	○	●	●	○	○	○	●	●		⊖	⊖			●			○
A/C			◑	⊖	○	○	⊖	⊖							○	⊖	●	●	○	○	○	⊖	⊖		●	⊖			⊖			⊖
Suspension			⊖	⊖	⊖	⊖	⊖	⊖							⊖	⊖	○	⊖	○	⊖	⊖	⊖	⊖		○	⊖			●			⊖
Brakes			◑	○	⊖	⊖	⊖	⊖							⊖	⊖	⊖	⊖	⊖	⊖	⊖	⊖	⊖		⊖	⊖			⊖			⊖
Exhaust			◑	⊖	⊖	⊖	⊖	⊖							⊖	⊖	○	⊖	⊖	⊖	⊖	⊖	⊖		⊖	⊖			⊖			⊖
Body rust			◑	⊖	⊖	⊖	⊖	⊖							⊖	⊖	⊖	⊖	⊖	⊖	⊖	⊖	⊖		⊖	⊖			⊖			⊖
Paint/trim			○	⊖	⊖	⊖	⊖	⊖							⊖	⊖	⊖	⊖	⊖	⊖	⊖	⊖	⊖		⊖	⊖			⊖			⊖
Integrity			○	○	○	○	⊖	⊖							⊖	⊖	⊖	⊖	⊖	⊖	⊖	⊖	⊖		⊖	○			○			⊖
Hardware			○	○	○	○	○	○							○	○	○	○	○	○	○	⊖	○		⊖	○			●			⊖

Note: Mercedes-Benz E-Class column 95 and Mercedes-Benz S-Class columns 90, 91, 93, 94 marked "Insufficient data".

Legend: Few ⊖ ⊖ ○ ◑ ● Many (Problems) · * Insufficient data

Top section

	Mercury Cougar V6	Mercury Cougar V8	TROUBLE SPOTS	Mercury Grand Marquis	Mercury Mystique
Years	88 89 90 91 92 93 94 95	88 89 90 91 92 93 94 95		88 89 90 91 92 93 94 95	88 89 90 91 92 93 94 95
			Engine		
			Cooling		
			Fuel		
			Ignition		
			Auto. trans.		
	★ ★		Man. trans.		
	★ ★		Clutch		
	(Insufficient data)		Electrical		
			A/C		
			Suspension		
			Brakes		
			Exhaust		
			Body rust		
			Paint/trim		
			Integrity		
			Hardware		

Bottom section

	Mercury Sable	Mercury Topaz	TROUBLE SPOTS	Mercury Tracer	Mercury Villager Van
Years	88 89 90 91 92 93 94 95	88 89 90 91 92 93 94 95		88 89 90 91 92 93 94 95	88 89 90 91 92 93 94 95
			Engine		
			Cooling		
			Fuel		
			Ignition		
			Auto. trans.		
		★ ★ ★ ★	Man. trans.	★ ★ ★	
		★ ★ ★ ★	Clutch	★ ★ ★	
			Electrical	(Insufficient data)	
			A/C		
			Suspension		
			Brakes		
			Exhaust		
			Body rust		
			Paint/trim		
			Integrity		
			Hardware		

Top section

TROUBLE SPOTS	Mitsubishi 3000GT (2WD) 88 89 90 91 92 93 94 95	Mitsubishi Eclipse (2WD) 88 89 90 91 92 93 94 95	Mitsubishi Expo LRV 88 89 90 91 92 93 94 95	Mitsubishi Galant 4 88 89 90 91 92 93 94 95
Engine				
Cooling				
Fuel				
Ignition				
Auto. trans.				
Man. trans.				
Clutch				
Electrical				
A/C				
Suspension				
Brakes				
Exhaust				
Body rust				
Paint/trim				
Integrity				
Hardware				

Bottom section

TROUBLE SPOTS	Mitsubishi Mirage 88 89 90 91 92 93 94 95	Mitsubishi Montero 88 89 90 91 92 93 94 95	Mitsubishi Diamante 88 89 90 91 92 93 94 95	Nissan 240SX 88 89 90 91 92 93 94 95
Engine				
Cooling				
Fuel				
Ignition				
Auto. trans.				
Man. trans.				
Clutch				
Electrical				
A/C				
Suspension				
Brakes				
Exhaust				
Body rust				
Paint/trim				
Integrity				
Hardware				

Insufficient data

Legend: ⊖ ⊖ ○ ◒ ● Few ← Problems → Many   ★ Insufficient data

Top table

	Nissan 300ZX								Nissan Altima								TROUBLE SPOTS	Nissan Maxima								Nissan Pathfinder							
	88	89	90	91	92	93	94	95	88	89	90	91	92	93	94	95		88	89	90	91	92	93	94	95	88	89	90	91	92	93	94	95
Engine	⊖		○		⊖									⊖	⊖	⊖	Engine	⊖	⊖	⊖	⊖	⊖	⊖	⊖	⊖	⊖	⊖	⊖	⊖	⊖	⊖	⊖	⊖
Cooling	⊖		○		⊖									⊖	⊖	⊖	Cooling	⊖	⊖	⊖	⊖	⊖	⊖	⊖	⊖	○	⊖	⊖	⊖	⊖	⊖	⊖	⊖
Fuel	⊖		○		○									⊖	⊖	⊖	Fuel	○	⊖	○	⊖	⊖	⊖	⊖	⊖	○	⊖	⊖	⊖	⊖	⊖	⊖	⊖
Ignition	⊖		○		○									⊖	⊖	⊖	Ignition	⊖	⊖	⊖	⊖	⊖	⊖	⊖	⊖	⊖	⊖	⊖	⊖	⊖	⊖	⊖	⊖
Auto. trans.	★		◐		★									⊖	⊖	⊖	Auto. trans.	○	○	○	⊖	⊖	⊖	⊖	⊖	○	★	⊖	○	○	○	⊖	⊖
Man. trans.	★		●●		★									⊖	⊖	⊖	Man. trans.	○	○	⊖	⊖	⊖	★	⊖	⊖	⊖	⊖	⊖	⊖	⊖	⊖	⊖	★
Clutch	★		●●		★									⊖	⊖	⊖	Clutch	●	●	○	○	⊖	⊖	★	⊖	○	○	⊖	⊖	⊖	⊖	⊖	★
Electrical	●		●●		⊖									○	○	⊖	Electrical	●	●	○	○	○	○	⊖	⊖	⊖	○	⊖	⊖	⊖	⊖	⊖	⊖
A/C	○		⊖○		○									⊖	⊖	⊖	A/C	⊖	○	⊖	⊖	⊖	⊖	⊖	⊖	○	⊖	⊖	⊖	⊖	⊖	⊖	⊖
Suspension	○		⊖○		⊖									⊖	⊖	⊖	Suspension	○	⊖	⊖	⊖	⊖	⊖	⊖	⊖	○	○	⊖	⊖	○	⊖	⊖	⊖
Brakes	⊖		●●		⊖									○	○	⊖	Brakes	●	●	⊖	⊖	○	○	○	⊖	⊖	○	○	⊖	⊖	⊖	⊖	⊖
Exhaust	○		⊖○		⊖									⊖	⊖	⊖	Exhaust	●	⊖	⊖	⊖	⊖	⊖	⊖	⊖	●	●	●	⊖	⊖	⊖	⊖	⊖
Body rust	○		⊖○		⊖									⊖	⊖	⊖	Body rust	⊖	⊖	⊖	⊖	⊖	⊖	⊖	⊖	⊖	○	⊖	⊖	⊖	⊖	⊖	⊖
Paint/trim	⊖		○○		○									⊖	⊖	⊖	Paint/trim	○	○	⊖	⊖	⊖	⊖	⊖	⊖	⊖	○	○	⊖	⊖	○	○	⊖
Integrity	⊖		○○		⊖									○	○	⊖	Integrity	○	⊖	⊖	⊖	⊖	⊖	⊖	⊖	⊖	○	⊖	○	○	○	○	⊖
Hardware	⊖		○○		⊖									○	○	⊖	Hardware	○	⊖	○	○	○	⊖	⊖	⊖	⊖	⊖	○	○	○	○	⊖	⊖

Note: Nissan 300ZX columns 89, 91, 93, 94, 95 marked "Insufficient data."

Bottom table

	Nissan Pickup (2WD)								Nissan Pickup (4WD)								TROUBLE SPOTS	Nissan Quest Van								Nissan Sentra							
	88	89	90	91	92	93	94	95	88	89	90	91	92	93	94	95		88	89	90	91	92	93	94	95	88	89	90	91	92	93	94	95
Engine	⊖	⊖	⊖	⊖	⊖	⊖	⊖	⊖	⊖	⊖	○	⊖			⊖	⊖	Engine						⊖	⊖	⊖	⊖	○	○	⊖	⊖	⊖	⊖	⊖
Cooling	○	⊖	⊖	⊖	⊖	⊖	⊖	⊖	⊖	⊖	⊖	⊖			⊖	⊖	Cooling						⊖	⊖	⊖	○	⊖	⊖	⊖	○	⊖	⊖	⊖
Fuel	○	⊖	⊖	⊖	⊖	⊖	⊖	⊖	⊖	⊖	○	⊖			⊖	⊖	Fuel						⊖	⊖	⊖	○	⊖	○	○	⊖	⊖	⊖	⊖
Ignition	⊖	⊖	⊖	⊖	⊖	⊖	⊖	⊖	⊖	⊖	○	⊖			⊖	⊖	Ignition						⊖	⊖	⊖	⊖	⊖	⊖	⊖	⊖	⊖	⊖	⊖
Auto. trans.	★	○	⊖	⊖	⊖	⊖	⊖	★	★	★	★	★			★	★	Auto. trans.						⊖	⊖	⊖	●	⊖	⊖	⊖	⊖	⊖	⊖	⊖
Man. trans.	⊖	⊖	⊖	⊖	⊖	⊖	⊖	★	★	○	★	○			⊖	⊖	Man. trans.									⊖	⊖	⊖	⊖	⊖	⊖	⊖	⊖
Clutch	⊖	○	○	⊖	⊖	⊖	⊖	★	★	○	★	○			⊖	⊖	Clutch									⊖	○	○	○	⊖	⊖	⊖	⊖
Electrical	○	○	○	○	⊖	⊖	⊖	⊖	○	○	○	⊖			⊖	⊖	Electrical						○	⊖	⊖	⊖	○	○	○	⊖	⊖	⊖	⊖
A/C	○	⊖	⊖	⊖	⊖	⊖	⊖	⊖	★	★	★	★			⊖	⊖	A/C						○	⊖	⊖	⊖	⊖	⊖	⊖	⊖	⊖	⊖	⊖
Suspension	○	○	⊖	⊖	⊖	⊖	⊖	⊖	○	○	⊖	○			○	○	Suspension						⊖	⊖	⊖	⊖	○	○	⊖	○	⊖	⊖	⊖
Brakes	○	○	⊖	⊖	⊖	⊖	⊖	⊖	⊖	⊖	⊖	○			⊖	⊖	Brakes						○	⊖	⊖	●	●	⊖	○	○	⊖	⊖	⊖
Exhaust	⊖	⊖	⊖	○	⊖	⊖	⊖	⊖	●	●	⊖	○			⊖	⊖	Exhaust						⊖	⊖	⊖	●	●	⊖	○	⊖	⊖	⊖	⊖
Body rust	⊖	○	⊖	⊖	⊖	⊖	⊖	⊖	●	●	⊖	○			⊖	⊖	Body rust						⊖	⊖	⊖	⊖	○	⊖	⊖	⊖	⊖	⊖	⊖
Paint/trim	⊖	●	○	⊖	⊖	⊖	⊖	⊖	●	●	⊖	⊖			⊖	⊖	Paint/trim						⊖	⊖	⊖	⊖	○	○	⊖	⊖	⊖	⊖	⊖
Integrity	⊖	⊖	⊖	⊖	○	○	○	○	○	○	⊖	○			⊖	○	Integrity						⊖	⊖	○	⊖	○	○	⊖	⊖	⊖	⊖	⊖
Hardware	○	○	⊖	○	○	○	⊖	⊖	⊖	○	⊖	⊖			⊖	⊖	Hardware						⊖	⊖	○	⊖	⊖	○	○	⊖	⊖	⊖	⊖

Note: Nissan Pickup (4WD) columns 92–93 marked "Insufficient data"; Nissan Sentra marked "Insufficient data" in later columns; Nissan Quest Van marked "Insufficient data."

Nissan Stanza

TROUBLE SPOTS	88	89	90	91	92	93	94	95
Engine	○	○	⊖	⊖	⊖			
Cooling	○	⊖	⊖	⊖	⊖			
Fuel	⊖	⊖	⊖	⊖	⊖			
Ignition	⊖	⊖	⊖	⊖	⊖			
Auto. trans.	○	○	⊖	⊖	⊖			
Man. trans.	◐	★	○	⊖				
Clutch	◐	★	○	○				
Electrical	●	⊖	○	⊖	⊖			
A/C	○	○	⊖	⊖	⊖			
Suspension	⊖	○	⊖	⊖	⊖			
Brakes	◐	○	●	◐	⊖			
Exhaust	●	⊖	◐	⊖	⊖			
Body rust	⊖	⊖	⊖	⊖	⊖			
Paint/trim	○	○	○	⊖	⊖			
Integrity	◐	○	⊖	⊖	⊖			
Hardware	●	○	○	○	◐			

Oldsmobile 88

TROUBLE SPOTS	88	89	90	91	92	93	94	95
Engine	⊖	⊖	⊖	⊖	⊖	⊖	⊖	⊖
Cooling	○	○	◐	○	○	○	⊖	⊖
Fuel	○	○	○	○	⊖	○	⊖	⊖
Ignition	○	○	○	○	⊖	⊖	⊖	⊖
Auto. trans.	○	○	○	⊖	⊖	⊖	⊖	⊖
Man. trans.								
Clutch								
Electrical	●	●	●	●	●	○	○	○
A/C	○	○	○	○	○	○	⊖	⊖
Suspension	●	○	◐	⊖	⊖	⊖	⊖	⊖
Brakes	●	●	●	●	●	◐	⊖	⊖
Exhaust	⊖	⊖	◐	⊖	⊖	⊖	⊖	⊖
Body rust	◐	⊖	⊖	⊖	⊖	⊖	⊖	⊖
Paint/trim	●	○	○	○	○	⊖	⊖	⊖
Integrity	◐	○	◐	○	○	◐	○	○
Hardware	●	◐	◐	◐	◐	◐	◐	⊖

Oldsmobile 98

TROUBLE SPOTS	88	89	90	91	92	93	94	95
Engine	⊖	⊖	⊖	⊖	⊖	⊖	⊖	⊖
Cooling	○	○	○	⊖	⊖	⊖	⊖	⊖
Fuel	○	○	○	⊖	⊖	⊖	⊖	⊖
Ignition	○	○	○	○	⊖	⊖	⊖	⊖
Auto. trans.	◐	○	○	⊖	⊖	⊖	⊖	⊖
Man. trans.								
Clutch								
Electrical	●	●	●	●	●	●	○	○
A/C	○	⊖	○	○	○	⊖	⊖	○
Suspension	⊖	○	⊖	⊖	⊖	⊖	⊖	⊖
Brakes	●	●	◐	○	○	○	⊖	⊖
Exhaust	⊖	⊖	⊖	⊖	⊖	⊖	⊖	⊖
Body rust	⊖	⊖	⊖	⊖	⊖	⊖	⊖	⊖
Paint/trim	○	⊖	○	○	⊖	⊖	⊖	⊖
Integrity	○	○	⊖	○	◐	○	◐	○
Hardware	○	◐	⊖	◐	⊖	◐	⊖	○

Oldsmobile Achieva

TROUBLE SPOTS	88	89	90	91	92	93	94	95
Engine					⊖	⊖	⊖	
Cooling					○	⊖	⊖	
Fuel					⊖	⊖	⊖	
Ignition					⊖	⊖	⊖	
Auto. trans.					⊖	⊖	⊖	
Man. trans.					★	★	★	
Clutch					★	★	★	
Electrical					○	○	○	
A/C					⊖	⊖	⊖	
Suspension					○	⊖	⊖	
Brakes					●	○	○	
Exhaust					⊖	⊖	⊖	
Body rust					⊖	⊖	⊖	
Paint/trim					○	⊖	⊖	
Integrity					⊖	⊖	⊖	
Hardware					●	●	⊖	

Insufficient data

Oldsmobile Aurora

TROUBLE SPOTS	88	89	90	91	92	93	94	95
Engine								⊖
Cooling								⊖
Fuel								⊖
Ignition								⊖
Auto. trans.								⊖
Man. trans.								
Clutch								
Electrical								○
A/C								⊖
Suspension								⊖
Brakes								⊖
Exhaust								⊖
Body rust								⊖
Paint/trim								⊖
Integrity								○
Hardware								⊖

Oldsmobile Bravada

TROUBLE SPOTS	88	89	90	91	92	93	94	95
Engine				⊖	○	○	⊖	
Cooling				⊖	⊖	⊖	⊖	
Fuel				⊖	○	○	⊖	
Ignition				○	⊖	⊖	⊖	
Auto. trans.				⊖	⊖	◐	⊖	
Man. trans.								
Clutch								
Electrical				●	●	◐	⊖	
A/C				⊖	⊖	⊖	⊖	
Suspension				○	○	⊖	⊖	
Brakes				●	●	◐	○	
Exhaust				○	⊖	⊖	⊖	
Body rust				○	⊖	⊖	⊖	
Paint/trim				●	◐	◐	○	
Integrity				●	◐	◐	○	
Hardware				●	●	●	○	

Oldsmobile Custom Cruiser Wagon

TROUBLE SPOTS	88	89	90	91	92	93	94	95
Engine	●	◐	○	⊖				
Cooling	○	●	○	○				
Fuel	○	○	⊖	⊖				
Ignition	⊖	○	⊖	○				
Auto. trans.	○	◐	⊖	⊖				
Man. trans.								
Clutch								
Electrical	●	●	◐	●				
A/C	○	○	○	⊖				
Suspension	○	○	◐	⊖				
Brakes	●	◐	●	○				
Exhaust	●	◐	●	○				
Body rust	●	◐	●	○				
Paint/trim	●	●	◐	○				
Integrity	●	◐	●	○				
Hardware	●	●	●	●				

Insufficient data

Oldsmobile Cutlass Calais

TROUBLE SPOTS	88	89	90	91	92	93	94	95
Engine	●	●	●	◐				
Cooling	⊖	●	◐	○				
Fuel	●	◐	○	⊖				
Ignition	●	◐	○	⊖				
Auto. trans.	⊖	○	○	⊖				
Man. trans.	★	★	★	★				
Clutch	★	★	★	★				
Electrical	●	●	●	●				
A/C	⊖	○	○	⊖				
Suspension	⊖	○	○	○				
Brakes	●	●	●	●				
Exhaust	●	●	●	◐				
Body rust	●	●	●	⊖				
Paint/trim	●	●	●	◐				
Integrity	⊖	○	○	○				
Hardware	⊖	●	●	⊖				

⊖ ⊖ ○ ◐ ●
Few ← Problems → Many

★
Insufficient data

Top section

Oldsmobile Cutlass Ciera	Oldsmobile Cutlass Supreme	TROUBLE SPOTS	Oldsmobile Silhouette Van	Plymouth Acclaim
88 89 90 91 92 93 94 95	88 89 90 91 92 93 94 95		88 89 90 91 92 93 94 95	88 89 90 91 92 93 94 95
		Engine		
		Cooling		
		Fuel		
		Ignition		
		Auto. trans.		
	★ ★ ★ ★ ★	Man. trans.		★ ★ ★ ★ ★
	★ ★ ★ ★ ★	Clutch		★ ★ ★ ★ ★
		Electrical		
		A/C		
		Suspension		
		Brakes		
		Exhaust		
		Body rust		
		Paint/trim		
		Integrity		
		Hardware		

Bottom section

Plymouth Colt, Colt Wagon	Plymouth Grand Voyager V6 (2WD)	TROUBLE SPOTS	Plymouth Grand Voyager V6 (4WD)	Plymouth Horizon, America
88 89 90 91 92 93 94 95	88 89 90 91 92 93 94 95		88 89 90 91 92 93 94 95	88 89 90 91 92 93 94 95
		Engine		
		Cooling		
		Fuel		
		Ignition		
		Auto. trans.		★
		Man. trans.		★ ★
		Clutch		★ ★
Insufficient data		Electrical	Insufficient data	
		A/C		★
		Suspension		
		Brakes		
		Exhaust		
		Body rust		
		Paint/trim		
		Integrity		
		Hardware		

300 RELIABILITY RECORDS

Plymouth Laser (2WD)

Trouble Spot	88	89	90	91	92	93	94	95
Engine			○	◑	◑	◑	⊖	⊖
Cooling			⊖	⊖	⊖	⊖	⊖	
Fuel			⊖	⊖	⊖	⊖	⊖	
Ignition			⊖	○	⊖	⊖	⊖	
Auto. trans.			○	○	○	⊖	★	★
Man. trans.			○	○	○	○	⊖	★
Clutch			○	⊖	⊖	⊖	⊖	★
Electrical			◑	◑	◑	○	○	
A/C			⊖	⊖	⊖	⊖	○	
Suspension			⊖	⊖	⊖	⊖	⊖	
Brakes			⊖	◑	○	○	○	
Exhaust			⊖	⊖	⊖	⊖	⊖	
Body rust			⊖	⊖	⊖	⊖	⊖	
Paint/trim			○	○	○	○	○	
Integrity			○	○	○	○	○	
Hardware			○	◑	◑	○	○	

Plymouth Neon

Trouble Spot	88	89	90	91	92	93	94	95
Engine								⊖
Cooling								⊖
Fuel								⊖
Ignition								⊖
Auto. trans.								⊖
Man. trans.								⊖
Clutch								⊖
Electrical								○
A/C								⊖
Suspension								⊖
Brakes								⊖
Exhaust								⊖
Body rust								⊖
Paint/trim								⊖
Integrity								⊖
Hardware								○

Plymouth Sundance

Trouble Spot	88	89	90	91	92	93	94	95
Engine	●	●	◑	○	○	○	○	⊖
Cooling	●	●	◑	○	○	⊖	⊖	
Fuel	○	⊖	○	○	○	○	⊖	⊖
Ignition	○	○	○	○	⊖	⊖	⊖	
Auto. trans.	○	○	⊖	⊖	⊖	⊖	○	
Man. trans.	★	★	★	★	★	⊖	⊖	★
Clutch	★	★	★	★	⊖	⊖	⊖	★
Electrical	●	●	●	●	●	⊖	○	
A/C	●	●	●	○	○	⊖	⊖	
Suspension	⊖	●	○	○	○	⊖	⊖	
Brakes	●	●	●	○	⊖	⊖	⊖	
Exhaust	○	⊖	⊖	●	○	⊖	⊖	
Body rust	○	○	⊖	⊖	⊖	⊖	⊖	
Paint/trim	●	●	○	○	○	⊖	⊖	
Integrity	⊖	⊖	○	○	○	⊖	⊖	
Hardware	●	●	○	○	○	○	○	

Plymouth Voyager V6 (2WD)

Trouble Spot	88	89	90	91	92	93	94	95
Engine	●	●	○	○	○	○	⊖	⊖
Cooling	●	●	◑	○	○	⊖	⊖	⊖
Fuel	●	○	○	○	⊖	⊖	⊖	⊖
Ignition	○	⊖	⊖	⊖	⊖	⊖	⊖	⊖
Auto. trans.	◑	◑	●	◑	○	○	⊖	⊖
Man. trans.								
Clutch								
Electrical	●	●	◑	●	○	○	⊖	⊖
A/C	●	●	◑	○	○	⊖	⊖	
Suspension	●	◑	○	○	○	⊖	⊖	
Brakes	●	●	●	○	○	⊖	⊖	
Exhaust	●	●	○	○	⊖	⊖	⊖	
Body rust	○	●	⊖	⊖	⊖	⊖	⊖	
Paint/trim	●	●	◑	○	○	○	○	
Integrity	⊖	⊖	⊖	⊖	⊖	⊖	⊖	
Hardware	●	●	◑	○	○	○	⊖	⊖

Pontiac 6000

Trouble Spot	88	89	90	91	92	93	94	95
Engine	⊖	○	○	○	⊖			
Cooling	●	○	○	○				
Fuel	⊖	○	⊖	⊖				
Ignition	⊖	○	⊖	⊖				
Auto. trans.	○	○	⊖	⊖				
Man. trans.	★							
Clutch	★							
Electrical	●	●	●	◑				
A/C	○	○	⊖	⊖				
Suspension	○	○	○	⊖				
Brakes	●	●	●	○				
Exhaust	○	○	○	◑				
Body rust	○	◑	⊖	⊖				
Paint/trim	○	○	⊖	⊖				
Integrity	○	○	⊖	⊖				
Hardware	◑	○	⊖	⊖				

Pontiac Bonneville

Trouble Spot	88	89	90	91	92	93	94	95
Engine	○	⊖	⊖	⊖	⊖	⊖	⊖	⊖
Cooling	●	○	○	○	⊖	⊖	⊖	⊖
Fuel	⊖	○	○	○	○	⊖	⊖	⊖
Ignition	○	⊖	⊖	○	⊖	⊖	⊖	⊖
Auto. trans.	○	⊖	⊖	○	○	⊖	⊖	⊖
Man. trans.								
Clutch								
Electrical	●	●	●	●	●	○	○	⊖
A/C	⊖	○	○	○	○	⊖	⊖	⊖
Suspension	⊖	○	⊖	○	○	⊖	⊖	⊖
Brakes	●	●	●	●	◑	○	⊖	⊖
Exhaust	⊖	⊖	⊖	⊖	⊖	⊖	⊖	⊖
Body rust	⊖	○	⊖	⊖	⊖	⊖	⊖	⊖
Paint/trim	○	○	○	○	○	⊖	⊖	⊖
Integrity	○	○	○	○	○	⊖	⊖	⊖
Hardware	○	●	○	○	○	⊖	⊖	⊖

Pontiac Firebird

Trouble Spot	88	89	90	91	92	93	94	95
Engine	⊖	○		○			⊖	
Cooling	●	●		○			⊖	
Fuel	●	○		○			⊖	
Ignition	⊖	○		○			⊖	
Auto. trans.	★	★		★			⊖	
Man. trans.	★	★	_Insufficient data_	★	_Insufficient data_	_Insufficient data_	★	_Insufficient data_
Clutch	★	★		★			★	
Electrical	●	●		◑			⊖	
A/C	○	○		◑			⊖	
Suspension	○	○		◑			⊖	
Brakes	●	●		○			⊖	
Exhaust	●	●		◑			⊖	
Body rust	●	○		◑			⊖	
Paint/trim	●	●		◑			○	
Integrity	●	●		●			○	
Hardware	●	●		●			○	

Pontiac Grand Am

Trouble Spot	88	89	90	91	92	93	94	95
Engine	●	●	◑	◑	○	⊖	⊖	⊖
Cooling	●	●	◑	◑	○	○	⊖	⊖
Fuel	⊖	○	○	○	⊖	⊖	⊖	⊖
Ignition	○	○	⊖	⊖	⊖	⊖	⊖	⊖
Auto. trans.	○	○	○	⊖	⊖	⊖	⊖	⊖
Man. trans.	★	★	★	★	★	★	★	★
Clutch	★	★	★	★	★	★	★	★
Electrical	●	●	●	◑	○	○	○	○
A/C	⊖	○	○	○	⊖	⊖	⊖	⊖
Suspension	●	●	●	○	○	⊖	⊖	⊖
Brakes	●	●	●	●	○	○	⊖	⊖
Exhaust	●	●	◑	⊖	⊖	⊖	⊖	⊖
Body rust	●	●	◑	○	○	⊖	⊖	⊖
Paint/trim	●	●	◑	○	○	○	⊖	⊖
Integrity	⊖	○	○	○	○	⊖	⊖	⊖
Hardware	⊖	○	○	○	○	⊖	○	⊖

Few ← **Problems** → Many

★ Insufficient data

Symbol key used below: ● = much worse than average; ⊖ = mixed/average band; ○ = better than average; ★ = insufficient data / not applicable.

	Pontiac Grand Prix								Pontiac Sunbird								TROUBLE SPOTS	Pontiac Sunfire								Pontiac Trans Sport Van							
	88	89	90	91	92	93	94	95	88	89	90	91	92	93	94	95		88	89	90	91	92	93	94	95	88	89	90	91	92	93	94	95
Engine	⊖	○	○	○	⊖	⊖	⊖	⊖	●	●	●	⊖	○	⊖	⊖	⊖	Engine								⊖			○	⊖	⊖	⊖	⊖	⊖
Cooling	●	○	○	⊖	⊖	⊖	⊖	⊖	●	●	⊖	⊖	○	○	⊖		Cooling								⊖			●	○	○	⊖	⊖	⊖
Fuel	⊖	●	○	⊖	⊖	⊖	⊖	⊖	○	○	⊖	⊖	⊖	⊖	⊖		Fuel								⊖			⊖	⊖	⊖	⊖	⊖	⊖
Ignition	○	○	●	⊖	⊖	⊖	⊖	⊖	○	○	⊖	⊖	⊖	⊖	⊖		Ignition								⊖			⊖	⊖	⊖	⊖	⊖	⊖
Auto. trans.	⊖	○	○	⊖	⊖	⊖	⊖	⊖	⊖	⊖	⊖	⊖	⊖	⊖	★		Auto. trans.								⊖			⊖	⊖	⊖	⊖	⊖	⊖
Man. trans.	★	★	★	★	★	★			★	★	★	★	★	★	★		Man. trans.								★								
Clutch	★	★	★	★	★	★			★	★	★	★	★	★	★		Clutch								★								
Electrical	●	●	●	●	●	●	●	⊖	●	●	●	●	●	○	○		Electrical								⊖			●	●	●	●	○	○
A/C	⊖	○	○	○	⊖	⊖	⊖	⊖	⊖	○	○	⊖	⊖	⊖	⊖		A/C								⊖			○	○	○	○	⊖	⊖
Suspension	⊖	●	○	⊖	⊖	○	⊖	⊖	○	○	⊖	○	⊖	○	⊖		Suspension								⊖			○	⊖	⊖	⊖	⊖	⊖
Brakes	●	●	⊖	●	●	⊖	⊖	⊖	●	●	●	●	●	○	○		Brakes								⊖			●	●	●	○	○	⊖
Exhaust	⊖	⊖	⊖	⊖	⊖	⊖	⊖	⊖	⊖	⊖	⊖	⊖	⊖	⊖	⊖		Exhaust								⊖			⊖	⊖	⊖	⊖	⊖	⊖
Body rust	○	⊖	⊖	●	⊖	⊖	⊖	⊖	●	●	⊖	⊖	⊖	⊖	⊖		Body rust								⊖			⊖	⊖	⊖	⊖	⊖	⊖
Paint/trim	●	●	●	○	○	⊖	⊖	⊖	●	●	⊖	○	○	○	○		Paint/trim								⊖			●	●	○	○	○	⊖
Integrity	⊖	⊖	○	⊖	⊖	⊖	⊖	○	⊖	⊖	⊖	⊖	⊖	⊖	⊖		Integrity								⊖			⊖	○	○	⊖	⊖	○
Hardware	●	●	⊖	●	○	⊖	⊖	⊖	○	⊖	⊖	○	⊖	●	○		Hardware								⊖			●	●	●	⊖	⊖	○

	Saab 900 4								Saab 9000								TROUBLE SPOTS	Saturn SC Coupe								Saturn SL Sedan, SW Wagon							
	88	89	90	91	92	93	94	95	88	89	90	91	92	93	94	95		88	89	90	91	92	93	94	95	88	89	90	91	92	93	94	95
Engine	○	○	○	⊖	⊖		⊖	⊖	⊖	○		○	⊖	⊖	⊖	⊖	Engine					○	○	⊖	⊖					○	○	⊖	⊖
Cooling	●	●	⊖	○			⊖	⊖	⊖	●		○	⊖	⊖	⊖	⊖	Cooling					⊖	⊖	⊖	⊖					⊖	⊖	⊖	⊖
Fuel	⊖	○	⊖	⊖			⊖	⊖	⊖	○		⊖	⊖	○	⊖		Fuel					⊖	⊖	⊖	⊖					⊖	⊖	⊖	⊖
Ignition	⊖	○	⊖	⊖			⊖	⊖	⊖	⊖		⊖	⊖	⊖	⊖		Ignition					⊖	⊖	⊖	⊖					⊖	⊖	⊖	⊖
Auto. trans.	★	★	★	★			★	★	★	★		★	★	★	★		Auto. trans.					⊖	⊖	○	⊖					⊖	⊖	⊖	⊖
Man. trans.	○	⊖	★	★			⊖	★	★	★		★	★	★	★		Man. trans.					⊖	⊖	⊖	○					○	⊖	⊖	⊖
Clutch	○	⊖	★	★			⊖	★	★	★		★	★	★	★		Clutch					⊖	⊖	⊖	○					○	⊖	⊖	⊖
Electrical	●	●	●	○			○	⊖	●	●		⊖	●	●	●	○	Electrical					○	○	⊖	⊖					○	⊖	⊖	⊖
A/C	●	○	○	⊖			⊖	⊖	⊖	○		⊖	○	○	⊖		A/C					⊖	⊖	⊖	⊖					⊖	⊖	⊖	⊖
Suspension	○	○	⊖	⊖			⊖	⊖	○	⊖		⊖	⊖	⊖	⊖		Suspension					○	⊖	⊖	⊖					⊖	⊖	⊖	⊖
Brakes	⊖	○	⊖	⊖			○	⊖	⊖	●		○	○	⊖	⊖		Brakes					○	⊖	⊖	⊖					⊖	○	⊖	⊖
Exhaust	●	●	○	⊖			⊖	⊖	●	⊖		⊖	⊖	⊖	⊖		Exhaust					⊖	⊖	⊖	⊖					⊖	⊖	⊖	⊖
Body rust	⊖	⊖	○	⊖			⊖	⊖	⊖	⊖		⊖	⊖	⊖	⊖		Body rust					⊖	⊖	⊖	⊖					⊖	⊖	⊖	⊖
Paint/trim	○	○	⊖	○			⊖	⊖	⊖	○		⊖	⊖	⊖	⊖		Paint/trim					⊖	⊖	⊖	⊖					⊖	⊖	⊖	⊖
Integrity	⊖	⊖	⊖	○			○	○	○	○		⊖	⊖	⊖	○		Integrity					●	⊖	○	⊖					○	○	⊖	⊖
Hardware	●	○	○	⊖			⊖	⊖	●	●		⊖	⊖	⊖	○		Hardware					⊖	○	○	⊖					⊖	⊖	⊖	⊖

Note: In the Saab 900 4 and Saab 9000 columns the middle years (1992–1993) are marked "Insufficient data." The Saturn SC Coupe early years are also marked "Insufficient data."

Subaru Impreza

Trouble Spots	88	89	90	91	92	93	94	95
Engine						⊖	⊖	⊖
Cooling						⊖	⊖	⊖
Fuel						⊖	⊖	⊖
Ignition						⊖	⊖	⊖
Auto. trans.						⊖	★	⊖
Man. trans.						⊖	★	★
Clutch						⊖	★	★
Electrical						○	⊖	⊖
A/C						⊖	★	⊖
Suspension						⊖	⊖	⊖
Brakes						⊖	⊖	⊖
Exhaust						⊖	⊖	⊖
Body rust						⊖	⊖	⊖
Paint/trim						⊖	⊖	⊖
Integrity						⊖	⊖	⊖
Hardware						○	⊖	⊖

Subaru Legacy

Trouble Spots	88	89	90	91	92	93	94	95
Engine			⊖	⊖	⊖	⊖	⊖	⊖
Cooling			⊖	⊖	⊖	⊖	⊖	⊖
Fuel			⊖	⊖	⊖	⊖	⊖	⊖
Ignition			⊖	⊖	○	○	⊖	⊖
Auto. trans.			○	○	⊖	⊖	⊖	⊖
Man. trans.			⊖	⊖	⊖	⊖	⊖	★
Clutch			○	○	⊖	⊖	⊖	⊖
Electrical			○	⊖	⊖	⊖	⊖	⊖
A/C			○	⊖	⊖	⊖	⊖	⊖
Suspension			○	○	⊖	⊖	⊖	⊖
Brakes			●	○	⊖	⊖	⊖	⊖
Exhaust			⊖	⊖	○	⊖	⊖	⊖
Body rust			⊖	⊖	⊖	⊖	⊖	⊖
Paint/trim			○	○	⊖	⊖	⊖	⊖
Integrity			○	⊖	○	⊖	⊖	⊖
Hardware			●	○	○	⊖	⊖	⊖

Subaru, Subaru Loyale

Trouble Spots	88	89	90	91	92	93	94	95
Engine	●	●	●	●	●	○		
Cooling	●	○	○	○	⊖	⊖		
Fuel	⊖	○	○	○	⊖	⊖		
Ignition	⊖	⊖	○	○	⊖	⊖		
Auto. trans.	○	○	○	⊖	○	★		
Man. trans.	⊖	⊖	⊖	⊖	⊖	★		
Clutch	●	○	○	○	○	★		
Electrical	⊖	○	○	○	○	○		
A/C	◐	○	○	⊖	⊖	⊖		
Suspension	○	○	○	⊖	⊖	⊖		
Brakes	◐	○	○	○	⊖	⊖		
Exhaust	●	●	○	○	⊖	⊖		
Body rust	●	○	○	○	⊖	⊖		
Paint/trim	◐	○	⊖	⊖	⊖	⊖		
Integrity	○	○	○	○	○	◐		
Hardware	○	○	○	○	○	○		

(94–95: Insufficient data)

Suzuki Sidekick

Trouble Spots	88	89	90	91	92	93	94	95
Engine		●	○	○	⊖	⊖	⊖	⊖
Cooling		⊖	⊖	⊖	⊖	⊖	⊖	⊖
Fuel		⊖	⊖	⊖	⊖	⊖	⊖	⊖
Ignition		⊖	⊖	⊖	⊖	⊖	⊖	⊖
Auto. trans.			★	★	★	★	⊖	★
Man. trans.		★	★	★	⊖	⊖	⊖	★
Clutch		★	★	★	⊖	⊖	⊖	★
Electrical		⊖	○	○	○	○	⊖	⊖
A/C		★	★	★	○	⊖	⊖	★
Suspension		⊖	⊖	⊖	⊖	⊖	⊖	⊖
Brakes		●	●	◐	○	⊖	⊖	⊖
Exhaust		●	●	○	○	⊖	⊖	⊖
Body rust		○	○	⊖	○	⊖	⊖	⊖
Paint/trim		○	○	○	⊖	⊖	⊖	⊖
Integrity		○	○	⊖	⊖	⊖	◐	⊖
Hardware		●	○	○	◐	⊖	⊖	⊖

Suzuki Swift

Trouble Spots	88	89	90	91	92	93	94	95
Engine		○	⊖	⊖	⊖	⊖	⊖	
Cooling		⊖	⊖	⊖	⊖	⊖	⊖	
Fuel		○	○	⊖	⊖	⊖	⊖	
Ignition		⊖	⊖	⊖	⊖	⊖	⊖	
Auto. trans.		★	★	⊖	○	★	★	
Man. trans.		⊖	⊖	⊖	⊖	⊖	⊖	
Clutch		○	⊖	⊖	⊖	⊖	⊖	
Electrical		◐	○	○	◐	○	○	
A/C		★	●	○	⊖	○	⊖	
Suspension		○	⊖	⊖	⊖	⊖	⊖	
Brakes		●	○	○	○	⊖	⊖	
Exhaust		●	●	●	○	⊖	⊖	
Body rust		⊖	⊖	⊖	⊖	⊖	⊖	
Paint/trim		○	○	○	○	⊖	⊖	
Integrity		●	●	●	◐	○	○	
Hardware		●	●	●	◐	○	○	

(95: Insufficient data)

Toyota 4Runner

Trouble Spots	88	89	90	91	92	93	94	95
Engine	○	○	○	○	◐	⊖	⊖	⊖
Cooling	○	⊖	⊖	⊖	⊖	⊖	⊖	⊖
Fuel	⊖	⊖	⊖	⊖	⊖	⊖	⊖	⊖
Ignition	⊖	⊖	⊖	⊖	⊖	⊖	⊖	⊖
Auto. trans.	★	★	⊖	⊖	⊖	⊖	⊖	⊖
Man. trans.	⊖	⊖	○	⊖	⊖	⊖	⊖	★
Clutch	●	○	○	◐	○	⊖	⊖	★
Electrical	○	○	⊖	⊖	⊖	⊖	⊖	⊖
A/C	⊖	⊖	◐	○	○	⊖	⊖	⊖
Suspension	○	○	⊖	⊖	⊖	⊖	⊖	⊖
Brakes	○	◐	◐	○	○	○	⊖	⊖
Exhaust	●	○	○	⊖	⊖	⊖	⊖	⊖
Body rust	○	○	⊖	⊖	⊖	⊖	⊖	⊖
Paint/trim	○	○	⊖	⊖	⊖	⊖	⊖	⊖
Integrity	○	⊖	⊖	⊖	⊖	○	○	⊖
Hardware	○	○	○	◐	⊖	⊖	⊖	⊖

Toyota Avalon

Trouble Spots	88	89	90	91	92	93	94	95
Engine								⊖
Cooling								⊖
Fuel								⊖
Ignition								⊖
Auto. trans.								⊖
Man. trans.								
Clutch								
Electrical								⊖
A/C								⊖
Suspension								⊖
Brakes								⊖
Exhaust								⊖
Body rust								⊖
Paint/trim								⊖
Integrity								○
Hardware								⊖

Toyota Camry

Trouble Spots	88	89	90	91	92	93	94	95
Engine	○	⊖	⊖	⊖	⊖	⊖	⊖	⊖
Cooling	⊖	⊖	⊖	⊖	⊖	⊖	⊖	⊖
Fuel	⊖	⊖	⊖	⊖	⊖	⊖	⊖	⊖
Ignition	○	⊖	⊖	⊖	⊖	⊖	⊖	⊖
Auto. trans.	⊖	⊖	⊖	⊖	⊖	⊖	⊖	⊖
Man. trans.	⊖	⊖	⊖	⊖	⊖	⊖	⊖	★
Clutch	○	○	⊖	⊖	⊖	⊖	⊖	★
Electrical	●	○	○	○	○	○	⊖	⊖
A/C	⊖	⊖	⊖	○	⊖	⊖	⊖	⊖
Suspension	○	⊖	⊖	⊖	○	⊖	⊖	⊖
Brakes	●	●	○	○	◐	○	⊖	⊖
Exhaust	●	●	○	○	○	⊖	⊖	⊖
Body rust	○	○	⊖	⊖	⊖	⊖	⊖	⊖
Paint/trim	○	○	⊖	○	⊖	⊖	⊖	⊖
Integrity	○	⊖	⊖	⊖	⊖	○	⊖	⊖
Hardware	○	○	○	○	⊖	⊖	⊖	⊖

Legend: ⊖ ⊖ ○ ◐ ● — Few ← Problems → Many   ★ Insufficient data

Toyota Celica / Toyota Corolla / Toyota Cressida / Toyota Land Cruiser

TROUBLE SPOTS	Toyota Celica 88 89 90 91 92 93 94 95	Toyota Corolla 88 89 90 91 92 93 94 95	Toyota Cressida 88 89 90 91 92 93 94 95	Toyota Land Cruiser 88 89 90 91 92 93 94 95
Engine				
Cooling				
Fuel				
Ignition				
Auto. trans.				
Man. trans.				
Clutch				
Electrical				
A/C				
Suspension				
Brakes				
Exhaust				
Body rust				
Paint/trim				
Integrity				
Hardware				

Toyota Celica: insufficient data (94, 95). Toyota Cressida: insufficient data (92–95). Toyota Land Cruiser: insufficient data (88, 90, 92, 93, 94, 95).

Toyota Pickup / Toyota Previa Van / Toyota T100 Pickup / Toyota Tercel

TROUBLE SPOTS	Toyota Pickup 88 89 90 91 92 93 94 95	Toyota Previa Van 88 89 90 91 92 93 94 95	Toyota T100 Pickup 88 89 90 91 92 93 94 95	Toyota Tercel 88 89 90 91 92 93 94 95
Engine				
Cooling				
Fuel				
Ignition				
Auto. trans.				
Man. trans.				
Clutch				
Electrical				
A/C				
Suspension				
Brakes				
Exhaust				
Body rust				
Paint/trim				
Integrity				
Hardware				

Toyota Previa Van: insufficient data (88, 89). Toyota T100 Pickup: insufficient data (88–92). Toyota Tercel: insufficient data (94, 95).

Volkswagen Golf, GTI, Golf III 4								Volkswagen Jetta, Jetta III 4								TROUBLE SPOTS	Volkswagen Passat								Volvo 240 Series							
88	89	90	91	92	93	94	95	88	89	90	91	92	93	94	95		88	89	90	91	92	93	94	95	88	89	90	91	92	93	94	95
○	◒					⊖	⊖	⊖	○	○	○	○		⊖	⊖	Engine			◒	◒				⊖	⊖	⊖	⊖	⊖	⊖	⊖	⊖
●	●					⊖	⊖	●	◒	◒	○	◒		⊖	⊖	Cooling			◒	◒				⊖	⊖	○	○	⊖	○	⊖	⊖
◒	◒					⊖	⊖	◒	◒	◒	○	○		⊖	⊖	Fuel			○	○				⊖	⊖	○	○	⊖	⊖	⊖	⊖
○	◒					⊖	⊖	○	⊖	⊖	○	○		⊖	⊖	Ignition			⊖	○				⊖	⊖	⊖	⊖	⊖	⊖	⊖	⊖
★	★					⊖	★	★	★	★	★	★		⊖	★	Auto. trans.			★	★					★	○	⊖	⊖	⊖	○	⊖	⊖
⊖	⊖					⊖	⊖	⊖	⊖	⊖	⊖	★		⊖	⊖	Man. trans.			★	★					★	⊖	★	★	★	★	★	★
○	◒					⊖	⊖	○	○	⊖	⊖	★		⊖	○	Clutch			★	★					★	⊖	★	★	★	★	★	★
●	●					⊖	⊖	●	●	●	●	●		⊖	⊖	Electrical			●	●					○	●	●	●	●	●	●	●
○	◒					⊖	⊖	◒	●	◒	○	○		⊖	⊖	A/C			◒	○					⊖	●	●	○	⊖	⊖	⊖	⊖
⊖	◒					⊖	⊖	○	○	◒	○	○		⊖	⊖	Suspension			◒	⊖					⊖	○	○	⊖	⊖	⊖	⊖	⊖
◒	◒					⊖	⊖	●	◒	◒	○	○		⊖	⊖	Brakes			○	●					⊖	●	●	●	●	●	●	●
●	●					⊖	⊖	●	●	◒	○	◒		⊖	⊖	Exhaust			●	○					⊖	○	⊖	⊖	⊖	⊖	⊖	⊖
○	○					⊖	⊖	○	◒	◒	○	○		⊖	⊖	Body rust			⊖	⊖					⊖	⊖	⊖	⊖	⊖	⊖	⊖	⊖
○	○					⊖	⊖	○	⊖	⊖	○	○		⊖	⊖	Paint/trim			⊖	⊖					⊖	○	⊖	⊖	⊖	⊖	⊖	⊖
◒	●					○	⊖	●	◒	◒	●	◒		○	⊖	Integrity			⊖	◒					⊖	○	⊖	⊖	⊖	⊖	⊖	⊖
●	●					●	⊖	●	●	◒	●	●		●	⊖	Hardware			●	●					⊖	○	○	◒	○	⊖	⊖	○

Golf / GTI columns 90–93: Insufficient data. Jetta column 93: Insufficient data. Passat columns 92–94: Insufficient data.

Volvo 740 Series								Volvo 850 Series								TROUBLE SPOTS	Volvo 940 Series								Volvo 960 Series							
88	89	90	91	92	93	94	95	88	89	90	91	92	93	94	95		88	89	90	91	92	93	94	95	88	89	90	91	92	93	94	95
⊖	○	⊖	⊖	⊖									⊖	⊖	⊖	Engine			○	⊖	⊖	⊖								⊖	⊖	⊖
○	○	○	◒	○									⊖	⊖	⊖	Cooling			○	●	○	⊖								⊖	⊖	⊖
⊖	○	○	○	⊖									⊖	⊖	⊖	Fuel			⊖	⊖	⊖	⊖								⊖	⊖	⊖
⊖	⊖	⊖	⊖	⊖									⊖	⊖	⊖	Ignition			⊖	⊖	⊖	⊖								⊖	⊖	⊖
⊖	⊖	⊖	⊖	⊖									⊖	⊖	⊖	Auto. trans.			⊖	⊖	⊖	⊖								⊖	⊖	⊖
★	★	★	★										⊖	⊖	★	Man. trans.																
★	★	★	★										⊖	⊖	★	Clutch																
●	●	◒	◒	○									○	○	⊖	Electrical			○	○	◒	⊖								○	○	⊖
●	○	○	○	○									◒	◒	⊖	A/C			○	⊖	⊖	⊖								○	⊖	⊖
⊖	⊖	⊖	⊖	⊖									⊖	⊖	⊖	Suspension			⊖	⊖	⊖	⊖								⊖	⊖	⊖
●	●	●	◒	○									⊖	⊖	⊖	Brakes			◒	◒	○	⊖								○	⊖	⊖
○	○	○	○	○									⊖	⊖	⊖	Exhaust			⊖	⊖	⊖	⊖								⊖	⊖	⊖
⊖	⊖	⊖	⊖	⊖									⊖	⊖	⊖	Body rust			⊖	⊖	⊖	⊖								⊖	⊖	⊖
⊖	⊖	⊖	○	⊖									⊖	○	⊖	Paint/trim			⊖	⊖	○	⊖								⊖	⊖	⊖
◒	○	○	○	◒									○	○	⊖	Integrity			⊖	⊖	○	⊖								◒	⊖	⊖
●	◒	○	◒	○									○	○	⊖	Hardware			○	○	⊖	○								◒	⊖	⊖

Volvo 940 Series columns 94–95: Insufficient data.

⊖ ◒ ○ ◐ ●
Few ← **Problems** → Many

★ Insufficient data

Taking care of your car ——

Why do some cars keep running reliably when others of the same model, year, and mileage are ready for recycling? It's partly luck, but regular and diligent care plays a big part. Taking good care of a car means checking its systems and performing preventive maintenance regularly. It also means being alert for unusual noises, vibration, and other symptoms that presage trouble. Dealing with minor problems promptly can keep them from growing into major problems that can leave you stranded at the roadside.

Automakers' service recommendations vary. Below, we give some general advice. For detailed information on tune-ups, timing belt, tire rotation, shocks or struts, wheel alignment, wheel balancing, and other important tasks, check your owner's manual.

How you drive also matters. Besides helping your car last a long time, sensible driving habits save gasoline and help prevent accidents. Our driving tips can be summed up in one basic piece of advice: Do everything—accelerate, brake, turn—gently.

Weekly

Radiator coolant. Check the plastic overflow bottle, attached by a hose to the radiator. If the level is below the Full mark, add water and antifreeze in equal amounts. If the level keeps dropping, check for leaks.

Oil level. Park the car on level ground, wait a few minutes. Then pull out and wipe the dipstick and reinsert it. If the level is below the Add line, add enough oil to bring the level to Full mark. Don't overfill.

Keep the body clean. Dirt and pollutants are tough on paint. Wash the car every week, using enough water to avoid scratching the paint. Hose out the fender wells and undercarriage with a strong spray. When water beads on the body panels become larger than a quarter, wax the body to protect the paint from tree sap, bird droppings, and other damaging dirt.

Monthly

Tire pressure. Check with an accurate gauge when the tires are cold. (Don't trust the air-pump gauges at service stations; they tend to be very inaccurate and inconsistent.) See the owner's manual or the label in the glove compartment or on the driver's doorpost for recommended pressures. And don't forget the spare.

Automatic-transmission fluid. With the engine warmed up and running, check the fluid level and color, using the transmission dipstick. (See the owner's manual for details.) If the level is low, add fluid to between the Add and Full marks. If the fluid is brown or black or smells burnt, change the fluid and filter. If the fluid is sickly white or pale, the transmission oil-cooler may need repair.

Power-steering fluid. Check the level with the dipstick (usually attached to the fluid-reservoir cap). If the level is low, top it up and have the system checked for leaks.

Brake fluid. Check the level in the master cylinder. (Wipe the cap clean before removing it.) If the fluid level is low, top it up and have the system checked for leaks.

Battery. On a low-maintenance battery, pry off the covers or unscrew the caps; if necessary, add distilled water. If the battery has an "eye," check its color. If the eye is green or blue, the battery is OK; if it's black, have the battery tested and charged; if it's pale or yellow, replace the battery.

Once a year

Brakes. Remove all wheels and examine the brakes. Have excessively worn pads or linings replaced, and have badly scored rotors or drums machined or replaced. Have the wheel bearings greased.

Clean the radiator. To prevent overheating, wash the radiator with detergent solution; remove debris with a soft brush.

Clean the battery and terminals. Remove deposits with a wire brush, wash with a solution of baking soda and water, then rinse. Cover vent holes with tape during cleaning so baking soda doesn't get inside. If the deposits reappear, coat the terminals with grease.

Every two or four years

Fluids. Replace the automatic-transmission fluid and filter. Drain and flush the cooling system. Drain and flush the brake system.

Belts. Replace engine drive belts every four years, even if they don't show any wear. If a belt becomes noisy, have it adjusted promptly.

Each oil change

Tires. Check for cuts and bulges, signs of an imminent blowout.

Constant-velocity joint boots. On front-wheel-drive cars, examine the boots. If damaged or cut, have them replaced.

Differential fluid. On rear-wheel-drive cars, remove the plug in the differential and feel for fluid with your little finger. If you don't feel any, add fluid until you can and have the system checked.

Air filter. Remove the air-filter cover and hold the filter up to light. If you don't see light, replace the filter.

Cooling-system hoses. At each oil change, squeeze the hoses when the engine is cold. Replace hoses with cracks or hard or mushy areas. Also replace hoses that bulge with the engine running.

Exhaust system. Check if it becomes noisy and have rusted-through parts replaced. It may make sense to replace the entire exhaust system all at once rather than piecemeal.

Clean the driveshaft. On rear-wheel-drive cars, mud build-up can cause annoying vibration.

Lubricate the universal joints. Check the owner's manual to see if it's necessary.

Motor oil

None of the tested oils proved better than the others in our tests. Buy the viscosity grade recommended for your car, and look for a starburst emblem on the container.

Last CR report: *July 1996*
Price range: *$1 to $4*

Shopping strategy

In a 4½-million-mile test of 20 popular motor oils in 75 New York City taxicabs, no single oil proved better than any other. Unless you typically drive under more severe conditions than a New York cab does, you won't go wrong if you shop strictly by price or availability.

Even the expensive synthetics (typically, $3 or $4 a quart) worked no better than conventional motor oils. They might be worth considering only for extreme driving conditions, such as in very hot or very cold temperatures.

Our advice: Buy the viscosity grade recommended in your owner's manual, and look for the API starburst emblem that indicates that the oil meets the latest industry requirements for protection against deposits, wear, oxidation, and corrosion (known as service grade SH).

The grades

Ideally, motor oil should be thin enough to flow easily when the engine is cold and remain thick enough to protect the engine when it's hot. It's ability to flow, or viscosity, is translated into grades. Automakers specify grades according to the temperature range expected over the oil-change period. The two most commonly recommended are 10W-30 and 5W-30.

When we measured the viscosity of oils under high-temperature, high-stress conditions, we found no difference between 5W-30 oils and their 10W-30 brandmates. But at low temperatures, the 5W-30 oil flowed more easily.

Oil-change intervals

On the basis of our test results, we think that the commonly recommended 3000-mile oil-change interval is too conservative. For "normal" conditions 7500-mile intervals (or the interval rec-

ommended in your owner's manual) should be fine. For the taxis in our severe tests, a 6000-mile interval was adequate. If your car is used in very severe circumstances—frequent cold starts and short trips, dusty conditions, trailer towing— you may want to change the oil at shorter intervals. Note, too, that diesel engines, and turbocharged engines, which we didn't test, may need more frequent oil changes.

We don't recommend stretching the change interval beyond the automaker's recommendations, no matter what oil you use. Engine combustion contaminants could eventually build up and harm engine parts.

Where should you go?

We surveyed car owners who changed the oil themselves or had it done at a service station or garage, a new-car dealer, or a quick-lube center. The do-it-yourselfer might spend as little as $10 for the oil and filter. The price at service station ran from $20 to $30. It was about $30 at a new-car dealer and $15 to $33 at a quick-lube center.

According to our survey, the quick-lube centers can do an adequate job. A garage or the dealer might be the place to go when you also need other work done. Choose among quick-lube centers according to price and service—and be sure you tell the center what grade of oil your car needs. Discount coupons are common; you may never have to pay full price.

Change the oil yourself only if you have the tools and equipment and can safely dispose of the used oil.

Auto insurance

The cost of insurance is one of the biggest expenses of owning a car. You can save substantially by price-shopping and rethinking coverage amounts and deductibles.

The choices

An auto policy consists of several types of insurance. Some are mandatory and some are optional, depending on the laws in your state.

Liability. Most states require this type of coverage, which is commonly split into two parts: bodily injury and property damage.

Bodily-injury liability compensates victims of accidents caused by you or someone who drives your car. It can be "single limit" or "split limit." Single-limit coverage pays a specified amount per accident, no matter how many people are involved. CONSUMER REPORTS recommends split-limit coverage, which pays up to a certain amount to each person injured in an accident. The other part, property-damage liability, covers damage to another person's property.

The minimum coverage limits required by most states are inadequate for anyone with assets to protect. CONSUMER REPORTS recommends buying bodily-injury coverage of at least $100,000 per person and $300,000 per accident, and property-damage coverage of at least $50,000.

Uninsured-motorist coverage. Mandatory in some states. This insures you, your family, and your passengers for accidents caused by uninsured or hit-and-run drivers. Most policies cover only bodily injury; some pay for damage to your car as well. It's a good idea to buy amounts equal to your bodily-injury and property-damage coverage.

Underinsured-motorist coverage. This pays up to a stated limit any accident-related expenses that exceed the other driver's coverage.

Medical-payments insurance. Unlike typical health insurance, this coverage of accident-related medical and hospital expenses can be purchased without a deductible. It also covers some funeral bills, lost wages, and incidental expenses. If you have adequate health coverage, however, you probably don't need it.

Collision coverage. This pays for damage to your car. The law doesn't require it, but you'll probably have to buy it if you have a car loan or lease. Collision coverage usually has a deductible of at least $100 per accident. CONSUMER REPORTS recommends choosing the highest deductible you can afford.

Comprehensive coverage is usually required by lenders, too. It covers damage to your car from events other than crashes—fire, vandalism, theft, and falling trees, for example. It, too, carries a deductible.

Car-rental and towing coverage. Insurance that pays for a rental car while yours is laid up or that covers towing after an accident doesn't cost much. But you may not need such coverage if your repair shop gives loaners or if you have towing coverage through an auto club.

Shopping strategy

Price shop. You can save a bundle simply by getting quotes from as many companies as you can. One way to price-shop is by using listings in the Yellow

Pages. Be sure to ask each agent to quote rates for comparable coverage.

Residents of California, Florida, Illinois, New Jersey, New York, Pennsylvania, and Washington can use the Consumer Reports Auto Insurance Price Service. See page 359.

Ask about discounts. A defensive-driving course, for instance, can result in a discount on your premium. You may also be eligible for discounts if your car has air bags, built-in antitheft devices and antilock brakes.

Increase your deductible. Choosing a $500 or even $1000 deductible can sub-stantially lower collision and comprehensive premiums.

Drop collision coverage after four or five years, or as soon as the collision premium adds up to 10 percent of the car's market value.

Consider buying auto and homeowners' insurance from the same company to get a multi-policy discount.

Insure teen-agers on the family policy.

For a small savings, pay your premium in full, instead of by installments.

If you're choosing between two cars to buy, an insurance agent can tell you which is more or less expensive to insure.

Tires

Our tests show that neither brand nor price is an accurate gauge of quality.

Last CR report: *truck and SUV tires, January 1996; all-season car tires, February 1994; performance car tires, January 1995*
Ratings: *page 317*
Price range: *$60 to $150*

The types

When it's time to replace the tires on your car, you have a chance to improve their quality. Automakers meet Government fuel-economy standards in part by equipping new cars with tires that roll especially easily—and thus eke out an extra fraction of an mpg. They also tend to look for tires that ride softly, to make a brief test drive at the dealership more appealing. But the automaker's priorities needn't be yours.

Most tires sold today are all-season tires, designed to perform reasonably well in dry weather, rain, and snow. The all-season category includes several subcategories.

Basic all-season tires are standard equipment on most new family sedans. Consider that type if long tread life, a comfortable ride, and budget price are all-important. If you sometimes drive in snow, make sure the tire has "M+S" (mud and snow) on the sidewall. You can tell a basic all-season tire by the speed rating imprinted on its sidewall—an S (112 mph) or a T (118 mph), or sometimes no letter at all.

All-season touring tires are hyped by the industry as premium quality. But in practice, even manufacturers can't agree on a definition. Goodyear, which claims to have coined the term, once defined the breed as a "performance tire with manners." So-called touring tires are generally more expensive than basic all-season tires (although there's considerable overlap), but we haven't noted significant differences, overall. Most touring tires carry an S or a T speed rating.

All-season performance tires are a relatively new category. Consider them if you drive aggressively. Such tires offer superior braking and cornering, but at the expense of tread life and, often, the comfort of the ride. If they have an M+S rating, they retain one advantage of basic all-season tires: decent traction in snow. Performance tires have a low-profile sidewall and an H (130 mph) speed rating.

Ultra-high-performance tires provide the ultimate in handling and braking on wet and dry pavement, but they can ride harshly and wear out quickly, and they tend to be hopeless in snow. Such tires are very wide and squat and generally have a V (149 mph) or Z (149-plus) speed rating.

Light-truck tires are available for general road, on/off road, and off-road use. The off-road type has the chunkiest, most aggressive tread. Light-truck tires also come in regular road and, for hauling heavy cargo, extra-load types.

Snow tires are your best bet for areas with heavy snowfall—better than any all-season tires. But these tires ride noisily, particularly if they're studded, and grip relatively poorly on dry roads, so remove them for the summer.

Shopping strategy

Tires are sold in several different types of outlets:

Tire dealers. About half of all buyers shop at tire dealers, which offer a wide selection of brands, models, and sizes and, usually, knowledgeable salespeople. If they don't have what you want in stock, they can generally get it for you quickly.

Service stations. Your local garage will probably be very accommodating if you're a regular customer. But it may offer limited stock, and the staff may not be knowledgeable about tires.

Department stores, warehouse clubs, and auto-parts stores. The quality and selection vary at chain stores such as Costco, Sam's Club, and Sears. If you do find premium name-brand tires at such outlets, be sure to check the prices against those of other tire dealers.

Mail-order houses. These outlets generally offer the lowest prices and a very wide selection. Look for their ads in auto-buff magazines. Delivery generally takes only a few days, and you can have the tires shipped directly to your garage. But line up a garage willing to mount the tires before you order.

Decoding a tire

Size and shape. Typically, the tire size looks something like P185/70R14. The "P" means a passenger-car or light-truck tire; "LT" means a tire for light-truck use only. The next three digits tell you how wide the tire is, in millimeters (here, 185 mm). The two digits after the slash are the "aspect ratio"—the ratio of the height of the sidewall to the tire width. Here, the sidewall height is 70 percent of the width, or about 130 mm. The "R" simply means radial ply—a design used for virtually all tires these days. The two digits at the end are the diameter of the wheel, in inches.

Speed rating. Some tires have an additional letter either within the size designation, before the "R" (185/70SR14, say) or just after the wheel diameter; such letter codes reflect the maximum speed the tire is certified to sustain. Some typical speed ratings: S means 112 mph; T, 118 mph; H, 130 mph; V, 149 mph, Z, 149-plus.

Treadwear rating. This is the tiremaker's measure of how well a tire's tread will wear, compared with a "reference" tire graded at 100. Theoretically, a tire with a wear index of 450 (relatively high) should last three times as long as one with an index of 150 (relatively low).

Traction and temperature. Scores are for Government tests for stopping on a wet surface and resisting the effects of high temperatures. A is best, C is worst. Don't settle for less than a B.

Date of manufacture. Every tire has a Department of Transportation serial number—something like DOTDBUA A44 414 GCD 415. The last three digits tell you the week and year the tire was manufactured; thus, 415 indicates the 41st week of 1995. Don't buy a tire that's more than two or three years old.

Maximum pressure. The tire's highest safe inflation pressure, in pounds per square inch (for example, 35 PSI MAX PRESS). It's best to follow the inflation recommendations in the car owner's manual. In any case, don't exceed the maximum listed on the tire.

Child safety seats

Despite Federal standards, not all seats are safe; we rated three Not Acceptable in our last report.

Last CR report: *September 1995*
Ratings: *page 314*
Price range: *$30 to $100*

The types

Infant seats. These consist of a carrier and a V-shaped harness. A few come with a base that is installed with the vehicle's safety belt and remains in the car. The carrier snaps into and out of the base. Infant seats are installed in a semireclined position that faces rear to help support the baby's head, neck, and back.

Seats made through the end of 1995 are labeled for use by babies up to 20 pounds. Seats manufactured after that may be labeled for use by babies up to 22 pounds, the weight of a typical 1-year-old. In judging fit, remember that the baby's head must be completely contained within the carrier. Price: $30 to $75.

Convertible seats. These are designed for both babies and small children. For young babies, convertible seats are installed in the rear-facing position. For children weighing from 20 to about 40 pounds, the seat is installed facing forward. Harness designs vary (see "Key features," below). Price: $50 to $125.

Booster seats. These are for children who are too big for a convertible seat but too small to use a vehicle's safety belts. There are two basic designs: high-back and no-back. Both can come with a removable shield. High-back boosters used with the harness or shield are best for younger children who may not remain seated unless confined. Either design will boost a child so he or she fits the vehicle's safety belts. Price: $20 to $60.

Built-in seats. Some GM, Ford, Chrysler, and Volvo models offer an optional safety seat built into the vehicle's seat. Built-ins are suitable for children over 1 year or 20 pounds. Built-ins avoid the problems associated with safety-seat installation. They can't dislodge in a crash, and they place the child farther away from the front seat, reducing the risk of head injury. Built-in seats may lack head support for a sleeping child, but those in some new cars solve the problem by reclining.

What's new

In our September 1995 and October 1996 reports on child safety seats, we judged four models Not Acceptable because they failed our crash-tests. Here's the latest:

The *Evenflo Travel Tandem*, an infant seat, failed catastrophically when carrying a 20-pound test dummy and used with its base in a test simulating a 30-mph head-on crash. It passed our test when used without its base. Shortly after our report, Evenflo informed us it had modified the Travel Tandem earlier in the year, to accommodate new, stricter Federal safety tests. The company said it would offer a free reinforcing plate to owners of Travel Tandems made prior to April 1; call 800 448-6924. As soon as we obtain the plate, we'll test it and report the results.

The *Kolcraft Traveler 700* can be used facing rearward for infants, facing forward for toddlers. In our crash-tests, the buckle assembly and overhead shield broke when the seat was forward-facing. Such a failure could eject a child from the seat. Kolcraft will provide a replacement buckle to owners of *Traveler 700* seats made between November 1994 and August 1995; call 800 453-7673.

The replacement buckle assembly held tight in our follow-up crash-test. But the harness straps slipped on impact, so the test dummy's upper body wasn't restrained quite as well as we'd like. Nonetheless, parents who have installed the replacement buckle can feel confident that the buckle and shield will stay intact.

The *Evenflo On My Way 206* is an infant carrier that uses a base. It failed our tests when used without its base. The carrier broke where the safety belt hooks into it, so it was no longer secured to the car. Evenflo voluntarily devised a retrofit kit to solve the problem; call 800 225-3056.

The retrofit is supposed to reinforce the area where the safety belt threads through the carrier. But in our follow-up crash-test, although the safety belt continued to hold the carrier, the reinforcements dislodged and the carrier cracked in the same general area as in our first test. Therefore, we still recommend using the *Evenflo On My Way 206* safety seat only with its base, and securing the base with the car's safety belt.

Evenflo has discontinued the *On My Way 206*. Its replacement, the *On My Way 207*, performed well in our safety tests.

Century continues to deny that its *Century 590* infant seat has a safety problem. In our tests, the 590 performed well without its base. (It can also be bought without the base as model 565 for less.) When it was tested with the base, the carrier and dummy were ejected and the base broke in three out of four runs. In the fourth run, the carrier rotated backward enough to compromise an infant's safety.

The manufacturer has launched a publicity campaign to discredit our findings. But other tests also point to a safety problem. At our urging, the National Highway Traffic Safety Administration (NHTSA) began its own technical evaluation and crash-tested the 590; the base cracked much the way it did in our tests. In a test run by the Canadian government, the carrier was ejected from the base.

Following publication of our original report, several class-action law suits were filed against Century. And we have also learned of an accident in which a nine-week-old infant was ejected from the vehicle while still strapped to the 590 carrier, which broke away from its base. The infant was unharmed.

Our advice remains: Don't use the 590 with its base. We still believe Century should voluntarily recall the model. Failing that, the NHTSA should order a recall.

Shopping strategy

Safety, of course is a paramount concern. Except for the three Not Acceptable models, all the seats we've tested kept their test dummies safe even in slightly stricter tests than those currently mandated by the Government.

In the event of a recall, you can make

sure you're notified if you fill out and mail in the registration card that comes with every seat. To find out about recalls on any seat, call the NHTSA's Auto Safety Hot Line, 800 424-9393, with the seat's make, model, and date of manufacture.

We don't recommend buying or using a used seat. It may have been in a crash and, most likely, won't come with instructions.

Decide on the type. A seat designed specifically for infants is the best choice for a newborn or small baby. When the baby outgrows the infant seat, we recommend a convertible seat with a five-point harness, which protects a child's upper torso the best. Any booster seat can safely be used without its shield or harness to position a child to wear a vehicle's safety belts. For younger children who resist staying put, we recommend a high-backed child seat that has a harness or shield.

Decide on the features. The more convenient a seat is to use, the more likely it is to be used every time your child is in the car. See "Key features," below.

The easiest brands to find. Century and Evenflo are the two biggest-selling brands, followed by Cosco, Gerry, and Kolcraft.

Key features

Child safety seats usually come fully assembled. They include a locking clip to use with vehicle safety belts and removable, machine-washable pads. Accessories and fabrics vary.

Other features to consider:

Harness. Convertible seats offer three types of harnesses. The *five-point harness*, consisting of two shoulder straps, two leg straps, and a crotch strap, provides the best upper-torso protection for all children and the best fit for infants. It's easy to buckle and unbuckle, but the straps can get in the way when you seat the child.

The *T-shield* harness consists of a plastic yoke that draws the shoulder straps over the child and buckles to the seat at the crotch. It provides good protection and is easy to use. But it's not suitable for an infant whose head doesn't clear the shield.

An *overhead-shield* harness has a padded, traylike shield that swings down over the child's head. It's generally easy to use, but the shield may block your view of the buckle. The design doesn't protect against head injury as well as the other types and, like the T-shield, it isn't suitable for a baby whose head doesn't clear the shield.

Installation. The design of the vehicle and its safety belts, or the design of the safety seat itself, can cause problems. Deeply contoured seats or bucket seats tend to make safety seats hard to install. The center of the rear seat is usually the safest place to install a safety seat. But if that part of the cushion is elevated, the safety seat can wobble and slide.

In many vehicles, the center rear lap belt is too short to encompass a sizable safety seat. And in some cars, the distance between the belt anchors may be too narrow to fit a safety seat.

According to new Federal regulations, all cars built since September 1995 must be able to secure a child safety seat without any locking clips. Many lap-and-shoulder belts in older cars, however, need a locking clip. Some vehicles require a supplemental buckle or a replacement belt.

Don't put an infant seat in the front if the car has a passenger-side air bag. For installation instructions specific to the seat you bought, refer to the section on installation in the car owner's manual as well as the instructions that come with the safety seat. If either of the instructions aren't clear, call the automaker, the safety-seat manufacturer, or both.

Ratings *Child safety seats*
& Recommendations

The tests behind the Ratings

Safety scores are based on the seats' performance in our tests simulating a 30-mph head-on crash. Column headings list the "age" of the test dummies we used, the seats' orientation (front- or rear-facing), and (for boosters) whether we used the seats' harness or shield or lap-and-shoulder belts like those found in real vehicles. **Price** is approximate retail. **Model availability:** Ⓓ means model is discontinued.

Standard features for these models

• Adequate protection in a 30-mph head-on crash. • Fully assembled product, with adequate instructions. • Locking clip for use with vehicle safety belts, if needed. • Mail-in registration card in case of a recall. • Rear-facing convertibles require more space between safety belts than front-facing ones.

Recommendations

Except for the Not Acceptable Century 590, any model we tested would be a good choice, provided it fits your vehicle. The clear choices are the top-rated Century 565 infant seat, A CR Best Buy at $35, and the Century 1000 STE Classic convertible seat, A CR Best Buy at $55 (or one of the higher-rated models that use a five-point harness). Any tested booster seat can safely be used without its shield or harness to position a child to wear vehicle safety belts. For younger children in a booster who may not stay put: the Century Breverra 4880 (with harness or shield), $65.

Overall Ratings

E VG G F P
⊖ ⊖ ○ ◐ ●

Within types, listed primarily in order of performance in safety tests

Brand and model	Price	Safety	Ease of use	Instal- lation	Comments
INFANT SEATS		9-MO.			
Century 565, A CR BEST BUY	$35	⊖	⊖	○	V-shaped harness. Requires installation with each use.
Evenflo On My Way 207 Ⓓ	65	⊖	⊖	○	V-shaped harness. Detachable auto base.
Kolcraft Rock'n Ride 13100	30	⊖	⊖	⊖	V-shaped harness. Requires installation with each use.

Brand and model	Price	Safety		Ease of use	Installation	Comments
INFANT SEATS		**9-MO.**				
Gerry Guard With Glide 627	$56	⊖		⊖	○	V-shaped harness. Requires installation with each use. May not fit with short safety belts. Vehicle belts can be difficult to weave through the safety seat. Hard-to-adjust harness straps.
■ **NOT ACCEPTABLE** WHEN USED WITH THE BASE						
Century 590	55	②		⊖	○	V-shaped harness. Carrier released from base in our safety tests. See story, page 000. Without base, requires installation with each use.

CONVERTIBLE SEATS		**3-YR. FRONT FACING**	**9-MO. REAR-FACING**	Ease of use	Installation	Comments
■ *The following models are judged suitable for small infants as well as larger infants and small children.*						
Century 1000 STE Classic, **A CR BEST BUY**	55	⊖	③	⊖	○	5-point harness. Rear-facing, requires installation with each use and may not fit with short safety belts.
Century SmartMove 4710	115	⊖	⊖	○	○	5-point harness. Wide base may not fit some vehicles. Hard-to-operate reclining mechanism.
Cosco Touriva 02514	68	⊖	⑤	⊖	⊖	5-point harness.
Kolcraft Auto-Mate 13225	60	○	⊖	⊖	○	5-point harness. Harness-adjustment dials let straps slip somewhat. Rear-facing, requires installation with each use and may not fit with short safety belts.
Safeline Sit'n'Stroll 3240X	140	○	⊖	○	●	5-point harness. Requires installation with each use. Wide base may not fit some vehicles. When rear-facing, may not fit with short safety belts. Safety-belt pathway may restrict child's movement. Belts could be dislodged by child if not tight. Hard-to-adjust harness straps.
■ *The following are judged less suitable for small infants, but suitable for large infants & small children.*						
Century 2000 STE	65	⊖	③	⊖	○	T-shield. Rear-facing, requires installation with each use and may not fit vehicles short safety belts.
Evenflo Scout 225	63	⊖	④	⊖	○	T-shield. Vehicle safety belt may interfere with buckle on safety seat in rear-facing position.
Evenflo Champion 224	64	⊖	⊖	⊖	○	Overhead shield. Vehicle safety belt may interfere with buckle on safety seat in rear-facing position.
Century 5500 STE Prestige	85	○	⊖	⊖	○	Overhead shield. Rear-facing, requires installation with each use and may not fit vehicles with short safety belts.
Gerry Guard SecureLock 691	80	○	⊖	⊖	⊖	Overhead shield. Hard-to-operate reclining mechanism. Automatic harness straps.

Ratings continued ▶

316 CHILD SAFETY SEATS

Overall Ratings *Continued*

Legend: E ⊖ VG ⊖ G ○ F ⊖ P ●

Brand and model	Price	Safety	Ease of use	Instal- lation	Comments
■ The following are judged less suitable for small infants, but suitable for large infants & small children.					
Century 3000 STE	$65	○	⊖	⊖	○	Overhead shield. Rear-facing, requires installation with each use and may not fit with short safety belts.
Cosco Touriva 02045 ▣	90	○	⑤	⊖	⊖	Overhead shield.
Kolcraft Traveler 700 13405 ▣ ⑥	60	○	⊖⑦	○	○	Overhead shield. Buckle failure released harness and dummy. Instructions error may lead to incorrect harness usage for infants. Retrofit judged effective. See story, page 000. Rear-facing, requires installation with each use and may not fit with short safety belts.
Cosco Touriva 02014	60	○	○	⊖	⊖	Overhead shield.
Evenflo Ultara I 235	85	○	⊖	⊖	◗	Overhead shield. Wide base may not fit some vehicles. Vehicle belt may interfere with buckle on safety seat in rear-facing position. Overhead shield may not adjust tightly for small child.

BOOSTER SEATS		3-YR. +SHIELD	3-YR. +BELTS	6-YR. +SHIELD	6-YR. +BELTS		
Century Breverra Premiere 4885	65	⊖	⊖	⑧	⊖	○	◗	5-point harness. Vehicles belts may be hard to weave through safety seat. High-back.
Gerry Double Guard 675	60	○	⊖	●	⊖	◗	◗	Swing-out shield. Shield could pinch child or installer when being lowered. No back.

▣ Evenflo has discontinued 206, which we rated Not Acceptable when used without the base. We found the retrofit kit offered by the mfr. ineffective and advise use of the 206 only with the base.

▣ Without base, score is ⊖.

▣ Not tested rear-facing. Should perform similarly to Century 3000 STE.

▣ Not tested rear-facing. Should perform similarly to Evenflo Champion 224.

⑤ Not tested rear-facing. Should perform similarly to Cosco Touriva 02014.

⑥ Kolcraft is offering a replacement buckle for owners of seats made between November 1994 and August 1995. That allows the seat to safely be used in the forward-facing position.

⑦ Rear-facing score is ⊖.

⑧ Mfr. advises against using shield with children over 45 lb.

Ratings
& Recommendations

Sport-utility & pickup-truck tires

The tests behind the Ratings

These tires are logical replacements on vehicles such as the Jeep Grand Cherokee (which we used as our test car), Ford Explorer, Chevrolet C/K pickup, and Ford F-Series pickup. We bought standard-load, on/off-road tires in size P235/75R15. Note: Scores are not comparable across types. **Noise** level was recorded at 30 mph. **Price** is approximate retail.

Recommendations

There wasn't all that much difference, overall, from the best to the worst tires in this group. For most light-truck owners, we see little reason to consider any tire model except the Dunlop Radial Rover, A CR Best Buy at $83. It performed the best in all our braking tests and among the best in cornering and handling. It rode well and had good steering feel.

See report, page 309. Last time rated in Consumer Reports: January 1996.

Overall Ratings *Listed in order of overall score*   E VG G F P

Brand and model	Price	Overall score (0–100)	Cornering DRY	Cornering WET	Handling	Noise SMOOTH	Noise COARSE	Ride
Dunlop Radial Rover Metric, **A CR BEST BUY**	$83		⊖	⊖	⊖	⊖	○	⊖
Michelin LTX M/S	105		⊖	⊖	⊖	⊖	○	⊖
Michelin LTX A/T	114		⊖	○	⊖	⊖	○	⊖
Cooper Discoverer	85		⊖	⊖	⊖	⊖	○	○
Kelly Safari SJR	80		⊖	⊖	⊖	⊖	○	○
Bridgestone Dueler APT (Sears)	85		⊖	○	⊖	⊖	○	◐
General Grabber AP	84		⊖	○	⊖	⊖	○	○
Goodyear Wrangler Aquatred	120		⊖	○	⊖	⊖	◐	◐
Firestone ATX II	87		⊖	○	○	⊖	○	◐
Goodyear Wrangler Radial	100		⊖	○	⊖	⊖	●	○

Ratings continued »

Model details *Listed in order of overall score*

NOTES ON THE DETAILS: Braking distance is the average for stopping on dry pavement from 60 mph (the average was 139 ft.), on wet pavement at 40 mph with anti-lock brakes (ABS) (average: 72 ft.) and without (average: 93 ft.).

Dunlop Radial Rover Metric $83
A CR BEST BUY

Slightly outperformed the rest in braking, and among the best in dry and wet cornering. Safe and responsive handling and a comfortable ride. Highest treadwear rating in this group. Braking: at 60 mph on dry pavement, 137 feet; at 40 mph on wet pavement with ABS, 69 feet, and without ABS, 87 feet. Treadwear rating: 440.

Michelin LTX M/S $105

A good wet-weather performer with ABS, and very comfortable—softer and quieter than the others. Braking: at 60 mph on dry pavement, 142 feet; at 40 mph on wet pavement with ABS, 71 feet; without ABS, 96 feet. Treadwear rating: 400.

Michelin LTX A/T $114

Among the quietest tires on smooth pavement. Otherwise, average in most respects. Braking: at 60 mph on dry pavement, 139 feet; at 40 mph on wet pavement with ABS, 70 feet; without ABS, 93 feet. Treadwear rating: 400.

Cooper Discoverer $85

Showed strongest grip in dry cornering. Very predictable as it's about to lose its grip. Especially quiet on smooth pavement. Braking: at 60 mph on dry pavement, 138 feet; at 40 mph on wet pavement with ABS, 74 feet; without ABS, 93 feet. Treadwear rating: 400.

Kelly Safari SJR $80

Long stopping distances without ABS. Noisy on smooth pavement, relatively quiet on coarse. Braking: at 60 mph on dry pavement, 139 feet; at 40 mph on wet pavement with ABS, 72 feet; without ABS, 96 feet. Treadwear rating: 320.

Bridgestone Dueler APT $85

A performance-oriented tire, with a noisy, harsh ride. Very nimble and responsive, and second best in wet and dry braking. But doesn't grip as well as some on the wet skid pad. Worst in rolling resistance. Available only from Sears. Braking: at 60 mph on dry pavement, 137 feet; at 40 mph on wet pavement with ABS, 70 feet; without ABS, 90 feet. Treadwear rating: 300.

General Grabber AP $84

Cornered well on dry pavement, adequately on wet. Responds fairly slowly to steering. Reasonably quiet, but ride is only so-so. Braking: at 60 mph on dry pavement, 138 feet; at 40 mph on wet pavement with ABS, 72 feet; without ABS, 95 feet. Treadwear rating not available.

Goodyear Wrangler Aquatred $120

One of the longest wet stoppers with ABS; one of the shortest without ABS. In cornering, loses grip progressively rather than abruptly. Braking: at 60 mph on dry pavement, 142 feet; at 40 mph on wet pavement with ABS, 74 feet; without ABS, 91 feet. Treadwear rating: 360.

Firestone ATX II $87

Consistently scored at the bottom in cornering tests. Not an especially comfortable ride. Scored well in rolling resistance. Braking: at 60 mph on dry pavement, 139 feet; at 40 mph on wet pavement with ABS, 74 feet; without ABS, 94 feet. Treadwear rating not available.

Goodyear Wrangler Radial $100

A disappointing tire. Worst in wet braking, mediocre in dry braking and wet cornering. Not much steering feel, but handles precisely. Noisiest tire of the bunch. Braking: at 60 mph on dry pavement, 141 feet; at 40 mph on wet pavement with ABS, 76 feet; without ABS, 97 feet. Treadwear rating: 300.

Ratings
& Recommendations

All-season performance tires

The tests behind the Ratings
Most of the models in this group are still available. We tested size P205/60R15 tires, which fit many mid-sized and large cars. Test car: Pontiac Bonneville SSEi. Note: Scores are not comparable across types. **Braking** scores are for stopping distance on dry pavement from 60 mph, and average on wet payment at 40 mph with and without the anti-lock brake system working. **Price** is approximate retail.

Recommendations
The Goodyear Eagle Aquatred performed very well, but it emitted a constant drone and is pricey. The Yokohama Avid MD-H4 scored a close second; it's particularly good for cars without ABS. The BF Goodrich Comp T/A HR4 is also worth considering for cars without ABS.

See report, page 309. Last time rated in Consumer Reports: January 1995.

Overall Ratings *Listed in order of overall score*

Legend: E VG G F P

Brand and model	Price	Overall score (0–100)	Braking Dry	Braking Wet	Cornering Dry	Cornering Wet	Handling
Goodyear Eagle Aquatred	$150		⊖	⊖	⊖	○	⊖
Yokohama Avid MD-H4	98		⊖	⊖	⊖	◕	○
BF Goodrich Comp T/A HR4	82		⊖	⊖	⊖	⊖	⊖
Pirelli P4000 Super Touring	103		⊖	⊖	⊖	◕	⊖
General XP2000 H4	75		⊖	⊖	⊖	○	○
Firestone Firehawk GTA	88		⊖	⊖	⊖	○	○
Michelin XGT H4	105		○	○	⊖	○	○
Michelin MXV4 Green X	115		⊖	○	⊖	◕	⊖
Goodyear Eagle GA	140		⊖	○	⊖	◕	⊖

PRODUCT RECALLS

Products ranging from child safety seats to chain saws are recalled when there are safety defects. Various Federal agencies—the Consumer Product Safety Commission (CPSC), the National Highway Traffic Safety Administration, the U.S. Coast Guard, and the Food and Drug Administration—monitor consumer complaints and injuries and, when there's a problem, issue a recall.

However, the odds of your hearing about an unsafe product are slim. Manufacturers are reluctant to issue a recall in the first place because they can be costly. And getting the word out to consumers can be haphazard.

A selection of the most far-reaching recalls appear monthly in CONSUMER REPORTS.

The following pages gather together a year's worth of recalls published in the November 1995 through October 1996 issues of CONSUMER REPORTS. For the latest information, see the current issue of the magazine.

If you wish to report an unsafe product or get recall information, call the CPSC's hotline, 800 638-2772.

Recall notices about your automobile can be obtained from a new-car dealer or by calling the NHTSA hotline at 800 424-9393. Questions about food and drugs are handled by the FDA's Office of Consumer Affairs, 301 443-3170.

You can better assure yourself of getting a recall notice by returning the warranty cards that come with many products.

Children's products

Cosco Youth Options furniture
May tip over and injure anyone nearby if several drawers are opened at once or if heavy objects are placed in top drawers.

Products: 585,000 chifforobes (wardrobe/chest of drawers combinations) and 309,000 four-drawer dressers sold since '91. White laminated furniture was sold unassembled. Affected chifforobes, models 80813 and 88813, consist of closet on left side and two shelves and three drawers on right side; they measure 51 inches high, 46 inches wide, and 16 inches deep, and sold for $89-$109. Dressers, models 80413 and 88413, measure 38 inches high, 30 inches wide, and 16 inches deep; they sold for $79-$89. Both items came with round, black-plastic feet that can be attached to bottom of furniture; Cosco says feet make furniture tip easily.

What to do: Remove feet so furniture sits flat on floor.

Playskool 1-2-3 high chair
Plastic joints could crack and make chair collapse.

Products: 300,000 high chairs sold 5/94-10/95 for $75.

What to do: Inspect chair, especially plastic pivot joints, and call 800 752-9755. Company will send repair kit—or, if chair has cracks, company will replace chair.

Playskool Fold N' Travel infant carrier
Child could fall out and suffer serious injury.

Products: 38,000 lightweight plastic infant carriers, models 100, 101, 102, and 103, sold 4/91-'93 for $35. Carrier is blue or teal with fabric or vinyl pad. It measures 17 in. long folded, 26 in. fully extended. Carrier is adjustable in three positions—rocker, feeder, or sleeper—by pushing buttons on either side of handle where it attaches to shell. Device can be folded by squeezing levers underneath carrier.

What to do: Return carrier to store or to Playskool for refund. For prepaid shipping carton and return information, call 800 447-7707.

Fabric-covered foam chairs sold at Ames department stores
Child could unzip fabric cover, ingest thin plastic liner, and choke on it.

Products: 20,000 chairs, 11 in. high, 11 in. wide, and 15½ in. deep, sold 1/94-6/96 for $50. Fabric cover features pictures of animals and childlike drawings. Zipper is on bottom of chair, as is white label that reads, in part: "NOW PRODUCTS INC." Chairs were sold with matching ottomans and sofas.

What to do: Discontinue use and call Now Products at 800 535-3218, ext. 33, for free repair kit.

Gerry cribs
Mattress and underlying support could collapse if side rails are assembled improperly.

Products: 17,043 cribs, models 8200, 8300, and 8500, sold 5/94-8/94 for $90. Unassembled cribs came in various shades of natural wood and were packaged in brown cardboard box labeled, in part: "Gerry Fold-Away Crib....Compact crib that folds in seconds...." Fully assembled, crib is 39½ inches long, 25½ inches wide, and 38 inches high. Hazard exists when side rails are put on backwards, contrary to manufacturer's instructions.

What to do: Check manufacturer's date code on label attached to hinged mattress support; if crib is affected, call 800 525-2472; company will send supplemental instructions to help you determine whether crib was assembled properly.

Little Tykes Cozy Highback Swing
Could flip over and allow child to fall out.

Products: 245,000 swings, model no. 4637, designed for children nine months to three years and sold 1/96-4/96 for $15-$18. Bright blue plastic swing is 13 inches wide, 12 inches long, and 14 inches high. "Little Tykes" logo is on stationary front crossbar. Swing hangs from four yellow ropes.

What to do: Phone 800 321-0183 for replacement swing or comparable Little Tykes product.

Cosco cribs
Slats could come out of side rails and entrap child's head or allow child to fall out.

Products: 190,000 full-sized cribs made of welded red, white, blue, or multicolored tubular metal. One side rail is fixed; other one can be raised or lowered. Most cribs were sold 1/91-4/94 for $95-$150. Affected models include numbers 10T01, 10T04, 10T05, 10T06, 10T09, 10T11, and 10T14. Manufacturer's identification, which includes model number, is at bottom of either side rail.

What to do: Call 800 314-9327 for free repair kit.

'Christmas in the Manger,' book by Nola Buck & Felicia Bond
Plastic "jewels" on page showing Three Wise Men could come off and choke child.

Products: 46,500 books, measuring 6x6½ inches, published by HarperCollins and sold 9/94-11/15/94 for $10. Books with paper jewels instead of plastic ones are not being recalled.

What to do: Return book to store for refund.

Splish Splash & Fuzz & Fur books
Plastic bolts could come off binder, choking child.

Products: 11,300 books, written by Lizi Boyd, published by Chronicle Books of San Francisco, and sold 5/1/95-6/19/95 for $6. Books, which measure 7 by 6 inches, are made of heavy cardboard. Front and back covers have cutouts filled with fabric. Fuzz & Fur (item number ISBN 0-8118-0377-5) has juvenile drawings of child and bear on front and child on back. Cover of Splish Splash (item number ISBN 0-8118-0346-5) shows child and bathtub on front and child and duck on back. Both books were wrapped in clear plastic and labeled, in part: "$5.95, Chronicle Books, 275 Fifth Street, San Francisco, CA 94103, Happy Baby Books, Copyright 1995 by Lizi Boyd, Printed in the Philippines."

What to do: Return books to store for refund.

Playskool Color 'N Contrast 'Kitty and Friends' & 'Puppy and Friends' cloth crib books
Straight pins left in books during manufacturing process could injure child.

Products: 24,000 books sold 11/95-3/96 for $5. Books consist of five attached plush fabric panels, each with black-and-white picture on one side and color picture on other. Panels can be folded into one another, creating "book." First and last panels have Velcro tabs to attach unfolded book to crib. Books are 5¼ inches square when folded and open to 26 inches. "Kitty and Friends" has colored pictures of house, bear, duck, flower, and locomotive; black-and-white panels show rocking horse, four boxes with quarter moon, heart, triangle, star, boy's face, target, and cat. "Puppy and Friends" has colored panels showing fish, ball, butterfly, car, and apple; black-and-white pictures show sailboat, four boxes with two circular mazes and two square mazes, girl's face, and design with triangle, heart, circle, star, and dog. Label on fabric flap reads, in part: "Dutton Children's Books, a division of Penguin Books USA Inc . . . Playskool . . . Hasbro, Inc." and "ISBN 0-525-45468-3" or "ISBN 0-525-45469-1."

What to do: Return book to store or mail to Penguin USA, 100 Fabrite Rd., Newbern, Tenn. 38059-1334, Attn.: Cloth Book Dept., for refund of purchase price and postage.

Playskool Durasport Moon Bouncer inflatable vinyl toy
If toy is improperly inflated or placed on hard surface, child could fall or bounce out and suffer serious injury.

Products: 142,000 toys sold since 11/94 for $60. Toy is designed for children ages 3 to 6 to bounce and jump in. It has red circular base that inflates to 5½ feet in diameter. Side walls, resembling three stacked yellow rings, inflate to 16 inches from jumping surface.

What to do: Phone 800 683-5847 for free set of gauges and instructions to help assure proper inflation. Outdoors, place toy on energy-absorbing surface like sand or mulch. Indoors, use padded surface; carpeting may not be sufficient to prevent injury.

'Little Me' baseball uniform for infants
Wooden buttons can come off and choke child.

Products: 5000 one-piece, white-cotton jersey garments with thin blue stripes, sold during spring of '92 for $27. Red "24" is stitched onto left front of garment with blue thread. Outfit, which came with matching blue-and-white baseball cap, has three round wooden buttons, each measuring ¾-inch. Label on garment reads, in part: "Little Me...100% Cotton...Made in USA..."

What to do: Send garment to Schwab Co., P.O. Box 1742, Upper Potomac Industrial Park, Cumberland, Md. 21501, for refund, including shipping cost.

Gasoline-powered go-karts sold under various labels
Child's hair or clothing could get tangled in spinning rear axle, causing serious injury or death.

Products: 300,000 one- and two-seat go-karts made by Manco Prods. and sold 1/72-6/96 at department, power-equipment, hardware, and specialty stores for $600-$2000. Sears sold go-karts under Sears name from '77-'83; Western Auto stores sold them under Phoenix label since '87. Manco distributed them under Fox label since '90. Some models have brush bars to protect riders from low tree branches and foliage. All Manco go-karts with exposed rear axle are affected. To check, stand behind go-kart and, with engine off, push it by hand. If axle connecting rear wheels rotates, kart is affected.

What to do: Note serial number (on white label on floor pan in front of driver's seat) and model number, and call 800 293-0795 for free axle-guard kit and installation instructions, or ask Manco dealer where kart was bought to install guard kit free.

Pull-A-Long wooden snail pull toys
Could come apart and choke child.

Products: 4800 toys, model 3092, sold at flea markets and discount stores in Calif. and Ill. 5/94-1/95 for $1. Set includes train of three snails measuring 2½, 3¼, and 3¾ inches long, with 13-inch pull cord. Each snail has straight base and round, peg-like wheels. Two larger snails have natural-wood head and red antennae; smallest snail has red head and natural-wood antennae. Toys came with nine red, green, blue, and natural-wood disks that can be stacked on peg on snail's back to form shell. Cardboard box is labeled, in part: "Pull-A-Long Wooden Snail 3 Wagons Made in China."

What to do: Return toy to store for refund, or mail to Four Seasons General Merchandise, 2801 E. Vernon Ave., Vernon, Calif. 90058, for refund plus postage.

'SnackTime Stroller Toy Bar'

Rattle attached to bar could break apart, and child could inhale small beads inside.

Products: 99,000 toys sold 7/95-6/96 for $13-$15. Toy is 14 inches long and 3 inches wide and fits over front bar of stroller. It includes four plastic figures: green and pink flower, which doubles as cupholder; purple and pink caterpillar, with plastic rings that function as stacking teether; yellow bear, which holds rattle and jingle balloons and plays music; and frog. whose head opens into removable, spill-resistant bowl. Toy came in cardboard box with see-through window labeled, in part: "SnackTime Stroller Toy Bar, Model Number 669...Combines Snacktime and Playtime for babies on the go!...Easily attaches to stroller crossbars...KIDS II...For Ages Up To 3 Years..." Toys sold after 8/1/96 and bearing model numnber 683 and date code are not subject to recall.

What to do: Return toy to Kids II, 1015 Windward Ridge Parkway, Alpharetta, Ga. 30202, for replacement bar.

Liquid timer toys

Contain ethylene glycol and petroleum distillates, combustible chemicals that are toxic if swallowed.

Products: 1800 toys sold in Ariz., Calif., Tex., and Puerto Rico 7/94-4/95 for $5. Timers came in two types: Trio Water Timer, model 3491, has three plastic tubes, each 5 inches high and 1½ inches in diameter, divided into two compartments by clear-plastic shelves. Base and top of timer are pink and yellow plastic. Center tube contains pink honeylike substance; outer tubes contain green or blue liquid. Some timers have images of basketball, baseball, or football attached to spinning wheels inside tubes. Box is labeled, in part: "TRIO TIMER, Item No. WT-6, 1991 MADE IN TAIWAN." Other water timer, model 3494, has two separate rectangular cells, each 4-3/4 inches high and 1-1/2 inches wide, containing red or blue liquid. Clear-plastic spout divides each cell into two compartments. Each cell contains yellow plastic wheel with black-and-white spiral design on outside. When timer is inverted, colored liquid makes wheels spin. Blue-and-white polka-dot box reads: "WATER TIMER, MADE IN TAIWAN."

What to do: Return toy to store for refund, or mail to Four Seasons General Merchandise, 2801 E. Vernon Ave., Vernon, Calif. 90058, for refund plus postage.

Magic Diamond paperweight toy

Contains ethylene glycol and petroleum distillates, combustible chemicals that are toxic if swallowed.

Products: 864 toys sold in Ariz., Calif., and Colo. 1/4/95-1/18/95 for $1. Clear-plastic paperweight is 3½ inches in diameter and is filled with clear liquid and pieces of iridescent paper. Black box is labeled, in part: "MAGIC DIAMOND" ITEM NO. MD-1, 1991, WORLDWIDELY PAT."

What to do: Return toy to store for refund, or mail it to Four Seasons General Merchandise, 2801 E. Vernon Ave., Vernon, Calif. 90058, for refund plus postage.

Teddy Precious Indian Girl stuffed bear sold at Kay-Bee toy stores

Small beads that decorate Native American-style sash could come off and choke child.

Products: 11,600 light-brown stuffed bears sold 3/95-3/96 for $13. Bear is 18 inches long and comes with brown vinyl dress and headband trimmed with Native American embroidery. Pink label on bear's foot says, in part, "Teddy Precious." Blue-and-white tag on bear's lower back reads, in part, "DAN-DEE INTERNATIONAL LIMITED, JERSEY CITY, N.J. 07305 . . . MADE IN CHINA." Some tags also include "SKU #089318."

What to do: Return bear to Kay-Bee store for refund.

Toy boats with small people figures

Child could choke on small parts.

Products: 7000 toys sold 6/93-8/94 for $2. Toys are packaged in sets of three boats and three people. Plastic boats are 2 inches long and come in red, yellow, green, or blue. Plastic people are 1½ inches high, with green, red, yellow, or blue barrel-shaped body, round white head, and small hat. Multicolored label on blister pack reads, in part: "Funtasy... Made in China... Justen Products Itasca, IL 60143."

What to do: Return toy to store for refund.

Household products

Ariens & Tanaka gasoline-powered backpack leaf blowers
Fuel tank could leak and create fire hazard.

Products: 11,000 leaf blowers, Ariens model BB-430 and Tanaka models TBL-455 and TBL-500, sold 1/86-12/92 for $400-$460. Blowers are mounted on black metal backpack frame with padded shoulder strap, and have orange fuel tank and black blower tubes. Brand and model identification appears on fuel tank or recoil starter.
What to do: Have nearest authorized Tanaka service center replace fuel tank. For information, phone 800 313-5580.

Shindaiwa gasoline-powered backpack blower & chain saw
Fuel tank could leak, posing fire hazard.

Products: 18,500 blowers and 4970 chain saws sold 4/92-6/95 for $430 and $300, respectively. Red blower is mounted on black metal backpack frame with shoulder straps, black blower tubes, and white fuel tank with "Shindaiwa...model number EB-45" printed in center. Red chain saw has gray guide bar and "model number 300S" printed on pull-start housing.
What to do: Return tools to authorized Shindaiwa servicing dealer for free replacement of fuel tank. For location of dealer, call 800 521-7733.

Better Valu clear ammonia
Mislabeled bottle contains bleach. Accidentally mixing bleach with ammonia or other acidic substances can produce toxic gases.

Products: 3608 64-ounce white plastic containers sold 6/1/95-8/23/95 for $1 at Brookshires and other stores in Tex., Okla., and La. Label says: "Better Valu...Clear Ammonia...64 FL. OZ 2 QTS...79801 98767...E15295...PACKED FOR FEDERATED FOODS, INC. ARLINGTON HEIGHTS, IL 60005-1096..." Only bottles labeled "ammonia" and with 10-digit bar code "79801 98767" and 10-digit batch code beginning with "E15295" are being recalled.
What to do: Return product to store for refund.

Brinkmann Smoke'N Pit cooker barbecue grill
Lid could fall and injure user.

Products: 43,800 cookers sold mostly 11/92-3/94 for $100-$130. Smoke'N Pit Pitmaster, model 805-21-1-2, sold for $100-$130; Smoke'N Pit Professional, models 805-2101-0 and 805-2101-1, sold for $200-$250. Grills are black steel and have straight rather than angled smokestack. Cooking chamber of both types measures 34½ inches long by 16½ inches wide. Professional version also has 17-inch-long firebox attached on side. Not all cookers have manufacturer's identification. On those that do, it's near lid handle.
What to do: Call 800 675-5301 for free replacement smokestack that lets lid open wider, eliminating stability problem.

Char-Broil model 1200 tabletop LP gas grill
Debris could build up in regulator valve and make valve appear to be off when it's not, allowing gas to collect over time. If consumer then lights burner, grill could explode or burst into flames.

Products: 1.2 million grills sold 1/92-3/96 at hardware stores and home centers for $30. Black steel grill measures 11 in. wide, 18 in. long, and 9 in. deep (when closed).
What to do: Call Char-Broil at 800 241-7548 for free replacement regulator with internal filter that will prevent debris from interfering with its operation.

Gaslow LP gas-monitor gauge
Propane could leak and ignite or explode.

Products: 31,000 gauges sold 7/94-8/94 for $20-$25. L-shaped gauge attaches to portable LP tank used on gas grills, recreational vehicles, and boats. Valve on device acts as both refill indicator and leak detector. Unit has 3½-inch copper-colored base that screws into propane tank, and black dial with black, green, and yellow face. Gauge was sold in clear-plastic package with black label that reads, in part: "GASLOW LP GAS MONITOR GAUGE...with Refill Indicator Built-in Leak Detector...Model No. GS-1 Item No. 13742." Recalled gauges bear 03/94 or 04/94 date code stamped on square end.
What to do: Phone 800 666-8558 for free replacement.

Milwaukee sander/grinder
May turn on too easily or stick in On position.

Products: 9300 4½-inch Mag series tools sold 7/1/95-9/30/95 for $120. Number 6148 or 6151 appears on label.
What to do: Return tool to store or Milwaukee branch office/service center for replacement, or send via United Parcel Service to Milwaukee Electric Tool Corp., 8950 Hacks Cross Rd., Olive Branch, Miss. 38654. Company will reimburse shipping charges.

Dewalt one-hour battery chargers for cordless power tools
Plastic housing might not withstand hard impact. If housing breaks, live electrical components could become exposed and present shock hazard.

Products: 150,000 chargers, models DW9104 and DW9106, sold 8/95-4/96 for $39-$59. Affected units have black top and bottom sections and are stamped on bottom with date code between 9534 and 9615 (first two digits are yr. of manufacture, last two are week it was made). Device is 5 in. deep, 3 in. high, and 4 in. wide, and has label on top with yellow lettering that reads, in part: "DEWALT." A circular depression, 1⅜ in. in diameter, is located under center of label on top of housing. Chargers without the depression are not involved. Device was sold separately or in kits with some rechargeable cordless tools.

What to do: Return charger to Black & Decker/Dewalt service center for free replacement. For information or the name of nearest center, call company at 800 540-2626.

Various Porter-Cable power tools
Pose electrical-shock hazard.

Products: 1500 tools sold 9/95: tiger saw, model 9737, serial numbers 24049-27983; profile sander, model 9444/444, serial numbers 37515-40151; cutout tool, model 7499, serial nos. 20503-20754; circular saw, model 345, serial numbers 172580-173973; plate joiner, model 556, serial numbers 227431-227768 and 227819-228381; and jig saw, model 7549, serial numbers 127677-127750, 128263-128774, and 129310-129392. Model and serial number appear on tool housing.

What to do: Phone 800 487-8665 for free repair or replacement.

Ryobi & Sears Craftsman table saws
Power-switch safety lock could fail, posing risk to unauthorized user.

Products: 150,000 Ryobi model BT3000 and Sears Craftsman model 315.22185 10-inch table saws sold for $400 to $600. Ryobi model was sold since 5/91; Sears, since 7/94. Affected saws have large rectangular On/Off buttons and switch lock-off key. In some cases, if Off button isn't completely depressed, saw could be started without key. Affected Ryobi models have serial number (found on data plate on right side) whose last four digits are lower than 9608. Serial number is irrelevant for Sears units.

What to do: Call 800 867-9624 for free replacement switch lock-off key. Also make sure On button is fully released when you remove lock-off key, and unplug saw when it's not in use.

Stamina model PR-6050 exercise machine
Welds could break and cause seat or other parts to fail, resulting in possible injury.

Products: 21,500 exercise machines sold 11/95-2/96 for $99 through various venues, including Wal-Mart, Value Vision, Damark International, and QVC home shopping network. Black metal machine resembles bicycle without wheels. "Stamina" is printed in red on lower rear of frame. To operate, user pulls handlebars, which rocks seat forward. Machine adjusts under seat to increase resistance and provide more intense workout.

What to do: Contact Stamina Products at 800 375-7520 to arrange for refund or free replacement. Company will pay for shipping. Company can also be contacted by mail. Write to: Stamina at P.O. Box 1071, Springfield, Mo. 65801-1071.

CSA E-Force Cross Trainer exercise machine
Welds could break and cause parts to fail, resulting in possible injury.

Products: 300,000 silver metal exercise machines, model T1200, sold 3/95-6/96 at retail stores and through TV informercials for $180-$249. Model designation (T1200) appears only on product literature and packaging, not on exerciser itself. Device resembles bicycle without wheels and bears words "E-FORCE Cross Trainer" on black plastic guards below seat. To operate, consumers pull handlebars, which rocks seat forward. Recall does not pertain to E-Force Rider or E-Force Sport.

What to do: Stop using machine immediately and call CSA at 800 651-8090 for free repair kit. Before calling, note machine's lot no., located on permanent label by rollers at base behind seat.

Berko Electric baseboard heater
Wiring could arc, creating fire or shock hazard.

Products: 1.5 million permanently installed heaters sold 1/80-3/87. Affected units bear model numbers beginning with "MBB," followed by four numbers, and ending in "M" (for example, "MBB2-524-M"). Silver Berko label, containing model number, is inside heater on right side, below steel air deflector. Date of manufacture appears at right of label. Heaters have tan cover and are 2 to 10 feet long.

What to do: Call 800 545-8306. Berko will either provide new wire to repair heater or provide 60 percent discount toward new Berko heater. (If air deflector is discolored, disconnect heater immediately.)

Square D & Nelco Corp. electric baseboard heater

Wiring could deteriorate, creating fire hazard —and shock hazard, if heater isn't properly grounded.

Products: 920,000 permanently installed tan baseboard heaters, measuring 2 feet (500 watts) to 10 feet (2500 watts), sold '70-86. Model numbers of affected heaters begin with 18, 25, or 30, followed by four digits and ending in SER A or B (for example, 25242-4 SER A). Brown and white Square D or Nelco Corp. identification label with model number and UL listing number is on bottom left side of heater, just below heating element.

What to do: Check heater cover; if it's discolored, stop using heater immediately. Square D no longer sells these heaters. Another heater manufacturer has agreed to sell comparable heaters at 50-percent discount to owners of recalled Square D heaters. For discount, remove identification label and present it to participating dealer. For name of nearest dealer, call 800 666-7557.

Square D & Nelco Corp. electric in-wall heater

Fan could stop blowing, making coils overheat and creating fire hazard.

Products: 80,000 heaters, Series A and B, model numbers TW 1222, TW 2022, and TW 2422, sold '70-86. To identify affected units, remove grill and look for label bearing model information, on top edge of grill.

What to do: Square D no longer sells these heaters. Another heater manufacturer has agreed to sell comparable heaters at 50-percent discount to owners of recalled Square D heaters. For discount, remove ID label and present it to participating dealer. For name of nearest dealer, call 800 666-7557.

Turner LP-2440 portable propane heater

Could release deadly carbon monoxide gas.

Products: 20,000 radiant heaters sold '63 to early '64 for $30-$35. Heater has green metal cabinet about 8 inches wide, 3 inches deep, and 13 inches high. Model number appears on front of heater along with words, "PORTABLE radiant heater, TURNER CORPORATION."

What to do: Call 800 889-7672 for instructions on returning defective heater and receiving $250 reward.

Atlas indoor/outdoor halogen work light

Pose serious electric shock, fire, and burn hazards. Also, tripod-mounted models could tip easily.

Products: 15,600 lights sold since '95 for $12 to $36. All models are yellow and black. Model CLP150, sold since 7/95, is clip-on light; models PQ150WS and PQ500WS, sold since 2/95, consist of light mounted on small frame with handle on top; model ST500, sold since 2/95, is single light mounted on tripod; model TST500, sold since 6/95, consists of two lights on tripod. Lights came in white box labeled with Atlas logo and address, model designation, and words "Made in China."

What to do: Return light to store for refund. For information, call Atlas at 800 849-8485.

Emergency Lite 3-in-1 night-light

If light comes apart while plugged in, exposed wires can deliver lethal shock.

Products: 3200 white plastic lights sold at home supply stores 1/95-5/5/95 for $10-$15. Light is 5 ½ inches high, 3¼ inches wide. Opaque front cover has model name, the word "HomeSafe," and the model number, 334N. Light can be plugged into outlet or used with rechargeable battery as flashlight. It automatically turns on at dusk, off at dawn.

What to do: Phone 800 669-0415 for free replacement.

Sprint household extension cords in various lengths

Pose fire and shock hazards.

Products: 20,196 cords, 6 to 20 feet long, sold 1/94-12/95 in N. Y. and N.J. for $1-$3. Cords are brown and white. Six-foot cords are item AC-67-6; 12-foot cords, item AC-67-12; 15-foot cords, item AC-67-15; 20-foot cords, item AC-67-20. Cords are labeled, in part: "SPT-2 ... 18AWGX2C." Cords were packaged in cardboard sleeve labeled, in part: "SPRINT . . . HOUSEHOLD EXTENSION CORD."

What to do: Return cord to store for refund. For information, call 718 499-5511—or 800 955-3115 outside New York metropolitan area.

Nokia and AT&T cellular telephone plug-in charger

Plug prongs could break off and become stuck in outlet, where they could cause electrical shock.

Products: 65,800 chargers sold 7/95-11/95. Black plastic shell measures about 3x2½x1 inches. Label on recalled chargers bears model number ACH-4U, date code 9531 through 9546, and "Made in Norway."

What to do: Call 800 204-2567 for free replacement.

Texas Instruments battery charger for TravelMate 4000M notebook computer

Could overheat and cause fire.

Products: 3200 plug-in battery chargers sold as optional accessory 11/94-1/96 for $140. Gray plastic charger is 5 3/4 inches long, 3 3/4 inches wide, and 1 inch deep. Label on bottom of charger reads, "Texas Instruments...P/N 9792543-0001...Type BTC·01..." Date codes 10/7/94 to 3/20/95 appear on charger.
What to do: Phone 800 730-4235 for replacement charger or refund, at company's discretion.

Keller & Columbia fiberglass extension ladders (various models and lengths)

Could collapse.

Products: 29,691 Industrial Type I and Industrial Heavy Duty Type 1A fiberglass ladders, 16 to 40 feet long, sold at home centers and hardware stores for $150 to $500. Keller Type I ladders are yellow and include model 5016, made 3/1/93-12/31/94, and model 5028, made 3/1/93-12/31/95. Keller Type IA ladders are orange and include: model 5128, made 7/1/90-12/31/95; model 5132, made 7/1/90-5/31/94; and models 5136 and 5140, both made 3/1/91-12/31/95. Columbia Type I ladder is yellow, model EF4128, made 3/1/93-12/31/95. Columbia Type IA ladders are orange and include: model EF1028, made 7/1/90-12/31/95); model EF1032, made 7/1/90-5/31/94; and models EF1036 and EF1040, both made 3/1/91-12/31/95). Last two digits in model number determine length of ladder. For example, model 5016 is 16 feet long. Model number and date of manufacture appear on sticker or metal plate on ladder. Deciphering date code is tricky. Ignore first digit. Second two digits are month of manufacture plus 10 (for example, 13 represents March). Last two digits are year ladder was made.
What to do: Return ladder to store for replacement or refund, or call 800 353-9013 for replacement rung lock to eliminate hazard.

Square D brand secondary surge arresters used in circuit-breaker panel boards

Could cause fire.

Products: 4200 surge arresters, catalog no. SDT1175SB, made for use in Square D "Trilliant" panel boards, SDT Series 1 Home Power Systems, 100-200 amperes. Units are designed to protect home electrical-wiring systems from lightning or power surges. Viewed in circuit-breaker panel, gray-plastic device measures 2½ inches wide, ¾ inch high. Small green indicator light is on side of product. Nearby label says: "SURGEBREAKER. Light On

(with unit properly installed) - unit is working. Light Off or Flashing - replace unit."
What to do: Phone 800 666-7557 for free replacement.

Six-outlet power strips sold at Odd Lots, Big Lots, & All For One stores

Pose electrocution and fire hazards.

Products: 125,000 beige metal power strips, item 81488, sold 5/95-12/95 in East, South, and Midwest for $5. Power strip has six black receptacle outlets, red On/Off indicator switch, and black power cord. Device measures 12 inches long, 2 ¼ inches wide, and 1½ inches deep, and came in blue box labeled, in part: "FULL SURGE 6 OUTLET POWER STRIP . . . 6 RECEPTACLES. CIRCUIT BREAKER. 5 FT CORD . . . 15 AMPS MAX." Back of box reads, in part: "SURGE PROTECTED 6-OUTLET CENTER . . . SAFE-TY GUARD . . . MADE IN CHINA UNION FIELD INDUSTRIES LTD CITY OF INDUSTRY, CA 91789 . . . UPC code 0 83726 81488 5."
What to do: Return power strip to store for refund or exchange. For more information, phone 800 877-1253 and ask for Michael Schlonsky.

Handheld electric hair dryers sold at Bill's Dollar Stores

Lack immersion-protection plug that can prevent electrocution if dryer is dropped in water.

Products: 12,000 dryers sold 5/95-2/96 throughout the South for $5. Dryers were labeled either "International Professional Styler" or "Acesonic Professional Styler."
What to do: Return dryer to store for refund or exchange.

Sprint Compact Pro HD-150 hair dryer

Could catch fire. Also, lacks immersion-protection plug that can prevent electrocution if dryer is dropped in water with power on.

Products: 1160 dryers sold in New York metropolitan area 1/94-4/96 for $10. Dryers bear Sprint name and are labeled, in part: "HD-150 1250W . . . AC-110V 60HZ." Box reads, in part: "SPRINT. . . COM-PACT PRO HD-150...MADE IN CHINA."
What to do: Return dryer to store for refund. For information, call 718 499-5511, or 800 955-3115 outside New York metropolitan area.

Sinostone SC-01 CO detector
Alarm may not sound.

Products: 18,700 detectors sold 10/94-8/95 for $28. Gray plastic detector measures 5½ inches long, 3¼ inches wide, and 1½ inches deep, and has vertical vents and "Accusniffer" lettering in front. Green Power light and red Alarm light are in center of detector, above Test/Reset button. Model number and company name and address are on sticker on back of detector. Unit has white power cord and plug, and battery back-up system. Detectors were packaged in green box, labeled in part: "Accusniffer...110 Volt Plug-in plus Battery Backup...SC-01, Stand alone model..."

What to do: Company is out of business. Stop using detector and replace with device that meets UL Standard 2034. Also, see report, page 125.

Home Gas Sentry AC-powered CO detector
May not alarm to indicate dangerous level of deadly odorless and colorless gas.

Products: 6000 detectors, imported and distributed by Stanley Solar & Stove Inc., of Manchester, N.H., sold 2/88-5/96 for $80. Rectangular, off-white plastic device measures 4¾ in. long, 2½ in. wide, and 1¼ in. deep with "Gas Sentry" on front. Green "Power" light and red "Alarm" light appear in center of unit. Co. name, date of manufacture, and manufacturing no. appear on sticker on back of detector. Device has white power cord and plug. Coal and wood stove dealers sold detectors in Northeast. Unit came in white box labeled, in part: "Home Gas Sentry...120 Volts AC...Model Z-1604-KM..."

What to do: Stop using detector and replace it with device that meets Underwriters Laboratories Standard 2034, which was revised as of 10/1/95. This recall notice was issued unilaterally by the U.S. Consumer Product Safety Commission; the distributor/importer isn't participating, according to the CPSC.

Braun espresso/cappuccino makers
If filter holder is pushed past maximum setting, it could dislodge under pressure and break glass carafe, cutting or burning anyone nearby.

Products: 5000 plastic and metal espresso/cappuccino makers, models E20 and E25, type 3058, sold 8/94-12/94 for $49-$69. Affected machines bear production codes 426 through 450 stamped on bottom of base. Cardboard box says, in part: "BRAUN Espresso/Cappuccino Maker...Made in Switzerland."

What to do: Call 800 933-8363 for redesigned filter holder.

Juice Tiger electric juicers sold through TV commercials
Filter basket and plastic cover could shatter and injure anyone nearby.

Products: 77,000 juicers, model numbers 204-SP and JE-1000, sold 11/91-10/93 for $100 to $150. Model number is on underside of base. White plastic juicer has prominent Juice Tiger logo. Only models sold via TV are involved—not model 160, juicers with "Made in France" on bottom of unit, or those sold in retail stores.

What to do: Check juicer parts. If you see cracks, scratches, or other signs of wear, stop using juicer and call 800 947-4909 for free replacement filter basket/wire mesh grater. Distributor will also provide warning label to put on cover of juicer.

Snackmaster food dehydrators from American Harvest
Could overheat and create fire hazard.

Products: 56,843 food dehydrators, models 2200/FD-30, 2400/FD-50, and 2400T/FD-50T, sold 1/95-8/95 for up to $110. Serial number on bottom of base begins with 59, followed by B, C, D, F, G, H, or J and ending with ZB, ZC, ZD, ZF, or ZH. Recall also includes any Snackmaster dehydrator with white or cream-colored base cover that has been serviced since 10/94. Recall does not involve Snackmaster Jr. FD-20. Round, white plastic appliance is 13 inches in diameter and has 2-inch-thick base and white lid. Base says "American Harvest Snackmaster Dehydrator." Base is stacked with two or four 1¼-inch-deep trays with holes in center. Each tray has white plastic screen on which food can be dried. Model FD-30 has two trays; model FD-50 and 50T have four. FD-30 and FD-50 have gray dial on base to adjust temperature. Model FD-50T has digital readout and green rubber buttons for setting time and temperature.

What to do: Call 800 540-8118 for prepaid shipping container to return base for replacement.

Various brands of chest-style freezers
Lock could be opened without key. Child could become trapped inside and could suffocate.

Products: 345,775 freezers sold 1/91-2/96 for $200 to $550, under following brand names: Crosley, Danby, Estate, Quickfrez, Roper, Whirlpool, and Woods. Units are white or almond and came in 7-, 10-, 12, 15-, and 22-cubic-foot sizes.

What to do: Note brand, model, and serial number on right inside wall or on outside back wall next to temperature control, and phone 800 227-6874. If freezer is affected, company will send free modification kit. Until lock is modified, unlock lid and place key where child can't reach it.

Whirlpool & Sears dishwashers
Wiring in door latch could overheat and catch fire.

Product: 500,000 Whirlpool and Sears Kenmore models made between 6/91 and 10/92. Affected Whirlpool models have serial numbers beginning with DU8, DP8, DU9, GDP8. Affected Sears models carry a number beginning with 665, followed by a period and the model number. Serial numbers for both brands' models run from FA2400000 to FA5299999 and FB01000000 to FB1899999.

What to do: Stop using the dishwasher and keep the door unlatched. For free servicing of a model bought anywhere other than Sears, call Whirlpool at 800-874-9481. Sears says it will notify customers directly and schedule free repairs. Sears customers who want more information can call 800 927-1625.

Maytag dishwashers
Could overheat and start fire.

Products: 553,000 Maytag dishwashers sold 4/94-10/95. Affected models bear serial numbers ending in the following letter pairs: KF, KH, KK, KM, KQ, KS, KU, KW, KY, KZ, or MB. Serial number is in upper left corner of dishwasher tub, just below countertop.

What to do: Phone 800 462-9267 for free dishwasher inspection and, if necessary, repair.

Pfizer PureSilk Shave Gel for women
Inner liner of can could rupture. If so, person could be injured by flying plastic shards or sharp edges of metal can.

Products: 500,000 purple, 7-oz. cans sold 10/95-6/96 for $2-$2.50. Recalls pertains only to shaving gel, not cream version of product.

What to do: Stop using product immediately and discharge gel to reduce pressure within can. Before disposing of can, record lot no., which appears on bottom. To receive free replacement certificate or refund, send your name and address, along with container lot no., to: Pfizer Consumer Health Care - Consumer Relations Dept., 235 E. 42nd St., New York, N.Y. 10017-5755. For information, call Pfizer at 800 723-7529.

Sheer rayon scarves made in India
Scarves are dangerously flammable.

Products: 375,000 long and flowing, square, or oblong sheer rayon chiffon scarves sold for $2-$28. Scarves are solid colored or print; some have metallic threads, gold-paint designs, or sequin trim. All have label that says "Made in India" and "100 percent rayon" or "65 percent rayon/35 percent metallic."

Most bear "Fashionique II" label. Other labels include: "ATG" All that Glitters; Hastings & Smith; April Cornell for Cornell Trading; Casual Corner; Berkshire; Peppermint Bay; Sterling Styles; Putumayo; and Willis Hill for Accessories Int'l. Scarves without brand name have label with following numbers: RN13962, RN 36791, RN 52466, RN 62500, RN63408, RN 71290, RN 79756. But some scarves with above brand names or numbers may not be subject to recall; contact store where scarve was sold to find out. Scarves were sold by following stores: Bon-Worth, Burlington Coat Factory, Caldor, Cato, Hit or Miss, Mervyn's, Ross, T.J. Maxx, Simply 6/Simply Fashions, Venture Stores, and many others.

What to do: Return scarf to store for refund, credit, or information on replacement. For more information, call U.S. Consumer Product Safety Commission Hotline at 800 638-2772.

Women's long-sleeve cotton sweat shirts sold at Dots stores
Shirts are highly flammable.

Products: 18,300 sweat shirts sold 7/95-2/96 at Dots stores in East and Midwest for $10. Cotton, reverse-fleece shirts are gray, black, red, navy, cobalt, or wine, and have a crown and "#1 Strategy" printed across front. Labels on neck read, "RED CABIN . . . RN 65313 . . . Made in Pakistan." Hang tags read, "STYLE # 133033 . . . RED CABIN."

What to do: Return shirt to Dots store for refund, or mail it to Zip Zag Customer Service Center, Attention: Peter Luthria, 1422 Grand St., 3rd Floor, Hoboken, N.J. 07030 for refund plus postage.

'Northwest Territory' men's cotton fleece shirts sold at Kmart stores
Shirts are highly flammable.

Products: 11,756 long-sleeve, button-down cotton shirts sold 9/95-12/95 for $20. Shirts came in small, medium, large, and extra large sizes and four colors: burgundy, hunter green, dark blue, and gray. They were made in Korea and have "RN42000" and "NORTHWEST TERRITORY" labels sewn in at neck. Hang tag reads, "Rugged Sportswear...Northwest Territory," along with style number 8025, item number 8311, and size.

What to do: Return shirt to nearest Kmart for refund.

NuTone ST-1000 stereo-cassette player
Could overheat and create fire hazard.

Products: 25,000 combination radio/audio-cassette players sold 1/90-12/95. White or walnut-colored stereo measures $14\frac{1}{2}$ x $9\frac{1}{4}$ inches and can be mounted flush against wall and wired to remote speakers. "NuTone" and "Model ST-1000" appear on front of radio to left of station dial. Cassette deck is at lower right. Unit was sold at retail stores and was also installed in new homes. Basic player was sold for $200. Set with two speakers, wire, antenna, and transformer sold for $246.

What to do: Call 800 273-1124 to have local repairer inspect and, if necessary, fix radio without charge.

MTC TV sets
Could overheat and start fire.

Products: 45,000 13-inch color television sets sold since 11/92 for up to $150. "MTC" appears on lower left front of cabinet. Affected units bear following model designations and serial numbers on rear of cabinet: model MTV1428R (serial number beginning with 92); MTV1428RF and MTV1429RF (serial number beginning with 93); MTV1428CC (serial number beginning with 93, as well as serial numbers 9403 212 00001 - 9410 212 20160); and MTV1429CC (serial number beginning with 93, as well as serial numbers 9405 113 00001 - 9408 213 01680).

What to do: Phone 800 346-3931 for free repair.

Cambridge SoundWorks powered subwoofer loudspeaker
Could overheat and cause fire.

Products: 6450 loudspeakers sold since 6/92 for $600 to $700. Speaker is used in stereo and home-theater sound systems to reproduce deep bass notes. Speakers were sold through company's national catalog, at retail stores in New England and Northern California, and at Best Buy stores.

What to do: Unplug subwoofer and call 800 367-4434 for replacement fuses to prevent overheating and instructions. Or, if you bought speakers at Best Buy store, Cambridge will give you $30 rebate if you return to store for replacement fuses.

IBM Series 9527 color computer monitors
Could cause electric shock.

Products: 56,000 17-inch monitors, models 9527-001, 9527-011, 9527-T01, 9527-T21, 9527-005, and 9527-015, sold since 9/28/93 for $1000-$3000. Model number is inside front pull-down panel or on label on rear.

What to do: Call 800 426-7378 for free repair.

Panasonic laser printers
May cause electrical shock.

Products: 3000 printers, models KX-P6100 and KX-P6500, sold 4/95-10/95 for $400-$500. Model number is on front of printer, to left of On/Off indicator lights. Printers with colored dot on underside and on box they came in are not affected.

What to do: Phone 800 328-6394 for free inspection and, if necessary, replacement. You will also receive free toner cartridge.

Plastic lawn chairs distributed by Southern Patio
Lack of rubber feet on rear legs could allow legs to splay or break and cause chair to collapse.

Products: 900,000 white plastic chairs, in "Perla," "Althea," and "Malibu" styles, sold 1/92-9/95 at supermarkets and home centers including Winn Dixie, Cub Foods, and Scotty's, for $6. Chairs measure 22 in. deep, 22 in. wide, and 32 in. high. Label on front of seat includes chair style, manufacturer's name and address, and words "Distributed by Southern Patio."

What to do: Return chair to store for refund or replacement. For information, call Southern at 800 729-5033.

Swim n' Play above-ground pools
Swimmers could cut themselves on exposed sharp edges.

Products: 1465 pools, including Charter Oak, Holiday Isle, Monaco, New Yorker, Silverwood, Triumph, Wedgewood, and Windsor models. Pools were sold '80-94 in Northeast at A-1 Pools, Este, Harrows, M&M Distributors, and Norbert Pools.

What to do: Phone 800 631-3483 for free replacement covers to fit over sharp edges of pool's sheet-metal ledge.

Hammocks (various models)
Lacking spreader bars to hold them open, hammocks hang like a thin rope. They can twist around child's neck, causing strangulation.

Products: Three million lightweight, portable hammocks measuring 5 to 7 feet wide and 7 to 20 feet long. They were sold since early '70s for $4 to $10 in sporting-goods and outdoor-equipment stores, Army and Air Force PX and BX stores, department stores, and drug stores. Hammocks were made or imported by: Academy Broadway, Smithtown, N.Y.; Algoma Net Co., Algoma, Wis.; Avid Outdoor, Olathe, Kan.; Coghlan's, Minneapolis; E-Z Sales, Gardena, Calif.; Nelson/Weather-Rite, Lenexa, Kan.; Rochco, Smithtown, N.Y.; Schwarzman Export Import Co., Brooklyn, N.Y.; Standard Sales, Los Angeles; and Texsport, Houston.

What to do: Return hammock to store. E-Z Sales will provide replacement hammock with spreader bars. Other companies will give refund.

Global Hi-Back Tilter 3990 chair
Chair could pitch forward without warning.

Products: 7000 chairs, which were sold by Office Depot nationwide from April 1994 to Oct. 1, 1995. Chairs purchased after Oct 1, 1995, are not involved in the recall.
What to do: Phone 888 242-4778 for free replacement base. Note: CR tests indicate that new base does not solve problem.

Upholstered recliner chairs
Gap between seat and leg rest could trap child's head and cause strangulation.

Products: 100,000 recliners made by Golden Chair, Inc. of Houlka, Miss., and sold 1/87-12/95; also, 42,000 recliners made by Allen Mfg. of Benton, Tenn., and sold 1/88-12/95. Golden models have beige, blue, brown, or mauve fabric; label stapled beneath footrest says "Golden Chair, Inc." or "Golden Furniture Manufacturing Co." "Lic. No. NY 58770" may also appear on label. Also, serial number on wood rail is visible under chair when it's fully reclined. Allen recliners have fabric and vinyl in various colors. Label under footrest says "#VA-9300Tn."
What to do: If gap between seat and leg rest is greater than five inches, stop using chair and call Golden (800 965-1227) or Allen (888 338-0550) for free crossbar you can attach to reduce gap. Before calling, measure and note width of opening between seat and leg rest as well as distance between mechanisms that fasten leg rest to chair.

Ryobi electric lawn mowers
Starter button could stick in On position even when motor is off. Blade could engage unexpectedly during subsequent start-up and injure operator.

Products: 20,000 corded and battery-powered Ryobi Mulchinator mowers, models BMM 2400 and CMM 1200, sold for $350-$400. Mowers are gray; black data plate with serial number is on rear of housing. Affected mowers have 10-digit serial number, with last four digits (9240 through 9352) denoting year and week of manufacture (40th week of '92 through 52nd week of '93).
What to do: Phone 800 345-8746 for free repair.

White-Rodgers temperature controls for various brands of natural-gas water heaters
Soot could build up on burner element and create fire hazard.

Products: 1.6 million temperature controls, models 37 and 37C, sold since 4/94. Control came with water heater or was sold as replacement part. Device, which resembles small metal box, is above access-panel door of water heater. Model number, on white label on right side of box, begins with "37." Affected units bear date codes 9412 to 9440 (12th week of '94 to 40th week of '94). Use hand mirror to read date-code label, which is in upper left corner on back of unit.
What to do: Inspect water heater. If you note discoloration or black soot on lower outside surface of tank, pilot flame that keeps going out, or unusual burning odor, phone 800 426-3503 to arrange for inspection and, if necessary, replacement.

3M Series 4400 overhead projectors
Pose shock hazard.

Products: 30,000 projectors, model numbers 4405, 4406, 4407, 4410, and 4415, made before 11/10/95 and sold to schools and office-supply stores 4/94-11/95 for $300 to $390. Affected units bear serial number 200,001 to 247,741. Model and serial numbers, date of manufacture, and "3M" appear on nameplate on bottom of projector. Heat from projector lamp could deform reflector and allow it to fall. Reflector could then heat bottom of unit, melt power cord, and expose wires. Projectors made after 11/10/95, with serial numbers 247,742 or higher and Code C4, are not affected. In addition, all projectors already repaired by 3M will have round red tag with "R" imprint on bottom of unit.
What to do: Call 800 328-1371 for retrofit kit and for installation instructions or information on having technician install kit free. You will also receive free projection lamp.

Cars

'94-96 Audis (various models)
Electrical accessories, including lights, wipers, turn-signal indicators, power windows, and air-conditioner could malfunction when engine is started.

Models: 24,000 cars made 1/94-12/95 including the following models: 90, 100, A6, Cabriolet, S4, and S6.
What to do: Have dealer replace ignition switch.

'95 BMW 740i & 740iL, & '95-96 750iL
Fuel leak could cause fire hazard.

Models: 18,000 cars made 9/94-10/95.
What to do: Have dealer replace two fuel hoses, four metal fuel lines, and clamps.

'89-96 Buicks, Chevrolets, Oldsmobiles, & Pontiacs

Rear outboard safety belts may not hold in crash.

Models: 2.2 million cars made 4/88-8/95, including '89-96 Buick Century, '89-90 Chevrolet Celebrity, '89-96 Oldsmobile Ciera, and '89-91 Pontiac 6000.

What to do: Have dealer install new bolt and thread-locking adhesive for each belt. Dealer will also apply washer-like patch to each anchor point to reduce noise as belt pivots.

'92-93 Buick Le Sabre & Park Avenue, Oldsmobile Eighty Eight & Ninety Eight, & Pontiac Bonneville

In cold weather and under heavy load, transmission-cooler hose could leak and create fire hazard.

Models: 498,449 cars sold 8/91-7/95 in Alaska, Colo., Conn., Del., Ill., Ind., Iowa, Ky., Me., Md., Mass., Mich., Minn., Mo., Neb., N.H., N.J., N.Y., N.D., Ohio, Pa., R.I., S.D., Vt., W.Va., Wisc., and Wyo.

What to do: Have dealer replace hose.

'93-95 Buick Regal

Clear bulbs instead of amber ones may have been installed in side-marker lights. That could confuse other drivers.

Models: 39,849 cars made 6/91-2/95.

What to do: Have dealer replace bulbs.

'95 Buick Roadmaster, Cadillac Fleetwood, & Chevrolet Caprice

Shifter could be moved out of Park with ignition key removed. That could allow parked vehicle to roll away.

Models: 83,400 cars made 11/94-8/95.

What to do: Have dealer adjust transmission linkage.

'96 Buick Park Avenue & '97 Le Sabre

Safety belts may not latch properly and may not provide protection in crash.

Models: 15,122 cars made 1/96-2/96.

What to do: Have dealer inspect all safety belts and replace any incorrect parts.

'91-95 Cadillacs

With automatic climate-control system in use, exceeded Government limits on carbon-monoxide emissions.

Models: 470,000 cars with 4.9-liter V8 made through the 1995 model year.

What to do: Have dealer replace engine-control computer chip.

'96 Cadillac Concours & De Ville

Hood could pop open unexpectedly, block driver's view, and hit windshield.

Models: 12,783 cars made 7/95-9/95.

What to do: Have dealer adjust secondary hood latch.

'96 Cadillac Eldorado and Seville

Short circuit in dashboard could disable gauges and most warning indicators and could prevent engine from starting.

Models: 1408 cars made 10/95-11/95.

What to do: Have dealer inspect and, if necessary, replace instrument-panel cluster.

'95-96 Chrysler Cirrus and Dodge Stratus

Oil could leak from engine and create fire hazard.

Models: 40,000 cars, with 2.4-liter Four, made 12/94-9/95.

What to do: Have dealer install expansion plug and retaining bracket on cylinder head.

'95-96 Chrysler Cirrus, Dodge Stratus, & '96 Plymouth Breeze

Valves in antilock brake system could stick and cause car to veer to one side when stopping.

Models: 90,000 cars made 8/94-8/95.

What to do: Have dealer install a plate and inject silicone grease into solenoid cavity of ABS hydraulic control unit.

'95-96 Chrysler, Dodge, & Plymouth cars with 'ACR' competition package

Brake master cylinder could leak fluid, resulting in decreased stopping ability.

Models: 151,800 cars made 8/94-10/95 including '95-96 Chrysler Cirrus, Dodge Neon and Stratus, and Plymouth Neon, and '96 Plymouth Breeze.

What to do: Have dealer replace rear brake master-cylinder piston assembly.

'90-92 Dodge Monaco & '88-92 Eagle Premier

Automatic front shoulder belts could stop working.

Models: 90,000 cars made 5/88-12/91.

What to do: If shoulder belt becomes unusable, have dealer replace track and drive assembly.

'96 Dodge & Plymouth Neon

Engine-wiring harness could short and cause various electrical malfunctions, including engine stalling.

Models: 15,000 cars made 7/95-11/95 at Toluca, Mexico, assembly plant.

What to do: Have dealer replace damaged wire and reroute wiring harness away from exhaust-gas-recirculation tube.

'88-93 Ford, Lincoln, & Mercury cars & Ford trucks

Ignition switch could overheat and cause fire in the steering column area.

Models: '88-90 Ford Escort, '88 Ford EXP, '88-92 and early '93 Ford Mustang, Tempo, Thunderbird; Mercury Cougar, Topaz; '88-89 Ford Crown Victoria; Mercury Grand Marquis; Lincoln Town Car; '88-91 Ford Aerostar, Bronco, F-Series pickup trucks.

What to do: Have dealer replace ignition switch.

'95 Ford Contour & Mercury Mystique

Outside front safety belts might fail in crash.

Models: 229,500 cars made 7/94-5/95. A few cars made 9/4/95-9/8/95 in Ford's Mexican plant are also included.

What to do: Have dealer reinforce belts' anchor tabs—or, if tab is cracked, have dealer replace entire safety-belt assembly.

'95 Ford Crown Victoria & Mercury Grand Marquis

Improper circuit breaker could make headlights go out unexpectedly.

Models: 45,000 cars made 8/94-11/94.

What to do: Have dealer switch circuit breakers.

'95 Ford Crown Victoria and Mercury Grand Marquis

Rear left and right safety belts may not provide adequate protection in crash.

Models: 49,000 cars made 8/94-10/94.

What to do: Have dealer add reinforcement plate to rear safety-belt anchors.

'96 Ford Taurus & Mercury Sable

Warning indicator for low brake fluid could remain lit continuously or fail to light.

Models: 76,500 cars made 6/85-9/95.

What to do: Have dealer replace indicator light switch.

'96 Ford Thunderbird & Mercury Cougar with semi-automatic climate-control system

Climate-control blower could fail to defrost or defog windshield, reducing driver's vision.

Models: 10,600 cars made 8/95-12/95.

What to do: Have dealer replace temperature-control modules.

'94 Honda Civic del Sol

Air bag may not deploy properly in crash.

Models: 6476 cars made 8/93-10/93.

What to do: Have dealer install reinforcement brackets to secure air-bag module assembly.

'95 Hyundai Sonata GLS

Defective rear gas-filled shock absorbers could cause loss of control.

Models: 356 cars made 3/95-7/95.

What to do: Have dealer check and, if necessary, replace rear shock-absorber and spring-seat assemblies.

'91-92 Lincoln Town Car

Secondary hood latch may not engage properly. If primary latch fails, hood could fly up.

Models: 73,837 cars made 4/91-10/91.

What to do: Have dealer replace secondary latch assembly.

'95-96 Lincoln Continental

Headlights and other exterior lights could go out suddenly when "autolamp" system is being used.

Models: 40,000 cars made 11/94-11/95.

What to do: Have dealer replace "autolamp" control module. Until repair is made, use manual switch to turn on headlights.

'89-94 Nissan Maxima & '90-92 Nissan Stanza

Road salt could corrode fuel-tank filler tube, resulting in leak and, possibly, fire. Also, left rear safety belt could fail because of corrosion in wheel housing, where belt is anchored.

Models: 747,000 cars made 8/88-2/94 and registered in Conn., Del., Ill., Ind., Iowa, Me., Md., Mass., Mich., Minn., N.H., N.J., N.Y., Ohio, Pa., R.I., Vt., Wash., D.C., W. Va., and Wisc.

What to do: Have dealer inspect car for corrosion and make needed repairs.

'88-92 Peugeot 505 station wagon

Fuel tank could drop, creating fire hazard.

Models: 3561 vehicles made 2/87-7/91.

What to do: Have dealer replace cradle that secures fuel tank.

'95 Pontiac Sunfire with automatic transmission

Sagging trim plate could obscure lighted pointer indicating shifter position, and driver might inadvertently shift into wrong gear.

Models: 28,068 cars made 7/94-6/95.
What to do: Have dealer replace trim plate on instrument panel.

'93-95 Volkswagen Corrado, Golf, Jetta, & Passat

Radiator-fan motor could fail, making engine overheat and stall.

Models: 34,000 cars, with V6 engine, made 4/93-2/95.
What to do: Have dealer inspect and, if necessary, replace fan blade and lock nut or complete cooling-fan assembly.

'88-89 Volvo 744 and 745

Insulation on battery cables could wear away, causing electrical short and, possibly, fire.

Models: 49,397 sedans and station wagons with 4-cylinder engine, made 8/87-4/89.
What to do: Have dealer inspect battery-cable harness and make necessary repairs and adjustments.

Sport-utility vehicles, trucks & vans

'92-95 Chevrolet Lumina, Oldsmobile Silhouette, & Pontiac Trans Sport minivans

In cold weather and under heavy load, transmission-cooler hose could leak and create fire hazard.

Models: 86,733 minivans, with 3.8-liter V6, made 8/91-7/95 and sold in Alaska, Colo., Conn., Del., Ill., Ind., Iowa, Ky., Me., Md., Mass., Mich., Minn., Mo., Neb., N.H., N.J., N.Y. N.D., Ohio, Pa., R.I.,S.D., Vt., W. Va., Wisc., and Wyo.
What to do: Have dealer replace hose.

'93-94 Chevrolet & GMC extended-cab pickup trucks

Front seatbacks could recline suddenly and cause loss of control.

Models: 675,661 light-duty pickups, with high-back bucket seats or 60/40 split-bench seats, made 6/92-9/94, including: Chevrolet C10, C20, C30, K10, K20, K30, and GMC C15, C25, C35, K15, K25, K35.
What to do: Have dealer remove foam and fabric between recliner assembly and seat frame; install washers between recliner and frame; and replace attaching bolts.

'95 Chevrolet Blazer & S10 & GMC Jimmy & S15 pickup trucks & sport-utility vehicles

Radiator fan could break apart. If hood is open, blades could strike anyone nearby.

Models: 73,163 light-duty trucks and sport-utility vehicles with 4.3-liter V6 and air-conditioning, made 9/94-11/94.
What to do: Have dealer inspect and, if necessary, replace fan.

'95 Chevrolet Lumina & Pontiac Trans Sport minivans

Engine may not slow down sufficiently when accelerator is released.

Models: 6772 minivans, with 3.1-liter V6, made 5/95-9/95.
What to do: Have dealer replace throttle-cable support bracket.

'96 Chevrolet S10 & GMC S15 & Sonoma pickup trucks

Transmission could seize, lock up rear wheels, and cause loss of control.

Models: 24,906 two-wheel-drive pickups, with four-cylinder engine and 5-speed manual transmission, made 8/95-1/96.
What to do: Have dealer inspect and, if necessary, replace transmission.

'96 Chrysler, Dodge, & Plymouth minivans

Fuel tank could leak, creating fire hazard.

Models: 80,000 minivans made 1/95-8/95, including Chrysler Town & Country, Dodge Caravan and Grand Caravan, and Plymouth Voyager and Grand Voyager.
What to do: Have dealer install redesigned fuel-tank filler tube and reroute rollover-valve vapor hoses.

'96 Chrysler, Dodge, & Plymouth minivans

Fire or explosion could occur during refueling because of static buildup on fuel-filler tube.

Models: 265,000 minivans, including Chrysler Town & Country, Dodge Caravan and Grand Caravan, and Plymouth Voyager and Grand Voyager, made 1/95-12/95.
What to do: Have dealer install ground strap for filler tube.

'96 Dodge Caravan & Grand Caravan & Plymouth Voyager & Grand Voyager

Rear bench seat could could break loose in accident, increasing risk of injury.

Models: 20,000 minivans, made 10/95-11/95, with bench seat rather than captain's chairs in rear.

What to do: Check vehicle identification number atop dashboard or on registration certificate. If 11th character is letter "R," have dealer replace bolts connecting rear bench seat to riser.

'96 Dodge Ram

Sparking at generator-cartridge fuse could cause under-hood fire.

Models: 12,000 vans made 7/95-10/95.

What to do: Have dealer tighten fasteners that secure fuse to power-distribution center.

'91-94 Ford & Mazda sport-utility vehicles & pickup trucks

Brakes could fail.

Models: 108,000 '91-94 Ford Explorer sport-utility vehicles and Ford Ranger pickups, and 2500 '91-94 Mazda Navajo sport-utility vehicles and '94 Mazda B2300, B3000, and B4000 pickups made 3/91-11/93 and originally sold or now registered in these Southern California counties: Imperial, Kern, Los Angeles, Orange, Riverside, San Bernadino, San Diego, San Luis Obisbo, Santa Barbara, and Ventura.

What to do: Have dealer replace power-brake vacuum-booster assembly.

'92-93 Ford Explorer

Rear liftgate could open unexpectedly.

Models: Models: 364,784 sport-utility vehicles made 1/92-3/93.

What to do: Have dealer install reinforcement brackets.

'93-94 Ford Ranger

In extremely cold weather, ice buildup in fuel system could make engine keep racing even after accelerator pedal is released or cruise control is disengaged.

Models: 26,000 light-duty pickups, with 2.3-liter Four, built 8/92-12/94 and registered in Alaska, Me., Mich. (upper peninsula), Minn., Mont., N.H., N.Y., N.D., Vt., and Wisc.

What to do: Have dealer replace air-intake duct and valve assembly in fuel system.

'94 Ford E150 & Econoline vans converted by Show Trucks

"Battery Buddy" system could short out and create fire hazard.

Models: 68 conversion vans made 11/93-9/94.

What to do: Have dealer relocate "Battery Buddy" system.

'96 Ford Taurus & Mercury Sable sedans & Ford Windstar minivan

Vehicle could roll even when shifter is in Park position.

Models: 99,700 vehicles, which can be identified by contacting Ford's customer service-line at 800 392-3673 or any Ford dealer. Note vehicle identification number before you call.

What to do: Have dealer inspect and, if necessary, replace parking-pawl mechanism.

'95 Geo Prizm & Toyota Corolla cars & Toyota Tacoma pickup trucks

Defective terminal could cause dead battery and could make battery explode, spraying acid.

Models: 14,363 cars and trucks made 6/95-7/95.

What to do: Have dealer replace battery.

'95 Jeep Cherokee & Grand Cherokee

Release button could come off parking-brake handle, rendering brake inoperative.

Models: 135,000 sport-utility vehicles made 10/94-2/95.

What to do: Have dealer replace parking-brake handle assembly.

'96 Jeep Cherokee & Grand Cherokee

Sparking at alternator-circuit fuse could cause under-hood fire.

Models: 32,000 sport-utility vehicles made 7/95-8/95.

What to do: Have dealer replace fuse with fuse link and repair any damage to power-distribution center.

'93 Mercury Villager & Nissan Quest

Heater and air-conditioner can suck leaves and other debris into air intake. Buildup could cause noise, odors, and even fire.

Models: 48,053 Mercury and 27,000 Nissan minivans made 4/92-4/93.

What to do: Have dealer install additional screen in climate-control system.

'96 Nissan Pathfinder
Steering wheel could become difficult to turn in very cold weather. Also, carpeting on transmission tunnel could snag driver's foot and hamper braking.

Models: 1775 sport-utility vehicles made 8/95-1/96.
What to do: Have dealer install new steering-gear assembly with appropriate lubricant. Also, have dealer remove carpet padding on transmission tunnel near accelerator to prevent driver's foot from getting caught.

'87-91 Range Rover
Bottom of fuel tank could rust prematurely, creating fire hazard.

Models: 15,378 vehicles made 5/87-9/90.
What to do: Have dealer inspect and, if necessary, replace fuel tank.

'95 Range Rover 4.0SE
Power steering could fail and suddenly make steering much heavier.

Models: 2946 sport-utility vehicles made 6/94-7/95.
What to do: Have dealer replace idler pulley in engine serpentine-belt system.

'95 Range Rover
Flexible brake hose connecting hydraulic pump to antilock brake system could leak, severely hampering stopping ability and creating fire hazard.

Models: 2114 vehicles made 6/94-4/95.
What to do: Have dealer inspect and, if necessary, replace flexible hose.

Child safety seats

Kolcraft Traveler 700
Seat could fail in crash.

Product: About 100,000 seats made after 11/1/94.
What to do: Owners who mailed in registration cards will automatically receive replacement-buckle assembly. Owners who did not can call 800 453-7673..

Evenflo Travel Tandem
Seat failed CR crash tests when used with its base.

Product: Seats made prior to 4/1/96.
What to do: Call 800 448-6924 for reinforcing plate.

Century seats & strollers
Defective buckles may release upon impact.

Product: Century 560, 565, 590, and Smart Fit safety seats and Century 4-in-1 safety seat/strollers made between 9/12/95 and 5/13/96. The safety seats carry the following suffixes after the model number: 4525, 4535, 4560, 4575, and 4590. The safety seat/strollers carry these suffixes: 11-570, 11-597, 11-600, and 11-650. In addition, the affected buckles have date codes 255-95 through 365-95 and 001-96 through 131-96 stamped across the top.
What to do: Call 800 762-7463 for free replacement buckle kit and installation instructions.

Century SmartMove
In forward-facing mode, seat may not provide adequate protection in crash.

Products: 11,000 seats, model 4750, made 12/5/95-2/13/96. Model number (first four numbers) and date of manufacture (last six numbers) appear on label on side of seat base. Affected seats also have white label attached to black Y-shaped adjuster strap on back of seat that bears one of the following codes: WO#-136716-01; WO#-136716-02; WO#-136716-03; WO#-138442-01.
What to do: Phone 800 583-4093 for replacement latch assembly.

Cosco Dream Ride Ultra
May not protect child adequately in crash.

Products: 15,370 seats, model 02-719, made 4/8/94-6/15/95. Model number and date of manufacture appear on label on seat's shell. Unit can be used as conventional infant seat or as traveling bed. In rear-facing position, device could tip too far backward in crash, increasing risk of injury.
What to do: Phone 800 314-9327 for free repair kit.

Evenflo Trooper
With infant weighing less than 20 pounds, seat must be used only in rearward-facing position—not in forward-facing position as instructions imply.

Products: 10,423 seats with adjustable shield, models 219140, 219164, 219180, 219186, and 219188, made 11/95-1/96. Label bearing model number and manufacture date appears on seat.
What to do: Phone 800 837-4002 for new instruction pamphlet.

Motorcycles & bicycles

'95 Buell S2 Thunderbolt motorcycle
Fairing could come off, contact front fender, and cause loss of control.

Models: 970 motorcycles made 2/94-3/95.
What to do: Have dealer inspect motorcycle and install instrument-panel stabilizer. (Some motorcycles may already have stabilizer.)

'95 Ducati 916 motorcycle

Rear brake disc could loosen, causing loud noise and reducing stopping ability.

Models: 209 motorcycles made 3/94-5/94.

What to do: Have dealer remove, inspect, and clean screws and apply adhesive before reinstalling them.

'95 Ducati 916 motorcycle

Throttle could stick in partially open position and cause accident.

Models: 1000 motorcycles made 3/94-6/95.

What to do: Have dealer modify throttle-cable assembly by removing Teflon bushing in cable housing.

'94 Specialized Rockhopper & '95 Stumpjumper mountain bikes

Handlebars could break on Rockhopper, and front brakes could fail on Stumpjumper.

Models: 52,838 Rockhopper, Rockhopper Sport, Rockhopper GX, Rockhopper FS, Rockhopper Comp, and Rockhopper Comp FS bikes sold since 9/93. Also, 3585 Stumpjumper bikes sold since 9/94.

What to do: Have dealer replace handlebars on Rockhopper models and rigid steel fork on Stumpjumper models. For further information, call Specialized at 800 214-1467.

'95-96 Yamaha motorcycles

Rear shock absorber could break and cause loss of control.

Models: 4348 motorcycles made 2/94-5/95, including '95 models YZF600RG and YZF600RGC and '96 models YZF600RH and YZF600RHC.

What to do: Have dealer install redesigned shock-absorber assembly.

'94-95 Pacific Conquest, Cyclone, & Conqueror mountain bicycles with 'Posi Track' suspension fork

Fork could crack, causing rider to lose control and fall.

Models: 10,000 26-in. bicycles sold 5/94-8/95 at Toys "R" Us and Target stores. Metal forks have black "Posi Track" decal on each stanchion tube, which are attached to alloy crown with two allen head bolts. Forks with stanchions welded to crown are not part of recall, nor are forks with colored decals.

What to do: Stop riding bicycle and call manufacturer, Pacific Cycle, at 800 283-3303 for free replacement fork.

'93-94 Scott USA bicycles with Unishock suspension forks

Forks could crack or separate and cause loss of control.

Models: 5600 Scott bicycles, including '93-94 Comp Racing, Team Racing, Ultimate CST, and Unitrack ST. Also, '94 Unitrack CC, Unitrack FSR, and Ultimate CST. Bicycles were sold 8/92 to 6/95 for $669 to $2495. During same period, 8000 forks were sold as aftermarket equipment for $200 to $400. Forks have "SCOTT" logo on side of each leg. Sticker on front of each leg reads, "UNISHOCK" followed by "LF," "R," "S," "TX," or "VR." Forks with white legs bearing plural name "UNISHOCKS" are not subject to recall.

What to do: Return bicycle to any authorized Scott dealer for free replacement fork of comparable value. For more information, phone 800 745-5467.

Manitou Mach 5 mountain-bike forks

Fork can break and front wheel can come off, causing loss of control.

Models: Suspension forks sold 8/95-3/96 as original equipment on more than 27,000 Diamondback Fisher, Marin, Mongoose, Trek, and other high-end bicycles. Also, 41,000 forks were sold as aftermarket equipment for $270-$380. Forks have Manitou and Mach 5 logos on sides of lower legs.

What to do: Check serial number on back of lower part of fork leg. Forks with numbers below 5100086500 have outer leg castings that should be replaced. Forks with numbers between 5100086500 and 5100149464 should be inspected by authorized Answer Products dealer. Forks with red dots on inside of drop out have been inspected and are not subject to recall. Phone 800 670-7446 for more information.

Performance bicycles

Seat post could break and cause loss of control.

Models: 5000 bicycles sold 3/93-4/96 at Performance Bicycle Shops and through company's mail-order catalog for $300-$500. Recalled bicycles include models X203, X204, M603, M604, M704, and M705.

What to do: Return bicycle to nearest Performance Bicycle Shop for free replacement of seat-post clamp bolt. For information, phone 800 553-8324.

Motor homes

'95 Holiday Rambler Imperial travel trailer & fifth-wheel trailer

Slide-out room could open suddenly.

Models: 313 trailers, with one or two hydraulically operated slide-out rooms, made 6/94-11/94.

What to do: Have dealer remove remote power switches on hydraulic motor and limit operation of slide-out room to primary switches mounted inside trailer.

'95 Itasca Suncruiser motor home

Awning attached to slide-out room could unfurl, break loose, and cause accident.

Models: 424 motor homes made 8/94-4/95.

What to do: Have dealer install arm locks, antibillow studs and brackets, and wind deflectors.

'91-95 Fleetwood motor homes

Warning indicator may not come on if pressure in front-brake air reservoir falls below 60 psi. That could reduce braking performance or suddenly engage emergency-brake system.

Models: 1175 class-A motor homes on Spartan chassis, including '91-95 American Eagle and '94-95 American Dream models made 2/91-6/95.

What to do: Have dealer install wiring harness that properly connects low-pressure switch to warning indicator.

Cobra & Rockwood fifth-wheel & travel trailers

Chassis wire harness could be pinched or cut, causing loss of control or complete brake failure.

Models: 43,330 trailers made 5/87-8/95, including: '88-96 Cobra Salem and Sierra; '90-93 Cobra Cavalier; '90-96 Cobra Corsica and Sandpiper; '90-95 Cobra Scottsdale; '91-96 Cobra Lumina; '92-96 Cobra Sunrise; '91-96 Rockwood Prestige and Lumina; '91-95 Rockwood Royale; and '93-96 Rockwood Wildwood.

What to do: Have dealer take up slack in chassis wire harness and secure harness to frame of trailer with single eye wire loop.

Vehicle accessories

Dynamic Smartlock I auto antitheft device

Could short-circuit and start fire, or actuate starter motor and make parked car lurch unexpectedly if it's in gear.

Products: 60,000 professionally installed antitheft devices made 2/94-10/94.

What to do: Have dealer install a $\frac{1}{16}$-amp fuse in wiring or replace entire module.

Marshall automatic changeover LP regulator, model 250

Propane could leak and ignite or explode.

Products: 25,000 regulators made 1/94-7/94. Device is used to regulate pressure in LP tanks, commonly used in campers, boats, travel trailers, and barbecue grills. Affected units bear date codes 4 94 through 30 94. First digit or digits represent week of manufacture; last two, the year. Code appears in two small raised circles on back of unit.

What to do: Phone 800 396-1322 for name of nearest service center that will inspect and, if necessary, replace regulator free.

'96 Tracker boat trailers

Slide-axle assembly could shift, making trailer sway back and forth and causing loss of control.

Products: 438 boat trailers in 16-, 17-, 18-, 20-, and 21-foot lengths, with slide-axle assemblies, made 8/95-10/95. Following models are included: BB18, BB20, DV16, DV17, FB21, PB21, PRO18, and Targa 17.

What to do: Have dealer tighten bolts that secure slide-axle assemblies to trailer frame.

Food & drugs

CVS Sleep Caplets with diphenhydramine

Lacks child-resistant packaging as required by law. Diphenhydramine can cause serious or fatal reaction if ingested by child.

Products: 3798 bottles of the sleep aid sold at CVS stores 2/26-3/19/96 for $3.89. Recalled product is labeled: "CVS sleep caplets nighttime sleep aid 60 CAPLETS...Active Ingredient: Each caplet contains 25 mg. Diphenhydramine Hydrochloride." Outer box and bottles bear lot nos. D423 or D424. Bottles with closure labeled "SAVE A CHILD, CLOSE TIGHTLY, TO OPEN PUSH DOWN & TURN," are not involved in recall.

What to do: Return bottle to store for refund or exchange.

Jell-O 'chiller sticks' used to make frozen pudding bars

Could break into small parts that could choke child.

Products: 678,000 sets of six sticks each, distributed as part of a promotion for Jell-O Instant Pudding. Plastic sticks, used with a mold or cup to make handheld frozen pudding treats, are red or purple and measure 3 in. long. Sticks were available at supermarkets (buy three boxes of instant pudding and get the sticks for free) or by phone, via an 800 number to Kraft Foods, Jell-O's parent company.

What to do: Discard sticks immediately. For more information, call Kraft at 800 433-9363.

Manufacturers' telephone numbers

Below is an alphabetical list of brand names in this year's Buying Guide and the telephone numbers of their manufacturers. Use it to track down a specific model that you want to buy or for getting more information from the manufacturer about a product.

A
Accu-Chek 800 858-8072
Admiral 800 688-9920
Advance 800 526-3979
Advent..800 323-0707
Aiwa 800 289-2492
Allison 606 236-8298
Altec Lansing 800 548-0620
Amana...800 843-0304
American Sensors.........................800 387-4219
AND..800 726-9855
Answer 212 339-5000
Apple 800 767-2775
Ariens..800 678-5443
AT&T 800 222-3111

B
B.I.C..800 348-6492
Be Sure 800 854-6226
BellSouth 800 338-1694
BF Goodrich 800 847-3435
Bissell 800 237-7691
Black & Decker.............................800 231-9786
Boca 407 241-8088
Bodyguard...................................800 665-3407
Bose..800 444-2673
Boston Acoustics 508 538-5000
Breadman.....................................800 233-9054
Bridgestone..................................800 847-3272
Brother 800 284-4329

C
Caloric 800 843-0304
Cambridge....................................800 367-4434
    (Canada) 800 252-4434
Canon..800 828-4040
Chemstrip 800 858-8072
Carrier 800 227-7437
Century 800 837-4044
Cerwin Vega 805 584-9332
Clearblue 800 883-3279
Clearplan......................................800 883-3279
Cobra 312 889-3087
Conceive 800 524-1377
Confirm..800 827-0987
Cooper 800 854-6288
Cosco 800 544-1108
COSTAR CO..................................800 432-5599
Craftsman (Sears) ....Contact local store
Craig 800 926-0292
Creative Labs 800 998-1000
CSA...800 272-0136
Cub Cadet.....................................330 273-4550

D
DCM..800 878-8463
Denon 201 575-7810
Diamond 800 468-5846
DP 800 637-6031
Dunlop 800 548-4714

E
E.p.t. 800 378-1783
Electrolux.....................................800 243-9078
Emerson.......................................800 898-9020
enzone...800 448-0535
Epson 800 289-3776
Eureka 800 282-2886
Evenflo 800 233-5921
ExerHealth....................................800 504-0300

F
Fact Plus 800 526-3979
Fantom 800 276-0912
Fedders 908 725-0500
Firestone 800 356-4644
First Alert 800 323-9005
Fisher 800 421-5013
Friedrich.......................................210 225-2000
Frigidaire
    (washers, air-conditioners) 800 374-4432
Frigidaire (refrigerators)..................800 944-9044

G
General Electric (appliances)...........800 432-2737
General Electric (audio/video/comm.) 800 447-1700
General..800 847-3349
Genie...800 654-3643
Gerry 800 626-2996
Gibson...800 374-4432
Global Village 800 736-4821
Glucometer 800 445-5901
Goldstar 800 243-0000
Goodyear.....................................800 321-2136
Gran Prix......................................314 621-3314
GT 800 743-3248

H
Hayes..770 441-1617
HealthRider 800 504-0300
Hewlett Packard 800 752-0900
Hitachi...800 369-0422
Honda 800 426-7701
Hoover 800 944-9200
Hotpoint.......................................800 626-2000
Huffy 800 872-2453
Husqvarna....................................800 438-7297

I
Infinity 818 407-0228

Jenn Air 800 688-1100
John Deere.......................................800 537-8233
JVC 800 252-5722

Kelly Springfield..............................800 638-5112
Kenmore (Sears) ....Contact local Sears store
Kent...800 245-3123
Kenwood..800 536-9663
Kirby 800 437-7170
KitchenAid.......................................800 422-1230
Kolcraft 800 453-7673
Koss (headphones & speakers) 800 872-5677
Koss (stereos)..................................800 726-3801
Kubota...888 458-2682

Lawn Chief, MTD..............................800 892-6121
Lawn-Boy ....Contact local dealer
Lexmark...800 891-0331
Lifecycle..800 877-3867
Lifesaver 800 654-7665
Lifescan 800 227-8862
Lumiscope 800 221-5747

Macurco 303 781-4062
MAG 800 827-3998
Magic Chef 800 688-1120
Magna 800 551-0032
Magnavox 800 531-0039
Marantz 630 307-3100
Marshall 800 634-4350
Maytag 800 688-9900
MediSense 800 527-3339
Michelin 800 847-3435
Miele 800 694-4868
Miller & Kreisel 310 204-2854
MTD...800 800-7310
Montgomery Ward ....Contact local store
Motorola phones..............................800 331-6456
Motorola (pagers) 800 548-9954
Mr. Coffee (breadmakers) 800 672-6333
Muratec...214 403-3350
Murray 800 251-8007

Nanao 800 750-4100
NEC (printers, CD-ROM drives,
   monitors) 800 632-4636
NEC (pagers, cellular phones,
   fax machines)..............................800 421-2141
NHT...800 648-9993
Nighthawk 800 880-6788
Nilfisk..800 645-3475
Nokia...800 296-6542

Okidata..800 654-3282
Omron 800 634-4350
Onkyo..201 825-7950
Optimus...800 843-7422
Oreck...800 989-3535
Oster 800 528-7713
Ovukit..800 874-1517
OvuQuick...800 874-1517

Pacific...800 666-8813
Panasonic 800 742-8086
Paradigm..905 632-0180
Phase Technology 904 777-0700
Philips..800 531-0039
Pillsbury (breadmakers)....................800 858-3277
Pinnacle (N.Y.) 516 576-9052
   (out of N.Y.)..................................800 346-2863
Pioneer..800 746-6337
Pirelli...800 327-2442
Polk...800 377-7655
Precise 800 238-1000
Precor 800 786-8404
Proform 800 727-9777

Qasar 201 348-9090

RA Labs 800 651-7444
Radio Shack.....................................800 843-7422
Rainbow...810 643-7222
Rexair..810 643-7222
RCA...800 336-1900
Regal...800 998-8809
Regina...800 847-8336
Roadmaster......................................800 626-2811
Roper 800 447-6737
Ross...800 338-7677
Royce Union 800 888-2453
Royal...800 321-1134

S-Tech 800 203-7987
Safeline 800 829-1625
Samsung (camcorders, ext. 505).....800 767-4675
Sanyo (West) 818 998-7322
   (Central) 708 775-0505
   (East) 201 641-2333
Safety 1st 800 723-3065
Schwinn...303 473-9609
Sears.....................................Contact local store
Sennheiser.......................................860 434-9190
Sharp...800 237-4277
Sherwood...800 962-3203
Shop Vac 717 321-7056
Signet..905 474-9129
Singer 800 237-7691
Snapper 800 762-7737
Sony (phones) 800 222-7669
Sony (electronics, computer equip.) ..800 352-7669
Southwestern Bell 800 255-8480
Specialized 406 779-6229
Speed Queen....................................800 843-0304
Sunbeam..800 621-8854
Sunmark 800 634-1164
Supra 800 774-4965
Swatch 800 879-2824
Symphonic 201 228-2063

Tappan...800 537-5530
Technics 201 348-9090
Texas Instrument 800 848-3927
Toastmaster (breadmakers) 800 947-3744

Toro ....Contact local dealer
Toshiba 800 631-3811
Trek 800 369-8735
Troy-Bilt 800 828-5500
Tunturi..800 827-8717

U.S. Robotics................................800 342-5877
Uniden..800 297-1023

ViewSonic.....................................800 888-8583
Vitamaster..800 633-5730

Walgreens......................Contact local Walgreens
Welbilt (breadmakers).....................800 872-1656
Weslo...800 727-9777
West Bend (breadmakers)...............800 367-0111
Whirlpool 800 253-1301

White..800 949-4483
White Westinghouse
  (washers, vacs)...........................800 245-0600
White-Westinghouse
  (air-conditioners) 800 374-4432
White-Westinghouse
  (general no.) 614 792-2153

Xerox (ext. 2)................................800 832-6979

Yamaha...800 492-6242
Yard-Man 800 800-7310
Yokohama 800 366-8473

Zenith..847 391-8752
Zojirushi (breadmakers)..................800 733-6270
Zoom..800 631-3116

STATEMENT OF OWNERSHIP, MANAGEMENT, AND CIRCULATION
(Required by 39 U.S.C. 3685)

1. Publication Title: CONSUMER REPORTS. 2. Publication No: 0010-7174. 3. Filing Date: September 5, 1996. 4. Issue Frequency: Monthly, except semi-monthly in December. 5. No. of Issues Published Annually: 13. 6. Annual Subscription Price: $24.00. 7. Complete Mailing Address of Known Office of Publication: 101 Truman Avenue, Yonkers, New York 10703-1057. 8. Complete Mailing Address of Headquarters or General Business Office of Publisher: 101 Truman Avenue, Yonkers, New York 10703-1057. 9. Full Names and Complete Mailing Addresses of Publisher, Editor, and Managing Editor. Publisher: Consumers Union of United States, Inc., 101 Truman Avenue, Yonkers, New York 10703-1057. President: Rhoda H. Karpatkin; Editorial Director: Joel Gurin; Executive Editor: Eileen Denver. 10. Owner: (If the publication is published by a nonprofit organization, its name and address must be stated.) Full Name: Consumers Union of United States, Inc., a nonprofit organization. Complete Mailing Address: 101 Truman Avenue, Yonkers, New York 10703-1057. 11. Known Bondholders, Mortgagees, and Other Security Holders Owning or Holding 1 Percent or More of Total Amount of Bonds, Mortgages, or Other Securities. If none, so state: None. 12. For Completion by Nonprofit Organizations Authorized to Mail at Special Rates: The purpose, function, and nonprofit status of this organization and the exempt status for Federal Income tax purposes has not changed during preceding 12 months.

15. Extent and Nature of Circulation:

	Average no. copies each issue during past 12 mo.	Actual no. copies of single issue published nearest to filing date
A. Total no. of copies (net press run)	4,980,235	5,045,917
B. Paid and/or requested circulation		
1. Sales through dealers, carriers, street vendors, counter sales (not mailed)	132,113	114,630
2. Paid or Requested Mail subscription (Include Advertisers' Proof Copies/Exchange Copies)	4,597,459	4,712,377
C. Total paid and/or requested circulation (sum of 15b(1) and 15b(2)	4,729,572	4,827,007
D. Free distribution by mail (Samples, complimentary, and other free)	14,128	16,052
E. Free distribution Outside the Mail	0	0
F. Total Free distribution	14,128	16,052
G. Total distribution (sum of 15 and 15f)	4,743,700	4,843,059
H. Copies not distributed		
1. Office use, leftovers, spoiled	43,539	10,543
2. Return from news agents	192,996	192,315
I. TOTAL (sum of 15g, 15h(1) and 15h(2) shown in A)	4,980,235	5,045,917
J. Percent Paid and/or Requested Circulation	99.70%	99.67%

17. I certify that the statements made by me above are correct and complete.

Louis J. Milani, Senior Director, Strategic Marketing and Business Affairs

8-YEAR INDEX TO THE LAST FULL REPORT IN CONSUMER REPORTS

This index indicates when the last full report on a given subject was published in CONSUMER REPORTS. It covers 1989 through November 1996. Note that, beginning this year (volume 61), CONSUMER REPORTS is no longer paginated continuously throughout each volume year; instead, each issue begins on page 1. **Bold type** indicates Ratings reports or brand-name discussions; italic type indicates corrections, followups, or updates. Some reports are available by fax or mail from Consumer Reports by Request 24-hour service. To order a report, note the fax number at the left of the entry and call 800 896-7788 from a touch-tone phone. (No code means a report is not available by fax.) You can use MasterCard or Visa. Each report is $7.75.

* Profiles grouped by car size are available by fax or mail; call 800 999-2793 for the fax numbers.

BUYING GUIDE INDEX

This index covers all the reports, brand-name Ratings' charts, and Repair Histories in this year's Buying Guide. To find the last full report published in CONSUMER REPORTS, see the eight-year guide that starts on page 342.

"It's simply the best car-buying guide around." – BYTE, APRIL '96

WHAT YOU NEED TO KNOW FROM PURCHASE TO MAINTENANCE – ALL ON CD ROM !

Covers 1988-1997 New & Used Cars

- Includes reports on cars, minivans, pickups, and sport-utility vehicles
- Personal Car Selector lets you find the car that meets your needs
- Reliability histories and Consumer Reports unbiased Ratings

Tells You How to Get The Best Deal

- Interactive video lets you practice negotiating with the dealer
- What you should know if you're leasing

Includes Invaluable Car Care Tips

- How to keep your car running (almost) forever
- How to find a mechanic
- How to buy auto parts and accessories
- A Record Keeper to track your maintenance

Consumer Reports

Minimum System Requirements: 486DX2/66 or above running Windows 3.1/Win 95; 8 MB RAM; 7MB hard drive space, 256 color (8-bit), 640x480; SoundBlaster® or Windows-compatible sound card; double-speed CD-ROM.

Only
$19.95
(includes shipping and handling)

To order call
1-800-331-1369
Ext. 171
24 hours a day, 7 days a week
Visa, Mastercard, American Express or send your name, address and check payable to Consumer Reports Cars for $19.95 (includes shipping and handling) to:

Consumer Reports Cars
225 SW Broadway, Suite 600
Portland, OR 97205-9836

Other Consumers Union Publications for you

ZILLIONS

The one-of-a kind magazine for kids ages 10-14. It's enthusiastic, upbeat and packed with Zillions of things kids want to know about, like sneakers ... video games ... fast foods ... music ... and great advice on all sorts of "growing up" situations. Winner of four ED PRESS awards for excellence in publishing.

CONSUMER REPORTS TRAVEL LETTER

How to get the best deals on airfares, hotel rates, cruises, and car rentals. Inside travel information with specific recommendations, warnings about frauds & scams, and ways to avoid hassles. Plus, in every issue you'll receive a FLASH report announcing late-breaking, short-term travel promotions, deals, and discounts.

CONSUMER REPORTS ON HEALTH

Unbiased reporting on nutrition and fitness, important drugs, health frauds, medical breakthroughs and other issues critical to your personal health.

Look for more information and order cards in the pages of Consumer Reports.